Beginnings and Beyond

Foundations in Early Childhood Education

EIGHTH
EDITION

Beginnings and Beyond

Foundations in Early Childhood Education

Ann Miles Gordon

Kathryn Williams Browne
Skyline College

WADSWORTH
CENGAGE Learning™

Australia • Brazil • Japan • Korea • Mexico • Singapore • Spain • United Kingdom • United States

Beginnings and Beyond: Foundations in Early Childhood Education, Eighth Edition
Ann Miles Gordon and Kathryn Williams Browne

Education Editor: Christopher Shortt

Senior Development Editor: Lisa Mafrici

Assistant Editor: Caitlin Cox

Editorial Assistant: Linda Stewart

Media Editor: Dennis Fitzgerald

Marketing Manager: Kara Kindstrom Parsons

Marketing Assistant: Dimitri Hagnéré

Marketing Communications Manager: Martha Pfeiffer

Content Project Manager: Tanya Nigh

Creative Director: Rob Hugel

Art Director: Maria Epes

Print Buyer: Rebecca Cross

Rights Acquisitions Account Manager, Text: Margaret Chamberlain-Gaston

Rights Acquisitions Account Manager, Image: Leitha Etheridge-Sims

Production Service: Megan Greiner, Graphic World Inc.

Text Designer: Lisa Buckley

Photo Researcher: Sarah D'Stair, Pre-PressPMG

Copy Editor: Graphic World Inc.

Cover Designer: Lisa Buckley

Cover Image: Design Pics, Jupiter Images

Compositor: Graphic World Inc.

For product information and technology assistance, contact us at
**Cengage Learning Customer & Sales Support,
1-800-354-9706**
For permission to use material from this text or product, submit all requests online at
www.cengage.com/permissions
Further permissions questions can be e-mailed to
permissionrequest@cengage.com

Library of Congress Control Number: 2009942071

ISBN-13: 978-0-495-80817-6

ISBN-10: 0-495-80817-2

Wadsworth
20 Davis Drive
Belmont, CA 94002-3098
USA

Cengage Learning is a leading provider of customized learning solutions with office locations around the globe, including Singapore, the United Kingdom, Australia, Mexico, Brazil, and Japan. Locate your local office at **www.cengage.com/global.**

Cengage Learning products are represented in Canada by Nelson Education, Ltd.

To learn more about Wadsworth, visit **www.cengage.com/wadsworth**

Purchase any of our products at your local college store or at our preferred online store **www.CengageBrain.com**

Printed in the United States of America
1 2 3 4 5 6 7 13 12 11 10

Dedication

To Kate, my longtime friend, respected colleague, and coauthor for 25 years and four books. You are a consummate professional. — AMG

To the students and colleagues of Skyline College—a most inspiring mix of professionals and fellow learners on the path of higher education. — KWB

Contents

SECTION 2
Who Is the Young Child?

CHAPTER 3
Defining the Young Child

CHAPTER 4
Developmental and Learning Theories

SECTION 3
Who Are the Teachers?   157

SECTION 4
What Is Being Taught?   329

Preface

Our Viewpoint

The early childhood field is a dynamic profession full of many challenges and great rewards. Teachers being trained today have the opportunity to respond to and affect the critical issues facing early childhood educators now and in the future. Students will confront the challenge of teaching a diverse group of learners differentiated by their abilities, ethnic and cultural backgrounds, family support, values, and beliefs. They will learn to navigate the tension between standards and assessments and developmentally appropriate principles and practice. As the field experiences changes and growth, new teachers must understand the meaning of professionalism and how their personal development fosters their professional commitment. In order to accomplish this daunting but exciting task, students need a text that is current, comprehensive, and able to connect knowledge and theory to the classroom—one that has eclectic viewpoints and a variety of models and that deepens their understanding of themselves as members of a lively and fulfilling profession. *Beginnings and Beyond: Foundations in Early Childhood Education* accomplishes that goal.

The purpose of *Beginnings and Beyond* is to promote the competence and effectiveness of new teachers through a presentation of basic knowledge, skills, attitudes, and philosophies based on the premise that new teachers must have opportunities to learn fundamental skills as they begin their teaching experience. The text expresses a viewpoint about quality early education and what practices ensure excellence. In the area of cultural sensitivity and multicultural relationships, we promote a "both/and" attitude, following the National Association for the Education of Young Children (NAEYC) guidelines for Developmentally Appropriate Practices. This attitude is a change from an "either/or" approach to deciding what is appropriate practice and what is not. The "both/and" thinking provides a more flexible, non-polarizing approach to the complexities of early childhood practices. Readers will find the "both/and" influence throughout the text but especially in the areas of early literacy, spiritual development, discipline, diversity, and anti-bias strategies. The point of "both/and" is particularly emphasized in school and family relationships where cultural differences and distinctions are always at play.

Demographic issues drive the direction of early childhood programs, and the text reflects that fact. *Beginnings and Beyond* maintains the emphasis that every child and family is unique and that they deserve the respect and affirmation of their cultural identity. This edition, therefore, weaves a strong multicultural perspective and consciousness throughout the text in order to help prospective teachers and caregivers increase their sensitivity to different cultural practices and values. This feature has become one of the book's strongest points.

How Do We Meet the Needs of Today's Learners?

Beginnings and Beyond is intended for college students who are interested in young children, beginning teachers who plan to engage in early care and education, practitioners in direct service to children and families, and professionals in the workforce who are enlarging their knowledge base. Through our comprehensive chapter coverage and unique pedagogical features, we provide a resource that meets the needs of today's early child educators.

Chapter Organization

The overall organization of the book takes the student from the history of early childhood education to current issues and future trends. Four key themes emphasized in the beginning and ending chapters weave the past and present together as students learn about (1) social reform, (2) the importance of childhood, (3) transmitting values, and (4) professionalism.

Five basic questions set the tone for each section by asking the reader to reflect on the wide-ranging nature of early childhood education. The book's flexibility allows instructors to begin with any section that seems appropriate to meet the needs of their classes. The five sections and chapter descriptions are as follows:

- **What Is the Field of Early Childhood Education?** In Section 1, descriptions of early childhood history and the types of programs provide a basis for understanding the complexity of the field.

  Chapter 1 describes the origin of early education through history, which forms the theory on which students will base their teaching, and then students learn about events that have shaped the field. Students meet the many contributors to early childhood education, such as the famous (Rousseau, Dewey, & Hill), the ancient (the Greeks), and contemporary influences (Reggio Emilia).

  Chapter 2 moves the student directly into the variety of programs and the importance of developmentally appropriate practice (DAP) in creating good programs for young children. The principles of DAP are matched with examples of DAP in action so that students will see a direct correlation between the DAP criteria and classroom application.

- **Who Is the Young Child?** Section 2 begins with a discussion of the young child's growth, followed by an overview of the developmental and learning theories that form the cornerstone of our knowledge about children.

  Chapter 3 provides students with an understanding of the nature of the children they will teach and their common characteristics and wide individual differences. Word Pictures, which are age-level descriptions, are a popular feature with students who have used this text, as they enable students to anticipate children's needs and plan appropriate experiences to reorganization of key chapters.

  Chapter 4 gives the student a concise description of universal and life-span theories and other developmental topics on which sound teaching principles and practices are based. Play, as a cornerstone

of learning, and updated information on brain-based research provide further application of theory to classroom use.

- **Who Are the Teachers?** Section 3 defines the aggregate of influences that act as teachers in the early childhood setting. Each chapter enlarges the student's view of what makes up a professional teacher.

  Chapter 5 describes the roles and responsibilities of an early childhood teacher as "professionalism in action" and introduces students to a broader definition of teaching. Examples of everyday ethical dilemmas provide opportunities for students to discuss their own values and beliefs in response to the NAEYC Code of Ethical Conduct. The chapter also explores team-teaching situations and the importance of teacher evaluations.

  Chapter 6 enhances the student's ability to observe and record the behavior of young children. Along with a comprehensive description of observational tools and effective techniques, there are updated segments about child evaluation, early learning standards, and concerns about testing and screening.

  Chapter 7 demonstrates how guidance and behavior are critical factors in the life of a classroom teacher through vignettes that help the student understand how and why young children behave as they do. Problem solving, conflict resolution, and a wide range of guidance techniques give students the necessary tools to guide young children's behavior.

  Chapter 8 offers the student a perspective on the all-important collaboration of families and teachers in creating the best possible learning environment for young children. Discussions of the definition of a family, today's family structures, and challenges facing parents bring a relevancy to students.

  Chapter 9 defines the characteristics of high-quality environments that include elements of health, safety, and nutrition, as well as an anti-bias approach and the inclusion of children with varying abilities. Key dimensions of the physical, temporal, and interpersonal environments help students understand how the deliberate use of the environment serves as a teaching strategy for appropriate behavior and learning.

- **What Is Being Taught?** Section 4 is a composite answer to the all-important question, what are we teaching our children? The first chapter in the section, Chapter 10, discusses the role of the curriculum and is followed by four chapters that address individual developmental domains.

Chapter 10 is based on the premise that a play-based curriculum is the foundation for early childhood learning, and the chapter provides students with examples and models of developmentally and culturally appropriate approaches to a play-based curriculum. Students will learn the importance of play, how to develop emergent and integrated curricula, and how to create projects. They will understand how different learning styles can be applied to curriculum development and will look at five popular curriculum models.

Chapter 11 explores the physical and motor skills of young children, the importance of outdoor play, and basic skills children need to learn. This chapter helps the student plan appropriate experiences and curriculum that will strengthen children's physical growth.

Chapter 12 translates research in cognitive-developmental psychology, such as multiple intelligences and brain-based research, into curriculum practices that include constructive play, language/pre-reading, and math learning and special topic of computers.

Chapter 13 addresses the many ways teachers provide language experiences for children, with additional focus on dual language learners and special topic of literacy.

Chapter 14 offers conceptual information about the psychosocial domain (emotional, social, creative, and spiritual dimensions) and also additional information about emotional intelligence, resilience, bullying, and conflict resolution. A special topic on art is also included.

■ **How Do We Teach for Tomorrow?** Section 5, which encompasses Chapter 15, helps the student take a broad look at issues facing the early childhood field today. It also serves as a bookend to the first chapter, repeating the four basic themes of the text in light of current needs. (1) "Ethic of Social Reform" reflects current issues such as affordable child care, universal preschools, and the influence of No Child Left Behind. (2) "The Importance of Childhood" explores childhood stress, abuse and neglect, poverty, and divorce and their effects on children. (3) "Transmitting Values" includes the media culture, the effect of violence and disasters, and class differences. (4) In the "Professionalism" section, standards are discussed, as are wages and work conditions and child advocacy. In each of these sections, the students learn about the reality of children's lives and how early childhood professionals can help them prepare for the challenges and responsibilities of adult life.

Special Features and Pedagogy

We offer numerous learning aids and engaging features to enrich the learning experience of students and to connect theory to practice. These include:

■ **NEW—Preview Questions** at the beginning of the chapter match the main chapter headings to provide students with a clear road map to the topics they will encounter in each chapter.

■ **NEW—The NAEYC Code of Ethical Conduct,** which highlights core values, ideals, and principles that apply to the chapter content, is featured at the beginning of each chapter. This feature provides opportunities for students to become familiar with the Code of Ethical Conduct and see its direct application to the teaching experience.

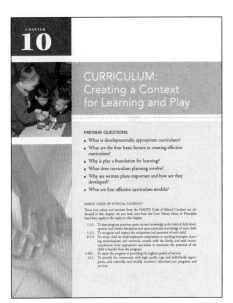

■ **NEW—TeachSource Video Case features** allow students and instructors to relate important chapter content to real-life scenarios in early child care settings. The Video Cases provide students with an opportunity to hear from real educators who are doing the work that they are preparing to do. The Video Cases and other engaging video clips provided on the premium website offer critical-thinking questions and give students ample opportunities for reflection and discussion.

■ **Insights from the Field** is a popular staple of each chapter. In order to engage the student more effectively, experienced practitioners in early childhood education write about an experience that illustrates a fundamental part of the chapter. Insight contributors to this edition are Scott Williams, the late Edith Dowley, Francis Wardle, Rosalind Charlesworth, Barbara Biglan, Kären Wiggins-Dowler, Elizabeth Crary, Libby Miles, Louise Cadwell, Marjorie Kostelnik, Rae Pica, Arleen Prairie, Wilma Robles de Meléndez, Sue Warford, and Sharon Kagan. They add a useful and relevant opinion to every chapter.

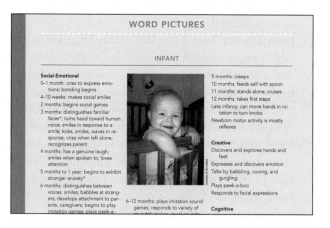

NEW—Developmentally Appropriate Practice (DAP) References are used throughout the text to emphasize material that represents a DAP. This feature, highlighted via a marginal icon and corresponding footnote, gives the student reader a concrete example of DAP in action. Culturally Appropriate Practice *and* Developmentally Appropriate Practice continue to be the subthemes of *Beginnings and Beyond*. We emphasize the importance of creating programs and building curricula based on an understanding of the nature of the child and the factors affecting a child's growth and development. We believe it is important that students realize the deep and crucial contributions that children's family, culture, and language make to development. NAEYC's years of experience in the definition and application of developmentally appropriate practice have given us further insights, which are reflected throughout the book.

■ The **What Do You Think?** box in each chapter brings attention to a relevant topic and invites the student to reflect on the concept in relation to his or her own life and learning.

What do you think are the most compelling arguments that play is a necessary part of any early childhood program? How would you respond to a kindergarten teacher who thought too much time was devoted to play and that the academics needed more emphasis? What would you say to a parent who was interested in enrolling a child into your program but wanted to know why so much time was devoted to play?

■ **The newly designed Word Pictures special section** in Chapter 3 describes the major characteristics of children from infancy through 8 years of age. This popular feature helps students become familiar with expected behaviors in young children as a frame of reference for creating programs and planning curriculum that responds to the children's interests as well as their abilities and needs.

■ **New and improved end-of-chapter aids** provide the student with an overall review of the material within the chapter. The Summary and Key Terms remind students of the most important concepts; the Review Questions are aligned to the Preview

Questions in the chapter opening; the Learning Activities suggest practical ways to integrate knowledge, theory, and experience; and the Helpful Websites and References provide added resources for students to expand their knowledge.

- **NEW—A correlation chart to the latest NAEYC Standards for Early Childhood Professional Preparation** is found on the back inside cover of this book. The handy chart makes it easier for students to see where the key standards in the field are addressed in specific chapters and topics throughout the text.

What's New in This Edition

The eighth edition of *Beginnings and Beyond* represents a completely updated work, both in the content and presentation. Some highlights of the new coverage and features include:

- Students will find **information that is presented in a truly accessible manner,** from the all-new chapter opening pedagogy and learning aids (such as the new Preview Questions keyed to chapter headings and the NAEYC Code of Ethics listings) to the comprehensive study and review materials at the end of the chapter. In addition, we streamlined and reorganized several key chapters for better comprehension.
- **Up-to-date Developmentally Appropriate Practice** (DAP) discussions and references are found throughout, including the **new DAP marginal icon** and footnotes in every chapter.
- **Updated coverage of standards and accountability,** which are important areas of concern for early childhood professionals. Chapter 6, in particular, has been completely updated to cover the latest in these key areas.
- **Expanded coverage of key content areas,** including play-based learning, children with special needs, behavior that is challenging, team teaching, diversity, emergent curriculum, brain-based learning, technology use, professionalism, and current issues and trends in the field.
- **New TeachSource Video features** integrated into each chapter to illustrate topics and best practices.
- **A completely new and improved design** to strengthen our presentation and to improve students' comprehension.

Accompanying Teaching and Learning Resources

The eighth edition of *Beginnings and Beyond* offers many ancillary materials that can support and enhance the text experience and an instructor's presentation of the course. From planning to presentation to testing, materials are available to provide students with an engaging and relevant exposure to the broad scope of topics in early childhood education.

Instructor's Manual

The updated instructor's manual provides a chapter-by-chapter plan for organizing a course using *Beginnings and Beyond*. In addition to chapter overviews, outlines, key terms, resource lists, discussion topics, and teaching tips, this manual will include a complete list of PowerPoint masters, arranged by chapter on the PowerLecture. Instructions for using the PowerLecture are also part of the manual.

Premium Website

The premium website offers students a variety of study tools and useful resources, such as additional information or activities, critical-thinking questions and activities for each "Insights from the Field" found in the text, and questions relevant to chapter learning objectives, which are presented for individual or group consideration. The website also offers access to the new **TeachSource Video Cases** and other video clips that are integrated into the text. The Video Cases are 4- to 6- minute video and audio modules presenting actual early childhood education scenarios, supported by viewing questions, teacher interviews, artifacts, and bonus videos that allow you to realistically and thoroughly analyze the problems and opportunities in the case. The Video Cases let you experience the complex and multiple dimensions of education that early childhood teachers face every day. Go to **http://www.cengage.com/login** to register or purchase access.

Professional Enhancement Series

An additional supplement to accompany the eighth edition is the *Introduction to Early Childhood Education Professional Enhancement* resource for students. This resource, which is part of Wadsworth Cengage Learning's Early Childhood Education Professional Enhancement Series, focuses on key topics of interest to future early childhood teachers, directors, and caregivers. This supplement, and other "primers" on key areas in early childhood education, can be bundled with this text upon request. Some of the tools provided are:

- tips for getting off to a great start in your new environment.
- suggestions for materials that promote development for children from infancy through primary grades.
- tools to assist in observing children and in gathering data to help set appropriate goals for individual children.
- case studies of relevant, realistic situations and best practices for successfully navigating them.
- insights into issues and trends facing early childhood educators today.

WebTutor Toolbox

WebTutor™ Toolbox for WebCT™ or Blackboard® provides access to all the content of this text's rich Book Companion Website from within your course management system. Robust communication tools—such as a course calendar, asynchronous discussion, real-time chat, a whiteboard, and an integrated e-mail system—make it easy for your students to stay connected to the course.

PowerLecture

A special new accompaniment to this edition of *Beginnings and Beyond* is our PowerLecture, which integrates Internet technology and early childhood education. The PowerLecture includes an electronic copy of the Instructor's Manual, PowerPoint Masters, and the ExamView Computerized Test Bank (CTB).

The updated computerized test bank allows instructors to create student exams composed of multiple choice, true/false, short answer, and completion questions for each chapter. The CTB provides approximately 1,000 questions in addition to the following features:

- Multiple methods of question selection
- Multiple outputs (print, ASCII, and Rich Text Format)
- Graphic support
- Random questioning output
- Special character support

About the Authors

Ann Miles Gordon has been an early childhood professional for more than 40 years as a teacher of young children, a teacher of parents, and a teacher of college students. She has taught in laboratory schools, church-related centers, and private and public preschool and kindergarten programs. Ann taught at the Bing Nursery School, the laboratory school for Stanford University's Department of Psychology, where she was a head teacher and lecturer in the Psychology Department. Ann also served as an adjunct faculty member in several community colleges, teaching the full gamut of early childhood courses. Ann served as executive director of the National Association of Episcopal Schools for 14 years, where more than 1,100 early childhood programs were a part of her network. Ann is semi-retired and a hands-on grandmother of two, through which she brings an enhanced perspective on infants and toddlers to *Beginnings and Beyond*, as well as up-to-date experience with center-based child care.

Kathryn Williams Browne has been teaching children, families, and students for more than 30 years. First a teacher of young children—nursery school, parent cooperative, full-day child care, pre-kindergarten, bilingual preschool, kindergarten, and first grade—she later moved to Stanford University's lab school, where she served as head teacher and psychology lecturer. Coauthoring *Beginnings and Beyond* with Ann was enhanced by Kate's role as a parent: her two children were born during the first two editions, so the book grew along with them. Her consultant and School Board experience offered perspectives into public policy and reform. Kate teaches in the California Community College system and the Early Childhood Mentor program, which offer the richness of a diverse student population coupled with the challenges of access and privilege that parallel those in the early education field itself. The balance of career and family, of work with children and for children, and of the special challenges of diversity and professionalism of early childhood education guide her work.

Ann and Kate are also coauthors of *To Teach Well: A Student Practicum Guide* (Merrill, 2009), *Guiding*

Young Children in a Diverse Society (Allyn & Bacon, in revision), and *Beginning Essentials in Early Childhood Education* (Delmar Cengage Learning, 2007).

Acknowledgments

We owe a great deal to the colleagues who contributed their thoughts through their "Insights from the Field" articles and we thank them for adding relevancy to this edition. Thanks also to Louise Boyd Cadwell for furnishing pictures of the St. Louis-Reggio Collaborative classrooms. At Cengage Learning, we would like to thank Lisa Mafrici, senior development editor, for her skillful guidance, constant encouragement, and gentle nudging; Chris Shortt, education editor, for having a new and refreshing vision for *Beginnings and Beyond* and making it a reality; and to the rest of the team at Cengage Learning for their professionalism and support.

Our reviewers, whose valuable gift of time and energy enhances the book's usefulness, have been superb with their insights and suggestions. We want to thank:

Linda Aiken, Southwestern Community College
Betty Ruth Baker, Baylor University
Audrey W. Beard, Albany State University
Wendy Bertoli, Lancaster Country Career and Technology Center
Diane E. Craig, Kent State University
Veronica Getskow, Los Angeles Valley College
Marilyn L. Haller, Oklahoma Baptist University
Kathy-Ann Hernandez, Temple University
Denise J. McConachie, Missouri Baptist University
Jean C. Murphy, Chicago State University

What Is the Field of Early Childhood Education?

© Cengage Learning

© Cengage Learning

History of Early Childhood Education

PREVIEW QUESTIONS

- What distinguishes early childhood education from other levels of education?

- Why is it important to know about the history of early childhood education?

- What are the major influences from abroad and in America?

- What nontraditional perspectives are included in our thinking?

- What impacts have other fields had on the development of the early childhood philosophy?

- What have been the basic themes in early childhood education throughout history?

- How do current political, social, and economic events affect the direction of early education?

Please refer to Figure 1-2, An Abbreviated Timeline for Early Childhood Education, and online for an expanded timeline as you read this chapter.

NAEYC CODE OF ETHICAL CONDUCT

These Core Values and sections from the NAEYC Code of Ethical Conduct are addressed in this chapter. As you read, note how the Core Values, Ideals, or Principles listed here apply to the topics in this chapter. (Reprinted with permission from the National Association for the Education of Young Children.)

Core Values: We have committed ourselves to helping children and adults reach their full potential in the context of relationships that are based on trust, respect, and mutual regard.

Section I: Ethical Responsibilities to Children—Childhood is a unique and valuable stage in the life cycle. We are committed to support children's development, respect individual difference, help children learn to live and work cooperatively, and promote health self-awareness, competence, self-worth and resiliency.

Section II: Ethical Responsibilities to Families—Families are of primary importance to children's development.

Section III: Ethical Responsibilities to Colleagues—In a caring, cooperative workplace, human dignity is respected, professional satisfaction is promoted, and positive relationships are modeled.

Section IV: Ethical Responsibilities to Community and Society—Early childhood programs operate within a context of an immediate community made up of families and other institutions concerned with children's welfare.

Introduction to the Field

Early childhood education has a rich and exciting history. In this chapter, the story of its development is also the chronicle of courageous people who took steps toward improving children's lives. Critical events have had a hand in shaping the history of early childhood education. As the images of the child change through the centuries, so, too, does the education of the young child and the educators themselves.

For the moment, imagine yourself as a time traveler. As you go back in time, you span the centuries and meet the people whose vision helped to shape our profession. You learn how Froebel's own unhappy childhood inspired a new way of teaching called the kindergarten. You see the passion and struggle of Montessori as she convinces the world that "slum children" can learn and succeed. In the 1960s, you witness the dedication of America to create a program for preschoolers known as "Head Start." You see early childhood teaching become a profession that includes infants and toddlers, as well as kindergarten and early primary grades.

New models are forged through necessity and innovation, thus changing what we know about children and their care and education. The energies of so many on behalf of children have produced bold ideas, creative models, even contrary beliefs and practices. Across the globe and through the centuries, the education of young children has evolved.

Why History?

Most early childhood students and many educators know little about the origins of their chosen profession. The names of Rousseau, Froebel, Montessori, and Dewey may not seem to have much significance at this time (although many teachers are familiar with some of their

techniques), but knowing something about the roots of this profession is important. Every time period has social and political events that influenced the reaction of people at the time, which then influenced how children were raised and educated. Further, most of these individuals were crusaders for education, often engaging in social reform and making the work of teaching into a legitimate profession. Their thinking was revolutionary, going against the mainstream of the time to emphasize the importance of childhood, and always offering insights that changed our ways of educating children and how we transmit our values to the next generation. Let their voices be heard, so you can develop your own.

What Do YOU Think? Do you currently work in a center or family child-care setting? What is its history? Which people or ideas inform the school's approach? Who of the historical figures in this chapter influences you as you arrange the environment? Plan the curriculum? Interact with children and their families?

There is a sense of *support* that comes from knowing that history. Contemporary education has its roots in the past; finding a suitable beginning point for that past helps provide an educator with perspective. New insights blend with ideas from past traditions, as the history of early childhood education is truly a history of rediscovery.

Think about this: the "education" of the 21st century actually stems from children's schooling thousands of years ago. For instance, works of Socrates, Plato, and Aristotle are part of the philosophical foundation on which our educational practices are built. Schools in ancient Greece and Rome taught literature, the arts, and science. These subjects are part of schools across the country today. One can see how traditional early childhood practices reflect and reinforce the European values and beliefs.

However, in order to recognize and respect all cultures of our children, we need to look beyond the dominant culture. Unfortunately, most common historical documents are works of Western Europe and European-American only. Searching for historical records from diverse cultures would be beneficial to understanding the full "American" educational experience. For instance, both oral and written records exist that describe education in Africa, particularly those cultures found in the Nile Valley (Hilliard, 1997). In more current terms, teachers must educate themselves about the culturally diverse roots of early educational practices.

Knowing that early childhood *philosophy* has deep roots can be an *inspiration* and helps teachers develop *professional expression*. As early childhood educators, we must learn to express our ideas, finding our own voice. **Professionalism** in education "relates to doing things well, at the right time, and for the right reason" (Spodek, Saracho, & Peters, 1988) and is one of the key themes of our field, as you will see at the end of the chapter. The past as well as the present and future must be considered when developing sound educational programs for young children. The *tenets* expressed by past educators help develop better methods of teaching. Looking at history gives an overview of how various ages looked at children and their learning based on the religious, political, and economic pressures of the time. Reviewing the professional record demonstrates how the needs of society affect education. Perhaps some of the mistakes of the past can be avoided if history is remembered.

Drawing upon knowledge of the past creates an awareness and understanding of changes in education. Into the fabric of early childhood education are woven many threads of influence that are responsible for current philosophies. By understanding and telling the story of the past, we are better equipped to interpret our own history, to have a sense of mission and purpose. "Doing history" is a good idea for early childhood educators, for Spodek tells us:

> When we [become] early childhood educators, each of us accepts as our own, either deliberately or implicitly, the mission that is central to our field: We are committed to enhancing the education, development, and well-being of young children. Our saga helps renew our sense of identity and commitment to our profession. (Spodek in Bauch, 1988)

We also get in touch with our own early childhood and education (see "Insights from the Field" by Scott Williams at the end of this chapter), thus connecting us to the children of long ago, ourselves, and those we care for every day.

All professions have a canon of beliefs and practices. As you acquire this knowledge, you begin to develop your own *philosophy of teaching* (based, in part, on information gathered in this chapter). As you do, be sure to constantly rethink your practices. All professionals should reexamine themselves on a regular basis, and each professional teacher must do the same. For while understanding historical records makes sense for professional development, recognizing that they are a reflection of certain cultural norms is also crucial. Remember that the voices you hear in these chapters are not from on high. Learn to be particularly suspect of the current proclaimed universal American practices that have to do with:

- Early attainment of individuality and independence.
- The necessity of early and free exploration.
- The critical importance of the early stimulation of intellect and language.

These are the three areas that previous research has seen as universal, which cross-cultural research has shown not to be. The first reflects a priority of many Western European cultures, but it is not a common practice in societies that promote group harmony and interdependence. Second, many indigenous groups hold their very young children close, carrying them along while they work; there is no data that indicate these children develop poorly. Third, while American educational systems of the early 21st century are building on increasing academic and intellectual standards, there is no universal mandate for an exclusive focus on this developmental domain in the early years. Figure 1-1 offers other traditional educational practices, their historical context, and alternatives to consider as you create your own educational philosophy.

As authors, we strive to offer a broader view of our DAP field, including its history. We recognize, for instance, that schools of the past were overwhelmingly created for boys and young men. This gender bias added to the underdevelopment of girls and women and prevails today in some parts of the world. By understanding the concepts of institutional and individual oppression, teachers can begin to examine their own notions and become "critical consumers" of information, both from the past and present. However, educational programs that included girls and the role of people of color in the early childhood movement are documented, if not always in the dominant literature of the time (see nontraditional perspectives later in this chapter).

DAP "Meet children where they are, as individuals and as a group," is a cornerstone of teaching children in developmentally appropriate ways.

Educational Practice	Historical Context and ECE Trend/Practice	Think Again . . .
Same-age grouping	K–12 schools in the United States since 1850s target curriculum goals.	■ Learning takes place with "guided collaboration," which often occurs with an older "expert." ■ Children learn when challenged to accommodate to higher level thinking, likely to occur with a mixed-age range. ■ Developing values of caring and responsibility happen best when children practice helping and protecting younger children. ■ Reduced family size indicates that multi-age experiences should happen in schooling. ■ Diversity (gender, culture, exceptionality, etc.) makes strict target goals unrealistic.
Daily schedules	Routines are the framework for programs, offering security and predictability.	■ Children's sense of time is unlike that of adults, so rigid schedules do not correspond to their development. ■ Brain research indicates a need for stimulation, change, and challenge rather than the same structure constantly.
Curriculum is at the center of good programs.	A plan for learning should be driven by specific outcomes in order to be assured that children are learning.	■ Not following an adult-planned and driven curriculum worked well for geniuses such as Einstein, Erikson, and Bill Gates. ■ Educators as diverse as Dewey and Steiner promoted curricula based on children's interests or innate spirit. ■ Children appear to learn well through a curriculum that emerges, following their interests and timetable.

FIGURE 1-1 As you develop a philosophy of teaching, be sure to examine common beliefs and practices of the profession.

Every culture has had and still does have the task of socializing and educating their young. So, although the written record may document a part of educational philosophy and teaching, there is no single monopoly on ideas about raising and educating children. Educational changes of a more recent nature follow. The impact of other disciplines, such as medicine and psychology, and the recurrent themes of early childhood education are also explored.

Defining the Terms

The term **early childhood education** refers to group settings deliberately intended to affect developmental changes in children from birth to 8 years of age. In school terms, it includes group settings for infants through the primary years of elementary school, kindergarten through 3rd or 4th grade in the United States. In programmatic terms, the education of young children includes formal and informal group settings regardless of their initial purpose. For instance, after-school programs for elementary ages are included, as are their formal academic sessions.

Early childhood educators thus build bridges between a child's two worlds: school (or group experience) and home. It is during these years that the foundation for future learning is set; these are the **building block years,** during which a child learns to walk, talk, establish an identity, print, and count. In later years, that same child builds on these skills to be able to climb mountains, speak a second language, learn to express and negotiate, write in cursive, and understand multiplication.

Influences from Abroad

When did early childhood education first begin? Refer to Figure 1-2, *An Abbreviated Timeline for Early Childhood Education,* and to the expanded timeline on the accompanying website, as you read this chapter. Getting a visual sense of when and where things happened can help you make sense of the various threads in our tapestry of early childhood educational history. It is impossible to pinpoint the origins of humankind because there are few records from millions of years ago. Some preparation for adult life was done informally, mostly through imitation. As language developed, communication occurred. Children learned dances, rituals, and ceremonies, and both boys and girls were taught skills for their respective roles in the tribe. Ancient historical documents seem to indicate that child-rearing practices were somewhat crude; DeMause (1974) even suggests that the further one goes back in history, the more likely the case of abandonment and brutality.

In Ancient Times

The definition of childhood has varied greatly throughout history. For example, in ancient times children were considered adults by age 7. A society's definition of childhood influences how it educates its children.

Many of our own practices are founded on those developed in Greece and Rome. Greek education—and virtually all classical European schooling—was provided for the boys of wealthy families, while girls and working-class children received training for domestic work or a trade.

Education began by age 6 or 7, although Plato and Aristotle both spoke of the need to educate the younger child. Some ancient Romans felt that education should begin at home as soon as a child began to talk, and they highlighted the use of rewards and the ineffectiveness of corporal punishment (Hewes, 1993).

Probably the first education in schools outside the home or homelike apprenticeship was in ancient Greek and Roman times. Plato (427 BC), Aristotle (384–323 BC), Cicero (143–106 BC), and Polybius (222–204 BC) founded schools, with the model of small-group tutoring, teaching wealthy boys thinking skills, governing, military strategy, and managing commerce. Our word *educate* comes from a Latin verb *educare*, through a French verb *educere*, to draw forth or to lead.

As the Roman Empire deteriorated and society fell apart (400–1200 AD), childhood lasted barely beyond infancy. Although education was the responsibility of parents, most were busy fighting for survival. Childhood was not seen as a separate time of life, and children were used in the labor force. People left villages and towns for the safety of a local baron or king, and schools ceased to exist. Few members of the ruling class could read or write their names, and the monastery schools were for priests and religious instruction only.

The education of children was fairly simple before the 15th century; there was no educational system, and the way of life was uncomplicated as well. The church control of school in the medieval period meant that education projected a view of children as basically evil in their natural state. The value of education was in preparation for an afterlife. Children learned mostly through their parents or by apprenticeship outside the family. The child was expected and encouraged to move into adulthood as fast as possible. Survival was the primary goal in life. Because the common religious belief was that people were naturally evil, children had to be directed, punished, and corrected constantly.

What little we know of systematic learning developed during the Dark Ages through the policies of Charlemagne—who proclaimed that the nobility should know their letters—and from monastery schools that maintained libraries. A new social class in the form of craft guilds began to grow as apprenticeships expanded. Although education was sparse, the seeds of learning were planted, including the introduction of the concepts of equality and brotherhood, a continuing concern of educators today.

European Renaissance and Reformation

The European Renaissance and Reformation (1400–1600) brought more ease and freedom for the common person. Children were seen as pure and good. The printing press, invented by Johannes Gutenberg in 1439,

An Abbreviated Timeline for Early Childhood Education

Authors' Note: A debt of gratitude is owed to D. Keith Osborn for his outstanding historical research and to James L. Hymes, Jr., for his generous time and perspective.

5th–3rd centuries BC to AD 1400s Few records exist concerning child-rearing practices; the development of cities gives rise to schooling on a larger scale.

1423 & 1439 The invention of printing and movable type allows knowledge to spread rapidly; ideas and techniques become available to large numbers of people; printing is credited with bringing about the end of the Middle Ages and the beginning of the Renaissance.

1657 *Orbis Pictus*, by Comenius, is the first children's book with pictures.

1690 John Locke published his essay, which postulated that children are born with a tabula rasa, or clean slate, on which all experiences are written.

1740–1860s Sabbath Schools and Clandestine Schools are established as facilities to educate African Americans in the United States.

1762 *Emile*, by Rousseau, proclaims the child's natural goodness.

1801 *How Gertrude Teaches Her Children*, by Pestalozzi, emphasizes home education.

1826 *Education of Man*, by Froebel, describes the first system of kindergarten education as a "child's garden," with activities known as "gifts from God."

1837 Froebel opens the first kindergarten in Blankenburgh, Germany.

1860 Elizabeth Peabody opens the first English-speaking kindergarten in Boston.

1861 Robert Owen sets up infant school in New Lanark, England, as an instrument of social reform for children of parent workers in his mills.

1871 The first public kindergarten in North America opens in Ontario, Canada. (First public American kindergarten: 1873).

1873 The Butler School at Hampton Institute is opened as a free school for black children, including kindergarten curriculum for five-year-olds.

1880 First teacher-training program for kindergartners, Oshkosh Normal School, Pennsylvania.

1892 International Kindergarten Union founded; becomes the Association for Childhood Education in 1930, increasing its scope to include elementary education.

1896 John Dewey establishes a laboratory school at the University of Chicago and develops a pragmatic approach to education, becoming the father of the Progressive Movement in American education.

1897 *My Pedagogic Creed* is published, detailing the opposition to rote learning and the philosophy of educating "the whole child."

1903 The Committee of Nineteen, a splinter group of the International Kindergarten Union, forms to report various philosophical concepts. Members include Patty Smith Hill, Lucy Wheelock, and Susan Blow.

1907 Casa di Bambini (Children's House) is opened by Maria Montessori in a slum district in Rome, Italy. She later develops an educational philosophy and program to guide children's growth through the senses and practical life experiences.

1909 First White House Conference on Children is held by Theodore Roosevelt, leading to the establishment of the Children's Bureau in 1912.

1911 Deptford School, an open-air school in the slums of London, is opened by Margaret McMillan. The school emphasizes health and play, thus coining the phrase "nursery school."

1915 First U.S. Montessori school opens in New York City.

1916 The Bureau of Educational Experiments, which becomes Bank Street College of Education (and laboratory school) in 1922, is founded by L. S. Mitchell, who is a leading proponent of progressive education at the early childhood level.

(continues)

FIGURE 1-2 An Abbreviated Timeline for Early Childhood Education (see the premium website for an expanded version).

1916   First Cooperative Nursery School opens at the University of Chicago.

1918   First public nursery schools are opened in England.

1921   A. S. Neill founds Summerhill school in England, which becomes a model for the "free school" movement (the book entitled *Summerhill* is published in 1960).

1922   Abigail Eliot opens Ruggles Street Nursery School and Training Center.

1925–1926   The National Committee on Nursery Schools is founded by Patty Smith Hill; it becomes NANE and eventually NAEYC.

1926   Gesell establishes the Clinic of Child Development at Yale University and studies norms of child growth and behavior.

1926–1927   Research facilities are founded at several American universities and colleges (e.g., Smith College, Vassar College, Yale University, and Mills College).

1927   Dorothy Howard establishes the first Black Nursery School in Washington, DC, and operates it for over 50 years.

1929   Lois Meeks Stolz names the first President of the National Association for Nursery Education (later to become National Association for the Education of Young Children), and joins the Teachers College (Columbia University) faculty to start the laboratory school and Child Development Institute. Stolz later becomes the Director of the Kaiser Child Service Centers during World War II.

1929   Susan Isaacs publishes *The Nursery Years*, which contradicts the more scientific psychological view of behavior shaping and emphasizes the child's viewpoint and the value of play.

1929–1931   Hampton Institute, Spellman College, and Bennett College open Black laboratory nursery schools, emphasizing child development principles as in other lab schools and serving as training centers.

1933   WPA (Works Projects Association) opens emergency nurseries for Depression relief of unemployed teachers.

1935   First toy lending library, Toy Loan, begins in Los Angeles.

1936   The first commercial telecast is shown in New York City, starring Felix the Cat.

1943–1945   Kaiser Shipyard Child Care Center, run by Lois Meeks Stolz, James Hymes, and Edith Dowley, operates 24-hour care in Portland, Oregon.

1944   *Young Children* is first published by NAEYC.

1946   Dr. Spock's *Baby and Child Care* is published. It advocates a more permissive attitude toward children's behavior and encourages exploratory behavior.

1946   Loris Malguzzi starts school of Reggio Emilia, Italy, emphasizing the child's individual creative expression.

1948   USNC OMEP, the United States National Committee of the World Organization for Early Childhood Education, is founded to promote the education of children internationally and begins to consult with UNICEF and UNESCO in the United Nations. It starts publishing a journal, *The International Journal of Early Childhood*, in 1969.

1956   La Leche League is established to provide mothers with information on breast-feeding, childbirth, infants, and child care.

1960   Katherine Whiteside Taylor founds the American Council of Parent Cooperatives, which later becomes the Parent Cooperative Pre-schools International.

1960   Nancy McCormick Rambusch founds the American Montessori movement.

1962   Perry Preschool Project, directed by David Weikart, opens in Ypsilanti, Michigan, and conducts longitudinal study to measure the effects of preschool education on later school and life.

1964–1965   The Economic Opportunity Act of 1964 passes, becoming the foundation of Head Start Programs in the United States, as part of a federal "War on Poverty."

1966   The Bureau of Education for the Handicapped is established.

1966   NANE becomes National Association for the Education of Young Children (NAEYC).

1969   Pediatrician T. Berry Brazelton publishes *Infants and Mothers*, along with several other books and numerous articles advocating a sensible and intimate relationship between parents and children.

FIGURE 1-2 *(continued)*

1969 The Ford Foundation, Carnegie Corporation, and the Department of Health, Education, and Welfare subsidize the Children's Television Workshop, which develops *Sesame Street.*

1971 Stride-Rite Corporation of Boston opens a children's program on site, becoming a vanguard for employer-supported child care.

1972 The Child Development Associate Consortium is started by Edward Ziegler to develop a professional teacher training program (now known as CDA).

1975 PL 94-142, the Education for All Handicapped Children bill, passes, mandating appropriate education for special needs children in the "least restrictive environment" possible, thus defining the concepts of "mainstreaming" and "full inclusion."

1979 The United Nations declares an International Year of the Child.

1982– Marion Wright Edelman establishes the Children's Defense Fund, a Washington-based lobby on behalf of children, and particularly children of poverty and color.

1984 NAEYC publishes a report entitled "Develomentally Appropriate Practices," which outlines what is meant by "quality" work with young children from infancy through age 8.

1985 NAEYC establishes a National Academy and a voluntary Accreditation system for centers, in an effort to improve the quality of children's lives, and confers its first accreditation the next year.

1986 U.S. Department of Education declares the Year of the Elementary School. PL 99-457, amending 94-142, establishes a national policy on early intervention for children as young as infants.

1990 The Child Care Development Block Grant is established to improve the quality, availability, and affordability of child care programs.

1990 U.N. Children's World Summit includes the following goals to be reached by the year 2000: (1) to reduce child mortality below age 5 by one third; (2) to provide universal access to basic education; and (3) to protect children in dangerous situations.

1990 The Americans with Disabilities Act (ADA) is passed, requiring programs of all sizes to care for and accommodate the needs of children with disabilities whenever they are reasonably able to do so.

1991 "Ready to Learn/America 2000," part of the U.S. government's educational strategy for reforming American public schools, is published.

1991 The first Worthy Wage Day, organized by the Child Care Employee Project, is held on April 9, drawing attention to the inadequate compensation of early childhood workers and how this affects the retention of a skilled and stable work force.

1993 The Family and Medical Leave Act (FMLA) passes, providing new parents with 12 weeks of unpaid, job-protected leave.

1996 The first "Stand for Children" demonstration is held in Washington, DC, drawing 200,000 participants.
Rethinking the Brain, published by the Family and Work Institute, summarizes the new research on children's brain development.

1997 The Child Development Permit Matrix is adopted by the California Commission on Teacher Credentialing, introducing the career ladder concept into early childhood public education.

1998 The 100,000th CDA Credential is awarded by Carol Brunson Phillips, Executive Director of the Council for Early Childhood Professionals.

2002 In the U.S., the "Leave No Child Behind" legislation is passed.

2003 Universal preschool is considered as a next step in providing equal access to quality early educational experiences for all children under 5 years of age.

2007 State-funded preschools rose in per-child funding, expanded access, and moved toward higher quality standards.

2008 12 states in the US still provide no state preschool for their children.

made books more available to the common person rather than exclusively to the domain of monks and church-sponsored schools. Martin Luther (1482–1546) urged parents to educate their children by teaching them morals and catechism.

The first humanist educators began to advocate a basic education for all children, including girls and the poor. The call for a *universal education* and *literacy* are two fundamental effects of this period on education as we know it today. Concern for the common man was on the rise, as skilled craftsmen formed a kind of middle class. By the 1500s, schools that taught subjects such as reading, writing, arithmetic, and bookkeeping were fairly common throughout Europe.

The German school system was established at this time and would influence education in all parts of Europe. People changed the way they looked at children and their education. Towns grew and expanded, and there was an opportunity to move to new lands. Living conditions improved and infant mortality waned. Children were living longer. The acquisition of knowledge and skills at an earlier age became important. If educated, children could be expected to help their family improve its situation. Parents found they needed help in teaching their children.

Into Modern Times

Comenius

John Amos Comenius (1592–1670), a Czech educator, wrote the first picture book for children. Called *Orbis Pictus* (*The World of Pictures*, 1658), it was a guide for teachers that included training of the senses and the study of nature. Comenius fostered the belief that education should follow the natural order of things. His ideas included the "school of the mother's lap," in which children's development follows a timetable of its own and their education should reflect that fact. Comenius advocated approaching learning based on the principles of nature. He believed that "in all the operations of nature, development is from within," so children should be allowed to learn at their own pace. He also proposed that teachers should work with children's own inclinations, for "what is natural takes place without compulsion." Teachers must observe and work with this natural order—the timetable—to ensure successful learning. This idea was later reflected in Montessori's sensitive periods and Piaget's stages of development. Today it is recognized as the issue of school **readiness.**

Comenius also stressed a basic concept that is now taken for granted: learning by doing. He encouraged parents to let their children play with other children of the same age. Rather than pushing a standard curriculum, Comenius said that "the desire to know and to learn should be excited … in every possible manner" (Keatinge, 1896). He also reflected the growing social reform that would educate the poor, as well as the rich.

In summary, probably the three most significant contributions of Comenius are *books with illustrations*, an emphasis on *education with the senses*, and the *social reform* potential of education.

Locke

An English philosopher of the 1600s, John Locke (1632–1714) is considered to be the founder of modern educational philosophy. He based his theory of education on the scientific method and the study of the mind and learning. Locke theorized the concept of **tabula rasa,** the

Cornix cornicatur, à à	A a	
The *Crow* crieth.		
Agnus balat, b è è è	B b	
The *Lamb* blaiteth.		
Cicàda stridet, cì cì	C c	
The *Grasshopper* chirpeth.		
Upupa dicit, du du	D d	
The *Whooppoo* saith.		
Infans ejulat, è è è	E e	
The *Infant* crieth.		
Ventus flat, fi fi	F f	
The *Wind* bloweth.		
Anser gingrit, ga ga	G g	
The *Goose* gagleth.		
Os halat, hà'h hà'h	H h	
The *Mouth* breatheth out.		
Mus mintrit, ì ì ì	I i	
The *Mouse* chirpeth.		
Anas tetrinnit, kha, kha	K k	
The *Duck* quaketh.		
Lupus ululat, lu ulu	L	
The *Wolf* howleth.		
[mum		
Ursus murmurat, mum-	M m	
The *Bear* grumbleth.		

Orbis Pictus, by John Comenius, is considered the first picture book written for children.

belief that the child is born neutral, rather than evil, and is a "clean slate" on which the experiences of parents, society, education, and the world are written. He based his theory on the scientific method and approached a child as a doctor would examine a patient. He was one of the first European educators to discuss the idea of individual differences gleaned from observing one child rather than simply teaching a group. Education needed to take the individual learner into account.

The purpose of education, he claimed, is to make man a reasoning creature. A working knowledge of the Bible and a counting ability sufficient to conduct business was the fundamental education required of adults, so children were taught those basics. Locke suggested that such instruction should be pleasant, with playful activities, as well as drills. Locke's influence on education was not felt strongly at the time. Later, however, his best ideas, such as the notion that the teacher must work through the senses to help children reach understanding, were popularized by Rousseau. Today, teachers still emphasize a sensory approach to learning.

In summary, Locke's contribution is felt most in our acceptance of *individual differences*, in *giving children reasons* as the basis for helping children to learn, and in his *theory of a "clean slate"* that points to the effect of the environment on learning.

Rousseau

After Comenius, new thoughts were everywhere in Europe. Locke offered some educational challenges, and Darwin brought a change to science. The time was ripe for new ideas about childhood. Jean Jacques Rousseau (1712–1778), a writer and philosopher, proposed that children were not inherently evil, but naturally good. He is best known for his book *Emile* (1761) in which he raised a hypothetical child to adulthood. He reasoned that education should reflect this goodness and allow spontaneous interests and activities of the children. "Let us lay it down as an incontrovertible rule that the first impulses of nature are always right; there is no original sin in the human heart … the only natural passion is self-love or selfishness taken in a wider sense."

Rousseau's ideas on education in and of themselves were nothing short of revolutionary for the times. Making what might be considered the first comprehensive attempt to describe a system of education according to nature, his concern for the learner led him to these ideas:

- The true object of education should not be primarily a vocational one.
- Children only really learn from firsthand information.

Rousseau advocated that children were naturally good and should have a flexible and less restrained school atmosphere.

- Children's views of the external world are quite different from those of adults.
- There are distinct phases of development of a child's mind and these should coincide with the various stages of education.
- Teachers must be aware of these phases and coordinate their instruction appropriately (Boyd, 1997).

Although he was not an educator, Rousseau suggested that school atmosphere should be less restrained and more flexible to meet the needs of the children. He insisted on using concrete teaching materials, leaving the abstract and symbolism for later years. His call to *naturalism* transformed education in such a way that led educators to eventually focus more on the early years. For instance, he encouraged others to "sacrifice a little time in early childhood, and it will be repaid to you with usury when your scholar is older" (*Emile*, 1761). Pestalozzi, Froebel, and Montessori were greatly influenced by him. The theories of developmental stages, such as of Jean Piaget and Arnold Gesell (see Chapter 4), support Rousseau's idea of natural development. In Europe, his ideas had a ripple effect that sent waves across the Atlantic Ocean.

Rousseau's ideas are still followed today in early childhood classes. *Free play* is based on Rousseau's belief in *children's inherent goodness* and ability to choose what they need to learn. Environments that stress autonomy and self-regulation have their roots in Rousseau's philosophy. Using *concrete rather than abstract materials* for young children is still one of the cornerstones of developmentally appropriate curriculum in the early years.

Pestalozzi

Johann Heinrich Pestalozzi (1746–1827) was a Swiss educator whose theories on education and caring have formed the basis of many common teaching practices of early childhood education. Like Rousseau, he used nature study as part of the curriculum and believed that good education meant the development of the senses. Rather than simply glorify nature, however, Pestalozzi became more pragmatic, including principles on how to teach basic skills and the idea of "caring" as well as "educating" the child. Pestalozzi stressed the idea of the **integrated curriculum** that would develop the whole child. He wanted education to be of the hand, the head, and the heart of the child. Teachers were to guide self-activity through intuition, exercise, and the senses. Along with intellectual content, he proposed that practical skills be taught in the schools. He differed from Rousseau in that he proposed teaching children in groups rather than using a tutor with an individual child. Pestalozzi's works, *How Gertrude Teaches Her Children* and *Book for Mothers*, detail some procedures for mothers to use at home with their children. Probably his greatest contribution is the blending of Rousseau's strong romantic ideals with his own egalitarian attitude: "I wish to wrest education from the outworn order of doddering old teaching hacks as well as from the new-fangled order of cheap, artificial teaching tricks, and entrust it to the eternal powers of nature herself" (in Silber, 1965).

In summary, Pestalozzi's contributions are strongest around the *integration of the curriculum* and *group teaching*. He initiated *sensory education* and blended both *freedom* and *limits* into working with children.

Froebel

Friedrich Wilhelm Froebel (1782–1852) is one of the major contributors to early childhood education, particularly in his organization of educational thought and ideas about learning, curriculum, and teacher training. He is known to us as the "Father of the Kindergarten," not only for giving it a name, but for devoting his life to the development of a system of education for young children. The German word **kindergarten** means **"children's garden,"** and that is what Froebel felt best expressed what he wanted for children less than six years of age. Because his own childhood had been unhappy, he resolved that early education should be pleasant. He attended a training institute run by Pestalozzi and left to promote children's right to play, to have toys, and to be with trained teachers by founding a Play and Activity Institute. Early childhood historian Dorothy Hewes (1993) notes:

> Froebel started his kindergarten in 1836, for children aged about two to six, after he had studied with Pestalozzi in Switzerland and had read the philosophy promoted by Comenius two hundred years earlier. His system was centered around self-activity and the development of children's self-esteem and self-

A Froebelian kindergarten at the end of the nineteenth century.

confidence. In his *Education of Man*, he wrote that "Play is the highest phase of child development—the representation of the inner necessity and impulse." He had the radical idea that both men and women should teach young children and that they should be friendly facilitators rather than stern disciplinarians.

Over 100 years ago, Froebel's kindergartens included blocks, pets, and finger plays. Froebel observed children and came to understand how they learned and what they liked to do. He developed the first educational toys, which he termed "gifts" (*gaben* in German) (Figure 1-3).

Angeline Brooks (1886), a teacher in an American Froebelian kindergarten in the late 1800s, described the gifts this way:

> Froebel regarded the whole of life as a school, and the whole world as a school-room for the education of the [human] race. The external things of nature he regarded as a means to making the race acquainted with the invisible things of the minds, as God's *gifts* for use in accomplishing the purpose of this temporal life. Regarding the child as the race in miniature, he selected a few objects which should epitomize the world of matter in its most salient attributes and arranged them in an order which should assist the child's development at successive stages of growth.

Some of his theories about children and their education later influenced Montessori and were reflected in the educational materials she developed.

Every day, teachers in centers and homes across the country practice the Froebelian belief that one's first educational experiences should be a *child's garden*: full of pleasant discoveries and delightful adventure, where the adults' role is to plant ideas and materials for children to use as they grow at their own pace.

Montessori

At the turn of the century, Maria Montessori (1870–1952) became the first female physician in Italy. She worked in the slums of Rome with poor children and with mentally retarded children. Sensing that what they lacked was proper motivation and environment, she opened a preschool, *Casa di Bambini*, in 1907. Her first class was 50 children from two to five years of age. The children were at the center all day while their parents worked. They were fed two meals a day, given a bath, and provided with medical attention. Montessori designed materials, classrooms, and a teaching procedure that proved her point to the astonishment of people all over Europe and America.

Before her, no one with medical or psychiatric training had articulated so clearly the needs of the growing child. Her medical background added credibility to her findings and helped her ideas gain recognition in this

Froebelian Gifts

When the children are just making friends with the teacher and with each other, it is very interesting and profitable for them to formulate their mite of knowledge into a sentence, each one holding his ball high in the air with the right hand and saying:

My ball is red like a cherry.
My ball is yellow like a lemon.
My ball is blue like the sky.
My ball is orange like a marigold.
My ball is green like the grass.
My ball is violet like a plum.

FIGURE 1-3 When introducing the gifts, the teacher in Froebelian settings would teach children rhymes and finger plays.

Maria Montessori designed materials, classrooms, and learning methods for young children.

Photo courtesy of the Archives of the Association Montessori Internationale country. The Montessori concept is both a philosophy of child development and a plan for guiding growth, believing that education begins at birth and the early years are of the utmost importance. During this time, children pass through "sensitive periods," in which their curiosity makes them ready for acquiring certain skills and knowledge.

Montessori was an especially observant person and used her observations to develop her program and philosophy. For instance, the manipulative materials she used were expensive so they were always kept in a locked cabinet. One day the cabinet was left unlocked, and the children took out the materials themselves and worked with them quietly and carefully. Afterward, Montessori removed the cabinet and replaced it with low open shelves. She noticed that children liked to sit on the floor so she bought little rugs to define the work areas. In analyzing how children learn, she concluded that they build themselves from what they find in their environment, so she designed the school around the size of the children. Because of her enlightenment, a carefully prepared environment with child-sized furniture and materials are common features of early educational classrooms.

By focusing on the *sequential steps of learning*, Montessori developed a set of learning materials still used widely today. One of her most valuable contributions was a theory of how children learn: children teach themselves if only we will dedicate ourselves to the self-creating process of the child. She believed that any task could be reduced to a series of small steps. By using this process, children could learn to sweep a floor, dress themselves, or multiply numbers.

After Montessori was introduced in the United States in 1909, her methods received poor reception and were often misunderstood. Chattin-McNichols (1993) notes that "adaptation of her methods in a variety of ways, a focus on academics by demanding middle-class parents, and a flood of 'trainers' and authors eager

to capitalize on Montessori contributed to a rapid downfall of Montessori schools in the United States by 1925 or so." A second American Montessori movement began in the late 1950s and early 1960s. Differences between European and American society and education generated the American Montessori Society, founded by Dr. Nancy McCormick Rambusch. According to Chattin-McNichols (1993):

> Today with a much wider range of children than ever before, the majority of Montessori schools are private preschools and child care centers, serving 3- to 6-year-old children. But there are many which also serve elementary students and a small (but growing) number of programs for infants, toddlers, and middle-school students. … The word *Montessori*, however, remains in the public domain, so that Montessori in the name of a school or teacher education program does not guarantee any adherence to Montessori's original ideas.

To summarize, Montessori's contributions were substantial to all we do in early childhood programs today. *A prepared environment*, **self-correcting** *and sequential materials*, teaching based on *observation*, and a trust in *children's innate drive to learn* all stem from her work. (Montessori education as a curriculum model is discussed in Chapter 10.)

Steiner

Rudolf Steiner (1861–1925) was an Austrian philosopher, scientist, and artist whose lectures for the German factories of Waldorf-Astoria led to the establishment of schools now known as Waldorf Schools. This system has influenced mainstream education in Europe, and its international reputation is felt in North America today. Steiner theorized that childhood is a phase of life important in its own right, and the environment must be carefully planned to protect and nurture the child (see Figure 1-4).

Steiner's Ages of Childhood

Age	Span	Child Learns by …	Emphasis
The Will	0-7	Imitation	Role models and beautiful environment
The Heart	7-14	Authority	Consistency with enthusiasm and feeling
The Head	14+	Challenge	Intellectual study for real mastery

FIGURE 1-4 Rudolf Steiner created a system of education in the early 1900s that was based on educational goals for the whole child and the transformation of the spirit/soul.

Steiner's philosophy, known as *anthroposophical spiritual science*, emphasized the children's spiritual development, imagination, and creative gifts. As did Froebel and Montessori, Steiner emphasized the whole child and believed that different areas of development and learning were connected into a kind of unity. The role of the teacher is that of a mother figure, and her goal is to allow the child's innate self-motivation to predominate. The teacher is to understand the temperament of each child, and to go with it; thus, play has a large place in Waldorf classrooms.

Self-discipline will emerge from the child's natural willingness to learn and initiate, and the classroom needs to support this self-regulation process. Yet, while the child's inner life is deeply valued by Steiner, experiences in early childhood must be carefully selected. For instance, fairy stories help children acquire time-honored wisdom; modern Waldorf followers insist that television be eliminated.

In summary, for Steiner, the people with whom the child interacts are of central importance. (Waldorf schools are addressed with curriculum models in Chapter 10.)

Nontraditional Perspectives

You can likely notice how traditional early childhood educational practices reinforce European-American values and beliefs. Education is often built from the knowledge base of its teachers; curriculum usually draws from the system—cultural, economic, or political—that is most familiar. If teachers are trained on European writings and the ideas of university-educated Americans, then their own teachings would likely reflect those philosophies.

But there have always been other influences on our child-rearing and educational practices, especially those of our own upbringing or of the communities whose children and families we teach. We know that there is more than one "right way" to care for and educate **DAP** children.

What nontraditional perspectives influenced early childhood education? As mentioned before, information about non-Western early childhood history is not easily accessible (see Additional Resources" for a reading list).

Gonzalez-Mena (2001) summarizes some of these perspectives in this way:

> Historically, attitudes toward childhood in China and Japan were influenced by Confucius' writings (551–479 B.C.), which stressed harmony. Children were seen as good and worthy of respect, a view not held in Europe until more recently.
>
> Native-American writings show close ties and interconnectedness, not only among families and within tribes but also between people and nature. Teaching children about relationships and interconnectedness are historical themes of early education among many indigenous peoples. Strong kinship networks are themes among both Africans and African Americans; people bond together and pool resources for the common good. Whether these contemporary tendencies come from ancient roots, historic, and modern oppression, or all three, remains unclear.

Latin American and Hispanic cultures value children highly and emphasize the importance of cooperation and sensitivity to authority figures. Families from the Pacific Islands stress the connection to family, as well as the importance of respecting one's elders.

Early education practices have been influenced by many of these perspectives. For instance, understanding and accepting each child's family and cultural perspectives includes a working knowledge of the variations in attitudes and child-rearing practices. Learning about nontraditional cultures and behaviors has become critical for professional teachers to honor diversity both in the classroom and in the larger societal context (see Chapters 3 and 9–15).

American Influences

Colonial Days

The American educational system began in the colonies. When thinking of Colonial America, people often envision the one-room schoolhouse. Indeed, this was the mainstay of education in the New England colonies. Although home-teaching of the Bible was common, children were sent to school primarily for religious reasons. Everyone needed to be able to read the Bible, the Puritan

---

DAP   Whether or not an activity or program is developmentally suited to a particular age or individual was put into more modern context in the mid-1980s when specific descriptions were required to support NAEYC's efforts to accredit early education programs. The dynamic nature of "DAP" allows for both basic principles and variation, reflecting the best thinking of the field, as well as requiring periodic evaluation and revision.

fathers reasoned. All children were sent to study, though historically boys were educated before girls. Not only was the Bible used in school, however; new materials like the *New England Primer* and the *Horn Book* were also used.

Early life in the New England colonies was difficult, and estimates run as high as 60 percent to 70 percent of children under age four dying in colonial towns during the "starving season." Discipline was harsh, and children were expected to obey immediately and without question. Parents may have loved their children, but Puritan families showed little overt affection. Children were important as economic tools, and they worked the land and were apprenticed into trades early.

In the South, it was a different story. Plantation owners imported tutors from England or opened small private schools to teach just their sons to read and write. Although the reasons were different from those in New England, the results were similar: a very high percentage of adult readers. From these came the leaders of the American Revolution and the new nation. History can provide us with reminders of the strides that have been made in American history and that the challenge of overcoming bias and unequal access continues.

The Revolutionary War brought the establishment of both the Union and religious freedom. By affirming fundamental principles of democratic liberty, the Founding Fathers paved the way for a system of free, common, public school systems, the first the world had seen (Cubberly, 1920). However, after the Revolutionary War, there were no significant advances in education until the late 1800s. Leaders such as Thomas Jefferson felt that knowledge ought to be available to all, but that opinion was not widely shared. Most of the post-Revolutionary period focused on growing crops and pioneering the frontier, not teaching and educating children. Even by the 1820s, education for the common man was not readily available. Industrialization in both the North and South did little to encourage reading and writing skills. Manual labor and machine-operating skills were more important. Although public schools were accepted in principle, in reality, no tax basis was established to support them.

Children in Enslavement

The first African Americans were not slaves but indentured servants, whose debts repaid by their labor would buy them their freedom. However, by 1620, Africans were brought to the New World as slaves. In many states, children of slaves were not valued as human beings but rather as property of the owner. During the Revolutionary War, many Americans turned against slavery because of the principles of the natural rights of the individual, as embodied in the Declaration of Independence and the United States Constitution. By the early 1800s, most northern owners had freed their slaves, although living conditions for them were generally poor.

Because of the high economic value of children as future laborers, there was a certain level of care given to pregnant women and babies. Osborn (1991) tells of a nursery on a South Carolina plantation around 1850 in which

> … infants and small children were left in a small cabin while the mothers worked in the fields nearby. An older woman was left in charge and assisted by several girls 8–10 years of age. The infants, for the most part, lay on the cabin floor or the porch—and once or twice daily, the mother would come in from the field to nurse the baby. Children of toddler age played on the porch or in the yard and, at times, the older girls might lead the group in singing and dancing.

Prior to the Civil War, education was severely limited for African Americans. Formal schools were scarce, and most education came through the establishment of "Sabbath schools." As part of religious instruction, slaves were often provided literary training. However, many plantation owners found these schools threatening and banned them by making laws prohibiting the teaching of slaves. Another facility then developed—the clandestine, or midnight, school. Because of its necessary secretive existence, few records are available, although it is reasonable to conclude that the curriculum was similar to that of the prohibited Sabbath schools.

After the Civil War, private and public schools were opened for African Americans. Major colleges and universities were founded by the end of the 1800s. Booker T. Washington, born into slavery, founded the Tuskegee Normal & Industrial Institute in Alabama in 1881 and emphasized practical education and intercultural understanding between the two races as a path to liberation. Many former slaves and graduates established schools for younger children. Of integrated schools, Osborn (1991) reports:

> Generally, however, if the schools accepted Blacks at all, it was on a strictly quota basis. … Blacks were often excluded from kindergartens. Thus as the early

Music time at Hampton Institute kindergarten.

childhood education movement began to grow and expand in the years following the Civil War, it grew along separate color lines.

Hampton Institute of Virginia established a laboratory kindergarten for African Americans in 1873, and by 1893, the Institute offered a kindergarten training school and courses in child care. The graduates of Hampton Institute became the teachers at the laboratory school because, in the words of its principal, "[the] students know the children and the influences surrounding them. … Their people are proud to see them teaching. They furnish what has always been a missing link between me and the parents" (Pleasant, 1992). It would be worth investigating whether all laboratory schools for African Americans copied European models, as did those of most American universities, or if they reflected some African influences.

A Progressive Era

By the end of the 1800s, however, a nationwide reform movement had begun. The Progressive Movement of the late 1800s and first half of the 20th century changed the course of education in both elementary and nursery schools in America. Coinciding with the political progressivism in this country, this philosophy emphasized a child-centered approach that gained advocates from both the scientific viewpoint (Dewey, Hall) and those of a psychoanalytic bent (Hill, Isaacs). Some of the major features of the educational progressive philosophy were:

1. We must recognize individual needs and individual differences in children.
2. Teachers [must be] more attentive to the needs of children.
3. Children learn best when they are highly motivated and have a genuine interest in the material.
4. Learning via rote memory is useless to children.
5. The teacher should be aware of the child's total development—social, physical, intellectual, and emotional.
6. Children learn best when they have direct contact with the material (Osborn, 1991).

These beliefs were instrumental in changing the old traditional schools from a strict and subject-based curriculum to one that centered on children's interests as the foundation for curriculum development. Progressives wanted educators to work on "how a school could become a cooperative community while developing in individuals their own capacities and satisfying their own needs" (Dewey, 1916). Although Dewey (1858–1952) and others did not reject the teaching of basic skills, the shift was away from such subject matter education.

Courtesy of Hampton University Archives

Dewey

John Dewey was the first real American influence on American education. Raised in Vermont, he became a professor of philosophy at both the University of Chicago and Columbia University. In the years that followed, Dewey was responsible for one of the greatest impacts on American education of all time.

Dewey believed that children were valuable and that childhood was an important part of their lives. Like Froebel, he felt that education should be integrated with life and should provide a training ground for cooperative living. As did Pestalozzi and Rousseau, Dewey felt that schools should focus on the nature of the child. Until this time, children were considered of little consequence. Childhood was rushed. Children as young as seven were a regular part of the work force—on the farms, in the mines, and in the factories. Dewey's beliefs about children and learning are summarized in Figure 1-5.

Dewey's ideas of schooling emerged from his own childhood and his family life as a parent. Jane Dewey, his sixth child, offered that "his own schooling had bored John; he'd disliked the rigid, passive way of learning forced on children by the pervasive lecture-recitation

method of that time" (Walker, 1997). Furthermore, the Deweys' parenting style caused a stir among friends and neighbors; the children were allowed to play actively in the same room as adult guests, to ignore wearing shoes and stockings, and even to "stand by during the birth [of brother Morris] while Mrs. Dewey explained the process" (Walker, 1997). His passionate belief in the innate goodness of children, in the principle of mind-body unity, and in the encouragement of experimentation shaped John Dewey's ideals.

A new kind of school emerged from these ideals. Even the buildings began to take on a different look. Movable furniture replaced rows of benches. Children's projects, some still under construction, were found everywhere. The curriculum of the school began to focus on all of the basics, not just on a few of the academics. If a group of six-year-olds decided to make a woodworking table, they would first have to learn to read to understand the directions. After calculating the cost, they would purchase the materials. In building the table, geometry, physics, and math were learned along the way. This was a group effort that encouraged children to work together in teams, so school became a society in miniature. Children's social

---

Dewey's Pedagogic Creed

My Pedagogic Creed—John Dewey	What It Means Today
1. "... I believe that only true education comes through the stimulation of the child's powers by the demands of the social situations in which he finds himself."	This tells us that children learn to manage themselves in groups, to make and share friendship, to solve problems, and to cooperate.
2. "... The child's own instinct and powers furnish the material and give the starting point for all education."	We need to create a place that is child-centered, a place that values the skills and interests of each child and each group.
3. "... I believe that education, therefore, is a process of living and not a preparation for future living."	Prepare children for what is to come by enriching and interpreting the present to them. Find educational implications in everyday experiences.
4. "... I believe that... the school life should grow gradually out of the home life ... it is the business of the school to deepen and extend ... the child's sense of the values bound up in his home life."	This sets the rationale for a relationship between teachers and parents. Values established and created in the home should be enhanced by teaching in the schools.
5. "... I believe, finally, that the teacher is engaged, not simply in the training of individuals, but in the formation of a proper social life. I believe that every teacher should realize the dignity of his calling."	This says that the work teachers do is important and valuable. They teach more than academic content; they teach how to live.

FIGURE 1-5 John Dewey expressed his ideas about education in an important document entitled "My Pedagogic Creed." (Washington, DC: The Progressive Education Association, 1897)

Reprinted with permission from Special Collections Research Center, Morris Library, Southern Illinois University Carbondale

John Dewey's lab school involved children in activities of a practical, real-life nature, such as weaving small rugs to use in the classroom.

skills were developed along with reading, science, and math. The teacher's role in the process was one of ongoing support, involvement, and encouragement.

The contribution of John Dewey to American education cannot be underestimated. Dewey's ideas are part of today's classrooms in several ways. His child-oriented schools are a model of child care centers and family child care homes, as learning and living are inseparable. As the following sections on kindergarten and nursery schools illustrate, John Dewey had a vision that is still alive today.

The Field Expands: Kindergarten

The word *kindergarten*—German for "children's garden"—is a delightful term. It brings to mind the image of young seedlings on the verge of blossoming. The similarity between caring for young plants and young children is not accidental. Froebel, the man who coined the word *kindergarten*, meant for that association to be made. As a flower opens from a bud, so too does a child go through a natural unfolding process. This idea—and ideal—are part of the kindergarten story.

The first kindergarten was a German school started by Froebel in 1837. Nearly 20 years later, in 1856, Margaretha Schurz, a student of Froebel, opened the first kindergarten in the United States. It was for German-speaking children and held in her home in Wisconsin. Schurz inspired Elizabeth Peabody (1804–1894) of Boston, who

opened the first English-speaking kindergarten there in 1860. Peabody, in turn, after studying kindergartens in Germany, influenced William Harris, superintendent of schools in St. Louis, Missouri. In 1873, Harris allowed Susan Blow (1843–1916) to open the first kindergarten in the United States that was associated with the public schools. By the 1880s, kindergarten teachers such as Eudora Hailmann were hard at work inventing wooden beads, paper weaving mats, and songbooks to use with active 5-year-old children.

Look at kindergarten in a historical perspective to trace the various purposes of this specialized educational experience. At first, Froebel's philosophy (see section on Froebel earlier in this chapter) was the mainstay of kindergarten education. At the same time, kindergartens began to become an instrument of social reform. Many of the kindergartens started in the late 1800s were established by churches and other agencies that worked with the poor and were called charity kindergartens. For instance, "in the early kindergartens, teachers conducted a morning class for about 15 children and made social calls on families during the afternoon. The children were taught to address the teachers as 'Auntie' to emphasize her sisterly relationship with their mothers" (Hewes, 1993).

Moreover, by early 1900, traditional kindergarten ideas had come under the scrutiny of G. Stanley Hall and others who were interested in a scientific approach to education. Dewey advocated a community-like (rather than garden-style) classroom. A classic clash of ideals developed between followers of Froebel (conservatives) and those of Dewey's new educational viewpoint (progressives). For those who saw kindergartens as a social service in an era of rising social conscience, the reasons for helping the less fortunate were similar to the rationale that led to the creation of Head Start 60 years later.

The emphasis in a Froebelian kindergarten was on teacher-directed learning. Dewey's followers preferred a more **child-centered approach,** with teachers serving as facilitators of children's learning. This is the same tension that exists today between the "back to basics" movement and the supporters of child-centered education. The progressives found fault with the "gifts" of Froebel's curriculum. Those who followed Dewey believed that "real objects and real situations within the child's own social setting" should be used (Read & Patterson, 1980). Froebel was viewed as too structured and too symbolic; Dewey was perceived as child-oriented and child-involved. Even the processes they used were different. Froebel believed in allowing the unfolding of the child's mind and learning, whereas Dewey stressed adult intervention in social interaction.

The reform of kindergarten education led to the creation of the modern American kindergarten. By the 1970s, the trend was to focus on the intellectual development of the child; thus there was an emphasis on academic goals for 5-year-olds. By the late 1990s, the concept of developmentally appropriate practices advocated a shift toward more holistic, broad planning for kindergarten. (Today's kindergarten programs are discussed in Chapter 2.)

Patty Smith Hill

Patty Smith Hill (1868–1946) of Teacher's College, Columbia University, was an outstanding innovator of the time and one of the Progressive Movement's most able leaders. It was she who wrote the song "Happy Birthday," created sets of large blocks (known as "Patty Hill blocks," now known as hollow and unit blocks) and founded the National Association for Nursery Education (NANE). The largest association of early childhood educators, it is known today as the National Association for the Education of Young Children (NAEYC). Trained originally in the Froebelian tradition, she worked closely with G. Stanley Hall and later with John Dewey. Thus her philosophy of classroom teaching was a blended one. She believed strongly in basing curricula and programs on the nature and needs of the children, and she was one of the major education experimenters of her day. She was:

… guided by principles of democracy and respect for individuals. She argued for freedom and initiative for children, as well as a curriculum relevant to children's lives. It was she who originated large-muscle equipment and materials suitable for climbing and construction, a departure from the prescribed small-muscle activities of the Froebelians. Patty Hill also urged unification of kindergarten and first-grade work, but her objective was not to start 5-year-olds on first grade work, as we today might readily assume. Rather, emphasis was on giving six-year-olds the opportunity for independent, creative activities before embarking on the three R's. (Cohen & Randolph, 1977)

These ideas became the backbone of kindergarten practice. Moreover, Hill did not work for kindergarten alone. In fact, during the 1920s, Hill rekindled Froebel's early ideas to promote nursery schools for children too young to attend kindergarten. Regardless of controversy within, kindergartens were still on the fringes of the educational establishments as a whole. In fact, Hill (1941) herself commented that "adjustment to public-school conditions came slowly … [and] until this happy adjustment took place, the promotion of the self-active kindergarten children into the grades has made it possible for the poorest and most formal first-grade teacher to criticize and condemn the work of the best kindergarten teacher as well as the kindergarten cause, because of the wide gap that existed between kindergarten and primary ideals at that time…"

As Hill and others prevailed and made continual improvements in teaching methods, materials, guidance, and curriculum, the interests of kindergarten and primary education could be seen as more unified.

Nursery Schools

Establishment in America

The very phrase "nursery school" conjures up images of a child's nursery, of a carefully tended garden, and of a gentle place of play and growing. In fact, the name was coined to describe a place where children were nurtured (see the section later in this chapter on the McMillan sisters). Nursery schools have always been a place of "care," for the physical needs, the intellectual stimulation, and the socio-emotional aspects of young children's lives.

Early childhood educators took Dewey's philosophy to heart. Their schools reflected the principles of a child-centered approach, active learning, and social coopera-

Reprinted with permission of the Golden Gate Kindergarten Association

Traditional nursery and kindergarten included circle time.

tion. By the 1920s and 1930s, early childhood education had reached a professional status in the United States. Nursery schools and day nurseries went beyond custodial health care. They fostered the child's total development. The children were enrolled from middle- and upper-class homes, as well as from working families. However, until the 1960s, nursery schools served few poor families.

Parent education was acknowledged as a vital function of the school and led to the establishment of **parent cooperative schools.** Brook Farm, a utopian cooperative community in the 1840s, had "the equivalent of an on-site child care center 'for the use of parents doing industrial work' or for mothers to use 'as a kindly relief to themselves when fatigued by the care of children'" (Hewes, 1993). The first of these parent participation schools was developed in 1915 at the University of Chicago, where a group of faculty wives started the Chicago Cooperative Nursery School. (Chapter 2 describes the parent cooperative model in detail.)

Research centers and child development laboratories were started in many colleges and universities from about 1915 to 1930. These laboratory schools were active in expanding the knowledge of how important a child's early years are. As Stolz (1978) describes it, "the [preschool] movement from the beginning was integrated with the movement for child development research. The purpose … was to improve nursery schools, and, therefore, we brought in the people who were studying children, who were learning more about them, so we could do a better job." It is noteworthy that professionals such as Hill, Stolz, Dowley, and others encouraged researchers to share their findings with classroom teachers to integrate these discoveries into the daily programs of children.

These schools followed one of two basic models. One model, patterned after the first psychological laboratory in Leipzig, Germany, in 1879, was formed to train psycholo-

gists in the systematic training of child study. This model adopted a scientific approach to the study of human beings, as the field of psychology itself attempted to become more like the biologic sciences. The second approach, like the Butler School of Hampton Institute and later Spelman College, was established primarily for training teachers. The latter model took its influence almost exclusively from educational leaders. The nursery school laboratory schools attempted a multidisciplinary approach, blending the voices from psychology and education with those of home economics, nursing, social work, and medicine. By 1950, when Katherine Read Baker first published *The Nursery School: A Human Relationships Laboratory* (now in its ninth printing and in seven languages), the emphasis of the nursery school was on understanding human behavior and then building programs, guidance techniques, and relationships accordingly. In her estimate,

> … the nursery school is a place where young children learn as they play and as they share experiences with other children. … It is also a place where adults learn about child development and human relationships as they observe and participate in the program of the school. … Anyone working in an educational program for children, even the most experienced person, needs to be learning as well as teaching. The two processes, learning and teaching, are inseparable.

Lucy Sprague Mitchell

Early childhood education in the United States grew out of John Dewey's progressive movement largely because of Lucy Sprague Mitchell (1878–1967) and her contemporaries. Raised in an environment of educational and social reform, Mitchell developed the idea of schools as community centers, as well as places for children to learn to think. As Greenberg (1987) explained, Mitchell gathered together, in a democratic, cooperative venture, many talented people to brainstorm, mastermind, and sponsor:

- A remarkable Bureau of Educational Experiments
- A school to implement and experiment with these principles
- A laboratory to record and analyze how and why they function as she knew they did (and as we know they do!)
- A teachers' college to promote them
- A workshop for writers of children's literature (a new genre—a number of currently famous authors of juvenile books attended)
- A bulletin to disseminate it all, as well as to disseminate what a plethora of progressive educators were up to elsewhere, *beginning* in 1916!

Strongly influenced by John Dewey, she became a major contributor to the idea of "educational experiments," that is, trying to plan with teachers the curriculum experiences that would then be observed and analyzed "for children's reactions to the various learning situations [and] the new teaching techniques" (Mitchell, 1951). For instance, Mitchell suggested that teachers expand on what they knew of children's "here-and-now" thinking by making

> ... trips with kindergarteners to see how work was done—work that was closely tied up with their personal lives ... the growth in thinking and attitudes of the teachers had moved far ... toward the conception of their role as a guide as differentiated from a dispenser of information.

By establishing Bank Street College of Education (and its laboratory school), Lucy Sprague Mitchell emphasized the link between theory and practice—namely, that the education of young children and the study of how children learn are intrinsically tied together.

Abigail Eliot

The nursery school movement was pioneered by Abigail Eliot (1892–1992). A graduate of Radcliffe College and Harvard University, Eliot had worked with the McMillan sisters (see section in this chapter) in the slums of London. A social worker by training, she became interested in children and their relationships with their parents. Eliot had a lively and clear view of what good schools for children could be. She is generally credited with bringing the nursery school movement to the United States. She founded the Ruggles Street Nursery School in the Roxbury section of Boston, teaching children and providing teacher training, and served as its director from 1922 to 1952, when it was incorporated into Tufts University. Today, it is known as the Eliot-Pearson Department of Child Study.

Eliot became the first woman to receive a doctoral degree from Harvard University's Graduate School of Education and, after retiring from Tufts, moved to California where she helped establish Pacific Oaks College. In all her work, she integrated Froebel's gifts, Montessori's equipment, and the McMillans' fresh air, as well as her own ideas. As she put it (Hymes, 1978):

> ... the new idea—was program. I had visited many day nurseries in Boston as a social worker. I can remember them even now: dull green walls, no light colors, nothing pretty—spotlessly clean places, with rows of white-faced listless little children sitting, doing nothing. In the new nursery school, the children were active, alive, choosing.

Celebrating a birthday in a WPA (Works Progress Administration) nursery program, provided by the Lanham Act for women in the workforce during World War II.

Courtesy of WPA (Works Progress Administration)

Midcentury Developments

Even as the economic crisis of the Depression and the political turmoil of World War II diverted attention from children's needs, both gave focus to adult needs for work. Out of this necessity came the Works Progress Administration (WPA) nurseries of the 1930s and the Lanham Act nurseries of the 1940s. The most renowned program of the midcentury was the Kaiser Child Care Centers.

Kaiser Child Care Centers

During World War II, funds were provided to deal with the common situation of mothers working in war-related industries. Further support came from industry during World War II. An excellent model for child care operated from 1943 to 1945 in Portland, Oregon. It was the Kaiser Child Care Centers. Kaiser became the world's largest such center and functioned "'round the clock" all year long. A number of services were made available on-site. An infirmary was located nearby for both mothers and children. Hot meals were made available for mothers to take home when they picked up their children. Lois Meek Stolz was the director of the centers, and James L. Hymes, Jr. was the manager. He describes the centers this way:

> … The centers were to have three distinctive qualities. One, they were to be located not out in the community but right at the entrance to the two

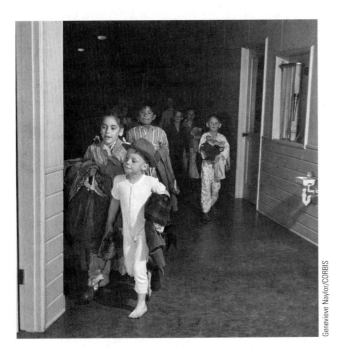

Kaiser Shipyard operated a model child care center during World War II.

Genevieve Naylor/CORBIS

shipyards, convenient to mothers on their way to and from work. They were to be industry-based, not neighborhood-centered. Two, the centers were to be operated by the shipyards, not by the public schools and not by community agencies. They were to be industrial child care centers, with the cost borne by the Kaiser Company and by parents using the service. Three, they were to be large centers, big enough to meet the need. In the original plan, each center was to serve a thousand preschool children on three shifts. (Hymes, 1978)

These centers served 3,811 children. As Hymes points out, they provided 249,268 child care days and freed 1,931,827 woman work-hours.

Once the war had ended, though, the workers left. Child care was no longer needed, and the centers closed. The Kaiser experience has never been equaled, either in the universal quality of care or in the variety of services. However, it left us a legacy, which Hymes has stressed ever since (in Dickerson, 1992): "It is no great trick to have an excellent child care program. It only requires a lot of money with most of it spent on *trained* staff."

The model Kaiser Child Care Centers provided for child care remains exemplary.

Equality in Education

As early as the beginning of the 20th century, the United States Supreme Court upheld laws concerning "the core of the Jim Crow system, the public schools in which white and black children first experienced the reality of segregation … Jim Crow schools—which taught their students only those skills needed for agricultural work and domestic service—fit the needs of the whole economy and society" (Irons, 2004). The term itself comes from a character in a late 1880s minstrel show and refers to the complete system of segregation.

World War I played an important role in moving large numbers of blacks from the rural South to the cities of the North and West, beginning what has been called the Great Migration. By 1930, the reported literacy rate for blacks had doubled from 1900 to just over 80 percent, but "the educational status of blacks in the Jim Crow states remained abysmally low in 1950" (Irons, 2004). The Depression was a particularly difficult time for African Americans, as the living standards for those Americans in poverty plummeted. Roosevelt's administration and the emerging industrial union movement gave impetus to blacks looking for both employment and political change. World War II continued the process of transformation for many adults, but for children, the situation was still bleak. The stage for another legal challenge to segregation was set. As Weinberg (1977) states, "Midcentury marked a turning point in the history of black America. The movement for equality came under black leadership, embraced unprecedented numbers of Negroes, and became national in scope. A persistent black initiative forced a reformulation of public policies in education."

The attack against the segregation system had begun. As seen in the historic cases of *McLaurin v Oklahoma* (1950) and *Brown v Board of Education of Topeka* (1954) the concept of "separate but equal" was overturned. Furthermore, the Civil Rights Act of 1964 continued to address the struggle for equality of opportunity and education, one that persists today in our schools and society (see "Ethic of Social Reform" later in this Chapter).

"Free School"

A. S. Neill (1883–1973) was the most famous proponent of the "free/natural school" movement of the mid-century. His book *Summerhill* describes 40 years of that educational program, of which he was headmaster. Neill claimed that most education was defective because it arose from the model of original sin. Assuming children were inherently evil caused educators to force children into doing what was contrary to their nature. Neill shared Rousseau's belief in noninterference, as he states, "I believe that a child is innately wise and realistic. If left to himself without adult suggestion of any kind, he will develop as far as he is capable of developing" (1960).

Neill's belief in freedom was practiced in his school, where children governed themselves and worked toward equal rights with adults. The benefits from such liberties were touted as highly therapeutic and natural, an escape from repression and guilt. Several influences are clear in these educational programs: Rousseau's belief in the *child's innate goodness*, Freud's idea of the *dangerous effects of guilt*, and some of the *social idealism* of Dewey and the Progressives.

Head Start

After the war, few innovations took place until a small piece of metal made its worldwide debut. Sputnik, the Soviet satellite, was successfully launched in 1957 and caused an upheaval in educational circles. Two questions were uppermost in the minds of most Americans: Why were we not first in space? What is wrong with our schools? The emphasis in education quickly settled on engineering, science, and math in the hope of catching up with Soviet technology.

Head Start is the largest publicly funded education program for young children in the United States.

The civil rights struggle in the early 1960s soon followed. In pointing out the plight of the poor, education was highlighted as a major stumbling block toward equality of all people. It was time to act, and Project Head Start was conceived as education's place to fight the "war on poverty." The same goals of Froebel and Montessori formed the basis of Head Start: helping disadvantaged preschool children. This was a revolution in American education, not seen since the short-lived child care programs during World War II. This project was the first large-scale effort by the government to focus on children of poverty.

Project Head Start began in 1965 as a demonstration program aimed at providing educational, social, medical, dental, nutritional, and mental health services to preschool children from a diverse population of low-income families. In 1972, it was transformed into a predominantly part-day, full-year program. Key features included offering health services, small groups, parent-teacher collaboration, and the thrill of communities getting involved with children in new ways. Osborn (1965) tells us:

> I wish I knew how to tell this part of the story ... the bus driver in West Virginia who took time off from his regular job and went to the Center to have juice and crackers with "his" children because they asked him to. ... The farmer who lived near an Indian Reservation and who each morning saddled his horse, forded a river and picked up an Indian child—who would not have attended a Center otherwise ... they represent the true flavor of Head Start.

Over the years, Head Start has provided comprehensive developmental services to more than 10 million children and their families.

This was an exciting time, a national recognition of the needs of young children and a hope for a better quality of life. Head Start was an attempt to make amends, to compensate poor children by preparing them for school and educational experiences. Parents, who were required to participate at all levels, were educated along with their children. The purpose of the community-based governing boards was to allow the program to reflect local values and concerns. Concurrently, underprivileged, poor people were being encouraged to take part in solving some of their own problems.

The spirit of Head Start was infectious. As a result of community interest in Head Start, there was a burst of enthusiasm for many programs for the young child. Thanks to Head Start, there is national attention to the need for providing good care and educational experiences for young children. The Head Start program is recognized as an effective means of providing comprehensive services to children and families, serving as a model for the development of the ABC Child Care Act. (The program is discussed in Chapter 2.)

Early Child Care for the Very Young

Some people say we are in the midst of a second child care revolution for young children, as two parents, single parents, and step-parents all leave the home to work in greater numbers than ever before. Parents must rely on educators to teach their children from a very young age, including infants. While many European industrialized nations have addressed these issues, the United States has not completely faced this reality or risen to the challenge.

The American public is unclear about what is the best way to raise our very young children, especially those under age 3. Women, by and large, are working outside of the home and are not available around the clock to care for infants and toddlers; men are not, by and large, electing to stay home or raise their children full time. There are not nearly enough properly funded centers or family child care homes for very small children, and the patchwork system of parents, extended family, and neighborhood adults fragments the care.

We need to look carefully at child care for infants and toddlers, questioning the relationship between child care and children's development. The women's movement of the 20th century brought attention to deeply held beliefs about child-rearing and early education practices. Then, when America was mobilized around World War II, chil-dren's care was addressed so as to enable mothers to work while fathers were in the armed forces. During the last 35 years, both parents have once again focused on work outside the home. Care for children by extended family, family child care homes, and centers is on the rise.

Interdisciplinary Influences

Several professions enrich the heritage of early childhood. This diversity was apparent from the beginning as the first nursery schools drew from six different professions: social work, home economics, nursing, psychology, education, and medicine. Three of the most consistent and influential of those disciplines were medicine, education, and child psychology.

Medicine

The medical field has contributed to the study of child growth through the work of several physicians. These doctors became interested in child development and extended their knowledge to the areas of child rearing and education.

Maria Montessori

Maria Montessori (1870–1952) was the first woman in Italy ever granted a medical degree. She began studying children's diseases and, through her work with mentally defective children, found education more appealing. (Her philosophy is discussed earlier in this chapter and will be part of the Chapter 10 curriculum models.)

Sigmund Freud

Sigmund Freud (1856–1939) made important contributions to all modern thinking. The father of personality theory, he drastically changed how we look at childhood. Freud reinforced two specific ideas: 1. a person is influenced by his early life in fundamental and dramatic ways, and 2. early experiences shape the way people live and behave as adults. Thus psychoanalytic theory is mostly about personality development and emotional problems. Freud's work set into motion one of the three major strands of psychological theory that influence the developmental and learning theories of early childhood today. Though he was not involved directly in education, Freud and psychoanalytic theory influenced education greatly. (Chapter 4 will expand on the theory and its application in early childhood education.)

Arnold Gesell

Arnold Gesell (1880–1961) was a physician who was concerned with growth from a medical point of view. Gesell began studying child development when he was a student of G. Stanley Hall, an early advocate of child study. He later established the Clinic of Child Development at Yale University, where the data he collected with his colleagues became the basis of the recognized norms of how children grow and develop. He was also instrumental in encouraging Abigail Eliot to study with the McMillan sisters in England.

Gesell's greatest contribution was in the area of child growth. He saw maturation as an innate and powerful force in development. "The total plan of growth," he said, "is beyond your control. It is too complex and mysterious to be altogether entrusted to human hands. So nature takes over most of the task, and simply invites your assistance" (Gesell, Ames, & Ilg, 1977).

Through the Gesell Institute, guides were published using this theory. With such experts as Dr. Frances Ilg and Dr. Louise Bates Ames, Gesell wrote articles that realistically portrayed the child's growth from birth to adolescence. These guides have sharp critics regarding their overuse and inappropriate application to children of cultures other than those studied. Moreover, their approach can be limiting, particularly as we think of developmentally appropriate practices and the importance of both individual variation and family and cultural diversity. Still, the "ages and stages" material (described in the Word Pictures of Chapter 3) is used widely as a yardstick of normal development. (Gesell's maturation theory is discussed in Chapter 4.)

Benjamin Spock

Benjamin Spock's book *Baby and Child Care* was a mainstay for parents in the 1940s and 1950s. In a detailed "how-to" format, Dr. Spock (1903–1998) preached a common-sense approach that helped shape the childhood of many of today's adults. By his death in 1998, the book had sold almost 50 million copies around the world and had been translated into 42 languages.

Spock saw himself as giving practical application to the theories of John Dewey (see this chapter) and Sigmund Freud (see Chapters 1 and 4), particularly in the ideas that children can learn to direct themselves, rather than needing to be constantly disciplined.

Medical doctors such as Benjamin Spock have contributed to early care and education in significant ways.

Spock suggested that mothers use the playpen less and allow children freedom to explore the world first-hand. To that end, he asked parents to "child proof" their homes—a radical thought at the time. The word *permissiveness*, as it relates to child-rearing, became associated with Dr. Spock's methods, although Spock himself described his advice as relaxed and sensible, while still advocating for firm parental leadership.

Dr. Spock became an outspoken advocate for causes that extended his ideas. He was an active critic of those forces—economic, social, or political—which destroy healthy development. Dr. Spock noted:

> Child care and home care, if well done, can be more creative, make a greater contribution to the world, [and] bring more pleasure to family members, than 9 out of 10 outside jobs. It is only our mixed-up, materialistic values that make so many of us think the other way around (1976).

T. Berry Brazelton

Dr. T Berry Brazelton (1918–) is a well-known pediatrician who supports and understands the development of infants and toddlers. He developed an evaluation tool called the Neonatal Behavioral Assessment Scale (the NBAS is also known as "the Brazelton") to assess newborns. Co-founder of the Children's Hospital Unit in Boston, professor emeritus of pediatrics at Harvard Medical School, and a former president of the Society for Research in Child Development, he is also a well-known author. His pediatric guides for parents deal with

DAP

DAP   One of the tenets of DAP is developing reciprocal relationships with families so that educators can better understand children's ages and stages in the context of their home, community, and cultural dimensions.

both physical and emotional growth. His writings speak to the parents' role in child-raising, such as setting limits, listening to what children say, and observing what they do, as in the following discussion:

> I think many working parents have a very tough time thinking about limits. They find it difficult to say no, to set behavior standards. … Parents tell me, "I can't stand to be away all day and then come home and be the disciplinarian." We have to realize how hard it is for parents to discipline these days. They need a lot of reinforcement to understand how important reasonable discipline is to the child. Teachers can be very important here, helping parents see the need to expect more adequate behavior (2001).

More recently, Brazelton has advocated a national parental leave standard and is involved in a federal lobbying group known as "Parent Action." He is also a popular TV personality, hosting the nationally syndicated show, *What Every Baby Knows*. He is co-founder of *Touchpoints*, an educational training center helping professionals engage and communicate with parents and their infants or toddlers.

Education

Early childhood is one part of the larger professional field known as education. This includes elementary, secondary, and college or postsecondary schools. Along with John Dewey and Abigail Eliot, several other influences from this field bear attention.

The McMillan Sisters

In the first three decades of this century, these two sisters pioneered in early education. Nursery schools in Britain and America probably were developed because of the drive and dedication of the McMillan sisters.

Both women had broad international backgrounds. They grew up in North America and Scotland. Margaret studied music and language in Europe. She was well read in philosophy, politics, and medicine. Rachel studied to become a health inspector in England.

Health studies of 1908 to 1910 showed that 80 percent of children were born in good health, but by the time they entered school, only 20 percent could be classified that way. Noticing the deplorable conditions for children under age 5, the McMillan sisters began a crusade for the slum children in England. Their concern extended beyond education to medical and dental care for young children. In 1910, they set up a clinic in Deptford,

Margaret McMillan, along with her sister Rachel, developed the "open-air" nursery school and training schools in England.

From Margaret McMillan: Portrait of a Pioneer, © 1989 Routledge. Reproduced by permission of Taylor & Francis Books UK

a London slum area, which became an open-air nursery a year later. The McMillans called it a "nurture school." Later, a training college nearby was named for Rachel. With no private financial resources, these two women faced tremendous hardships in keeping their school open. It is to their credit that Deptford still exists today.

The McMillans' theory of fresh air, sleep, and bathing proved successful. "When over seven hundred children between one and five died of measles, there was not one fatal case at Deptford School" (Deasey, 1978). From the school's inception, a primary function was to research the effects of poverty on children.

Of the two sisters, Margaret had the greatest influence at the school at Deptford. After Rachel died in 1917, Margaret continued to champion early education issues beyond Deptford. "Her clinics, night camps, camp school, baby camp, open-air nursery school, and training college all reflected her conviction that health was the handmaiden of education" (Bradburn, 2000). Abigail Eliot writes of her:

> Miss McMillan invented the name [nursery school]. She paid great attention to health: a daily inspec-

tion, the outdoor program, play, good food—what she called "nurture." But she saw that an educational problem was also involved and she set to work to establish her own method of education for young children. This was why she called it a "school" (Hymes, 1978).

Susan Isaacs

Susan Isaacs (1885–1948) was an educator of the early 20th century whose influence on nursery and progressive schools of the day was substantial. In 1929, she published *The Nursery Years*, which emphasized a different point of view than that of the behaviorist psychologists of the times. She interpreted Freudian theory for teachers and provided guidance for how schools could apply this new knowledge of the unconscious to the education of children. She proposed:

> ... the opportunity for free unhindered imaginative play not only as a means to discover the world but also as a way to reach the psychic equilibrium, in working through wishes, fears, and fantasies so as to integrate them into a living personality (Biber, 1984).

The teacher's role was different from that of a therapist, she asserted, in that teachers were "to attract mainly the forces of love, to be the good but regulating parent, to give opportunity to express aggression but in modified form, and not to attract herself to the negative explosive reactions of hatred and oppression" (Biber, 1984).

Isaacs's influence is felt today in schools whose philosophy emphasizes the child's point of view and the notion of play as the child's work.

The Child Study Movement

A survey of education influences is incomplete without mentioning the Child Study Movement in the United States beginning in the 1920s. It was through this movement that education and psychology began to have a common focus on children. Besides the Gesell Institute, many research centers and child development laboratories were established at colleges and universities around the country. The Merrill-Palmer Institute, for example, began in 1920 as a school to serve Detroit, Michigan's urban children and later served as a model for the Head Start Program; in addition, it sponsored research and training about children and families. These laboratory schools (discussed further in Chapter 2) reflect the interest of several disciplines in the growth of the young child. Schools of psychology looked for children to observe and study; schools of education wanted demon-

The history of early childhood education includes contributions from many ethnic groups. San Francisco's Golden Gate Kindergarten Association has provided nursery education for the city's various neighborhoods from the turn of the century to the present.

Reprinted with permission of Golden Gate Kindergarten Association

stration schools for their teachers-in-training and for student-teacher placement. Schools of home economics wanted their students to have firsthand experiences with children. Schools of education hoped to develop leadership from among its teaching and research staff (Harms & Tracy, 2006). These on-campus schools provided a place to gather information about child development, psychology, and educational innovation.

This period of educational experiments and child study led to an impressive collection of normative data by which we still measure ranges of ordinary development. Broman (1978) sums up the influence of the movement this way:

> From the beginning of the child study movement in the 1920s ... early childhood was not a major emphasis in education until after the War on Poverty and the establishment of Head Start in 1965. The child study movement, however, was the impetus that began the search for the most appropriate means of educating young children.

The British Infant Schools

Developed by Robert Owen in the early 19th century, the British infant schools had a strong commitment to social reform. Owen was a self-made businessman whose philosophy extended to the creation of an ideal community. Like Rousseau, he believed that people were naturally good but were corrupted by harsh environment and poor treatment. He took his ideas to the British House of Commons, speaking against the common practice of child labor. He then was invited to take over the building of a school in New Lanark, a 2000-person community near several textile mills. Once there, he stopped employment of children under ten, sent younger children to nursery and infant schools he built, and required the mills to allow secondary-age children to reduce their labor time to go to school. His son and a daughter immigrated to the United States and founded the community of New Harmony. Both utopian communities were built on Owen's ideas of a new social order built on experimentation and reform.

In England, the term *infant school* refers to the kindergarten and primary grades. In 1967, the Plowden Report proposed a series of reforms for the schools. These changes paralleled those of Owen and mainstream American early education. Three aspects of this **open school** style that received the most attention were:

1. *Vertical (or mixed age) groupings.* Children from 5 to 8 years of age are placed in the same classroom. Several teachers may combine their classes and work together in teaching teams. Children may be taught by the same teachers for two or three years.
2. *Integrated day.* The classroom is organized into various centers for math, science, and the arts. The teacher moves from one child or center to another as needed. Play is often the central activity, with an emphasis on follow-through with children's ideas and interests as they arise.
3. *Thinking over facts.* There is an underlying concept that the process of thinking takes precedence over the accumulation of facts. Learning how to think rather than stockpiling data is encouraged. How to identify and solve problems is valued more than having a finished product. Teachers focus on the child's current learning rather than on the future.

Just as Owen's ideas took hold in America in the 19th century, so, too, did the 20th century version of the infant school fire the imaginations of teachers in the United States. Their tenets of open education are developmentally appropriate for both preschool and primary schools.

Reggio Emilia

In the last part of this century, yet another educator and educational system have influenced early childhood thinking. Loris Malaguzzi (1920–1994) developed his theory of early childhood education from his work with infants, toddlers, and preschoolers while working as the founder and Director of Early Education in the town of Reggio Emilia, Italy. His philosophy includes creating "an amiable school" (Malaguzzi, 1993) that welcomes families and the community and invites relationships among teachers, children, and parents to intensify and deepen to strengthen a child's sense of identity. Malaguzzi continually asked teachers to question their own practices and listen to the children, as we can hear in his letter (Gandini, 1994) excerpted below:

> My thesis is that if we do not learn to listen to children, it will be difficult to learn the art of staying and conversing with them. … It will also be difficult, perhaps impossible, to understand how and why children think and speak; to understand what they do, ask, plan, theorize or desire. … Furthermore, what are the consequences of not listening? … We adults lose the capacity to marvel, to be surprised, to reflect, to be merry, and to take pleasure in children's words and actions.

Reggio Emilia has attracted the attention and interest of American educators because of its respect for children's work and creativity, its project approach, and its total community support. (Reggio Emilia serves as a model of early childhood curriculum in Chapters 2, 9, and 10.)

Psychology

The roots of early childhood education are wonderfully diverse, but one taproot is especially deep: the connection with the field of psychology. In this century particularly, the study of people and their behavior is linked with the study of children and their growth.

Initially, child development was mostly confined to the study of trends and descriptions of changes. Then, the scope and definition of child development began to change. Psychodynamic theories of Freud and Erikson were contrasted by Behaviorist theories of Watson and Skinner and by the Cognitive theories of Piaget and Vygotsky. Bowlby and Ainsworth studied attachment, Kohlberg and Eisenberg moral development, and Maccoby and Gilligan gender differences.

Developmental psychologists now study the processes associated with those changes. Specifically, child development focuses on language acquisition, the effect of early experiences on intellectual development, and the process of attachment to others. Most recently, social learning and self-efficacy along with brain-based research are included to describe these important influences in early education. Such is the world of early childhood—it is no wonder that we are so closely tied to the world of psychology. (This is discussed in depth in Chapter 4.)

Themes in Early Childhood Education

When we review the colorful and rich history of early childhood education, four major themes emerge. Each is reflected in the ensuing thought and theory of each age.

Ethic of Social Reform

The first theme, **the ethic of social reform,** expects that schooling for young children will lead to social change and improvement. Maria Montessori, Robert Owen, the McMillans, Patty Smith Hill, Abigail Eliot, and the Head Start program all tried to improve children's health and physical well-being by attending first to the physical and social welfare aspects of children's lives. Other more recent examples, including Marian Wright Edelman, Louise Derman Sparks, Robert Coles, and Jonathan Kozol, illustrate how important this theme is to our work.

Marian Wright Edelman is an outstanding children's advocate. A graduate of Spelman College and Yale Law School, Edelman began her career as a civil rights lawyer (the first black woman to be admitted to the Mississippi state bar). By the 1960s she had dedicated herself to the battle against poverty, moving to Washington, D.C., and founding a public interest law firm that eventually became the Children's Defense Fund (CDF). CDF has become the United States' strongest voice for children and families (see Figure 1-6).

The author of several books, including *Families in Peril, The Measure of Our Success,* and *The Sea Is So Wide and My Boat Is So Small,* Edelman advocates for equity in social reform:

> [We] seek to ensure that no child is left behind and that every child has a Healthy Start, a Head Start, a Fair Start, a Safe Start, and a Moral Start in life with the support of caring families and communities (Edelman, 2006).

CDF: Child Advocacy as Social Reform

1975	Assisted in passing the Education for All Handicapped Children Act
1979	Blocked attempts to eliminate $200 million for Social Services
1980	Supported Adoption Assistance & Child Welfare Act
1982	Helped forward the Children's Mental Health Program
1990	Supported Act for Better Child Care (Child Care & Development Block Grant)
1994	Reauthorized Head Start with Quality Improvements
1997	Promoted Children's Health Insurance Program (CHIP)
2001	Expanded Child Care Tax Credit
2002	Food Stamp provisions preserved
2003	Preserved CHIP funding to all states
2007	Evaluation of the CDF freedom schools, summer enrichment programs, find that children score higher on standardized reading achievement tests.
2008	Published its annual State of America's Children, reporting that it lags behind nearly all industrialized nations in key child indicators.

FIGURE 1-6 Children's Defense Fund, led by Marian Wright Edelman, has successfully advocated for children with research and persistence for more than three decades.

This reform work is being carried on by her son, Jonah, who now organizes the annual Washington, D.C., rally "Stand for Children."

Louise Derman Sparks, in collaboration with Betty Jones and the Anti-Bias Task Force of Pacific Oaks and Julia Olsten Edwards of Cabrillo College, has published several books and countless articles about anti-bias education. These works outline several areas in which children's behavior is influenced by biases in our society and suggests a host of ways that teachers (and parents) can begin addressing these issues. These professionals have added an important dimension to the notion of social reform, for they focus our attention on ourselves, the school environment, children's interactions, and the community of parents and colleagues in educational settings.

DAP

DAP   In planning appropriate curriculum for young children, teachers must make a comprehensive effort to plan for children's development and learning, including integrating cultural awareness and the effects of bias into their daily practices.

Finally, social reform in the last 20 years has been championed by educators and citizens beyond early childhood education. Robert Coles, a psychiatrist and educator, has written and lectured extensively about his observations and work with children of poverty and is best known for *Children of Crisis: A Study of Courage and Fear* (1971). Jonathan Kozol has spoken extensively about segregation in the schools, most notably in his books *Letters to a Young Teacher* (2007) and *Savage Inequalities: Children in America's Schools* (1991), in which he writes:

> Surely there is enough for everyone in this country. It is a tragedy that these good things are not more widely shared. All our children ought to be allowed a stake in the enormous richness of America. Whether they were born to poor white Appalachians or to wealthy Texans, to poor black people in the Bronx or to rich people in Manhasset or Winnetka, they are all quite wonderful and innocent when they are small. We soil them needlessly.

A challenge of our profession is to create funding mechanisms to provide early educational experience for *all* children regardless of family income. Founded in 1948, the Annie E. Casey Foundation, one of the largest private foundations in the United States, is based on helping vulnerable kids and families succeed. Educators today still assert that tired, undernourished children are not ready to learn or to be educated. Social reform can go a step further, such as with Universal Preschool (see Chapter 15), improving access to quality early childhood programs and involving the community in its efforts.

Importance of Childhood

The second theme is **the importance and uniqueness of childhood.** In fact, the entire notion of the importance of childhood rests on the concept of the child as a special part of human existence and, therefore, a valuable part of the life cycle. Before 1700 or so, Western society showed little concern for children. Infanticide was pervasive, if not actually accepted. Once families and society began to value children, life changed dramatically for the young.

The saying "As the twig is bent, so grows the tree" could apply to all children and their early childhood learning experiences, as well as to an individual child. When people accepted the importance of childhood, they began to take responsibility for a quality life for children. From Comenius, Rousseau, and Froebel of earlier centu-

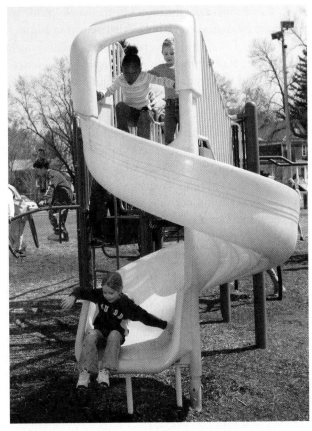

Childhood is a special time of life.

ries to Neill, Russell, and the Child Study Movement of the 1900s, society began to provide for the health and physical welfare of children and come to understand the necessity to care for their minds. Reflecting on public thinking about childhood over the last four centuries reveals these patterns (Mintz, 2004):

- pre modern childhood (through 17th century)—children as adults in training
- modern childhood (18th–20th centuries)—children as innocent and fragile creatures
- post modern childhood (late 20th to 21st centuries)—children as participants/consumers of culture and the common life

We believe the early years form the foundation for later development, physically, intellectually, socially, and emotionally. This viewpoint takes a holistic approach; that is, all developmental areas of a child matter and blend together to form a complete child. Teachers may "sort out" the various aspects of development to concentrate their focus. (Chapter 4 elaborates on developmental issues.) For instance, a teacher may profile the child's motor skills or level of language development.

Even so, we must take into account the whole child, for each part influences the whole. A current trend in our field to address the preservation of childhood is NAEYC's developmentally appropriate practices (DAP) and accompanying Program Accreditation movement. (Chapters 2 and 9 expand on DAP and Program Quality.)

Moreover, we must take the child in context. Children come to us with a genetic history and from, as Gonzalez Mena (2001) states, "a family that is part of a racial, ethnic, cultural, language, and socioeconomic group. We welcome not only the individual child into our classroom but also his or her family." (Chapter 8 develops this aspect further.)

Believing that childhood is a special time of life brings with it a commitment to honor what children do during this time. Childhood has always been a biological phase of human development, but "the ways in which childhood and adolescence are conceptualized and experienced are social and cultural constructions that have changed dramatically over time (Mintz, 2004). For example, we now believe that play is essential to children's development (see Chapters 3. 9, and 10), but this importance is not widely understood.

One trend that is of increasing concern to childhood advocates is the "pushing" of children toward adulthood too fast and away from childhood too quickly (see Chapters 12, 13, and 15 for a discussion of this trend). David Elkind wrote in the 1980s of a "hurried child" syndrome, in which children were pushed unnecessarily out of a relaxed childhood by a fast-paced society whose pressure to succeed and move fast put children of all ages at risk. As he emphasized (1982):

> We should appreciate the value of childhood with its special joys, sorrows, worries, and concerns. Valuing childhood does not mean seeing it as a happy, innocent period but rather as an important period of life to which children are entitled. They have a right to be children, to enjoy the pleasures and to suffer the trials of childhood that are infringed upon by hurrying. Childhood is the most basic human right of children.

Children need special attention during these years. Childhood is fundamentally different from adulthood; it needs to be understood and respected as such. Children's styles of learning, of letting the child "learn by doing" and "learn by discovery," are part of the essential respect for children and childhood. Public recognition of that need has created a wealth of programs for the young not dreamed of at any other time in history.

Transmitting Values

The third recurrent theme in our educational heritage is that of **transmitting values.** What children should ultimately *do* and *be* is at the core of all child-rearing practices, whether in the home or the school. Values—whether social, cultural, moral, or religious—have been the essence of education for centuries. For example, the Puritan fathers valued biblical theology. Therefore, schools of their time taught children to read in order to learn the Bible. Rousseau and Froebel valued childhood, so they created special places for children to express their innate goodness and uniqueness. The works of Montessori, Dewey, and Steiner reflected a belief in the worth and dignity of childhood. They transmitted these values into the educational practices we have inherited. Finally, the initiators of Head Start (see Chapter 2) and the Anti-Bias Curriculum (see Chapter 9) realized that the child's self-worth would be enhanced by valuing one's culture or origin. Awareness and appreciation of ethnic heritage are becoming a integral parts of the early childhood curriculum.

Many issues clamor for our attention. We live in a world of information overload and are barraged constantly by different social, political, economic, and media issues. Especially in the United States, where advertising and consumerism reign, we get distracted and have difficulty focusing on our values. "People are so overwhelmed," wrote Brazelton and Greenspan (2001). "While they're whirling around, they don't have time to stop and think, 'What are my values? Do my children really come first? Am I making time for them in my life?'" Many young families today are aware of this situation and are looking for spiritual and moral direction for themselves and their

Early educational experiences transmit society's values to children.

children. Look at "What do you think?" for an outline of issues that indicate priority areas.

We know that children learn what they live. Valuing and connecting home cultural knowledge with an early childhood program is challenging. Successful teaching practices must reflect teaching practices at home in substantial ways; blending basic life skills, ethics, culture, and traditions builds substance in our children and in our society. This teamwork is possible if (and this is a big *if*) adults can find a way to honor diversity and still form a cohesive culture. "An ability to reach unity in diversity will be the beauty and test of our civilization," said Mahatma Gandhi. It is our ethical responsibility to articulate our values as educators and to include those of the families we teach.

Teaching children to live in a democratic society has always been valued in the United States. In the curriculum from early education through college, this belief is reflected as we educate our children for citizenship. Being an early childhood educator provides you with the opportunity to be an agent for social change—to actually translate the values of democracy into practice. Valuing and connecting home cultural knowledge with a program is a challenge that brings together the adults critical to a child's development (Riojas-Cortz 2003). Successful teaching practices include the process of defining our values and working on how we teach them; both are the critical issues in education.

What Do YOU Think?

What are your values for young children? What do you think are priorities in your program? Compare your list with this one, by Brazelton and Greenspan (2001).

1. Ongoing nurturing relationships
2. Physical protection, safety, and regulation
3. Experiences tailored to individual differences
4. Developmentally appropriate experiences
5. Limit-setting, structure, and expectations
6. Stable, supportive communities and cultural continuity

Professionalism

The fourth recurrent theme is professionalism. "If you are thinking about working with young children as a career, perhaps you are wondering how early childhood

TeachSource Video

Watch the TeachSource Video Case entitled "Teaching as a Profession: An Early Childhood Teacher's Responsibilities and Development". After you study the video clip, view the artifacts, and read the teacher interviews and text, reflect upon the following questions:

1. How does pre-school teacher Samantha Brade show her sense of the importance of early childhood education, and what values is she trying to transmit?

2. How does Samantha demonstrate professionalism, and why should this inform one's teaching?

education compares in prestige and importance with elementary or secondary education," wrote Stanford's Edith Dowley (1985). As one of the original head teachers of the Kaiser Child Care Centers, Dowley had seen many changes in her nearly half-century in the field: "Is it truly a profession for growth and change? Can a student preparing to work with young children today look forward to a challenging, intellectually stimulating, and rewarding future in an early childhood profession?"

If you have read this chapter, then you already know the answer. The early years are a special time of life, and those who work with young children can openly declare their calling. There are four aspects of this sense of professionalism:

- *Sense of identity.* Early childhood professionals see themselves as caregivers who strive to educate the whole child, taking into consideration the body, the mind, and the heart and soul. (Chapter 3 explains this holistic focus.)
- *Purpose to engage in developmentally appropriate practices* (DAP). What constitutes quality care and education calls for blending three knowledge bases:

1. Child development and learning.
2. The strengths, interests, and needs of each child.
3. The social and cultural contexts in which children live.

(You will see DAP icons and comments throughout the text; Chapter 2 further defines it, and Chapters 9 through 14 demonstrate how to teach in this way.)

■ *Commitment to ethical teaching and to child advocacy.* Being a professional means behaving with a child's best interests in mind, keeping confidentiality when discussing issues in the classroom and about families, upholding a code of ethics, and taking themselves and their work seriously. (Chapter 5 elaborates on a teacher's role and includes our Code of Ethical Conduct.)

■ *Participation in the work as a legitimate livelihood.* Early childhood education is more than glorified babysitting; the people who provide care and education to young children deserve wages and working conditions that are worthy of their efforts. The Center for the Study of Child Care Employment, led by Marcy Whitebook and others, is attempting to both define and highlight the issues of labor and employment of early childhood workers as a profession. (Chapter 15 underscores the importance of compensation and working conditions.)

"In the last decade and a half, the boundaries of the profession have changed rather dramatically for teachers. As we have become a more complex and diverse society, the roles traditionally ascribed to teachers have taken new meaning and significance. In the case of teachers of young children, their role has expanded to encompass many, heretofore, duties and responsibilities that were often considered to be part of the home" (Cruz, 2008). The challenges we face in meeting our professional obligations are considerable. Cruz continues:

Aside from the traditional roles that teachers have assumed, they are now expected to serve as curriculum specialists, diagnosticians, health care providers, family counselors, adult educators, program managers, child development experts, child advocates, mental health specialists, nutrition specialists, and many others too numerous to list. At the same time, the teaching profession is confronting new notions of pedagogy and more intense scrutiny by professional groups. With the focus on standards, readiness initiatives, assessment, and other forms of accountability, the field of early education is truly being reinvented.

So where do we go from here? We have professional organizations to guide us. The National Association for the Education of Young Children (NAEYC) is the largest, best known organization. Two others are the Association for Childhood Education International (ACEI) and Society for Research in Child Development (SRCD). The Children's Defense Fund (CDF) advocates for children, particularly addressing the needs of poor and minority children and those with disabilities. These organizations have made improvements in the status of children, and they have begun to outline standards and practices for the people who call themselves "early childhood professionals." (See Figure 1-7.)

These four aspects—an ethic of social reform, the importance of childhood, the transmission of values, and professionalism of the field—have been have been at the center of early education for centuries. Occasionally one theme dominates, as it did in the 1960s when the desire for social reform led to the creation of Head Start. At other times, they seem indistinguishable from one another. Together, they have shaped the direction of early

Guides to the Early Childhood Profession

Document	Goal	Source/Access
Code of Ethical Conduct	Provide a moral compass for early childhood educators	Feeney & Freeman (1999) Appendix A
Developmentally Appropriate Practices	Provide guidance about current understandings, values, and goals for working with children in group settings	Bredekamp & Copple (1998) Chapters 2 and 9
Program Accreditation Criteria & Procedures	Establish recommended standards for practice, serving as benchmarks	NAEYC Academy (2006) Chapters 2 and 15
Early Childhood	Guidelines for teacher education	Hyson (2003)
Professional Preparation	Advancing careers in child development	Sharpe (2002)

■ **FIGURE 1-7** Documents that promote professionalism in early childhood education.

Insights *from the field*

A Delightful Story *by Scott M. Williams, M.S.*

The field of Early Child Education eagerly awaits, with hopeful expectation, your special contribution. "What could I possibly have to offer?" you ask. Your own history, or life story, is your greatest asset. Tucked away in your own early years are special experiences that can shape the lives of small children.

Your background is vitally important to the lives of others. The strengths and weaknesses of your life add a richness and diversity to the ever-growing tapestry of early child education. Your cultural heritage and life experiences enable you to touch children in a unique and powerful way.

A troubled childhood does not make you exempt from being a contributor. Remember Friedrich Froebel, the founder of kindergarten who was inspired to make a difference because of his unhappy childhood. The difficulties of our background can create an understanding and sensitivity to the challenges others face. If you were fortunate to be raised in a family with an abundance of love and resources, then children are waiting for you to share your gift with them.

Writing Your Own Story

A reflective search into your own early childhood can reveal these treasures. Writing is a powerful medium to accomplish this. Questions follow that will stimulate your thinking. For many of us, we may not have clear memories of these early stages of life. Therefore, draw upon the stories and memories that have been offered by your family and others who knew you then. If you find that you cannot answer a question, simply move onto the next, then plan on asking a family member who may be able to offer insight into your answer. We encourage you to write and save your answers for future reference. Addressing these questions later in your professional journey may provide fresh insights.

When finished with these questions, you may want to continue writing your story by responding to the phrase: "When I was a toddler ..." or "When I was six ...."

Regarding your early years:

1. What expectations does your culture have for young children? (Consider what messages society sends to families about the activities in which these children should participate.)

2. In which activities did you participate as a child less than eight years old? (Remember the toys with which you may have played or activities your family said you liked.)

3. Did you participate in preschool? If so, what was the setting? Was it in your home, the home of others, a neighborhood child care facility, or a larger group center? (You might consider how it was physically organized and the people involved.)

4. Were your contacts with others ethnically diverse or localized to one cultural group? (Cultural identity can be defined in many ways such as geographical, religious, racial, and so forth. Many of our identities include many cultures; that is, they are multicultural.)

5. What did you gain from those early years that will help you as an early childhood educator? (Look for a way this can be passed to others.)

6. Describe one way you would like to improve the early childhood education you received. (By rethinking what you did not receive, you can change this in the lives of those you are involved with.)

Your personal story and love of children can be your greatest motivators in this field. Return often to your story to find fresh treasures to share with those young people you serve.

Scott M. Williams is on the faculty of California State University at Northridge in the Human Development department and is in private practice as a marriage, family, and child counselor.

- -

childhood education as we know it today. As we learn more about children, society, and ourselves, the 21st century will be a time to reconsider and redefine our aims and directions. It is a formidable challenge—and a worthy one. "Ours is a profession that is constantly growing," reminds Dowley, "branching out in many directions and ready to meet emerging challenges in flexible, innovative ways."

SUMMARY

The history of early childhood education is like a tapestry—woven of many influences. A broad field such as medicine is a thread in this cloth, as is the passion of a Patty Smith Hill or a Lucy Sprague Mitchell. The history forms the theory on which we base our teaching. Every child, every class, and every experience translates our history into educational practice and makes another thread in this grand cloth.

Events of history have had a hand in shaping early childhood education. Forces such as war (which produced the Kaiser Shipyards project), political movements (such as progressivism), and the state of the economy (which brought the War on Poverty and Head Start) bring about change and development in how children are cared for in this country. The ingredients that early childhood educators consider essential today—that care and education are inseparable, that teaching practices are developmentally appropriate, and that adequate funding is critical for success—all stem from historical events and people.

Several fields of study and a number of professions have added to our knowledge of children and thus have affected educational theory. From the professions of education, medicine, and psychology, early childhood education has developed ideas of what is best for children. These influences will be described at length in Chapter 4.

The individuals who created our history have had a profound effect on early childhood theory and practices.

Their strong and passionate beliefs have captured our imaginations and fueled our commitment to enhancing the well-being of children. What John Comenius, Maria Montessori, and Marian Wright Edelman all had in common was a drive to extend themselves on behalf of young children. Thus, early childhood theory has a *personal* component, an emotional investment that gives each of you a sense of belonging to a larger cause. The work that has gone before goes on through us and extends beyond us—to children of all ages and any era.

Each historical figure posed questions about the nature of childhood, of children, and of teaching. The answers have influenced educational philosophy and practice, and, in turn, have been affected by the social, political, religious, and economic forces of the day. Early childhood education itself is an interdisciplinary field, with important contributions from medicine, education, and psychology. From a child's garden to the child care model, each innovation has added to our "story." The four themes—the ethic of social reform, the importance of childhood, transmitting values, and professionalism—shape our ideas of ourselves in our work.

The contributions of many pioneers leave us dreams for the young children of our society. This can give meaning to our lives as teachers as we continue to create a climate for the child who will make history tomorrow.

KEY TERMS

professionalism
early childhood education
building block years
readiness
tabula rasa
integrated curriculum

kindergarten/children's garden
self-correcting
child-centered approach
parent cooperative schools
open school
vertical groupings (mixed age)

integrated day
ethic of social reform
importance and uniqueness
   of childhood
transmitting values

REVIEW QUESTIONS

1. Identify and describe five key people who influenced the field of early childhood education. With whom would you like to have studied or worked? Why?

2. Match the name with the appropriate phrase. Put them in the order that best matches your own theory of early childhood education. State your reasons.
   Rousseau   "prepared environment"
   Montessori   "nurture" school

Froebel	children are naturally good
Malaguzzi	father of kindergarten
Dewey	common-sense approach
Spock	first picture book for children
McMillan sisters	Progressive Movement
Comenius	Reggio Emilia

3. Define early childhood education in your own words. Include age ranges and what you believe to be its purpose. Contrast this to the text definition and defend your position.

4. Name three institutions or living persons who are influencing the history of early childhood today. Describe your reactions to each and how they have influenced your educational philosophy.

5. Read the list below of some nontraditional and mainstream perspectives as described in the chapter. After each, trace its original root and put at least one example of how this perspective could be practiced in an early childhood classroom today.

Perspective	Roots in Early Childhood Practice
Harmony	
Kinship networks	
Close ties to nature	
Respect for elders	
Cooperative work	
Expressiveness	

6. Maria Montessori made several contributions to education. What are some of her theories, and how did she adapt them for classroom use? How are Montessori materials or teaching methods used in your classroom?

7. Name the four themes that have guided early childhood education throughout its history.

LEARNING ACTIVITIES

1. Find out when and by whom the school or center in which you are teaching was started. What were some of the social, economic, and political issues of those times? How might they have affected the philosophy of the school?

2. Write your own pedagogic creed. List five of what you consider to be the most important beliefs you hold about educating young children. How do you see those beliefs expressed in school today?

3. Make a list of the values you think are important to teach children. In an adjoining column, add the ways in which you would help children learn those values. In other words, list the materials and curriculum you would use.

4. Consider an informal interview with the director. What philosophies are important? Ask to look at any old photos, handbooks, or newspaper clippings. Do you think starting a history of your program would be useful?

HELPFUL WEBSITES

American Federation of Teachers Educational Foundation   **http://www.aft.org**

Annie E. Casey Foundation   **http://www.aecf.org**

Association for Childhood Education International   **http://www.acei.org**

British Infant School   **http://www.sparatcus.schoolnet.co.uk**

Center for the Study of the Child Care Workforce   **http://www.irle.berkeley.edu/cscce**

The Children's Defense Fund http://www.childrensdefense.org

National Association for the Education of Young Children http://www.naeyc.org

National Center for Children and Poverty http://www.nccp.org

National Institute for Early Education Research http://www.nieer.org

North American Reggio Emilia Alliance http://www.reggioalliance.org

Society for Research in Child Development http://www.srcd.org

Waldorf Schools http://www.waldorfanswers.org

 Additional resources including the TeachSource Videos can be found on the premium website for this book. Go to **http://www.cengage.com/login** to register your access code.

REFERENCES

Aries, P. (1962). *Centuries of childhood*. New York: Knopf.

Bain, W. E. (1967). *75 years of concern for children*. Washington, DC: Association for Childhood Education International.

Baker, K. R. (1950). *The nursery school: A human relationships laboratory*. New York: Saunders.

Biber, B. (1984). *Early education and psychological development*. New Haven, CT: Yale University Press.

Boyd, D. (1997). Jean Jacques Rousseau. Unpublished paper. Redwood City, CA: Canada College.

Bradburn, E. (2000). Margaret MacMillan: 1860-1933. In A. Gordon & K. W Browne (Eds.), *Beginnings and beyond* (5th Ed.). Clifton Park, NY: Thomson Delmar Learning.

Brazelton, T. B., & Greenspan, S. (2001). *The irreducible needs of young children: what every child must have to grow, learn and flourish*. Cambridge, MA: DaCapo Press.

Bredekamp, S., & Copple, C. (Ed.). (1998). *Developmentally appropriate practice in early childhood programs*. Washington, DC: NAEYC.

Broman, B. L. (1978). *The early years in childhood education*. Chicago: Rand McNally College Publishing.

Brooks, A. (1886). *Four active workers*. Springfield, MA: Milton Bradley.

Caniff, D. I. (1990, November 28). Why the "Waldorf" movement is thriving in Eastern Europe. *Education Week*, X(13).

Chattin-McNichols, J. (1993). In A. Gordon & K. W Browne (Eds.), *Beginnings and beyond* (3rd Ed.). Clifton Park, NY: Thomson Delmar Learning.

Cohen, D. H., & Randolph, M. (1977). *Kindergarten and early schooling*. Englewood Cliffs, NJ: Prentice-Hall.

Coles, R. (1971). *Children of crisis: A study of courage and fear*. New York, NY: Houghton Mifflin.

Comenius, (1658). *Orbis Pictus* (The World of Pictures).

Copple, C., & Bredekamp, S. (2006). *Basics of developmentally appropriate practice*. Washington, DC: NAEYC.

Cottrol, R.J., Diamond, R.T., & Ware, L.B. (2004, Summer). The Decline of the Idea of Caste: Setting the Stage for *Brown v. Board of Education*. American Educator, AFT.

Cubberly, E. P. (1920). *A brief history of education*. Boston: Houghton Mifflin.

Deasey, D. (1978). *Education under six*. New York: St. Martin's Press.

DeMause, L. (1974). *The history of childhood*. New York: Psychohistory Press.

Derman Sparks, L. (1988). *The anti-bias curriculum*. Washington, DC: NAEYC.

Derman-Sparks, L. & Olsen Edwards, J. (2010) *Anti-bias education for young children and ourselves*. Washington, DC: NAEYC.

Dewey, J. (1897, 1916). *My pedagogic creed*. Washington, DC: The Progressive Education Association and Democracy and Education.

Dickerson, M. (1992, Spring). James L. Hymes, Jr.: Advocate for young children. *Childhood Education*.

Dowley, E. (1985). Early childhood education in the shipyards. In A. Gordon & K. W Browne, *Beginnings and beyond* (1st Ed.). Clifton Park, NY: Thomson Delmar Learning.

DuBois, W E. B. (1995). The talented tenth. Published in The Negro Problem (1903), excerpted in F. Schultz (Ed.), Sources: *Notable selection in education*. Guilford, CT: Dushkin.

Edelman, M. W (2006). *The state of America's children*. Washington, DC: Children's Defense Fund.

Elkind, D. (1982). *The hurried child.* Reading, MA: Addison-Wesley.

Feeney, S., & Freeman, N. K. (1999). *Ethics and the early childhood educator: Using the NAEYC Code.* Washington, DC: NAEYC.

Froebel, F. (1887). *The education of man* (M. W Hailman, Trans.). New York: D. Appleton.

Gandini, L. (1994, July). Tribute to Loris Malaguzzi. *Young Children, 49*(5).

Gesell, A. L., Ames, L. A., & Ilg, F L. (1977). *The child from five to ten.* New York: Harper & Row.

Gonzalez-Mena, J. (2001). *Foundations: Early childhood education in a diverse society.* Mountain View, CA: Mayfield.

Greenberg, P. (1987, July). Lucy Sprague Mitchell: A major missing link between early childhood education in the 1980s and progressive education in the 1890s-1930s. *Young Children, 42*(5).

Harms, T. & Tracy, R. (2006, July). University Laboratory Schools in Early Childhood Education. *Young Children, 61* (4).

Hewes, D. (1993). On doing history. In A. Gordon & K. W Browne (Eds.), *Beginnings and beyond* (3rd Ed.). Clifton Park, NY: Thomson Delmar Learning.

Hill, P. S. (1996). Kindergarten. From the American Educator Encyclopedia (1941). In Paciorek & Munro. Sources: *Notable selections in early childhood education.* Guildford, CT: Dushkin.

Hilliard, A. G., III. (1997, September). Teacher education from an African American perspective. In J. Irvine (Ed.), *Critical knowledge for diverse teachers and learners.* Washington, DC: AACTE.

Hymes, J. L., Jr. (1978-79). *Living history interviews (Books 1-3).* Carmel, CA: Hacienda Press.

Hyson, M. (Ed.) (2003). *Preparing early childhood professionals: NAEYC's standards for programs.* Washington, DC: NAEYC.

Irons, P. (2004, Summer). Jim Crow's Schools. *American Educator,* AFT.

Kauerz, K. (2005, March). State kindergarten policies: Straddling early learning and early elementary school. *Young Children* on the Web: Beyond the Journal.

Keatinge, M. W (1896). *The great didactic of John Amos Comenius* (Trans. and with introductions). London: Adams and Charles Black.

Kozol, J. (1991). *Savage inequalities: Children in America's schools.* New York: Crown Publishers.

Malaguzzi, L. (1993, November). For an education based on relationships. *Young Children.*

McMillan, M. (1919). *The nursery school.* London and Toronto: J. M. Dent & Sons; New York: E. P. Dutton.

Mintz, S. (2004). *Huck's raft: A history of American childhood.* Cambridge, MA: Belknap Press of Harvard University.

Mitchell, L. S. (1951). *Our children and our schools.* New York: Simon & Schuster.

Montessori, M. (1967). *The Montessori method* (Trans. A. E. George). Cambridge, MA.

National Academy. (2006). *Accreditation criteria & procedures (Revised).* Washington, DC: NAEYC.

Neill, A. S. (1960). *Summerhill: A radical approach to child rearing.* New York: Hart.

Osborn, D. K. (1991). *Early childhood education in historical perspective* (3rd Ed.). Athens, GA: Education Associates.

Pleasant, M. B. B. (1992). *Hampton University: Our home by the sea.* Virginia Beach, VA: Donning.

Read, K., & Patterson, J. (1980). *The nursery school & Kindergarten: Relationships and learning* (7th Ed.). New York: Holt, Rinehart, & Winston.

Riojas-Cortez, M., Flores, B.B., & Clark, E.R. (2003, November). Valuing and connecting home cultural knowledge with an early childhood program. *Young Children* on the Web: Beyond the Journal.

Rousseau, J. J. (1761). *Emile* (Trans. by B. Foxley). London and Toronto: J. M. Dent & Sons.

Sharpe, C. (2002). *Advancing careers in child development in California.* Pasadena, CA: Pacific Oaks College & Children's School.

Silber, K. (1965). *Pestalozzi: The man and his works.* (2nd Ed.). London: Routledge and Kegan Paul.

Sparks, L. D. (1989). *Anti-bias curriculum: Tools for empowering young children.* Washington DC: National Association for the Education of Young Children.

Spock, B. (1947). *The common sense book of baby and child care.* New York: Duell, Sloan & Pierce.

Spock, B. (1976, April). Taking care of a child and a home: An honorable profession for men and women. *Redbook Magazine.*

Spodek, B., Saracho, O. N., & Peters, D. L. (Eds.) (1988). *Professionalism and the early childhood practitioner.* New York: Teachers College Press.

Steiner, R. (1926). *The essentials of education.* London: Anthroposophical Publishing.

Stolz, L. M. (1978). In Hymes, J. *Living history interviews.* Carmel, CA: Hacienda Press.

Walker, L. R. (1997, Fall). John Dewey at Michigan. *Michigan Today.*

Weinberg, M. (1977). *A chance to learn: The history of race and education in the United States.* Cambridge, MA: Cambridge University Press.

Courtesy of the author

Types of Programs

PREVIEW QUESTIONS

- What is meant by "developmentally appropriate practices" (DAP)?

- How do early childhood programs serve diverse needs?

- What are the core programs of early childhood education?

- What are some of the variations in early care and education?

- How is the age range extended in early childhood programs?

- What are factors that influence program quality?

- Why and how are programs evaluated?

NAEYC CODE OF ETHICAL CONDUCT

These Core Values and sections from the NAEYC Code of Ethical Conduct are addressed in this chapter. As you read, note how the Core Values, Ideals, or Principles listed here apply to the topics in this chapter. (Reprinted with permission from the National Association for the Education of Young Children.)

Section I:
I-1.2   To base program practices upon current knowledge in the field of child development and related disciplines and upon particular knowledge of each child.

P-1.4   For every child we shall implement adaptations to teaching strategies, learning environment, and curricula, consult with the family, and seek recommendations from appropriate specialists to maximize the potential of the child to benefit from the program.

Section II:
I-2.5   To interpret each child's progress to parents within the framework of a developmental perspective and to help families understand and appreciate the value of developmentally appropriate early childhood practices.

P-2.2 We shall inform families of program philosophy, policies, and personnel qualifications, and explain why we teach as we do, which should be in accordance with our ethical responsibilities to children.

Section IV:
I.4.1 To provide the community with high quality (age and individually appropriate, and culturally and socially sensitive) education/care programs and services.
P.4-7 We shall be familiar with laws and regulations that serve to protect the children in our programs.

Developmentally Appropriate Practice in Early Childhood Programs

Throughout this text and whenever NAEYC principles are discussed, we use the term *developmentally appropriate practice*. What exactly is **developmentally appropriate practice,** or **DAP,** as it is more familiarly known?

More than 20 years ago, NAEYC published a position paper, which articulated standards for high quality care and education for young children. The guidelines were a response to the need for a set of unified standards for accreditation through NAEYC's newly established National Academy of Early Childhood, and gave a necessary antidote to the more teacher-directed, academic preparation and skills-teaching methods that were encroaching on many early childhood programs.

The DAP approach stressed the need for activity-based learning environments based on what we know about children through years of child development research and what we observe of their interests, abilities, and needs. The position paper was revised by NAEYC in 1996, 2005, and 2009 to be more inclusive by moving away from an "either/or" point of view to that of "both/and." In other words, there are many right ways to apply DAP principles.

Three Core Considerations of DAP

The position statement of "Developmentally Appropriate Practice in Early Childhood Programs Serving Children from Birth through Age 8" (NAEYC, 2009) cites three core considerations on which teachers and caregivers should base their decisions about young children's growth and development:

1. *What is known about child development and learning*—knowledge of age-related characteristics that permit general predictions about what experiences are likely to best promote children's learning and development. This is the core around which the idea of *developmentally appropriate* is built.
2. *What is known about each child as an individual*—what practitioners learn about each child that has implications for how best to adapt and be responsive to individual variations.
3. *What is known about the social and cultural contexts in which children live*—the values, expectations, and behavioral and linguistic conventions that shape children's lives at home and in their communities that practitioners must strive to understand in order to ensure that learning experiences in the program or school are meaningful, relevant, and respectful for each child and family.

The following scenario shows how these core considerations are applied when planning a developmentally appropriate program for toddlers:

1. *What does child development tell us about toddlers?* We know that toddlers express their need to do everything by themselves, usually more than they can actually achieve. They like to feel independent and learn quickly if given a little help and then encouraged to do what they can for themselves (see Chapters 3 and 4 for more detail).
2. *What do we know about each child as an individual?* Many of these toddlers rely on their parents to help them put on their clothes, feed them, or put their toys away. Others are being taught these tasks at home. Most of the children come to the teachers for assistance and a few ask for help. One toddler will persist at a dressing task for nearly five minutes while another will throw shoes across the floor if they do not fit the first time.
3. *What do we know about the social and cultural context in each child's life?* Most of the children in this group come from homes in which help is readily available from siblings and extended family members. The group's dominant cultural values and child-rearing practices reinforce dependence and community, although there is a smaller group of families that want their children to become independent as soon as possible.

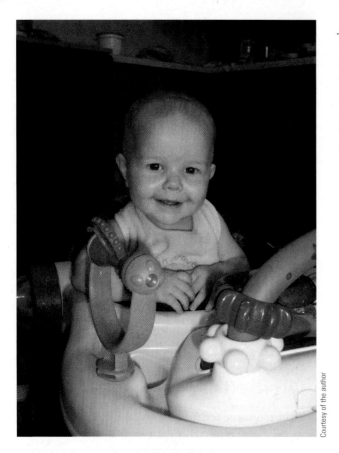

Courtesy of the author

A developmentally appropriate program takes into consideration this child's age, individual abilities, and the culture of her home and family.

By looking at all three core considerations together, we have some decisions to make about setting goals toward greater independence for the toddlers. Respecting cultural and social contexts means we begin by talking to families, perhaps at a parent meeting, in which families are invited to share their child-rearing practices from their cultural viewpoint. Once we have an understanding of what families expect and want, we have an opportunity to work together to find a solution that will be beneficial both for the toddlers and for the families. This is what Hyun (1998) refers to as "negotiable curriculum, where teachers are no longer the ultimate power holders in any decision-making." When developmentally appropriate elements are taken into consideration, the bonds between families and teachers are strengthened and the best interests of the children prevail.

Guidelines for DAP

DAP provides the context for learning environments in which children's abilities are matched to the developmental tasks they need to learn. Programs are designed

for young children based on what is known *about* young children (Bredekamp & Copple, 1997). To that mix, we add what we know about the individual children and their families. This collective knowledge is applied to each decision that is made about the program. Copple and Bredekamp (2009) suggest five key areas of practice that guide the decision-making process, with references to locations in this text that address these key areas:

1. *Creating a Caring Community of Learners.* As noted in Chapter 1, from the earliest beginnings, teachers have been encouraged to blend education and care and to create child-centered environments; this chapter defines programs that support and value all children, regardless of age, ability, gender, or racial and ethnic background. Chapter 3 describes the many ways children are alike, yet different and unique. Using the Word Pictures, teachers can develop programs that support a learning community that includes children with special needs. Chapters 7 and 8 discuss the respectful, cooperative, and positive relationships that lead to optimum learning conditions. Chapter 9 defines the total learning environment that has a secure, comfortable, and positive emotional climate to support the learning community.

2. *Teaching to Enhance Development and Learning.* Chapter 4 provides the theoretical foundation that influences learning, and Chapter 5 defines teaching practices and relationships that create challenging learning experiences. Chapters 10 to 14 demonstrate how teaching across the developmental domains and disciplines strengthens children's learning.

3. *Planning Curriculum to Achieve Important Goals.* Chapter 10 defines and elaborates how to create curriculum based on the goals that are set for children's learning. Chapters 11 to 14 articulate the learning potential through physical growth, language, cognition, and social/emotional experience that children need.

4. *Assessing Children's Development and Learning.* Observation is a key element in evaluating children's learning, and Chapter 6 provides many models to follow. The same chapter also explores the meaning of assessment in order to implement the practices and programs that will guide teaching and learning.

5. *Establishing Reciprocal Relationships with Families.* The focus of Chapter 8 is developing collaborative relationships with families that promote a sense of partnership based on mutual need, understanding, and negotiation.

Each chapter of this text, individually and collectively, supports and demonstrates these five guidelines for developmentally appropriate practices in developmentally appropriate programs.

DAP

DAP in Action

Developmentally appropriate principles are reflected when:

- Programs and curriculum respond to the children's interests as well as their needs.
  Example: While digging in the sand pit, four children uncover water. Others rush to see it. The teacher sees their interest and asks them about the bridges and tunnels they are starting to build. A project in the making: children conduct research, experiment, build, and learn.
- Children are actively involved in their own learning, choosing from a variety of materials and equipment.
  Example: Some children search the yard for materials that will bridge the water. Others go inside to find the big book on bridges. Still others dig in other areas of the sandpit to find more water and to try building tunnels for the water. One child finds a walnut shell and floats it on the water. The teacher encourages and supports each child's involvement.
- Play is the primary context in which young children learn and grow.
  Example: Each day, the children rush outside to see their bridges and tunnels. The teacher has helped them find materials that will act as a cover over the bridge. Inside, several children are making dolls from twigs and fabric scraps to use in the project.
- Teachers apply what they know about each child and use a variety of strategies, materials, and learning experiences to be responsive to individual children.
  Example: Josephina is drawing a picture of the bridge and is having trouble with the arches. Knowing that Josephina is somewhat shy and uneasy in large groups, the teacher asks Aldo (who is easygoing and loves to draw) to look at Josephina's picture to see if he might help her. The two children focus on the drawing, each making observations that help Josephina take the next step in her artwork.
- Teachers consider widely held expectations about each age group and temper that with challenging yet achievable learning goals.
  Example: In preparation for a field trip to see two bridges that are near the school, the teacher sets out her expectations (walk with a buddy, stay together, stay on the sidewalk, do not run, etc.). Because this is their first field trip of the school year, the teacher rehearses the children for several days prior to the trip. Music and rhythm accompany them as they practice walking with a friend and play number games of "two-by-two" during group times.
- Teachers understand that any activity has the potential for different children to realize different learning from the same experience.
  Example: After the field trip, Josephina draws a different type of arch for her bridges. Selena, Gracie, and Sam take over the block corner to build bridges and tunnels; three others join them. Maddie finds a book on flowers; they look like some of the flowers she saw on the way to the bridges. Reilly wants to play London Bridge at group time.
- All aspects of development—physical, social/emotional, cognitive, and language—are integrated in the activities and opportunities of the program.
  Example: The bridge project promoted physical (walking, digging), cognitive (learning how bridges and tunnels are built, researching in books), language (construction terms, such as piers, spans, suspension), social-emotional (pairing up two-by-two), and creative (drawing a bridge, adding flowers, trying tunnels).

Each of these examples shows how to meet the needs of all children, no matter their abilities and background. Keep in mind that while each principle defines one particular factor, all of the principles are interrelated and that cultural and social differences, for instance, will be a factor in all of the principles.

How DAP Benefits Children's Learning

Developmentally appropriate principles benefit children in many ways including the following:

1. In constructing children's own understandings of concepts and benefit from instruction by more competent peers and adults.
2. Through opportunities to see connections across disciplines through integration of curriculum and from opportunities to engage in in-depth study.
3. With a predictable structure and routine in the learning environment and from the teacher's flexibility and spontaneity in responding to their emerging ideas, needs, and interests.

DAP The broad principles of DAP fit all programs and are based on the decisions that utilize all five of these interrelated guidelines.

4. By making meaningful choices about what children will do.
5. From situations that challenge children to work at the edge of their capacities and from ample opportunities to practice newly acquired skills.

Developmentally and Culturally Appropriate Practice (DCAP)

Culturally appropriate practice is the ability to go beyond one's own **sociocultural** background to ensure equal and fair teaching and learning experiences for all. This concept, developed by Hyun, expands DAP to address cultural influences that emphasize the adult's ability to develop a "multiple/multiethnic perspective" (1998). Preparing teachers and caregivers for multiculturalism is not just about becoming sensitive to race, gender, ethnicity, religion, socioeconomic status, or sexual orientation, according to Hyun. It is also related to an understanding of the way individual histories, families of origin, and ethnic family cultures make us similar to and yet different from others. Through such insights, teachers will be able to respond positively to the individual child's unique expressions of growth, change, learning styles, culture, language, problem-solving skills, feelings, and communication styles (Hyun, 1998).

Hyun stresses the need for "cultural congruency" between a child's home and school experience and suggests the following questions as a way to begin addressing the issue:

1. What relationships do children see between the activity and work they do in class and the lives they lead outside of school?
2. Is it possible to incorporate aspects of children's culture into the work of schooling without simply confirming what they already know?
3. Can this incorporation be practiced without devaluing the objects or relationships important to the children?
4. Can this practice succeed without ignoring particular groups of people as "other" within a "dominant" culture? (1998)

A consistency between home and school would "allow for children to express and show the importance of their own family culture and identity" by "using children's personal experience, family culture, and diverse language

DAP

TeachSource Video ▶❚❚

Watch the TeachSource Video Case entitled "Curriculum Planning: Implementing Developmentally Appropriate Practice in an Early Childhood Program." After you study the video clip, view the artifacts, and read the teacher interviews and text, reflect upon the following questions:

1. What examples of Developmentally Appropriate Practices did you see or hear mentioned by preschool teacher Ke Nguyen and her colleagues? Compare and contrast your observations with the text.

2. How would you judge the quality of this program? What are some of the criteria you would use?

---

expressions as important sources of learning and teaching" (Hyun, 1998).

The third core component of DAP, addressing the social and cultural contexts in which children live, highlights the importance of connecting a child's sense of cultural continuity between home and school.

Early Childhood Programs: Serving Diverse Needs

From the types available, to the numbers of children who attend these schools, the name of the game in early childhood programs is diversity. The range can encompass a morning nursery school for toddlers, a primary school classroom, an infant-parent stimulation program, or a full child care service for 3- to 6-year-olds. Some programs run for only a half-day; others are open from 6:00 a.m. until 7:00 p.m. Still other centers, such as hospitals, accept children on a drop-in basis or for 24-hour care. Child care arrangements can range from informal home-based care to more formal school or center settings. Religious institutions, school districts, community-action groups, parents, governments, private social agencies, and businesses may run schools.

DAP Schools may be the first place where families and children experience cultures different from their own. It is important that children learn facts and not stereotypes about other cultures.

Individual attention and warm relationships are essential components of every program.

Factors That Determine Types of Programs

Programs in early childhood settings are defined by many factors, and each is an integral part of the mission of the program. Any given program is a combination of these factors and each has an impact on the quality and type of learning that takes place. Some of the factors that influence programs are:

1. Ages of the children who are being served
2. Philosophical, theoretical, or theological ideals
3. Goals of the program
4. Purpose for which the program was established
5. Requirements of sponsoring agency
6. Quality and training of teaching staff
7. Shape, size, and location of physical environment
8. Cultural, ethnic, economic, and social make-up of the community
9. Financial stability

Programs for young children also exist to serve a number of needs, which impact programs goals and mission. Some of these are:

- Caring for children while parents work (e.g., family child care homes or child care centers)

- Enrichment programs for children (e.g., half-day nursery school or laboratory school)
- Educational programs for parent and child (e.g., parent cooperatives, parent–child public school programs, or high school parent classes)
- An activity arena for children (e.g., most early childhood programs)
- Academic or Readiness instruction (e.g., primary grades and many pre-kindergarten programs)
- Culturally or religiously specific programs (e.g., a school setting with a definitive ethnic focus or a church-related school that teaches religious dogma)

These programs generally reflect the needs of society as a whole. Millions of mothers of children under age 6 are in the labor force as never before. Early childhood schools provide a wide range of services for children from infancy through 8 years of age to meet the demands of today's working mothers. Approximately two of every three mothers of preschool age children and three of every four mothers of school-age children are in the labor force (Children's Defense Fund, 2008).

Special Program Features

A program usually has any number of goals or missions. One mission may be to encourage children to learn from one another. This philosophy has two important features that are reflected in many early childhood programs. The following two sections describe how mixed-age groupings and looping contribute to the goals of the program.

Mixed-Age Groupings

Placing children of several age levels into the same classroom is called **mixed-age grouping.** In these classes, younger children learn from older children and older children learn by teaching younger children. This practice is often referred to as family, heterogeneous, vertical, or ungraded grouping (Katz, Evangelou, & Hartman, 1990) and, though not new, is an area of considerable interest to early childhood educators.

The age range among children in mixed-age groups is usually wider than one year to capitalize on the difference in age, experience, knowledge, and abilities of the children (Katz, 1995). Mixed-age groupings have been a practice in Montessori programs, in the schools of Reggio Emilia, and in one-room schoolhouses for many years. Advocates of mixed-age groups point to a number of developmental advantages when children interact with peers above and below their age level:

- The child's own developmental level and pace are accommodated, allowing children to advance as they are ready.

- Age and competition are de-emphasized as cooperative learning is enhanced.
- Caring and helping behaviors toward younger children and a sense of responsibility toward one another are fostered.
- Diverse learning styles and multiple intelligences are accepted.
- A variety and number of different models for learning and for friendships are available.
- Children grow in independence in their work and in socialization.

Katz (1995) further asserts that teachers and children alike tolerate a wider range of individual differences and behaviors in a mixed-age group, and cooperation, sharing, and giving help to one another are more frequent. Younger children participate in and contribute to more complex projects and activities than they would otherwise. Older children seem to spontaneously help and assist the younger ones (Chase & Doan, 1994).

There are risks associated with mixed-age groupings. The potential for older children to take over and/or overwhelm the younger ones is real, as is the possibility that younger children will pester the older children. This requires monitoring by the teaching staff, and the Reggio Emilia schools offer a good model of this process. In these Italian programs, older children have the responsibility to work with the younger children, explaining things and helping them find appropriate roles to take in their projects.

The academic and social advantages of mixed-age grouping cannot occur without a variety of activities from which children may freely choose and the opportunity for small groups of children to work together. Teachers must be intentional about encouraging children to work with others who have skills and knowledge they do not yet possess. Other considerations are the optimal age range, the proportion of older to younger children, the amount of time spent in mixed-age groups, and the implementation of a project-oriented curriculum (Katz, Evangelou, & Hartman, 1990).

It is easy to see how mixed-age groupings reflect the principles of Dewey, Piaget, Gardner, and Vygotsky, whose "zone of proximal development" is made more available through the interactions of peers as well as adults. The practice of mixed-age grouping has much to commend it and must be seriously addressed as an issue in programs for young children.

Looping

The practice of keeping a teacher and the same group of children together in the same class for at least two years is called **looping.** As with mixed-aged grouping, it is an old idea revisited. Today, looping is customary in the Waldorf Schools, Reggio Emilia programs, and Montessori, and it has emerged in other programs for a number of reasons. Proponents of looping suggest that it:

- Offers stability and emotional security to children.
- Gives teachers a greater opportunity to get to know children and therefore be able to individualize the program for them.
- Provides more instructional time without time spent at the beginning of the school year on routines of procedures and familiarization.
- Fosters better social interactions among children.
- Enhances a sense of family and community within the classroom (Bellis, 1999; Chapman, 1999).

In the schools in Reggio Emilia, infants and toddlers are kept in the same class with the same teachers for three years to provide a family-like environment. Looping is often paired with multi-aged classrooms, which further extends the natural, family-like atmosphere.

Critics of looping cite the need for experienced teachers who enjoy teaching across the age levels and who can work with the same children over an extended period of time. Looping does not fit all teachers and all children, and it could be offered as an option for parents and teachers to meet the needs of those who believe its advantages are worthwhile (Bellis, 1999; Chapman, 1999).

Any of the following early childhood programs may include mixed-age groups and looping. The educational and philosophical goals of the program will determine what features to include.

The Core of Programs of Early Childhood Education

The following sections explore the different types of programs available to families. Each has unique characteristics, emphases, and challenges.

Traditional Nursery School

The **traditional nursery school** (often called preschool) exemplifies a developmental approach to learning in which children actively explore materials and in which activity or learning centers are organized to meet the developing skills and interests of the child. Most of these programs serve children from 2½ to 5 years of age.

The philosophy of these schools is best described by Katherine Read Baker in her now classic book *The Nursery School: A Human Relationships Laboratory* (1950). First published over sixty years ago, this book serves as an encyclopedia of the traditional nursery school, its methods, and its philosophy, reflecting the influence of Comenius, Locke, Rousseau, Pestalozzi, Froebel, and Montessori.

The idea of a school as a place of human activity mirrors the thoughts of Dewey, Piaget, Erikson, and others. Baker develops this philosophy fully with an educational model that emphasizes the human needs, growth patterns, and relationships in a young child's life.

Developmentally, a traditional nursery school focuses on social competence and emotional well-being. The curriculum encourages self-expression through language, creativity, intellectual skill, and physical activity. The basic underlying belief is the importance of interpersonal connections children make with themselves, each other, and adults.

The daily schedule (see Figure 2-1) reflects these beliefs. Large blocks of time are devoted to free play, a time when children are free to initiate their own activities and become deeply involved without interruptions, emphasizing the importance of play. In this way, children learn to make their own choices, select their own playmates, and work on their interests and issues at their own rate. A dominant belief is that children learn best in an atmosphere free from excessive restraint and direction.

Typically, there is a balance of activities (indoors and out, free choice, and teacher-directed times) and a wide variety of activities (large- and small-muscle games, intellectual choices, creative arts, and social play opportunities).

A nursery school is often a half-day program, but many offer extended hours.

Half-Day Schedule	
9:00	Children arrive at school
9:00–9:45	Free play (indoors)
9:45	Cleanup
10:00	Singing time (large group)
10:15–10:30	Toileting/snack time (small group)
10:30–11:30	Free play (outdoors)
11:30	Cleanup
11:45	Story time
12:00	Children leave for home

FIGURE 2-1 A sample schedule for traditional half-day nursery schools is the core of early education programs.

The Role of the Teacher

The role of the teacher and methods of teaching are important factors in a traditional nursery school. They assume that young children need individual attention and should have personal, warm relationships with important adults. Therefore, the groups of children are generally small, often fewer than 20 in a class. The teacher–child ratio is low, as few as 6 to 10 children for each teacher. Teachers learn about children's development and needs by observation and direct interaction, rather than from formalized testing. They work with children individually and in small groups and often teach through conversation and materials. Teachers encourage children to express themselves, their feelings, and their thinking. Such rapport between teacher and pupil fosters self-confidence, security, and belonging. Proponents of the traditional nursery school believe that these feelings promote positive self-image, healthy relationships, and an encouraging learning environment.

Child Care Centers

By definition, a **child care center** is a place for children who need care for a greater portion of the day than what the traditional nursery school offers. The school schedule is extended to fit the hours of working parents. A longer day means that ordinary routines such as meals and naps are woven into the program. These full-day options are also educational settings, echoing but extending the curriculum of a half-day program.

Child care needs are met in many ways, from center-based care to family settings. Child care centers can include preschools, employer-sponsored care, Head Start, for-profit and non-profit institutions, religious institutions, colleges, YMCAs, public schools, social service agencies, and family child care.

Full-day child care is not a modern phenomenon. Some of the first nursery schools in England operated from 8:00 a.m. until 4:00 or 5:00 p.m. (as noted in Chapter 1). At the end of this chapter, an "Insights From the Field" article by the late Edith Dowley tells the fascinating story of the child care centers established in the Kaiser Shipyards in Portland, Oregon, during World War II. They are a prime example of the kind of business and political support that is needed to support children and their families today.

Child care centers often serve infants and toddlers, as well as 2½- to 5-year-olds. Many offer kindergarten, before- and after-school options, and summer programs.

Routines, such as eating, provide a balance to an active and busy day at the child care center.

Scheduling

Compare the nursery school schedule (Figure 2-1) with the child care schedule (Figure 2-2). The morning starts slowly. Children arrive early because their parents must go to work or school. The center may supply breakfast, midmorning and midafternoon snacks, and a noon lunch. A nap period for one to two hours for all the children gives a needed rest and balances their active, social day with quiet, solitary time. The program also includes ex-

Full-Day Schedule

Time	Activity
7:00–8:30	Arrival/breakfast; limited indoor play
8:30	Large group meeting
8:45–9:45	Free play (inside)
9:45	Cleanup/toileting
10:00	Snack time (small groups)
10:15–11:30	Free play (outside)
11:30	Cleanup/hand-washing
12:00	Lunch
12:30	Toothbrushing/toileting
1:00–2:00	Nap time
2:00–3:00	Free play (outside)
3:00	Group time
3:15	Snack time (small groups)
3:30–5:00	Inside and outside free play/library hour
5:00	Cleanup
5:15–5:30	Departure

FIGURE 2-2 A typical full-day care schedule. Most child care programs combine education and caring for basic needs.

tended experiences outside the school—field trips, library story hour, or swimming lessons—because children spend the major portion of their waking hours on-site. As the day draws to a close, children gather together quietly, with less energy and activity.

Licensing

Licensing is the process of fulfilling the legal requirements, standards, and regulations for operating child care facilities. There are no national standards or policies regarding licensing of child care facilities in the United States. Many local and state governments require licensing of child care centers and family child care homes, but there is no central licensing agency in every state. Depending on the state, a license may be issued by the Department of Health, Department of Education, or Department of Social Welfare. Certification of child care workers is also left to local standards.

Early childhood professional groups are calling for increased standardization of licensing procedures to ensure that children are receiving the best possible care in safe and healthy environments. The same minimum standards would apply to adult–child ratios, suitable safety precautions, health and nutrition needs, and the amount of training and preparation required of caregivers.

Children are spending longer hours in child care, and there are more programs sponsored by a variety of agencies such as churches, public schools, and private for-profit firms. With this diverse mix, a common set of standards for licensing is imperative to ensure the best possible care for all children who need these services.

An NAEYC position paper (NAEYC, 1998a) in support of licensing and regulation of early care and education programs recommends that:

- All programs providing care and education for two or more unrelated families should be regulated and that there be no exception or exemptions from this requirement.
- All centers or schools serving 10 or more children that provide services to the public should be licensed.
- States should establish licenses for individuals, such as teachers, caregivers, and program administrators.
- Licensing regulations should address health and safety, group size, adult–child ratios, and preservice and inservice standards.

Staffing

The staff in a full-day setting is often called on to deal with the parenting side of teaching. Children in full-day care may need more nurturing and clearer consistency in behavioral limits. At the same time, they need individual flexibility, understanding, and regular private time with caring adults.

Parents' needs also may be greater and require more of the teachers' time. Child care parents may require extra effort; they have full-time jobs as well as child-rearing responsibilities draining their energies. It takes a strong team effort on the part of the teacher and the parent to make sure the lines of communication stay open and that families and schools are mutually supported.

The teaching staff undoubtedly has staggered schedules, perhaps a morning and an afternoon shift. Administration of this type of program is therefore more complex. An effort must be made to ensure that all teachers get together on a regular basis to share the information and details about the children in their care. Both shifts must be aware of what happens when they are not on-site to run the program consistently. (See Chapter 15 for further discussion on child care issues.)

Family Child Care

In **family child care,** the provider takes care of a small number of children in a family residence. The group size can range from two to 12, but most homes keep a low adult–child ratio, enrolling fewer than 6 children. It is reminiscent of an extended family grouping.

Nearly 20 percent of working mothers with children under age 5 select family child care (U. S. Census Bureau, 2005). The home setting, sometimes right within the child's own neighborhood, offers an intimate, flexible, and convenient service for working parents. There are more than one million family child care providers in the United States today (National Association for Family Child Care, 2005). Children in a family child care home can range from infants to school-age children who are cared for after regular school hours.

The developmental ranges that family child care providers must meet may range from infancy up to 12 years, which poses a challenge to develop experiences and activities for a mixed-age group of children. Family child care providers work and live in the same environment posing logistical problems of storage, space definition, and activity space. Often, family child care providers care for their own children within their programs, leading to problems with separation and autonomy of their children and providing enough time to the child as a parent. Family child care providers are administrators and managers, as well as teachers and caregivers, faced with budgets and fee collections.

Advantages

Family child care is good for children who do well in small groups or whose parents prefer to place them in a family-style setting. This is especially true for infants and toddlers. Family child care homes often schedule flexible hours to meet the needs of parents who work. The wide age range can be advantageous as well. Consistency and stability from a single caregiver throughout the child's early years and a family grouping of children provide a homelike atmosphere that is especially appropriate for infants and toddlers.

Family child care providers own and operate their own small business in their homes. Providing child care is a way for women who want to remain at home with their children to contribute to the family income. Meeting the requirements for licensing, fulfilling all the administrative tasks of a business and an educational program, and keeping current with the local, state, and federal tax requirements are part of the professionalism required for this type of child care arrangement.

Challenges

Many homes are unregulated; that is, they are not under any sponsorship or agency that enforces quality care, and many are exempt from state licensing. Family child care providers often lack knowledge of child development and early education and are not required to take courses. The National Association for Family Child Care has established an accreditation system and promotes high-quality family child care through professional development, public education, and policy initiatives (NAFCC, 2009).

Family child care providers can feel isolated from others in the child care field. A hopeful sign, however, is that more articles on family child care are being included in professional publications, and early childhood conferences and workshops are now including issues related to the family child care provider. This type of care could be a star in the galaxy of child care options. Small and personalized, it offers parents an appealing choice of home-based care. It is obvious, though, that further regulation of standards, availability of training for providers, and an awareness of the advantages of family child care need to be addressed. For those who need child care, this should be a viable alternative; for those who want to work at home, this type of career should be given serious consideration.

The options for child care are many. In Figure 2-3, the choices that parents make when looking for child care are addressed.

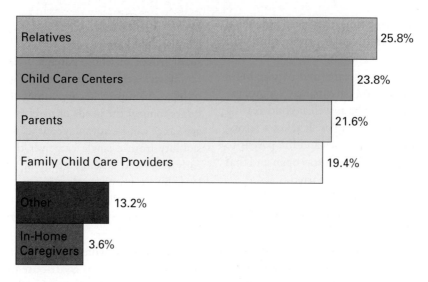

FIGURE 2-3 Child care options (Data from: U.S. Bureau of Census. *"Who's Minding the Kids?"* Childcare Arrangements, Spring, 2005. Survey of Income and Program Participation.

Head Start: An Early Intervention Model

In 1965, the federal government created the largest publicly funded education program for young children ever. Head Start began as part of this country's social action in the "war on poverty," and the implications of the program were clear: If at-risk poverty-stricken children could be exposed to a program that enhanced their schooling, their intellectual functions might increase, and these gains would help break the poverty cycle.

Over the last 45 years, Head Start has served more than 25 million children and their families (Head Start, 2009). The success of Head Start can be attributed to its guiding objectives and principles, most notably expressed through:

- *Its comprehensive nature.* The child is seen as a whole, requiring medical, dental, and nutritional assessment, as well as intellectual growth. Extensive health, education, and social services are offered to children and their families.
- *Parent participation and involvement.* Head Start expects parents to serve as active participants and get involved in the program at all levels: in the classroom as teacher aides, on governing boards making decisions about the program, and as bus drivers and cooks.
- *Services to families.* Many of the comprehensive services offered to children are extended to parents as well to assist them in their fight against poverty.

Paid jobs in the program, continuing education, job training, and health care are some of the support services families received.

- *Community collaboration.* Interest and support from the local community help Head Start respond to the needs of the children and families it serves. Public schools, religious institutions, libraries, service clubs, and local industry and businesses help to foster responsible attitudes toward society and provide opportunities for the poor to work with members of the community in solving problems.
- *Multicultural/multiracial education.* Since its inception, Head Start has sought to provide a curriculum that reflects the culture, language, and values of the children in the program. Head Start efforts in this regard have been the models for other early childhood programs.
- *Inclusion of children with special needs.* Since 1972, Head Start has pioneered the inclusion of children with disabilities in its classrooms. Head Start has the distinction of being the first and largest federally funded program for children with special needs (Greenberg, 1990).
- *Ecology of the family.* Head Start programs look at children within the context of the family in which they live and view the family in the context of the neighborhood and community. This concept of taking the many forces that work against low-income families and viewing them as interrelated is a key factor in Head Start's success. (See also Chapters 1 and 15.)

© Cengage Learning

There are similarities among all programs, but the relationship among parents, children, and caregiver is the universal consideration.

A Picture of Head Start

Enrollment
   908,412 children

Ages Enrolled
5-year-olds:	3%
4-year-olds:	51%
3-year-olds:	36%
Under 3:	10%

Race/Ethnic Population
Native American/Alaskan Native:	4%
Hispanic/Latino:	35%
Black/African American:	30.1%
White:	39.7%
Asian/Pacific Islander:	2.5%
Biracial/Multiracial:	4.9%
Other:	18.8%

FIGURE 2-4 Head Start continues to be a vital program that serves the needs of a diverse population. This information is for the fiscal year 2007. (U.S. Department of Health and Human Services, the Office of Head Start, 2009.)

The success of Head Start led to the creation of three specific programs that furthered the goals of Head Start: Parent & Child Centers, which serve infants and toddlers and their families; the Child and Family Resource Programs, which provide family support services; and the Child Development Associate credential, which provides early childhood training and education for Head Start teachers.

It should be noted that, at the beginning, one aim of Head Start was to change the language and behavior patterns of the low-income children served, many of whom came from minority groups, and to resocialize them into cultural patterns and values of the mainstream, middle class. Head Start was a "compensatory" program, and the implications were that children from poor or minority families were unprepared for the demands of school in terms of language and cognitive skills, achievement, and motivation. This widely held perspective of the 1960s was known as the "cultural disadvantage" model, which suggests that any language, cognitive, or relational style that differs from the Anglo, mainstream, middle-class style is necessarily detrimental to rather than supportive of the educational process.

Contrast this view with the more recent, pluralistic perspective, called the "cultural difference" model, which affirms that no one way of "behaving and believing" should be required for successful participation in school or society. Figure 2-4 summarizes today's Head Start programs.

Early Head Start

Early Head Start was established in 1994 as part of the Head Start Reauthorization Act. This program serves low-income families with infants and toddlers and pregnant women and is based on Head Start's four cornerstones: child development, family development, staff development, and community building.

Nine principles guide the efforts of Early Head Start: (1) high quality; (2) prevention of developmental concerns and promotion of healthy child development; (3) positive relationships and continuity in care-giving; (4) parent involvement; (5) inclusion; (6) culture; (7) comprehensiveness, flexibility, responsiveness and intensity to respond to families needs; (8) smooth transitions into Head Start programs; and (9) collaboration with local communities to maximize resources available to families.

Evaluating Early Intervention Effectiveness

Two studies have helped highlight Head Start's impact over the years. One, the Consortium for Longitudinal Studies, pooled data from a number of smaller studies in the hope that clear trends regarding early intervention could be identified. Brown (1985) noted two significant findings: (1) that Head Start children were less likely to be placed in special education classes, and (2) that early intervention programs were associated with a significant increase in IQ and school achievement.

The second study, the High/Scope Perry Preschool Project, was not of a Head Start program but had an enormous impact on policy makers and government officials and affected Head Start funding in significant ways.

The High/Scope Perry Preschool Study. This project presented the most convincing evidence to date of the effectiveness of early intervention programs for low-income children. Started in the 1960s, it is the first longitudinal study to measure the effects of preschool education and to track the children from preschool years through age 27.

Children from one randomly assigned group were placed in high quality early childhood programs at age 3; the other group did not attend preschool. The results showed great differences between the children who had the advantage of a high quality program and those who did not. Low-income children who had attended preschool significantly outperformed those who had not.

The children attending the preschool program were better educated, spent fewer than half as many years in special education programs, had higher earnings, were less likely to receive welfare, and were five times less likely to be arrested (Schweinhart & Weikart, 1993).

Gender differences were also noted. Preschool program girls had a significantly higher rate of graduation than did the girls who did not attend preschool, whereas, in comparison, preschool program boys completed slightly less schooling than nonpreschool boys (Cohen, 1993b).

Not only does this study underscore the need for high quality preschool programs for children who live in poverty, but it also demonstrates the potential impact that Head Start has on the country's future. It is the first study of its kind to suggest the economic impact of early intervention. Because most of the children in the high quality early childhood program required less remedial education, had better earning prospects, and were less costly to the welfare and justice systems, early intervention in education was shown to be cost-effective.

Head Start Today

Head Start has had a rocky history, its contributions notwithstanding. Struggling against budget cuts and controversy over its effectiveness, Head Start has undergone program improvements and expansions.

The original vision of Head Start was improved and expanded for the 1990s as a model that challenges the effects of poverty and promotes physically and mentally healthy families. Head Start has a formidable challenge ahead as it protects the high quality of its original charter while expanding and increasing services.

Variations on Early Childhood Core Programs

There are many variations of the core programs that provide care and education for young children. These programs differ primarily due to the sponsoring agencies, the children they serve, their underlying mission, and whether or not they are non-profit or for-profit organizations.

Universal Preschools

Increasing numbers of school districts offer prekindergarten programs for 4-year-olds, although some include 3-year-olds as well. Depending on their goal, these programs fall somewhere between traditional nursery schools and not quite full-day care. For some, the focus is on school readiness; others give priority to children at risk for school failure, children who come from families in which English is not spoken, or low-income families. In states in which early education has achieved a level of support, all 4-year-olds are eligible for enrollment, regardless of income. More than one million children attend these state-funded preschools in 38 states plus the District of Columbia (Barnett et al, 2007). The concept for universal preschools is and will be a continuing issue. (See Chapter 15 for further discussion.)

Laboratory Schools

The college and university **laboratory schools** were among the first preschools established in the United States. They focus on teacher training, research, and innovative education.

As part of the Child Study Movement, laboratory schools gathered information previously unknown about children and child development. Early schools include the Hampton Institute which began in 1873, the University of Chicago founded by John Dewey in 1896, the Bank Street School in 1919 which was started by Harriet Johnson, and the laboratory nursery school at Columbia University's Teachers College, started in 1921 by Patty Smith Hill. In the late 1920s, Vassar, Smith, and Mills colleges all opened laboratory schools. Shortly after World War II, the Bing Nursery School at Stanford University opened. More recently, community college campuses have followed the lead of these pioneers. **Campus child care centers** are beginning to combine child care services with the laboratory function of teacher training in one setting. The types and roles of the schools vary, depending on the educational philosophy and needs of the college and its students.

Regardless of their specific purposes, laboratory schools increase our understanding of children. They are often excellent places for beginning teachers to learn good teaching practices. They encourage the joining of psychology, medicine, and other related fields to early education, and they serve as professional models for the public as to what is good in child care and education.

Parent Cooperatives

Parent cooperative schools are organized and run by parents. This type of early childhood setting offers a unique opportunity for parents to be involved in the education of their child. Faculty wives at the University of Chicago started the first parent cooperative, the Chicago Cooperative Nursery School, in 1915.

Parent cooperative schools may offer half-day or full-day child care programs and are usually nonprofit organizations. They are similar to other nursery schools, with two notable exceptions. First, parents organize and maintain the school: they hire the teachers, buy supplies and equipment, recruit members, raise funds, influence school philosophy, and manage the budget.

Second, parents or their substitutes are required to participate in the classroom on a regular basis. In light of current family work patterns and the unavailability of many parents, this requirement has been modified in some programs. Professional teachers are hired, or other parents who are available are paid to substitute for parents who cannot work at the center.

Cooperative schools work well for many reasons. Popular with young families, they have low operating costs, offer interaction with parents in similar circumstances, and offer the mutual support generated among members of a co-op. Friendships grow among parents who share child rearing as participants in their own and in their child's education. But what a co-op does not cost in dollars, it may cost in time. By their very nature, cooperatives can exclude working parents unless another adult is able to substitute for them in classroom participation. Maintenance is very much the parents' responsibility; co-ops must regularly schedule work parties to refurbish the facility.

Depending on the size of the school, parents hire one or more professional teachers. These teachers must be able to work well with adults, have curriculum-building skills, and model good guidance and discipline techniques. Because many parent cooperatives require a

A mother arrives at the co-op school for her day of participation.

weekly or monthly parent meeting, the teaching staff must also be competent in parent education. Child development and child-rearing topics are part of almost any cooperative nursery school discussion and require the leadership of a practiced teacher. The role of the teacher in this setting, then, is twofold: to provide for a sound educational experience for young children and to guide and direct parents in their own learning.

Employer-Sponsored Child Care

Employer-sponsored child care refers to child care facilities on or near the job site and supported by the business or industry. Hospitals, factories, colleges, and military bases often provide this service.

The number of women working outside the home and the increase in single-parent families encourage us to look at the workplace as a logical solution for child care needs. Employers who have implemented child care claim that the benefits are increased employee morale and better recruitment and retention of employees. For parents, there is the added appeal of having their children close by and being part of their educational process.

Industry responded to the need to create a supportive structure for workers to combine work and family. Child care has become a corporate issue, with both large and small corporations participating. Government agencies are among the largest employers offering child care options, primarily for use by military personnel (Neugebauer, 2001).

More companies are hiring management organizations to operate their child care facilities rather than maintaining them themselves. Employers are also insisting on quality, and centers are being accredited through NAEYC. The rising cost and upgraded professional requirements of the recent NAEYC accreditation process has caused some companies to look for alternate measures of quality (Neugebauer, 2008).

Benefits to employees may include the option for one or more of the following: parental leave, flexible hours, corporate group discounts at local centers or family child care homes, resource and referral services, pretax salary reductions for child care, vouchers to purchase child care, and reserved spaces in specific child care settings supported by the company. Companies located near each other may collaborate on the costs of these benefits. An extra benefit is that employers may provide a 25 percent tax credit for costs associated with providing child care and a 10 percent tax credit for child care resource and referral (Neugebauer, 2001).

While employers have continued to support child care assistance for their employees, the Families and Work Institute (2008) reports that the percentage of employers providing child care has not changed from 1998 to 2008. The recent economic upheaval is causing employers to question whether or not they can still afford to support this program (Neugebauer, 2008).

For-Profit Child Care

Sometimes called "proprietary child care," the for-profit establishments comprise over one third of all child care centers. A number of national chains of child care centers developed rapidly over the last 40 years, with some controlling anywhere from seven to 2400 centers (Neugebauer, 2006).

For-profit child care is viewed as a good investment opportunity. A few very large companies dominate the scene, creating child care chains across the country, primarily as managers of employer-sponsored programs or franchisers of centers.

For-profit centers offer a variety of programs to meet parents' needs. Infant and toddler programs, preschools, kindergartens, before-school and after-school care, and summer sessions accommodate working parents. Many programs are expanding into kindergarten and primary grades. The major concerns of the chief executives of the nation's for-profit child care organizations are the shortage of qualified teachers, public school early childhood programs, and the economy (Neugebauer, 2006).

Nanny Care

Nannies are professional in-home child care providers. Originating in England, the nanny movement became popular during the 1980s as a child care option for parents who could afford to have child care in their homes.

The International Nanny Association emphasizes training and professionalism and provides training and mentoring programs, publications, and a Nanny Credential exam. Nanny training programs can be found in community colleges and vocational schools where their training may include child development, nutrition, and family relationships. Living arrangements vary; nannies may or may not live in the child's home and they may or may not be responsible for housekeeping or meal preparation.

It should be noted that everyone who is called a "nanny" does not have the professional training and knowledge that is necessary to qualify as a professional nanny.

Au pairs differ from nannies in that they are allowed to spend only one year in the United States and do not receive any special training for their child care role.

Programs in Religious Facilities

Throughout this nation's history, religious institutions have demonstrated their concern for the welfare of children and their families. It was the religious institutions that established many of the early schools, advocating the education of children. At the turn of the last century, day nurseries and settlement houses sponsored by religious groups cared for children of immigrants and poor working mothers. Later, hospitals and orphanages were founded, and religious leaders spoke out for children's rights and the creation of child labor laws. In each era, depending on social and economic conditions, the religious community has responded to the needs of children.

Programs in religious facilities fall into two groups. A **faith-based** early childhood program expresses its religious beliefs within the context of the program and curriculum. Other programs sponsored by religious organizations do not include religious dogma as a part of their program. As one of the largest single providers of child care in the United States, religious-based centers provide a variety of early childhood programs and their numbers continue to grow (Neugebauer, 2008).

The curriculum in religious facilities depends on the program's philosophy and the involvement of the congregational leadership. Many faith-based programs include Bible study as an integral part of the curriculum. Each setting is different, even within the same denomination. Some programs integrate philosophies from Reggio Emilia, Bank Street, High/Scope, and Waldorf into their curriculum.

A program can be the direct operation of an individual congregation that has full and programmatic control over the center. A program can also be an indirect operation where the congregation incorporates the center as a separate, nonprofit agency but maintains representation on the governing board. A third option is an independent operation where the congregation rents out space to a secular or nonprofit center (Hampton, 2002).

Most programs that operate in religious facilities acknowledge four purposes for housing an early childhood program (Hampton, 2002):

1. *Pastoral Care*—as a service to families within the congregation.
2. *Community Service*—as a service to families within the local community.
3. *Education/Enculturation*—to teach religious beliefs.
4. *Social Justice*—as an outreach to low-income families or those with special needs.

In some child care centers, parents and teachers communicate by writing notes.

Known as "benign landlords" (Lindner, et al., 1983), programs in religious institutions typically offer free or reduced-cost rent and may subsidize utilities, maintenance services, repairs, and some insurance. Their nonprofit tax-exempt status is usually applied to child care programs that exist as part of the congregation's ministry. Programs housed in religious facilities, however, suffer the same difficulties as other child care facilities, such as low staff wages and poor or nonexistent benefits.

Common problems that arise in religious facilities include sharing space with other congregational programs, frequent changes in leadership in the congregation's governing body, unclear policies and procedures regarding decision-making groups within the congregation, and inappropriate governance structures regulating the operation of the child care program.

For those families who seek alternative education in a religious context, religious-based schools fill the need. Many denominations serve children from early childhood through high school. The relationship with the individual religious organizations and the academic philosophy will vary from setting to setting.

Other Programs

Teen Parent Programs

Many high schools now have on-campus child care programs. Some serve as laboratory facilities to introduce adolescents to child care principles and practices before they become parents. Others are part of a growing trend to provide support services to teenage parents. Young parents are encouraged to complete their high school education by returning to campus with their children. In addition to their regular academic classes, parents are required to participate in parent education classes, in which they discuss child-rearing practices and parenting concerns. They also spend time in the children's classroom, applying their skills under the supervision of early childhood professionals.

The aim of these programs is to help meet the long-term needs of adolescent parents by providing educational skills necessary to secure a job. At the same time, valuable support and training for parenthood help teenagers deal with the reality of the young children in their lives.

Early Intervention and Special Education Programs

Programs for children with special needs offer a combination of educational, medical, and therapeutic services. Early Childhood Special Education (ECSE) is a relatively new field and includes programs for early intervention for infants and toddlers through age 2, and preschool special education for 3 to 5-year-old children with exceptionalities or developmental delays. A team of professionals, including early childhood special educators, social workers, and physical, language, and occupational therapists, work together with parents to enhance each child's progress.

Any inclusive early childhood program may be an appropriate setting for children with special needs as long as there is adequate planning and support (Allen & Cowdery, 2009). (Further discussion of programs for children with special needs follows in Chapter 3.)

Migrant Children's Programs

Early childhood programs serve the needs of migrant farm families and rural poor families. Often migrant farm worker mothers are employed to work alongside the early childhood professionals. The focus of these programs is often on improving the child's primary language skills and developing a second language, job training, and access to health care and social services.

Hospital Settings

Hospitals may provide group settings for children who are confined for a period of time. Many hospitals provide on-site child care for their employees as well.

Meeting the Needs of Children Who are Homeless

In any given year, approximately 1.35 million children will experience homelessness (National Coalition for the Homeless, 2007). These children may attend schools closest to the shelter in which they stay for a brief time and then change schools when their parents move to another shelter. Many times these are children who already experience problems and failures in school. State and federal legislation is now being enacted to ensure full and equal educational opportunities for children who are homeless. (See Chapter 15, "Endangered Childhood," for a discussion of children at risk from abuse or neglect.)

Extending the Age Range

Early childhood programs throughout the country deliver services to a wide range of ages in a variety of programs geared to various age levels and needs. As children move into kindergarten and primary school, their early childhood experiences change.

Infant/Toddler Programs

The inclusion of infants and toddlers in group care is the result of more mothers in the workforce. Infant/toddler programs may be full-day centers or they may be part-time. Most are a combination of physical care coupled with intellectual simulation and development.

Parent relationships are an especially important part of any program for babies and toddlers. The general intention of these centers is to provide care that is supplemental to family life and that supports the child's family structure. To do that, the caregiver at an infant/toddler center involves the parents in the everyday decisions about the care of their child, provides them with information about the child's day, and strengthens the child's sense of belonging to that particular family.

Philosophy of Infant/Toddler Care

Through the insights of Piaget and Erikson (see Chapter 4), we have come to view the infant more and more as an involved person, one who experiences a wide range of intellectual and emotional abilities. Although they may appear to be helpless beings, babies are in fact persons with feelings, rights, and an individual nature. The caregiver in a quality infant/toddler center understands that feeding, diapering, and playing are the curriculum of this age group.

Caregiving routines are at the heart of the infant/toddler program. The challenge is to find ways to use these daily routines to interact, develop trust and security, and provide educational opportunities. In many cases, the caregiver's role extends to helping parents use these same common occurrences to promote the optimal development of their child. Magda Gerber, a pioneer in infant care, coined the term **educaring** to describe the relationship between an infant and an adult. Observing, listening, and reading babies' cues are key elements in educaring.

Gerber's philosophy is based on the use of responsive and reciprocal interactions in which baby and caregiver learn about each other. Communicating through care giving routines (diapering, feeding) in one-to-one intense and focused interactions is a foundation of Gerber's approach to caring for infants and toddlers (Gerber, 1979).

Program Differences

Infant and toddler programs differ from preschool programs in a number of ways. The young infant (birth to 9 months) needs *security*; mobile infants from 8 to

18 months need opportunities for *exploration*; toddlers (16–36 months) are in the process of forming their *identity* (Copple & Bredekamp, 2009). Infant and toddler programs reflect these needs by:

- Creating a stable environment with low staff turnover and low caregiver–child ratios.
- Providing more one-to-one physical care.
- Ensuring immediate response from adults.
- Following up with parents and families on a daily basis.
- Using ordinary routines as learning opportunities.
- Developing skills that go beyond teaching: mothering, being a playmate.
- Promoting intentional rather than discovery learning.
- Developing finely tuned interpretation skills to recognize need and distress signals in young children.
- Understanding the significance of cultural sensitivity as children gain a sense of their own identity.

The distinction between programs for infants and those for toddlers is also important. Just as a scaled-down version of preschool is not a toddler program, neither is a scaled-down version of a good day for toddlers an appropriate model for infants. The mobility of the toddler, for instance, requires different amounts of space and time in the schedule than those required for infants. Babies sleep more their first year of life; their rhythm of eating, sleeping, and playing must be met. They thrive when someone responds to their smiles and developing skills. Common routines provide the caregivers time to talk with the babies about what they are doing and what is happening to them. They get babies to focus on themselves through gentle, extensively personal involvement. Good programs for babies recognize their capacities and the extent of their awareness of themselves and others in their environment.

Routines are also the focus of the toddler's day but in a somewhat different way. Mealtimes and toileting provide daily opportunities for toddlers to explore and to express their emerging sense of self. Handwashing—even eating—becomes a time to fill, to taste, to dump, and to pick up. Again, the curriculum emerges from a developmental need toddlers have of "Me! Mine!" To foster that independence, that wanting to "do it myself," routines that allow for experimentation, mistakes, and messes make a good toddler curriculum. Good programs for infants and toddlers, then, are distinctly arranged for their developmental needs and are not simply modified versions of what works well in a program for 3-year-olds.

Infant Care and Attachment

An important consideration in infant care is the daily separation of parent and child. As you will learn in Chapter 4, **attachment** is the deep bond and personal relationship that connects infants to the important people in their lives, such as parents and caregivers. The more secure the attachment, the more positive effects it has on the child. Research on the influence of daily separation suggests that it is the *quality* of care that impacts attachment security (Berk, 2009). When the caregiver–infant ratio is low and the caregiver's interactions are warm, positive, and knowledgeable about child development, children's cognitive, social, and emotional development thrive (McCartney et al, 2007).

Kindergarten

The kindergarten year is one of transition from early childhood programs into a more formal school setting. While some kindergartens extend the "learning through play" philosophy found in developmental preschool programs, others become more focused on the academic skills of 5-year-olds and less on developmentally appropriate practices.

Kindergarten programs abound throughout the United States. They are found in elementary public and private schools, religious institutions, and as part of preschool child care centers. Ninety-five percent of all 5-year-olds are enrolled in a kindergarten program (National Center for Education Statistics, 2008).

© Cengage Learning

Active involvement with people and objects helps infants and toddlers develop feelings of self-identity, curiosity, and creativity.

Length of Day

The length of kindergarten programs is under debate in many states and schools districts. Nine states require a full-day kindergarten and 43 states offer only half-day kindergarten. Seven states do not offer kindergarten at all. Nationally, approximately 60 percent of kindergarteners attend a full-day program (Education Commission of the States, 2006).

Too often the arguments regarding the costs of such programs overshadow a more basic question: What are the best and most appropriate kindergarten programs, teaching methods, and curricula, regardless of the length of day? The following should be considered in response to this question:

- *The purpose of the kindergarten program.* How will the kindergarten program foster the goals in appropriate curricula and adapt to the needs of children? The goal should begin with the child and build the program to fit the child's needs, skills, and developing abilities.
- *The effects of a full day on children.* Many children have already been in a child care setting for up to 10 hours a day and have shown they thrive in programs that are suited to their ages, development styles, and needs. There is no question that most children can handle a full-day kindergarten program, providing it is adapted to their age, interests, and abilities.
- *The needs and concerns of families.* Some families may want a full-day program because they work and need a safe and nurturing place for their children. Others who do not work outside the home may want to keep their children with them a while longer. Families need to have a choice about the type of program that best suits their family.
- *The effect on teachers.* A full-day kindergarten means that class is extended for a longer period of time, providing opportunities to improve the quality of the program by individualizing the curriculum. Teachers in half-day kindergartens often teach one class in the morning and one in the afternoon. The negative effects on planning, continuity, parent relationships, and individualizing curriculum are obvious, not to mention the risk of teacher burnout.
- *The concerns of the administration.* The cost effectiveness of extending a kindergarten program all day will undoubtedly require more staff, more supplies and equipment, and greater food-service costs. The policy makers in any school setting must take these into account along with the other issues, but one would hope they would not be limited by them.

- *The nature and quality of the extended-day program.* Often, in programs in which children are in half-day kindergarten, the quality of the extended-care part of their day is not equal to their school experience. In many extended-day programs, the staff is untrained, has a high turnover rate, and does not reflect the same program goals for the kindergartener.

School Entry Age

Most states establish an arbitrary date (e.g., December 1) by which children must be a certain age to enter kindergarten. In the United States, compulsory age for kindergarten ranges from 5 to 8; most children are age 5½ at the beginning of the school year. A few of the states have a cutoff date of August 15, ensuring that all of the children are 5 years old as they enter kindergarten (Kagan & Kauerz, 2006).

What Do YOU Think? Do you think that all kindergartens should be full day? Why? Should half-day kindergartens be retained? Why? Are "transitional" or "developmental" kindergartens useful? How? What do you think about the use of more testing as a way to assess kindergartners' success in school?

Several trends are adding to the discussions about kindergarten. Lowering and raising the age for beginning kindergarten is debated frequently. Some parents hold children out of kindergarten for one year and enroll them when they are age 6, a practice called "redshirting" (Katz, 2000). Teachers retain many children each year in kindergarten; and administrators have created an array of kindergarten-substitute programs such as "developmental," "extra-year," or "transitional" kindergartens. By the time they finally reach kindergarten, children are now in class with late 4-year-olds, 5- and 6-year-olds—a vast developmental span under one roof. Research shows mixed results for these practices.

Some of the methods used to create more homogeneous kindergarten classrooms or to raise expectations for kindergarten admittance are:

- Inappropriate uses of screening and readiness tests.
- Discouragement and/or denial of entrance for eligible children.

- Creation of transitional classes for those who are considered not ready for kindergarten.
- An increasing use of retention (NAECS/ NAEYC, 2001).

Curriculum: Developmental or Academic

Critical issues such as school-entry age and length of school day are deeply related to kindergarten curriculum issues. Kindergarten programs range from relatively traditional classes to highly structured, academically oriented classes. Over the last 20 years, the push to teach separate skills, such as reading, writing, and math, has created more and more academically focused kindergartens in which worksheets and teacher-directed lessons are the norm. As kindergartens have changed, there is greater pressure on teachers to accelerate children's learning. Hatch (2005) cites three specific changes that have altered the course of kindergarten programs:

1. Children today experience very different childhoods than even a decade ago.
2. Knowledge of how children learn and develop has expanded.
3. The standards-based reform movement has changed expectations for kindergarteners by imposing arbitrary standards of performance. This increases the academic expectations on them and the pressure on teachers to comply with regulations.

Hatch recommends a more balanced approach to kindergarten teaching that would merge the traditional and emerging knowledge and understanding of what children are like with what they need to meet the challenges of the accountability movement.

It is clear that some of Froebel's "children's garden" has wandered far from its child development roots. Curricula in which play is not respected as a vehicle for learning, reading is taught as a separate skill, and attempts are made to accelerate children's learning are at odds with kindergarten history. Revisit Chapter 1 and read again about Froebel, Dewey, Piaget, Patty Smith Hill, Susan Isaacs, and other pioneers and their approach to learning. Educating the whole child is very much in evidence in their work as is their basic connection to child development theory and research. (For further discussion on the negative effects of early academics, see Chapter 3 for developmental ranges and Word Pictures for appropriate expectations. In Chapter 6, the related questions of standardized testing and screening are discussed. In Chapters 10 and 15, related issues are explored.)

Kagan and Kauerz (Gullo, 2006) provide four reflections on what kindergartens can and should be in the future. They integrate concerns about the developmentally appropriate integrity of kindergartens and the domination of imposed standards and testing:

1. Kindergarten must remain "special," that unique year in which play is a legitimate medium for establishing children's learning patterns, and in which curriculum, standards, and assessments are in sync with preschool and first grade.
2. Kindergarten must keep the child front and center, even with the new emphasis on content. Curriculum must address the full range of developmental domains (social, emotional, cognitive, and physical) to prepare children for more formally taught content. Children's curiosity, enthusiasm, initiative, and willingness to learn must be nurtured to enhance their overall ability to learn.
3. Kindergarten must acknowledge and support differences in the needs of children and their families. Different learning styles in children must be addressed as well as family needs for flexibility in the structure, such as full- or half-day sessions.
4. Kindergarten must foster positive relationships between the children and their teachers, between families and the school, and between the school and the community. The success of these relationships can help establish trust and respect that last throughout the child's school years.

Kindergarten is a significant transition in the lives of children and families and a critical year in a child's

© Cengage Learning

Kindergarteners are able to enjoy close friendships.

growth and development. It should be made available and accessible to all children in the United States.

Primary Grades

Early childhood is defined as children from birth through age 8. Primary grades, in both public and private schools, focus on the basic academic skills of reading, writing, math, science, social studies, art and drama, health and safety, and physical education. While these subjects are usually taught separately, the curriculum should be integrated so that children learn subject matter through a variety of activities.

Dramatic changes are taking place in the primary-age child. Children this age are eager to learn and are developing logic and reasoning skills as they move from Piaget's preoperational stage to one of concrete operations (see Chapter 4). Their learning tasks are more difficult than in kindergarten and require greater persistence and effort. Starting at about age 6, children begin to plan out and think through their actions and take others' views into consideration. As they grow more independent in their learning, primary-age children like choosing their own tasks, working cooperatively in small groups with their classmates, and participating in planning each day's work. Group discussions and planning projects address the child's needs to be part of the planning process. Enhancing the child's enthusiasm for learning is a primary task for the teachers of this age group.

Play for the primary-age child now revolves around rules that accompany organized games, board games, and cards. Learning still takes place through independent exploration and manipulation of materials, so classroom centers are an important part of the environment. The classroom itself may be more structured but it is important that developmentally appropriate early childhood principles, practices, and environments are applied through third grade.

Teaching in the primary grades presents more challenges due to the pressure of local, state, or national standards that dictate what children need to learn at this age and grade level. All states now have these standards for each grade level and each subject matter. As a result, teachers may have little or no control over what they teach and the unfortunate result may be a curriculum that "teaches to the test;" that is, one that stresses only the subject matter on which the child will be tested. As Copple and Bredekamp (2009) note, teachers should "include balancing children's need for focused instruction about a specific subject area or concept with children's need to build on what they already

know." The best curriculum for the primary child is one that is in **alignment** with the standards so that the subject matter matches what the standards say children should know and do at this grade and subject level. Accountability through learning standards will continue to have a strong impact on the early elementary years. (Further discussion of early learning standards and their effect on teaching and learning will follow in Chapter 6.)

School-Age Child Care

Before-school and after-school programs are designed for children before they start or after they finish their regular academic day. This type of care is usually available for children from ages 5 to 12. The most common nonparental care arrangements for school-age children are center-or school-based programs (Lawrence et al, 2006).

Staff for after-school programs comes from a variety of backgrounds, most of which include some experience with children, such as teachers, recreation specialists, or specialists within the arts. As with most child care programs, however, high turnover and low wages affect the quality of the service. Finding qualified staff is the major challenge facing school-age providers, along with finding space and funding (Neugebauer, 2007).

Two national organizations, the National School-Age Care Alliance and the School-Age Child Care Project (now called the National Institute on Out-of-School Time) joined forces to create an accreditation system for after-school care. Their goals are to set professional standards, accredit high quality programs, and support program improvement.

There is a critical need for safe, recreational programs for after-school care. Six percent of children ages 5 to 11 and 33 percent of children ages 12 to 14 regularly care for themselves (U.S. Census Bureau, 2005). *America After 3 PM* reports that 14.3 million children are in **self-care** in the afternoons. Too often, these children go home with a house key around their neck or in their pocket. They are instructed to look after themselves and possibly a younger sibling until the parent (or parents) comes home from work. These self-care children are a young and vulnerable population.

Children need the safety, the creative opportunity, and the emotionally supportive relationships that out-of-school care can provide. A quality after-school program has the potential to increase school attendance and positively affect learning. These programs are natural extensions of responsible child care and are essential services to children and their families.

Homeschooling

The homeschool movement began in the 1950s as an alternative to public education and was illegal in many states (Cloud & Morse, 2001). Homeschooling is now legal in all 50 states and the District of Columbia. Today, approximately 1.5 million students are homeschooled (National Center for Education Statistics, 2008), reflecting a diverse range of participants. About 75 percent are non-Hispanic whites in contrast to 65 percent in public schools. Nearly four percent are African American and another four percent are Hispanic (Bieleck, Chandler, & Broughman, 2001).

Three reasons why parents select homeschooling are school environment, to provide religious instruction, and dissatisfaction with the academic instruction available elsewhere. From 2003 to 2007, the percentage of students whose parents reported that religious instruction was the most important factor increased from 73 to 83 percent (National Center for Education Statistics, 2008).

The educational philosophies and methods used in homeschooling are widely diverse and range from prepackaged curriculum that parents buy to "relaxed homeschooling" and "unschooling" (Cloud & Morse, 2001). The "relaxed" or "natural" homeschooling method involves real-life projects as teaching opportunities, such as taking care of the farm animals or building a table. Using real life's teachable moments, the education is often tailored to the child's interests and abilities. About seven percent of homeschoolers use no curriculum plans, and children pursue their own interests in the method called "unschooling" (Cloud & Morse, 2001). If some of this seems familiar, you might want to look back at Chapter 1 and review the various educational philosophies on which early childhood programs are based.

There are a number of concerns expressed by educators regarding homeschool educational programs which include: (1) lack of quality control due to varying regulations; (2) lack of socialization opportunities for students; (3) lack of sports opportunities; (4) the extreme time commitment demanded of parents; (5) lack of accountability, regulations, and policies surrounding homeschooling; and (6) the loss of revenue for public education.

The Issue Is Quality

Each day, nearly 12 million children under the age of 5 are in some type of child care arrangement (U.S. Census Bureau, 2007) and each of these early childhood settings will differ in the level of quality they provide. What does it mean to have a "high quality" program that benefits children and their families?

Indicators of Quality

Early childhood programs vary greatly in their educational goals and practices, their methods of instruction, and even in the kind of social "mood" or atmosphere they create.

Yet the quality of these programs is based on three essential factors:

1. The teacher–child ratio; that is, the number of children cared for by each staff member (see Chapter 9)
2. The total size of the group or class
3. The education, experience, and training of the staff (see Chapter 5)

The importance of these three factors cannot be underestimated, and they underscore each of the principles that follow.

The National Association for the Education of Young Children (NAEYC), has established a list of criteria for high-quality early childhood programs, based on a consensus of thousands of early childhood professionals (NAEYC, 2005). The criteria that serve as a standard of excellence for any group program for young children follows. After each one is a reference to the chapter(s) in this text in which the topic is more fully developed. NAEYC's (2005) 10 essentials for high quality programs are:

1. *Relationships*. Positive relationships help children develop personal responsibility, self-regulation, constructive interactions, and academic mastery. Warm sensitive relationships help children feel secure, develop a positive sense of self, respect for others, and the ability to cooperate. (Chapters 3, 5, 7, 8, 10, and 14)
2. *Curriculum*. The curriculum draws on research for concepts, skills, and methodology that fosters children's learning and maximizes learning through time and materials as well as provides learning opportunities for children individually and in groups. (Chapters 4, 10, 11, 12, 13 and 14)
3. *Teaching*. Developmentally, linguistically, and culturally appropriate teaching practices enhance children's learning, as does multiple instructional methods, including teacher-directed, child-

DAP Each early childhood center has its own culture that reflects their mission, philosophy, and beliefs. The culture of a program influences its commitment to quality.

directed, and structured and unstructured learning opportunities. Teachers reflect the children's backgrounds, needs, interests, and capabilities in their instructional approaches. When more than one teacher is in the classroom, a team teaching approach is used. (Chapters 5, 8, and 10)

4. *Assessment of Child Progress.* Appropriate and systematic assessment measures, which are culturally sensitive, inform needs. Assessments aid in identifying children who need additional instruction and/or intervention and further assessment. (Chapters 3, 6, and 10)

5. *Health and Safety.* A healthy state of well-being enhances a child's ability to learn. Adults help protect children from illness and injury and help them make healthy choices for themselves. (Chapters 9 and 15)

6. *Teachers.* The teaching staff is educationally qualified, knowledgeable, and professionally committed to support children's learning and development, as well as families' diverse needs and interests. The teachers who have specific preparation in child development and early childhood education are more likely to have warm, positive interactions with children, promote richer language experiences, and create a higher quality learning environment. Ongoing professional development ensures that teachers will reflect current research and best practices. (Chapters 2, 5, 9, and 10)

7. *Families.* Good family relationships are collaborations between home and school and reflect family composition, language, and culture. They are based on mutual trust and respect in recognition of the primacy of the family in the life of the child. (Chapters 8 and 15)

8. *Community Relationships.* The program establishes relationships with and uses the resources of the community to realize program goals. By helping to connect families with a variety of resources, the children's health and development is enhanced. (Chapters 2, 3, 9, and 15)

9. *Physical Environment.* A safe, healthy, and accessible environment and well-maintained indoor and outdoor areas fosters learning, health, and safety for young children. The design of the facilities and the activities support a high-quality program. (Chapters 2, 9, 10 and 11)

10. *Leadership and Management.* The program effectively administers policies, procedures, and systems that support a stable staff, strong personnel, fiscal, and program management. Effective governance and structure, program accountability, positive community relations, and a supportive workplace create a high-quality environment for all. (Chapters 2, 5, and 15)

Quality early care and education contribute to the healthy cognitive, social, and emotional development of all children but particularly those from low-income families. The cost of child care is disproportionately high for poor families, so that those who might benefit the most have the most difficult time affording quality care. Good, affordable, accessible child care that will meet the increasing needs of American families is one of today's most crucial issues.

Three Studies on Quality

Every day, scores of parents search for affordable programs and reliable providers. A study by the National Association of Child Care resource and Referral Agencies (NACCRRA, 2008) polled over 1000 parents nationwide to find out what parents want in child care. Quality was mentioned more than any other issue. Parents want their children safe, able to learn, and in child care that is affordable.

Highlights from three other studies underscore the quality issue:

1. The Carolina Abecedarian Project (1999), conducted by the Frank Porter Graham Child Development Center in Chapel Hill, North Carolina, is the first study to track participants from infancy to age 21. The children were considered at risk for potential school failure. The study showed the strong influence of high quality child care when comparing those who were enrolled full time in a quality early childhood program from infancy to age 5 versus those who did not attend a preschool program, although all attended comparable public schools beginning with kindergarten.

    Important factors in determining quality were in place to ensure success: staff experience and education, little or no staff turnover, small teacher–student ratios, group size, and parent participation. Significant benefits for the children enrolled in the program included the likelihood of attending a four-year college and delaying parenthood until after high school. Moreover:

    ▪ At age 21, 65 percent of the child care graduates either had a good job or were in college, compared to 40 percent of the non-child-care subjects.

- By age 15, twice as many of the children who did not receive intervention services had been placed in special education programs than those who had been in child care.
- Only 30 percent of the child care children had to repeat a grade in school compared with 56 percent of the others.

2. The Cost, Quality, and Child Outcomes Study (CQCOS, 1995) found that the average child care is mediocre in quality and that some were of such poor quality that they threatened children's emotional and intellectual development. Infants and toddlers were most likely to be at risk for poor care in these centers; nearly half of their settings failed to meet basic health and safety needs.

   A follow-up study, The Children of the Cost, Quality, and Outcomes Study Go to School (Whitebook, Sakai, Gerber, & Howes, 2001), tracked the children through second grade. The findings noted that:
   - Children who receive good, quality child care had better social and cognitive skills in kindergarten and beyond.
   - Children who were at risk gained the most from positive child care experiences and sustained these gains through second grade.
   - Children who had closer relationships with their child care teachers had better behavior and social skills through second grade.

3. A study by the RAND Corporation (Karoly & Bigelow, 2005) for the first time reported the economic returns of one state's (California) investment in quality preschools for all 4-year-old children. The study projected that for every dollar invested in a quality universal program, society would get between $2 and $4 back. The benefits include:
   - Major increase in lifetime earnings ($2.7 billion per class year of children served)
   - Improved K–12 schools (19 percent reduction in grade repetition per class year; 15 percent fewer special education years; 15 percent reduction in high school dropouts)
   - Significant reductions in violent juvenile offenses, arrests, and incarceration

Issues That Affect Quality

The focus of the child care issues centers on a few core problems that threaten the *quality* of child care throughout the country:

- The annual turnover rate for child care staff is over 30 percent (Whitebook, Sakai, Gerber, & Howes,

2001). Minimal benefits, lack of healthcare, and low wages account for this high rate of turnover.
- Thirty-two states do not require prior training to teach in child care centers, and 39 states and the District of Columbia do not require training of family child care providers (Children's Defense Fund, 2005).
- Hourly earnings of child care workers averaged $10.53 in 2006, much less than the average of $16.76 throughout private industry (Bureau of Labor Statistics, 2009). The mean annual wage is approximately $19,670 (Bureau of Labor Statistics, 2007).

Bredekamp and Glowacki (1996) succinctly summarize the primary issues in child care today: "The economics of child care continue to create a trilemma—quality for children, affordability for families, and adequate compensation for staff."

The triple threats to child care—quality, cost, and compensation—will be discussed further in Chapter 15.

Evaluating Programs for Quality

As educators, we are constantly evaluating, judging, and rating, areas such as:

- *Curriculum.* Will this language game help develop the listening skills of 3-year-olds?
- *Materials and equipment.* If we order the terrarium, will there be enough money for the math lab?
- *The environment.* Should the children begin school with free play or a group time? Where can we store the nap cots? Do the cubbies create a hazard out in the hallway?
- *Children's behavior.* Evan and Francie interrupt each other too much. Should they be placed in separate work groups?
- *Teacher effectiveness.* Yolanda still finds it difficult to lead a group time. How can she be supportively challenged?

Evaluation Is a Process

As a process, **evaluation** is at once a definition, an assessment, and a plan. Evaluation involves making decisions, choices, and selections. In its simplest form, it is a process of appraisal. A good evaluation encourages positive change. It is easy to continue the same program, the same

© Cengage Learning

Evaluations are part of everyday life in an early childhood setting. How are these children learning to listen? To relate to the teacher?

teaching techniques, year after year when a school is operating smoothly. Sometimes it is not clear what—or how—improvements could be made. A regular evaluation process keeps a system alive and growing. Evaluations help give meaning and perspective to children, teachers, and programs. An assessment that helps clarify issues and ideas brings renewed dedication and inspiration.

Programs may be evaluated by taking an inventory of a school's curriculum and educational materials. Program evaluation involves analyzing children, teachers, parents, and administrations to see how they all work together to meet the goals of the program.

Evaluation Essentials

1. *Setting goals.* Without evaluation, goals are meaningless. Evaluation helps shape a goal into a meaningful plan of action. To be useful, an evaluation must include suggestions for improving the performance or behavior. The assessment tool that only describes a situation is an unfinished evaluation; goals for improvement must be established.
2. *Expectations.* In every early childhood setting, more than one set of expectations is at work. The director has job expectations of all the teachers. Teachers

have standards of performance for themselves, the children, and parents. Parents have some expectations about what their children will do in school and about the role of the teachers. Children develop expectations regarding themselves, their parents, teachers, and the school.

3. *The degree to which expectations are met.* A good evaluation tool outlines clearly and specifically how expectations have been met in a system of mutual accountability. Evaluation is a way to look at where and how improvements can be made, to challenge methods, assumptions, and purposes. Total programs are evaluated to see if they accomplish their objectives. Evaluations provide information by which to rate performance, define areas of difficulty, look for possible solutions, and plan for the future.
4. *The degree of inclusion.* A good evaluation instrument should be culturally appropriate and recognize the many ways that a program can be multicultural and anti-biased in its operations. In Chapter 9, you will learn about anti-bias and inclusive environments. (See Figure 9.4 for a checklist for creating an inclusive setting.)

Why Evaluate?

There are four major reasons for making an annual evaluation of a program for young children.

To Gain an Overview

Evaluating a program gives an overview of how all the various components function together. The fundamental questions are: Is this a good place for children? Would you want your child to be here? What is a high quality program for young children?

Looking at children, teachers, and the total environment, a program evaluation reveals the environment as an integrated whole. These assessments add an awareness of how one area is related to another and how the parts mesh in a particular setting. Such evaluations, then, are the standards of quality and include:

DAP

- Children's progress
- Teacher performance
- Curriculum development
- The financial structure
- Family involvement
- The community at large
- The governing organization of the school

DAP Program accountability enhances the daily life of the program and helps sustain a high level of quality.

In program evaluations, each of these is assessed for how it functions alone and how each works in concert with the others.

To Establish Accountability

A program evaluation establishes **accountability.** This refers to a program's ability to answer to a controlling group or agency, for instance, the school board or the government office or the parents and the community in which the program operates. These groups want to know how their funds are being spent and how their philosophy is being expressed through the overall program.

To Make Improvements

Program evaluations are an opportunity to take an objective look at how the goals of the school are being met. A good evaluation will support the strengths of the existing program and suggest areas in which changes might improve overall effectiveness. An in-depth assessment increases the likelihood that program goals and visions will be realized. The evaluation helps determine the direction the program may take in the future.

To Acquire Accreditation

Evaluations are a necessary step for some schools that wish to be approved for certification or accreditation by various organizations or government agencies. Such groups require that a school meet certain evaluation standards before the necessary permits are issued or membership is granted. Agencies, such as a state department of social services or department of education, often license family child care homes, while private schools may need to follow certain criteria to be affiliated with a larger organization (such as the American Montessori Society).

The National Academy of Early Childhood Programs, a division of NAEYC, has established an accreditation system for improving the quality of life for young children and their families. The accreditation system articulates standards for physical, social, emotional, and cognitive development of children in-group care. The academy established goals for accreditation around 10 criteria, which are outlined in Figure 2-5.

How to Evaluate a Program

There are three important steps to take when evaluating a program that will ensure a successful evaluation process. Each is a necessary ingredient for a good evaluation, and together they provide a realistic picture of the individual program.

Define the Objectives

A program evaluation begins with a definition of the program's objectives. Knowing why a program is to be evaluated indicates how to tailor the procedure to the needs and characteristics of an individual school. With the objectives defined, the choice of evaluation instrument becomes clear. If, for example, a program objective is to provide a healthy environment for children, the evaluation tool used must address the issues of health, safety, and nutrition.

Choose an Evaluation Instrument

Evaluation instruments vary with the purpose of the program evaluation. NAEYC's accreditation guidelines are effective (described as 10 essentials for high quality programs on pages 61–62), as are four rating scales developed by the Frank Porter Graham Child Development Institute at the University of North Carolina at Chapel Hill. Each focuses on a specific early childhood setting:

- Infant/Toddler Environment Rating Scale (ITERS-R) which is designed to assess programs for children from birth to 2+ years of age
- Early Childhood Environment Rating Scale (ECERS-R) for preschool through kindergarten programs serving children 2+ through 5 years of age
- Family Child Care Environment Rating Scale (FCCERS-R) for use in home that serve infants through school-age
- School-Age Care Environment Rating Scale (SACERS) that assesses group care programs for children from 5 to 12 years of age

See Chapter 9 for details of how these elements are used in planning environments. Figure 2-5 is a checklist that includes the program areas to include in an evaluation.

Implement the Findings

The evaluation process is complete when the results are tabulated and goals are set to meet the recommendations of the evaluation. Program administrators meet with the teaching staff to discuss the challenges highlighted by the evaluation. A process is put into place for addressing the issues, a calendar is established to create a timeline for improvement, the appropriate staff members are assigned the responsibility for making the changes, and the process begins anew. Evaluations are only as useful as the implementation plan. They can help identify specific concerns, determine the areas of growth and potential development, and be a blueprint for the future.

Checklist for Program Evaluation

The Physical Environment

____ Are the facilities clean, comfortable, safe?

____ Are room arrangements orderly and attractive?

____ Are materials and equipment in good repair and maintained?

____ Is there a variety of materials, appropriate to age levels?

____ Are activity areas well-defined?

____ Are cleanup and room restoration a part of the daily schedule?

____ Are samples of children's work on display?

____ Is play space adequate, both inside and out?

____ Is personal space (e.g., cubby) provided for each child?

The Staff

____ Are there enough teachers for the number of children?

____ How is this determined?

____ Are the teachers qualified? What criteria are used?

____ Is the staff evaluated periodically? By whom and how?

____ Does the school provide/encourage in-service training and continuing education?

____ Do the teachers encourage the children to be independent and self-sufficient?

____ Are the teachers genuinely interested in children?

____ Are teachers aware of children's individual abilities and limitations?

____ What guidance and disciplinary techniques are used?

____ Do teachers observe, record, and write reports on children's progress?

____ Are teachers skilled in working with individual children, small groups, and large groups?

____ Does the teaching staff give the children a feeling of stability and belonging?

____ Do teachers provide curriculum that is age-appropriate and challenging?

____ How would you describe the teachers' relationships with other adults in the setting? Who does this include, and how?

____ Can the teaching staff articulate good early education principles and relate them to their teaching?

Parent Relationships

____ How does the classroom include parents?

____ Are parents welcome to observe, discuss policies, make suggestions, help in the class?

____ Are different needs of parents taken into account?

____ Where and how do parents have a voice in the school?

____ Are parent-teacher conferences scheduled?

____ Does the school attempt to use community resources and social service agencies in meeting parents' needs?

The Organization and Administration

____ Does the school maintain and keep records?

____ Are scholarships or subsidies available?

____ What socioeconomic, cultural, and religious groups does the school serve?

____ What is the funding agency, and what role does it play?

____ Is there a school board, and how is it chosen?

____ Does the school serve children with special needs or handicaps?

____ Is the classroom group homo- or heterogeneous?

____ What hours is the school open?

____ What age range is served?

____ Are there both full- and part-day options?

____ Is after-school care available?

____ Does the school conduct research or train teachers?

____ What is the teacher-child ratio?

The Overall Program

____ Does the school have a written, stated educational philosophy?

____ Are there developmental goals for the children's physical, social, intellectual, and emotional growth?

____ Are the children evaluated periodically?

(continues)

❚ **FIGURE 2-5** Checklist for areas of program evaluation.

____ Is the program capable of being individualized to fit the needs of all the children?

____ Does the program include time for a variety of free, spontaneous activities?

____ Is the curriculum varied to include music, art, science, nature, math, language, social studies, motor skills, etc.?

____ Are there ample opportunities to learn through a variety of media and types of equipment and materials?

____ Is there ample outdoor activity?

____ Is there a daily provision for routines: eating, sleeping, toileting, play?

____ Is the major emphasis in activities on concrete experiences?

____ Are the materials and equipment capable of stimulating and sustaining interest?

____ Are field trips offered?

____ Do children have a chance to be alone? In small groups? In large groups?

Cultural Responsiveness

____ Are multicultural perspectives already incorporated throughout the school, classroom curriculum, and classroom environment?

____ Do my attitudes (and those of all staff) indicate a willingness to accept and respect cultural diversity? How is this demonstrated?

____ Do classroom materials recognize the value of cultural diversity, gender, and social class equity?

____ Do curricular activities and methods provide children opportunities to work and play together cooperatively? In mixed groups of their choice or at teacher direction?

____ Do schoolwide activities reflect cultural diversity? How is this noticed?

____ Does the program planning reflect the reality (views and opinions) of families and the community?

____ Does the curriculum include planning for language diversity? For full inclusion? (Adapted from Baruth and Manning, 1992, and de Melendez and Ostertag, 1997.)

▌ **FIGURE 2-5** (continued)

Insights *from the field*

EARLY CHILDHOOD EDUCATION IN THE SHIPYARDS *by Edith M. Dowley*

This editorial is about an unforgettable experience I had with young children in a period of national crisis. It occurred during World War II, in an innovative project that not only was a remarkable solution to a problem for those times, but that also has special relevance and appropriateness, I believe, for the 21st century.

In early 1943, the Kaiser Shipbuilding Corporation was faced with the necessity of employing more women to meet the stepped-up schedule for producing warships in their two shipyards in Portland, Oregon. Of the 12,000 women already employed, one-third of them were mothers who had no place to leave their preschool children while they worked. Absenteeism among women was running 50 percent higher than among men and was contributing to slow-downs in production that seriously affected the war effort. The reasons most women gave for being late or for missing work were that the babysitter did not show up or a child was ill and could not be left at home until seen by a doctor. Henry Kaiser, reportedly in typical fashion, responded to the dilemma by saying that if mothers were worried about leaving their children, he would provide them with nurseries. He resolved to build the finest child care centers in the country.

Within a few weeks, architects were drawing plans for two child service centers to be placed at the entrances to the shipyards—one at Swan Island and the other at Oregon Yard. Paid for by the United States Maritime Commission and absorbed as part of the cost of building ships, these centers turned out to be not only very fine centers, but also the largest child care centers in the world.

Dr. Lois Meek Stolz, a well-known leader in the fields of child development and early childhood education, was chosen by Edgar Kaiser to direct the two child service centers. She planned the entire children's program and made provisions for staffing the centers. She brought James L. Hymes, Jr., former editor of *Progressive Education*, to the program as manager of the Child Service Centers, and she recruited Dr. Miriam Lowenberg, a well-known nutritionist, to be responsible for the children's nutritional needs.

The Staff

Each center had a supervisor who was responsible for the total operation over all three shifts—day, swing, and graveyard. There were group supervisors, head teachers, assistant teachers, dieticians, and nurses under her direction. In addition, each center had a social worker who served as a liaison between the teachers in the centers and the parents in the shipyard. All of the staff members were recruited from nursery school training centers throughout the United States. All of the teachers had college degrees, and the supervisors and most of the head teachers had master's degrees and years of experience with children. They were young, energetic women "chosen for their comfortable qualities as well as for their scientific knowledge" (Jean Muir, from an article she wrote for the *Oregon Journal*, Sunday, December 12, 1943).

The Setting

The teaching staff began arriving in late October as the finishing touches were being made on the buildings. They found, to their delight, that the centers, although temporary, were beautifully and functionally designed. Each center was built around a large, octagonally shaped courtyard with four wading pools where children could play away from the hazards of traffic. The courtyard itself was grass-covered, with a hard-surfaced area designed for wheel toys that extended around the perimeter. Because of the long rainy season in Portland, covered porches, equipped with jungle gyms, climbing boxes, slides, and large, hollow blocks, connected the interior rooms to the grassy areas. Children could thus enjoy vigorous outdoor play every day of the year, regardless of the weather.

A cog-wheel plan of architecture provided for 15 rectangular playrooms (26' by 49') extending out from a central circular corridor. Between and opposite every two playrooms were smaller rooms for teachers' meetings, special play, or story times. Each of the 15 playrooms had windows on two sides to provide light and interesting views of the outside world. Window seats, low enough for children to sit on, were built so that the children could curl up on them and watch the ships, cars, trucks, and cranes in the busy shipyard below where their parents were working. This proved to be a special delight as darkness came and the yards were lighted, showing the outlines of the ships and their reflections in the water.

The interior colors were soft pastel shades of blue, yellow, and apricot, depending on the exposure of the individual room. Adult-height counterspace covered the expansive shelving where children could readily reach the many unit blocks, toys, games, books, and puzzles that were neatly and meaningfully stored there. Children's lockers, arranged like a dressing room unit, provided hooks for coats and jackets, a shelf for caps, mittens, and art work to take home, and a place for safekeeping of special possessions. Each room had its own toilet room with toilets and wash basins scaled to child size. Wash cloths and towels provided by the center were hung on hooks within the children's reach and marked with individual symbols matching the ones on their lockers.

There was a large room in each center, separated from the playrooms, where children could be cared for when they were ill. Comfortable cribs, like those used in children's hospitals, were placed in glass-sided cubicles that allowed children quiet places to sleep, eat, or sit up and play while recovering from colds, coughs, earaches, or upset tummies. A registered nurse was on duty at all times in the infirmary, and teachers planned and provided the play materials and projects for both the bed patients and those who were up and about.

Each center had a fully equipped, large, modern kitchen that was adequate for serving meals and snacks, over a 24-hour day, to some 400 children and their teachers. Large, heated rolling carts were available to deliver the china, silverware, and food to each room, where children were served at small, low tables. Usually, five children and a teacher dined together each day as a "family."

The architects thoughtfully included one additional feature: several large, square bathtubs raised two steps above the floor. These tubs allowed teachers, when necessary or desirable, to bathe a child without bending over. These tubs also provided safe places for children to "swim" and splash and engage in relaxing water play.

Opening Days

Oregon Center, where I was a group supervisor, opened its doors on November 8, 1943, to children, age 18 months to six years, of parents working on the day and swing shifts. On that day, a total of 67 children came to the center. We were, of course, very disappointed in this turnout. We realized, however, that the majority of people in the area had never even heard of a nursery school and were not able to imagine a children's center that would stay open twelve months a year, six days a week, and twenty-four hours a day! So we planned "open house" on Sundays and invited the public to tour the centers. We went down into the shipyards to talk to the workers about the child services available. Feature articles with many photographs appeared in the local newspapers. Gradually, more children were enrolled. By Christmas of that year, there were over 100 children being cared for in the center. In January, the graveyard shift was started, as was a Saturday and after-school program for older children. By August 27th, when Oregon Shipyard went on a seven-day work week, the Center was operating seven days a week, with an average daily attendance of 370 children.

Everything possible was done to keep workers on the job of building ships. Parents paid only nominal fees for child service: 75 cents a day for one child in a family and 50 cents for each additional child, paid by the week. If a child came seven days a week, parents were only charged for six days.

The Children

Mothers or fathers brought the children to their rooms at the Center each day before their shifts began, and picked them up after the shift ended. Day-shift children often spent nine or more hours in the Center as that was the longest shift. Day-shift parents were always in a hurry, it seemed, and were less able to spend time helping their children make the transition from home to school. Separating from their mothers and fathers was painful for some children at first.

After working out in the cold and rain for long hours at a stretch, day-shift parents were very tired and in a hurry at the end of the day when they came to pick up their children. Some were cross and impatient as they hurried their preschoolers to avoid missing the bus or car-pool ride. There was no time to talk over their child's day with the teacher. So, teachers communicated with parents about their children by writing brief comments next to a child's name on a chart hung outside the playroom door. These comments had to be worded with great tact, we discovered. Even such comments as "John didn't finish his lunch" or "Betsy didn't take a nap today" could result in angry scolding or slapping of the child. We tried to emphasize the positive behaviors in our messages in order to make each child appear more lovable and interesting to parents.

For the children on the swing shift, life was quite different. They usually arrived early after a leisurely day at home or out shopping with their parents. Mothers and fathers on their way to work often stayed for a while at the center, reading stories or looking at toys or interesting things the children described to them the night before. There was a more relaxed atmosphere in the playrooms during the swing shift than during the day shift. This was evident in the conversations between children, and especially in their dramatic play.

Swing-shift children were served supper as a group, after which they had time to play, listen to stories, enjoy music and play games, paint pictures and, in summertime, play outside until dark. They then undressed and went to bed. The children were then awakened and dressed before their tired parents arrived.

Additional Services

The Center also tried to provide time-saving services to parents that might relieve some of the stresses under which they worked. Home Service Foods began in January of 1944. Precooked meals, planned by Dr. Lowenberg, were prepared in the centers' kitchens. Priced at fifty cents each, one order was ample for a working man or woman, and a single portion would serve two preschool children. These ready-packaged meals were ordered two or more days in advance and contained the main course and dessert, the foods that usually required the most preparation time. Directions were included for heating and serving, and suggestions for additional foods to round out the meal were offered.

In time, other services were added, such as mending children's clothes, buying their shoelaces, and haircutting. In February, a program of immunizations was begun. Children whose parents had not been able to arrange for the necessary shots required for nursery school attendance were able to receive their shots at the Center. Teachers, in the absence of parents, brought children in turn to the Center's physician, holding them on their laps to reassure and comfort them while they got their shots.

Parent-Teacher Interactions

Parent-teacher conferences were usually difficult to arrange. We found ways to talk briefly with a mother by walking with her to a waiting bus or car. Teachers invited parents into the playrooms to see the artwork of their children or to view special block buildings preserved for their admiration.

Parent meetings took place occasionally when dinner was served to the mothers and fathers in one room while their children had dinner in another. Group supervisors went down into the shipyard to talk to a parent when it seemed necessary. On these occasions, I found myself surrounded by fathers and mothers who eagerly asked "What was my child doing when you left?" As parents realized how much teachers knew and cared about their children, they made time for interviews and shared their problems and pleasures with them.

Program Results

Many good things happened in the Child Service Centers in the Kaiser Shipyards—for children, for parents, for the industry, for all of us. We all had a part in winning the war as "cham-

pion shipbuilders," as we were told, and for that we were proud. The head of the Maritime Commission told the teachers that, without their help, it would have been impossible to keep the shipyards in production seven days a week. Parents told us that when they were tired and tempted to sleep late on Sunday morning, their children would awaken them, saying "Get up, get up. If you don't go to work, we don't get to go to school." When the centers were closed in 1945 at the end of the war, records showed that "3,811 children were taken care of—a total of 250,000 child care days—which freed almost 2 million working hours for the women" (Stanford University Campus Report, Interview with Lois Stolz, March 30,1983).

But I think the most remarkable, the best thing that happened was that, in a time of war, when mothers of preschool children worked eight and nine hours a day, six or seven days a week, the lives of almost 4,000 children were made happy, healthy, and in some ways, better than they ever were before. This could only happen as a combination of skillful professional planning, strong professional leadership, and some of the best teachers the nursery school profession has ever prepared. I believe that all children deserve to benefit from that combination, especially in their early years.

We must wonder if, in the future, there will be enough professionally prepared specialists in the field to provide leadership. Will there be enough teachers who are knowledgeable about the nature and development of infants and young children and sensitive to their individual needs? Will there be enough enlightened and caring personnel to license and monitor (with in-service education) facilities and programs for an entire nation's children? You—and those who follow in your footsteps—hold the answers to these questions.

Edith M. Dowley was involved in early childhood education for fifty years. She was a group supervisor in the Kaiser Child Service Centers, and later became the first director of Stanford University's Bing Nursery School, a position she retained until 1975. She served as a national consultant to Project Head Start from 1965 to 1968, and from 1971 to 1972 she was a member of the California Task Force on Early Childhood Education. The late Dr. Dowley was most recently Professor Emerita of Psychology and Education at Stanford University.

SUMMARY

High-quality early childhood programs reflect the core elements of developmentally appropriate practices (DAP) by basing the program on what is known about child development and learning, what is known about each individual child, and what is known about the child's social and cultural context. By following DAP guidelines, early childhood programs maximize the benefits children gain from attending an early education program. Following the guidelines for Developmentally and Culturally Appropriate Practice (DCAP) ensures equal and fair teaching and learning experiences for all students.

Educational facilities for young children reach a broad population. They serve children from infancy through elementary-school age. An array of programs is available; each varies for philosophical reasons as well as because of the ages of children enrolled. Early childhood teachers have a wide range of programs from which to choose—as do parents.

The traditional nursery school and its sister programs of child care centers and family child care form the core of early childhood programs. There are many sponsors of early childhood programs, including universities, employers, religious institutions, profit and non-profit groups, parents, public schools, high schools, hospitals, and governmental agencies. Head Start and Early Head Start are two successful examples of government sponsored attempts to provide early education and intervention to children caught in poverty's cycle.

Reflecting the needs of society, extended day programs provide for group care before and after school hours. Infant/toddler programs are common, and school-age care is a service that meets the demands for good, safe, and challenging programs for children who need care on either side of their school day.

Quality is a primary issue in all early childhood programs. The trilemma of finding and keeping qualified teachers and supporting them with equitable wages and benefits is challenging while attempting to keep a program financially accessible to those who need it.

A good evaluation process includes a clear purpose, knowing who and what will be evaluated, and what use will be made of the results. Any program designed to meet the needs of children must be evaluated on a regular basis. Teachers, children, and the program must be assessed individually and then evaluated as a whole. Each supports and depends upon the other; an evaluation is a way to look at how these relationships are working. The result is a better prepared staff and a program of greater quality.

For more activities and information, visit our website at http://www.EarlyChildEd.delmar.com

KEY TERMS

developmentally appropriate practice (DAP)
sociocultural
mixed-age grouping
looping
traditional nursery school
child care center

family child care
laboratory schools
parent cooperative schools
employer-sponsored child care
faith-based programs
educaring

attachment
alignment
self-care
evaluation
accountability

REVIEW QUESTIONS

1. What are the three core considerations of developmentally appropriate practices?

2. What factors determine how a program serves diverse needs?

3. What are the core programs of early childhood education?

4. What are the variations of the core programs and who do they serve?

5. The age range of early childhood programs is extended in what ways?

6. What are the three most important factors that determine the quality of an early childhood program?

7. What are the reasons for evaluating early childhood programs?

LEARNING ACTIVITIES

1. Choose one program and describe why you would like to teach in it. What are the most attractive elements of the program? What are some of the challenges you would have working in such a program?

2. Visit a family child care home. Look at the home as if you were a prospective parent. What did you like most? Least? Is the home licensed? If so, for how many children? After talking with the family child care provider, what do you think are the disadvantages of this type of program? What do you think are possible solutions to these problems?

3. What are the licensing regulations for child care in your area? Describe the steps necessary in your town to open a nursery school, child care center, and a family child care home.

4. Visit a Head Start program and a local Kindergarten. Compare their programs in terms of appropriate or inappropriate curriculum. What are the major concerns of the teaching staff in each type of setting? What are the controversies about each of these programs in your community?

5. Does your own setting have an evaluation plan? Analyze the goals of your setting and note where the implementation meets (or does not meet) the goals.

6. Visit an NAEYC accredited program. Discuss the following with the director or supervisor: How did the staff respond to the process? What were some of the most difficult issues to address? What was the role of parents in the process? What have been the benefits of accreditation?

HELPFUL WEBSITES

Bureau of Labor Statistics   **http://www.stats.bls.gov**

U.S. Department of Education   **http://www.edu.gov**

Families and Work Institute   **http://www.familiesandwork.org**

National Institute on Out-of-School Time   **http://www.niost.org**

National Network for Child Care   **http://www.nncc.org**

National Association for Family Child Care   **http://www.nafcc.org**

Child Care Information Exchange   **http://www.ccie.com**

National Center for Education Statistics   **http://www.nces.ed.gov**

Culturally and Linguistically Appropriate Services   **http://www.clas.uiuc.edu**

Center for Child Care Workforce   **http://www.ccw.org**

International Nanny's Association   **http://www.nanny.org**

Head Start/Early Head Start   **http://www.acf.hhs.gov/programs/ohs**

ChildStats   **http://www.childstats.gov**

U.S. Census Bureau   **http://www.census.gov**

Children's Defense Fund   **http://www.childrensdefense.org**

About Homeschooling   **http://www.homeschooling.about.com**

National Association for the Education of Young Children   **http://www.naeyc.org**

 Additional resources including the TeachSource Videos can be found on the premium website for this book. Go to **http://www.cengage.com/login** to register your access code.

REFERENCES

Afterschool Alliance. Working families and afterschool. A special report from *America After 3 PM*. Retrieved from http://www.afterschoolalliance.org/research America3PM.cfm.

Allen, K. E., & Cowdery, G. (2009). *The exceptional child: Inclusion in early childhood education*. Clifton Park, NY: Delmar Learning.

Baker, K. R. (1950). *The nursery school: A human relationships laboratory*. Philadelphia, PA: Saunders.

Barnett, W. S., Hustedt, J. T., Friedman, A. H., Boyd, J. S., & Ainsworth, P. 2007. *The state of preschool, 2007 yearbook*. National Institute for Early Education Research (NIEER).

Bellis, M. (1999, May). Look before you loop. *Young Children*, pp. 70–72.

Berk, L. E. (2009). *Child Development*. Boston: Allyn & Bacon.

Bieleck, S., Chandler, K., & Broughman, S. (2001). Homeschooling in the United States: 1999. *Education Statistics Quarterly* (NCES 2001-033). U.S. Department of Education, Washington, DC.

Bredekamp, S., & Glowacki, S. (1996). The first decade of NAEYC accreditation: Growth and impact on the field. In S. Bredkamp & B. A. Willer (Eds.), *NAEYC accreditation: A decade of learning and the years ahead*. Washington, DC: National Association for the Education of Young Children.

Brown, B. (1985, July). Head Start-How research changed public policy. *Young Children*, pp. 9-13.

Bureau of Labor Statistics. Occupational Employment Statistics, May, 2007. 39-9011 Child Care Workers. Retrieved from website March, 2009: www.bureau oflabor.gov.

(The) Carolina Abecedarian Project. (1999). The Frank Porter Graham Child Development Institute. The University of North Carolina at Chapel Hill: Author.

Chapman, J. (1999, May). A looping journey. *Young Children*, pp. 80–83.

Chase, P., & Doan, J. (Eds.). (1994). *Full circle: A new look at multi-age education*. Portsmouth, NH: Heineman Publishers.

Children's Defense Fund. (2005). *The state of America's children, yearbook 2051*. Washington, DC: Author.

Children's Defense Fund (2008). *The state of American's children, yearbook, 2008*.

Cloud, J., & Morse, J. (August 27, 2001). Home sweet school. *Time*, pp. 47–54.

Cohen, D. L. (1993b, April 21). Perry preschool graduates show dramatic new social gains at 27. *Education Week*, p. 1.

Copple, C., & Bredekamp, S. (2009). *Developmentally appropriate practice in early childhood programs serving children from birth through age 8*. Washington, DC: National Association for the Education of Young Children.

Cost, Quality, and Child Outcomes Study Team (1995). *Cost, quality and child outcomes in child care centers*. Denver: Department of Economics, University of Colorado at Denver.

Education Commission of the States (ECS). 2008. Retrieved from website 2/20/09. www.ecs.org/kindergarten.

Education Commission of the States (ECS). 2006. Retrieved from website 2/21/09. www.ecs.org/kindergarten.

Families and Work Institute (2008). 2008 National Study of Employers. Retrieved from www.families andwork.org.

Gerber, M. (1979). Respecting infants: The Loczy model of infant care. In E. Jones (Ed.), *Supporting the growth of infants, toddlers, and parents*. Pasadena, CA: Pacific Oaks.

Greenberg, P. (1990, September). Before the beginning: A participant's view. *Young Children*, pp. 41–52.

Gullo, D.F. (Ed.) 2006. *Teaching and learning in the kindergarten year*. Washington, DC: National Association for the Education of Young Children.

Hampton, D. (April 2002). Executive Director, Ecumenical Child Care Network. Speech delivered to Delaware Valley Child Care Council, Philadelphia, PA.

Harms, T, Clifford, R. M., & Cryer, D. (1998). *Early Childhood Environmental Rating Scale* (Rev. Ed.). New York: Teachers College Press.

Hatch, J. A. (2005). *Teaching in the new kindergarten*. Clifton Park, NY: Thomson Delmar Learning.

Head Start (2009). *2009 Head Start fact sheet.* Washington, DC: Head Start Bureau, Department of Health and Human Services.

Hyun, E. (1998). *Making sense of developmentally and culturally appropriate practice (DCAP) in early childhood education.* New York: Peter Lang.

Kagan. S. L., & Kauerz, K. (2006). Making the most of kindergarten: Trends and policy issues. In D. F. Gullo (Ed.) *Teaching and learning in the kindergarten year.* Washington, DC: National Association for the Education of Young Children.

Karoly, L. A., & Bigelow, J. H. (2005). *The economics of investing in universal preschool education in California.* Santa Monica, CA: RAND (Research and Development Corporation).

Katz, L. (1995, May). The benefits of mixed-age grouping. *ERIC Digest.* (EDO-PS-95–8)

Katz, L. (2000, August). Academic redshirting and young children. *ERIC Digest.* (EDO-PS-00-13)

Katz, L. G., Evangelou, D., & Hartman, J. A. (1990). *The case for mixed-age groupings in early education.* Washington, DC: National Association for the Education of Young Children.

Lawrence, S., & Kreader, J. K. (2006). School-age child care arrangements. *Child Care & Early Education Research Connections* at www.research connections.org.

Lindner, E., Mattis, M. C, & Rogers, J. (1983). *When churches mind the children.* Ypsilanti, MI: High/Scope Press.

McCartney, K., Dearing, E., Taylor, B., & Bub, K. (2007). Quality childcare supports the achievement of low-income children: Direct and indirect pathways through caregiving and the home environment. *Journal of Applied Developmental Psychology, 28,* 411-426.

National Association of Child Care Resources and Referral Agencies (NACCRRA). (2008). Child Care in America. Retrieved from website February, 2009.

National Association for Family Child Care. (2005). *NAFCC accreditation and information.* Salt Lake City, UT: Author.

National Association for the Education of Young Children Position Statement. (2009). Developmentally appropriate practice in early childhood programs serving children from birth through age 8. In Copple. C. & Bredekamp, S. (Eds.), *Developmentally appropriate practice in early childhood programs.* Washington, DC: National Association for the Education of Young Children.

National Association for the Education of Young Children. (1998a, January). NAEYC position statement on licensing and public regulation of early childhood programs. *Young Children,* pp. 43–50.

National Association for the Education of Young Children. (1998b). *Accreditation criteria and procedures of the National Academy of Early Childhood Programs.* Washington, DC: Author.

National Association for the Education of Young Children. (2005). *NAEYC early childhood program standards & accreditation criteria.* Washington, DC: National Association for the Education of Young Children.

National Association of Early Childhood Specialists in State Departments of Education and the National Association of Education for Young Children. (2001, September). Still unacceptable trends in kindergarten entry and placement. *Young Children,* pp. 59–62.

National Center for Education Statistics (2008). All levels of education. In *Digest of Education Statistics, 2007 (NCES 2008-022).* Washington, DC: U.S. Department of Education.

National Coalition for the Homeless (2007). *How many people experience homelessness?* NCH Fact Sheet #2. National Coalition for the Homeless, June, 2008.

Neugebauer, R. (2001, September). Employer child care growth and consolidation issues. *Child Care Information Exchange,* pp. 14–17.

Neugebauer, R. , Wilson, M., & Ballas, T. (2007, September/October). School-age child care trend, part II. *Child Care Information Exchange,* pp. 28-39.

Neugebauer, R. (2008, July/August). Employer child care organizations eye changing economics: Employer child care status report # 16. *Child Care Information Exchange,* pp. 78-79.

Neugebauer, R. (2008). For profit child care: Four decades of growth: Ninteenth annual status report on for profit child care. *Child Care Information Exchange.* Retrieved from website March, 2009.

United States Census Bureau (2007). *Who's minding the kids? Child care arrangements: Spring, 2005.* Survey of Income and Program Participation (SIPP). Internet release date February 2008. Washington, DC U. S. Bureau of the Census: Author.

Schweinhart, L. J., & Weikart, D. P. (1993, November). Success by empowerment: The High/Scope Perry preschool study through age 27. *Young Children,* pp. 54–58.

Suro, R. (1992, January 5). Holding back to get ahead. *The New York Times,* 4A, pp. 30–32.

Whitebook, M., Sakai, L., Gerber, E., & Howes, C. (2001). *Then and now: Changes in child care staffing, 1994–2000.* Washington, DC: Center for the Child Care Workforce.

Who Is the Young Child?

© Cengage Learning

Defining the Young Child

PREVIEW QUESTIONS

- What is meant by "the whole child"?
- How are children alike?
- What is the value of Word Pictures?
- How do children differ?
- Who are children with special needs, and how are they accommodated in early childhood classrooms?
- Who is the gifted and talented child?
- What are some of the cultural, ethnic, and racial considerations in working with young children?

NAEYC CODE OF ETHICAL CONDUCT

These Core Values and sections from the NAEYC Code of Ethical Conduct are addressed in this chapter. As you read, note how the Core Values, Ideals, or Principles listed here apply to the topics in this chapter. (Reprinted with permission from the National Association for the Education of Young Children.)

Ideals:

I-1.1   To be familiar with the knowledge base of early childhood care and education.

I-1.2   To base program practices upon current knowledge in the field of child development and related disciplines and upon particular knowledge of each child.

I-1.3   To recognize and respect the uniqueness and potential of each child.

I-1.6   To support the right of each child to play and learn in inclusive early childhood programs to the fullest extent consistent with the best interests of all involved.

I-1.7   To ensure that children with disabilities have access to appropriate and convenient support services and to advocate for the resources necessary to provide the most appropriate settings for all children.

Principles:

P-1.   We shall not participate in practices that discriminate against children by denying benefits, giving special advantages, or excluding them from programs or activities on the basis of their race, ethnicity, religion, sex, national origin, language, ability, or the status, behavior, or beliefs of their parents.

The Whole Child

The concept of "the whole child" is based on the accepted principle that all areas of human growth and development are integrated. It is only for the purpose of studying one area or another in depth that such categories are created. The six developmental areas labeled in the Word Pictures in Figure 3-1 help us focus on certain aspects of a child's normal development. In reality, all areas of growth are "intertwined and mutually supportive" (Allen & Marotz, 2007).

Each Child Is Unique

Each child is unique, the sum total of a multitude of parts, and, as such, is different from anyone else. Individual natures and learning styles affect the way teachers will teach any two children of the same age in the same class.

We often define children by their physical characteristics; their differences are most obvious by the way they look:

Eric is a tall blond. He is much larger than his just-3 age would indicate. He has long slender fingers and arms to match. His movements are fluid; he lopes across the room toward the easel.

Lamar's short stocky build and constant swagger lend the impression that he is a pretty tough character at age 6. His twinkling eyes and infectious smile offset that image.

Natalie at 4 is a study in perpetual motion. Green eyes flashing, arms and legs waving, she ignores the bulk of her diaper as she propels herself

down the slide. There is little indication that the mild case of spina bifida she has inhibits her motor activities. It certainly has not affected her daring.

Nothing heightens an awareness of the individuality of each child more than working in the classroom. Teachers quickly learn what makes each child special as we learn what children look like when they move their bodies, change expressions, and assume a posture. A teacher can sense whether Sonja is happy, hurt, or hurried by the way she moves and how she looks. Rodrigo's face mirrors his distress or his delight. The observant teacher learns to read children for evidence of their social, emotional, physical, and intellectual growth. Children quite naturally express these characteristics with their whole body, and each child's response is unique.

Growth Is Interrelated

One area of development affects the other. Figure 3-1 helps us to look at this concept of development visually. Think of each area of development as a circle. There are six of them: physical-motor, language, intellectual, social-emotional, cultural awareness, and creative.

Think how each area might affect or interact with the others:

- Physical development affects how children feel about themselves. Children who appreciate their body and its power feel confident in what they can do (social-emotional).
- Intellectual skills interact with language development and creativity. When children have mastered

FIGURE 3-1 How areas of growth are interrelated: each area of growth is affected by and influences every other area of development.

LANGUAGE
CREATIVE
PHYSICAL-MOTOR
CULTURAL AWARENESS
SOCIAL-EMOTIONAL
COGNITIVE

Children: alike, yet different.

their primary language, they can then clarify some of their thought processes.

- The kindergartner who masters using scissors (physical) is ready to try printing. The fine-motor skills enhance the cognitive task of learning the alphabet.
- A child with a hearing loss is likely to have language delay as well; thus the physical development affects the language part of growth.
- The child who has trouble making friends (social) is likely to exhibit his unhappiness (emotional) in the school yard (physical) and in the math period (intellectual).

Valuing Wholeness

The concept of the whole child strongly suggests the uniqueness of the person. Although they are often discussed separately, the areas of development (social-emotional, physical, language, cultural awareness, intellectual, and creative) cannot be isolated from one another. They each make a valuable contribution to the total child.

How Children Are Alike

The similarities of the many children in a class are striking. Teachers can see the differences, yet there are common characteristics within the age group itself. Six toddlers working on an art project exhibit six different personal styles, yet typically, they all become distracted and leave their projects half finished.

Observation of children—how they look and how they act—helps a teacher see each child as an individual (see Chapter 6). At the same time, there is enough standard behavior appropriate to certain age levels that allows for some generalizations about children's behavior.

Caldwell (1993) cites three universal characteristics that unite children of the world. Each child is like every other in that: (1) they all have the same needs, the most important of which are food, shelter, and care; (2) they all go through the same developmental stages; and (3) they all have the same developmental goals, although the timing and the cultural influences will differ.

The Value of Word Pictures

Each developmental phase has characteristic traits. These traits can be characterized in a series of developmental profiles, or **Word Pictures.** In the following pages some of the classic normative data collected by Gesell (see Chap-

ter 1) and Ilg (1943) are combined with theories of Piaget, Elkind, Erikson, and Vygotsky (see Chapter 4) to demonstrate what children have in common at various ages. Despite the wide range of individual differences at all ages, common behaviors lend a perspective to help teachers prescribe programs, plan activities, and create curricula.

In Behavior and Guidance

Guidance and discipline are based on an awareness of the expected behaviors common to a given age range. Many so-called problem behaviors are normal behaviors of the age at which they occur: for example, the difficulty some toddlers and 2-year-olds have with sharing their toys. Knowing this does not imply a passive approach; teachers and parents do not ignore undesirable behavior because the child is "going through a stage." Instead, adults seek to guide and direct children in ways that enhance their ability to learn more effective behavior. Four-year-olds test limits and are resistant to controls. The wise teacher accepts the testing of power and individuality, yet still maintains necessary limits to behavior.

Word Pictures of a child, taken from age-level charts, help teachers know what to expect and when to expect it. By using the charts as a reference, teachers lessen the risk of expecting too much or too little of children at any given age. If, for instance, 4-year-olds typically "tell tall tales," teachers' responses to their stories reflect an awareness of that tendency. The fun of making up a story and the use of imagination are acknowledged, but there is not a concern that the child is lying. **Age-level characteristics** give a frame of reference with which to handle daily situations and a basis for planning appropriate guidance measures.

Adults see children through many filters. What is it like to look through children's eyes?

In Curriculum

Word Pictures can be used to tailor curriculum planning to an individual child or a particular class or group on the basis of known developmental standards. A group cooking experience, for instance, allows children to choose their level of comfort and involvement. As an early reader at age 4, Darragh loves to read the recipe to others. Lourdes's favorite activity is to mix the ingredients together, refining her small motor skills. Von, who loves to play with mud and clay, spreads the cookie sheet with oil while Felicity helps the teacher adjust the oven temperature. When planning an activity, the teacher takes into account what she knows about each child's development and the age group. Cooking is always a fun activity but serves a greater purpose when planned with individual children in mind. The skills and abilities of the specific age group helps to determine the kind of activities at which children can succeed while still taking the next steps in their development. See the next section for guidelines on using the Word Pictures as tools for planning. Chapters 10 through 14 have more practical applications and examples for planning curricula.

In Cultural Awareness

Derman-Sparks and Edwards (2010) point out that children become aware of and form attitudes about racial and cultural differences at a very early age. Their experiences with their bodies, social environment, and cognitive development combine to help them form their own identity and attitudes. As they develop cognitively, children become aware of differences and similarities in people.

These cultural milestones are included in the Word Pictures to indicate how, as children come to a sense of themselves as individuals, their attitudes and behaviors towards others can be influenced.

Using Word Pictures

Age-level charts describe common behaviors and characteristics in the course of normal development. When used appropriately, Word Pictures can be a valuable teaching tool.

Six Developmental Areas

Six basic developmental areas are included in the Word Pictures:

- *Social-Emotional Development.* This includes a child's relationship with himself and others, self-concept, self-esteem, and the ability to express feelings.
- *Language Development.* This includes a child's utterances, pronunciation, vocabulary, and sentence length, as well as the ability to express ideas, needs, and feelings. It includes receptive language (do they understand what they hear?) and verbal levels (what do they say?).
- *Physical-Motor Development.* This includes gross motor, fine motor, and perceptual motor development.
- *Cognitive Development.* This includes curiosity, the ability to perceive and think, memory, attention span, general knowledge, problem solving, analytical thinking, beginning reading, computing skills, and other cognitive processes.
- *Cultural Identity Development.* This suggests the interconnections between developmental stages and a growing awareness of one's attitudes toward others of differing cultures. Various cultural milestones appear in each age group *highlighted by an asterisk*, which, when appropriately fostered, can increase a child's sensitivity to differences. These characteristics cut across all of the other developmental areas.
- *Creative Development.* This includes creative activities such as movement, dance, music, and painting, as well as originality, imagination, divergent thinking, and problem solving.

How Word Pictures Help Teachers

The Word Pictures are designed to help classroom teachers. They focus on the critical issues that teachers address when planning for a group of children. These are:

- Behaviors most common to the age group.
- Those that have implications for children in group settings.
- Those that suggest guidance and disciplinary measures.
- Those that have implications for planning a developmentally appropriate curriculum.
- Those that are cultural milestones, *which are highlighted by an asterisk* to suggest the interaction of children's development and their awareness of attitudes toward race and culture.

DAP In order to build attitudes that go beyond mere tolerance, we must help children gain more accurate pictures of persons and cultures different from their own.

WORD PICTURES

INFANT

Social-Emotional

0–1 month: cries to express emotions; bonding begins

4–10 weeks: makes social smiles

2 months: begins social games

3 months: distinguishes familiar faces*; turns head toward human voice; smiles in response to a smile; kicks, smiles, waves in response; cries when left alone; recognizes parent

4 months: has a genuine laugh; smiles when spoken to; loves attention

5 months to 1 year: begins to exhibit stranger anxiety*

6 months: distinguishes between voices: smiles; babbles at strangers; develops attachment to parents, caregivers; begins to play imitation games; plays peek-a-boo; sensitive to parental moods

8 months: laughs out loud

9 months: screams to get own way

Play is activity only for present moment

Fears unfamiliar: people, places, things*

Beginning sense of separate self*

Language

0–1 month: turns head in response to voices; cries to express needs

6–8 weeks: coos; gestures to communicate: pushes objects away; squirms; reaches out to people*; pouts; smacks lips; shrieks; points

2 months: makes voluntary vocal sounds

3 months: babbles

Courtesy of the author

6–12 months: plays imitation sound games; responds to variety of sounds*; makes vowel sounds; acquires receptive language*; cries to communicate

12 months: says first words

Physical-Motor

By 1 year: grows 10 to 12 inches; triples birth weight; lengthens by 40 percent; doubles brain size; grows full head of hair; bounces in crib; uses whole-body motions

4 months: sees, grasps objects

5 months: examines fingers; sits when propped

6 months: rolls over; discovers feet; teething begins

7 months: crawls

8 months: sits up unaided; pulls to standing position; pincer grasp established

9 months: creeps

10 months: feeds self with spoon

11 months: stands alone; cruises

12 months: takes first steps

Late infancy: can move hands in rotation to turn knobs

Newborn motor activity is mostly reflexes

Creative

Discovers and explores hands and feet

Expresses and discovers emotion

Talks by babbling, cooing, and gurgling

Plays peek-a-boo

Responds to facial expressions

Cognitive

0–1 month: responds to mother's voice; aware of senses, especially pain, touch*

10 weeks: memory is evident*

4 months: makes smiles of recognition

7–10 months: solves simple problems (knocks over box to get toy)

8 months: begins to believe in permanence of objects; follows a simple instruction

8–12 months: becoming intentional in behavior

11 months: begins trial-error experimentation

12 months: plays drop/retrieve games, pat-a-cake

Explores with hands and fingers

Smiles, vocalizes at image in mirror*

*Key characteristics of cultural awareness or identity.

TODDLER

Social-Emotional

Almost totally egocentric

Likes to be noticed; loves an audience

Lacks inhibitions

Insists on own way, assertive

Likes doing things by self

Independent, has self-identity*

Adapts easily

Refers to self by name

Laughs loudly at peek-at-boo

Cries when left alone

Curious*

Relates to adults better than children

Active, eager

Talks mostly to self

Usually friendly

Strong sense of ownership

Mimics adult behavior*

Experiences and shows shame*

Language

Some two-word phrases

Enjoys vocalizing to self

Babbles in own jargon

Uses "eh-eh" or "uh-uh" with gestures

Names closest relatives*

Repeats adults' words*

Points to communicate needs, wants

Shakes head "no" to respond*

Responds to directions to fetch, point

Obeys verbal requests

Asks "What's that?" or "Whassat?"*

Understands simple phrases

Uses five to 50 words

Physical-Motor

Awkward coordination; chubby body

Tottering stance

Creeps when in a hurry

Walks with increasing confidence

Walks with feet wide apart, arms out, head forward

Finds it difficult to turn corners

Goes up and down stairs holding on

Backs into chair to sit down

Can squat for long periods of time

In constant motion

Loves to pull/push objects

Runs with stiff, flat gait

Uses whole-arm movements

Carry and dump becomes a favorite activity

Scribbles

Turns pages two or three at a time

Zips/unzips large zipper

Likes holding objects in both hands

Creative

Responds to mood of music

Freely examines every object

Sings phrases of nursery rhymes

Courtesy of the author

Loves to finger-paint and explore texture

Stares; takes it all in

"The age of exploration"

Makes up nonsense syllables

Cognitive

Points to objects in a book

Matches similar objects

Fits round block in round hole

Loves opposites: up/down, yes/no*

Imitates simple tasks

Interest shifts quickly

Short attention span

Follows one direction

Gives up easily but easily engaged*

Conclusions are important: closes doors, shuts books

Thinks with feet; action-oriented

Builds tower of three or four small blocks

*Key characteristics of cultural awareness or identity.

© Cengage Learning

Social-Emotional

Self-centered

Unable to share, possessive

Clings to familiar; resistant to change*

Ritualistic; insists on routines*

Dependent

Likes one adult at a time*

Quits readily; easily frustrated

Goes to extremes

Impulsive; shifts activities suddenly

Easily distracted

Pushes, shoves

Finicky, fussy eater; some food jags

Refers to self by given name*

Treats people as inanimate objects*

Dawdles; slow-geared

Plays parallel to other children

Watches others*

Likes people*

Excited about own capabilities

Language

Uses two- or three-word sentences

Telegraphic sentences: "Throw ball"

Has difficulty in pronunciation

"Me," "Mine" most prominent pronouns*

Spontaneous language; rhythmic, repetitive

Constant talking; interested in sound

Sings phrases of song, not on pitch

Cannot articulate feelings

Frustrated when not understood

May stutter

Asks "Whassat?" about pictures*

Can match words with objects

Repeats words and phrases

Uses 50 to 300 words

Physical-Motor

Uses whole-body action: pushes, pulls, pokes

Climbs into things

Leans forward while running

Climbs stairs one by one

Dependent on adults for dressing

Can help dress/undress

Has reached one-half potential height

Bladder/bowel control begins

Feeds self

Thumb-forefinger opposition complete

Grasps cup with two hands

Awkward with small objects

Lugs, tumbles, topples; unsteady

Alternates hands; hand preference is developing

Can rotate to fit objects

Expresses emotions bodily*

Sensory-oriented

Cuts last teeth

Has difficulty relaxing

Creative

Imitates other children

Combines parallel play and fantasy play

Plays with sounds; repeats syllables over and over

Enjoys simple finger plays

Can follow simple melodies

Learns to scribble

Uses art for sensory pleasure

Cognitive

Recognizes, explores physical characteristics of objects*

Investigates with touch and taste

Intrigued by water, washing

Likes to fill and empty things

Has limited attention span

Lives in present

Understands familiar concepts*

Can tell difference between black and white*

Needs own name used

Likes simple make-believe

Does one thing at a time

Remembers orders of routines

Recalls where toys are left

Classifies people by gender*

Names familiar objects in books

*Key characteristics of cultural awareness or identity.

THREE-YEAR-OLD

Social-Emotional

Highly imitative of adults*

Wants to please adults; conforms*

Responds to verbal suggestions

Easily prompted, redirected

Can be bargained with, reasoned with

Begins to share, take turns, wait

Avid "me-too"-er*

Exuberant, talkative, humorous

Has an imaginary companion

Has nightmares, animal phobias

Plays consciously, cooperatively with others*

Plays spontaneously in groups

Demonstrates fears

Goes after desires; fights for them

Asserts independence often

Often stymied, frustrated, jealous

Sympathizes*

Strong sex-role stereotypes*

Language

Talkative with or without a listener

Can listen to learn*

Likes new words*

Increases use of pronouns, prepositions

Uses "s" to indicate plural nouns

Uses "ed" to indicate past tense

Uses sentences of three or more words

Says "Is that all right?" a lot

Talks about nonpresent situations

Puts words into action

Moves and talks at the same time

Substitutes letters in speech: "w" for "r"

Intrigued by whispering

Uses 300 to 1000 words

© Cengage Learning

Physical-Motor

Has well-balanced body lines

Walks erect; nimble on feet

Gallops in wide, high steps

Alternates feet in stair climbing

Suddenly starts, stops

Turns corners rapidly

Swings arms when walking

Jumps up and down with ease

Uses toilet alone

Loses baby fat

Achieves bladder control

Rides a tricycle

Puts on, takes off wraps with help

Unbuttons buttons

Has some finger control with small objects

Grasps with thumb and index finger

Holds cup in one hand

Pours easily from small pitcher

Washes hands unassisted

Can carry liquids

Has activity with drive and purpose

Can balance on one foot

Creative

Dramatizes play

Enjoys slap-stick humor

Laughs at the ridiculous

Experiments with silly language

Imaginary companion may appear

Tricycle becomes many objects in dramatic play

Acts out own version of favorite story

Enjoys simple poems

Learns color concepts

Cognitive

Matches people according to physical characteristics*

Estimates "how many"

Enjoys making simple choices

Alert, excited, curious

Asks "why?" constantly*

Understands "It's time to…"

Understands "Let's pretend…"

Enjoys guessing games, riddles

Has lively imagination*

Often over generalizes*

Carries out two to four directions in sequence

Often colors pages one color

Can't combine two activities

Names and matches simple colors

Has number concept of one and two

Sees vague cause-and-effect relationships*

Can recognize simple melodies

Distinguishes between night and day

Understands size and shape comparisons

*Key characteristics of cultural awareness or identity.

FOUR-YEAR-OLD

Social-Emotional

Mood changes rapidly

Tries out feelings of power

Dominates; can be bossy, boastful, belligerent

Assertive, argumentative

Shows off; is cocky, noisy

Can fight own battles

Hits, grabs, insists on desires

Explosive, destructive

Easily over stimulated; excitable

Impatient in large groups*

Cooperates in groups of two or three*

Develops "special" friends* but shifts loyalties often

May exclude others from play*

Resistant; tests limits

Exaggerates, tells tall tales

Alibis frequently

Teases, outwits; has terrific humor

May have scary dreams

Tattles frequently

Has food jags, food strikes

Language

Has more words than knowledge

A great talker, questioner

Likes words, plays with them

Has high interest in poetry

Able to talk to solve conflicts*

Responds to verbal directions

Enjoys taking turns to sing along

Interested in dramatizing songs, stories

Exaggerates, practices words

Uses voice control, pitch, rhythm

Asks "when?" "why?" "how?"*

Joins sentences together

Loves being read to

Physical-Motor

Longer, leaner body build

Vigorous, dynamic, acrobatic

Active until exhausted

"Works": builds, drives, pilots

Can jump own height and land upright

Hops, skips

Throws large ball, kicks accurately

Hops and stands on one foot

Jumps over objects

Walks in a straight line

Races up and down stairs

Turns somersaults

Walks backward toe-heel

Accurate, rash body movements

Copies shapes such as a cross, square

Can draw a stick figure

Holds paint brush in adult manner, pencil in fisted grasp

Can lace shoes

Dresses self except back buttons, ties

Has sureness and control in finger activities

Alternates feet going down stairs

Creative

Is adventurous

Shows vivid imagination

Displays great interest in violence in imaginary play

Loves anything new

Demonstrates more elaborate dramatic play

Makes up new words, sounds, and stories

Enjoys complexity in book illustrations

Exaggerates and goes to extreme

Likes funny poetry

© Cengage Learning

Tells spontaneous story with artwork

Can put on elaborate plays with puppets

Finds ways to solve problems

Combines words and ideas

Cognitive

Does some naming and representative art

Gives art products personal value

Can work for a goal*

Questions constantly*

Interested in how things work

Interested in life-death concepts

Has an extended attention span

Can do two things at once

Dramatic play is closer to reality*

Judges which of two objects is larger

Has concept of three; can name more

Has accurate sense of time

Full of ideas

Begins to generalize; often faulty*

Likes a variety of materials

Calls people names*

Has dynamic intellectual drive*

Has imaginary playmates

Recognizes several printed words

*Key characteristics of cultural awareness or identity.

FIVE-YEAR-OLD

© Cengage Learning

Takes turn in conversation

Has clear ideas and articulates them*

Insists "I already know that"

Asks questions to learn answers*

Makes up songs

Enjoys dictating stories

Uses 1500 words

Tells a familiar story

Defines simple words

Answers telephone, takes a message

Thinks out loud*

Physical-Motor

Completely coordinated

Has adult-like posture

Has tremendous physical drive

Likes to use fine-motor skills

Has accuracy, skill with simple tools

Draws a recognizable person*

Handedness is evident

Dresses self completely

Cuts on a line with scissors

Begins to color within the lines

Catches ball from three feet away

Skips using alternate feet

Enjoys jumping, running, doing stunts

Rides a two-wheeler

Balances on a balance beam

Jumps rope, skips

Runs lightly on toes

Likes to dance; is graceful, rhythmic

Sometimes roughhouses, fights

Creative

Explores variety of art processes

Becomes engrossed in details of painting, blocks

Fantasy is more active, less verbal

Thinks out loud

Has ideas; loves to talk about them

Can learn simple dance routine

Enjoys making patterns, designs

Puts on simple plays

Has idea of what to draw—wants to make something recognizable

Cognitive

Curious about everything*

Wants to know "how?" and "why?"*

Likes to display new knowledge, skills

Somewhat conscious of own ignorance*

Knows tomorrow, yesterday

Can count 10 objects, rote counts to 20

Sorts objects by single characteristic*

Knows own name, address, town

Makes a plan, follows it, centers on task

Sorts objects by color, shape

Concepts of smallest, less than, one-half

May tell time accurately, on the hour

Knows what a calendar is used for

Seldom sees things from another's point of view

Social-Emotional

Poised, self-confident, self-contained

Sensitive to ridicule*

Has to be right; persistent

Has sense of self-identity*

May get silly, high, wild

Enjoys pointless riddles, jokes

Enjoys group play, competitive games*

Aware of rules, defines them for others*

Chooses own friends; is sociable*

Gets involved with group decisions*

Insists on fair play*

Likes adult companionship*

Accepts, respects authority*

Asks permission

Remains calm in emergencies

Language

Uses big words and complete sentences

Can define some words

Spells out simple words

*Key characteristics of cultural awareness or identity.

Social-Emotional
Six-year-old

Likes to work, yet often does so in spurts

Does not show persistence

Tends to be a know-it-all

Free with opinions and advice

Brings home evidence of good schoolwork

Observes family rules*

Gender-role stereotypes are rigid*

Friends easily gained, easily lost*

Tests and measures self against peers*

Makes social connections through play*

Friends are of same sex*

Believes in rules except for self*

Active, outgoing

Charming

Proud of accomplishments

Shows aggression through insults, name-calling*

Seven-year-old

More serious

Sensitive to others' reactions*

Eager for home responsibilities

Complaining, pensive, impatient

Shame is common emotion*

Leaves rather than face criticism, ridicule, disapproval*

Complains of unfair treatment, not being liked*

Shows politeness and consideration for adults*

Enjoys solitary activities

First peer pressure: needs to be "in"*

Wants to be one of the gang*

Relates physical competence to self-concept*

Self-absorbed; self-conscious

Language
Six- and seven-year-olds

Enjoy putting language skill to paper

Talk with adults rather than to them*

Chatter incessantly

Dominate conversations

Speech irregularities still common

Learning to print/write

Acquisition of new words tapers off

Bilingual capacities nearly complete* if English is second language

Ability to learn new language still present*

Physical-Motor
Six- and seven-year-olds

Basic skills need refinement

Like to test limits of own body

Value physical competence*

Work at self-imposed tasks

Need daily legitimate channels for high energy

Learn to ride two-wheeler, skate, ski

Use motor skills as a tool for socializing

Boisterous, enjoy stunts and rough-housing

Susceptible to fatigue

Visual acuity reaches normal

Hungry at short intervals, like sweets

Chew pencils, fingernails, hair

Creative
Six-year-old

Tries out artistic exploration seriously for the first time

Industrious

Greater interest in process, not product

Eager, curious, enthusiastic

Loves jokes and guessing games

Loves to color, paint

Understands cause and effect

Likes cooperative projects, activities, tasks

Interested in skill and technique

Courtesy of the author

Seven-year-old

Likes to be alone listening to music

Wants work to look good

The age for starting music lessons

Driven by curiosity, desire to discover and invent

Intensely interested in how things work; takes apart, puts back together

Uses symbols in both writing and drawing

Interested in all sorts of codes

Likes to select and sort objects

Cognitive
Six- and seven-year-olds

Work in spurts, not persistent

Letter and word reversal common

Learn to read, beginning math skills

Can consider others' points of view*

Use logic, systematic thinking*

Can plan ahead

Enjoy collecting: sorting, classifying

Can sequence events and retell stories

Concepts of winning and losing are difficult*

Like games with simple rules*

May cheat or change rules*

Want "real" things: watches and cameras that work

Sift and sort information*

Can conceptualize situations*

Enjoy exploring culture of classmates*

*Key characteristics of cultural awareness or identity.

EIGHT-YEAR-OLD

Social-Emotional

Outgoing, enthusiastic

Enormously curious about people and things*

Socially expansive*

Judgmental and critical of self and others*

Ambivalent about growing up

Often hostile but attracted to opposite sex

Growing self-confidence

Learns about self through others: peers, parents*

Is aware of and sensitive to differences from other children*

Begins to evaluate self and others through clothing, physical attraction, social status*

Likes to meet new people, go new places*

Has emerging sensitivity to personality traits of others*

Eager for peer approval and acceptance*

Growing sense of moral responsibility

Joins clubs

Chooses same-sex playmates

Struggles with feelings of inferiority

Likes to work cooperatively

Responds to studies of other cultures*

Has growing interest in fairness and justice issues*

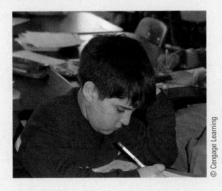
© Cengage Learning

Language

Talks with adults

Attentive and responsive to adult communication*

Teases members of opposite sex

Talks about "self*

Talkative, exaggerates

Likes to explain ideas

Imitates language of peers

Enjoys storytelling and writing short stories

Physical-Motor

Beginning to engage in team sports*

Often a growth-spurt year

Speedy, works fast

Restless, energetic, needs physical release

Plays hard, exhausts self

Eye-hand coordination matures; learning cursive handwriting

Enjoys competitive sports*

Hearty appetite, few food dislikes

Repeatedly practices new skills to perfect them

Creative

Has great imagination

Enjoys riddles, limericks, knock-knock jokes

Likes to explain ideas

Visual acuity and fine motor skills come together

Is most productive in groups

Shows interest in process and product

Cognitive

Criticizes abilities in all academic areas

Seeks new experiences*

Likes to barter, bargain, trade

Enjoys creating collections of things

Interested in how children from other countries live*

Thinks beyond the here-and-now boundaries of time and space

Enjoys role-playing character parts*

Tests out parents to learn more about them

Needs direction, focus

Enjoys all types of humor

Full of ideas, plans

Gaining competence in basic skills

Industrious, but overestimates abilities

Interested in process as well as product of schoolwork

Growing interest in logic and the way things work

Takes responsibility seriously*

*Key characteristics of cultural awareness or identity.

In Chapter 4, you will come to appreciate the importance of research and significant theories from which these Word Pictures are drawn.

Guidelines for Using Word Pictures

It is important to use these age-level charts with discretion. The following six guidelines will help:

1. Balance your impression of the Word Pictures with your own experiences with children. *Example: Toddlers are always on the move and prefer standing and squatting to sitting in a chair. Observe a toddler story time to see how many children are sitting on the floor, how many are standing, and how many are squatting on their haunches.*

2. Make a profile of the whole child and resist the tendency to categorize or stereotype. *Example: Chad, like most 7-year-olds, likes music and reflects his age group's creative characteristics. He has the physical motor skills and cognitive abilities of an 8-year-old and the social-emotional needs of a 6-year-old. This portrait of Chad helps his teachers plan for his individual needs.*

3. Get perspective on the range of developmental norms a child exhibits over time. *Example: Children have varying levels of development at any point in time. Look at the Word Pictures for the group just above and just below the age level of the child you are observing. A typical child may have the physical development of a 3-year-old, the language skills of a 4-year-old, and the social coping skills of a 2-year-old. Children will exhibit some of the behaviors appropriate to all three ages.*

4. Remember that these norms of development refer to average or typical behavior. They should not be applied too literally. *Example: Allen and Marotz (2007) caution, "…these age specifications are only approximate markers derived from averages or norms… midpoints not intended to represent any one child."*

5. Keep in mind that children go through most of the stages described and in the same sequence, but they will do so at their own rates of growth. *Example: Individual differences occur as development follows its own orderly and predictable path as children acquire the abilities and skills that are necessary to succeed in the next stages.*

6. Focus on what the child can do rather than on what he or she cannot do. Use the characteristics to compare the child's own rate of growth. *Example: In observing Dwayne, it is important to assess where he is in relation to other 4-year-olds, but it is more important to know where he is six months from now, a year from now, and what he was like a year ago. From this, a clear picture of his rate of growth emerges.*

How Children Differ

Watching and working with children exposes how very different each child is. Why is this when they have so many features in common? Megan gives the tire swing a big push. Ariel shrieks with delight, but Hans bursts into tears and screams to get off. What accounts for the wide range of behaviors?

Developmental Differences

You are aware by now that children grow and develop at different rates. Each child has an inner timetable that is unique, which means that each child is ready to learn according to his or her maturation process.

This readiness factor is to be respected and may or may not coincide with the rest of the children in the class. This is what makes teaching exciting and challenging.

While the rate of development may vary, it follows a sequence in all children, even those with special needs. Physical development, for instance, tends to be from the head downward (notice how large a newborn baby's head is in comparison to the rest of the body) and the center outward (young children gain control over arm movements before mastering finger control).

Other Factors

Genetic Makeup

Each child has a unique combination of genes that determine eye and hair color, height, body shape, personality traits, and intelligence. Certain diseases, such as Tay Sachs, cystic fibrosis, and sickle cell anemia, are linked through heredity (Berk, 2009).

Environment

Genetics (nature) may account for some of the differences among children but not all. The environment (nurture) has great impact throughout development.

DAP

DAP Think of both the universal and individual characteristics of children, and honor each child's uniqueness.

From conception, the brain is affected by environmental conditions. An individual child's rate and sequence of development reflects "an ongoing dialogue between the brain, the body, and the physical and social environment" (Berk, 2009).

The attitudes with which children are raised, their culture, their socioeconomic status, the kinds of caregiving they experience, and their community combine in countless ways to affect growth. In Chapter 15, this subject is more thoroughly discussed. Nutrition, safety, play space, adult relationships, neighborhood, and family stability affect individual development. Whether a child lives in relative poverty or riches, environmental factors interact with genes to create a single, individual person.

Gender and Race Differences

Girls and boys differ in both the rate and the pattern of growth, especially during adolescence. Ethnic variations in growth are common. African American and Asian American children seem to mature faster than do North American Caucasian children (Berk, 2009). Growth "norms" should be used with caution and with respect to ethnic differences.

Learning Styles

Children exhibit a number of different approaches to learning that must be accounted for when planning programs. Some are quiet; others move around and talk, while others seem never to listen. While on a field trip to the farm, these children demonstrate three common learning styles:

- Lorenzo watches, looks around, and visually absorbs the environment. He calls to others, "See the goat!" and "Look at that." Lorenzo is a **visual learner.**
- Olivia chatters away to her friends as they enter the barnyard. "Listen to all the noise the sheep are making." "Hear the horses?" While she enjoys listening to what others have to say, Olivia has difficulty waiting for her turn to talk. Olivia is an **auditory learner.**
- As she runs ahead of the other children, Anna calls out, "Get over here so we can touch them!" Looking up at the teacher, she begs, "Take me closer. I want to see what sheep feel like." Anna is **a tactile learner.**

Each of the children responds to the experience in a way that reflects an individual learning style. Lorenzo will interpret the field trip in pictures, by drawing or painting what he saw. Olivia will repeat stories from her experience over and over again as she integrates her experience at the farm. Anna will play out her farm experience by making clay animals or dancing an "animal dance." (In Chapters 4 and 10, learning styles are further discussed in terms of Gardner's Multiple Intelligences.)

Grouping children by rigid age levels seems contrary to our understanding of individual learning styles, rates of growth, readiness factors, and wide ranges of abilities. It is a convenient, though arbitrary, system of teaching children. The implication for teachers, however, is clear: programs are planned to meet the needs and challenges of the whole group. Individual differences are incorporated into the planning. Activities are selected to allow for a variety of responses from children at different stages of development and learning styles.

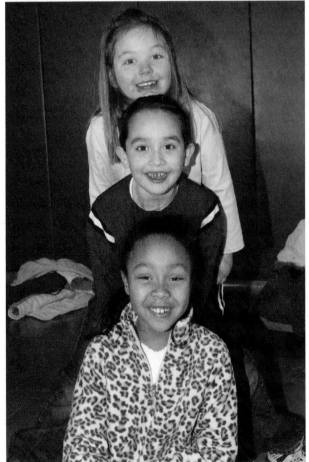

In our diverse world, teachers should be sensitive to the influence of sex, race, and individual patterns of development.

See Chapter 5 for specific suggestions on how teachers plan to accommodate the individuality of children, particularly these sections: Self-awareness, Attitudes and Biases, Ten Essentials to Successful Teaching, and A Student Teacher's Guidelines for Beginning. The curriculum chapters, 10 through 15, demonstrate other examples of planning for a wide range of skills. It might be useful, too, to read Chapter 9, particularly the self-help environment and the anti-bias curriculum.

Planning for Developmental Differences

When teachers are aware of the range of developmental differences and learning styles of the children in the class, they can incorporate those variations into the planning process. The following are some strategies for how to plan for these types of variations:

- Plan individual and group activities according to the age level of the class, considering the behavior patterns and learning styles that exist. Make sure the materials and activities are in a variety of formats so that children can choose the ones that support their style of learning.
- Plan for all age levels with the understanding and appreciation of the variations within a one-year age span.
- Know the individual children, their strengths, and their challenges by observing their growth (see Chapter 6). Remember that families bring further knowledge of each child and that is added into the mix when assessing children's progress.
- Plan around the known similarities, the developmental tasks, and age-appropriate behavior common to that group of children, including those with special needs. The needs, interests, abilities, and unique characteristics of all the children in the class must be considered.
- Set group and activity goals based on the general characteristics of the age group, but change the goals as needed. Small group work may help all children in reaching the goals.
- Modify activities to make them more accessible or appropriate for children with special needs. Tables can be made higher or lower for wheelchair access; or a teacher may spend extra time in the dramatic play area to help individual children learn social skills.

Planning for the differences in children's skills and abilities takes time, but it is one of the most important challenges teachers face. Thorough knowledge of each child is the foundation for developmentally appropriate planning that meets the needs of all the children in the class.

Children with Special Needs

Approximately 15 to 20 percent of all children in the United States will exhibit some form of atypical development and need special services (Bee & Boyd, 2006). These are children who did not develop according to normal developmental patterns.

DAP

They exhibit a wide range of atypical conditions ranging from short-term behavior problems to long-term physical, mental, and emotional problems.

Two types of children come under the category of children with special needs: children who have some sort of exceptionality and children who are gifted. They extend the definition of "Who is the child?" and are discussed separately in this section.

Children with Exceptionalities

- Five-year-old Pete, blind from birth, has been in nursery school for three years.
- Chrissy, a 4-year-old with multiple **exceptionalities,** has her daily program in a special school supplemented by attending the child care center three afternoons each week.
- Travis is a child with Down syndrome, and this is his first experience in a school not restricted to atypical children.

These children have some obvious characteristics that qualify them for special-needs status. Other children with less apparent exceptionalities also fall into this category. The term "**special needs**" includes a great many conditions that may or may not be noticeable. Allen and Cowdery (2009) suggest three conditions under which a child is considered exceptional: A child's normal growth and development is (1) delayed; (2) distorted, atypical, or abnormal; or (3) severely or negatively affected. This definition includes the physical, mental, emotional, and social areas of development. Figure 3-2 highlights many of the exceptionalities a teacher may encounter.

DAP   Remember that planning for children with special needs cuts across social, economic, and cultural lines and always begins by looking at typical development.

In the course of normal development, any one area of a child's growth is affected by the development of the whole child, and this holds true for children who do not develop according to the norms. Any single exceptionality may lead to other multi-handicapping conditions:

- A child with a profound hearing loss is often delayed in speech production or language abilities and suffers social isolation due to the inability to hear and speak with peers.
- A child with a speech impairment or cleft palate may have the intellectual capacity to put simple puzzles together but may not yet have the language to engage verbally in songs and finger play.
- A child with **Down syndrome** may have congenital heart defects, intellectual impairments, eye abnormalities, or poor physical coordination.
- Children who have cerebral palsy, a central nervous system disorder, often have other exceptionalities, such as intellectual delays, epilepsy, and hearing, visual, and speech problems (Kiernan, et al).

Figure 3-2 lists a number of exceptionalities, from mild to severe, that teachers of young children may encounter.

Learning Disabilities

Children with learning disabilities are found in almost every classroom; they have no discernable condition but, nevertheless, are having problems with one or more basic skills or learning. According to Berk (2009), five to ten percent of school-age children have some kind of learning difficulty. They may have, among other things, poor memory skills, difficulty in following directions, hand-eye coordination problems, and trouble discriminating between letters, numbers, and sounds, which keep them from storing, processing, and producing information.

Dyslexia, the most common specific learning disability, occurs when children have difficulty in learning to read. They may reverse letters (such as *d* and *b*) or words (such as *was* and *saw*), although many children do this who are not dyslexic. A child with a learning disability may have strength in another area, such as math, and yet have a learning difficulty with language. A learning disability does not mean that a child is intellectually impaired or delayed.

Learning difficulties are usually not a singular dysfunction. Children who exhibit problems with reading and writing will often have difficulties with spatial relationships and body coordination. Observations of these behaviors can give teachers some of the first warning signs of learning disorders.

There is continuing controversy on how to define and identify these children. Although some experts consider minimal brain damage to be the cause of learning disabilities, there is no consensus yet on why children have these conditions.

A child with a learning disability usually has a normal or above normal IQ (Allen & Cowdery, 2009) and

Teachers of Young Children May Encounter a Variety of Disabilities

- *Speech and language:* hearing impairment, stuttering, articulation problems, cleft palate, chronic voice disorders, learning disabilities.
- *Physical-motor:* visual impairment, blindness, perceptual motor deficits, orthopedic disabilities such as cerebral palsy, spina bifida, loss of limbs, muscular dystrophy.
- *Intellectual:* cognitive delays, brain injury, brain dysfunction, dyslexia, and learning disabilities.
- *Social-emotional:* self-destructive behavior, severe withdrawal, dangerous aggression toward self and others, noncommunicativeness, moodiness, tantrums, attention-deficit hyperactivity disorder, severe anxiety, depression, phobias, psychosis, autism.
- *Health impairments:* severe asthma, epilepsy, hemophilia, congenital heart defects, severe anemia, malnutrition, diabetes, tuberculosis, cystic fibrosis, Down's syndrome, sickle cell anemia, Tay-Sachs disease, AIDS.
- *Specific learning disabilities:* difficulties with language use and acquisition, spoken and written language affected, perceptual handicaps, brain injury, minimal brain dysfunction, dyslexia, developmental aphasia.

FIGURE 3-2 These disorders may range from mild to severe, and children will exhibit a wide variety of abilities and needs even if they are diagnosed with the same condition. For further information concerning a specific one, the student will want to consult a special education textbook.

tends to develop normally, but the task of reading seems to highlight several areas of difficulty: problems of visual perception, inability to integrate visual and auditory information, impaired memory, problems with language, and difficulty distinguishing the separate sounds in words. This wide range of symptoms, the number of potential causes, and the varying degrees to which children exhibit the symptoms make learning exceptionalities difficult to diagnose.

As noted earlier in this chapter, young children differ in their individual rate of growth, and many differences and delays are still within the normal range of development.

Attention-Deficit/Hyperactivity Disorder (ADHD)

Do you remember a classmate who could never sit still—one who was constantly on the move, talked excessively, and disrupted classroom activities? This behavior is typical of children with a condition known as **attention-deficit/hyperactivity disorder (ADHD)**, which, according to Berk (2009), affects up to three to five percent of all school-age children, more often boys than girls.

ADHD (previously called hyperactivity) is a condition affecting children and adults and appears to be hereditary. The National Resource Center on ADHD (2009) notes three subtypes of ADHD that are common today:

1. ADHD predominately inattentive type (ADHD-1)
   - Makes careless mistakes
   - Does not pay close attention to details
   - Easily distracted; hard to maintain attention
   - Does not appear to listen; seems forgetful
   - Has trouble with follow-through
   - Loses things; has difficulty with organization
   - Might avoid tasks that take prolonged intellectual effort
2. ADHD predominately hyperactive-impulsive (ADHD-HI)
   - Fidgets, squirms
   - Has trouble staying seated, runs about
   - Talks excessively; difficulty with being quiet during activities
   - Blurts out answers; interrupts; intrudes on others
   - Has difficulty waiting to take turns
3. ADHD combined type (ADHD-C)
   - Child or adult meets criteria from both categories listed above.

Children with ADHD are difficult to manage both at home and in the classroom. They are prone to restlessness, anxiety, short attention spans, and impulsiveness. Their constellation of behaviors may apply at some level to many children, but teachers must be cautious about labeling the normally active, somewhat disruptive child as having ADHD. The child with ADHD exhibits these behaviors in extreme, usually before age 7 (Berk, 2009).

Strock (2006) has noted that certain other disorders can accompany ADHD, such as learning disabilities in 20 to 30 percent of children; oppositional defiant disorder (ODD), which occurs mostly in boys; conduct disorder (CD), which includes stealing, lying, and fighting and may occur in 20 to 40 percent of children with ADHD; and bipolar disorder.

Medication is a common treatment for children with ADHD, but because its effects are short term and its side effects can be serious, it is controversial. The most effective approach appears to be a combination of medication and individual behavior management strategies (Allen & Cowdery, 2009; Berk, 2009). There is no easy solution for dealing with children who have ADHD; further research into the cause of this disability and development of safe effective treatments are clearly needed.

Guidance techniques that are good for children with ADHD include:

- Maintain regular and consistent routines and rules: "Remember, Sitara, we always wash hands before eating snacks."
- Have realistic expectations: "I know it is hard for you to wait. Why don't you go over to the other cabinet and see if the pencils you want are in there?"
- Make eye contact when giving directions using clear and simple explanations: "Look at me, Toby, so I know that you are listening. Good. Now let's go over the assignment together."
- Allow time for transitions by giving a plan for the next step: "In three minutes it will be time to get ready to go home. When the other children begin to leave, I want you to get your coat and come back here to sit with us."
- Select jobs in which the child can be successful: "Connie, please pass out the napkins to this table today."
- Recognize accomplishments: "Good work, Connie. You gave everyone a red napkin and then sat down with one for yourself."

Guidance techniques that work well with children who have ADHD are also successful with children who have a variety of behavioral conditions, proving again that children are more alike than they are different.

Asperger Syndrome

Asperger syndrome (AS) is a developmental condition that is part of Autism Spectrum Disorder and is characterized by a lack of social skills, poor concentration, self-absorption, and limited interests (Allen & Cowdery, 2009). The difference between autism and AS is the level of mental functioning. Most children with AS have normal or above normal intelligence and often learn how to communicate and behave in appropriate ways (Willis, 2009).

Gallagher and Gallagher (2002) explain the four separate categories of AS defined by the American Psychological Association:

1. Impaired social functioning; inability to make friends or show empathy, avoids eye contact.
2. Restricted and stereotyped behaviors and interests; overly intense interest in one area; repetitive hand movements and compulsive repetition, often long passages memorized from television or the movies.
3. Average or above average language development; normal use of vocabulary, yet may use language in such a complex manner that it makes no sense. They lack the language of social communication with others.
4. Average or above average cognitive development; ranges anywhere from average to highly gifted.

Many children with AS attend schools with normally developing children. Their behaviors may seem odd to their peers and disruptive to the class. Allen and Cowdery (2009) suggest the following strategies for working with children with AS:

- Simple and direct communication.
- Combine objects and actions: show the child the book and demonstrate where it goes in the shelf.
- Provide peer interactions with other children who are disabled and have similar levels of language and social development.
- Establish a predictable routine and environment; minimize distractions.
- Improve communication skills by having the child ask for something rather than point.
- Encourage frequent communication with the family.

Family Support

Parents are usually the first to notice that their child is not developing according to the norms. They may ask the child's teacher to watch for signs of hearing impairments, lack of necessary motor skills, or language imperfections. Because early diagnosis and intervention are important, teachers will want to assess the child's overall skills. As you will learn in Chapter 6, early childhood educators need to be skilled in carefully observing and documenting the growth and development of individual children. Teachers will then plan appropriate follow-through with the family. This may include a consultation with a physician for further developmental screening and testing. If both the family and the teachers feel there is a potential problem, the task is to help identify it and secure the services needed.

The teacher's role is to observe the child and provide current information, to support the family through their concern, to help them find appropriate resources (such as social service agencies, public health offices, private and public schools), to assist with future placement for child care, and to be available for consultation with others who are working in the best interests of the child. The early childhood professional is not an expert in diagnosing learning exceptionalities but can be effective in helping families secure proper referrals and treatment.

Public Recognition

Since the mid-1960s, there has been significant public recognition of and the advent of public funding for the education programs for persons with special needs. Prior to that, public and private attitudes seemed to be ones of shame and segregation. Past generations hid adults and children with special needs in their homes or secluded them in institutions. Keeping special populations out of sight gave way to providing separate opportunities for them. Schools, classes, and recreational programs were started exclusively for people with special needs. Public consciousness is now sufficient to understand that not all people with special needs are necessarily mentally impaired. The current practice of integrating children with varying exceptionalities into ongoing programs in schools—the mainstream of American life—is not only more humane but practical as well. Highlights of the nearly 40 years include:

- In 1972, Head Start required that a minimum of 10 percent of its enrollment be reserved for children with special needs. Head Start led the way toward large-scale inclusion.
- In 1975, Public Law 94-142, the Education for All Handicapped Children Act, was passed. This so-called "Bill of Rights for the Handicapped" guarantees free public education to disabled persons from 3 to 21 years of age "in the least restrictive environ-

ment." An individualized program (IEP) for each person is mandatory, to be worked out with the child's family. This provides a more family-centered approach in which the strengths and the needs of the family are taken into consideration. The success of P.L. 94-142 means that thousands of children with special needs who would have been denied any educational opportunities are now in school with typically developing children.

- P.L. 99-457, the Education of the Handicapped Amendments Act of 1986, has had an even more profound impact for early childhood educators. Sections of this law provide funding for children who were not included in the previous law: infants, toddlers, and 3- to 5-year-olds. This law also allows for the inclusion of "developmentally delayed" youngsters and leaves local agencies the opportunity to include "at risk" children in that definition. The vague definitions give local agencies the right to define disabling conditions in terms of local needs.

- In 1990, Congress reauthorized P.L. 94-142 and renamed it the Individuals with Disabilities Education Act (IDEA) (P.L. 101-576). Two new categories, autism and traumatic brain injury, were included, and children from birth to age 5 years were now eligible to receive services. IDEA was updated in 2004. It now details extensive changes in qualifications for special education teachers, extends services for children who are homeless, and extends services to children until they reach kindergarten age. IDEA 2004 also requires educators/guardians to encourage appropriate classroom behavior through positive guidance strategies.

- Many programs may be affected by another piece of legislation, P.L. 101-336, the American with Disabilities Act (ADA), which was passed in 1990. This civil rights act makes it unlawful to discriminate against people with special needs because of their exceptionality and requires that people with special needs have equal access to public and private services, as well as reasonable accommodations. This law has had an impact on hiring practices in early childhood centers and family child care homes and may require adaptations to facilities and work environments to make them more accessible to individuals with special needs. Although not specifically an education law, ADA is another step toward respecting the dignity and worth of all individuals.

Legislation makes strong demands on the family to be intimately involved with their child's program. Family involvement greatly improves the child's chances for success (Allen & Marotz, 2007). Teachers and families work together on a planned, consistent set of expectations. The child's confidence is reinforced at home and at school for the same achievements. Families of children with special needs find support from other parents as they share common child-rearing concerns. Teachers learn a great deal about children's exceptionalities from the families of the children who have special needs. This helps them become more effective teachers and be aware of the individual needs of the child.

The importance of all of this legislation cannot be underestimated by those in and entering the field of early childhood. The integration and transition of children with special needs into early childhood programs require knowledgeable teachers. Early childhood educators would be wise to avail themselves of special education courses now to meet this challenge. Many states require such course work before certification; others will surely follow to fulfill these mandates.

The Inclusive Classroom

Allen and Cowdery (2009) differentiate between the terms **inclusion** and **mainstreaming.** In the past, children with special needs were integrated into classrooms only after they had met certain standards and expectations. Often they were assigned to separate special education classes. When ready, they were mainstreamed into classrooms with typically developing children. Inclusion means that a child with special needs is a full-time member of a regular classroom, a more natural environment, with children who do, as well as those who do not, have special needs.

More than a word definition is at stake, however. Allen and Cowdery (2009) go on to point out that inclusion is about belonging, having worth, and having choices;

TeachSource Video ▶❚❚

Watch the TeachSource Video entitled, "Five-Eleven Years: Developmental Disabilities in Middle Childhood." After you study the video clip, reflect on the following questions:

1. How did this teaching staff and environment adapt in order to include children with special needs?

2. What examples did you observe that foster children's interactions with children with special needs, and how successful do you think they were?

an inclusive classroom is about "accepting and valuing human diversity and providing support so that all children and families can participate in the program of their choice." Teachers are a key factor in the successful integration of children with exceptionalities. Their attitude is critical; they must be committed to teaching all children with equal caring and concern, regardless of their intelligence or skill levels. To enhance inclusion, Allen and Cowdery (2009) suggest that teachers:

All children, regardless of abilities, learn and grow through play.

- Promote healthy social relationships between children who have special needs and those who do not so that they participate in a wide variety of activities together.
- Recognize that every child with special needs has strengths as well as deficits and build on those strengths through a rich learning environment that fosters appropriate behavior.
- Receive training and guidance in the critical task of working with children who have special needs and are developmentally challenged and with other professionals who work within the inclusion process.
- Work with families to plan and implement the child's individualized program.
- See that children with special needs are actively involved and accepted in the total program with individualized activities that meet each child's needs and abilities.
- Help children with special needs to take advantage of, to the fullest extent of their capabilities, all the activities the school has to offer by including materials and activities that support the growth of the lowest-functioning children and challenges those who are high-functioning.
- Use play as a medium for learning, but recognize that some children with special needs have to be taught play skills.

What Do YOU Think? What would be your biggest challenge when working in a classroom with children who have special needs, as well as children who do not? Have you ever had friends, relatives, or neighbors who are with special needs? How would that experience inform your attitude about working in an inclusive classroom?

Inclusion is an important concept for all children. For typically developing children, it is an opportunity to learn to accept differences in people. In the early education center, much of the curriculum is directed toward fostering the child's self-esteem and self-worth. Teaching is dedicated to helping youngsters see themselves and others as important and valuable. Inclusion presents an opportunity to extend that principle to the full range of human characteristics.

For the child with special needs, the large numbers of typically developing children who serve as age-appropriate behavior models is important. Some children with special needs may not have an opportunity to hear the language of their normal peer group. They may not know how to play with another child or how to communicate in socially acceptable ways. In the inclusive classroom, with sensitive and knowledgeable teachers, children with exceptionalities are helped to realize their potential as growing and learning children.

Fortunately, the preschool teacher rarely needs to face the task of inclusiveness alone. Many early childhood centers have access to a team of professionals who can provide the child, the family, and the teaching staff with effective therapeutic activities. Their combined knowledge helps teachers understand the specific exceptionality and plan an appropriate curriculum for each child. Together, teachers, clinicians, and parents work out a well-rounded program. This is called an interdisciplinary approach to teaching.

In 1998, NAEYC endorsed a Position on Inclusion written by the Division of Early Childhood of the Council for Exceptional Children. This statement, which you can read on the student website, offers guidelines for implementation.

There is a significant point about teaching young children with diverse behaviors and the labels or categories that define their exceptionality. "It is not how a child is classified," according to Allen and Cowdry (2009), "but how the child is cared for and taught as an individual, that is the most important issue in addressing behavior and learning problems in young children."

Children Who Are Gifted and Talented

The U.S. Department of Education's most recent definition of **gifted and talented** students is: "children and youth with outstanding talent who perform or show the potential for performing at remarkably high levels of accomplishment when compared with others of their age, experience, or environment. These children and youth exhibit high performance capacity in intellectual, creative and/or artistic areas, and unusual leadership capacity, or excel in specific academic fields. They require services of activities not ordinarily provided by the schools. Outstanding talents are present in children and youth from all cultural groups, across all economic strata, and in all areas of human endeavor." The National Association for Gifted Children (2009) defines a gifted person as "someone who shows, or has the potential for showing, an exceptional level of performance in one or more areas of expression."

Traditionally, children have been identified as gifted if they score between 130 and 150 on standard IQ Tests. The definitions above, however, indicate a broader basis for identifying children who are gifted and include those who exhibit exceptional talent in other than just intellectual superiority. Ford and others (2002) have long promoted the view that the percentage of Blacks and Hispanics are underrepresented in identification as gifted and that this oversight is linked to standardized

tests which are often culturally and linguistically inappropriate for many students. Ford (1995) also notes that many Black students with high achievement scores were not included in gifted programs because teachers did not refer them for screening and calls for greater multicultural competence in those who teach gifted students (Ford et al, 2000). To that end, The National Association for Gifted Children (2009) proposed standards that all teachers who work in gifted programs must have formal and specific training.

Ford (et al, 2002) further notes that the inclusion of the word "potential" in the definition of gifted is a critical factor that will enhance the inclusion of children who are ethnically and culturally in the minority, children with special needs, and children of poverty. It serves as a reminder that giftedness is a trait that cuts across all socioeconomic and cultural groups.

Early childhood teachers should be aware of some traits children who are gifted display so they can recognize potentially gifted children in their care. Further, since the majority of children in the early years are too young for IQ or standardized tests, teachers are likely to have unidentified gifted children in their programs. These are listed in Figure 3-3.

Teaching Children Who Are Gifted and Talented

The teacher's role with children who are gifted is that of providing challenge and stimulation. Children who are gifted may need scaffolding strategies to support their learning. In some cases, the children who are gifted may be advanced to an older group, moving on to kindergarten or first grade, or spend part of the day in special classes where they can interact with like-minded peers (Berk, 2009). A more common approach in early child-

---

Characteristic Traits of Children Who Are Gifted and Talented

- *Language:* advanced verbal skills and vocabulary; experiments with words; expresses ideas easily; inventive with songs and stories
- *Intellectually:* long attention span and ability to concentrate; learns rapidly and has a strong memory; imaginative and original; plans and organizes well; problem-solves; questions; understands abstract concepts; creative thinker; advanced sense of humor
- *Socially:* independent and content to be alone in purposeful activity; heightened awareness of people and environments, especially changes; social relationships sometimes difficult
- *Overall:* exceptional gift or talent is evident in at least one area of development

FIGURE 3-3 Children who are gifted and talented exhibit a wide range of exceptional behaviors. (Adapted from Allen & Cowderly, 2009; Berk, 2009.)

hood has been in the area of curriculum enrichment. In this way, the child remains with age-level peers to develop social skills. Children who are gifted often feel isolated from their non-gifted peers and may have social and/or emotional difficulties. These factors must also be considered in planning programs.

Curriculum areas are developed in more complex ways. The child who is gifted needs a learning environment that supports intellectual risk-taking, the use of logic and abstract concepts, and curiosity and enhances their specific talents. All the children in the classroom benefit from this enrichment; each responds according to his or her abilities and a rich curriculum benefits the whole class.

This brings to mind Gardner's multiple intelligences (MI) (Gardner, 1993). The eight different kinds of knowing that Gardner developed seem appropriate for teaching children who are gifted and talented. (See Multiple Intelligences in Chapters 4 and 10, especially Figures 4-12 and 10-5.) A variety of meaningful activities across the MI spectrum helps children learn according to their strengths and primary intelligence and suggests curriculum that will help develop new skills and knowledge. Concepts, knowledge, and information are presented in multiple ways so that each child will succeed in learning through the most meaningful method.

Families of children who are gifted will need support and encouragement as well as guidance in dealing with their child's exceptionality. Together, teachers and parents can explore what will best suit each individual child so that this giftedness may be nurtured and challenged at home and at school.

Dealing with Bias and Stereotypes

One of the most important issues for a child with special needs is to be accepted. Young children are known for their forthrightness in commenting on and asking questions about what confuses or frightens them. Children without special needs may be anxious about what another child's exceptionality may mean to them. Although this is a common reaction and age appropriate, we cannot allow an individual to be rejected on the basis of his or her abilities. Derman-Sparks and Edwards (2010) suggests the following strategies:

- The rejection must be handled immediately with support and assurance give to the child who was rejected that this type of behavior will not be permitted.
  Example: "No, Rachel. You cannot tell Gina that she can't play because she is in a wheelchair. Let's look at ways you can include her in your play."

- It is important to help children recognize how they are different and how they are alike.
  Example: "Gina is very good at writing stories, just like you, Rachel. Perhaps you could write a story together."

- Children need to have their fears about other children's abilities and exceptionalities taken seriously and to have adults understand their concerns.
  Example: "I'm glad you told me that Emma frightened you because she is blind. You don't have to be afraid that you, too, will be blind. Emily was born without sight and when you were born, you were able to see. You could use your eyes to help Emily walk to the playground."

- Questions must be answered promptly, truthfully, and simply. Use the children's own curiosity, and let the child with special needs answer questions, whenever possible.
  Example: "Yes, Emily, Janice has some questions about being blind. Would you like to tell her how you are able to read with Braille?"

All children benefit when adults are willing to confront bias and deal with children's prejudice and misconceptions. When we provide opportunities for children to interact with people who look and act differently than they do, we actively foster acceptance and respect for the individual. (More gender diversity issues are found in Chapter 15.)

Culture, Race, and Ethnic Considerations

The answer to "Who is the young child?" takes on new meaning as we look at the ethnic mix of American life. A multicultural explosion has swept across the nation, filling early childhood programs with children from many different cultural backgrounds. There are more students in the classroom who are culturally and linguistically different from the teaching staff and from each other. Unless teachers are informed and educated about these differences, they may misinterpret a child's abilities, learning, and needs. Too often, language barriers between a teacher and a child lead to the conclusion that the child is a slow learner or has a disability.

Working with families will become more challenging to a teacher's ingenuity and communication skills. Many families are unfamiliar with school culture in the United States and the expectations schools have about family involvement and participation. Some parents are illiterate in their own language. An informed and sup-portive teacher can help children succeed under these circumstances.

A lack of understanding about the culture, history, beliefs, and values of the children is harmful to a child's self-concept (see Derman-Sparks and Edwards, 2010, and other references in this book). When there are no assessment tools or instructional materials in the language of the children or depict their native heritage, children are placed at a distinct disadvantage and often eliminated from programs and services that could help them succeed.

Children of Mixed Heritage

One group of children and families who have often been neglected in the discussion of race, ethnicity, and culture are those who are biracial or interracial. The number of children of mixed heritage is increasing, and their needs are unique. As Wardle (1993) notes, interracial families are a "natural extension of our multicultural society."

Biracial children have parents who are of different races, for instance, a child of a Native American and a white person. All combinations of races can produce a biracial child, such as a Korean/African American child, or a Chinese American/ Japanese American child. **Interracial** children have parents who represent more than two racial or ethnic backgrounds. These terms also apply

to children who are adopted by parents of a different race.

Kelly (2009), a Black woman married to a White man, writes about her newborn son, reflecting some of the emotion tied to children of mixed heritage: "I was worried that our son would be so light-skinned as to appear Caucasian, and I wanted him to look Black. ... I wanted to claim [him] for "my" side—in league with [me] against small minds, casual racism, and discrimination ... at seven months after his birth, [my son] is the exact shade you'd get if you mixed his father and me up in a paint can—a color I call golden." The election of Barack Obama, who is biracial, as President of the United States has evoked needed conversations that bring to light many of the issues facing children and families who are interracial.

A Core Value of the NAEYC's Code of Ethical Conduct is respecting the dignity, worth, and uniqueness of each individual. Throughout the Code, the vulnerability and uniqueness of the child is stressed. The time has come to apply these principles to provide a supporting environment that affirms interracial families.

Self-esteem and self-identity can become issues as biracial and interracial children reach adolescence (Berk, 2009). People who have an interracial heritage often choose to identify with one parent, most often the parent of color (Wardle, 1987). It is important to help interracial children gain a positive self-concept and identity at an early age. Classrooms environments and curricula should intentionally reflect images of interracial children and families to help children recognize and connect with people who share their heritages so that they learn to see and understand themselves. In the "Insights from the Field" at the end of the chapter, Wardle suggests a number of ways to begin this process.

Educators need to encourage open discussions of racial identification and give children some positive experiences in talking about their heritage. Consult with families about how they handle their mixed heritage and how they identify themselves and their children. Focus on their needs as a family in order to help them nurture their child in an interracial context.

Cultural Sensitivity

Cultural sensitivity means that each child's heritage is honored, that it is understood as unique from other cultures, and that it is respected. It means that teachers must become familiar with the cultural norms of the children in their classes and build bridges for children and their families into the more dominant culture.

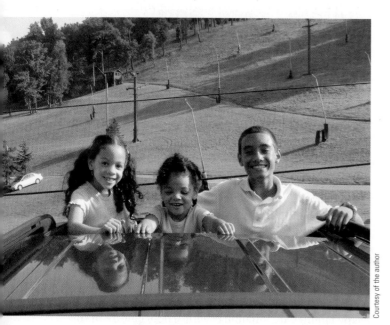

Courtesy of the author

Educators must help all children develop a pride in their cultural heritage.

The culturally sensitive teacher will get to know each of the families as a separate entity and become familiar with their individual expressions of culture and values. Today's teacher will recognize that one family does not represent the totality of the culture (which would be stereotyping) and will be careful not to overgeneralize from one example. The effective teacher will be called on to integrate these insights into curriculum planning as well as in their relationships with the children's families in order to serve the best interests of the young child.

Insights *from the field*

CHILDREN OF MIXED HERITAGE *by Francis Wardle, M.S., Ph.D.*

Trell's first-grade teacher asked him to research the life of one of his grandparents for a Black History Month project. Trell enthusiastically collected photographs, old letters, and newspaper clippings of his favorite grandfather. He asked his parents for anecdotal information; he also remembered his favorite times with his grandfather. He spent hours preparing.

Before the important day, Trell went over the report with his teacher. He knew she would be as excited as he was about his grandfather, who had been a famous politician in his day. Much to Trell's disappointment, his teacher rejected his report. Trell, a biracial boy, had chosen to tell about his white/Carib grandfather. The teacher wanted only black people presented. Trell was devastated.

Anti-bias, multicultural education has found a permanent place in our early childhood programs. Psychologists have recognized that a crucial part of children's self-esteem is contingent on a positive view of their racial and ethnic heritage and that children with high self-esteem do better in school. So programs now provide materials, books, dolls, activities, content, and discussion to help support the ethnic and racial identity of their children.

Multicultural approaches place children within five distinctive groups: African American, Hispanic/Latino, Native American, Asian American, and white. Programs then respond to children on the basis of the group to which they belong. For children like Trell, whose parents represent more than one of these categories, this does not work. And teachers who work with the growing number of multiracial and multiethnic students find themselves without tools to support these children. Where do they fit in?

Children of mixed heritage—multiracial and multiethnic—have a racial and cultural heritage that includes both biological parents' complete backgrounds. Educators must carefully help these children develop a pride and positive self-esteem in their *total* multiracial heritage, culture, and identity.

There are no multiracial holidays, no heroes, no puzzles of multiracial families, very few books, no posters, and no curriculum activities. Here are a few suggestions to help teachers begin to fill this void:

- Use interracial and interethnic families in your program to help with information, photographs, holidays, stories, histories, and curriculum resources.

- Create your own posters, materials, and books that show interracial families (including foster, adoptive, and blended families).

- Pressure companies that provide books and curriculum materials to include multiracial and multiethnic materials in their selections.

- Provide an immediate response to any language or behavior that in any way negates a multiethnic or multiracial child's identity, heritage, or pride. This includes comments implying that the child cannot embrace his full multiracial identity.

- Research multiracial and multiethnic heroes (e.g., composer Gottschalk, ornithologist Audubon) and present material to your class.

- Never celebrate activity that requires a child to select only part of his heritage. If you celebrate cultural days, such as Cinco de Mayo and Martin Luther King Day, present them in a way all children can benefit. Make sure a multiracial child is comfortable identifying both with Cinco de Mayo and Martin Luther King Day, if the child has those combined heritages.

- Contact a local multiracial support group to get ideas, information, and advice.

- Do not teach about race, ethnicity, and culture in a way that excludes children and people. We should teach about culture and heritage to be inclusive, and as a way to give individuals strength, traditions, and values, not to group and exclude people.

Francis Wardle, M.S., Ph.D., is Executive Director of the Center for the Study of Biracial Children. He has written extensively on this topic, including Proposal: An Anti-Bias and Ecological Model for Multicultural Education, an article that presents a multicultural model inclusive of children with multiracial and multiethnic heritages, and Meeting the Needs of Multiethnic & Multiracial Children in Schools, a 2004 Allyn & Bacon publication written with Maria Cruz-Janzen.

SUMMARY

The child in early childhood programs ranges from the dependent infant to the outgoing 8-year-old. In those few short years, teachers witness tremendous physical, intellectual, social, and emotional gains. The child learns to crawl, walk, run, climb, throw a ball, write with a pencil, use scissors, hold a spoon, and manipulate toys. Both large and small muscles are called into play throughout each stage of development.

Language development is equally impressive. The babbling infant becomes fluent, sometimes in more than one language. Intellectual gains coincide as children become able to express thoughts, solve problems, and exhibit growth in their reasoning powers.

Socially, the child learns to relate to family members, schoolmates, teachers, and other adults. Every range of human emotion is developed during these early years as children learn appropriate ways to express and release their feelings.

Teachers notice that children share many common characteristics while displaying wide individual differences. Profile charts—Word Pictures—describing normal development help teachers understand when a particular behavior is likely to occur. With advance notice, then, teachers can plan activities and curricula that appeal to children at every age level; disciplinary and guidance measures can match the child's specific level of development.

Yet it is obvious that growth and development do not proceed normally for all children. Two groups of children have special needs within the early childhood classroom. Children with exceptionalities require particular attention to their particular exceptionality and teachers need special skills to teach them. Children who are gifted also require attention; their exceptional abilities must be challenged and stimulated within the regular early childhood program.

The changing demographics that bring more and more culturally and linguistically diverse children into early childhood settings require that teachers become familiar with the specific cultural norms represented in America today. This includes the special developmental and social needs of children of mixed heritage. This will call for new teaching strategies, culturally appropriate curriculum, and special efforts to work with parents from a multicultural perspective.

KEY TERMS

Word Pictures
age-level characteristics
visual learner
auditory learner
tactile learner
exceptionalities

special needs
Down syndrome
attention-deficit/hyperactivity
 disorder (ADHD)
Asperger's syndrome
inclusion

mainstreaming
gifted and talented children
biracial
multiracial
interracial

REVIEW QUESTIONS

1. What are some of the reasons for using the concept of the whole child in early education? How is each child unique?

2. Name four ways children are alike.

3. How can Word Pictures be a valuable tool for planning programs for young children? What are some of the guidelines for using Word Pictures?

4. How do children differ? What accounts for these differences and how does this affect curriculum planning?

5. Who are the children with special needs? Why is it important for teachers to know about the variety of special needs? What are some of the difficulties that must be overcome for successful inclusion of children with special needs?

6. What do educators need to consider when teaching children who are gifted and/or talented?

7. How important is it to know and understand the cultures and heritage of children we teach?

LEARNING ACTIVITIES

1. Select two children who are approximately the same age. Compare their physical, cognitive, language, creative, and social development. How are they alike? How are they different? What conclusions do you draw about their developmental level?

2. Look at the Word Picture for a 3-year-old. Compare it with a 3-year-old you know. What behavior do you observe in the real 3-year-old that falls within the range of the chart? What is different? Are there cultural differences?

3. Observe a class of children with special needs in an inclusive classroom. What would you do to foster interactions between the children who have exceptionalities and the children who do not? What verbalizations are used about a child's exceptional condition, and do other children seem to understand how their friends are similar to them as well as different?

4. Survey a classroom for its cultural, racial, and ethnic mix. How do the classroom and the curriculum reflect the various heritages of each child? What suggestions would you make to enhance cultural sensitivity in this class?

HELPFUL WEBSITES

Children and Adults with ADHD   http://www.chadd.org

National Dissemination Center for Children with Disabilities (NICHCY)   http://www.nichcy.org

Individuals with Disabilities Education Act   http://www.idea.ed.gov

Council for Exceptional Children   http://www.cec.sped.org

The Division of Early Childhood for Exceptional Children   http://www.dec-sped.org

The ARC (formerly National Association of Retarded Citizens)   http://www.thearc.org

Circle of Inclusion   http://www.circleofinclusion.org

National Association for Gifted Children   http://www.nagc.org

The Center for the Study of Biracial Children   http://csbchome.org

 Additional resources including the TeachSource Videos can be found on the premium website for this book. Go to http://www.cengage.com/login to register your access code.

REFERENCES

Allen, K. E., & Cowdery, G. (2009). *The exceptional child: Inclusion in early childhood education.* Clifton Park, NY: Delmar Learning.

Allen, K. E., & Marotz, L. (2007). *Developmental profiles: Birth to eight.* Clifton Park, NY: Delmar Learning.

Bee, H. , & Boyd, D. (2006). *The developing child.* (9th Ed.). Harper Collins: New York.

Berk, L. E. (2009). *Child development.* Boston: Allyn & Bacon.

Caldwell, B. M. (1993). One world of children. In A. Gordon & K. W. Browne (Eds.), *Beginnings and beyond: Foundations in early childhood education* (3rd Ed.). Clifton Park, NY: Thomson Delmar Learning.

Derman-Sparks, L., & Olsen Edwards, J. (2010). *Antibias education for young children and ourselves.* Washington DC: NAEYC.

Ford, D. Y. (1995). A study of underachievement among gifted, potentially gifted, and general education students. Storrs: National Research Center of the Gifted and Talented, University of Connecticut.

Ford, D. Y. Howard, T. C., Harris, J. J., & Tyson, C. A. (2000). Creating culturally responsive classrooms for gifted African American students. *Journal for the Education of the Gifted, 23,* 397-427.

Ford, D.Y., Harris III, J. J., Tyson, C. A., & Frazier Trotman, M. (2002, revised). *Theory into practice: Providing access for culturally diverse gifted students: from deficit to dynamic thinking.* Columbus: The Ohio State University, on behalf of its College of Education (2003).

Gallagher, S. A., & Gallagher, J. J. (2002). Understanding our gifted. 42 (2), Winter 2002. Boulder, CO: Open Space Communications.

Gardner, H. (1993). *Frames of mind: The theory of multiple intelligences.* New York: Basic Books.

Gesell, A., and Ilg, F. L. (1943). *Infant and child in the culture of today.* New York: Harper Brothers.

Kelly, R. Beyond just black and white. (February 2, 2009). *Newsweek,* Volume CLIII, 41.

Kiernan, S., et al. (not dated). *Mainstreaming preschoolers: Children with orthopedic handicaps.* Washington, DC: U.S. Department of Health, Education, and Welfare.

National Association for Gifted and Talented. What is Giftedness? NACG website, retrieved January 30, 2009.

National Resource Center on ADHD. (2006). The disorder named ADHD. What We Know Series K1. Chadd website.

Strock, M. (2006). Attention deficit hyperactivity disorder (NIH publication No. 3572). Available from http://www.nimh.nih.gov/publicat/adhd.

United States Department of Education website. The Jacob K. Javits Gifted and Talented Student Education Act of 2001, Section 5464. Retrieved January 30, 2009.

Wardle, F. (January, 1987). Are you sensitive to interracial children's special identity needs? *Young Children,* 53-59. The National Association for the Education of Young Children.

Warlde, F. (1990). Supporting the healthy development of adopted, multiracial children. *The Interracial Family Circle Newsletter,* 6 (3), 11-17.

Wardle, F. (March, 1993). Interracial families and biracial children. *Exchange,* 45-48.

Developmental and Learning Theories

PREVIEW QUESTIONS

- What is a learning theory, and what does it do?
- What are the developmental domains?
- What are the eight major theories of child development and learning?
- Which key developmental topics impact early education?
- How can educators use developmental theory and research?

NAEYC CODE OF ETHICAL CONDUCT

These Core Values and sections from the NAEYC Code of Ethical Conduct are addressed in this chapter. As you read, note how the Core Values, Ideals, or Principles listed here apply to the topics in this chapter. (Reprinted with permission from the National Association for the Education of Young Children.)

Core Values: We have committed ourselves to: (1) appreciating childhood as a unique and valuable stage of the human life cycle; and (2) basing our work with children on knowledge of child development.

Ideals:

I-1.1   To be familiar with the knowledge base of early childhood care and education and keep current through continuing education and in-service training.

I-1.2   To base program practices upon current knowledge in the field of child development and related disciplines and upon particular knowledge of the individual child.

Introduction

While taking a routine report at an elementary school, a police officer was interrupted by a girl of about 6 years old. Looking the officer up and down, she asked, "Are you a cop?" "Yes," said the woman, and continued writing the report. "My mother said if I ever needed help I should ask the police. Is that right?" "Yes, again," replied the officer. "Well, then," she said as she extended her foot forward, "would you please tie my shoe?"

What was this child thinking? Can you see how she took in information from her mother and then applied it to her own life? How do children do that? What is the process of listening, thinking, and then doing?

While working for an organization that delivers lunches to elderly shut-ins, a mother used to take her preschool son on the afternoon rounds. He was always intrigued by the various appliances there, particularly the canes, walkers, and wheelchairs. One day, she saw him staring at a pair of false teeth soaking in a glass. He turned to her and whispered, "The tooth fairy will never believe this!"

Look how this child applied his fantasy world to what he encountered. During the years from birth to middle childhood, how do young children come to understand the world? How do they make sense of what they see, touch, and experience?

The father of 6-month-old Michiko puts one end of a toy monkey in his mouth and dangles it in front of her. Michiko gazes intently, getting still and wide-eyed, finally reaching up tentatively to touch the doll. Yet, when Keith's nanny tries the same thing with him, the 9-month-old smiles and laughs as he grabs it and tries to shove it back into her mouth.

How is it that two children can respond so differently? Is this simply a few months' age difference? Is it because of their gender or ethnic differences? Or has one child played this game before and not the other?

Theories

So many remarkable transformations take place in the early years. Development, the orderly set of changes in the life span, occurs as individuals move from conception to death. So much changes over time, and those of us curious about children want to know the nature of these changes and the reasons why things happen. What are the theories? What has research told us?

A developmental theory is a "systematic statement of principles and generalizations that provides a coherent framework for understanding how and why people change as they grow older" (Berger, 2008). A learning theory attempts to explain how learning takes place. By observing children, theorists try to make sense out of what they see, looking for patterns and variations to make a kind of story that explains the reasons or causes of the details. Research allows us to look at many children or a group of children over time, even one child with intense scrutiny, to seek these explanations.

Early childhood education draws from several fields of study. Much of what we know about children today comes from child development and child psychology research. Our knowledge base comes directly from psychological studies that ask questions such as:

- How do children develop?
- What do they learn and in what order?
- What do children need to be ready to learn?
- What affects learning?
- Do all children develop in the same ways?
- What are the similarities and differences in growth and development?

To begin to answer these questions, we need some way to look for information and then choose and organize the facts so that we can understand what we see. In other words, we need a **theory.** Psychologists and educators have been doing just that for years, and, in the last hundred years, a great deal has been discovered about these issues.

Theories are especially useful in providing a broad and consistent view of the complexity of human development. Berger (2008) offers these points:

- Theories produce hypotheses. They allow us to make an educated guess (called a **hypothesis**) about children's behavior and development.
- Theories generate discoveries. Because these theories are based on experience, teachers can check their validity as they observe children every day.
- Theories offer practical guidance. The theories you read of form the foundation of developmentally appropriate practice (DAP) that is a guide for teachers at all levels of early education. (See "Insights from the Field" by Rosalind Charlesworth at the end of the chapter.)

The basic quest for sound theories about development and knowledge and for systematic statements about behavior and development has given educators much to consider in forming their own ideas about children.

Yet, why do we need to know anything about theory or research? Is direct experience with children not enough to plan good programs? Certainly the practical aspects of teaching young children are important. However, only with a genuine understanding of why a practice is conducted can early educators successfully plan and achieve meaningful and effective intervention. If the processes involved in development are not random, then we must try to know them. As complex as the system of children's growth, thinking, feeling, and behaving may be, we cannot consider ourselves responsible professionals until we understand the theory behind the practice.

The Nature of Development

A child is a blend of many parts that interrelate in different ways and change with growth over time. Such complexity and dynamic change is difficult to describe, much less predict.

Developmental Domains

The study of human development requires insight and information from many disciplines because each person develops simultaneously in body, mind, and spirit.

(Berger, 2008); thus, we usually divide development into three domains to make it easier to study. We try to consider separately the three aspects that make up the whole of development (Figure 4-1). We can then better understand the major processes of development that parallel these developmental areas:

- Biological processes describe changes in the body.
- Cognitive processes are those changes in one's thought, intelligence, and language.
- Socio-emotional processes reflect changes in an individual's relationships with other people, emotions, and personality.

Questions about Development

Major issues are raised in the study of development. The science of development seeks to understand why and how people change or remain the same over time; as a science, it depends on theories, research methods, and critical analyses to understand the what, how, and why of development. Because of this, all kinds of children—younger and older, rich and poor, of various ethnicities, backgrounds, culture and experience—must be studied. Critical to this study is to observe change

FIGURE 4-1 The various domains of child growth and development are interrelated and interdependent.

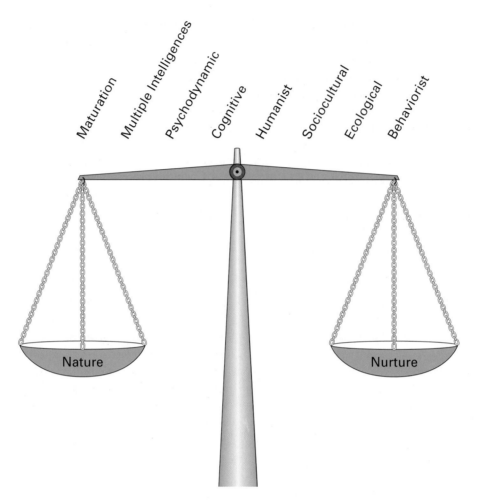

Maturation Multiple Intelligences Psychodynamic Cognitive Humanist Sociocultural Ecological Behaviorist

Nature

Nurture

| **FIGURE 4-2** Development is a combination of the forces of nature and nurture. Each theory offers its own emphasis on heredity/prenatal conditions and environmental/life experiences.

over time. The following are three very common development questions:

1. *Is children's development due more to maturation or experience?* The changes we see in children over time may be due to internal or external influences. Some theories claim children change because of innate, biologic, or genetic patterns built into the human being; others claim that they are shaped by the environment and experiences (such as parents, materials, TV, school, and so on) of life. This argument is often referred to as the **nature/nurture controversy,** also known as the problem of heredity versus environment. As you will remember from Chapter 1, this issue has been discussed for centuries. On the "nature" side, Rousseau argued that the child is born with natural, or innate, goodness. Locke, however, asserted that it was "nurture" that mattered. He contended that children entered the world with a *tabula*

rasa, or clean slate, on which all experience and learning was then written. Today, most psychologists and educators agree that the patterns of development and learning are complex and not so simply explained. Modern theories are not set in such black-and-white terms but rather focus on variations that emphasize one or the other (see Figure 4-2).

2. *Is growth smooth and continuous or more stage-like?* Some theories emphasize a gradual, cumulative kind of growth, more like "from an acorn, a giant oak will grow." This continuity of development is usually the viewpoint of theories that emphasize experience (nurture). Others see children growing in stages that are clearly marked by distinct changes. "This view sees each of us as passing through a sequence of stages in which change is qualitative rather than quantitative. As an oak moves from seedling to giant tree, it becomes more oak-like and its development is continuous. As a

caterpillar changes into a butterfly, it does not become more caterpillar, but, instead, becomes a different kind of organism" (Santrock, 2001). This viewpoint emphasizes the innate nature of development. Figure 4-2 shows the relative orientations of each theory presented in the chapter.

3. *What can theory and research do for early childhood educators?* Science has opened our eyes to the amazing complexity of the mind and the wondrous path of growth in the body. This was not always so. In previous generations, little scientific information was available by which parents (and teachers) could assess the validity of theories. Many beliefs were espoused by adults about children, such as "You'll spoil the baby if you respond to his demands too quickly," or "Children who suffer early neglect and deprivation will not realize their normal potential." These statements can be powerful, particularly as they are passed on to you by your family and culture. However, some ideas are rooted in myth rather than reality. Child development researchers and theorists have accumulated a rich store of knowledge, based on scientific hypothesis that is then tested with evidence. They can help sort fact from fiction.

Initially, the study of child development was mostly confined to the study of trends and descriptions of age changes. As the 20th century progressed, the scope and definition of child development changed radically. Developmental psychologists studied how psychological processes begin, change, and develop. Child development focused on language acquisition, various early effects on later intellectual development, and the process of attachment to others. Now, developmentalists are taking a life-span approach to development, taking into considerations the many directions and contexts of development, understanding the power of culture and the resilience and plasticity of individual growth, and using new tools of technology to unlock the secrets of the brain.

Early childhood teachers should know how children develop and how they learn. Knowing how children develop is critical in making the daily decisions about curriculum, the classroom setting, and children. To be effective with children, teachers need a thoughtful philosophy and approach that is based on what we know about how children develop and what works to help them learn and understand. The teacher who is well versed in theory has invaluable tools to work with parents, advise the family of the range of typical behavior, and talk to parents about concerns that are beyond the norms. Therefore, it is important to have a background in both developmental psychology and learning theories.

Major Theories and Key Topics

No one set of principles encompasses all developmental and learning theories. We have chosen eight theories. Some are grand theories that describe either universal processes or the entire span of development (psychodynamic, behaviorist, cognitive). Others are mini-theories that explain just a part of development (multiple intelligences, maturation, humanistic). A few are emergent theories (sociocultural, ecological) that are relatively new. They are commonly known as (1) psychodynamic theory, (2) behaviorist theory, (3) cognitive theory, (4) sociocultural theory, (5) ecological theory, (6) multiple intelligences theory, (7) maturation theory, and (8) humanistic theory.

In addition, there are several special topics for educators in the study of child development. The chapter ends with a discussion of (1) ethnicity and culture, (2) attachment, (3) play, (4) gender, (5) moral development, and (6) brain-based research.

While writing this chapter, we were reminded of this children's incident:

> While playing "school" in the dramatic play area, Noemi insisted on wearing pretend glasses, as her favorite teacher did. "No!" cried Venecia. "They will make you mad and crabby!" (In fact, her teacher only wore the glasses when she was too tired to wear contact lenses.) "Yes, I will," replied Noemi. "She wears them cuz they makes her smarty-pants." (This is another viewpoint and a kind of myth about intelligence and eyewear.) "You're both wrong," called out Charly. "Everybody knows you have to wear glasses and hoop earrings to be a teacher." (As a matter of fact, the teacher did look like this.) Everyone looked puzzled, and then the play resumed.

Just like these children, not all the experts agree or even think alike. Because the field of child development is broad, encompassing a wide variety of opinion and fact, there is no one theory that describes everything. Moreover, these theories arose at different time periods, in various countries. Each theory describes children and their processes in different ways. It is up to you, the educator, to decide which ones best describe children and their growth. Read carefully, and then compare your experiences with the theories and concepts you read here. As a teacher, you have a diversity of thought on which to establish a professional philosophy.

Psychodynamic Theory

Psychodynamic theory is about personality development and emotional problems. **Psychodynamic,** or psychoanalytic, theories look at development in terms of internal drives that are often **unconscious,** or hidden from our awareness. These motives are the underlying forces that influence human thinking and behavior and provide the foundation for universal stages of development. In psychoanalytic terms, children's behavior can be interpreted by knowing the various stages and tasks within those stages.

Sigmund Freud

Sigmund Freud began his career as a medical doctor and became interested in the irrational side of human behavior as he treated "hysterics." His technique, asking people to recline on a couch and talk about everything, was ridiculed by the medical establishment as the "talking cure." Then, as patients revealed their thoughts, fantasies, and problems, he began to see patterns.

Psychoanalytic Theory

According to Freud, people possess three basic drives: the sexual drive, survival instincts, and a drive for destructiveness. Of the first, childhood sexuality, Freud outlined development in terms of psychosexual stages, each characterized by a particular part of the body (see Figure 4-3). In each stage, the sensual satisfaction associated with each body part is linked to major challenges of that age. For instance, think about how some of the issues of toddlers, such as biting or thumb sucking, and the preschool concerns with "doctor play," masturbation, or gender identifica-

tion in the dress-up corner might be seen in a psychosexual context. Each stage also has its own conflicts between child and parent, and how the child experiences those conflicts will determine basic personality and behavior patterns.

Freud (1920) put forth this theory, and his ideas were expanded on by Anna Freud (his daughter), Carl Jung, Karen Horney, and others. Although Freud's interest was abnormal adult behavior and its causes, his conclusions have had a major effect on our conception of childhood and its place in the life span.

To Freud, the personality was the most important aspect of development, more central to human growth than language, perception, or cognition. Personality was defined by three structures:

1. Id—the instinctive part that drives a person to seek satisfaction
2. Ego—the rational structure that forms a person's sense of self
3. Superego—the moral side that informs the person of right and wrong

He thought that the personality developed in a fixed pattern of stages that emerged as the body matured naturally. But even though the sequence of the stages might be firm, how children were treated while going through those stages determined whether they developed healthy or abnormal personalities. In particular, the mother–child relationship was important in each stage. Thus, the interaction between the child's wishes and needs and how these were treated (by the mother or other adults) was a focal point for proper development.

All psychoanalytic explanations of human development emphasize the critical importance of relation-

Freudian Stages of Childhood Psychosexual Development

Stage	Age	Description/Major Area
Oral	Birth to 2	Mouth (sucking, biting) source of pleasure Eating and teething
Anal	2–3	Bowel movements source of pleasure Toilet learning
Phallic	3–6	Genitals source of pleasure Sex role identification and conscience development
Latency	6–12	Sexual forces dormant Energy put into schoolwork and sports
Genital	12–18	Genitals source of pleasure Stimulation and satisfaction from relationships

FIGURE 4-3 Freud's psychoanalytic theory of childhood development. Psychoanalytic theory contends that each stage has its own area of pleasure and crisis between the child and parent of society.

ships with people and the sequence, or stages, of personality development. The psychoanalyst Erik Erikson expanded and refined Freud's theory of development. It is Erikson whose ideas have most affected early childhood education.

Erik Erikson

Erik Homberg Erikson is perhaps the most influential psychoanalyst of the modern era and certainly a key figure in the study of children and development. His interests in children and education included a teaching background in progressive and Montessori schools in Europe. After clinical training in psychoanalysis, he remained interested in the connections between psychotherapy and education. His books, *Childhood and Society* (1950) about his version of Freud's theory, and Pulitzer Prize–winning *Gandhi's Truth* (1969), helped him become well known in the United States. Erikson became the first child analyst in the Boston area and worked for both University of California at Berkeley and Stanford University.

Psychosocial Theory

Erikson's theory of human development, like those of Freud and Piaget, states that life is a series of stages through which each person passes, with each stage growing from the previous ones. He proposes eight stages of **psychosocial** development, each representing a critical period for the development of an important strength. Positive growth allows the individual to integrate his or her physical and biologic development with the challenges that the social institutions and culture present. Each stage is characterized by an emotional challenge. Erikson gave us the term *identity crisis* to describe how people struggle with a pair of contrasting issues at each stage as they try to answer, "Who am I?" (see Figure 4-4).

FIGURE 4-4 Eriksonian crisis in a young child's life. Psychosocial theory claims that conflicts are opportunities to balance competing urges. The child who takes initiative (grabbing a toy) can also feel guilt (returning it).

A second key point of Erikson's theory is balance. In Erikson's framework, balancing a child's wishes and the demands of the environment with a mentally healthy dose of each emotion is essential for personality strength.

In other words, every growing organism passes through certain developmental stages. A stage is a period during which certain changes occur. What one achieves in each stage is based on the developments of the previous stages, and each stage presents the child with certain kinds of problems to be solved. When children succeed, they go on to attack new problems and grow through solving them.

Erikson differed from Freud in some fundamental ways. First, he emphasized the drive for identity and meaning in a social context rather than the Freudian notion of sexual and aggressive drives. Second, development occurs throughout the life span, in contrast with the notion that personality is shaped only in childhood. Finally, the developmental struggles that occur during one's life can be overcome later. You can go back; while it is true that the first four stages play a key role in developing ego identity, problems of childhood can be dealt with in later stages so the adult can achieve vitality.

Everyone has certain biologic, social, and psychological needs that must be satisfied to grow in a healthy manner. Medicine has learned much about physical needs—diet, rest, and exercise. Basic intellectual, social, and emotional needs also must be met for an organism to be healthy. Eriksonian theory speaks to these needs. Whether these needs are met or left unfulfilled affects development.

Erikson's stage theory is expanded here because of its importance to the field of early childhood education. Figure 4-5 names all 8 stages; the text elaborates on the first four in the early childhood period.

Stage 1: Trust versus Mistrust (Birth to 1 Year)

Erikson's first stage is roughly the first year of life and parallels Freud's oral-sensory stage. Attitudes important to development are the capacity to trust—or mistrust—inner and outer experiences. By providing consistent care, parents help an infant develop a basic sense of trust in self and an ability to trust other people. They give affection and emotional security as well as provide for physical needs. Inconsistent or inadequate care creates mistrust. In extreme cases, as shown by Spitz's classic studies on infant deprivation, lack of care actually led to infant death (Spitz & Wolf, 1946). A less extreme case might form isolation or distrust of others. Given a solid base in early trust, though, the typical infant develops the virtue, or strength, of hope.

Psychosocial Stages of Erikson's Theory

Stage	Description	Challenge	Strength
Stage One	Newborns	Trust vs. Mistrust	Hope
Stage Two	Toddlers	Autonomy vs. Shame and Doubt	Willpower
Stage Three	Childhood	Initiative vs. Guilt	Purpose
Stage Four	School	Competence (or industry) vs. Inferiority	Competence
Stage Five	Adolescence	Search for identity vs. Role confusion	Fidelity
Stage Six	Young adulthood	Intimacy (love and friendship) vs. Isolation (loneliness)	Love
Stage Seven	Grown-ups	Generativity (caring for the next generation) vs. Stagnation	Care
Stage Eight	Old age	Integrity vs. Despair	Wisdom

FIGURE 4-5 Erikson's theory of psychosocial development. Centering on basic crises at each stage of development, the theory proposes that these conflicts are part of the life process and that successful handling of these issues can give a person the "ego strength" to face life positively.

Babies must learn trust at two levels: "external, a belief that significant adults will be present to meet their needs, and internal, a belief in their own power to affect changes and cope with a variety of circumstances" (Mooney, 2000). As adults engage with infants, they encourage attachment by holding babies close when feeding them and responding right away to their distress when they cry (see "Developmental Topics" at the end of this chapter).

When working with infants and toddlers, teachers must take special care to provide a predictable environment and consistent caregiving. Babies are totally dependent on adults to meet their needs; they are particularly vulnerable to difficulties because they have few skills for coping with discomfort and stress. Therefore, it is critical that they be cared for by warm, positive adults who are sensitive and respond affectionately to an infant's needs as soon as they arise. In this way, the very young develop the trust in the world that will support their growth into the next stage.

Stage 2: Autonomy versus Doubt (2 to 3 Years)

The second stage, corresponding to the second and third years of life, parallels the muscular-anal period in Freudian theory. The child learns to manage and control impulses and to use both motor and mental skills. To help a child develop a healthy balance between **autonomy** and doubt, parents should consider how to handle their toddlers' toilet learning and growing curiosity to explore. Restrictive or compulsive parents may give the child a feeling of shame and doubt, causing a sense of insecurity. Successful growth in this stage gives children strength of will. "This stage, therefore, becomes decisive for the ratio of love and hate, cooperation and willfulness, freedom of self-expression and its suppression. From a sense of self-control without loss of self-esteem comes a lasting sense of good will and pride; from a sense of loss of self-control and of foreign over-control comes a lasting propensity for doubt and shame" (Erikson, 1963).

Encouraging a sense of autonomy while teaching limits without shaming is a delicate balance. According to Mooney (2000), adults foster independence in toddlers by:

Giving children simple choices	"Milk or juice today?"
Not giving false choices	"Do you want to get in your car seat?"
Setting clear, consistent, reasonable limits	"People are not for biting."
Accepting children's swings between independence and dependence	"Sometimes you want to play by yourself, and sometimes near me; both are ok."

Chapter 7 elaborates on how to help guide children using positive discipline.

Budding curiosity means high energy, so the daily schedule should include plenty of time for active movement and flexibility to deal with fluctuating energy and mood. Toileting is a learned behavior just as dressing, painting, and singing are; a relaxed attitude about this area helps the child gain mastery without shame. Allowing for plenty of "two steps forward, one back" acknowledges the child's natural doubts and the balancing that happens in this stage.

Stage 3: Initiative versus Guilt (3 to 5 or 6 Years)

The third stage of Eriksonian theory corresponds to the preschool and kindergarten years and parallels Freud's phallic stage of development. The developmental task is to develop a sense of purpose. Out of autonomy comes initiative, and from healthy doubt can come a conscience. For example, a preschooler grabs another's toy; he may run and hide when the crying begins. The teacher gently leads the child to give it back and allows the regret to be expressed through making amends. Another example comes from noticing that the kindergarten girls have great ideas about putting on a play but are disorganized about planning, so the teacher guides them to choose a title, various roles, and a "to do" list so they can execute in constructive and cooperative ways. An overly restrictive adult may end up with a child who is easily discouraged and inhibited. On the other hand, parents or teachers signaling no restraints give the child no clear idea of what is socially acceptable and what is not. The key strength that grows out of this stage is purpose.

Teaching children of this age is both exhilarating and exasperating. Many find this stage easier physically than the previous two but more challenging socially. It is a time when children move in two opposing directions: accomplishment or destruction. To support children's development of initiative with reasonable expectations, teachers can:

- Encourage children to be as independent as possible.
- Focus on gains and attempts rather than on mistakes.
- Set expectations aligned with a child's individual abilities.
- Focus curriculum on real things and on doing instead of simply listening.

Section 4 of this book concentrates on environmental and curricular issues.

Remember, the child who takes initiative is ready to meet the world head-on and wants to do it "all by myself." This may include both putting on a jacket and hitting someone who has said something unkind. An environment that can respond to a child's interests, both in theme and at the moment, will be interesting and successful. At the same time, teachers must be prepared with a small set of logical limits (or "rules") and the means to follow through kindly and firmly when those limits are tested. Socializing at this age is the very point of the emotional states of initiative and guilt; children must have enough freedom to develop their own ways to deal with one another and still develop a sense of fairness and conscience. Chapter 7 offers strategies for setting and maintaining limits at this age.

Stage 4: Industry versus Inferiority (6 to 12 Years)

Erikson's fourth stage, beginning with the primary school years and ending with puberty, parallels Freud's latency period. The major theme in this stage is mastery of life, primarily by adapting to laws of society (people, laws and rules, relationships) and objects (tools, machines, the physical world). This is the child's most enthusiastic time for learning. The stage is "the end of early childhood's period of expansive imagination. The danger in the elementary school years is the development of a sense of inferiority—of feeling incompetent and unproductive" (Santrock, 2001). It is also a time of great adventure. Children begin to think of being big and to identify with people whose work or whose personality they can understand and admire.

- *Find a place in my own school:* Be the line leader on the way to the cafeteria, the goalie on the soccer field, scribe at a scout meeting.
- *Applying myself to something new:* Try organizing and serving snacks at the after-school center.
- *Handling the "tools of the tribe":* Learn to use colored pencils, to read aloud, to fill out forms, to check out balls and bats.

Problems arise if the child feels inadequate and inferior to such tasks. A parent or teacher who overemphasizes children's mistakes could make them despair of ever learning, for instance, the multiplication tables or cursive handwriting. This is particularly sensitive for the child with special needs and for those who are learning a second language. At the same time, adults must encourage children to work toward mastery. Adults should "mildly but firmly coerce children into the adventure of finding out that one can learn to accomplish things which one would never have thought possible by oneself" (Erikson, 1963). Parents must not let their children restrict their own horizons by doing only what they already know. Particularly in social situations, it is essential for children to learn to do things with others, as difficult and unfair as this may sometimes be.

Applying Psychosocial Theory to Work with Children

First, Erikson has a clear message about the importance of play. Second, the theory offers guidelines for the role of adults in children's lives.

Play is a critical part of children's total development. Most schools for children under age 6 have periods of time allotted for play called "choice time" or "free play." Erikson supports these ideas explicitly by stating that the senses of autonomy and of initiative are developed mainly through social and fantasy play. He suggests that child's play is "the infantile form of the human ability to deal with experiences by creating model situations and to master reality by experiment and planning. ... To 'play it out' in play is the most natural self-healing measure childhood affords" (Erikson, 1964). (See the Developmental Topic on "Play" later in this chapter.)

The adult is primarily an emotional base and a social mediator for the child. Teachers become interpreters of feelings, actions, reasons, and solutions. We help children understand situations and motives so that they can solve their own problems. Look at each child's emotional makeup and monitor his or her progress through developmental crises; each crisis is a turning point of increased vulnerability and also enhanced potential. Allow the child, in Erikson's words:

> ... to experience over and over again that he is a person who is permitted to make choices. He has to have the right to choose, for example, whether to sit or whether to stand, whether to approach a visitor or to lean against his mother's knee ... whether to use the toilet or to wet his pants. At the same time he must learn some of the boundaries of self-determination. He inevitably finds that there are some walls he cannot climb, that there are objects out of reach, that above all, there are innumerable commands enforced by powerful adults. (1969)

In preschool and kindergarten, a teacher allows children to take initiative and does not interfere with the results of those actions. At the same time, teachers and parents provide clear limits so that the children can learn what behaviors are unacceptable to society. For example, the kindergartners at a birthday party are laughing and shouting in the bedroom, when suddenly the birthday girl emerges in tears with several others in tow trying to tell what happened. The adult who can help them take turns in the telling and declare how scary it was when someone fell off the bouncing bed and bumped her head helps the children acknowledge real feelings and learn to interact around social challenges.

The issues of early childhood, from Erikson's theory, are really human issues. The remnants of these stages stay with us all our lives, and teachers who are aware of their own processes can fully appreciate the struggles of children.

In Erikson's theory, the adult serves as a social mediator for the child.

Behaviorist Theory

Behaviorism is the most pragmatic and functional of the modern psychological ideologies. Behaviorist theories describe both development and learning. Initiated during the 1920s and continually modified today, behaviorism is "the most distinctively American contribution to psychology" (Suransky, 1982). Countless developmental psychologists and researchers have defined and expanded on this idea, several of whom are mentioned later in this chapter. To summarize the behaviorist theory, we have chosen five theorists: Ivan Pavlov, John Watson, Edward Thorndike, B. F. Skinner, and Albert Bandura.

The Behaviorists

What is known today as "behaviorism" begins with the notion that a child is born with a "clean slate," a *tabula rasa* in Locke's words, on which events are written throughout life. The conditions of those events cause all important human behavior. Behaviorists often insist that only what can actually be observed will be accepted as fact. Only behavior can be treated, they say, not feelings or internal states. This contrasts to the psychodynamic approach, which insists that behavior is just an indirect clue to the "real" self, that of inner feelings and thoughts.

Ivan Pavlov, a Russian physiologist, was working in a laboratory, studying how animals digest food. He noticed that the dogs in his laboratory would anticipate their meals when they heard or saw their attendants making preparations. Instead of starting to salivate just when food was set in front of them, the dogs would salivate to a number of stimuli associated with food. He identified this simple form of learning as respondent conditioning. The association of involuntary reflexes with other environmental conditions became known as classical conditioning, a cornerstone of behaviorist theory.

John B. Watson was an American theorist who studied Pavlov's experiments, then translated those ideas of conditioning into human terms. In the first quarter of the 20th century, Watson made sweeping claims about the powers of this classical conditioning. He declared that he could shape a person's entire life by controlling exactly the events of an infant's first year. One of his ideas was to discourage emotional ties between parents and children because they interfered with the child's direct learning from the environment (though he later modified this). Nonetheless, he gave scientific validity to the idea that teachers should set conditions for learning and reward proper responses.

Edward L. Thorndike also studied the conditions of learning. Known as the "godfather of standardized testing," Thorndike helped develop scales to measure student achievement and usher in the era of standardized educational testing (see Chapter 6). He set forth the famous **stimulus-response** technique. A stimulus will recall a response in a person; this forms learned habits. Therefore, it is wise to pay close attention to the consequences of behavior and to the various kinds of **reinforcement.**

B. F. Skinner took the idea of *tabula rasa* one step further to create the doctrine of the "empty organism." That is, a person is like a vessel to be filled by carefully designed experiences. All behavior is under the control of one or more aspects of the environment. Furthermore, Skinner maintained that there is no behavior that cannot be modified. Some people argue that Skinnerian concepts tend to depersonalize the learning process and treat people as puppets. Others say that behaviorist psychology has made us develop new ways to help people learn and cope effectively with the world.

Albert Bandura refined behaviorism beyond conditioning into a social learning theory. **Socialization** is the process of learning to conform to social rules. Social-learning theorists watch how children learn these rules and use them in groups. They study the patterns of reinforcement and reward in socially appropriate and unacceptable behavior and how children learn:

> Children acquire most of their social concepts—the rules by which they live—from models whom they observe in the course of daily life, particularly parents, caregivers, teachers, and peers. Social learning theory [suggests] the models most likely to be imitated are individuals who are nurturant—warm, rewarding, and affectionate. Attachment also affects the process: The most significant or influential models are people to whom the child is emotionally tied. (Bandura in Fong & Resnick, 1986)

From this arose a new concept known as **modeling.** This is what used to be known as learning and teaching by example. For instance, children who see their parents smoking will likely smoke themselves, and those who witness kindness to others are likely to imitate it. In fact, Bandura's studies provided "strong evidence that exposure to filmed aggression heightens aggressive reactions in children. Subjects who viewed the aggressive human and cartoon models on film exhibited nearly twice as much aggression than did subjects in the control group who were not exposed to the aggressive film content" (Bandura, 1963). This work suggests that pictorial mass media—television, video games, and computer activities—serve as important sources of social behavior. Any behavior can be learned by watching it, from language (listening to others talk) to fighting (watching violence on television).

Bandura's theory has expanded into a cognitive model, theorizing that children think hard about what they see and feel. Social learning is also related to self-understanding and a belief in one's own abilities, known as **self-efficacy.** Thus, personal and cognitive factors influence behavior, as does the environment, and, in turn, children's behavior can affect the environment around them. Adding the factors of modeling and reflective thinking to behaviorist theory links it to Piaget's cognitive theory (next in this chapter).

Theory of Behaviorism and Social Learning

What is behavior, or learning, theory all about? Learning occurs when an organism interacts with the environment. Through experience, behavior is modified or changed. In the behaviorist's eyes, three types of learning occur: (1) classical conditioning; (2) operant conditioning; and

(3) **observational learning** or modeling. The first two are based on the idea that learning is mostly the development of habit. What people learn is a series of associations, forming a connection between a stimulus and response that did not exist before. The third is based on a social approach. Figure 4-6 summarizes these three types of behaviorist learning processes.

Classical Conditioning

Classical conditioning can be explained by reviewing Pavlov's original experiments. A dog normally salivates at the sight of food but not when he hears a bell. When the sound of a bell is paired with the sight of food, the dog "learns" to salivate when he hears the bell, whether or not food is nearby. Thus, the dog has been conditioned to salivate (give the response) for both the food (unconditioned stimulus) and the bell (conditioned stimulus). Similarly, when the school bell rings in the afternoon, children begin to gather their papers into backpacks to go home. They have been conditioned to the sound of the bell; ask any teacher who has had to deal with a broken bell system how strong this conditioning is. Classical conditioning can also account for the development of phobias. Watson used a young boy in a laboratory to test this theory. He showed the boy a white rat, then sounded a loud noise. After only seven pairings, the boy would cringe at the sight of the rat without the bell sounding at all. Only a few painful visits to a childhood dentist can teach a lifetime fear of dental health professionals.

Operant Conditioning

Operant conditioning is slightly different from classical conditioning in that it focuses on the response rather than the stimulus. In operant conditioning, the process that makes it more likely that a behavior will recur is called reinforcement. A stimulus that increases the likelihood of repeated behavior is called a **reinforcer.** Most people are likely to increase what gives them pleasure (be it food or attention) and decrease what gives them displeasure (such as punishment, pain, or the withdrawal of food or attention). The behaviorist tries to influence the organism by controlling these kinds of reinforcement.

A positive reinforcer is something that the learner views as desirable:

"social reinforcers"	attention, praise, smiles or hugs
"nonsocial reinforcers"	tokens, toys, food, stickers

For example, you would like Claire to begin to use a spoon instead of her hands to eat. Before conditioning, you talk to her whenever she eats. During the conditioning period, you can give attention (a positive reinforcer) each time she picks up a spoon during feeding times and ignore her when she uses her hands. Afterward, she is more likely to use a spoon and less often her hands. This is an example of a positive reinforcer, something that increases the likelihood of the desired response.

The reinforcers can be either positive or negative. A negative reinforcer is removal of an unpleasant stimulus as a result of some particular behavior. Circle time is Jimmy's favorite activity at school. Yet he has difficulty controlling his behavior and consistently disrupts the group. Before conditioning, he is told that if he talks to his neighbors and shouts responses at the teacher, he will be asked to leave the circle. During the conditioning period, Jimmy is praised whenever he pays attention, sings songs, and does not bother those around him (positive reinforcement). When he begins to shout, he is told to leave and return when he can sing without shouting (negative reinforcement). A negative reinforcer is used to stop children from behaving in a particular way by arranging for them to end a mildly aversive situation immediately (in this case, the boy has to leave the group) by improving their behavior. Jimmy, by controlling his own behavior, could end his isolation from the group.

Behaviorist Learning Processes

	Classical Conditioning	Operant Conditioning	Modeling
Kind of behavior	Reflexive	Voluntary	Voluntary
Type of learning	Learning through association	Learning through reinforcement	Learning through observation and imitation
Role of learner	Passive	Active or passive	Active

FIGURE 4-6 Behaviorist learning processes. Classical conditioning, operant conditioning, and modeling are three ways of learning, describing how behavior is learned and the role of the learner in each process.

Punishment is different from negative reinforcement. Punishment is an unpleasant event that makes the behavior less likely to be repeated; that is, if Jimmy were spanked every time he shouted, then his shouting would be the punished behavior and it is likely he would begin to shout less. However, when leaving the group is the reinforcer for shouting, he tries to stop shouting to increase the likelihood of being able to stay, and not being taken away from the group. Negative reinforcement thus increases the likelihood that the desired behavior will be repeated (staying in the group) and removes attention from the less desirable behavior (the shouting). The "time-out" chair, for instance, could be viewed as either a punishment or a negative reinforcer. If used as exclusion from the group or a withdrawal of playing privileges, a child would find the time-out as a punishment. On the other hand, if a child could leave the time-out more quickly by exhibiting certain behaviors (instead of the "bad" behavior), it might be seen as a negative reinforcer.

Reinforcement, both positive and negative, is a powerful tool. It is important for adults to realize that it can be misused. It is wise to be careful, particularly in the case of negative reinforcement. An adult may not be gentle with a negative reinforcer when angry with a child's inappropriate behavior. Educators and parents should be aware of the possibilities and check their own responses.

Modeling

The third kind of conditioning is called observational learning or modeling. Social behavior is particularly noteworthy to early childhood professionals, as most work with children in groups and thus witness social behavior constantly. Any behavior that involves more than one person can be considered social. One of the most negative social behaviors is aggression. It is this type that Albert Bandura researched, finding that much of it is learned by watching others.

Aggression is a complex issue, involving various definitions and behaviors. To illustrate social learning theory, Bandura defines aggression as behavior intended to inflict harm or discomfort to another person or object. Bandura showed a short film of aggressive behavior to young children. The original mid-1960s studies are summarized below:

Each child in Bandura's experiment viewed one of three films. In all three films, an adult hit, kicked, and verbally abused an inflated Bobo doll in ways that young children are unlikely to do spontane-

© Cengage Learning

Modeling is a special kind of observational learning in which children watch others and then pattern their behavior after what they have seen.

ously. The films differed in what happened to the model after the aggressive sequence. In one film, the model was lavishly rewarded with praise and foods that appealed to preschoolers, such as candy and caramel popcorn. In another film, the model was punished in a dramatic way, including severe scolding and a spanking. The third film simply ended after the model's aggressive behavior, with no consequences following the aggression. After viewing one film, each child in the experiment was allowed to play in a room with a Bobo doll, all the toys used in the aggression film, and a variety of other toys.

The results are most impressive, especially to those working with young children. The level of aggression expressed by each child was directly related to what the children saw as the consequences in the film. When offered prizes, they imitated almost exactly what their model had done. Also, children appeared more likely to attack one another after viewing the attacks on the Bobo doll in film. Further studies have shown that children's levels of aggression are higher right after viewing the film but less so when shown it again six months later (Berger, 2005). Regardless of the controversy that may surround any study of children's aggression or the effects of watching filmed violence on youngsters, the social-learning theory deserves serious consideration. The effect of television and media viewing on children is discussed in Chapter 15.

Applying Behaviorist Theory to Work with Children

Behaviorist theories make a strong case for how the environment influences our behavior:

- *Physical environment:* A teacher arranges the room so that positive learning is enhanced.
- *Daily schedule:* Routines and sequence of events are planned to encourage habits.
- *Teacher/child interaction:* Teachers respond carefully to children to shape their behavior.

Adults are powerful reinforcers and models for children. A learning situation comprises many cues; it is up to adults to know what those cues are and how to control them. Teachers who use behavior modification techniques know both what children are to do and how they will be reinforced for their behavior. The ethics and usefulness of using this kind of control bring up important criticism and concern (see Kohn in "What Do You Think?"). Each teacher and program must consider the impact of this theory and how to apply it to classroom and client. Chapter 7 has examples of behavior modification techniques and a discussion about their limitations.

What Do YOU Think?

Alfie Kohn, a nationally known educator and author, is a strong critic of behaviorism. He cites research showing that rewards decrease motivation; in fact, the more rewards are used, the more they seem to be needed. Punishment and negative reinforcement produce short-term compliance only, and often disregard feelings, needs, and intentions. "Skinnerian thinking—caring only about behaviors—has narrowed our understanding of children and warped the way we deal with them . . . In a nutshell, it's the child who engages in the behavior, not the behavior itself, who matters" (Kohn, 2005).

1. Do you think children end up being "punished by rewards"?
2. How do you shape children's behavior?
3. How much of what we do with children can be explained by behaviorism?

What children learn is shaped by the circumstances surrounding the learning. Experiences that are enjoyable are reinforcing. From the peek-a-boo game with an infant to a 7-year-old's first ride on a skateboard, an experience is more likely to be repeated and learned if it is pleasant. Social learning is particularly powerful in the lives of young children. Adults must be mindful of their own behavior; watching children as young as 2 years old play "family" or "school" will convince the most skeptical critic that any behavior is learnable and can become part of children's behavioral repertoire.

Cognitive Theory

Adult: What does it mean to be alive?
Child: It means you can move about, play—that you can do all kinds of things.
Adult: Is a mountain alive?
Child: Yes, because it has grown by itself.
Adult: Is a cloud alive?
Child: Yes, because it sends water.
Adult: Is wind alive?
Child: Yes, because it pushes things.

How do children learn to think, and what do they think about? Cognitive theory describes the structure and development of human thought processes and how those processes affect the way a person understands and perceives the world. Piaget's theory of cognition forms a cornerstone of early childhood educational concepts about children; others have developed this theory further into a constructivist theory of learning.

Jean Piaget

Jean Jacques Piaget was one of the most exciting research theorists in child development. A major force in child psychology, he studied both thought processes and how they change with age. Piaget's ideas serve as our guide to the cognitive theory because of the thoroughness of his work. He had great influence on child psychology, theories of learning, intellectual development, and even philosophy. He became the foremost expert on the development of knowledge from birth to adulthood.

How did Piaget find out about such matters? A short review of his life and ideas reveals a staggering volume of work and a wide scope of interests. Born at the turn of the century, Piaget built on his childhood curiosity in science and philosophy by working with Dr. Simon at the Binet Laboratory (Simon and Binet devised the first intelligence test). While recording children's abilities to answer questions correctly, he became fascinated with children's incorrect responses. He noticed that children tended to give similar kinds of wrong answers at certain ages.

Thus, Piaget launched into a lifelong study of intelligence. He believed that children think in fundamentally different ways from adults. He also developed a new method for studying thought processes. Rather than using a standardized test, he adapted the psychiatric method of question and response. Called the *methode clinique*, it is a technique in which adults ask questions and then adapt their teaching and further inquiries based on children's answers. This method of observation and assessment is discussed in detail in Chapter 6.

Piaget then began studying children's thought processes. With his wife, one of his former students, he observed his own children. He also began to look closely at how actively children engage in their own development. Prolific his entire life, Piaget gave us a complex theory of intelligence and child development. He recorded, in a systematic way, how children learn, when they learn, and what they learn (Elkind & Flavell, 1996).

Theory of Cognitive Development

While others thought that the development of thinking was either intrinsic (nature) or extrinsic (nurture), Piaget thought that neither position offered a full explanation for a child's amazing and complex behaviors.

His theory relies on both maturational and environmental factors. It is called maturational because it sets out a sequence of cognitive (thinking) stages that is governed by heredity. For example, heredity affects our learning by (1) how the body is structured biologically and (2) automatic, or instinctive, behavior, such as an infant's sucking at birth. It is an environmental theory because the experiences children have will directly influence how they develop. Piaget claimed that children build their own knowledge and that "construction is superior to instruction" (Santrock, 2001).

Theory Basics

Thinking and learning is a process of interaction between a person and the environment. Piaget also believed that all species inherit a basic tendency to organize their lives and adapt to the world around them. This is known as a constructivist theory (see later in this chapter); that is, children actively construct knowledge on an ongoing basis. They are developing and constantly revising their own knowledge. As they experience the world, they take in new information and either absorb it into what they already know (**assimilation**) or create a new place for it (**accommodation**), thus returning to a sense of balance (**equilibration**). In doing so, all organisms "figure out" what the world is all about and then work toward surviving in that world. Piaget believed children learn best when they are actually doing the work (or play) themselves, rather than being told, shown, or explained to, which were the dominant teaching methods of the day. Having studied Montessori methods, Piaget concluded that teachers could prepare a stimulating environment and also interact with the children to enhance their thinking.

Regardless of their age, all people develop **schemas,** or mental concepts, as a general way of thinking about, or interacting with, ideas and objects in the environment. Very young children learn perceptual schemas as they taste and feel; preschool children use language and pretend play to create their understanding; older children develop more abstract ones, such as morality schemas, which help them determine how to act.

Throughout, we use three basic processes to think: these are known as the adaptive processes of assimilation and accommodation and the balancing process of equilibration. Figure 4-7 demonstrates how these work.

Piaget theorized that thinking develops in a certain general pattern in all human beings. These stages of thinking are the psychological structures that go along with adapting to the environment. Piaget identified four major stages of cognitive development:

Sensorimotor stage	0 to 2 years
Preoperational stage	2 to 6 or 7 years
Concrete operational stage	6 to 12 years
Formal operational stage	12 years to adulthood

Each person of normal intelligence will go through these stages in this order, although the rate will change depending on the individual and his or her experiences. Each stage of development has critical lessons for the child to learn in order to think and make sense of the world. Figure 4-8 illustrates key experiences at each stage of cognitive development in the early years. Piaget's work has been a major influence in early childhood programs.

Piaget's theories revolutionized our thinking about children's thinking and challenged psychologists and educators to focus less on *what* children know than the *ways* they come to know. But was Piaget right? Researchers have been exploring and debating the ideas of cognitive theory for many years, often engaging in what Piaget himself called "the American question": Can you speed up the rate in which children pass through these intellectual stages of development?

Piaget's Three Processes of Cognitive Adaptation

Assimilation: Taking new information and organizing it in such a way that it fits with what the person already knows.

Example: Juanita sees an airplane while walking outside with her father. She knows that birds fly. So, never having seen this flying thing before, she calls it a "bird (pájaro)." This is what we call *assimilation.* She is taking in this new information and making it fit into what she already knows. Children assimilate what they are taught into their own worlds when they play "school" by taking turns and "house" with their dolls and toys or other people.

Accommodation: Taking new information and changing what is already thought to fit the new information.

Example: Aaron is at the grocery store with his mother and newborn baby. He calls the woman in the line ahead of them "pregnant" although she is simply overweight. After being corrected, he asks the next person he sees, "Are you pregnant or just fat?" This is what we call *accommodation.* Having learned that not all people with large bellies are pregnant, he changes his knowledge base to include new information. Children accommodate to the world as they are taught to use a spoon, the toilet, or a computer.

Equilibration: A mental process to achieve a mental balance, whereby a person takes new information and continually attempts to make sense of the experiences and perceptions.

Example: Colby, age seven, gets two glasses from the cupboard for his friend Ajit and himself. After putting apple juice into his short, wide glass he decides he'd rather have milk, so he pours it into Ajit's tall, thin glass. "Look, now I have more than you!" says his friend. This puzzles Colby, who is distressed (in "disequilibrium"): How could it be more when he just poured it out of his glass? He thinks about the inconsistency (and pours the juice several times back and forth) and begins to get the notion that pouring liquid into different containers does not change the amount (the conservation liquids). "No, it isn't," he says, "it's just a different shape!" Thus, Colby learns to make sense of it in a new way and achieve equilibrium in his thinking. Children do this whenever they get new information that asks them to change the actual schemas, making new ones to fit new experiences.

FIGURE 4-7 In Piagetian theory, the processes of assimilation, accommodation, and equilibration are basic to how people think (cognition) and learn.

Now, developmental psychologists believe that Piaget's theory of distinct stages is not correct, but the idea of a sequence in thinking is. Furthermore, current research on the brain supports Piagetian theory. Brain maturation, as reflected in **myelination,** a process that speeds transmission of nerve impulses between neurons, seems to follow a sequence that parallels the various thinking stages of development. Brain-based research and its implications for early childhood teachers are discussed at the end of this chapter.

What we do know is that children progress from one stage to the next, changing their thinking depending on their level of maturation and experience with the environment. Certain physical skills, such as fine-motor coordination, determine how much a child is capable of doing. Certain environmental factors, such as the kinds of experiences the world and adults provide, influence the rate of growth. Yet throughout the process, children take in new knowledge and decide how it fits with what they already know. As new information comes in, the child learns and grows.

What Do YOU Think?

There are two main criticisms of Piaget's theory: the age and the stage.

1. *The Age:* He seems to have been wrong about just how early many cognitive skills develop. For example, virtually all the achievements of the concrete operational period are present in at least rudimentary or fragmentary form in the preschool years. This might simply mean that Piaget just had the ages wrong—that the concrete operations stage really begins at age 3 or 4.

2. *The Stage:* Research on expertise now shows that specific knowledge makes a huge difference. Children and adults who know a lot about some subject or some set of materials (dinosaurs, baseball cards, mathematics, or whatever) not only categorize information in that topic area in more complex and hierarchical ways; they are also better at remembering new information on that topic and better at applying more advanced forms of logic to material in that area.

So, was Piaget right? And about what?

Stages of Early Childhood Cognitive Development

© Cengage Learning

As a baby

Sensorimotor Period

Key concept

Object permanence

Definition

—the understanding that objects continue to exist even when they are out of sight
—essential to understanding the physical world

Explanation

—Birth to four months, infants respond to objects but stop tracking them if they are covered.
—Four to eight months, infants will reach for an object if it is partially covered.
—By eight to twelve months, infants will search for hidden objects randomly, anywhere.
—By 12 to 18 months, toddlers will search for an object where they last saw it.
—By 18 to 24 months, toddlers will search for hidden objects in systematic way.

As a preschooler

Preoperational

Key concept

Symbolic play and language

Definition

—the use of ideas, images, sounds, or symbols to stand for objects and events = symbolic play
—the use of an abstract, rule-governed system of symbols that can be combined to communicate information = language
—essential to developing the capacity to think

Explanation

—From 14 to 19 months, representational ability emerges.
—By 24 months, most can use substitute objects in pretend play.
—Nine to twelve months, infants begin to use conventional social gestures.
—Around one year, first words emerge.
—18 to 24 months, first sentences appear.

As a primary child

Concrete Operational

Key concept

Reasoning

Definition

—Actions can be carried out mentally.
—Logical reasoning replaces intuitive thinking in concrete situations.
—Classification skills develop.
—Essential to ability to think logically.

Explanation

—can coordinate several characteristics rather than a single property
—reversibility emerges; can see the same problem from several perspectives
—can divide things into sets and reason about their relationships
—Conservation skills emerge; an amount of liquid remains the same, no matter the container.

FIGURE 4-8 During each stage of cognitive development, children learn a key concept that enhances their thinking and reasoning.

Constructivist Theory

For more than a century, there has been regular debate about how children learn and concerning the best methods of teaching. Traditional methods of teaching, particularly for school-age children, are based on behaviorist views of learning. Articulated by Thorndike and Skinner (see the behaviorist section in this chapter), these methods emphasize learning by association and in a stimulus-response manner. With this **transmission model** of teaching, the teacher possesses the knowledge and transmits it directly to the children.

In contrast, a method called **constructivism** has emerged. Based on ideas from Dewey and Piaget and supported by socio-cultural theory, this **transactional model** of teaching actively engages a child in tasks designed to create personal meaning. Learning is an active process, based on the belief that knowledge is constructed by the learner rather than transferred from the teacher to the child.

"Constructivism is a theory of learning which states that individuals learn through adaptation. What they learn or adapt to is directly influenced by the people, materials and situations with which they come into contact" (Meade-Roberts & Spitz, 1998). People build on preexisting knowledge, be it intellectual, social, or moral. One of its basic tenets is that "knowledge is subjective; that is, everyone creates his own meaning of any particular experience, including what he hears or reads" (Heuwinkel, 1996). Another fundamental idea is that children learn by taking new ideas and integrating them into their existing knowledge base. This is exactly in line with Piaget's processes of assimilation and accommodation.

The teacher's role is to build an environment that is stimulating and conducive to the process of constructing meaning and knowledge. The preprimary schools of Reggio Emilia (see Chapters 2, 9, 10, and 14) encourage children to create their own material representations of their understanding by using many types of media (drawing, sculpture, stories, puppets, paper). At kindergarten and school-age levels, learning literacy and mathematics is considered a developmental process that the teacher "facilitates by providing modeling, authentic experiences, mini-lessons on specific topics and frequent opportunities for students to consult with and learn from each other" (Heuwinkel, 1996). Many constructivist classrooms work on creating community through rule-creating; in fact, those teachers would tell us that "the only way to help students become ethical people, as opposed to people who merely do what they are told, is to have them construct moral meaning" (Kohn, 2005).

Constructivist classrooms look diverse because the style and cultures of the teacher and children will prevail. Furthermore, a constructivist class is often noisy. Children will have choices and make decisions on significant parts of their learning. There may be more "arguments" about how children are to play and build, with children leading discussions and many participating in solutions. The teacher is a facilitator and does less talking while the learners do more, and provides more guidance and written observations rather than enforcing rules or giving tests.

Although there may still be some direct instruction and demonstrations as there are in classes based on behaviorist views, a constructivist program has fundamental differences about teaching and learning, about how children learn best, who and how they should be taught, and who has the answers. Constructivist classrooms may do a better job promoting children's social, cognitive, and moral development than do more teacher-centered programs. It is a theory used extensively in emergent curriculum programs (see Chapters 10–14).

Applying Cognitive Theory to Work with Children

What can teachers learn from the complicated cognitive theory? Piaget's writings do not apply directly to classroom methods or subject matter per se, and therefore, careful interpretation is required. In fact, he never claimed to be an educator. However, Piaget's theories provide a framework, or philosophy, about children's thinking. Piagetian theory has some implications for both environment and interactions.

Materials

Children need many objects to explore so that they can later incorporate these into their symbolic thinking. Such materials need to be balanced among open-ended ones (such as sand and water activities, basic art and construction materials), guided ones (cooking with recipes, conducting experiments, classification and seriated materials), and self-correcting ones (puzzles, matching games, such as some of the Montessori materials). It is important to remember that young children need to be involved with concrete objects and to explore and use them in their own ways, which include both sensorimotor and beginning symbolic play.

Scheduling

Children need lots of time to explore their own reality, especially through the use of play. A Piagetian classroom would have large periods of time for children to "act out" their own ideas. Also, time should be scheduled for imitation of adult-given ideas (songs, finger plays, and stories).

Teachers

Children need teachers who understand and agree with a developmental point of view. The teacher who knows the stages and levels of thinking of the children will be one who can guide that class into new and challenging opportunities to learn and grow.

In working with children under age 5, we must remember that, because they do not understand mental representations very well, they will have trouble recognizing that another person may view or interpret things differently than they do. This **egocentric** viewpoint is both natural and normal but must be factored into teachers' thoughts as they work with children. For instance, you may be able to ask a 6- or 7-year-old: "How would you feel if you were in that situation?" For a younger child, the question is incomprehensible. For the same reason, the younger child may have trouble distinguishing how things seem or appear from how they really are (see Figure 4-9). As Flavell puts it,

> For them, if something seems dangerous (the menacing-looking shadow in their unlit bedroom), it is dangerous, and if it seems nondangerous (the friendly acting stranger), it is nondangerous. We often think of young children as naive, credulous, gullible, trusting, and the like. Their inadequate understanding that things may not be as they appear might be partly responsible for this impression. (Flavell, Green, & Flavell, 1989)

FIGURE 4-9 Children's ideas, or mental representations, change with age. The older child recognizes that, although the contents of the box are only one thing out in the world, they can be represented in people's heads in more than one way—a possibility that escapes the younger child. (Special thanks to John Flavell for the example and the research. Reprinted by permission of John Flavell.)

To encourage thinking and learning, teachers should refrain from telling children exactly how to solve a problem. Rather, the teacher should ask questions that encourage children to observe and pay attention to their own ideas. Teachers should:

- Use or create situations that are personally meaningful to children.
- Provide opportunities for them to make decisions.
- Provide opportunities for them to exchange viewpoints with their peers.

Awareness

Perhaps more important is the awareness on the part of all adults that all children have the capability to reason and be thinkers if they are given appropriate materials for their stage of development. Teachers must remember that young children:

1. Think differently from adults.
2. Need many materials to explore and describe.
3. Think in a concrete manner and often cannot think out things in their heads.
4. Come to conclusions and decisions based on what they see, rather than on what is sensible and adult-logical.
5. Need challenging questions and the time to make their own decisions and find their own answers.

DAP

The thoughts and ideas of Piaget are impressive, both in quantity and quality. The collective works of this man are extremely complex, often difficult to understand. Yet they have given us a valuable blueprint. Clearly, he has provided unique and important insights into the development of intelligence and children:

> It is Piaget's genius for empathy with children, together with true intellectual genius, that has made him the outstanding child psychologist in the world today and one destined to stand beside Freud with respect to his contributions to psychology, education, and related disciplines. Just as Freud's discoveries of unconscious motivation, infantile sexuality, and the stages of psychosexual growth changed our ways of thinking about human personality, so Piaget's discoveries of children's implicit philosophies, the construction of reality by the infant, and the stages of mental development have altered our ways of thinking about human intelligence (Elkind, 1977).

Sociocultural Theory

In the last two decades, many American early educators have turned their attention to another theorist. Because of the interest in the programs at Reggio Emilia, Italy, we now look closer at the works of Vygotsky. His sociocultural theory focuses on the child as a whole and incorporates ideas of culture and values into child development, particularly the areas of language and self-identity. In his view, children's development was more than just a response to personal experience. Rather, children are influenced in fundamental ways by their family, community, and socioeconomic status. Vygotsky also emphasized the deep role of culture in learning. This theoretical framework and the ecological theory (the next section) have shifted mainstream thinking to encompass more than a child's individual experiences. Work by Janice Hale (see Chapter 3) has identified and applied sociocultural theory to the development of the African American child. Ramirez and Castaneda (1974) have identified particular cognitive and language patterns among young children in selected Hispanic populations. In both cases, these patterns are linked to family and cultural styles of relating and problem solving.

Lev Vygotsky

Born in 1896 in Byelorussia, Lev Vygotsky graduated from Moscow University with a degree in literature in 1917. For the next six years, he taught literature and psychology and directed adult theater as well as founding a literary journal. In 1924, he began work at the Institute of Psychology in Moscow, where he focused on the problems of educational practice, particularly those of handicapped children. Toward that end, he gathered a group of young scientists during the late 1920s and early 1930s to look more closely at psychology and mental abnormality, including medical connections. Unfortunately, his career was cut short by tuberculosis; he died in 1934 at age 38. Yet in that short time, he studied the works of Freud, Piaget, and Montessori. His theory is also rooted in experimental psychology, the American philosopher William James, and contemporaries Pavlov and Watson (see the behaviorist theory section of this chapter).

DAP Children are active learners, drawing on physical and social experience as well as culturally transmitted knowledge to construct their own understandings of the world around them.

Sociocultural Theory

Vygotsky's work is called **sociocultural** because it focuses on how values, beliefs, skills and traditions are transmitted to the next generation. Like Erikson, Vygotsky believed in the connection between culture and development, particularly the interpersonal connection between the child and other important people. Like Maslow (see later in this chapter), he considered the child as a whole, taking a humanistic, more qualitative approach to studying children. Though he understood the primary behaviorists of his day, he differed from them in that he emphasized family, social interaction, and play as primary influences in children's lives, rather than the stimulus-response and schedules of reinforcement that were becoming so popular in his day.

Vygotsky believed that the child is embedded in the family and culture of his community and that much of a child's development is culturally specific. Rather than moving through certain stages or sequences (as Piaget proposed), children's mastery and interaction differ from culture to culture. Adults, Vygotsky noted, teach socially valued skills at a very early age; children's learning is, therefore, quite influenced by what their social world values. There are three ways culture is passed on: The first is imitative learning (like Bandura); the second by instructed learning (such as following directions as in the elementary school classroom); and the third by collaborative learning (involving working together, such as in guided help or in play).

Like Piaget, Vygotsky asserted that much of children's learning takes place during play. This is because language and development build upon each other, and the best way to develop competency is through interaction with others in a special way. According to Vygotsky, children learn through guided participation with others, especially in a kind of apprenticeship in which a tutor supports the novice not only by instruction but also by doing.

Social interactions lead to continuous step-by-step changes in children's thoughts and behavior, so relationships between a teacher and a learner both impart skills and provide the context and cultural values of that skill, as well as teaching how to build relationships and use language: Engaging together matters.

When a mentor senses that the learner is ready for a new challenge—or simply wants the learner to come along—he or she draws the novice into a **zone of proximal development (ZPD),** which is the range of learning that would be beyond what the novice could learn alone but could grasp with help. For example, Sergio can ride a tricycle alone, and has hopped onto his sister's two-wheeler. Surely he will fall. But if his uncle runs alongside and helps him get balanced, he can do more. Of course, it will take many attempts, but with assistance, Sergio can increase his ZPD and eventually ride on his own.

Who can help a child's ZPD? Initially, of course, it is the family. For instance, a young girl is carried even as a toddler to the open market with her mother. There, she watches and is guided toward learning how to touch cloth, smell herbs, taste food, and weigh and compare amounts. Is it any wonder she learns advanced math skills and the language of bargaining early?

The reciprocal relationships in the child's ZPD can also include the teacher. Think about your role, for example, in helping a child in your program learn problem-solving skills in completing a puzzle, putting on mittens, or resolving a conflict. Finally, other children—older ones who have more expertise or peers who may have superior skills or simply offer help—can help a child's learning. "Cooperative learning, in which small groups of peers at varying levels of competence work toward a common goal, also fosters more advanced thinking," writes Berk (2000). "In a Vygotskian classroom, learning is highly interactive and simultaneously considers where children are and what they are capable of becoming."

Other people create a kind of **scaffolding**, or helpful structure, to support the child in learning. Although not originally used by Vygotsky, the term helps define the most important components of tutoring. Just as a physical scaffold surrounds a building so that it might be worked on, so does the child get hints, advice, and structure in order to master a skill or an activity. This can be seen in children's developing speech, in guidance, and in ordinary tasks, as learning to ride a bike. Adults can arouse interest in a task, simplify it—scaffold it—so that it is within the child's ability, and teach enthusiasm by helping the task get accomplished (Rogoff, 1990).

Sociocultural theory dictates that learning is active and constructed, as does cognitive theory. Vygotsky differs from Piaget, however, in the nature and importance of interaction. Piaget insisted that, although children needed to interact with people and objects to learn, the stages of thinking were still bound by maturation. Vygotsky claimed that interaction and direct teaching were critical aspects of a child's cognitive development and that a child's level of thinking could be advanced by just such interaction.

Vygotsky believed that language, even in its earliest forms, was socially based. Rather than egocentric or immature, children's speech and language development during the years of 3 to 7 is merged and tied to what children are thinking. During these transitional years, the child talks aloud to herself; after a while, this self-talk becomes internalized so that the child can act without talking aloud. Vygotsky contended that children speak to themselves for self-guidance and self-direction and that this private speech helps children think about their behavior and plan for action. With age, **private (inner) speech** (once called "egocentric speech"), which goes from out loud to whispers to lip movement, is critical to a child's self-regulation.

Applying Sociocultural Theory to Work with Children

Sociocultural theory has five implications for the classroom teacher:

1. *A child's family and culture need to be incorporated into a child's schooling.* Teachers must genuinely embrace (rather than give lip service) to the concept that the child's first teacher is the family. Each family may emphasize certain skills—vocabulary development, cooperation with siblings, self-care, and independence—that serve as the sociocultural context for learning. For instance, children of color in American society are socialized to operate in two worlds and thus must achieve a kind of **bicognitive development,** (along with bicultural and perhaps bilingual skills). Such work led the way for the pop-

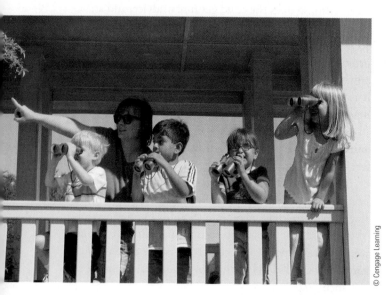

In Vygotsky's sociocultural theory, children learn as other people create a kind of scaffolding to support the children.

© Cengage Learning

ular "learning styles" movement of the 1970s and 1980s. Research done with different cultural groups has reinforced the importance of looking at culture as part of the context in which the child lives and learns (Tatum, 1995; York, 2005).

2. *Teacher/child relationships are vital to learning.* The teacher and learner adjust to one another; teachers use what they know about children to guide their teaching and plan their curriculum. Sociocultural theory supports both emergent curriculum (see Chapter 10) and spontaneous, teachable moments of the anti-bias curriculum (see Chapter 9). Of course, young children need adults to help create curriculum and set an environmental stage for learning. But they also need teachers to mediate social relationships and conflicts, to ask questions and know where a child is headed. Adults help children learn by seeing the challenge, giving assistance when needed, and noticing when the task is mastered and the child is ready for a new challenge.

3. *Pay close attention to the psychological and cultural "tools" used to learn.* For example, some American children are taught to tie a string around their fingers as a memory device whereas in Russia they tie a knot in their handkerchief. Tunes can aid learning (like the alphabet song); the higher mental functions need the help of a person who knows the tools of the society to learn.

4. *Play is valuable.* It is in play that the child can practice operating the symbols and tools of the culture. Vygotsky (1978) puts it this way:

   Action in the imaginative sphere, in an imaginary situation, the creation of voluntary intentions, the formation of real-life plans and volitional motives—all appear in play and make it the highest level of preschool development. The child moves forward essentially through play activity. Only in this sense can play be considered a leading activity that determines the child's development.

   For instance, children might build a structure with blocks; the teacher encourages them to draw the building and then map the entire block corner as a village or neighborhood. The adult serves an important role as an intellectual mediator, continually shifting to another set of symbols to give children a different way of looking at the same thing.

5. *Individual differences are important.* In a Vygotskian classroom there will be activity and an awareness of individual differences. Plan activities that encourage both assisted and cooperative learning. Observe for

opportunities to increase an individual's ZPD by planning experiences for extending the upper limit. Classrooms work best with multi-aged grouping, or at least with plenty of opportunity for older "buddies" to lead and younger ones to help.

Ecological Theory

As with sociocultural theory, the ecological theory is based on the premise that development is greatly influenced by forces outside the child. "No person can be understood in isolation, at just one moment in time. Urie Bronfenbrenner deserves credit for recognizing this fact" (Berger, 2008). He applied a general systems theory to human development in the 1970s, as the ecology movement began in America and Europe. Development is "a joint function of person and environment and human ecosystems include both physical factors—climate, space, home, and school—and the social environment—family, culture, and the larger society" (Bronfenbrenner, 2000).

Urie Bronfenbrenner

Born in the former Soviet Union, Bronfenbrenner immigrated to the United States at age 6, settling in New York. After studying psychology and music at Cornell University, he did graduate work in developmental psychology. He served as a clinical psychologist in the United States Army during World War II. When he returned to civilian life, he worked on the faculties of the University of Michigan and Cornell University, where he crafted this well-known theory (Bronfenbrenner, 1979).

Ecological Systems Theory

Bronfenbrenner's model describes four systems that influence human development, nested within each other like a circle of rings. With the child at the center, these four are the settings in which a child spends a significant period of time, the relationships of those settings, the societal structures, and then the larger contexts in which these systems operate. Figure 4-10 illustrates these

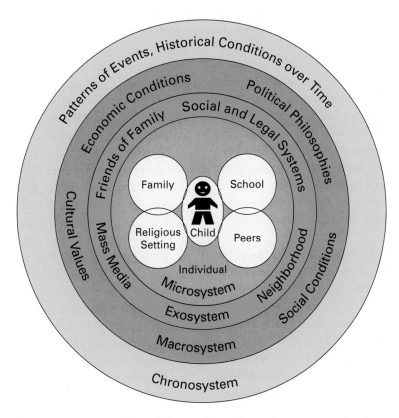

FIGURE 4-10 Ecological theory shows the various systems that influence in a child's development.

systems. The influences between and within these systems is critical to acknowledge: Just as in nature, activity in one part will affect all the other parts. For example, a sudden income drop will affect the family in many ways: The parents may be preoccupied and unavailable to the child, who may then need more attention from the caregivers at school, who in turn may ask for more resources from the community for the family.

Applying Ecological Theory to Work with Children

The usefulness of this theory is in its combining of many methods—multidisciplinary, multicultural, and multidirectional—to understand the developing child. The values of the community (the exosystem) can influence social conditions (the macrosystem) and, in turn, be influenced by the individual family or program (microsystem). For example, think of an area where several families with young children move into the neighborhood. The community priorities shift to incorporate more family interests; parents get everyone involved in creating a neighborhood playground. In doing so, the city council lobbies the state legislature to adopt more "family-friendly" political policies. The many systems in those children's worlds thus have a profound effect, both directly and indirectly, on their development. Imagine a situation in which the parents had very little voice in their community, or the town council was unresponsive to their needs. The playground would never have been built, the children would have little visibility in the neighborhood except to be troublesome, and the families would feel like outsiders in the community. Thus, the dynamic nature of many systems is described well in ecological theory.

The ecological theory underscores the need for working partnerships between early childhood programs, the families they serve, and the societal structures children need to grow. The mesosystem, for instance, involves all the connections between the microsystems. Put the young child in the center (see Figure 4-10), and it includes all the communication processes between the child's family and teachers. Therefore, letters home, parent–teacher conferences, chats upon arrival and departure, and phone calls would all contribute to the child's mesosystem. In this regard, the ecological theory possibly best encompasses most of the questions about the nature of development posed at the beginning of the chapter.

Multiple Intelligences Theory

Howard Gardner

Howard Gardner, a professor of human development at the Harvard Graduate School of Education, has been very influential in the ongoing debate about the nature of intelligence. Born in Pennsylvania, he earned both bachelor and doctorate degrees at Harvard University, and was fortunate to have Erikson as a tutor. Influenced by the works of Piaget and working with Jerome Bruner, Gardner became part of the Harvard's Project Zero research center for education. His ideas are best read in the books *Frames of Mind: The Theory of Multiple Intelligences* (1983) and *Multiple Intelligences: The Theory in Practice* (1993). Gardner currently teaches at Harvard in education and Boston University in neurology.

Theory of Multiple Intelligences

The century-old argument that Gardner presents is whether intelligence is a single, broad ability (as measured by an IQ test) or is a set of specific abilities (more than one intelligence). His theory of **multiple intelligences** asserts that there is strong evidence, both from the brain-based research (see discussion in this chapter) and from the study of genius, that there are at least eight basic different intelligences.

Gardner's view of the mind claims that "human cognitive competence is better described in terms of sets of abilities, talents, or mental skills, which we call 'intelligences.' All normal individuals possess each of these skills to some extent; individuals differ in the degree of skill and the nature of their combination" (1993). Multiple intelligences theory thus pluralizes the traditional concept of intelligence, which becomes the ability to solve a problem or to create a product.

Solving a problem includes the ability to do so in a particular cultural setting or community. The skill needed and developed depends very much on the context in which the child lives. For example, we all know now that certain parts of the brain are designated for perception, bodily movement, language, or spatial processing. Everyone who has a functional brain will be able to demonstrate some skill in these areas. But the child who has special "musical intelligence," for instance, will hear a concert and insist on a violin (as did Yehudi Menuhin). Or the child whose culture depends on running for its

How Are You Smart?

Area	Definition	Example
Musical Intelligence	The capacity to think in music, to be able to hear patterns, recognize them, and then remember them.	Gardner cites the importance of music in cultures worldwide, as well as its role in Stone Age societies, as evidence of this.
Bodily-Kinesthetic Intelligence	The capacity to use parts or all of your body to solve a problem or make something.	We can see this in a person's ability in sport (to play a game), in dance (to express a feeling, music or rhythm), in acting, or in making a product.
Logical-Mathematical Intelligence	The capacity to think in a logical, often linear, pattern and to understand principles of a system; most common intelligence tested with standard "IQ" tests.	Problem solving is often remarkably rapid (as in gifted children), and this thinking is often nonverbal (the familiar "Aha!" phenomenon).
Linguistic Intelligence	The capacity to use language to express thoughts, ideas, and feelings and the ability to understand other people and their words.	The gift of language is universal; spoken language is constant across cultures, and the development of graphic language is one of the hallmarks of human activity.
Spatial Intelligence	The capacity to represent the world internally in spatial terms, as in problem navigation, in the use of maps, and in relying on drawings to build something.	Playing games such as chess and all the visual arts—painting, sculpting, drawing—use spatial intelligence, as do the sciences such as anatomy, architecture, and engineering.
Interpersonal Intelligence	The capacity to understand other people and focus on contrasts in moods, temperaments, motivations, and intentions.	Master players in school notice how others are playing before entering; some children seem to be born leaders; teachers, therapists, religious or political leaders, and many parents seem to have the capacity to notice distinctions among others.
Intrapersonal Intelligence	The capacity to understand yourself, knowing who you are, how you react, and the internal aspects of one's self.	Often having access to their own feeling life, they draw on a range of emotions as a means of understanding and guiding their own behavior. Children with an innate sense of what they can and cannot do and often know when they need help.
Naturalist Intelligence	The capacity to discriminate among living things (plants, animals), as well as a sensitivity to other features of the natural world (clouds, rock configurations).	This intelligence is valuable for hunters, gatherers, and farmers and is important to those who are botanists or chefs.

FIGURE 4-11 Gardner's multiple intelligences theory describes a new way of looking at intelligence.

daily living (as do some people of Kenya) is more likely to have children well developed in that area of intelligence. Gardner writes of Anne Sullivan, teacher of blind and deaf Helen Keller, as an example of interpersonal intelligence, for she could understand what Helen needed in a way no one else could.

Gardner's descriptions of the various intelligences are described in Figure 4-11.

Applying Multiple Intelligences Theory to Work with Children

Gardner's theory of multiple intelligences has had a big impact on schools, transforming curricula and teaching methods from preschool to high school (Gardner, 2000). Even *Sesame Street* has taken to applying the theory to developing its programs. Teachers in early childhood use the theory daily as they individualize their environments, curricula, and approaches. The child whose facility with puzzles excels that of his classmates is given a chance to try more complex ones. The children who thrive in dramatic play are offered a time to put on a puppet show for the class. The child whose mind works especially musically, logically, or interpersonally is encouraged to develop those special gifts.

At the same time, there is no one right way to implement multiple intelligences. The theory is both culture and context specific so that, in a similar way to a constructivist classroom, "multiple intelligence classes" would have teachers developing their own strategies, developing curricula and assessment methods based on both their own and their children's culture and priorities and on the individual children's intelligences. (Chapters 12 and 13 will give examples of the multiple intelligences curriculum.)

Maturation Theory

Arnold Gesell

As noted in Chapter 1, Arnold Gesell was a physician intrigued with the notion that children's internal clock seemed to govern their growth and behavior. In the 1940s and 1950s, Gesell established norms for several areas of growth and the behaviors that accompany such development. The Gesell Institute, which fosters the work of Dr. Louise Bates Ames (1979) and others, continues to provide guidelines for how children mature from birth to puberty. The Word Pictures in Chapter 3 are an excellent example of the information maturational theory and research have provided.

Theory of Maturation

Maturation, by definition, is the process of physical and mental growth that is determined by heredity. The maturation sequence occurs in relatively stable and orderly ways. Maturation theory holds that much growth is genetically determined from conception. This theory differs from behaviorism, which asserts that growth is determined by environmental conditions and experiences, and from cognitive theory, which states that growth and behavior are a reflection of both maturation and learning.

Maturation and growth are interrelated and occur together. Maturation describes the quality of growth; that is, while a child grows in inches and pounds, the nature (or quality) of that growth changes. Maturation is qualitative, describing the way a baby moves into walking, rather than simply the age at which the baby took the first step. Growth is *what* happens; maturation is *how* it happens.

Studies have established that the maturation sequence is the same for all children, regardless of culture, country of origin, or learning environment. But there are two vital points to remember:

- Although maturation determines the sequence of development, the precise age is *approximate*. The sequence of developmental stages may be universal, but the rate at which a child moves through the stages varies tremendously.
- Growth is *uneven*. Children grow in spurts. Motor development may be slow in some stages, fast in others. For instance, a baby may gain an ounce a day for two months, then only half a pound in an entire month. Usually there is a growth spurt at puberty, with some children at 13 nearly their adult height, others not yet five feet tall. This unpredictability brings, again, much individual variation.

Applying Maturation Theory to Work with Children

Maturation theory is most useful in describing children's growth and typical behavior. In Chapter 3, these normative data are used to develop Word Pictures that describe common characteristics of children at different ages. Such charts will help adults understand behavior better and will keep them from expecting too much or too little.

At the same time, be cautious not to overgeneralize from the normative charts. The photo on page 129 illustrates this variation. Remember that there is great individual variation and uneven growth. Gesell's initial data were focused on a narrow portion of the population and were derived from American children only. Further work in the last three decades has adjusted the ranges with succeeding generations of children and an ever larger and more diverse population. Maturation theory has inspired developmental norms that help parents, teachers, and physicians alike determine whether a child's growth is *within* the normal range.

Humanistic Theory

The Humanists

As the field of psychology began to develop, various schools of thought arose. By the middle of this century, two "camps" dominated the American psychological circles. The first (psychodynamic) included the Freudians and is best known to us through the works of Erik Erikson. The second (behaviorism) began with Watson and Thorndike and was later expanded by Skinner and Bandura.

In 1954, Abraham Maslow published a book that articulated another set of ideas. He called it the "Third Force" (or Humanistic Psychology), which focused on what motivated people to be well, successful, and mentally healthy.

This humanist theory has a place in early childhood education because it attempts to explain how people are motivated. Specifically, humanistic theory is centered on people's needs, goals, and successes. This was a change from the study of mental illness, as in psychotherapy, or the study of animal behavior, in the case of much behaviorist research. Instead, Dr. Maslow studied exceptionally mature and successful people. Others, such as Carl Rogers, Fritz Perls, Alan Watts, and Erich Fromm, added to what was known about healthy personalities.

The humanists developed a comprehensive theory of human behavior based on mental health. Maslow's theory of human needs is clearly a "Western" philosophy, although it is often presented as a universal set of ideas. In fact, other cultures would see life differently. An African worldview might see the good of the community as the essential goal of being fully human. Cultures with more of a "collective" orientation, rather than an emphasis on the individual or self, would see serving the family or group as the ultimate goal of humanity. Humanistic psychology can also be seen as being at odds with cultures and religions that seek ultimate reliance on a supreme deity, putting "God" rather than "self" at the top of the hierarchy. One must always question the underlying values of a theory, and humanist theory is no exception.

Maslow's Theory of Human Needs

Maslow's theory of **self-actualization** is a set of ideas about what people need to become and stay healthy. He asserts that every human being is motivated by a number of basic needs, regardless of age, gender, race, culture, or

The maturational sequence is the same for all children, although the precise age is approximate, so there is tremendous individual variation in children of a particular age.

geographic location. According to Maslow (1954), a basic need is something:

- Whose absence breeds illness.
- Whose presence prevents illness.
- Whose restoration cures illness.
- Preferred by the deprived person over other satisfactions, under certain conditions (such as very complex, free-choice instances).
- Found to be inactive, at low ebb, or functionally absent in the healthy person.

These needs, not to be denied, form a theory of human motivation. It is a hierarchy, or pyramid, because there is a certain way these needs are interrelated, and because the most critical needs form the foundation from which the other needs can be met. Figure 4-12 illustrates the hierarchy, or pyramid, of Maslow's theory.

Applying Humanistic Theory to Work with Children

The **basic needs** are sometimes called **deficiency needs** because they are critical for a person's survival, and a deficiency can cause a person to die. Until those are met, no other significant growth can take place. How well a teacher knows that a hungry child will ignore a lesson, or simply be unable to concentrate. A tired child often pushes aside learning materials and experiences until rested. The child who is deprived of basic physiologic needs may be able to think of those needs only; in fact,

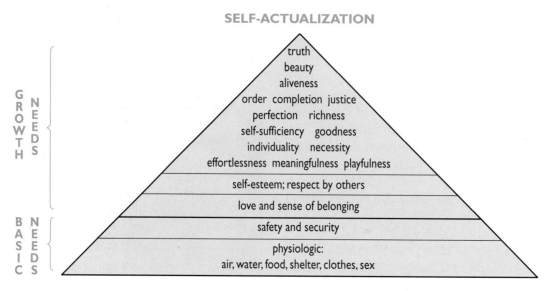

SELF-ACTUALIZATION

GROWTH NEEDS

truth
beauty
aliveness
order   completion   justice
perfection   richness
self-sufficiency   goodness
individuality   necessity
effortlessness   meaningfulness   playfulness

self-esteem; respect by others

love and sense of belonging

BASIC NEEDS

safety and security

physiologic:
air, water, food, shelter, clothes, sex

FIGURE 4-12 Maslow studied healthy personalities and theorized that what people need for growth is a hierarchy of basic and growth needs. (Adapted from Maslow, 1954.)

"such a man can fairly be said to live by bread alone" (Maslow, 1954). The humanists would strongly advocate a school breakfast or lunch program and would support regular rest and nap times in programs with long hours.

Once the physiologic needs are satisfied, the need for safety and security will emerge. Maslow points at insecure and neurotic people as examples of what happens when these needs are left unfulfilled. These people act as if a disaster is about to occur, as if a spanking is on the way. Given an unpredictable home or school, a child cannot find any sense of consistency and so is preoccupied with worrying and anxiety. Maslow would advise teachers to give freedom within limits, rather than either total neglect or permissiveness.

The **growth needs** can emerge when the basic needs have been met. Higher needs are dependent on those primary ones. They are what we strive for to become more satisfied and healthy people.

The *need for love and belonging* is often expressed directly and clearly by the young children in our care. A lack of love and sense of belonging stifles growth. To learn to give love later in life, one has to learn about love by receiving it as a child. This means learning early about the responsibilities of giving as well as receiving love.

The *need for esteem* can be divided into two categories: self-respect and esteem from others. "Self-esteem includes such needs as a desire for confidence, competence, mastery, adequacy, achievement, independence, and freedom. Respect from others includes such concepts as prestige, recognition, acceptance, attention, status, reputation, and appreciation" (Goble, 1970).

Self-actualization is what gives a person satisfaction in life. From the desire to know and understand the world and people around us comes a renewal of self-knowledge. For the early childhood educator, these needs are expressed in the enthusiasm, curiosity, and natural "drive" to learn and try. In meeting these needs, a person finds meaning for life, an eagerness to live, and a willingness to do so. Figure 4-12 describes both basic and growth needs in detail.

Children must have their physical and basic emotional needs met before these requirements of higher cognitive learning can be fulfilled. Moreover, the child who seems stuck in a particular "needs area" will likely stay there until that basic need is satisfied. A hungry, insecure, or hurt child is a poor learner. Teachers must continually advocate better physical and social conditions for all children.

Maslow's theory has important implications for child care. Children's basic needs are teachers' first concern: Teachers must ensure that children are properly clothed, fed, and rested as well as safe and secure. Only then are they ready to address curriculum and skill development.

Developmental Topics

To complete the chapter on developmental and learning theories, we need to expand our knowledge of child development to include several important topics. The teacher well versed in these developmental topics will be able to make better decisions concerning classrooms and curricula. Moreover, they will be able to connect with families around those points and those people most important to them: the children.

Ethnicity and Cultural Diversity

"Human nature is a cultural process. As a biological species, humans are defined in terms of our cultural participation. We are prepared by both our cultural and biological heritage to use language and other cultural tools and to learn from each other" (Rogoff, 2003). Development can be fully understood only when it is viewed in the larger cultural context. We can readily see the importance of culture in child rearing and family interaction, yet we often overlook its effect on education. We must know about children in their own setting, their own context, to understand them well enough to teach them. The ecology of a child's life must be acknowledged and brought into our work. These international examples show the influence of cultural orientation:

> The primary curricular emphasis in England is upon children's social development until age 3, after which academic competence is emphasized. Swedish educators focus on developmental issues, particularly socio-emotional development. In Asian countries where children's physical well-being and primary health care have improved to the point where they are no longer issues, the focus is upon academic achievement and excellence. While academic achievement is not stressed in the Czech Republic, young children are taught the value and importance of work and aesthetics, and they participate in cultural programs by the time they are 3.

Let us turn to the United States. "[I]nterpersonal episodes [are] absolutely saturated with cultural assumptions about the right way to think, feel, and behave. There are some real cultural differences about how to be a good parent and how to be a good child," states Stanford University's Hazel Markus (2005). For example:

- A mom leaned over a stroller, handed a silent 3-year-old a juice drink and announced, "It's hot. You must be thirsty."
- A 7-year-old ran up to his mother and grandmother and tried to get the younger woman's attention. She said, "I don't care how excited you are—don't interrupt your grandmother when she's speaking."
- A dad, sounding exasperated, told his 18-month-son, "Okay, now, you have a choice: either you wear this hat or we put on sunscreen. Which do you want?" The child replied, "I want juice."

These conversations reflect values—middle-class Euro-American, Latino, or East Asian. Ethnicity and cultural identity clearly play an important role in child development. Culturally competent teachers understand different patterns of ideas and practices.

Three important issues for teachers arise from this topic. First is the fact that "large numbers of children are members of one cultural group while being taught or cared for by members of other cultural groups. Although this need not create problems, research shows that special problems can arise in many cross-cultural teaching settings" (Hilliard & Vaughn-Scott, 1982). In fact, Lightfoot (1978) has documented four problems that tend to develop:

1. There are problems when the *language* that is spoken by the child is not understood by caregivers from another culture.
2. There are problems when caregivers have low *expectations* for children based largely on the children's membership in a low-status cultural group, rather than on the actual abilities of the children.
3. There are problems when caregivers are unprepared to deal with children whose general behavioral *style* is different from that of the caregivers.
4. There are problems when standard *testing* and *assessment* techniques are applied to certain cultural groups with insufficient recognition of, or respect for, the cultural patterns of the group.

Second, most early theories were based on observations of male or white subjects. This risks a skewed view of development. We encourage you to read studies of development that include other ethnic populations, such as Rogoff (2003), Garcia Coll (2005), Gura (1994), and York (2005). Ethnic minority children have been ignored in past research or viewed as variations from the norm. Often the group studied is given an ethnic label (such as Latino) that assumes the group is homogeneous and glosses over critical differences among the people in the group. Also, when ethnic groups are studied, often the focus is on children's problems. The range of existing differences makes more research—and also more teacher interest in individual family cultures—essential. Without such knowledge, teachers may misunderstand children with cultural patterns that are different from the mainstream and children and their families, in turn, may misunderstand the larger society (Bowman, 2007) or a school's practices and a teacher's behaviors.

Third, theories have their limits. As Nakahata (Hironaka Cowee, 2001) states:

> In the critical early childhood years, children begin to develop a sense of self as families hand down be-

liefs, attitudes, and behaviors. Much of what is handed down is unspoken and is acquired through social interactions. In this way, adults pass on their culture and shape children's understandings of themselves, their world, and their place in it. As children are forming their identity and self-worth, they often struggle with conflicting messages from home, media, school, and peers about who they are and what they are worth.

Theories can foster a global outlook about children in general, but these theories must be viewed in light of both cultural diversity and a respect for individuality. For example, language acquisition is universal. "All children, unless there is something really wrong in their environments or in their biology, learn how to speak. What language they speak, how much they use language to communicate, how large is their vocabulary in said languages is more context specific" (Garcia Coll, 2003).

Knowing what child development information to use across cultures and what varies among cultures helps teachers apply theories (see Figure 4-13). Chapter 3 helps you identify these universals. While reading all these theories, try to look beyond any one model, and define a set of principles that are fundamental to good practice and that can incorporate varied cultural patterns and values.

Attachment

Attachment is a term used particularly in the works of John Bowlby and Mary Ainsworth and a concept used in Burton White's descriptive work and Magda Gerber's Resources for Infant Educarers (RIE) programs for infants and toddlers. Attachment is the emotional connection, an "affectional tie that one person or animal forms between himself and another specific one—a tie that binds them together in space and endures over time" (Ainsworth, 1979). The child or adult who is attached to another uses that person as a "safe base" from which to venture out into the world, a source of comfort when distressed or stressed, and a support for encouragement. Attachment behaviors are anything that allows a person to get and stay attached, such as smiling, eye contact, talking, touching, even clinging and crying.

"It is an essential part of the ground plan of the human species—as well as that of many other species—for an infant to become attached to a mother figure. This figure need not be the natural mother but can be anyone who plays the role of the principal caregiver" (Ainsworth, 1979). Freud believed infants became attached to those

Children: All, Some, One

All children are alike . . .
- have the same needs and rights
- go through the same developmental stages
- have the same developmental goals

Some children are alike . . .
- similar cultural and social expectations will create commonalities
- rate of vocabulary increase is similar within groups with priority of language expression
- children show similar helping behaviors from families who value harmony

Each child is unique . . .
- genetic makeup
- temperament
- sensory sensitivity
- interests
- motivation

FIGURE 4-13 Make child development theories useful without overgeneralizing (patterned after Caldwell, 1983).

who fed them. Erikson asserted that the first year of life was critical for attachment, in the stage of trust versus mistrust.

Research does show that human and animal babies do indeed send signals to their mothers very early. Infants begin the social smile at 6 weeks and positive reactions to familiar people by 3 months. The human infant's early signals include crying and gazing, both of which are powerful to adults, and a kind of rhythmic sucking that appears to keep the mother engaged. Soon after appears the synchrony, a coordinated interaction between an infant and caring adult that connects the two. Becoming more frequent and elaborate as time goes on, it helps the infant express feelings and the sensitive adult to respond.

Developmentally, children develop an initial bond and then proceed to develop real mutuality—that is, to learn and practice almost a "dance" between themselves and their favored loved one. Ainsworth found that, although virtually all infants develop attachments, including to multiple caregivers, they differ in how secure they are in those attachments. Furthermore, attachment can be measured in the infant and toddler, as seen in children's response to a stranger both in and out of the parent's presence (see Figure 4-14).

Not everyone believes that attachment is so important to later competence and identity. Kagan (1987) believes infants are resilient and that children can grow positively within wide variations of parenting. Researchers have found cultural variations in attachment. German babies are more likely than American babies to be categorized as avoidant, but this might be because the

culture encourages early independence. Japanese babies are more likely to be seen as avoidant, but this could also be a factor of the method used to record it, which calls for children to be left in a room without the mother, a situation that rarely occurs for most Japanese infants.

Some developmentalists claim the theory ignores the context and diversity of how children are socialized, and by whom. "I believe that European Americans are obsessed with attachment because we hold our babies less than almost any other cultural group in the world," writes a colleague (Saxton, 2001). "Attachment does not seem to be an issue, much less a concept, in cultures in which children are carried, held, or sleep with their parents for the better part of the first three years." Attachment to a primary caregiver is another example of the dual nature of development: "Unless something is really wrong in their environment or their biology, all children

Patterns of Attachment

	Exploratory Behavior Before Separation	Behavior During Separation	Reunion Behavior	Behavior with Stranger
Secure	Separates to explore toys; shares play with mother; friendly toward stranger when mother is present, touches "home base" periodically.	May cry; play is subdued for a while; usually recovers and is able to play.	If distressed during separation, contact ends distress; if not distressed, greets mother warmly; initiates interaction.	Somewhat friendly; may play with stranger after initial distress reaction.
Anxious/ambivalent (resistant)	Has difficulty separating to explore toys even when mother is present; wary of novel situations and people; stays close to mother and away from stranger.	Very distressed; hysterical crying does not quickly diminish.	Seeks comfort and rejects it, continues to cry or fuss; may be passive—no greeting made.	Wary of stranger; rejects stranger's offers to play.
Anxious/avoidant	Readily separates to explore toys; does not share play with parent; shows little preference for parent versus stranger.	Does not show distress; continues to play; interacts with the stranger.	Ignores mother—turns or moves away; avoidance is more extreme at the second reunion.	No avoidance of stranger.

SOURCE: Compiled from Ainsworth, M. D. S., & Wittig, B. A. (1969). Attachment and Exploratory Behavior of One-Year-Olds in a Strange Situation. In B. M. Foss (Ed.), *Determinants of Infant Behavior* (Vol. 4). London: Methuen.

FIGURE 4-14 Patterns of attachment. (From Ainsworth's "Strange Situation" in 12- to 18-month olds.) (From *Understanding Children*, by Judith Schickendanz, © 1993 by Mayfield Publishing Company. Reprinted with permission of McGraw-Hill Companies.)

get attached to a primary caregiver. In most cases it is the mother, but cultures differ in if it is the father, or there are multiple caregivers, grandparents, etc., who are part of the daily life of the child" (Garcia Coll, 2005).

Researchers have found that a majority of American infants tested in the stranger situation demonstrated secure attachment. Still, when attachment fails, children are placed at tremendous risk. Failure of attachment can come from:

- parents who did not have secure attachments as children
- neglectful conditions, such as depression, abject poverty
- abusive parents that discourage bonding
- premature infants with underdeveloped systems
- blind infants who cannot engage in gazing

Intervention can help unattached persons learn the skills to connect, teaching specific interactive techniques with ongoing supports such as crisis hotlines and personal counseling.

Parents and researchers have asked careful questions about full-day child care, particularly for infants, wondering if such care undermines children's attachment to their parents. The debate has spurred research into both parent–child attachment and child care programs. Whether concerns about infant child care prove valid or not, as of this date, we can conclude that children are not at any higher risk in high-quality child care. This highlights the need for such programs, as will be addressed further in Chapters 9 and 15.

Play

Play! What a wonderful word! It calls up images from the past, those childhood years when playing was the focus of our waking hours. "Will you play with me?" is one of the most expressive, expectant questions known. It carries with it hope and anticipation about a world of fun and make-believe, a world of adventure and exploration, a world of the young child.

City streets, parks and fields, tenements, huts, empty rooms, and backyards are all settings for play. Play is a way of life for children; it is their natural response. It is what children do and it is serious business to them. Any activity children choose to engage in is play; it is never ending.

Play is the essence of creativity in children throughout the world. Play is universal and knows no national or cultural boundaries. Educators and psychologists have called play a reflection of the child's growth, the essence of the child's life, a window into the child's world (Frost, Wortham, & Reifel, 2007). It is a self-satisfying activity through which children gain control and come to understand life. Play teaches children about themselves; they learn how tall—or short—they are, what words to use to get a turn on the swing, and where to put their hands when climbing a ladder. Through play, children learn about the world: what the color purple is, how to make matzo balls, and how to be a friend. Play helps children define who they are.

Types of Play

Play takes many forms. Children play when they sing, dig in the mud, build a block tower, or dress up. Play can be purely physical (running, climbing, ball throwing) or highly intellectual (solving an intricate puzzle, remembering the words to a song). Play is creative when crayons and paint are used. Its emotional form is expressed when children pretend to be mommies, daddies, or babies. Skipping rope with a friend, playing tag, and sharing a book are examples of the social side of play.

There is a general sequence to the development of social play. Babies and toddlers have a clearly defined social self. Infant play begins with patterns established at birth: babies gaze, smile, and make sociable sounds in response to the quality and frequency of attention from a parent or caregiver. Socialization of infants occurs through interaction. By the end of their first year, infants smile at and touch one another and vocalize in a sociable effort. Toddlers play well on their own (*solitary play*) or with adults. They begin solitary pretend play around 1 year of age. They still watch others (*onlooker*). During the toddler years, as children become more aware of one another, they begin to play side by side, without interacting (*parallel play*). They are aware of and pleased about but not directly involved with the other person. It is during this year that toddlers begin some form of coordinated play, doing something with another child. The preschool years bring many changes for children in relation to social development. The number and quality of relationships increase as does the ability to play with other children. At first, this is accomplished just by a child's presence in a group: playing at the water table with four other children or joining a circle for finger plays (*associative play*). When children join forces with one another in an active way, when they verbalize, plan, and carry out play, group play is established, and can be characterized as "Let's do it together," whether building a house for the farm animals or engaging in rough-and-tumble wrestling. *Cooperative play* is the most common type of peer interaction during the preschool years and into the school-age period. Figure 4-15 shows Parten's classic 1932 study of children's play patterns, also described in Chapter 6.

Keep in mind that children's play always portrays their own social values and family ethnic practices (Hyun, 1998). Developmentally and culturally appropriate practice would remind us that our understanding and knowledge about play have been based on Euro-American cultural patterns. Wise early childhood practitioners will incorporate this perspective into their work with children.

Most play is unstructured and happens naturally when the curriculum is designed for play. Spontaneous play is the unplanned, self-selected activity in which children freely participate. Children's natural inclinations are toward play materials and experiences that are developmentally appropriate. Therefore, when they are allowed to make choices in a free play situation, children will choose activities that express their individual interests, needs, and readiness levels.

Dramatic play—or imaginative or pretend play—is a common form of spontaneous play. Three- and four-year-olds are at the peak of their interest in this type of activity. In dramatic play, children assume the roles of different characters, both animate and inanimate. Children identify themselves with another person or thing,

Play Categories

Unoccupied Play

- May stand in one spot
- Looks around the area
- Performs random movements that have no apparent goal

Solitary Play

- Plays alone
- Plays independently of others

Onlooker Play

- May watch while others play
- May talk but does not enter play
- Shows active interest in the play

Parallel Play

- Plays alongside others
- Plays separately from others but with toys or actions that are similar to the others

Associative Play

- Play involves social interaction but little or no organization
- Interested in each other without an agreed-upon plan

Cooperative Play

- Socially interacts in a group with a sense of group identity
- Joins an organized activity, a prototype for games

FIGURE 4-15 Parten's play categories, developed by observing free play patterns in nursery school settings.

playing out situations that interest or frighten them. Dramatic play reveals children's attitudes and concepts toward people and things in their environment. Much of the play is wishful thinking, pretending great strength and deeds. This is the way children cope with their smallness or lack of strength and is considered important in psychodynamic theory.

Two types of dramatic play are noteworthy:

1. **Superhero play** is appealing to children because it so readily addresses their sense of helplessness and inferiority. Pretending to be Wonder Woman makes it easier to understand and accept the limitations of the real world. It helps children learn about power and friendship, allows them a way to test their physical limits and explore feelings, and answer the "big questions about the world, such as 'what is right and wrong, what is good and bad, what is fair and unfair, what is life and death, what is a boy and a girl, and what is real and fantasy'" (Hoffman, 2004).

   At the same time, this kind of play makes many adults uncomfortable, since the children's play is often loud, disruptive, filled with conflict and problems, and solved with violence. Children sometimes end up in stereotypical, repetitive play that seems to ignore other learning. Chapters 14 and 15 address how to set the stage and support superhero play in ways that foster positive growth.

2. **Sociodramatic play** happens when at least two children cooperate in dramatic play. Dramatic play provides the means for children to work out their difficulties by themselves. By doing so, they become free to pursue other tasks and more formal learning. Both types of play involve two basic elements: imitation and make-believe:

   Pretending to be a firefighter, Sherry grabs a piece of rope and runs toward the playhouse, saying "shhshhshshshshsh" while pretending to squirt water on the fire. She shouts to her playmates, "Over here! Come over here! The fire is on this side."

Sherry's make-believe scenario and her ability to follow the rules of behavior common to firefighters (grabbing hoses, calling for help) are the two critical factors from Vygotsky's point of view: That firefighting scene supports his theory that cognitive skills develop through social interactions. Sherry exemplifies a child moving from concrete to abstract thought because she did not require realistic objects (a hose and water) but imagined them with a rope and her ability to create the sound of water.

This ability to separate thoughts from actions and objects will stand Sherry in good stead when she studies math concepts. Rules that children follow in make-believe play teach them to make choices, to think and plan about what they will do, and to show willingness toward self-restraint, as children learn to follow the social rules of pretend play. This is important preparation for real-life situations.

Values of Play

For the first half of the 20th century, interest in children's play focused on emotional causes and effects (Bowman, 1990). The main theme was the emotional releases that play provided children. Psychodynamic theory recommended play as a suitable outlet for expressing negative feelings, hostility, and aggression. Clay can be pounded, balls can be kicked and thrown, and dolls can be spanked. Young children give free expression to a wide range of emotions, playing them out and releasing tension.

But play is more than an avenue for emotional release. Play is universal to childhood experiences because it is intrinsically motivated; that is, it is naturally satisfying to children. In addition,

- Play is relatively free of rules except for those children will impose on themselves.

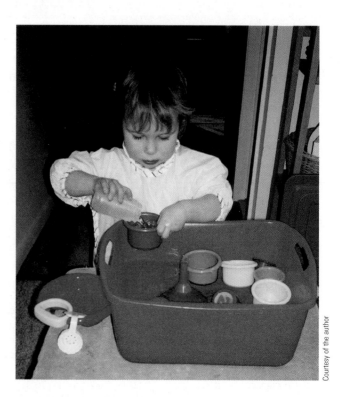

Learning through play takes many forms and happens naturally in unplanned, self-selected activities.

Courtesy of the author

- Play is controlled and dominated by the children.
- Play is carried out as if the activity were real life.
- Play focuses on the activity—the doing—rather than on the end result or product.
- Play requires the interaction and involvement of the children. (Rubin, Fein, & Vandenberg 1983)

Play promotes learning for the whole child, providing benefits for all developmental domains (American Academy of Pediatrics, 2006; Elkind, 2007).

Play as the Cornerstone of Learning

Outside of child development circles, there has been little appreciation in the United States culture for the value and importance of play for young children. In times of rising expectations and academic standards, educators and families feel pressured to focus on activities related to school readiness. Yet a growing body of research shows that every school success indicator is enhanced by play (Isenberg & Quisenberry, 2002; Singer, 2006).

Jones (2000) states the case aptly: "But if children are just playing, how will they learn? Each child learns by asking his or her own next questions and trying out the answers. Often both the questions and the answers take the form of actions rather than words. Children learn by doing." In summing up, Jones adds, "In play, children are autonomous; they're independent. They make decisions, solve the problems, deal with the consequences." Early childhood specialists must become adept at speaking out on the value of play and its relationship to what children learn. "Play is viewed by some as the opposite of work; play does not mean learning. Play is often trivialized by sayings like 'That is mere child's play' or 'He is only playing' as if to say play is unimportant" (Klein, Wirth, & Linas, 2003).

To reclaim play as a special activity crucial to children's development, we should look at play as the foundation from which children venture forth to investigate, to test out. Curriculum takes on expression through play; teachers plan curriculum that uses play as the medium for learning. As they mature, children integrate and assimilate their play experiences. What started out as play—the sheer fun of it—is transformed into learning experiences. Curiosity about magnets at age 5 nourishes a scientific attitude for the later years, as well as a foundation for studying gravity, planetary movements, and the like. Feeling free to sing out at group time at age 3 can prepare a child to be an active participant in the kindergarten classroom at age 6.

Teachers want children to learn about themselves, to learn about the world around them, and to learn how to

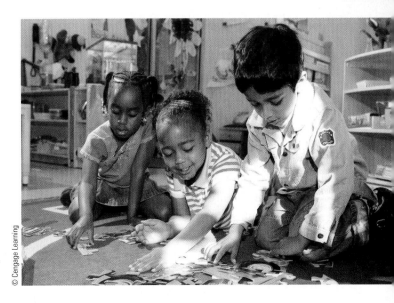

© Cengage Learning

Play is the cornerstone for learning.

solve problems. A childhood filled with play opportunities should culminate in these three types of learning:

1. *Learning about themselves* includes developing a positive self-image and a sense of competence. Children should know and feel good about themselves as learners. They should develop a sense of independence, a measure of self-discipline, and knowledge based on full use of their sensory skills.

2. *To learn about others and the world around them* means developing an awareness of other people. Teachers want children to perfect their communication and social skills so that they will be more sensitive participants in the world in which they live. This means that children learn and appreciate the values of their parents, the community, and society at large. When children become aware of the demands of living in today's society, that awareness can help them become more responsible citizens. The emphasis on social interaction and group relationships in the early childhood setting underscores this goal.

3. *To learn to solve problems,* children need to be accomplished in observation and investigation. When exploring a puzzle, for example, children need to know how to manipulate it, take it apart, and put it back together, to see how other people solve puzzles, and to know how to get help when the pieces just do not seem to fit together. They should know how to predict and experiment. What will happen, wonders a kindergartner, when a glass is placed over a glowing candle? How will that change if the glass is

large or small? What is the effect if the glass is left over the candle for a long time or for a second? Young children also need to learn how to negotiate, discuss, compromise, and stand their ground, particularly when they encounter and solve problems socially. "I want the red cart and someone already has it," thinks the preschooler. "Now what? How can I get it? What if the other person says no? Will the plan that works with my best friend work with someone else? When do I ask for help? Will crying make a difference?" To be effective problem solvers, children must know and experience themselves and others.

Play in the early years is a key to school success and solid development.

Gender

Are girls and boys different in terms of development and learning? What are these differences, and how do they occur? What differences are caused by "nature" and which ones by "nurture?" Should we treat our girls and boys the same or differently? The realities and the myths surrounding sex differences and their effect on behavior from infancy to adulthood is the subject of interest, controversy, and research.

Definitions

Sex differences are the biological differences between males and females; **gender differences** are culturally imposed distinctions in the roles and behaviors. While boys and girls are about the same size and shape in childhood, gender differences and adult distinctions are more significant.

There are two aspects of gender development that are particularly important in the early years: **gender identity** (the sense of being female or male, which most children acquire by age 3), and **gender role** (the set of expectations that define how a male or female should behave, think, and feel). Gender is important to some developmental and learning theories.

Theories and Research

Freud asserted that behavior was directly related to reproductive processes. His stages of psychosexual development reflect the belief that gender and sexual behavior are instinctual. Erikson also claimed that anatomy was destiny: Males were more intrusive because of genital structure, and females were more inclusive. He later modified his view, saying that women were overcoming

their biological heritage. These identification theories come from the view that the preschool child will find the opposite-sex parent attractive but will steer away from this by identifying with the same-sex parent.

Bandura and Piaget emphasize that children learn through observation and imitation, and that through reinforcement, children learn gender-appropriate behavior. Proponents of this view point to how parents encourage girls and boys to engage in certain activities and types of play. Certainly the media communicates sexist messages; this theory would claim that such stereotyping influences the development of gender roles.

The works of Eleanor Maccoby (1998) and others have provided both hard data and an open forum for discussions about how people grow and the complex interaction between heredity and environment that makes child development so fascinating. These findings help teachers understand gender identity and its implications for education:

- By age 2, children name themselves as girl or boy and can identify adult strangers as daddies or mommies.
- By age 4, children will label toys (dolls, trucks) and some roles (soldier, nurse) appropriate for one gender and not the other.
- Children develop gender stability (the understanding of staying the same sex throughout life) by age 4 and gender constancy (a person keeps the same gender regardless of appearance) by about 5 or 6.
- Sex-typed behavior begins to appear at age 2 or 3, when children tend to choose same-sex playmates and sex-typed toy preferences, and children become more selective and exclusive as they mature.
- By elementary school, the playground is like a "gender school," with children showing a clear preference for same-sex peers.

Developmental Differences

What are the real differences between girls and boys? Physically, males grow to be 10 percent taller than females, and girls are less likely to develop physical or mental disorders than are boys. Boys are also more active than girls and physically more aggressive overall. However, there are fewer differences in verbal aggression, although males do show less self-regulation than females (Eisenberg, Martin, & Fabes, 1996). There are no significant differences between girls and boys in intelligence or reasoning behavior. Some cognitive functioning and personality differences do exist, but overall the differences are small and there is no overall pattern.

Teachers and parents, as well as researchers, have observed that boys and girls seem to show distinct differences in their play choices, play behavior, and toy selection from an early age. Although biology certainly plays a part, it would seem that parents and society exert powerful influences. The toys parents and teachers choose (dolls for girls, trucks for boys), the predominance of females in early childhood settings, television shows and advertising, and toy store displays combine to communicate a very strong reinforcement of traditional sex-role expectations.

Gender Stereotyping

To break through the restrictiveness of gender stereotyping, teachers need to pay careful attention to the messages they give children. One challenge we face is the female culture of early childhood programs. Women dominate the early childhood education workforce, so children are often only exposed to women's interaction styles (Wardle, 2004). If boys struggle in our programs, we must be alert to the activities and schedules we establish, behaviors we may reward or punish, the "goodness of fit" for both boys and girls in our programs. In the environments we prepare for them, the materials they use, and the examples we model, children create their own ideas and learn behavior that works for them in the world.

Moral Development

People used to assume that young children needed to be taught exactly what was "right" and "wrong" and that was enough. In the last 30 years, research has shown that moral development is a more complex process with both a cognitive and an emotional side to it. Several theorists and researchers have proposed how to think about children's moral development. The theories of Jean Piaget, Lawrence Kohlberg, Nancy Eisenberg, and Carol Gilligan are discussed here.

Piaget (1965) investigated children's moral reasoning by presenting children with pairs of stories and asking them which child was "naughtier." From this, he discovered that children under age 6 base their judgment on the amount of damage done, not the child's intentions. By middle childhood, children are beginning to take intent into account so that one can begin to see a shift in moral reasoning toward the end of the early childhood period from objective judgments based on physical results and concrete amounts to more subjective considerations (such as the purpose of the perpetrator or psychological factors). The connections to children's cognitive

stage of development is interesting, and adults might consider that a child's protests over wrongdoing ("I didn't mean to do it!") may very well signal a new level of reasoning, with the realization that one's intentions do matter.

Lawrence Kohlberg (1981) is best known as a theorist in social development, addressing educational practice and gender constancy as well. Building on Piagetian dimensions, Kohlberg's theory of moral development involves both social growth and intellectual reasoning. People move from stage to stage as a result of their own reasoning power, and they see for themselves the contradictions in their own beliefs. As with Erikson and Piaget, Kohlberg's stages are hierarchical—a person moves forward one by one, and no stage can be skipped. On the basis of children's responses to moral dilemmas similar to those of Piaget, Kohlberg identified three levels of moral development, as illustrated in Figure 4-16. For early childhood educators, research shows that preconventional reasoning (stages 1 and 2) is dominant into elementary school.

Kohlberg's theory has been criticized for placing too much emphasis on moral thought and not enough of moral behavior. Further, many point out that his view is culturally biased and the stories asked are not applicable to all children. Western moral doctrine emphasizes individual rights; other cultures focus on a greater respect for traditional codes and practices. (See Figure 4-17 for an example of such differences.)

Most of the stories, or dilemmas, that Piaget and Kohlberg used were about stealing, lying, disobeying rules, and the like. Researcher and theorist Nancy Eisenberg (1983) has explored the kinds of reasoning children use to justify good (**prosocial**) behavior. She asks children what they would do in situations with a moral dilemma. One of her stories involves a child on the way to a friend's birthday party. The child encounters someone who has fallen and is hurt. What should the child do: help the hurt child and miss cake and ice cream, or leave the child and go on to the party?

Such questions brought to light several levels of prosocial reasoning. In the early childhood years, children seem to be engaged in level one (*hedonistic reasoning*), in which the individual's own needs are put first. In the case mentioned earlier, the child would leave the hurt person and go to the party ("I won't help because I have to go to the party"). As children move through middle childhood, they tend to move to level two, in which the needs of another begin to be considered and to increase in importance. Answers to the story would begin to shift toward including others ("I'd help because they'd help me

Kohlberg's Stages of Moral Development

I. Preconventional Morality

Stage 1:   Punishment and obedience orientation
Might makes right; obey authority and avoid punishment.

Stage 2:   Individualism and relativist orientation
Look out for number one; be nice to others so they will be nice to you.

II. Conventional Morality

Stage 3:   Mutual interpersonal expectations
"Good girl, nice boy"; approval more important than any reward.

Stage 4:   Social system and conscience
"Law and order"; contributing to society's good is important.

III. Postconventional Morality

Stage 5:   Social contract
Rules are to benefit all, by mutual agreement; may be changed same way; the greatest good for the greatest number.

Stage 6:   Universal ethical principles
Values established by individual reflection, may contradict other laws.

FIGURE 4-16 Kohlberg's Stages of Moral Development. Cross-cultural data and extensive American research indicate a persuasive universality and a strong sequence of stage development in children's moral development.

next time"). Eisenberg's stages roughly parallel Kohlberg's and help broaden these concepts without contradicting the fundamental arguments.

Carol Gilligan (1982) challenges Kohlberg's strong emphasis on justice and fairness and his omission of caring for others. In her book *In a Different Voice* (1982), Gilligan points out that mostly males were studied for such work and that, because girls and boys are socialized differently, their moral judgments will be quite different. For instance, boys may be raised with the idea that justice and fairness are the key moral bases, whereas girls may be taught that caring and responsibility to others are central. Buzzelli (1992) has also worked extensively on young children's moral understanding and has applied recent research to children's development of peer relationships. Although this claim of different moral ideas based on gender differences has yet to be fully researched, it is an important thought to keep in mind, particularly when teaching and raising young children.

Moral development is often deleted from the curriculum in American schools. Further, one aspect of moral development that has been studied very little is that of children's spirituality and faith. Because of the separation of church and state in American public schools, many educators shy away from discussions of anything that might be considered "religious." In doing so, educational programs also find themselves staying out of anything that helps children understand who they are and the greater questions of life and its meaning. Yet even John Dewey called moral education the "hidden curriculum," conveyed through the atmosphere of every program. Elementary schools occasionally have some kind of teaching for "character education," or a values clarification class. In addition, most caregivers will tell you what children notice about life and death issues and about caring for others is part of everyday experiences.

Brain-Based Research

Some of the most exciting research discoveries in the last two decades have been in the area of brain-based research. Neuroscience research has developed sophisticated technologies, such as ultrasound, magnetic resonance imaging (MRI), position emission tomography (PET), and effective, noninvasive ways to study brain chemistry (such as the steroid hormone cortisol). Brain scans and other technologies have made it possible to investigate the intricate circuitry of the brain.

Moral Reasoning: Cultural Implications

Disagreement: Brahman children think it is right;
American children think it is wrong:

—Hitting an errant child with a cane
—Eating with one's hands
—Father opening a son's letter

Disagreement: Brahman children think it is wrong;
American children think it is right:

—Addressing one's father by his first name
—Eating beef
—Cutting one's hair and eating chicken after father's death

Agreement: Brahman and American children think it is wrong:

—Ignoring a beggar
—Destroying another's picture
—Kicking a harmless animal
—Stealing flowers

Agreement: Brahman and American children think it is right:

—Men holding hands.

FIGURE 4-17 Children's moral reasoning has a cultural aspect, as shown by comparing children in the United States and India. (From *Child Development*, 9th ed., by J. W. Santrock, © 2001 McGraw-Hill Companies. Reprinted with permission of McGraw-Hill Companies.)

No aspect of biological growth is more critical than the rapid growth of the brain. "A newborn's skull is disproportionately large, because it must be big enough to hold the brain, which at birth is 25 percent of its adult weight. The neonate's body, by comparison, is typically only five percent of adult weight. By age 2, the brain is almost 75 percent of adult brain weight; the child's body is only about 20 percent as big as it will be" (Berger, 2008). During childhood, the brain develops faster than any other part of the body so that by age 7 it is almost fully grown.

We once believed that brains were entirely formed by genes and prenatal influences. Today, neuroscientists believe in plasticity, the concept that growth changes throughout life for a variety of reasons. Still, early childhood is a critical time for brain development. The timing and quality of early experiences combine to shape brain architecture (Shonkoff, et al, 2008).

What We Have Learned

At least three important conclusions can be made at this time:

1. *The brain seems to operate on a "use it or lose it" principle.* At birth, one has about 100 billion brain cells and 50 trillion connections among them. With use, these cells grow branches (**dendrites**) that reach out to make connections with other cells. With impoverishments, you may lose the dendrites. By age 2, most pruning of dendrites has already occurred. Established patterns of behavior are increasingly difficult to change as individuals get older; it is more effective and efficient to get things right the first time than to try and fix them later.

2. *As children move from toddlers to preschool, brain functions are developed.* Myelination speeds transmission of nerve impulses between neurons and enables children to think and react faster. Fast and complex communication can now occur.

   The system of acquiring cultural knowledge is more open in the early stages of life than later. This has implications for both emotional attachment and language development:

   - "Patterns (not quantity but quality) of interactive experience for the young child's life are important in shaping both pruning and possible synaptic growth during the early years of life" (Siegel, 1999). We should work to provide a quality attachment to at least one important and consistent adult in the early years.
   - "The best time to learn a second language is before 7 years of age. We know that babies lose their ability to discriminate some phonetic distinctions as a function of the language they are exposed to by 12 months of age (Garcia Coll, 2003). Therefore, culture, language, communication, and social interactions are ingrained very early on.

3. *By age 7, the brain has grown to its adult size, and the basic areas of sensory and motor cortexes are functioning.* Now is the time to add experiences that encourage the dendrites to reach out to neurons. The brain's two hemispheres are connecting, and the brain can now become more efficient in its functions. As Galinsky (1997) tells us, "The connections that have been reinforced by repeated experience tend to remain while those that are not are discarded. Thus, a child's early experiences—both positive and negative—help shape the brain, affecting to some degree how he thinks, feels, and relates to oth-

ers throughout his life." Figure 4-18 summarizes these research findings with connections to theories and advice for educators.

Early Stress

Every environment has opportunities for interaction with a variety of objects, people, and circumstances that can stimulate brain growth. Conversely, any environment can be impoverished. This is less about toys than it is about interactions and the atmosphere. Repeated exposure to extreme stress kills some neurons and prevents others from developing properly (Sanchez, Ladd, & Plotsky, 2001). When the brain perceives a threat or stress, the body reacts. Stress can trigger a flood of hormones, particularly **cortisol,** that may create an overreaction. Or, as in some abused children, a blunted stress response may occur (Gunnar & Vasquez, 2001). Since brain circuits are formed especially in infancy and toddlerhood, early mistreatment can cause damage. In later childhood, the chronic threat of emotional embarrassment, social disrespect, or simply hurried, restrictive time settings can all trigger stress responses.

Applications to the Classroom

Applying brain research to the early childhood classroom is a challenge. Early in life, neural connections form rapidly in the brain and tail off during adolescence—but why? Does anything we do make much of a difference, when this pattern has presumably taken place over eons of time? "Neuroscientists know very little about how learning, particularly school learning, affects the brain at the synaptic level," claims (Bruer, 1998). "We should be skeptical of any claims that suggest they do." Thirty years of research has shown that critical periods are quite complex; the brain can reorganize itself throughout our lifetimes, so we do not yet understand what brain-based research might mean for education. For now, this framework for action gives us some general advice:

- *First, do no harm.* Let us do everything to help parents and caregivers form strong, secure attachments. At the same time, we need to provide parent education and information about what does help their children's brain and well-being to grow. "An infant's attachment with the primary caregiver dur-

Brain-Based Research Findings

Key Finding:	Theories That Support It:	Implications for Educators:
1. "Human development hinges on the interplay between nature and nurture."	This finding shows how both nature and nurture work together and points to the dynamic interplay between the environment and learning that is a hallmark of cognitive/constructivist thought and sociocultural theory.	The brain is affected by all kinds of environmental and interactive conditions. The impact is both specific and dramatic, influencing both the general direction and the actual circuitry of the brain.
2. "Early care has a decisive and long-lasting impact on how people develop, their ability to learn, and their capacity to regulate their own emotions."	This finding confirms the work on attachment (see this chapter) and underscores the importance of warm and responsive care.	The daily interaction with nurturing adults helps children develop the network of brain cells so they can learn to regulate and calm themselves, which actually helps the brain turn off a stress-sensitive response quickly and efficiently.
3. "The human brain has a remarkable capacity to change, but timing is crucial."	Montessori's sensitive periods and Steiner's belief in a seven-year cycle of growth (see Chapter 1) both stress the notion of timing.	Experiments have proven that there are certain "windows of opportunity" for the proper development of vision and language, and studies show certain effective times in the learning of music. There are limits to the brain's ability to create itself, and researchers have found that these limitations have some time periods to them that we ought not to ignore.

FIGURE 4-18 Decades of brain-based research is summarized here from the 1996 Conference of Brain Development in Young Children, sponsored by the Families and Work Institute (Shore, 1997).

ing these early years is crucial for healthy development, and poor attachment, along with abuse or neglect, can alter the brain's structural path, predisposing a child to lack empathy or to being aggressive" (Schore in Waters, 2004). We must educate ourselves so the quality of child care and early education is ensured.

- *Second, prevention is best, but when a child needs help, intervene quickly and intensively.* The brain is a work in progress, and children can recover from serious stress. "For humans, even in an early developing system like vision, these periods can last until early childhood. For language, the critical period for learning to speak without an accent ends in early childhood, but the critical period for learning language's grammar does not end until around age 16" (Bruer, 1998). But the list of preventable conditions is clear, and it is everyone's job to work toward eliminating the unnecessary traumas.

- *Third, promote the healthy development and learning of every child.* "Risk is not destiny," reminds Shore (1997), "The medical, psychological, and educational literatures contain a sufficient number of examples of people who develop or recover significant capacities after critical periods have passed to sustain hope for every individual."

Using Developmental and Learning Theories

As a teacher, you must think about what you believe about children, development, and learning. This chapter gives much food for thought in this regard, and students are often overwhelmed. Two critical questions arise: (1) Why do contradictions exist among the theories? and (2) How can I decide which is the "right" one?

To answer the first question, remember that each theory addresses a particular aspect of development. For instance, psychodynamic theory focuses on the development of personality, behaviorist on the conditions of learning, cognitive on how children think and learn, maturation on how development progresses, and humanist on the conditions for overall health. Each has its avid proponents with a body of research that supports it. Because every theory has its own focus and advocates, each viewpoint is rather subjective and somewhat narrow. In other words, no one theory tells us everything . . . and that is the answer to the second question.

Thoughtful teachers develop their own viewpoints. Begin to decide what you believe about children, learning,

and education. Try to avoid the pitfall of taking sides. Instead, integrate theory into your teaching practices by comparing the major developmental and learning theories with your own daily experiences with young children. Figure 4-19 reviews the highlights of each theory.

Most early childhood educators are eclectic in their theoretical biases. That is, they have developed their own philosophies of education based on a little of each theory. Each teacher has an obligation to develop a clear set of ideas of how children grow and learn. We are fortunate to have choices.

Basic Tenets

Most educators agree on some basic tenets based, in part, on theories of development and learning:

1. *Basic needs.* Children's basic physiologic needs and their needs for physical and psychological safety

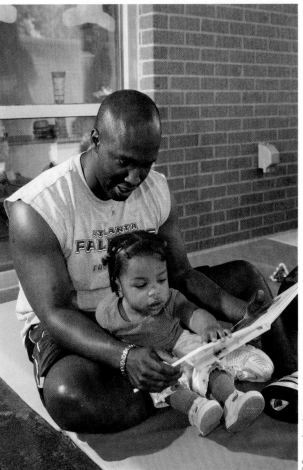

One of the conclusions of research and theory is that children's interactions with significant people in their lives play a major role in development.

© Cengage Learning

Summary of Major Theories

Theory	Major Theorists	Important Facts
Psychosocial	Erik Erikson	Maturational emphasis Stage theory of social and emotional development Crises at each level Teacher: Emotional base, social mediator
Behaviorist	John Watson Edward Thorndike B. F. Skinner Albert Bandura	Environmental emphasis Stimulus–response Conditioning (classical and operant) Reinforcement (positive and negative) Modeling Teacher: Arranger of environment and reinforcer of behavior
Cognitive	Jean Piaget	Maturational and environmental emphasis Assimilation and accommodation Stage theory of cognitive development Teacher: Provider of materials and time and supporter of children's unique ways of thinking
Sociocultural	Lev Vygotsky	Zone of proximal development Private speech Collaborative/assisted learning
Multiple intelligences	Howard Gardner	Many kinds of intelligence Problem-solving and product-creating
Maturation	Arnold Gesell	Emphasis on heredity Normative data Teacher: Guider of behavior based on what is typical and normal
Humanist	Abraham Maslow	Environmental emphasis Mental health model Hierarchy of human needs Teacher: Provider of basic and growth needs
Others	Mary Ainsworth John Bowlby Nancy Eisenberg Carol Gilligan Lawrence Kohlberg Eleanor Maccoby	Attachment and categories research Attachment theory Expands moral development to prosocial Questions categories of moral development Moral, cognitive, and sex-role development Sex differences research
Brain-based research	Bruce Perry Daniel Siegel Albert Schore	New insights into early development "Use it or lose it" principle Warm and responsive care matters

FIGURE 4-19 The major theories of and research on development and learning describe children and their growth in different ways.

must be met satisfactorily before they can experience and respond to "growth motives." [Humanist, Brain-based research]

2. *Factors in development.* Children develop unevenly and not in a linear fashion as they grow toward psychosocial maturity and psychological well-being. A wide variety of factors in children's lives, as well as the manner in which they interpret their own experiences, will have a bearing on the pattern and rate of progress toward greater social and emotional maturity. [Psychosocial, Behaviorist, Maturation, Ethnicity/Culture]

3. *Crises in Childhood.* Developmental crises that occur in the normal process of growing up may offer maximum opportunities for psychological growth, but these crises are also full of possibilities for re-

gression or even negative adaptation. [Psychosocial, Cognitive, Ecological, Play, Moral Development]

4. *Striving for Mastery.* Children strive for mastery over their own private inner worlds as well as for mastery of the world outside of them. [Psychosocial, Cognitive, Multiple Intelligences, Play]

5. *Relationships and Interactions.* The child's interactions with significant persons in his life play a major part in his development. [Psychosocial, Behaviorist, Sociocultural, Humanist, Attachment, Gender Identity, Brain-Based]

Look at the following "What Do You Think?" box and consider your own theoretical base.

What Do YOU Think?

Decision making in teaching can be difficult. Can theory help us?

It is 10 a.m. at the infant-toddler center. Fifteen-month-olds Kenya and Peter are crying and fussy this morning. Neither has eaten since breakfast. They have been indoors all morning.

Theory: *Maturation theory.* Children's physical developmental needs affect their emotional states.

Plan: Schedule regular times for active movement. Be sure to offer food and watch for signs of hunger.

Mario and Therese, both in wheelchairs, joined the first grade last month, but their parents report that neither wants to come to school. Their academic work is at grade level but they participate very little. They seem familiar with their teacher.

Theory: *Sociocultural theory.* Children need to feel part of the class culture in order to learn well.

Theory: *Psychosocial theory.* The children can identify with the teacher and become successful but may feel incompetent with unfriendly or indifferent classmates.

Theory: *Cognitive theory.* They can understand other points of view as long as it is in real situations.

Plan: Put each child in a small group to design and build wheel toys for pets. Building upon the newcomers' expertise in a cooperative activity gives all the children the scaffolding needed to be successful and helps the new children become accepted into the class.

Preschoolers Jared and Panya have been arguing about who has brought the "best" toy to child care. Others have heard the ruckus and have stopped to watch the two start a fight.

Theory: *Cognitive theory.* Their egocentric thinking prevents them from seeing any view other than their own. Also, they are unable to hold two ideas at the same time, so they cannot see that both toys are "good."

Theory: *Behaviorist theory.* The children can learn from watching others and applying other's example to their own behavior.

Plan: The teacher engages the children in a conflict resolution method that gets all children to express their own ideas, both about the problem and for some solutions, so they can practice hearing another's ideas while still holding their own. The teacher models praising each child's positive characteristics in the other's presence, showing other ways to behave appropriately and how the children and their toys can play together.

Developmental Research Conclusions

Research, and the information it yields, must serve the needs of the practitioner to be useful. Teachers can combine researchers' systematic data with personal observations and experiences, including the significance of relationships, language and thinking, biologic factors, and special needs (see also Chapters 6 and 12–14). To keep in mind the real child underneath all these theories, teachers apply developmental research to their own classroom settings. Figure 4-20 consolidates what developmental research has found and how it can be put into practical use with young children.

There is so much information now about children and their development. It is easy to feel overwhelmed, and easier still to believe what we read. Santrock (2001) advises us:

- Be cautious about what is reported in the popular media.
- Do not assume that group research applies to an individual.
- Do not generalize about a small or clinical sample.
- Do not take a single study as the defining word.
- Do not accept causal conclusions from correlational studies.
- Always consider the source of the information and evaluate its credibility.

Conditions for Learning

Caring for children means providing for total growth, creating optimal conditions for learning in the best possible environment. Developmental theory helps define conditions that enhance learning and from which positive learning environments are created. Research on all theories extends the knowledge of children and learning. Coupled with practical application, both theory and research have helped all to recognize that:

1. *Learning must be real.* We teach about the children's bodies, their families, their neighborhoods, and their school. We start with who children are and expand this to include the world, in their terms. We give them the words, the ideas, the ways to question and figure things out for themselves.

2. *Learning must be rewarding.* Practice makes better, but only if it is all right to practice, to stumble and try again. We include the time to do all this by providing an atmosphere of acceptance and of immediate feedback as to what was accomplished (even what boundary was just overstepped). Also, practice can make a good experience even better, as it reminds children in their terms of what they can do.

3. *Learning must build on children's lives.* We help connect the family to the child and the teacher. We realize that children learn about culture from family and knowledgeable members of the community, such as teachers, librarians, grocers, and the like. We know important family events and help the family support happenings at school. For children, learning goes on wherever they may be, awake and asleep. Parents can learn to value learning and help it happen for their child.

4. *Learning needs a good stage.* Healthy bodies make for alert minds, so good education means caring for children's health. This includes physical, emotional, and mental health. Psychological safety and well-being are theoretical terms for the insight, availability, and awareness teachers bring to their classrooms. On the lookout for each child's successes, we prevent distractions in the way furniture is arranged, how noisy it is, and how many strangers are around. Mental health is both emotional and intellectual. We try to have a variety of materials and experiences, and a flexible schedule when someone is pursuing an idea, building a project, or finishing a disagreement.

As long as we care for children, we will have our hands full. With the theoretical underpinnings presented here, we have the tools with which to make our own way into the world of children and of early childhood education.

DAP

DAP Recognize that what makes something challenging and achievable will vary, depending on the individual learner's development in all areas: the store of experiences, knowledge, and skills; and the context within which the learning opportunity takes place.

Developmental Research Tells Us	Teachers Can
1. Growth occurs in a sequence.	Think about the steps children will take when planning projects. Know the sequence of growth in their children's age group.
2. Children in any age group will behave similarly in certain ways.	Plan for activities in relation to age range of children. Know the characteristics of their children's age group.
3. Children grow through certain stages.	Know the stages of growth in their class. Let family know of any behavior that is inconsistent with general stages of development.
4. Growth occurs in four interrelated areas.	Understand that work in one area can help in another.
5. Intellectual growth:	
Children learn through their senses.	Have activities in looking, smelling, tasting, hearing, and touching.
Children learn by doing and need concrete experiences.	Realize that talking is abstract; have children touch.
Cognitive growth happens in four areas: Perception (visual, auditory, etc.)	Provide materials and activities in matching, finding same/different, putting a picture with a sound, taste, or with a symbol. Provide opportunities to find and label things, talk with grown-ups, friends, tell what it "looks like," smells like, etc.
Language	Know that memory is helped by seeing, holding objects, and people.
Memory	Recognize that reasoning ability is just beginning, so children judge on what they see rather than what you may want them to realize.
Reasoning	Be sure adult explanations aid in understanding reasons. Practice finding "answers" to open-ended questions such as "How can you tell when you are tired?"
6. Social growth:	
The world is only from the child's viewpoint.	Expect that children will think of only their own ideas at first. Be aware that the rights of others are minimal to them.
Seeing is believing.	Remember that if they cannot see the situation, they may not be able to talk about it.
Group play is developing.	Provide free-play sessions, with places to play socially. Understand that group play in structured situations is difficult because of "self" orientation.
Independence increases as competence grows.	Know that children test to see how far they can go. Realize that children will vary from independent to dependent (both among the group and within one child).
People are born not knowing when it is safe to go on.	Understand that children will need to learn by trial and error.
Adult attention is very important.	Know the children individually.
Young children are not born with an internal mechanism that says "slow down."	Move into a situation before children lose control.
7. Emotional growth:	
Self-image is developing.	Be alert for each child's self-image that may be developing. Give praise to enhance good feelings about oneself. Know that giving children responsibilities helps self-image. Talk to children at eye level. Children learn by example. Model appropriate behavior by doing yourself what you want the children to do.
8. Physical growth:	
Muscle development is not complete.	Do not expect perfection, in either small- or large-muscle activity.
Muscles cannot stay still for long.	Plan short times for children to sit.
Large muscles are better developed than small ones.	Give lots of chances to move about; be gentle with expectations for hand work.
Hand preference is being established.	Watch to see how children decide their handedness. Let children trade hands in their play.
A skill must be done several times before it is internalized.	Have materials available to be used often. Plan projects to use the same skill over and over.
Bowel and bladder control is not completely internalized.	Be understanding of "accidents." If possible, have toilet facilities available always, and keep them attractive.

FIGURE 4-20 Developmental research tests theories of growth and learning to find out about children and childhood.

Insights *from the field*

Developmental Theory: The Foundation of Developmentally Appropriate Practice *by Rosalind Charlesworth*

Developmental theory serves as a guide for developmentally appropriate practice (DAP). Age appropriateness and individual appropriateness were the original basic dimensions for DAP (Bredekamp, 1987). Age appropriateness is based on "what is known about child development and learning" and individual appropriateness on "what is known about the strengths, interests, and needs of each individual child." Developmental theories can provide clues as to where individuals or groups of children may be developmentally. Cultural appropriateness is a third critical dimension that was included in the 1997 revision edited by Bredekamp and Copple. Cultural appropriateness is based on "knowledge of the social and cultural contexts in which children live." The major developmental theories were based on observations of children in each theorist's particular culture. Therefore, modifications must be considered relative to the multitude of cultures to which DAP might be applied in our ever more diverse society.

Theories of child development can serve as guides for assessing the developmental levels of any children. They can help us know what children's competencies are and where we should begin instruction. Theories of development can serve as guides for planning instruction for individuals and for groups. The constructivist theories of Piaget and Vygotsky are especially helpful in guiding us to developmentally appropriate instructional practice. Concepts such as that of children constructing knowledge through their exploration of the world while adults determine their zone of proximal development and scaffold their learning experiences within the zone are invaluable guides. Piaget's periods of cognitive development provide clues to interpreting children's thinking as they move from sensorimotor to preoperational to concrete operational thought during early childhood. The period from ages five to seven, known as the *five to seven shift*, is very critical in assessing and planning for kindergartners and first graders (Golbeck, 2006). Erikson's stages help us understand the social/emotional development and behavior of young children beginning with basic trust, then the need for autonomy and independence and the need to be productive. These theorists all support the importance of play as the major vehicle for learning during early childhood. Other theorists also influence DAP. Maslow's hierarchy of human needs, Rogers' views on development of the self-concept, and Bandura's theories of social learning have all been applied to teaching practice. Interpretations of these theoretical guidelines may differ across cultures but provide a foundation for early childhood planning and practice.

Theory provides direction for program structure. Structure is necessary for any program in several areas: classroom space, guidance techniques, instructional methods, materials, curriculum, and assessment. Structure based on the development of young children includes some of the following factors that can be related to developmental theory:

- Classroom space is clearly divided into a variety of learning areas. The space includes table areas, a soft carpeted area, floor areas used as instructional space, and centers with open shelves where children can select materials (Piaget and Erikson).

- Guidance techniques should be clear, consistent, positive and inductive; time blocks are broad and flexible but follow a consistent routine; children have choices of activities that fit their competencies, interests, and learning styles; children are involved in rule making (Rogers, Bandura, Erikson, Piaget, and Vygotsky).

- Instructional methods include whole class, small group, and individual activities as appropriate; children are encouraged to construct their own knowledge; focus is on creative thinking and problem solving, peer interaction is encouraged, and play is the major vehicle for learning (Piaget and Vygotsky).

- Materials are organized in space, are concrete and open-ended and promote creativity, and first-hand experiences are provided (Piaget).

- Curriculum is guided by standards and scope and sequence but adapted for individual children's development, content is integrated, and there is equal emphasis on cognitive, affective, and psychomotor areas of development (Piaget, Vygotsky, and Erikson).

- Assessment is done in an organized manner, mainly through observations and individual interviews as children work with appropriate materials. Observations are done on a daily basis to obtain information used for planning. Information for planning is obtained regarding children's current competencies and interests. Planning can then focus on age, individually, and culturally appropriate teaching strategies (Piaget and Vygotsky).

Culture, the third dimension of DAP, has been at the center of many arguments against developmental theory as the foundation of DAP. Historically, in the United States and other Western cultures, an individualistic approach to education and development has been valued. "Individualism stresses independence and individual achievement, focusing on the needs of the individual, self-expression, and personal choice" (Zepeda, Rothstein-Fisch, Gonzales-Mena, & Trumbull, 2006).

Most other cultures (about 70 percent) value a more collectivist approach (Zepeda et al., 2006). Zepeda and others (2006) define collectivism as follows:

... most of the world tends to focus on the interdependence of groups and individuals. ... Collectivism emphasizes social responsibility and the priority of group needs over individual needs. It stresses respect for authority and obligation to group norms.

They provide several examples of how these two views might result in different beliefs. For example, in the area of play and learning the individualistic view would see "Learning is child centered and involves play, exploration, and individual choice," while the collectivist view would be that "Learning is adult directed and depends more on observation than play, exploration, and child choice." The individualistic view appears to fit with Piaget and Erikson, the collectivist view with some of Vygotsky's and Bandura's ideas. Perhaps differences between collectivism and individualism can be bridged in order to provide a developmentally appropriate program for young children, one that considers culture and fully involves families in a partnership that respects cultural beliefs and child-rearing methods.

Just as DAP is a guide to practice, developmental and learning theories are *guides* to DAP, not rules. Planning for children is very complicated because children and families are complex and diverse. Many variables must be considered; one size doesn't fit all.

References

Bredekamp, S. (Ed.). (1987). *Developmentally appropriate practice in early childhood programs serving children from birth through age eight* (expanded edition). Washington, DC: National Association for the Education of Young Children.

Bredekamp, S., & Copple, C. (Eds.). (1997). *Developmentally appropriate practice in early childhood programs* (revised edition). Washington, DC: National Association for the Education of Young Children.

Charlesworth, R. (2008). *Understanding child development* (7th Ed). Clifton Park, NY: Delmar Learning.

Golbeck, S. L. (2006). Developing key cognitive skills. In D. F. Gullo, Ed., *Kindergarten today*, pp. 37–46. Washington, DC: National Association for the Education of Young Children.

Zepeda, M., Rothstein-Fisch, C., Gonzales-Mena, J., & Trumbull, E. (2006). *Bridging cultures in early care and education: A training module*. Mahwah, NJ: Erlbaum.

Rosalind Charlesworth is professor and department chair in the Department of Child and Family Studies at Weber State University in Ogden, Utah.

SUMMARY

Developmental and learning theories form the cornerstone of our knowledge about children. What we know about how children grow, learn, and adapt to the world around them is critical in our quest for understanding.

Our field is greater for the contributions of several schools of study. *Freud* reminds us of the importance of early experiences. *Erikson's* theory of psychosocial development gives us insight into children's feelings and how their emotional and social lives affect their learning. The *behaviorists*, a distinctively American group of psychologists, demonstrate how much we can learn of human affairs by applying the methods of science. *Piaget*, a "giant in the nursery school" (Elkind, 1977), opens our eyes to a stage theory of growth and shows us how active children are in their own learning. *Vygotsky* reminds us of how values, beliefs, skills, and traditions are transmitted to the next generation within a "zone of proximal development" based on relationships with other people. The *ecological*

theory is very useful in highlighting the complex influences on children's development. Gardner suggests multiple kinds of intelligence, rather than seeing the mind as a static "black box" or empty vessel. *Gesell* offers us developmental norms. *Maslow*, a humanistic psychologist, establishes a hierarchy of needs, reminding us that the basic physical and psychological needs must be met before higher learning can take place. The developmental topics of *ethnicity and culture* reverberate through the study of *attachment*, *play*, *gender identity*, and *moral development*. The *brain-based research* opens doors to new vistas of possibility and better teaching and learning.

In learning about these theories, we are more able to formulate our own philosophy of education. By consistently applying the insights from research and theory, we show our willingness to make a commitment to children. What we know about growth and development helps us fight for our most important resource—our children.

KEY TERMS

theory
hypothesis
nature/nurture controversy
psychodynamic theory
unconscious
psychosocial
autonomy
stimulus-response
reinforcement
socialization
modeling
self-efficacy
observational learning
classical conditioning
operant conditioning
reinforcers

punishment
assimilation
accommodation
equilibration
schema
myelination
transmission model
constructivism
transactional model
egocentric
sociocultural
zone of proximal development
  (ZPD)
scaffolding
private (inner) speech
bicognitive development

multiple intelligences
maturation theory
self-actualization
basic needs (deficiency needs)
growth needs
attachment
superhero play
sociodramatic play
sex differences
gender differences
gender identity
gender role
prosocial
dendrites
cortisol

REVIEW QUESTIONS

1. Match the theorist with the appropriate description:

B. F. Skinner	Ecological theory
Abraham Maslow	Multiple intelligences
Jean Piaget	Sex differences
Albert Bandura	Attachment
Mary Ainsworth	Social learning
Eleanor Maccoby	Zone of proximal development
Erik Erikson	Psychosocial development
Arnold Gesell	Behaviorism
Lev Vygotsky	Developmental norms
Howard Gardner	Cognitive theory
Uric Bronfenbrenner	Self-actualization

2. Describe Piaget's stages of cognitive development and their implications for early childhood education.

3. Name at least three psychologists who have contributed to the knowledge of development. Describe your reaction to each.

4. How is play beneficial to the child's development?

5. Define the common stages of play, and state at what chronological age each is likely to appear.

6. Given the eight theories of learning and development, which one would most likely advocate large blocks of free play? An early academic program? Open-ended questioning by teachers? Regular early mealtime?

7. Who said it? Match the theorist to the relevant quotation.

Lev Vygotsky	"The first organ to make its appearance as an erogenous zone and to make libidinal demands upon the mind is, from the time of birth onwards, the mouth."
Erik Erikson	"There are problems when caregivers have low expectations for children based largely upon the children's membership in a low-status cultural group, rather than on the actual abilities of the children."
Jean Piaget	"From a sense of self-control without loss of self-esteem comes a lasting sense of good will and pride; from a sense of loss of self-control and of over-control comes a lasting propensity for doubt and shame."
Sigmund Freud	"Children acquire most of their concepts—the rules by which they live—from models who they observe in the course of daily life."
Sara Lawrence Lightfoot	"The young child's thinking manifests considerable activity that is frequently original and unpredictable. It is remarkable not only by virtue of the way it differs from adult thinking but also by virtue of what it teaches us."
Albert Bandura	"No matter how we approach the controversial problem of the relationship between thought and speech, we shall have to deal extensively with inner speech."

LEARNING ACTIVITIES

1. You are a teacher in a large urban child care center. Your children arrive by 7:00 a.m. and usually stay until after 5:00 p.m. each day. What would you do first thing in the morning? Use Maslow's hierarchy of needs to justify your answer.

2. What do you think of the influence of television on children's behavior? Consider the typical cartoons that the children you know are watching. From a social learning perspective, what are they learning? What else would you have them watch?

3. You are a teacher in a middle-class suburban preschool. What do you know about your group's needs and developmental stages? What assumptions, if any, can you make about development and social class? What does their cultural background tell you about what to teach? How will you find out about what each child is ready to learn?

4. Observe children in a child care center as they say goodbye to their parents. What can your observations tell you about their attachment levels? What can teachers do to support attachment and also help children separate?

5. Observe teachers as children play. What is the difference in play when (1) a teacher interacts with children in their play and (2) a teacher intervenes? What happens to the play immediately after teacher contact is made? How long does the play last? What is your conclusion?

6. Write a defense of play as a hallmark of early childhood philosophy and curriculum. How would you adapt the paper for parents? For a student of early childhood education? For teachers?

HELPFUL WEBSITES

Alliance for Childhood   http://www.allianceforchildhood.org

American Educational Research Association   http://www.area.net

AskEric   http://ericir.syr.edu

ERIC (Educational Resources Information Center)   http://www.eric.ed.gov

Early Childhood Research Quarterly   http://www.naeyc.org/publications/ecrq

Gesell Institute   http://www.gesellinstitute.org

National Association for the Education of Young Children   http://www.naeyc.org

Society for Research in Child Development   http://www.srcd.org/

 Additional resources including the TeachSource Videos can be found on the premium website for this book. Go to http://www.cengage.com/login to register your access code.

REFERENCES

General Texts

Berger, K. S. (2008). *The developing person* (8th Ed). New York: Worth.

Berk, L. (2007). *Infants, children, and adolescents* (6th Ed). Boston: Allyn & Bacon.

Fong, B., & Resnick, M. (1986). *The child: Development through adolescence.* Palo Alto, CA: Mayfield.

Santrock, J. W. (2007). *Child development* (11th Ed). Boston, MA: McGraw Hill.

Psychodynamic Theory

Erikson, E. H. (1963). *Childhood and society* (2nd Ed). New York: Norton.

Erikson, E. H. (1964). Toys and reasons. In M. R. Haworth (Ed.), *Child psychotherapy: Practice and theory*. New York: Basic Books.

Erikson, E. H. (1969). A healthy personality for every child. In P. H. Mussen, J. J. Conger, & J. Kagan (Eds.), *Child development and personality* (3rd Ed). New York: Harper & Row.

Erikson, E.H. (1969). *Gandhi's truth*. New York: W.W. Norton & Company.

Freud, S., & Hall, G. Stanley. (1920). *A general introduction to psychoanalysis*. New York: Boni & Liveright

Mooney, C. G. (2000). *Theories of childhood*. Beltsville, MD: Redleaf Press.

Spitz, R. A., & Wolf, K. M. (1946). Analytic depression: An inquiry into the genesis of psychiatric conditions in early childhood, II. In A. Freud, et al. (Eds.), *The psychoanalytic study of the child (Vol. II)*. New York: International Universities Press.

Behaviorist Theory

Bandura, A. (1963). Imitation of film-mediated aggressive models. *Journal of Abnormal and Social Psychology*.

Bandura, A. (1986). *Social foundations of thought and action: A social cognitive theory*. New York: Prentice Hall.

Kohn, A. (1999) *Punished by rewards*. New York: Basic Books.

Skinner, B. F. (1953). *Science and human behavior*. New York, NY: MacMillan Co.

Suransky, V. P. (1982, Autumn). A tyranny of experts. *Wilson Quarterly*, 53–60.

Cognitive Theory

DeVries, R., & Kohlberg, L. (1990). *Constructivist early education: An overview and comparison with other programs*. Washington, DC: National Association for Education of Young Children.

Elkind, D. (1977). Giant in the nursery school—Jean Piaget. In E. M. Hetherington & R. D. Parke (Eds.), *Contemporary readings in psychology*. New York: McGraw-Hill.

Elkind, D., & Flavell, J. (Eds.). (1996). *Essays in honor of Jean Piaget*. New York: Oxford University Press.

Flavell, J. H, Green, F. L., & Flavell, E. R. (1989). Young children's ability to differentiate appearance-reality. *Child Development*, 60, 201–213.

Heuwinkel, M. K. (1996, Fall). New ways of learning = new ways of teaching. *Childhood Education*, 313–342.

Kohn, A. (2005). *Unconditional parenting*. New York: Atria Books.

Meade-Roberts, J., & Spitz, G. (1998). *Under construction*. Unpublished documents.

Sociocultural Theory

Berk, L. Vygotsky's sociocultural theory. In A. Gordon & K. W. Browne (2000), *Beginnings and beyond* (5th Ed). Clifton Park, NY: Thomson Delmar Learning.

Hale, J. (1986). *Black children: Their roots, culture and learning styles*. Baltimore, MD: The Johns Hopkins University Press.

Ramirez, M., & Castaneda, A. (1974). *Cultural democracy, biocognitive development and education*. New York: Academic Press.

Rogoff, B. (1990). *Appreciation in thinking: Cognitive development in a social context*. New York: Oxford University Press.

Tatum, B. D. (1995, February). Stages of racial/ethnic identity development in the United States. Paper presented at the National Association for Multicultural Education, Washington, DC.

Vygotsky, L. S. (1978). *Mind in society: The development of higher psychological processes*. Cambridge, MA: Harvard University Press.

York, S. (2005). *Roots and wings: Affirming culture in early childhood programs*. St. Paul, MN: Redleaf Press.

Ecological Theory

Berger, K.S. *The developing person* (8th Ed). New York: Worth.

Bronfenbrenner, U. (2000). Ecological system theory. In A. Kazdin (Ed.), *Encyclopedia of Psychology*. Washington, DC: American Psychological Association and Oxford Press.

Bronfenbrenner, U. (1979) *The ecology of human development: Experiments by nature and design*. Cambridge, MA: Harvard University Press.

Multiple Intelligences Theory

Gardner, H. (1983). *Frames of mind*. New York: Basic Books.

Gardner, H. (1991). *The unschooled mind*. New York: Basic Books.

Gardner, H. (1993). *Multiple intelligences*. New York: Basic Books.

Gardner, H. (2000). *Intelligence reframed: Multiple intelligences for the 21st century*. New York: Basic Books.

Maturation Theory

Ames, L. B., & Ilg, F. (1979). *The Gesell Institute's child from one to six; The Gesell Institute's child from five to ten; The infant in today's culture.* New York: Harper & Row.

Gesell, A. (1940). *The first five years of life.* New York: Harper & Row.

Humanist Theory

Goble, F. G. (1970). *The third force: The psychology of Abraham Maslow.* New York: Grossman.

Maslow, A. H. (1954). *Motivation and personality.* New York: Harper & Row.

Developmental Topics
Ethnicity and Cultural Diversity

Bowman, B. (2007). The effects of culture on thinking. *Exchange Magazine,* May/June, 2007.

Caldwell, B. (1983). *Child development and cultural diversity.* Geneva, Switzerland: OMEP World Assembly.

Garcia Coll, C, et al. (2005). In Cooper, et al. (Eds.). *Developmental attitudes and pathways through middle childhood: Rethinking diversity and contexts as resources.* NY: Lawrence Erlbaum Associates.

Gura, P. (1994). Childhood: A multiple reality. *Early Childhood Development and Care,* 98.

Hilliard, A., & Vaughn-Scott, M. (1982). The quest for the 'minority' child. In S. Moore & C. Cooper (Eds.), *The young child: Review of research* (Vol. 3). Washington, DC: National Association for Education of Young Children.

Hironaka Cowee, M. (2001). *Identity tied to culture.* CAEYC: Connections.

Lightfoot, S. L. (1978). *Worlds apart.* New York: Basic Books.

Markus, H., in Vaughan, L. J. Culture as sculptor: Markus explores 'Models of Self.' Stanford University, *The Bing Times,* November, 2005.

Rodd, J. (1996). Children, culture and education. *Childhood Education, International Focus Issue.*

Rogoff, B. (2003). *The cultural nature of human development.* New York: Oxford University Press.

Attachment

Ainsworth, M. (1979, October). Infant-mother attachment. *American Psychologist,* 131–142.

Bowlby, J. (1969,1973). *Attachment and loss (Vols. I and II).* New York: Basic Books.

Kagan, J. (1987). Perspectives on infancy. In J. D. Godowsky (Ed.), *Handbook on infant development* (2nd Ed). New York: John Wiley & Sons, Inc.

Saxton, R. (2001). *Personal communication.*

White, Burton L. (1995) *The new first three years, revised.* NY: Fireside Publications.

Play

American Academy of Pediatrics: Ginsberg, K.R., Committee on Communications, and Committee on Psychosocial Aspects of Child & Family Health (2006). Clinical report: The importance of play in promoting healthy child development. http://www.aap.org/pressroom/playFINAL.pdf.

Bowman, B. (1990). Play in teacher education: The United States perspective. In E. Klugman & S. Smilansky (Eds.), *Children's play and learning.* New York: Teachers College Press.

Elkind, D. (2007). *The power of play.* Cambridge, MA: DaCapo Press.

Frost, J. L. (1996). *Play and playscapes.* Clifton Park, NY: Delmar Learning.

Frost, J. L., Wortham, S.C., & Reifel, S. (2007). *Play and child development* (3rd Ed). Upper Saddle River, NJ: Prentice Hall.

Hoffman, E. (2004). *Magic capes, amazing powers: Transforming play in the classroom.* St. Paul, MN: Redleaf Press.

Isenberg, J., & Quisenberry, N. (2002). Play: Essential for all children. A position paper of the Association for Childhood Education International. http://www.acei.org/playpaper.htm.

Jones, E. (2000). What is the point of play? In A. Gordon & K. W. Browne, *Beginning and beyond: Foundations in early childhood education.* Clifton Park, NY: Thomson Delmar Learning.

Klein, T. P., Wirth, D., & Linas, K. (2003). Play: Children's context for development. *Young Children, (58)*3.

Rubin, K. H., Fein, G. G., & Vandenberg, B. (1983). Play. In E. M. Heatherington (Ed.), *Handbook of child psychology (Vol. 4, Socialization, personality and social development).* New York: Wiley.

Singer, D.G., Golinkoff, R., & Hirsh-Pasekm, K. (Eds.) (2006) *Play=Learning.* NY: Oxford University Press.

Gender

Eisenberg, N., Martin, C. L., & Fabes, R. A. (1996). Gender development and gender effects. In D. C. Berliner & R. C. Calfee (Eds.), *Handbook of educational psychology.* New York: Macmillan.

Maccoby, E. E. (1998). *The two sexes.* Cambridge, MA: Harvard University Press.

Wardle, F. (2004). The challenge of boys in our early childhood programs. *Early Childhood News* (January-February, 2004).

Moral Development

Buzzelli, C. A. (1992, September). Young children's moral understanding: Learning about right and wrong. *Young Children,* 47–53.

Eisenberg, N., Lenon, R., & Roth, K. (1983). Prosocial development in middle childhood: A longitudinal study. *Developmental Psychology, 23,* 712–718.

Gilligan, C. (1982). *In a different voice.* Cambridge, MA: Harvard University Press.

Kohlberg, L. (1981). *The philosophy of moral development.* New York: Harper & Row.

Piaget, J. (1965) *The moral judgment of the child.* NY: Free Press.

Brain-Based Research

Bruer, J.T (1998). Brain science, brain fiction. *Educational Leadership,* (56)3.

Galinsky, E. (1997, Winter). New research on the brain development of young children. *CAEYC Connections.*

Garcia Coll, C. (2003). Cultural perspectives on parenting. http://www.extension.institute.edu [12/04/03].

Gunnar, M. R., & Vasquez, D. M. (2001). Low cortisol and a flattening of expected daytime rhythm: Potential indices of risk in human development. *Development and Psychopathology, 13,* 515–538.

Sanchez, M., Ladd, C.O., & Plotsky, P. M. (2001). Early adverse experience as a developmental risk factor for later psychopathology. *Development and Psychopathology, 13,* 413–450.

Schore, A., in Waters, R. (2004) The baby brain connection. *San Francisco Chronicle Magazine,* 16-27.

Siegel, D. J. (1999). Relationships and the developing mind. *Exchange Magazine,* 11/99, 48-50.

Shonkoff, J.P., et al (2008). The timing and quality of early experiences combine to shape brain architecture: working paper 5. Cambridge, MA: Harvard University Center on the Developing Child.

Shore, R. (1997). *Rethinking the brain: New insights into early development.* New York: Families and Work Institute.

Who Are the Teachers?

© Cengage Learning

© Cengage Learning

Teaching: A Professional Commitment

PREVIEW QUESTIONS

- Who are the early childhood teachers and how does their teaching differ from other teachers?

- What are the eight essential attributes for successful teaching?

- What is a professional code of ethics, and why should we have one?

- What are some of the roles and responsibilities of early childhood teaching?

- What does it mean to be a member of a teaching team?

- Why are evaluations important?

- How can a beginning teacher ensure a positive start?

NAEYC CODE OF ETHICAL CONDUCT

These Core Values and sections from the NAEYC Code of Ethical Conduct are addressed in this chapter. As you read, note how the Core Values, Ideals, or Principles listed here apply to the topics in this chapter. (Reprinted with permission from the National Association for the Education of Young Children.)

A. Responsibility to coworkers

Ideals:

I-3A.1   To establish and maintain relationships of respect, trust, and cooperation with coworkers.

I-3A.2   To share resources and information with coworkers.

I-3A.3   To support coworkers in meeting their professional needs and in their professional development.

I-3A.4   To accord coworkers due recognition of professional achievements.

B. Responsibilities to employers

Ideals:

I-3B.1 To assist the program in providing the highest quality of service.

I-3B.2 To do nothing that diminishes the reputation of the program in which we work, unless it is violating laws and regulations designed to protect children or the provisions of this Code.

C. Responsibilities to employees

Ideals:

I-3C.1 To promote policies and working conditions that foster mutual respect, competence, well-being, and positive self-esteem in staff members.

I-3C.2 To create a climate of trust and candor that will enable staff to speak and act in the best interests of children, families, and the field of early childhood care and education.

I-3C.3 To strive to secure equitable compensation (salary and benefits) for those who work with or on behalf of children.

Who Are the Teachers of the Young Child?

Margarita had always wanted to be an early childhood teacher. Right after high school she went to a community college and earned her A.A. degree. Shortly after her first child was born, she became a licensed family child care provider, and she now cares for infants and toddlers in her own home. It is important to Margarita that she feels she is making a contribution to the family's well-being, as well as enjoying a satisfying career. She plans to pursue her B.A. degree in the evenings when her children are older.

Paul recently spent several years teaching in a school for children with severe developmental delays. He has been a lead teacher for 4-year-olds at the child care center for two years, gaining experience with children whose developmental patterns are typical. Paul wants to remain a teacher but is concerned about the salary levels. He has given himself one more year before he will make a decision to stay or leave the field.

Kendra's four children were in parent-cooperative nursery schools, where she enjoyed the companionship of many other parents of young children. After a few years of teaching elementary school, she is now director of a parent co-op and teaches children from ages 2 to 5. She particularly enjoys leading weekly parent discussion groups.

Elva was the most sought-after parent aide in the school after she began helping out when her two boys were ages 4 and 5. This success stimulated her to get an A.A. degree in early childhood education, then a bachelor's degree in child

development. She is now a certified first grade teacher in a bilingual program and is working on her Master's degree.

All of these people had different motivations, yet they all were drawn to the early childhood classroom. They may teach in different settings and have different educational backgrounds and skills, yet they do share common everyday experiences of the teacher of young children. They plan, observe, listen, help, learn, play, console, discipline, confer, comfort, and teach the children and adults who make up their particular world of early childhood.

Teacher Diversity

According to the U.S. Bureau of Labor Statistics (2008), the teachers of young children represent the population in the following percentages:

Teaching Level	White	Black	Asian	Hispanic/ Latino
Child Care Worker	78.9	16.0	2.7	16.8
Preschool and Kindergarten	80.0	14.3	3.0	10.4
Elementary and Middle School	86.6	10.3	1.6	6.9

These statistics tell us that today's diverse demographics are not equitably represented in the teaching population. A 2001 study in three California communities from 1994 to 2000 (Whitebrook, et al) noted that while 50 percent of the classrooms in the study had Chinese-speaking children, only 7 percent had a staff member who spoke Cantonese or Mandarin. Forty-four percent of the classrooms had Spanish-speaking children, yet only half were staffed by Spanish-speaking teachers or caregivers. It is no wonder that parents in these programs reported difficulty in communicating with the staff because of language barriers. This raises the question of how the early childhood field is upholding the Code of Ethical Conduct as it relates to children and their families, hiring practices, and employment opportunities.

Comparison with Teaching in Other Educational Settings

The nature of teaching in the early years is unlike that of other age groups. At first glance, the differences in teaching preschool and older children may outweigh any similarities. There are some common elements, however, that link the two:

- Early childhood teachers teach what other teachers teach. The curriculum in the early years is rich in math, science, social studies, history, language, art, and geography, as it is in any other grade.
- Early childhood teachers and their elementary and high school counterparts share many of the frustrations of the teaching profession—long hours, low pay, and a people-intensive workplace.
- They also share the joy of teaching—the opportunity to influence children's lives and the satisfaction of meeting the daily challenges that teaching children provides.

Figure 5-1 highlights the similarities and differences between early childhood teachers and others.

The Beginnings of Professionalism

NAEYC has developed standards for the field of early childhood education to ensure that teachers receive the best possible professional preparation available. "Teachers are the key," says Hyson (2003), who goes on to say that it is the high quality early childhood professional, not the curriculum, assessments, and strategies, that has the greatest effect on children's learning and development.

Early Childhood Teachers: Differences and Similarities

Elements of Teaching and Learning	Early Childhood Settings	Elementary and High School Settings
How teaching and learning occur	Through teacher–child interactions and concrete use of materials	Through lectures and demonstrations that are often teacher dominated
	Guides children toward discovery	Teaches subject matter
Play opportunities	Primary learning medium is play	Usually just at recess
Opportunity for child to make choices	Many choices throughout the day both inside and outside	Few options—all students do same activity most of the day
Classroom environment	Abundant floor space, many activity centers, variety of materials for play	Rows of desks and tables
Daily schedule	Large blocks of time for unlimited exploration of materials and for play	45-minute to 1-hour periods on subject matter
Small group interactions	Majority of teaching	Much less frequent
Large group interactions	Few times a day	Majority of teaching
Outdoor activity	Teachers involved as intensively as they are in the classroom	Others usually supervise play yard—little direct teacher interaction
Parent relationships	Frequent, if not daily, contact	May see them once a year as child grows older
Working with other adults	Often works with aide, assistant teachers, and parents	Usually teaches alone or with part-time aide
Educational materials	Toys, games, natural materials, blocks	Textbooks and worksheets
Evaluating students	Observational and anecdotal assessments, portfolios	Grades, tests, and report cards
	Emphasis on growth of whole child	Standardized academic assessment
Age range of students	May have two- to two-and-a-half-year age span or greater	Usually same age
Art, music, and physical education	Available throughout the day as an ongoing part of curriculum	Restricted to a special class, time, or teacher
Teacher training	Strong child development foundation	Emphasis on subject matter

FIGURE 5-1 The nature of teaching in the early years is unlike that of other age groups.

A set of standards for professional preparation provides the vision for how teacher training programs and professional development will help teachers pursue the education, specialized training, and ongoing professional development they need. These standards echo the professional values found in the Code of Ethical Conduct and include the diversity of age ranges and programs in the early childhood field. The standards identify common expectations for professional knowledge and skills and emphasize a multidiscipline approach to educating teachers. The importance of outcomes, which indicate what early childhood professionals should know and do, are stressed throughout the standards, as are the continual assessment of these outcomes. Figure 5-2 outlines the five aspects of NAEYC's **professional standards.**

Eight essential attributes of a professional teacher are:

1. knowledge and skills
2. abiding by a code of ethics
3. continuing education and professional development
4. professional affiliations
5. knowledge of career options
6. cultural competency
7. advocacy
8. becoming a whole teacher

Knowledge and Skills

There is a body of knowledge and educational foundation that is assumed of anyone entering the early childhood profession, as noted in Figure 5-2: the NAEYC's Standards. Some basic teaching skills are also necessary. These include methods and techniques appropriate for teaching the very young child.

The NAEYC Standards for Early Childhood Professional Preparation outline key elements that begin with having a common background with others in the field. This includes studying child development and human behavior, family relations, parent education and development, and curriculum planning, as noted in key elements in Standard 1.

Some practical teaching experience under the guidance of a master teacher is expected, as is familiarity with observation and recording techniques. The key elements in Standard 3 provide the framework for professional development as teachers acquire further skills on the job. Key elements in Standard 5 encourage lifelong learning that will advance teaching practices.

Becoming a professional teacher involves progressing along a continuum of development. The state you live in may or may not have regulations for early childhood teachers; some states offer a specialized certification for

NAEYC's Standards

What Today's Teachers Should Know and Do

1. Promote child development and learning. Well-prepared early childhood professionals should:
   - understand what young children are like
   - understand what influences their development
   - use this understanding to create great environments where all children can thrive

2. Build family and community relationships. Well-prepared early childhood professionals should:
   - understand and value children's families and communities
   - create respectful, reciprocal relationships
   - involve all families in their children's development and learning

3. Observe, document, and assess. Well-prepared early childhood professionals should:
   - understand the purposes of assessment
   - use effective assessment strategies
   - use assessment responsibly, to positively influence children's development and learning

4. Teach and learn. Well-prepared early childhood professionals should:
   - build close relationships with children and families
   - use developmentally effective teaching and learning strategies
   - have sound knowledge of academic disciplines or content areas
   - combine all of these to give children experiences that promote development and learning

5. Become a professional. Well-prepared early childhood professionals should:
   - identify themselves with the early childhood profession
   - be guided by ethical and other professional standards
   - be continuous, collaborative learners
   - think reflectively and critically
   - advocate for children, families, and the profession

FIGURE 5-2 What today's teachers should know and do. (NAEYC, 2003. Reprinted with permission from the National Association for the Education of Young Children.)

those in the early childhood field. Professional expectations mandated by the states provide some degree of professionalization of early childhood teachers.

Figure 5-3 is an example of the California statewide certification program. This *career matrix* has a number of levels, each with alternative qualifications for meeting the requirements. Within each level, there are a variety of teaching roles. Each state defines its own certification standards. Information is available through the state's department of education.

Look back to the teachers you met at the beginning of the chapter. Margarita is making plans to move from being a licensed home caregiver to pursuing a bachelor's degree. Match her plans with Figure 5-3 to see what other options she will have. Elva's story demonstrates how education and experiences work together.

Experience and education work together to refine the skills and knowledge of the early childhood professional as shown in Figure 5-3. In addition, Figure 5-4 has some

A Career Lattice: Child Development Permit Matrix

Level	Education Requirement	Experience Requirement
Assistant	6 units of ECE or CD	None
Associate teacher	12 units ECE/CD, including core courses	50 days of 3+ hours/day within 2 years
Teacher	24 units ECE/CD, including core courses + 16 general education (GE) units	175 days of 3+ hours/day within 4 years
Master teacher	24 units ECE/CD, including 16 GE units + 6 specialization units + 2 units adult supervision	350 days of 3+ hours/day within 4 years
Site supervisor	A.A. (or 60 units) with 24 ECE/CD units, including core + 6 units administration + 2 units adult supervision	350 days of 4+ hours/day including at least 100 days of supervising adults
Program director	B.A. with 24 ECE/CD units, including core + 6 units administration + 2 units adult supervision	Site supervisor status and one program year of site supervisor experience

FIGURE 5-3 A combination of education and experience work together to form a career ladder for early childhood professionals in California who want a child development permit.

General Role Definitions for the Early Childhood Teacher

Title	Description	Minimum Qualifications
Apprentice/ Teacher Aide	Is responsible to teacher for implementing program	Entry level, no previous formal training but enrolled in early childhood education classes
Assistant or Associate Teacher	Is part of the teaching team under the direction of teacher; may implement curriculum, supervise children, and communicate with parents.	Child Development Associate (CDA) credential
Teacher	Is coleader who plans and implements curriculum, works with parents, and evaluates children's progress	Associate's degree in early childhood education or related field
Lead Teacher	Creates a model classroom, applies good early childhood education practices, supervises other team members, develops new curriculum, provides leadership to team	Bachelor's degree in early childhood education or related field; supervised teaching experience; additional coursework work in family life, assessment, supervision, etc.

FIGURE 5-4 There are many ways to reach the top of a career ladder. Each role has its own job description that will vary with the type of early childhood education setting. The qualifications will also be based on individual programs and their needs. (Adapted from *Blueprint for Action: Achieving Center-Based Change through Staff Development,* by P. J. Bloom, © 2005 New Horizons.)

useful descriptions of the various roles teachers have in early childhood programs. This chart also shows how the progression from teacher aide to master teacher is matched to increasing responsibilities and education.

Abides by a Code of Ethical Conduct

As teachers mature, they turn their attention to issues and concerns outside themselves. Many of these issues are related to ethical conflicts and moral principles. The NAEYC Standard 5 points out that professionals are guided by ethical and other standards of behavior. Teachers are, after all, human beings, and that entails genuine conflict about behavior. Doing what is right becomes difficult at times; knowing what is right may be elusive. Even identifying what is right—an ethical conflict—may not be obvious. NAEYC's Code of Ethical Conduct (see Appendix A and the beginning of each chapter) is an important resource for all teachers and caregivers.

Every day, situations arise with parents, children, other teachers, and administrators that require teachers to make some hard choices. Some cases are clearly ethical dilemmas: suspected child abuse by a parent or teacher, talking about children and their families outside of school, or the firing of a staff member without due cause. Others, some of which are common occurrences, may not seem as obvious. Some everyday examples are:

When parents:

- ask you to advance their child into the next class against your advice.
- want you to use discipline practices common to their family and culture but at odds with your own sense of what children need.
- attempt to gossip with you about another child, staff member, or family.

When another teacher:

- suggests a private staff meeting outside of school with a select group of teachers.
- refuses to take a turn cleaning out the animal cages.
- regularly misses staff meetings.
- disagrees with the school's educational philosophy and continues to teach in ways that differ from the approved methods in that setting.
- goes to the school administrator with a complaint about a staff team member.

When the administrator:

- insists on adding one more child to an already over-enrolled class.

- makes personnel decisions based on friendship, not performance.
- backs a parent who complains about a teacher without hearing the teacher's side of the story.

Teachers may find it helpful to discuss their ethical concerns with colleagues. Some centers provide in-service programs for the staff in which these issues are raised. Other schools have a code of ethics for their employees to follow.

Just what are **ethics**? Essentially, they are the moral guidelines by which we govern our own behavior and that of society. "Ethics—in the form of knowledge and skill in making responsible professional decisions—is one of the most fundamental qualities of a competent early childhood educator" (Smith, in Feeney & Freeman, 1999).

We can strictly define ethics as *the system or code of morals of a particular philosopher, religion, group, or profession.* This definition suggests that a personal code of ethics can be supported by a professional code of ethics. A code of ethics is a set of statements that helps us deal with the temptations inherent in our occupations. It helps us act in terms of what is right rather than what is expedient (Katz & Ward, 1991).

Why might the early childhood profession need such a code? A primary reason is that the choices teachers make should be based not simply on personal values and preferences but "on values, judgments, and ethical commitments shared by the professional society or association of which they are a member" (Katz & Ward, 1991).

A code of ethics provides collective wisdom and advice from a broad base in the profession. It states the principles by which each individual can measure and govern professional behavior. It says that a group or association has recognized the moral dimensions of its work. It provides teachers with a known, defined core of professional values—those basic commitments that any early childhood educator should consider inviolate. This protects teachers and administrators from having to make hard ethical decisions on the spur of the moment, possibly on the basis of personal bias. An established professional code supports the teacher's choice by saying, "It isn't that I won't act this way: No early childhood educator should act this way" (Kipnis, 1987).

NAEYC adopted a Code of Ethical Conduct and Statement of Commitment in 1989. It has since been revised, most recently in 1997. The four sections of the Code are: (1) Ethical responsibilities to children; (2) Ethical responsibilities to families; (3) Ethical re-

Core Values of NAEYC's Code of Ethical Conduct

- Appreciating childhood as a unique and valuable stage of the human life cycle.
- Basing our work with children on knowledge of child development.
- Appreciating and supporting the close ties between the child and family.
- Recognizing that children are best understood in the context of family, culture, and society.
- Respecting the dignity, worth, and uniqueness of each individual (child, family member, and colleague).
- Helping children and adults achieve their full potential in the context of relationships that are based on trust, respect, and positive regard.

FIGURE 5-5 These core values form the basis of agreement in the profession about standards of ethical behavior. See Appendix A for a full version.

sponsibilities to colleagues; and (4) Ethical responsibilities to community and society. The Code of Ethical Conduct and Statement of Commitment may be found in Appendix A at the back of this text. Figure 5-5 shows a basic list of core values that has emerged from this work, values "that are deeply rooted in the history of our field" (NAEYC, 1997).

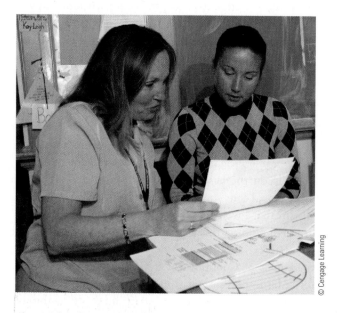

© Cengage Learning

The Code of Ethical Conduct is shared with all members of the center or school staff.

Continuing Education and Professional Development

Creative and stimulating classrooms are the product of teachers who continue to learn more about how to teach. After the initial stage of teaching, many teachers begin to seek new challenges and new ways to improve the quality of their teaching. Usually this search leads to some form of **continuing education,** such as participation in workshops, courses, or seminars. Standard 5 reinforces the concept of teachers as life-long learners.

Katz (1999) describes four distinct stages of teacher development, ranging from Survival to Maturity. The beginning teacher often feels inadequate and ill-prepared during the first year of teaching (Survival) but soon begins to focus on individual children and specific behavior problems (Consolidation). By the third or fourth year (Renewal) the teacher is ready to explore new ideas and resources and, within another year or two, has come to terms with teaching and searches for insights and perspectives (Maturity). At each stage, teachers need differing degrees of on-site support (mentoring), with increased exposure to professional conferences and organizations.

If time to pursue continuing education is not built into a teacher's schedule, there may be other options:

- In-service training programs may be brought into the school setting. Resource people can be invited to lead the staff in discussions about children's behavior, family relationships, assessment charts, science curricula, and creating multicultural classrooms.
- Members of the teaching staff can develop a program of their own, offering their expertise to fellow faculty at an in-service meeting.
- A computer specialist, art resource teacher, or multicultural expert can be invited to visit the classrooms, instructing children and providing staff with some useful ideas and plans.
- A family therapist can be invited to speak at a staff meeting about strategies for supporting families in crisis.
- A library for teachers, stocked with professional books, journals (such as *Young Children*), newspapers (such as *Education Week*), and e-letters such as *Exchange Every Day*, can provide a teacher with the means to keep up with current trends and practices and to improve teaching skills in the classroom.
- Parents who are professionals in a variety of fields can be utilized whenever possible to enrich the knowledge and skills of the staff.

Look back at the career matrix (Figure 5-3) and see how many opportunities there are for advancement with the

TeachSource Video ▶ⅠⅠ

Watch the TeachSource Video Case entitled "Teaching as a Profession: An Early Childhood Teacher's Responsibilities and Development." After you study the video clip, view the artifacts, and read the teacher interviews and text, reflect upon the following questions:

1. One of the primary values in the NAEYC Code of Ethical Conduct is that children are best understood in the context of their family, culture, and society. Where and how does teacher Samantha Brade weave this into the interview?

2. In the case, Samantha defines many roles and responsibilities that challenge her as a professional. Comment on her ability to be self-reflective as she talks about teaching.

and best practices within the field. One of the largest, the National Association for the Education of Young Children (NAEYC), has local and state affiliate groups through which one can become a member. NAEYC offers a range of services to its members, including conferences and publications such as the journal *Young Children*. The Association for Childhood Education International (ACEI) has a similar function, whereas the Society for Research in Child Development (SRCD) focuses on child psychology, research, and development.

There are a number of organizations concerned with young children, teachers, and issues related to the early childhood profession. Abundant resources are available from these groups, and their websites are at the end of this chapter and on the textbook website.

right education and experience. As you achieve each level, there are challenges to be met. A course in group dynamics, cultural sensitivity, or adult assessment portfolios will enhance your chances to move into more satisfying work and enlarge your contributions to those you work with and to the profession as a whole.

Professional Affiliations

Early childhood professionals may choose to join one of the professional organizations related to the early childhood field. In doing so, they meet the criteria for Standard 5 to identify themselves with the early childhood profession and become continually aware of the research

Knowledge of Career Options

The need for quality programs for young children has never been greater, and the demand for early childhood specialists will continue, fostered by national attention to the issues of children and families. If you are considering a career in early childhood education (ECE), the options are many and varied. Several of the Standards point to specific early childhood careers. For instance, Standard 1 suggests a teaching and /or consulting job, or Standard 2 may lead toward a calling as a family–child therapist or community organizer. Figure 5-6 lists some of the possibilities that exist in this profession.

Cultural Competency

Throughout this text, you will be exposed to cultural awareness and sensitivity in many contexts: in Chapter 1—diversity, immigrant children, class differences; in Chapter 3—cultural sensitivity and family cultural influences; in Chapter 7—culturally appropriate guidance; in Chapter 8—the changing American family; in Chapter 10—culturally appropriate curriculum, inclusive curriculum, multicultural curriculum, and culturally responsive teachers; and in Chapter 15—multicultural education, bilingual education, the challenges for immigrants, class differences, equal play and gender issues, and sexuality.

The culturally competent early childhood professional must be aware of the issues addressed in those chapters. The population trends within the United States have changed dramatically over the last few decades and the ability to adapt to a diversified group of families will be the challenge for the teachers of the 21st century. DAP

What Do YOU Think? Look at the situations described on page 163. How do you see the Code of Ethical Conduct supporting resolutions to those dilemmas? How does the Code of Ethics relate to your own sense of moral and ethical teaching behaviors?

DAP One of the values in NAEYC's Code of Ethical Conduct is the recognition that children are best understood in the context of family, culture, and society.

Career Options in Early Childhood Education

Direct Services to Children and Families

Teacher in early childhood program
Director of child care facility nursery school,
    Montessori program
Family day-care provider
Nanny or au pair
Foster parent
Social worker/adoption agent
Pediatric nurse/school nurse
Family therapist/parent educator
Pediatrician
Parent educator
Early intervention specialist
Recreation leader
Play group leader
Home visitor

Community Involvement

State/local licensing worker
Legislative advocate
Child care law specialist
ECE environmental consultant
Interior designer for children's spaces
Government planning agent on children's issues
Consultant in bilingual education, multiculturalism
Nutrition specialist for children
Child care referral counselor

Indirect Services to Children and Families

Curriculum specialist
Instructional specialist—computers
Child development researcher
ECE specialist
Program consultant
Consumer advocate
Teacher trainer, two- and four-year colleges
Consultant
Resource and referral programs
State and national departments of education and/or
    human services

Other Options

Communications consultant
Script writer/editor
Freelance writer
Children's book author
Children's photographer
Microcomputer specialist/program consultant

FIGURE 5-6 There are many challenges in a variety of careers awaiting the early child-hood professional. (Adapted from "Career Options in Early Childhood Education" by Dianne Widmeyer Eyer. In *Beginnings & Beyond: Foundations in Early Childhood Education* (3rd Ed), p. 170. Clifton Park, NY: Thomson Delmar Learning.)

Today's teachers should be able to build strong family and community relationships (Standards 2, 4, 5) across all types of cultural diversity.

DAP This requires a pluralistic mindset and an ability to communicate across cultures and individual circumstances. We will make our own personal and professional journey through these remarkable times to prepare children to live in a world of diversity.

Advocacy

Children of America need advocates to speak for them and their families on issues ranging from health care to education to poverty to professional quality, staff, and wages. It is up to the early childhood professional to give voice to the issues concerning our young children and to educate the public about those issues. Public policy mak-

ers on the local, state, and national level need to hear from those who can speak out for those who cannot. Part of the role of a professional early childhood educator is to join the voices that support educational and teaching reforms as specifically stated in Standard 5. Volunteer with a local organization and make a difference in the lives of teachers and caregivers. Local NAEYC affiliates need volunteers to support *The Week of the Young Child* campaign each year and to monitor public policy at the local and state levels. Some early childhood professionals find it useful to sit on the boards of childcare and health organizations.

Becoming a Whole Teacher

At some point, teachers emerge with their own point of view about teaching, based on self-knowledge of what calls them to teaching, why they teach the way they do,

DAP Children get emotional support and a sense of belonging when they see that their family culture is valued.

and what they know of the children they teach. This integration of knowledge and training, experience and life, is referred to by several names. Some say "real" teachers. Others refer to the "total" teacher. A common phrase is the "whole" teacher. Any one of these terms is an apt reflection of the relationship between how teachers view children and how they see themselves. There is a meshing of the emotional, physical, intellectual, and social aspects of each human being, adult, or child.

Something happens when this blending occurs. During the first few years in the classroom, teachers consolidate their various official functions—merging their teacher training and experience with their personal style and nature. To discover and define the role of a teacher means to develop a personal teaching style. This is the sum of one's response to teaching, and it is unique to each teacher. When it happens, a beginning teacher becomes aware of "feeling" like a teacher. The strengths and convictions one has as a person blend with those one has as a teacher; they become inseparable. What teachers do and what teachers are become woven together. In adding the personal teacher to the professional teacher, the sum becomes greater than two, allowing the whole teacher the freedom to grow in insight and understanding.

The Teacher's Role: Professionalism in Action

Defining the Early Childhood Teacher's Roles

The variety of roles early childhood teachers perform has been described in many ways:

Storyteller	Traffic director	Conflict mediator
Custodian	File clerk	Mediator
Carpenter	Poet	Plumber
Adult educator	Parent	Musician
Purchasing	Resource	Faculty member
Agent	Nurse	Program
Staff supervisor	Business	Planner
Personnel	Manager	Treasurer
Director	Employee	Employer
Psychologist	Sociologist	Scientist

This diversity is exactly what makes teaching in the early years so appealing. The multiple roles a teacher plays add challenge to the job. (The role of the teacher in relation-ship to parents and programs is discussed further in Chapter 8.)

Two prominent early childhood teacher educators state the value of having teachers who have a theoretical and historical grounding. Jones (1994) tells us that teachers, like young children, are constructivists. The complexity and unpredictability of teaching, she says, call for on-the-spot decisions, and those decisions are based on developmental and learning theory and constructed from the teacher's own experience and practice. Teachers also need to know the theory, history, and traditions of the field and the social and political climate of the day.

Phillips (1994) defines teaching as those "daily acts of creation" that are constructed from the teacher's own repertoire of skills, knowledge, and training added to what he or she observes about children and his or her interactions with their families. The teacher as a collaborator is a significant part of the teacher's role definition in the schools of Reggio Emilia, Italy (see Chapter 10). Collaboration reinforces the notion underlying many definitions that teachers are, first and foremost, lifelong teachers.

In "Insights from the Field" at the end of this chapter, Barbara Biglan tells a story of how students in an early childhood course learn a unique way to identify the many roles of an early childhood professional.

What teachers do with children is not all there is to teaching. Some of the work occurs outside the classroom. It is helpful to look at the teacher's role in another way. What are the things a teacher does with children? What are the things a teacher does after the children go home? How does the teacher interact with other adults in the early childhood setting?

Professionalism in the Classroom

Interacting with Children

Teachers find their greatest satisfaction and challenges in their first role—who and what they are with children. The teacher–child interactions, the spur-of-the-moment crises, the intense activity, the on-the-spot decisions, the loving and nurturing, go far in making one "feel" like a real teacher. Helping Rhonda get a good grip on the hammer, soothing Josh and Benno after they bump heads, and talking with Alexa about her drawing are at the heart of teaching young children. These encounters are enjoyable and provide moments for interactive teaching opportunities. These times help to establish good relationships with

© Cengage Learning

Teachers model learning, listening, and loving.

the children. It is during these spontaneous, anything-can-happen-and-probably-will times that teachers display their craftsmanship and professionalism.

The art of teaching comes alive on the floor of the classroom. All teaching skills are utilized. Responses are automatic and ingrained. Teachers intuitively use their knowledge base, their experience, and their proven techniques. Almost unconsciously, they reach back in their minds for all those things they know about children. Throughout the school day they apply that combination of knowledge and know-how.

Managing the Classroom

Being a successful manager is a little like being a successful juggler. Both require the ability to think about and react to more than three things at once. With a simple gesture, a significant look, or merely moving nearby, the teacher maintains the ongoing activity.

Anticipating a clash between Nathan and Julie, the teacher, Miriam, intervenes, redirects them, and

moves away. At the same time, she has kept a watchful eye on Bobby at the bathroom sink. Passing close to Francie, she touches the child's shoulder in brief acknowledgment, smiling down as Francie struggles with the doll's dress. Miguel and Lea run up to her, grab her by the skirt and hand, and pull her toward the science display. They need to ask her something about the snake … *now!* Jake, the handyman, has come into the classroom wanting to know exactly which of the climbers needs repair. Sarah, the parent volunteer, waves to her; it's time to check on the corn bread baking in the kitchen. Quickly, the teacher files a mental note of the names of the children who accompany Sarah to the kitchen. As she reaches for a copy of *Ranger Rick* (the one with the great snake pictures in it), she observes Angie and her father entering the room. They both look upset. Telling Miguel and Lea she will return, the teacher walks over to greet the latecomers. As she moves past Doug, the student teacher, she comments on how well his language game is going and suggests he continue for another five minutes. Glancing at the clock, she realizes it is almost cleanup time. Her assistant, Chuck, watches her. She looks his way, and a nonverbal signal passes between them. Without a word, they both understand that snacks will be a little late today. Angie's father begins to explain their delay as the teacher bends down to invite the child to come and look at the new snake cage with her.

In this setting, the teacher has a major role in supervising a number of people. Aides and volunteers, student teachers, and visitors add to the richness of a program. But it is the teacher who coordinates and supervises their various functions. From the description, it is clear that the teacher's role as a supervisor and manager includes:

- caretaker for a safe environment
- observer of and listener to children
- on-the-spot teacher trainer for students, aides, and volunteers
- on-site supervisor for student teachers
- liaison and communicator with parents

Setting the Tone

Teachers are responsible for what occurs in the classroom, so they must have a finger on its pulse at all times and take the pulse while moving around the classroom or yard. From the moment of arrival, the teacher puts into effect another vital element by setting the tone, creating an atmosphere in which teachers and children will work and play. The skill with which this is done can make the critical difference between a classroom that is alive and supportive and one that is chaotic or tense.

The teacher establishes what will be the **emotional framework**. This is done with body movements, by the tone of voice, facial expressions or lack of them, and nonverbal as well as verbal gestures. The way the children respond reflects this tone. This interaction between the atmosphere the teacher creates and the child's behavior sets the tone.

DAP

Young children are very sensitive to adult moods and attitudes. A teacher who exudes calm and confidence, strength and support, will inspire a more relaxed, comfortable atmosphere in which children can learn and grow. If the teacher is punitive and harsh, the tone of the classroom will reflect that. On the other hand, if teachers act on their beliefs that children deserve respect and are intelligent, capable human beings, they will create an entirely different climate—and the children will respond in kind.

Normal behavior for the young child includes tantrums, crying, resistance, curiosity, impatience, emotional swings, noise, and self-centeredness. This is the time to achieve a sense of his or her own separate self. Children need a place to work through the developmental stages that their needs and nature indicate. The atmosphere that a teacher creates is a key element in that process.

The way teachers handle conflict, react to tears, the words they use, and the voices raised communicate a direct message to the child. The understanding, the soothing, the warmth, and the acceptance create a climate where children feel safe, secure, and guided. This requires teachers who respect childhood, the individuality of children, their growing patterns, their emerging feelings, and their special capacity to learn. Today we would also stress the need for teachers to become culturally competent: to accept and understand cultural differences, have a working knowledge of the cultural backgrounds of the children in the class, and appreciate that this may be the children's first experience outside their own culture. The end result is that preschoolers will thrive in an atmosphere influenced by teachers who understand this time of tension and growth in their lives.

Planning and Evaluating Curriculum

As teachers move through the school day interacting with children, managing the classroom, and sensing the tone, they consciously or unconsciously evaluate what is happening:

- The relay race outdoors produced more tears than cheers; most of the children were interested in par-

ticipating when the game started but drifted away. Why?
- The Cuisenaire™ rods were never touched today. How can we make this a more inviting activity?
- The toddlers are beginning to participate fully in the "Eensy Weensy Spider" finger play. What might they like to learn next?
- Several children have asked why Sasha "talks funny." When would be a good time to talk about his language and teach the class a few words in Russian?

The teacher notes where and how children played, the quality of their interactions, and possible "next steps" in curriculum. These notes are then discussed with other staff members at the end of the day or in weekly planning sessions. Effective ways to develop curriculum planning are discussed in Chapter 10.

It is important to note that the process has its roots in what the teacher sees happening in the classroom as children play and learn. It is constructivist theory in action: teachers watching and observing children to give meaning and support to their learning. Early childhood teachers use their observation skills, collect data as they work with children, and build emergent curriculum around their knowledge of actual classroom practice and behavior.

Out-of-Class Responsibilities

Good classroom management is often dependent on how teachers spend their time away from the children. Many of the tasks that give added strength and depth to a teacher's curriculum are those that, out of necessity, must be accomplished after hours. The two most obvious jobs that fall into this category are record keeping and meetings.

Record Keeping

Early childhood teachers and caregivers keep a variety of records; the type and kind will vary from school to school. Although report writing and record keeping may be considered time-consuming, they are essential to any good early childhood program. Record keeping is based on a number of factors:

- *The purpose for which the records will be used.* In schools that rely on government funding, record keeping is not optional. The children's progress, the teacher's performance, and the program itself must

DAP A caring community of learners is based on the relationships among its members. Teachers, children, and families all have a responsibility to support and care for one another.

be evaluated on a regular basis to ensure continued funding.

- *The philosophy of the school.* In many settings, but especially in laboratory schools and teacher-training centers, teachers write periodical progress reports on the children to guide them in planning.
- *As part of a teacher-training process.* Documentation is critical for accreditation of early childhood programs. CDA (Child Development Associates) candidates submit a written portfolio of their experiences in the classroom as supportive evidence of their competency as teachers of young children.
- *As part of an accreditation process.* NAEYC's accreditation procedures require extensive documentation of the school's operation, ranging from governance and management issues to teacher effectiveness, space usage, parent involvement, school philosophy, and curriculum.
- *As a commitment to quality and appropriate child development practices.* Recording children's social and emotional growth provides information from which insights and interpretation can develop. It may be just a brief note taken on the run, a thoughtful anecdote written at length after class, or a checklist of the child's playmates for one day. All of these give teachers a greater understanding of the role they play in children's development.
- *As a means of family information and education.* Recorded observations, notes, and similar data collected over a six-month period may show that Abraham is not participating in any strenuous physical activity and studiously avoids activities that involve balancing and climbing. This information, when shared with parents, could lead to a medical evaluation and diagnosis of possible perceptual problems.
- *As a means of developing curriculum.* Emergent curriculum plans and learning activities sprout from such reports and records. It was not until such data were collected for entry into first grade that the kindergarten teacher realized most of the children in the class were not sufficiently proficient with scissors. A project approach remedied the need and the class learned a necessary skill.

Attending Meetings

Meetings are probably the most time-consuming of all out-of-class jobs. The teacher may need to communicate with the other people who are involved in the lives of the children, directly or indirectly. Families, other teachers, babysitters, doctors, and social workers are some of the people with whom a teacher may want to confer. Teachers also attend professional meetings. Figure 5-7 lists the most common types of meetings.

Organizing and Collecting Materials

Some of a teacher's after-hours activities are intended to fortify and vitalize the classroom. Therefore, teachers organize and collect materials for use in class. They might

---

Common Types of Meetings

Staff Meetings

Held usually once a week for individual teaching teams. Purpose is to plan curriculum, set goals, and discuss children's progress. Faculty meetings for all school personnel may be held less frequently.

Parent–Teacher Conferences

May be offered on a scheduled basis or they may be called by either parents or teachers as needed. Each school defines its own policy as to the number and frequency of parent contacts.

Parent Education Meetings

Many schools offer evening programs for parents. Teacher attendance may or may not be required.

Professional Meetings

Attendance at workshops, seminars, in-service training. Local, state, and national conferences are sponsored by the National Association for the Education of Young Children, Association for Childhood Education International, and Child Care Coordinating Council.

Student–Teacher Conferences

In schools used as training sites, teachers arrange time with individual students assigned to their classes.

Home Visits[1]

May or may not be optional. Some schools schedule them before opening day. Otherwise teachers must arrange them on their own time.

[1] Many parents welcome teacher's visits. Others may fear criticism or judgement about their home environment or family practices.

FIGURE 5-7 Teachers attend many different types of meetings, which help them create better programs, learn more about children, and learn how to become better teachers.

Sharing insights with colleagues helps the early childhood professional become more self-aware.

collect space shuttle books from the library, find out if the bagel factory will allow field trips, or cut 18 pumpkin shapes. They might add pictures to the bulletin board, obtain new books and records, or replenish curriculum materials.

Teachers may also need to purchase materials and equipment. The kitchen needs new mixing bowls, the supply room is low on red construction paper, and someone has to pick up fabric for pillow covers. In some settings, teachers will serve on committees and assist with ordering supplies and materials. All of these responsibilities fall to the family childcare provider.

Making Contacts

Teachers may call or e-mail families to check on children who are sick or absent, return calls from parents and colleagues, or update a parent about a child's progress. For children with special needs, teachers may need to contact doctors, therapists, and other specialists. The popularity of e-mail has made some communications with families much faster and easier.

Working with Families

Working with families may include working on multicultural events and curriculum or organizing class fairs or school fund-raising events. These duties are a part of the job of teaching young children but many will be shared with other teachers on the team or at the school. Though time-consuming, these responsibilities add to the creativity and care that teachers express for the children and their families. Chapter 8 discusses the teacher–family relationship in depth.

Personal Qualities of Early Childhood Educators

Dedication, compassion, insight, a sense of humor, flexibility, patience, energy, and self-confidence are the hallmarks of a good teacher. Physical and mental well-being are important, as is a demonstrated sense of ethical responsibility and reliability. Teachers should be fairminded, showing concern for all the people they meet in an early childhood setting. A good teacher knows how to be kind, warm, and loving yet firm and consistent.

The well-rounded teacher, while maintaining a professional commitment, has other interests as well. Good teachers have an involvement with the world outside the walls of the early childhood setting. They want to help children understand some of the real-life issues and concerns. They know that their interest in the world at large transmits itself to children.

In addition to working with children, teachers support parents when they keep in touch. A brief, friendly phone call can make a family feel included in their child's education process.

Self-Awareness

To be the best teacher possible, understanding and accepting oneself is vital. **Self-awareness** will make a difference in the way teachers relate to children. Each teacher must ask: Who and what and why am I? And how does knowing this bring some meaning into my life? How does it affect my life as a teacher? What guides my moral and ethical decisions? Good teachers are the ones who are trying every day to become more than they are and who demonstrate to their students that this quest to learn and to grow, to accept failure and go on to new challenges, is what life is all about (LeShan, 1992). Teachers who think like this have learned the importance of reflective and critical thinking in their own lives.

Implicit in the NAEYC's standards in Figure 5-2 is that early childhood professionals are life-long learners, pursuing the skills and knowledge they need through avenues such as coursework, professional development, degree programs, training, and licensing. Good teachers find out what they need to know in order to provide what young children need to develop and learn.

Teachers communicate an authentic appreciation of learning when they have a sense of it in their own lives and ask themselves: Do I see myself as a learner? Where does my learning take place? How? What happens to me when something is difficult or when I make a mistake? Do I learn from other teachers? Do I learn from children?

Asking—and then answering—these questions helps teachers gain insights into their own behavior as adults and as professionals who work with children. Pausing to look at their own behavior when faced with a difficult task or in handling a mistake helps teachers remember what children experience each day.

Opening themselves up to the possibility of learning from students stretches teachers' capacity to grow into relationships with children based on mutual respect and trust. This is especially important when teachers do not share the same cultural background or have no experience with a particular disability.

Opening themselves to learning from other teachers creates a foundation for mutual support, collegiality, professional mind-stretching, and deepening of friendships.

Self-knowledge—examining values and personal qualities—takes courage and a willingness to risk oneself. Accepting oneself is where to begin in accepting children. When teachers take the time to look at their own style of behavior and how it affects others, they place themselves on a par with children as learning, growing people.

Attitudes and Biases

A person's values and attitudes weave their way into every relationship and are an indication of the ethical framework that guides the way they live and teach. This can be both positive and negative. Personal beliefs concerning race, culture, gender, abilities, and economic status may negatively affect our teaching in ways of which we are not aware. Facing prejudices about children and families based on long-held beliefs may be one of the most difficult things for a teacher to do. Most teachers will not have lived through the significant and powerful experience of adapting to a new culture, learning a new language, surviving on food stamps and aid to support dependent children, or living in a wheelchair; therefore, they may be uncomfortable with people who are labeled "different" because they have faced these issues.

Adults have opinions, born of their own experiences, of what is "good" or "naughty" behavior. Personal histories are filled with biases. Children who are messy, who have odors, whose clothes are too big or too small, who eat strange food, who don't do what girls or boys are supposed to do, may bother some teachers. Some of these biases can be resolved, but only if a teacher takes the time to examine personal beliefs and biases.

The **anti-bias** approach to teaching young children (Derman-Sparks & Edwards, 2010) is as important today as it was when it was first presented because of significant changes in the ethnic makeup in the United States. Widespread racial and ethnic prejudice is still prevalent in this country and concern remains on the part of early childhood educators about the harm to children's self-identity and self-esteem.

The anti-bias movement promotes the concept that all children are worthy of our respect and challenges teachers to examine beliefs, attitudes, and actions that might deny any child that unconditional respect. (See sections in Chapters 9, 11, and 15 for further discussion.)

The anti-bias approach affords teachers an opportunity to confront their own anxieties and biases. As you work with families of various religious and ethnic minorities, you learn other cultural norms and practices and are better able to promote greater global understanding with the children you teach.

As a way to begin, you might ponder these questions:

- Am I aware of my own identity and its influences on my beliefs and behaviors?
- Do I have a set of ethical beliefs I follow? Is there a system of ethical behaviors related to working with children and families that I could learn?
- Do I foster a respect for the value of those who are somehow different from me? How?
- Do I examine my biases and look at ways I can change my own attitudes? When? How?
- Do I show a preference for children who most closely fit my own ethnic, cultural, and religious background? When? How?
- Do I somehow pass along my biases to the children I teach? When? How? With whom?
- Do I truly enjoy differences in human beings? When? With whom?

Kuster (1994) notes some critical issues teachers face when they work with families whose primary language is other than English:

1. Fluency in the child's language is critical for maximizing the child's learning experience.
2. Learn to value the family's child-rearing practices.
3. Preserve and enhance the child's culture by learning and valuing your own.
4. Confront your own personal attitudes and biases.

These suggestions reinforce the need for teachers to become more sensitive to their own attitudes about cultures other than their own.

© Cengage Learning

Teachers' values and attitudes are reflected in the way they work with children.

Teacher Burnout

Teacher burnout is an occupational hazard of substantial proportion. Burnout often results when a teacher is faced with a demanding workload, uncertain or inadequate rewards, and other pressures that damage work effectiveness. At its most extreme, teacher burnout can drive a good professional out of the field altogether, a common situation in early childhood settings and one that creates *one of the highest occupational turnover rates in the nation.*

When teachers feel that their efforts are not appreciated or they are not making the kind of impact with children and families, the results are low morale, stress, and disillusionment in a profession in which staff quality is the most important single factor in program quality. Some consider that the No Child Left Behind plan (see Chapter 15) is causing increased stress with its emphasis on what they see as inappropriate state-induced standards that do not focus on the development of the whole child. This creates a conflict in values and in their ability to meet the requirements of their job.

A major issue for the early childhood professional is financial. Child care teachers make an average of $9/hour, and preschool teachers a little over $12, whereas kindergarten teachers make over $20/hour (Carter, 2008). Low wages lead to high levels of staff turnover, which then affects the quality of the program. These issues are further explored in Chapter 15 and play a significant part in teacher burnout.

In a climate in which teachers can meet children's needs and program goals can be effectively addressed, feelings of job satisfaction and productivity will prevail.

Bloom (2005) cites 10 characteristics that produce a healthy and positive school climate that, in turn, promote high morale among the teaching staff:

- friendly, supportive, and trusting staff relationships
- emphasis on personal and professional growth
- leadership with clear expectations that encourages and supports staff
- clearly defined roles and policies
- fairness and equity regarding promotions, raises, and other rewards
- staff involvement in decision making
- agreement among staff on philosophy, goals, and objectives
- emphasis on efficiency and good planning
- a physical environment that promotes responsible teaching and learning
- the ability to adapt to change and solve problems.

Teachers and staff must take the responsibility to work together to create the kind of climate that enhances success and satisfaction in the workplace. (Related discussions are in Chapters 10 and 15.)

A Collaborative Effort: Team Teaching

The heart of teaching is what happens when you begin to work in a classroom every day with adults, as well as children. Numerous adults are included in the total teaching picture. Some of these people may be:

- other teachers, aides, and student teachers
- volunteers
- program directors and administrators
- school support personnel: clerical and janitorial staffs, food-service workers, bus drivers
- families
- consultants and specialists.

That list defines the broader meaning of **team teaching.** The majority of classroom interactions, however, will be with other teachers, and these relationships are among the most important a teacher can have. The beginning teacher may join a team of teachers or may teach in a small class alone. This will depend on:

- the age level of the children
- licensing or accrediting requirements
- the size of the classroom
- the school's philosophy and practices

Team teaching is defined as two or more adults working together in one classroom with one group of children (Browne & Gordon, 2009). The team approach is common in many nursery schools and childcare centers where larger groups of children attend. Kindergarten and first- and second-grade teachers generally teach alone in self-contained classrooms, sometimes with an aide. In extended-day and after-school programs, high school and college students may make up the rest of the team.

Team Composition

Most teams are composed of people with varying skills, experience, and training. A typical group will have a lead or head teacher—someone who is trained in child development or early childhood education. Assistants with less experience and training add support. Student teachers, interns, and volunteers may round out the group. A resource teacher—someone who specializes in art, music, or physical development, for instance—may also be available on a part-time basis.

Many state regulations mandate a minimum number of adults in the early childhood setting, and this minimum varies with the ages of the children. In infant programs, for instance, there is a higher ratio of adults per child (NAEYC suggests an optimal a ratio of 1:4), so it is more likely there will be several teachers in one classroom. Together the teachers will shape, direct, and participate in that program as a team of teachers.

The prescribed ratio of adult to children changes as the children mature and become able to function in more independent ways. (See Chapter 2 for more examples.)

Role Definition and Satisfaction

To teach successfully, each person on the team must have a satisfying role to play and to be appreciated for the special something he or she brings to the team. All teachers want to know how their special talents and experiences contribute to the success of this program.

A written job description helps teachers understand the scope of their own position, as well as those of other staff members. Clearly defined roles also serve as a guard against legal and ethical problems, especially if children are injured at school. A clear understanding of the roles and responsibilities a teacher has is essential for the teacher's own sense of well-being and for the smooth functioning of the program.

Flexibility

It is important to adapt to the varying needs of children and equally important to respond to the needs of other staff members. Flexibility involves a willingness to offer and accept negotiation and compromise to preserve the effectiveness of the whole staff's effort. A professional teacher demonstrates a willingness to change with the changing needs of coworkers, to be open to new ideas proposed by others, and to help children become comfortable with flexibility and change.

Open and Frequent Communication

The ability to communicate thoughts, concerns, and feelings to others honestly and openly is perhaps the most important factor in promoting good personal relationships. Communication takes many forms: verbal and nonverbal, written and spoken, and body language.

The three basic reasons for developing successful communication links with others on the teaching staff are:

1. *To share information*—about children and their families ("Sheila's grandmother died yesterday"), about changes in the schedule ("The dentist is unable to visit today; who wants to conduct group time?"), and about child development strategies ("Remember, we are all going to observe Leah's gross motor skills this week").
2. *To contribute new ideas*—teachers encourage one another to keep teaching fresh and alive when they

Professional attitudes and behaviors enhance team teaching.

share a recent article of interest, reports from a conference they attended, or a successful art activity.
3. *To solve problems*—accepting differences in opinions, approaches, personality, and style among people is part of the challenge of working closely with others. Open communication is an ongoing process in which people have honest and frequent discussions of their differences, respecting each other's feelings and integrity and working together for mutually agreeable solutions. Section P-3A.1 of the Code of Ethical Conduct states that when we have concerns about the professional behavior of a co-worker, we let that person know of our concerns and attempt to resolve the problem in a collegial manner.

Who Am I?

As noted earlier, self-awareness is a prerequisite to becoming a professional teacher. The kind of self-knowledge that contributes to success as a member of a faculty or teaching team knows how your strengths and weakness complement or conflict with other team members and in which teaching situations you feel comfortable or uneasy. How you perceive yourself as a leader and your ability to follow others can affect team relationships. Be aware of what you have done lately that caused you to learn more about yourself, especially as a member of a teaching team.

Mutual Respect and Acceptance

Appreciating and accepting the individuality of other team members are as important to the success of the program as are appreciating and accepting the individuality of each child. The climate of trust and the nonthreatening atmosphere gained through mutual respect allow each staff member to contribute openly and innovatively to the program. It helps to know what you have in common with your co-workers, whether or not their teaching philosophies differ from you and from one another, and what values they hold dear. You will want to be clear about what you want them to respect and accept about you as well. Section P-3B.1 of the Code of Ethical Conduct makes it clear that when we do not agree with program policies, we first work within the organizational structure to affect change.

Collegiality

A sense of being a team does not happen by accident, but by conscious effort. Every member of the staff must be committed to working together on a daily basis, as well

© Cengage Learning

as to the long-term goals of the program. Jorde-Bloom (2005) defines collegiality as the extent to which a team is friendly, supportive, and trusting of one another.

Showing empathy for the feelings and needs of co-workers suggests that you reflect on how you might show support or offer help to another staff member in order to promote and sustain high morale among your fellow teachers.

Sharing the Spotlight

Tension among staff members can arise from a sense of competition. Good team members learn how to share their strengths in ways that support the team without creating a competitive atmosphere. There must be a feeling of shared success when things work well, just as there is a shared responsibility when problems arise. One of the challenges of working on a team is to deal with feelings that may come from judging another teacher's abilities and/or successes. It helps to know how you feel and react when a parent praises another teacher in front of you or a child prefers another teacher to you. Section P-3A.2 of the Code of Ethical Conduct reminds us to base our views regarding the personal attributes or professional conduct of others on firsthand knowledge and its relevancy to the children and the program.

Evaluation

Evaluations are part of the privilege of claiming membership in the teaching profession. No teacher can become truly successful unless provisions are made for ongoing evaluations that provide a clear picture that confirms strengths and pinpoints areas for growth. The evaluation process is discussed in depth later in this chapter.

Advantages of Team Teaching

There are many reasons why teaching in teams is such an integral part of so many early childhood programs. The advantages are numerous:

- *Variety of adult role models.* Teachers who are male, female, disabled, young, middle-aged, older, and varying in ethnic backgrounds bring equally diverse attitudes, approaches to children, interests, skills, and knowledge to share. This teaches children to accept differences in people as they watch adults interact with others on the teaching team.
- *Support for children.* The absence of one teacher is not as disruptive when the children can count on other familiar faces. This enables children to learn to trust the teaching environment because someone they know is always there.

- *Collegiality.* Teachers can find support from one another as they share planning problems and achievements and grow in admiration and respect for one another.
- *Lightened workload.* There is a sharing of all the teaching tasks, from curriculum planning and cleanup to parent conferencing and record keeping.
- *Enriched program.* Talents and resources of the team are used to best advantage so that team members will teach to their strengths, adding richness to the program.

Challenges

Good teachers are "complicated human beings with strengths and weaknesses, talents and limitations, good days and bad days" (LeShan, 1992). They work at becoming good teachers by developing skills in interpersonal relationships with other adults, just as they promote good social relationships among the young children they teach. Most of the disadvantages of team teaching stem from communication problems among team members.

Communication problems and conflicts arise in every teaching situation. The Code of Ethical Conduct provides a road map for navigating some of the issues that create conflicts. The Code outlines clear expectations for professional and collegial behavior among staff members and employers. Review them in Appendix A.

The previous section, "The Beginnings of Professionalism," is particularly useful for team situations. Teachers new to the team-teaching process will want to discuss it with other team members ranging from health care to education to poverty to professional quality, staff, and wages. It is up to the early childhood professional to give voice to the issues concerning our young children and to educate the public about those issues. Public policy makers on the local, state, and national level need to hear from those who can speak out for those who cannot. Part of the role of a professional early childhood educator is to join the voices that support educational and teaching reforms. Volunteer with a local organization and make a difference in the lives of teachers and caregivers.

Evaluating Teachers: A Key to Quality

Teachers are the single most important factor in determining program quality. What makes "the effective teacher" has no one simple answer. Earlier sections in this chapter describe important attributes of the teacher.

How these can be assessed is complicated, but assessing them is necessary to guide teachers toward more effective teaching in their work with children, co-workers, parents, and administrators.

Think of teachers as conductors of a symphony orchestra. They do not compose the music. They do not design or build the instruments, nor do they decide which ones will be played in the orchestra pit. They may even have limited choice of the music that will be played. Yet it is their job to lead a group of musicians through a medley of songs, bringing out the best in each musician, all under the intense scrutiny of a critical audience. Teachers must do this with care and expertise under the watchful eyes of parents and families, boards, supervisors, and funding agencies. Through the process of evaluation, the teacher as conductor sets and achieves the goals to create a harmonious effect. Reread the introduction to evaluation in Chapter 2, on pages 63–65, for other insights.

© Cengage Learning

Evaluations are a professional responsibility that help to clarify job performance, professional growth, and challenges.

Why Evaluate?

Most early childhood programs require an annual assessment of the teaching staff. An evaluation is not only a professional expectation, but it also reflects the NAEYC's Standards for a well-prepared early childhood professional. Evaluations support a teacher's life-long learning and ability to become reflective about their teaching experiences.

There are six reasons that an evaluation process is important:

1. to describe job responsibilities
2. to monitor job effectiveness
3. to clarify strengths and challenges
4. to create a plan for professional development
5. to determine employment
6. to meet accreditation requirements

To Describe Job Responsibilities

It is essential for teachers to understand their job to do it well. A good job description outlines what is expected. One purpose of an evaluation is to see how those expectations are being met.

In an infant and toddler center, for example, teachers try to help children learn to separate comfortably from their parents. Evaluation in this setting could focus on the exact skills needed to implement this goal, such as how a teacher helps a parent separate from a young child, what environmental cues are used, how the child is comforted, and what teaching strategies were or were not successful.

Evaluation for specifying job responsibilities is a part of one's professional self-definition, as well as a clarification of actual duties. Studying ourselves helps us know who we are and what we do. Assessing job responsibilities aids in this process.

To Monitor Job Effectiveness

Once clear guidelines are set for teaching expectations, a method is needed to monitor actual teaching. Most evaluation systems attempt to check teacher effectiveness. This process may vary from school to school. In some schools, teaching effectiveness is measured, in part, by child achievement, such as how children score on tests. Other centers may solicit parent opinion.

A teacher's co-workers may be part of an assessment team. For the most part, an evaluation for job effectiveness will include an observation of teaching time with children.

To Clarify Strengths and Challenges

Many teachers prefer an evaluation process that identifies specific areas of strength and challenges. Feedback about actual teaching and other job responsibilities is helpful to all teachers, whether beginners or experienced personnel. An assessment that offers teachers information about how to perform their job better contributes to job competence and satisfaction. By recognizing strengths, teachers receive positive feedback for high-quality work. By identifying areas of concern, they can begin to set realistic goals for improvement.

To Create a Plan for Professional Development

One function of teacher evaluation is to foster professional development. Teachers do not become "good" and then stay that way for life. Regardless of their stage of development, teachers need goals in order to continually improve.

To be effective, goal setting must be embedded in an on-going system of professional development. Caruso and Fawcett (1999) note that staff development must also be integrated with the overall goals of the center or program for which a teacher is being evaluated.

Professional development takes into consideration the various stages of expertise and development of the individuals on the staff. A career-ladder plan, adopted by NAEYC in 1993, takes into account the diversity of education, training, and experience of early childhood professionals. The ladder sets out steps individuals can take to assume more responsibility as they become more qualified and prepared. This lattice framework promotes a system of professional development that can motivate early childhood professionals at all levels toward professional growth (Willer, 1994).

To Determine Employment

An evaluation can also be used to decide whether teachers should be retained, promoted, or released. Assessment procedures are an administrator's most valuable tools in making that decision. A clear and effective evaluation tool enables the administrator to monitor performance and target specific areas for improvement. The administrator then has a fair and equitable way to determine the promotional status of each employee.

To Meet Accreditation Requirements

Many programs seek accreditation by organizations whose standards they embrace. NAEYC is the leading accrediting body for early childhood programs through its National Academy of Early Childhood Programs. The self-study aspect of the accreditation process includes a teacher's self-assessment, the director's assessment of the teaching staff, and the teacher's assessment of the director. The criteria in the self-study provide the standards by which these evaluations are made, providing concrete ways to measure quality.

Components of an Effective Evaluation

An effective evaluation process helps to challenge methods and assumptions and to identify ways to provide support for growth and change. Certain elements are common to all evaluations. The following criteria serve as a guideline to an effective evaluation process:

- *Select who and what will be evaluated.* Decide how often and under what circumstances the evaluation will take place.
- *Have a clear purpose or motive.* Know the reasons for making an evaluation and consider who and what will benefit from the process. State what you expect to gain from it.
- *Decide how the data will be collected.* Have a good understanding of the process or format that will be used. Be clear about who will collect the data and make the report. Some sample evaluations are found in this chapter.
- *Know what use will be made of the evaluation.* Be aware of what decisions will be made from the results. Know who receives this information and how they will interpret it.
- *State goals clearly.* Evaluators should make sure goals and objectives are outlined in ways that can be measured and observed easily and state behavioral goals in terms of what the person will do. The person being evaluated should be equally clear in his or her responses to the evaluation instrument(s).
- *Make a plan.* Be prepared to act. Use the results to motivate people to put into action what they have learned from the evaluation. Set new goals based on the evaluation. Set up a timetable to check progress on a regular basis.

The important point to remember is that evaluation should be a continuous process, for without follow-through, long-lasting improvement is unlikely to occur. Take a look at Figure 5-8 to see how a **feedback loop** works for an evaluation process.

Issues in Teacher Evaluations

How to evaluate is an important issue in teacher assessment. A system for evaluating employees can be one of trust and mutual respect or of anxiety and tension. The method often determines how successful the entire evaluation will be.

Preliminary Steps

To begin with, a school follows the same guidelines for developing a teacher evaluation as for child assessment (see Chapter 6). That is, the process includes determining a purpose, establishing who will collect the data and how, and clarifying how the evaluation will be used. In the assessment of teachers, the important components are: purpose (as described in Chapter 2), evaluators, process, and follow-through.

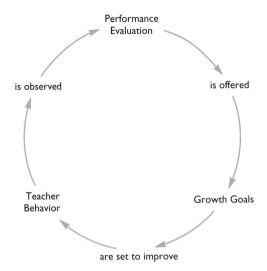

Performance Evaluation

is observed → is offered

Teacher Behavior → Growth Goals

are set to improve

FIGURE 5-8 A feedback loop is a continuous cycle in which teacher behavior is observed for a performance evaluation. The evaluation is offered through growth goals, which are set in order to affect teacher behavior. Thus, the circle is continuous, with each part helping the next.

Evaluators

Several models have been developed around the issue of who will assess teacher performance.

Self-Evaluation. Self-assessment is used in the Child Development Associate's evaluation system for these reasons (Ward & CDA staff, 1976):

- The candidate is a valid source of information for use in assessment. Certain information is available only from the candidate's perspective.
- The candidate is able to clarify information on his or her performance, thereby adding to the assessment team's evidence for a valid decision.
- The candidate is better able to identify strengths and weaknesses and to receive recommendations for continued professional growth.

Figure 5-9 is an example of a staff evaluation form, which can also be used as a self-assessment tool. A less formal technique is to ask questions about yourself and your job, such as:

- How do I approach parent/family relationships?
- Have my guidance techniques been working well?
- Am I in a comfortable working relationship with my colleagues?
- What should be my next professional goals?
- How do I help children learn?

A teacher's self-evaluation provides an opportunity to improve his or her effectiveness with children.

- Do I have a supportive relationship with my supervisor?

The answers to these few questions can provide a solid base for discussion between teacher and supervisor or assessment team.

One drawback of self-assessment is its subjectivity. We see ourselves too closely and too personally to be able to be entirely objective about our teaching. Therefore, self-assessment must be accompanied by other evaluating feedback.

Supervisory Evaluation. Job performance is an administrator's responsibility; therefore, teachers can expect their supervisor, director, or head teacher to be involved in their evaluation. Supervisors often use a single form combining a teacher's self-assessment and the supervisor's evaluation, such as Figure 5-9. This kind of form simplifies the paperwork and assures both teacher and supervisor that both are using the same criteria for evaluation. Caruso and Fawcett (1999) suggest a variety of formats used for evaluations; observations, conferences, videotapes, reports, portfolios, and storytelling are some of the ways to accomplish an assessment.

When selecting an appropriate format or tool, look for a balance in the categories on which a teacher is being evaluated. These usually include some of the following:

- knowledge and application of child development principles
- planning
- behavior management
- interactions with children

DAP

	C (90–100%)	F (60–89%)	O (30–59%)	N (0–29%)
General Work Habits				
1. Arrives on time				
2. Reliable in attendance; gives ample notice for absences				
3. Responsible in job duties				
4. Alert in health and safety matters				
5. Follows the center's philosophy				
6. Open to new ideas				
7. Flexible with assignments and schedule				
8. Comes to work with a positive attitude				
9. Looks for ways to improve the program				
10. Remains calm in a tense situation				
11. Completes required written communication on time				
Professional Development, Attitude, and Efforts				
1. Takes job seriously and seeks to improve skills				
2. Participates in workshops, classes, groups				
3. Reads and discusses distributed handouts				
4. Is self-reflective with goals for ongoing development				
Attitude and Skills with Children				
1. Friendly, warm, and affectionate				
2. Bends low for child level interactions				
3. Uses a modulated, appropriate voice				
4. Knows and shows respect for individuals				
5. Is aware of development levels/changes				
6. Encourages independence/self-help				
7. Promotes self-esteem in communication				
8. Limits interventions in problem solving				
9. Avoids stereotyping and labeling				
10. Reinforces positive behavior				
11. Minimal use of time out				
12. Regularly records observations of children				
Attitude and Skills with Parents				
1. Available to parents and approachable				
2. Listens and responds well to parents				
3. Is tactful with negative information				
4. Maintains confidentiality				
5. Seeks a partnership with parents				
6. Regularly communicates with parents				
7. Conducts parent conferences on schedule				
Attitude and Skills with Class				
1. Creates an inviting learning environment				
2. Provides developmentally appropriate activities				
3. Develops plans from observation and portfolio entries				
4. Provides materials for all curriculum components				
5. Provides an appropriate role model				
6. Anticipates problems and redirects				
7. Is flexible and responsive to child's interests				
8. Is prepared for day's activities				
9. Handles transitions well				
Attitude and Skills with Co-Workers				
1. Is friendly and respectful with others				
2. Strives to assume a fair share of work				
3. Offers and shares ideas and materials				
4. Communicates directly and avoids gossip				
5. Approaches criticism with learning attitude				
6. Looks for ways to be helpful				

Comments:

FIGURE 5-9 The quality and effectiveness of teaching is affected by the quality and effectiveness of the evaluation process. This form is useful for a self-evaluation and supervisory evaluation. (From *The Visionary Director: A Handbook for Dreaming, Organizing, and Improving Your Center*, by Margie Carter and Deb Curtis, pp. 266–277. Copyright © 1998 by Margie Carter and Deb Curtis. Reprinted with permission from Redleaf Press, St. Paul, Minnesota, www.redleafpress.org.

- interactions with adults (other teachers, administrators, and parents)
- interpersonal communication
- professionalism
- dependency
- cultural sensitivity
- respect for individual differences in adults and children
- preparing and maintaining appropriate learning environments
- health and safety
- personal qualities

Peer Evaluation. Evaluation by others associated with the teachers is a welcome addition to the evaluation process. Often a system includes more than a teacher's supervisor. Possible combinations are:

- Teacher (self-evaluation) and supervisor
- Teacher, supervisor, and parent
- Teacher, supervisor, and another team member (teacher, aide, student teacher)

A team evaluation is a more collaborative approach. More information is collected on the teacher's performance. A team approach may be more valid and balanced because a decision about teaching will be made by consensus and discussion rather than individual, perhaps arbitrary, methods. Figure 5-10 is an example of a peer observation form that might be used.

Peer Observation

Name of colleague observed _____ Date _____

As you observe, please note comments about the following aspects of the classroom environment: interactions between teacher and children; interactions between the teacher and other co-workers or volunteers; interactions between the teacher and parents; the physical arrangement of space; the curriculum; and health, nutrition, and safety aspects of the classroom.

Aspects of this classroom I was impressed with include...

1. _____

_____

2. _____

_____

3. _____

_____

Aspects of this classroom that might be improved include...

1. _____

_____

2. _____

_____

3. _____

_____

Signed _____

FIGURE 5-10 An evaluation will have a wider perspective when it comes from more than one viewpoint. (Adapted from *Blueprint for Action: Achieving Center-Based Change through Staff Development,* by P. J. Bloom, © 2005 New Horizons.)

Peer or team evaluation does have its disadvantages, however. It is a time-consuming process because more than one person is asked to evaluate a teacher. Feedback may be contradictory; what one evaluator sees as a strength, another may view as a shortcoming. The system can be complicated to implement (i.e., finding time for teachers to evaluate another team member, finding funds to bring in substitutes, and confidentiality issues when a parent is part of the evaluation team). Clearly, a school must weigh these issues carefully as evaluation systems are devised.

A Systematic Process

Many evaluations are based on observable, specific information about a teacher's activities and responsibilities. This is known as a **performance-based assessment.** Figure 5-11 is an example of performance-based assessment in regard to a teacher's work with children. When paired with specific goals and expectations, this system is known as **competency-based assessment.**

Competency-based assessments outline exactly what teachers must do to demonstrate their competency, or skill, in their job responsibilities. Criteria are set as a teacher begins working. Areas are targeted that pinpoint what knowledge, skills, and behaviors the teacher must acquire.

The evaluation tools or format determine how valid the information gathered will be. Informal techniques may result in unreliable conclusions. A process that is formalized and systematic, related to goal setting and professional development, has a greater chance of success. While it is important to select an appropriate method and assessment tool, keep in mind that it is the process through which the evaluation is conducted that matters most.

Portfolio-based assessments are becoming a popular tool for helping teachers make sense of the experiences that help them become better teachers. A **portfolio** is not an assessment tool in and of itself. It is the display or collection system used to demonstrate evidence of professional growth. Folders, boxes, files, and binders are all used to house the collection of data. It is an intentional compilation of materials and resources collected over a period of time that provides evidence for others to review. Campbell, Cignetti, Melenyzer, Nettles, and Wyman (1997) define a portfolio as "an organized, goal-driven documentation of your professional growth and achieved competence in the complex act called teaching."

Documentation is systematic and an important part of creating the portfolio. Concrete evidence of how a teacher understands and implements the best teaching practices, translates theory into action, and demonstrates knowledge of the nature of teaching is the ultimate goal.

A portfolio is ever changing and reflects the individuality of the teacher by virtue of what it contains. As an assessment tool, the portfolio is useful in many ways. It helps teachers clarify their values, keeps them focused on the goals they have set, provides an avenue for self-

Performance-Based Assessment

Teacher Goal	Example
To help each child develop a positive self-concept	I greet each child with a smile and a personal comment.
To help each child develop socially, emotionally, cognitively, and physically	I have goals for each child in each developmental area, fall and spring.
To help provide many opportunities for each child to be successful	My parent conference sheets have examples; for instance, Charlie didn't want to come to group time, so I had him pick the story and help me read it—he comes every day now!
To encourage creativity, questioning, and problem solving	This is my weak point. I tend to talk too much and tell them what to do.
To foster enjoyment for learning in each child	I do great group times and give everyone turns.
To facilitate children's development of a healthy identity and inclusive social skills	I participated in our center's self-study and am taking an anti-bias curriculum class.

FIGURE 5-11 Performance-based assessment ties the goals of the program to the teacher's work. This example asks the teacher to do a self-assessment; a director, parent, or peer could observe and make a second assessment.

reflection, and demonstrates growth. By what is included and what is omitted, a portfolio shows an evaluator tangible evidence of a teacher's abilities, provides a framework for setting new goals, and gives a more personal sense of the teacher's commitment and professionalism. Figure 5-12 lists some of the items often included in a teacher's portfolio.

Cultural Awareness and Sensitivity

Cultural awareness has an effect on how a teacher relates to children, and this needs to be taken into consideration when assessing a teacher's performance. Insight about a teacher's social and cultural background is particularly useful if the evaluator is a member of the majority population and the teacher is not.

There are five specific cultural factors that can affect communication, particularly where supervisors and staff members are concerned (Caruso and Fawcett, 1999). They are:

1. *Time sense.* Being on time and doing tasks in a timely fashion are high priorities for many people raised in mainstream American culture. Each culture has its own concept of time, and the teacher who is always late for meetings may be reflecting the cultural context in which he or she was raised.

2. *Space.* How close you get to someone while talking is also a function of cultural context. In some cultures, invading another's personal space (the "com-fort zone") is considered rude. If a teacher backs away, she may be considered cold and unfriendly. If the teacher is the one getting too close, he may be seen as forward and aggressive. These perceptions may be innocent reactions based on their cultural sensibilities and should be viewed in that light.

3. *Verbal and nonverbal communication.* Eye contact is seen in some cultures to be disrespectful if prolonged; to others it may be a sign of interest and attentiveness. Other facial expressions, such as smiling (or not), gestures, and body language, communicate different things from culture to culture. Silence, too, is used in different cultures in a variety of ways with an assortment of meanings. Speaking loudly may be a cultural norm or it may communicate anger and accusations. Teachers and their supervisors need to learn each other's communication styles and be particularly aware of those that are culture-bound.

4. *Values.* Our values drive our behavior and responses. If a teacher comes from a background that emphasizes dependency in the early years and the school philosophy is one that encourages early independence, a cultural conflict can erupt and affect a teacher's evaluation adversely. Supervisors and teachers must understand each other's value system and what causes each of them to make certain decisions.

5. *Concepts of authority.* The way people deal with authority is also culture-specific. Early childhood professionals who supervise and evaluate staff members from cultures different than their own need to be aware of what cultural expectations surround the issue of authority. In some instances, authority figures are often male, and females are raised not to question authority. A correct answer may be more culturally appropriate than expressing one's true feelings or ideas. The supervisor can avoid misunderstandings if he or she is aware that the teacher is used to an authoritarian style of leadership from supervisors and thus gear the conversation accordingly.

The evaluator has a rare opportunity to create bridges of understanding between and among many cultures. By seeing the connection "between their own cultural knowledge and their behavior as professionals in an early childhood setting," children can become "cultural brokers," notes Jones (1993). Within their school community, they can create a two-way interchange about culturally relevant issues with children, parents, and other teachers.

What's in a Portfolio?

Materials developed by the teacher, such as, but not limited to:

A videotape of the teacher in the classroom

Lesson plans and evaluation of a specific activity

Samples of materials and resources developed for the classroom

Articles written for parents or newsletters

Journal of teaching experiences

Photos of field trips or projects

Self-reflective notes on teaching

Professional articles

Other _____

FIGURE 5-12 A portfolio is a personalized assessment tool and contains a variety of materials and resources that reflect a teacher's professional growth. Some centers have their own criteria for a portfolio.

Follow-Through

What follows an evaluation is critical to the overall success of an evaluation system. For instance, after gathering information for an evaluation session, a supervisor and teacher might discuss and evaluate concrete examples and live performance. Together they can establish goals for changing what may be ineffective or problematic.

Follow-through is the final part of the continuous feedback loop in a good evaluation system. Data are collected on teacher behavior and given to the teacher in person. Goals are set to improve teaching. A follow-up check is done periodically to see how—and if—goals are being met. Teaching improves as recommendations are put into practice.

Follow-through makes the feedback loop complete as information about improvement is communicated. Refer back to Figure 5-6, which illustrates this cycle.

Techniques for Productive Evaluation Sessions

Evaluations take hard work, time, and dedication to a higher quality of teaching. It is also a shared responsibility. The supervisor must be explicit about a teacher's performance and be able to identify for the teacher what is effective and what is problematic.

Teachers themselves must value the process and understand its implications for their professional growth. The benefits of productive evaluation sessions are clear. They range from improved self-esteem, higher levels of job effectiveness, and less absenteeism and turnover to assessment-related salary raises and other job benefits. Certain techniques help make evaluation sessions productive for teachers:

1. Become involved from the beginning as the evaluation procedure is established. Know what is expected and how you will be evaluated.
2. Set a specific meeting time for your evaluation. Ask your supervisor for a time that works for you both.
3. Set some goals for yourself before meeting with your supervisor. If you know what you want to work on, you are more likely to get help achieving your goals.
4. Develop a plan for action. Be prepared to set a timeline for when and how you will work on your goals.
5. Establish a feedback loop (see Figure 5-6). Make a follow-up date, and make copies of your goal sheet for both you and your supervisor.
6. Approach the meeting with a sense of trust, respect, and openness. Planning ahead promotes these attitudes.

Better teaching and continued professional growth are the results of a good evaluation process. No two teachers are identical, so each evaluation must be interpreted in terms of the behavior and stage of development of the individual person. As teachers become more effective in their work with children, the quality of the entire program is improved.

The Beginning Teacher

Beginning teachers of young children cannot expect to successfully blend all of the many facets of teaching at once. However, beginning teachers must be committed to the time and energy needed to become proficient at their craft.

Beginning teaching can be a great deal of fun, as well as a unique learning experience. Textbook theories come alive as children live out child development concepts. New teachers expect to learn about individual child growth and development; many are surprised to discover that they also learn how children function in groups and with adults. Working with an experienced teacher who models highly polished skills is an important part of the new teacher's experience.

Yet we know that first-time teaching is not always fun. It is a time for intensive self-searching and self-revelations. Many teachers' own school experiences loom before them and undermine their confidence. There may still be doubts about becoming a teacher at all. It is uncomfortable to feel judged and criticized by others. This is a time of anxiety for most beginning teachers. But remember, even the poised, confident, and always-does-the-right-thing master teacher was once a beginner.

The Student Teacher

Many teacher-training programs require a formal period of supervised work with young children either in the college's child development center or in early childhood programs throughout the community. For students in such a program, practice teaching may be the first hands-on opportunity to work with children.

Beginnings for student teachers are just as important as they are for young children. A child's first days of school are planned very carefully; likewise, there are some strategies for easing the transition from student to student teacher. The following guidelines will help to

Through experience, teachers learn how to handle large groups of children. Learning to develop story time and reading skills is an ongoing process.

make the first days of student teaching a satisfying and positive experience:

- Contact the teacher and meet before school begins. Find out what time school begins, where the classroom is located, what the age group is, the size and makeup of the class, the daily schedule, and what hours you are expected to be on site. Ask if there are children with special needs and if there are cultural considerations of which you should be aware. Find out what is expected of you the first few days. Be sure to meet the other administrative staff of the school.
- Visit the classroom to which you are assigned to become acquainted with its layout. Tour the yard as well. Find out where the janitor's room, kitchen, nurse's office, and storeroom are located.
- Share with the master teacher any special skills or talents you may have; let the teacher help you use

these skills in new ways with young children. Let the teacher know about any other experiences with children: baby-sitting or camp counseling. Be sure to let the teacher know of any course requirements you must meet by this experience.

- Together, you, the master teacher, and your college instructor in student teaching will set goals and expectations for your student teaching experience. This will define more concretely what you would like to get out of the time you spend in the classroom, whether it is gaining experience with a group of children or learning to lead a group time by the end of the semester. By establishing common goals, the master teacher will be able to help guide a course so that these goals will be realized. An evaluation process related to those goals should be agreed on so that you will learn whether you have met the expectations of the teacher, the school, and the program.

Insights *from the field*

Teaching: A Professional Commitment *by Barbara Biglan, M.A., Ph.D.*

As early childhood educators, we play many roles. We are surrogate parents, new friends, sources of comfort and support, providers of new and exciting learning experiences, and active learners committed to professional growth. All of these roles are played by the dedicated individuals who work with young children in a variety of educational settings.

In our class, Early Childhood Curriculum, we developed metaphors to explore these diverse roles of a teacher, to gain insight into the development of professional behaviors, and to understand the meaning of commitment to the education of young children. There were common threads running through these descriptions: reflective learning, strategies for practice, and appreciating culture and diversity.

One metaphor that engaged all of us was that of the early childhood teacher as an artist. We worked as a class to add and expand the description. It became for us a way to think about our personal and collective commitment to the education of young children.

In our metaphor of teacher as artist, the canvas is the foundation knowledge required as a theoretical base for developmentally appropriate practice. The brushes are the variety of methods and strategies used to plan and implement educational activities. The composition of the work of art involves the balance of respect for each child, family, and culture, and provision of opportunities for each child to achieve the full potential of his or her unique talents in the context of a community of learners. Each artist uses color to express his or her own unique blend of talents. Bright yellows and reds express the excitement involved in new learning experiences, the blues and purples show the loving and supportive daily interactions, the earth tones provide the background of a team of colleagues with a well-grounded sense of mission, and the greens remind all of us to keep growing in knowledge and ability. The final "professional" product is a result of talent, training, experience, and evaluation.

As we grow in our professional commitment, we will each "create" many works of art. Each work of art will express our belief that all children can learn and should be treated with dignity and respect. Each work of art will represent our journey of growth and development as teachers of young children.

We hope that all who prepare to become early childhood educators will find a meaningful metaphor to guide their growth and professional commitment to teaching.

Barbara Biglan, M.A., Ph.D., has been a classroom teacher, computer coordinator, the headmistress of an independent school (pre-K–6), and a college professor. She is currently a faculty member in the Education Department at Chatham College in Pittsburgh, Pennsylvania, and the higher education project director for the Math Science Partnership of Southwest Pennsylvania, an NSF funded initiative to improve the teaching and learning of science and math K–16. She started life as an educator 40 years ago with a BS in science as a junior high school science teacher, earned a master's in Education and then a Ph.D. in Science Education K–12.

SUMMARY

Teachers of young children share with other teachers a variety of subject matter. The curriculum in the early childhood school is rich in math, science, language, social studies, geography, and the like. The format for these learning experiences is a "hands-on" approach. Teachers set out materials, equipment, and activities that invite children's interest and interaction.

Becoming a professional teacher means that there are professional guidelines and standards to follow. NAEYC's Standards for Professional Preparation serve as a challenge for what today's and tomorrow's teachers should know and be able to do. The Code of Ethical Conduct fosters professionalism throughout the field as teachers apply its ideals and principles to everyday situations.

In some areas, the early childhood teacher differs from others in the field of education. Team teaching, teacher–child interactions, small group emphasis, and adult relationships are more common in the early years than in other types of schools. The teaching role is not restricted to working just with children. Teachers must learn to interact with numerous adults—primarily parents, other teachers, and administrators. Teaching roles will vary, depending on whether you teach alone or on a team. Team teaching is common in many early childhood programs and has many advantages. By keeping in mind the 10 essentials for successful teaching, all early childhood teachers can ensure themselves of optimal working conditions in their setting.

Early childhood teachers have multiple roles. They supervise and manage the classroom, interact with children and a number of adults, and set the emotional tone. Much of what they do occurs away from children. There are meetings to attend, reports to write, parent conferences to hold, and materials to purchase. These after-hours duties add to the depth of classroom experiences the teacher provides for the children.

Ethical situations arise frequently, calling on the teacher or administrator to make difficult choices about children and their lives. A professional code of ethics sets out standards of behavior based on core values and commitments all early childhood professionals share. It can support decisions individuals have to make in the best interests of children.

A systematic teacher evaluation process that is linked to professional growth opportunities is important. The process should include a self-evaluation by the teacher who, with a supervisor, sets appropriate professional goals. An evaluation by a supervisor and goal setting that relates to the program's philosophy and mission are also part of the process. Continuing growth within the professional field includes understanding the cultural context from which teachers relate to the children, families, other staff members, and supervisors.

The student teacher gains valuable experience working directly with children under the supervision of a mature teacher. As they grow and gain confidence, teachers pass through several stages of professional development and search for ways to be more effectively challenged. As they integrate teaching style and personality, they become whole teachers.

KEY TERMS

professional standards	self-awareness	performance-based assessment
ethics	anti-bias	competency-based assessment
continuing education	team teaching	portfolio-based assessment
emotional framework	feedback loop	portfolio

REVIEW QUESTIONS

1. What do you think are the most important reasons for becoming an early childhood teacher?

2. How do the eight essential attributes for successful teaching foster a sense of professionalism?

3. How does a Code of Ethical Conduct help teachers?

4. Name four in-class and five out-of-class responsibilities in the teacher's role.

5. Give five reasons why team teaching is important in the early years.

6. Describe a good evaluation process.

7. What are some of the difficulties a beginning teacher faces?

LEARNING ACTIVITIES

1. Draw a picture of the first classroom you remember. Place furniture in it, and note where your friends sat, where you sat, and where the teacher sat. Down one side of the paper write one-word descriptions of what you felt when you were in that classroom.

2. Survey a classroom where you teach or observe. How many different cultures are represented? How does the teacher respond to the cultural diversity?

3. Have you ever had a teacher who was "different"? Describe the person. What did you like most about that teacher? What did you like least? Would you hire that teacher? Why?

4. Write your own code of ethics.

5. Read the ethical situations posed in the section, "Abiding by a Code of Ethical Conduct." Think about how you would solve them. Discuss your answers with a member of your class, a teacher, and a parent.

6. Observe a teacher working in a team situation and one who works alone in a classroom. What seem to be the advantages of each? Disadvantages? Which would you prefer for your first year of teaching? Why? Your third year? Your seventh year?

7. Do you disagree with any core values listed in the section on code of ethical conduct? What are they? How would you change them? Discuss your response with another teacher, another student, or your class instructor.

8. In small groups, discuss the popular images of teachers as reflected in current movies and literature. Is there a consensus of the portrait of teachers today? Where do early childhood professionals fit into the picture? Are issues raised about teachers being addressed anywhere? Where? How? By whom? What would you conclude about your role as a member of the teaching profession?

9. What elements would you add to Figure 5-1 on the basis of your observation of early childhood programs and teachers?

10. Try to establish goals for your own growth as a professional in the following areas:

Area	Goal	Objectives/Implementation	Timeline
Programmatic			
Administrative			
Staff Relations			
Professional Growth			

Ask your supervisor or a colleague to help you make a realistic timeline for each goal.

HELPFUL WEBSITES

Center for Child Care Workforce   http: ///www.ccw.org

Council for Professional Recognition (CDA)   http: //www.cdacouncil.org

National Association for the Education of Young Children   http: //www.naeyc.org

Association for Childhood Education International   http: //www.acei.org

Child Care Information Exchange   http: //www.ccie.com

ERIC Clearinghouse on Elementary and Early Childhood Education   http: //www.eric.ed.gov

National Black Child Development Institute   http: //www.nbcdi.org

Wheelock College Institute for Leadership and Career Initiatives   http: //www.institute.wheelock.edu

 Additional resources including the TeachSource Videos can be found on the premium website for this book. Go to **http://www.cengage.com/login** to register your access code.

REFERENCES

Bloom, P. J. (2005). *Blueprint for action: Achieving center-based change through staff development.* Lake Forest, IL: New Horizons.

Browne, K. W., & Gordon, A. M. (2009). *To teach well: An early childhood practicum guide.* Upper Saddle River, N.J.: Prentice.

Campbell, D. M., Cignetti, P. B., Melenyzer, B. J., Nettles, D. H., & Wyman, R. M. (1997). *How to develop a professional portfolio: A manual for teachers.* Boston: Allyn & Bacon.

Carter, M. (2008). Assessing quality: What are we doing? Where are we going? *Exchange,* November/December, 2008. Volume 30, Issue 6, No. 184, 32-36.

Caruso, J. J., & Fawcett, M. T. (1999). *Supervision in early childhood education: A developmental perspective.* New York: Teachers College Press.

Derman-Sparks, L., & Edwards, J. O. (2010). *Anti-bias education for young children and ourselves.* Washington, DC: National Association for Education of Young Children.

Eyer, D. (1989). Career options in early childhood education. In A. Gordon & K. W. Browne (Eds.), *Beginnings and beyond: Foundations in early childhood education.* Clifton Park, NY: Thomson Delmar Learning.

Hyson, M. (Ed.) (2003). *Preparing early childhood professionals: NAEYC standards for Programs.* Washington, DC: National Association for the Education of Young Children.

Jones, E. (Ed.) (1993). *Growing teachers: Partnerships in staff development.* Washington, DC: National Association for the Education of Young Children.

Jones, E. (1994). Breaking the ice: Confronting status differences among professions. In J. Johnson & J. B. McCracken (Eds.), *The early childhood career lattice: Perspectives on professional development.* Washington, DC: National Association for the Education of Young Children.

Jorde Bloom, P. (1988b, September). Teachers need TLC too. *Young Children.*

Katz, L. G. (1999). *Talks with teachers of young children.* Norwood, NJ: Ablex.

Katz, L. G., & Ward, E. H. (1991). *Ethical behavior in early childhood education.* (Expanded Ed.). Washington, DC: National Association for Education of Young Children.

Kipnis, K. (1987, May). How to discuss professional ethics. *Young Children,* 26-30.

Kuster, C. A. (1994). Language and cultural competence. In J. Johnson & J. B. McCracken (Eds.), *The early childhood career lattice: Perspectives on professional development.* Washington, DC: National Association for the Education of Young Children.

LeShan, E. (1992). *When your child drives you crazy.* New York: St. Martin's Press.

National Association for the Education of Young Children. (1997). *Code of ethical conduct.* Washington, DC: National Association for the Education of Young Children.

Phillips, C. B. (1994). What every early childhood professional should know. In J. Johnson & J. B. McCracken (Eds.), *The early childhood career lattice: Perspectives on professional development.* Washington, DC: National Association for the Education of Young Children.

Ramsey, P. G. (2004). *Teaching and learning in a diverse world* (3rd Ed). New York: Teachers College Press.

Smith, M. M. (1999). "Foreword" in S. Feene, & N. K. Freeman, *Ethics and the early childhood educator using the NAEYC code*. Washington, DC: National Association for the Education of Young Children.

Spodek, B. (1994). The knowledge base for baccalaureate early childhood teacher education programs. In J. Johnson and J. B. McCracken (Eds.), *The early childhood career lattice: Perspectives on professional development*. Washington, DC: National Association for the Education of Young Children.

U.S. Bureau of Labor Statistics. (2008). *Labor force characteristics by race & ethnicity, 2007*. Report # 1005. Washington, DC: U.S. Government Printing Office.

Ward, E. H., & CDA Staff. (1976, May). The Child Development Association Consortium's Assessment System. *Young Children*, 244-255.

Whitebrook, M., Sakai, L., Gerber, E., & Howes, C. (2001). *Then and now: Changes in child care staffing, 1994-2000*. Washington, DC: Center for the Child Care Workforce.

Willer, B. (Ed.). (1994). A conceptual framework for early childhood professional development: NAEYC Position Statement, adopted November 1993. In J. Johnson & J. B. McCracken (Eds.), *The early childhood career lattice: Perspectives on professional development*. Washington, DC: National Association for the Education of Young Children.

Observation and Assessment of Children

© Cengage Learning

PREVIEW QUESTIONS

- What does it mean to see children through observation?
- How can observation help us understand children?
- How can we record what we see?
- Why and how can young children's learning be assessed?

NAEYC CODE OF ETHICAL CONDUCT

These Core Values and sections from the NAEYC Code of Ethical Conduct are addressed in this chapter. As you read, note how the Core Values, Ideals, or Principles listed here apply to the topics in this chapter. (Reprinted with permission from the National Association for the Education of Young Children.)

Core Values: Helping children and adults achieve their full potential in the context of relationships that are based on trust, respect, and positive regard.

Section I:
- P-1.4. For every child we shall implement adaptations in teaching strategies, learning environment and curriculum, consult with the families and seek recommendations from appropriate specialists to maximize the potential of the child to benefit from the program.

Section II:
- I-2.5. To interpret each child's progress to parents within the framework of a developmental perspective and to help families understand and appreciate the value of developmentally appropriate early childhood practices.

Seeing Children through Observation

Children are fascinating. They are charming, needful, busy, creative, unpredictable, and emotional. At school, at home, in the grocery store, and in the park, children demonstrate a variety of behaviors. There is the happy child who toddles toward the swing. The angry, defiant child grabs a book or toy and runs away. The studious child works seriously on a puzzle.

These pictures of children working, playing, and living together flash through the mind, caught for an instant as if by a camera. Good observational skills can help teachers capture both typical and exceptional moments in a child's life. Memory leaves just the impression. Documentation with visual samples and the written word are opportunities to check impressions and opinions against the facts. In this chapter, you will learn about observing and recording the behavior of young children and how to apply these skills to assess children, to collect their work in a way that reflects each of them, and to evaluate their growth.

What Is Observation?

Teachers learn to make mental notes of the important details in each interaction:

> That's the first time I've seen Karen playing with Bryce. They are laughing together as they build with blocks.
>
> For five minutes now, Teddy has been standing on the fringes of the sand area where the toddler group is playing. He has ignored the children's smiles and refused the teacher's invitation to join in the play.
>
> Antonio stops climbing each time he reaches the top of the climbing frame. He looks quickly around and if he catches a teacher's eye, he scrambles down and runs away.

Through their behavior, these three children reveal much about their personalities. The teacher's responsibility is to notice all the clues and put them together in meaningful ways. The teacher sees the obvious clues, as well as the more subtle ones. The way observations are put together with other pertinent information becomes critical.

> Karen has been looking for a special friend. Now that she has learned some ways to approach other children that don't frighten and overwhelm them, children want to play with her.

Teddy's parents divorced two weeks ago. It appears he is just beginning to feel some of that pain and has become withdrawn at school.

At home, Antonio is expected to do things right the first time. Because climbing over the top of the frame might be tricky, he does not attempt it at all. At school, he generally attempts only what he knows he can do without making a mistake.

These simple observations, made in the midst of a busy day at school, give vital information about each child's abilities, needs, and concerns. It is a more developed picture. Children are complex human beings who respond in many ways. Teachers can observe these responses and use their skills to help each child grow and learn. The ability to observe—to "read" the child, understand a group, "see" a situation—is one of the most important and satisfying skills a teacher can have. As Curtis (2008) states:

> Learning to see children takes time and practice, both when I am with them and when I take time to reflect on my work. The extra effort is worthwhile as it is much better to share in children's insatiable curiosity, deep feelings, and pure delight than it is to be the toddler police, focusing only on fixing behaviors, teaching to outcomes, or checking boxes on official forms.

A consistent practice of observation will help teachers develop what Feeney, Christensen, and Moravcik (2001) describe as "child-sense—a feeling for how individual children and groups of children are feeling and functioning."

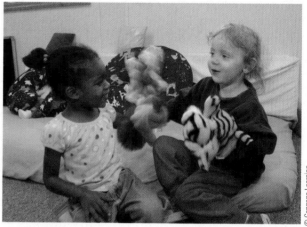

These two children are seen playing together for the first time. What can teachers learn by observing them regarding their use of materials? The way they make friends? How they solve problems?

Observation is the basis of so much of a teacher's work. It influences how a teacher sets up the environment and how and when it will be changed. It helps a teacher create the daily schedule, planning appropriate time periods for various activities. It allows the teacher to make sense of and respond well to the many interpersonal exchanges that mean so much to parents and caregivers alike. Observation also plays an important role in **assessment,** either by replacing (in the case of young children) or by supplementing standardized **evaluation** tools (for elementary-aged children). In fact, assessing children can be done only on the basis of good observations. In more reflective and less structured ways, teachers will observe how they react and feel, observing themselves and their own values. Observations are used in nearly every chapter of this book.

Observation is more than ordinary looking. It takes energy and concentration to become an accurate observer. Teachers must train themselves to record what they see on a regular basis. They need to discipline themselves to distinguish between detail and trivia and learn to spot biases that might invalidate observation. Once acquired, objective observation techniques help give a scientific and professional character to the role of early childhood educator.

Play is the work of childhood. It is the way children express themselves and how they show what they are really like. By observing play, teachers can see children as they are and as they see themselves. Much of what children do gives clues to their inner beings. The stage is set; the action begins as soon as the first child enters the room. Here, teachers can see children in action and watch for important behavior. All that is needed is to be alert to the clues and make note of them:

> Sierra, a toddler, walks up to Brooke. Sierra grabs Brooke's toy, a shape sorter, away from her. Then she begins to place shapes into the sorter. She has difficulty placing the shapes into the container. Sierra then throws the shapes, her face turns red, and she kicks the container away from her.
>
> Nico kneels on the chair placed at the puzzle table, selecting a 10-piece puzzle. He turns the puzzle upside down, allowing the pieces to fall on the table. He selects one piece at a time with his left hand and successfully puts every piece in the frame the first time. He raises both hands in the air and yells, "I did it!"

What are children telling us about themselves? Which actions are most important to note? Understanding children is difficult because so many factors influence their behavior. A child's stage of development, culture,

health, fatigue, and hunger can all make a difference in how a child behaves. Additionally, environmental factors such as the noise level, congestion, or time of day can add to the complex character of children's actions. Therefore, the teacher must make it a point to observe children at critical moments.

First, *notice the way a child begins each day.* Karen always clings to her blanket after her dad leaves her at school. Teddy bounces in each day ready to play the moment he walks in the door. Antonio says good-bye to his grandmother and then circles the room, hugging each adult before settling into an activity. These children show something about their needs. A good observer will continue to watch, taking note of these early morning scenes. One can interpret these behaviors later, seeing how they apply to each child and how behavior changes over time.

Second, *watch how children use their bodies.* The basic routines of eating, napping, toileting, and dressing show how they take care of themselves. Whether or not Nico knows how to put his jacket on by himself may indicate his skills in other areas that require initiative and self-sufficiency. It may also indicate how he is developing an awareness of himself as a separate, independent being.

Third, *focus on how children relate to other people.* Teachers see Sierra choose Brooke as a playmate even when she fights with her, but she seems to avoid the other toddlers. The observant teacher will also make note of the adults in each child's life. Who does Sierra seek for comfort? For answering questions? Who takes care of the child outside of school? Who picks the child up from school each day?

Finally, check for *what children like to do, how well they use the environment,* and *what they avoid.* Specific observations about the various areas of skill development—physical-motor, intellectual, affective—can be mirrors of growth. Teachers observe whether a child picks materials that are challenging or exhibits the tendency toward the novel or the familiar. Teddy starts each morning in the art area and then plays with puzzles before taking care of the animals. Karen prefers the blocks and dramatic play areas and lately has been spending more time in the cooking corner. Observing children at play and at work can tell us how they learn and what methods they use to gain information.

Why Observe?

Classrooms are busy places, especially for teachers who plan many activities and share in hundreds of interactions every day. There is so much that demands attention and response; at the same time, by building in systematic observation, teachers can improve their teaching, construct theory, assess children, assist families, and solve problems.

Improve Your Teaching

It is difficult to monitor our behavior while we are in the midst of working with children and time-consuming to reflect on that behavior afterward. Yet, we know that teachers who are most effective are those who are thorough in their preparation and systematic in evaluating their own work. It takes a certain level of awareness—of self, of the children, and of the environment—to monitor our own progress. This includes carefully checking what is happening, looking for feedback, and then acting on it. Teachers can do this by asking others to observe them through videotaping, by observing each other at work with the children, and by self-observation.

Bias and Objectivity. Observing children helps teachers become more objective about the children in their care. When making observational notes, teachers look first at what the child is doing. This is different from looking at how a child ought to be doing something. The teacher becomes like a camera, recording what is seen without immediately judging it. This **objectivity** can balance the intense, personal side of teaching.

Bias is inherent in all our perceptions. We must acknowledge this truth without falling prey to the notion that because our efforts will be flawed, they are worthless. Observing is not a precise or wholly objective act (see Figure 6-2). No two people will see something in identical ways. For instance, reread the segments about Sierra and Nico. One teacher sees in Sierra a child demonstrating an age-appropriate response to frustration; another sees someone who is too aggressive; a third focuses on Brooke as a victim, rushing to comfort her and ignores Sierra altogether. And Nico? One teacher sees a 5-year-old boy who is flaunting his "power" over everyone at the table, and another sees a child swept up in the pride of accomplishment. As Seefeldt and Barbour (1997) state:

> It is a fact. Observing can never be totally objective or independent of the observer. Whatever is observed passes through the filter of the observer's beliefs, biases, assumptions, history, understanding, and knowledge. The individual observer's biases, beliefs, and ideas dictate what is observed, how, where, and when. The individual always brings his or her perception and interpretation to the observation.

Teachers are influenced in their work by their own early childhood experiences. They have notions about how children learn, play, grow, or behave because of the way they were raised and trained. For example, the same behaviors might be labeled "assertive and independent" by one teacher and "bossy and uncooperative" by another. The same applies to parents. "'My husband and I just completed behavior rating scales for one of our children,' a colleague writes. 'Imagine my surprise at the disparity between our ratings on several characteristics. We live with the same child daily! How could we have made such different observations or inferences about the same child?'" (Saxton, 1998).

To pull back, take some notes, and make an observation give the teacher a chance to see the larger scene. Team teaching can help. One teacher can step in and manage a situation so another can get out of the thick of activity and observe from a distance. Teammates can help each other gain perspective by comparing notes on the class, an individual, or a time of the day. Observations can be a means of validating one teacher's point of view or changing it by checking out an opinion or idea through systematic observation.

Additionally, all teachers develop ideas and impressions about children when they spend time with them. Some children seem shy, some helpful, some affectionate, aggressive, cooperative, stubborn, and so on. These opinions influence the way teachers behave and interact with children. The child thought to be aggressive, for instance, is more likely to be blamed for starting the quarrel when one occurs nearby. Children who teachers consider polite are often given special consideration. Teacher bias may cause assumptions that stereotype rather than illuminate the child (or the group).

Guidelines. Three guidelines come to mind as one begins to observe, and these guidelines are illustrated in the second part of Figure 6-3:

1. *Practice "intensive waiting."* Cultivate an ability to wait and see what is really happening instead of rushing to conclusions about what it means, where such behavior comes from, or what should be done. These hurried impressions hinder a teacher's work toward understanding. Try to suspend expectations and be open to what is really happening, whether this concerns behavior, feelings, or patterns.
2. *Become "part scientist"* (Cohen, Stern, and Balaban, 1997). A good observer makes a clear distinction between fact and inference, between real behavior and an impression or conclusion drawn from it. Awareness of the difference between what actually

What we see is in the eye of the beholder. What do you behold?

A two-year-old screams "Mine!" and fends off a boy trying to grab the blanket she's holding.

You see: "She's obviously protecting her security blanket; she is standing up for herself."

*Believing in private property.

Or: "Look at that selfish child; she disturbs the group and is unkind."

*Believing in group harmony.

A four-year-old shouts at another, "No; don't knock it down; we just built it ourselves!"

You see: "He's protecting his space; he takes pride in what he creates."

*Believing in self-expression and low frustration tolerance.

Or: "He is rude; he hurts others' feelings and is unfriendly."

*Believing in group affiliation and building community.

Kindergartners are sifting and sorting rice at a sensory table.

You see: "They are learning pre-math concepts through their senses."

*Believing children learn best by doing, by using their hands.

Or: "They are playing with food, and rice is sacred."

*Believing people must take care of food and treat it with respect.

Infants sleeping in cribs in a child care center.

You see: "It is wonderful how the room is set up for quiet napping."

*Believing in children sleeping independently, on their own.

Or: "How sad that the babies are left alone like that."

*Believing in children being held, cared for always.

FIGURE 6-1 Observers watching the same scene, seeing the same behavior, think of it in very different terms. Seeing through a different pair of cultural eyes, each of us is thus affected in our reactions and assessments. Excerpted from Gonzalez-Mena, J., in *Beginnings and Beyond* (5th Ed), by A. Gordon & H. W. Browne. © 2000. Reprinted with permission of Delmar Learning, a division of Thomson Learning: www.thomsonrights.com. Fax 800-730-2215.)

Can You Spot the Bias?

Poor Observation

Julio walked over to the coat rack and dropped his sweater on the floor. He is *shy* (1) of teachers, so he didn't ask anyone to help him pick it up. He walked over to Cynthia *because she's his best friend* (2). *He wasn't nice* (3) to the other children when he started being *pushy and bossy* (4). *He wanted their attention* (5), so he *nagged* (6) them into leaving the table and going to the blocks *like four-year-old boys do* (7).

Good Observation

Emilio pulled out a puzzle from the rack with his right hand, then carried it with both hands to the table nearby. Using both hands, he methodically took each piece out of the frame and set it to his left. Sara, who had been seated across from Emilio with some table toys in front of her, reached out and pushed all the puzzle pieces onto the floor. Emilio's face reddened as he stared directly at Sara with his mouth in a taut line. His hands turned into fists, his brow furrowed, and he yelled at Sara in a forceful tone, "Stop it! I hate you!"

Analysis and Comments

1. Inference of a general characteristic.
2. Inference of a child's emotion.
3. Observer's opinion.
4. Inference with no physical evidence stated.
5. Opinion of child's motivation.
6. Observer's inference.
7. Overgeneralization; stereotyping.

Analysis and Comments

Emilio was clearly *angry* as demonstrated in his facial expressions, hand gestures, and body movements. The way a child speaks is as revealing as what a child says when one wants to determine what a child is feeling. Muscular tension is another clue to the child's emotions. But the physical attitude of the child is not enough; one must also consider the context. Just seeing a child sitting in a chair with a red face, one doesn't know if he is embarrassed, angry, feverish, or overstimulated. We need to know the events that led to this appearance. Then we can correctly assess the entire situation. By being open to what is happening without judging it first, we begin to see children more clearly.

FIGURE 6-2 Two observations. The first example contains numerous biases, which are numbered in the left column and explained in the right column. The second example has clear descriptions and is relatively free of biases.

happens and one's opinion and conclusions about those events is critical to good teaching.

3. *Engage in "slowing down"* (Jones and Reynolds, 1992) so that teachers ask themselves some of these questions as they teach:

- What is happening for this child in this play?
- What is his agenda?
- Does he have the skills and materials he needs to accomplish his intent?

No one can be free from bias, nor is that the point. The impressions and influences made can provide valuable insights into children. This can be done only with an awareness of one's own biases. Knowing personal influences and prejudices, coupled with observation and recording skills, prepares teachers to focus on actual behaviors. By separating what happens from what you *think* about it or how you *feel* about it, you are able to distinguish between fact and inference. This does not mean teachers have to become aloof; your body language can reflect both warmth and a measure of objectivity at the same time.

Construct Theory

Observations are a link between theory and practice. All teachers gain from making this connection. New teachers can see the pages of a textbook come alive as they watch a group of children. They can match what they see with what they read. By putting together psychology and medical research with in-class experiences, teachers gain a deeper understanding of the nature of children.

Early childhood education is the one level of education that systematically bases its teaching on child development. If we are to develop programs that work for young children—what they can do, how they think and communicate, and what they feel—we need to be able to apply sound child development knowledge to the classroom. Your theory and image of the child are where your teaching begins. Malaguzzi (1993) advised the teachers of Reggio Emilia:

Each one of you has inside yourself an image of the child that directs you as you begin to relate to a child. This theory within you pushes you to behave in certain ways; it orients you as you talk to the child. …We must move beyond just looking at the child to become better observers, able to penetrate into the child to understand each child's resources and potential and present state of mind. We need to compare theirs with our own in order to work well together.

Use as an Assessment Tool

Recording observations often takes the form of written or visual documentation that serve as informal ways to assess children's skills and capabilities. Assessment is a critical part of a teacher's job, and evaluating children includes observing and assessing their behavior and their development. **Authentic assessment,** done when children are in their natural setting and performing real tasks, fits best with the overall goal of developmentally appropriate practice. Portfolio use and other kinds of work-sampling systems are discussed later in this chapter.

Observation can be used as a tool for teachers to assess the accuracy of their own impressions. Comparing notes with others refines a teacher's own objective observation skills. The results lead directly into environmental design, daily scheduling, and curriculum planning as demonstrated below:

- Does the traffic flow easily or are children stuck in areas and unable to get out?
- When and where does the trouble start at clean up? Who participates or avoids it?
- Since sorting and classifying is a math concept goal for the group, what are children doing to show what they know and have yet to master?

By using observation to assess children and the program, teachers are accountable to their clients: the children, the parents, and the public. Assessment issues and early learning standards are described later in this chapter.

Assist Families

Families benefit from teacher observations. Detailed records collected over time reveal growth in many areas and can be used in school–family conferences. The teacher shares fresh, meaningful examples that demonstrate the child's growth and abilities. Families then know more about the child as a *school-person* and are reassured that the teachers value and understand their child. The child's teachers also gain a perspective when families share their personal stories and ideas about the child as a *home-person*. Problems become clearer, and plans can be made to work together. Results can be further tested through continuing observation. Chapter 8 discusses family–school relationships in detail.

Wonder Why and Solve a Problem

In the spirit of being a kind of scientist, teachers can become researchers in their own classrooms. A scientist, like a child, sees something and wonders why. This curiosity leads to thinking about the various components of a problem and looking at the parts as well as the whole. Next comes the "head-scratching" part—a time of reflection, developing hunches or intuitions about the problem, and generating alternatives. The teacher is then ready to try out an alternative, known in scientific terms as testing the hypothesis. Finally, the teacher gets results, which feeds back into rethinking the problem or celebrating the solution.

Using observation to research a problem can turn frustration into a more productive approach. For example, Curtis and Carter (2000) suggest posing children's noisy play into a research question: "How do children use sounds in their play and what might this mean?" Without extensive training, teachers can engage in a kind of scientific thinking for "action research" that is easily adaptable to teaching.

Understanding What We Observe

The goal of observing children is to understand them better. Teachers, students, and parents collect a great deal of information by watching children. Observational data help adults know children in several significant ways.

Children as Individuals

How do children spend their time at school? What activities are difficult? Who is the child's best friend? Observing is watching a child with the purpose of trying to understand that child from the inside out—to see the world from that child's viewpoint and how it is experienced. By watching individual children, teachers help them learn at their own pace, at their own rate of development, in their own time. When teachers know who each child is, they can choose activities and materials to match interests and skills. This is called **individualized curriculum:** tailoring what is taught to what a child is ready and willing to learn.

This kind of curriculum gives children educational experiences that offer **connected knowledge:** a curriculum that is real and relevant to the individual child and is part of developmentally appropriate practices (see Chapters 1, 2, 9, and 10). It is also part of a program for children with special needs; in these cases, an individualized education plan (IEP) is developed jointly by teachers, education specialists, and parents to better serve the child.

Observing helps a teacher spot a child's strengths and areas of difficulty. Once these are known, teachers plan **intervention** measures, helping to make the school experience successful for the child. The **accommodations** made on behalf of individual needs are important for all developmentally appropriate programs and crucial for children with special needs. See "What Do You Think?" and Figure 6-3.)

Dowley (not dated) suggests that an observation of a child can be made on three levels. First, a teacher tries to report exactly what the child does: Note exactly what actions the child takes. Second, express how the child seems to feel about what happened: Note facial expressions, body language, and quality of the behavior. Third, include your own interpretations: Add as a last and separate step some of your own personal responses and impressions. Figure 6-4, later in this chapter, includes this last level.

Children in General

When recording behavior, teachers see growth patterns emerge. These trends reflect the nature of human development. Both Piaget and Erikson used this technique to learn how children think and develop socially and emotionally. Gesell studied large numbers of children to get developmental **norms** of physical growth. Parten (1932) and Dawes (1934) watched hundreds of preschoolers and arrived at the definitive description of children's play patterns and quarreling behavior. For today's early childhood educator, observing children can provide the answer to these questions:

- What might you expect when a 2-year-old pours juice?
- How will the second grade class respond to a field trip?
- What kind of social play is typical for the 4-year-old?
- How does an infant move from crawling to walking upright?

Observation gives a feeling for group behavior, as well as a developmental yardstick to compare individuals within the group. Teachers determine age-appropriate expectations from this. It is important, for example, to know that most children cannot tie their own shoes at age 4 but can be expected to pull them on by themselves. A general understanding aids in planning a thoughtful and challenging curriculum. Teachers in a class of 3-year-olds, for instance, know that many children are ready for 8- to 10-piece puzzles but that the 20-piece jigsaw will most likely be dumped on the table and quickly abandoned.

Observation and Analysis

Gabriel [2.4 years]: Observations of Psychosocial Development-Temperament

I have seen patterns of quiet and timid behavior all throughout the course of my observation. I suppose that Gabriel belongs to the "slow to warm up" temperament cluster. From what I've observed, Gabriel usually withdraws from the crowd. He prefers to play alone, preferably in quiet spaces. He also likes to play with toys as if they are his own. In one situation, a fellow toddler approaches while Gabriel is playing with an abacus. The fellow toddler tries to participate and play with quiet Gabriel, but as soon as this other kid starts playing with the beads, Gabriel quickly grabs the abacus, knocks it down, picks it up, walks away, and plays it alone for himself.

Gabriel also appears "slow to adapt." When introduced in playtime situations with others, he does not respond promptly to what the others are asking him to do. His usual response would be a stare, or sometimes, no response at all. For example, two children were playing a game of filling up buckets with sand. When they saw Gabriel, one of them gave him a bucket; he held it without movement for a minute, then dropped it and wandered away. In another scenario, one of the caregivers pushed a child in a cart; Gabriel watched closely and seemed to wait for her to play with him. The caregiver, however, suggests Gabriel push the cart and play with the kid. In response, he just looks blankly, and afterwards, complies but reluctantly begins to push the cart and only while the caregiver watches.

FIGURE 6-3 Making an observation involves three levels: reporting exactly what the child does, how the child seems to feel, and your own interpretations. (Notes courtesy of M. Duraliza, 2007.)

Finally, knowledge of children in general gives teachers a solid foundation on which to base decisions about individuals. From observing many children comes an awareness of each child's progression along the developmental scale. Experienced teachers of toddlers will not put out watercolor sets, but the second grade teacher will do so routinely. Teachers learn that it is typical of 4- and 5-year-olds to exclude others from their play because they will have seen it happen countless times. The 3½-year-old who is sure she is "too little" to use the toilet will not concern the knowledgeable teacher, who knows that this is developmentally appropriate behavior. Decisions about single children come from watching and knowing many children. This understanding is a valuable asset when talking to parents.

DAP

Developmental Relationships

Observing brings about an understanding of the various developmental areas and how they are related. Development is at once specific and integrated. Children's behavior is a mix of several distinct developmental domains (see Chapters 4 and 11–14) and, at the same time, an integrated whole with parts that influence each other. When we say the *whole child*, we mean a consideration of how development works in unison.

When observing children, one must focus on the major domains of physical-motor, cognitive/language, and socio-emotional development. Thus, preschool teachers look to ascertain the language abilities of 3-year-olds and also the social skills that preschool children acquire. They need to know which self-help skills children can learn before age 6 and the expectations and experiences the children have at home. They must observe how fine motor development may interact with intellectual growth, or if gross motor skill affects successful cognitive learning. Overarching for all, teachers observe how self-concept relates to all of the other areas.

Observing helps teachers see how the pieces fit together. For instance, when given a set of blocks in various sizes, colors, and shapes, a 4-year-old will have no difficulty finding the red ones or square ones, but (s)he may be puzzled when asked to find those that are both red and square. No wonder that same child has difficulty understanding that someone can be their best friend and someone else's at the same time.

Practiced observation will show that a child's skills are multiple and varied and have only limited connection to age. Karen has the physical coordination of a 4½-year-old, the language skills of a 6-year-old, and the social skills of a 2-year-old—all bound up in a body that just turned 3. Sharing the picture of this whole child between parents and teachers can be helpful to both.

Influences on Behavior

Careful observation gives us insight into the influences and dynamics of behavior:

> Boaz has a hard time when he enters his child care each morning, yet he is competent and says he likes school. Close observation reveals that his favorite areas are climbing outdoor games and the sandbox. Boaz feels least successful in the construction and creative arts areas, the primary choices indoors, where his school day begins.
>
> Mari, on the other hand, starts the day happily but cries frequently throughout the day. Is there a pattern to her outbursts? Watch what happens to Mari when free play is over and group time begins. She falls apart readily when it is time to move outdoors to play, time to have snacks, time to nap, and so on.

The environment influences both these children. The classroom arrangement and daily schedule impact children's behavior, because children are directly affected by the restraints imposed by their activities and their time. Boaz feels unsure of himself in those activities that are offered as he starts his day. Seeing only these choices as he enters the room causes him discomfort, which he shows by crying and clinging to his dad. By adding something he enjoys, such as a sand table indoors, the teacher changes the physical environment to be more appealing and positive. Boaz's difficulties in saying goodbye disappear as he finds he can be successful and comfortable at the beginning of his day.

The cause of Mari's problem is more difficult to detect. The physical environment seems to interest and appeal to her. On closer observation, her crying and her disruptive behavior appear to happen just at the point of change, regardless of the activities before or afterward. It is the time aspect of the environment that causes diffi-

---

DAP The methods of assessment are appropriate to the developmental status and experiences of young children, and they recognize individual variation in learners and allow children to demonstrate their competence in different ways. Methods appropriate to the classroom assessment of young children, therefore, include results of teachers' observations of children, clinical interviews, collections of children's work samples, and their performance on authentic activities.

culty for her. The teacher makes a special effort to signal upcoming transitions and to involve her in bringing them about. Telling Mari, "Five more minutes until naptime" or "After you wash your hands, go to the snack table" gives her the clues she needs to anticipate the process of change. Asking her to announce clean up time to the class lets her be in control of that transition.

Adult behavior affects and influences children. Kindergartner Annika has days of intense activity and involvement with materials; on other days she appears sluggish and uninterested. After a week of observation, teachers find a direct correlation with the presence of Chip, the student teacher. On his participation days, Annika calls out to him to see her artwork and watch her various accomplishments; when Chip is absent, Annika's activity level falls. Once a pattern is noticed, the teacher acts on these observations. Chip offers Annika ideas for activities she could work on to show him when he returns to class. When he is absent, the teacher lets her write him a note or draw him a picture and then reminds Annika of the plan and gets her started.

Children also influence one another in powerful ways. Anyone who has worked with toddlers knows how attractive a toy becomes to a child once another has it. The first grader who suddenly dislikes school may be feeling left out of a friendship group. Teachers need to carefully observe the social dynamics of the class as they seek to understand and figure out how to handle problem situations.

Understanding of Self

Observing children can be a key to understanding ourselves. People who develop observational skills notice human behavior more accurately. They become skilled at seeing small but important facets of human personality. They learn to differentiate between what is fact and what is inference. This increases an awareness of self as a teacher and how one's biases affect perceptions about children. Teachers who become keen observers of children apply these skills to themselves. As Feeney and colleagues (2008) note:

> In a less structured but no less important way, you also observe yourself, your values, your relationships, and your own feelings and reactions. When you apply what you know about observation to yourself, you gain greater self-awareness. It is difficult to be objective about yourself, but as you watch your own behavior and interactions you can learn more about how you feel and respond in various situations and realize the impact of your behavior on others.

The values and benefits of observation are long-lasting. Only by practicing observations—what it takes to look, to see, to become more sensitive—will teachers be able to record children's behavior fully and vividly, capturing the unique qualities, culture and personality of each child. The challenge of observation is high, but the benefits are well worth the effort.

Recording What We See

Once teachers and students understand why observing is important, they must then learn how to record what they see. Although children are constantly under the teacher's eyes, so much happens so fast that critical events are lost in the daily routine of classrooms. Systematic observations aid in recording events and help teachers make sense of them.

In recording what you observe, you need to learn how to look and to learn the language of recording. These are the "nuts and bolts" of observing and assessment. Learning to look, however, requires a certain willingness to become aware and to do more than simply watch. Although it is true that teachers rarely have the luxury of observing uninterrupted for long periods of time, they can often plan shorter segments. Practice by paying attention to the content of children's play during free periods—theirs and yours.

© Cengage Learning

Learning to look requires a certain awareness so that the teacher does more than simply watch or become completely involved in an activity.

Next, try your hand at jotting some notes about that play. It is easy to get discouraged, especially if you are unaccustomed to writing. The language of recording gets easier as you practice finding synonyms for common words. For instance, children are active creatures—how many ways do they run? They may gallop, dart, whirl, saunter, skip, or hop. Or think of the various ways children talk to you: they shriek, whisper, whine, shout, demand, whimper, lisp, or roar. Once you have a certain mastery of the language (and be sure to record what you see in the language that comes easiest to you), describing the important nuances of children's behavior will become easier. For an example of such descriptions, look at Figure 6-6.

Common Elements of Observations

The key ingredients in all types of observations used in recording children's behavior are (1) defining and describing the behaviors and (2) repeating the observation in terms of several factors such as time, number of children, or activities. All observational systems have certain elements in common:

Focus

- What do you want to know?
- Whom/what do you want to observe? Child? Teacher? Environment? Group?
- What aspects of behavior do you want to know about? Motor skills? Social development? Problem solving?
- What is your purpose? Study the environment? Observe the daily schedule? Evaluate a child's skills? Deal with negative behavior? Analyze transitions?

System

- What will you do?
- How will you define the terms?
- How will you record the information you need? How detailed will your record be? Will you need units of measure? What kind?
- For how long will you record?

Tools

- What will you need for your observations?
- How will you record what you want to know?
- Environment
- Where will you watch? Classroom? Yard? Home?
- What restraints are inherent in the setting?

In particular, the tools for observation and documentation are crucial, reminds MacDonald (2006), "because

you will miss everything that is happening if you have to scramble to find what you need to record what is right in front of you." Technology has brought new tools into the recording aspect of observation. MacDonald suggests the following list:

Pencil and paper, clipboards
Recorders with batteries
Camera with film (or digital camera with memory cards)
Video camera
Computer or laptop

Using these building blocks of observational systems, teachers seek a method that yields a collection of observable data that helps them focus more clearly on a child or situation.

Four major methods of observing and two additional information-gathering techniques will be discussed. They are:

1. Narratives
2. Samplings
3. Ratings
4. Modified child study techniques

Types of Observations

There are several types of observations you can conduct, depending on the situation or purpose you are trying to achieve. Several of the most common ones are described in this section.

Narratives

At once the most valuable and most difficult of records, **narratives** are attempts to record nearly everything that happens. In the case of a young child, this means all that the child does, says, gestures, appears to think about and seems to feel. Narratives maintain a **running record** of the excitement and tension of the interaction while remaining an accurate, objective account of the events and behavior. Narratives are an attempt to actually recreate the scene by recording it in thorough and vivid language. Observers put into words what they see, hear, and know about an event or a person. The result is a full and dynamic report.

Running records and narratives are the oldest and often most informative kind of report. Historically, as Arnold Gesell reported (see Chapters 1 and 3), they were used to set basic developmental norms. They are a standard technique in anthropology and the biologic sciences. Irwin and Bushnell (1980) provide a detailed historical background that traces the narrative back to Pestalozzi (1700s) and Darwin (1800s). Jean Piaget watched and recorded in minute detail his own children's growth. His observations resulted in a full report on children's thought processes and development of intelligence. Baby biographies, narratives written by parents, were some of the first methods used in child study and reached their peak of popularity in the early 1900s.

Diary descriptions are another form of narrative. Just as the term implies, it is, in diary form, a consecutive record of everything children do and say and how they do it. The process is a natural one. In the classroom, this means describing every action observed within a given time period. It might be a five minute period during free play to watch and record what one child does. The child who is a loner, the child who is a wanderer, and the child who is aggressive are prime candidates for a diary description. Another way to use this type of running record is to watch an area of the yard or room, then to record who is there and how they are using the materials.

Specimen descriptions, a modified version of a running record as it is often called in research, are a more common form of the narrative. The procedure is to take on-the-spot notes of a specific child each day. This task lends itself easily to most early childhood settings. The teachers carry with them a small notebook and pencil,

tucked in a pocket. They jot down whatever seems important or noteworthy during the day. These anecdotal notes are the most familiar form of recording observations (see Figure 6-4). They often focus on one item at a time:

- A part of the environment—how is the science area used?
- A particular time of day—what happens right after nap?
- A specific child—why is a child hitting others?

This system may be even less structured, with all the teachers taking "on-the-hoof" notes as daily incidents occur. These notes then become a rich source of information for report writing and parent conferences.

Logs or **journals** are the final forms of the narrative. Teachers write in details about each child or a critical incident. Because this is time-consuming and needs to be done without interruption, it helps to write immediately after the program is over. Sometimes teaching teams organize themselves to enable one member of the staff to observe and record in the journal during class time. The important point is that children's behavior is recorded either while it is happening or soon afterward.

The challenging part of this recording technique, the narrative, is to have enough detail so the reader will be able to picture whole situations later. Using language as

The Child Alone

Unoccupied Behavior. SH slowly walks from the classroom to the outside play area, looking up each time one of the children swishes by. SH stops when reaching the table and benches and begins pulling the string on the sweatshirt. Still standing SH looks around the yard for a minute, then wanders slowly over to the seesaw. Leaning against it, SH touches the seesaw gingerly, then trails both hands over it while looking out into the yard. (Interpretive comments: This unoccupied behavior is probably due to two reasons: SH is overweight and has limited language skills compared with the other children. Pulling at the sweatshirt string is something to do to pass the time since the overweight body is awkward and not especially skillful.)

Onlooker Behavior. J is standing next to the slide watching her classmates using this piece of equipment. She looks up and says, "Hi." Her eyes open wider as she watches the children go down the slide. P calls to J to join them but J shakes her head "no." (Interpretive comments: J is interested in the slide but is reluctant to use it. She has a concerned look on her face when the others slide down; it seems too much of a challenge for J.)

Solitary Play. L comes running into the yard holding two paintbrushes and a bucket filled with water. He stops about three feet away from a group of children playing with cars, trucks, and buses in the sandbox and sits down. He drops the brushes into the bucket and laughs when the water splashes his face. He begins swishing the water around with the brushes and then starts wiggling his fingers in it. (Interpretive comments: L is very energetic and seems to thoroughly enjoy his outside playtime with water. He adds creative touches to his pleasurable experience.)

FIGURE 6-4 The narrative form of observation gives a rich sample of children's behavior; even though it risks teacher bias, it still records valuable information.

a descriptive tool requires a large vocabulary and skillful recorder. Whatever notes the teachers use, however brief, need to be both clear and accurate. Figure 6-4 is an example of the narrative type of observation.

At the same time teachers are recording in a graphic way, they need to be aware of the personal biases that can influence observations. When we look at children, what we see is in part a result of our personal experiences, the theories we hold, and the assumptions we make. Teaching is an intensely personal activity, and what the children look like, do, and say may arouse strong feelings and reactions. Figure 6-2 compares two observations to illustrate this point. By becoming aware of our biases and assumptions, we can become more accurate and objective in our work as teachers.

There are many advantages to this type of observation. Narratives are rich in information, provide detailed behavioral accounts, and are relatively easy to record. With a minimum of equipment and training, teachers can learn to take notes on what children do and say. To write down everything is impossible, so some selection is necessary. These "judgment calls" can warp the narrative. The main disadvantages of narratives are the time they can take, the language and the vocabulary that must be used, and the biases the recorder may have. Even though the narrative remains one of the most widely used and effective methods of observing young children today, many teachers prefer more structured procedures. These more definite, more precise techniques still involve some personal interpretation, but the area of individual judgment is diminished. The observational techniques discussed in the following sections also tend to be less time-consuming than the narrative.

Samplings

Sampling methods examine specific types of behavior and divide the observation into measurable units. Two types of this observational method are time sampling and event sampling.

A **time sampling** is an observation of what happens within a given period of time. Time sampling appears to have originated with research in child development. It has been used to record autonomy, dependency, task persistence, aggression, and social involvement. Developed as an observational strategy in laboratory schools in the 1920s, time sampling was used to collect data on large numbers of children and to get a sense of normative behaviors for particular age groups or sexes. It has been used to study play patterns and to record nervous habits of school children, such as nail biting and hair twisting (Irwin & Bushnell, 1980). The definitive study using

time sampling is Mildred Parten's observation in the 1930s of children's play. The codes developed in this study have become classic play patterns: solitary, parallel, associative, and cooperative play. These codes are used throughout this text (see Chapters 3, 10, and 14), as well as in the professional field to describe the interactions of children.

In a time sample, behavior is recorded at regular time intervals. To use this method, one needs to sample what occurs fairly frequently. It makes sense to choose those behaviors that might occur, say, at least once every 10 minutes. Figure 6-5 demonstrates a time-sampling procedure.

Time sampling has its own advantages and disadvantages. The process itself helps teachers define exactly what it is they want to observe. Certainly, it helps focus on specific behaviors and how often they occur. Time sampling is ideal for collecting information about the group as a whole. Finally, defining behaviors clearly and developing a category and coding system reduce the problem of observer bias.

Yet, by diminishing this bias, one also eliminates some of the richness and quality of information. It is difficult to get the whole picture when one divides it into artificial time units and with only a few categories. The key is to decide what it is teachers want to know and then choose the observational method that best suits those needs. When narratives or time samplings will not suffice, perhaps an event sampling will.

An **event sampling** is another sampling method. With this method, the observer defines an event, devises a system for describing and coding it, then waits for it to happen. As soon as it does, the recorder moves into action. Thus, the behavior is recorded as it occurs naturally.

The events that are chosen can be quite interesting and diverse. Consider Helen C. Dawes's classic analysis of preschool children's quarrels. Whenever a quarrel began, the observer recorded it. She recorded how long the quarrel lasted, what was happening when it started, what behaviors happened during the quarrel (including what was done and said), what the outcome was, and what happened afterward. Her format for recording included the duration (*x* number of seconds), a narrative for the situation, verbal or motor activity, and checklists for the quarrel behavior, outcome, and aftereffects (Irwin & Bushnell, 1980).

Other researchers have studied dominance and emotions. Teachers can use event sampling to look at these and other behaviors such as bossiness, avoidance of teacher requests, or withdrawal. Like time sampling,

PLAY WITH OTHERS

P = Parallel
A = Associative
C = Cooperative

Child	Time Unit												Totals		
	9:00			9:15			9:30			9:45					
	P	A	C	P	A	C	P	A	C	P	A	C	P	A	C
Jamal															
Marty															
Dahlia															
Keith															
Rosa															
Cameron															
Hannah															

FIGURE 6-5 Time sampling of play with others involves defining the behavior and making a coding sheet to tally observations.

Problems in the Classroom

1. Behavior to be observed: *children's accidents [spills, knockovers, falls].*
2. Information you want to know: *[who, where, when, causes, results].*
3. Recording sheet. *[use M–F morning for 2 weeks]*

© Cengage Learning

Time	Children	Place	Cause	Outcome
8:50	Shelley, Mike	play dough	M steps on S toes	S cries, runs to Tchr
9:33	Tasauna, Yuki	blocks	T runs through, knocks over Y's tower	Y hits T, both cry
9:56	Spencer	yard	S turns trike too sharply, falls off	S cries, wants mom
10:28	Lorena, Shelley	doll corner	L bumps table, spills pitcher that S has just set there	S cries, runs to Tchr
Totals and Analysis: 4 problems	*Shelley-2 Mike, Yuki, Tasauna, Spencer, Lorena-1*	*Inside: Pd, Bk, Dolls Outside: trike*	*Property: 1 Territory: 2 Power: 1?*	*Crying: 4 Seeking Tchr: 2 Seeking Parent: 1*

FIGURE 6-6 Event sampling can be helpful in determining how frequently a specific event takes place. For instance, sampling the number and types of accidents for a given child or time frame helps teachers see what is happening in class.

event sampling looks at a particular behavior or occurrence. But the unit is the event rather than a prescribed time interval. Here again, the behavior must be clearly defined and the recording sheet easy to use. Unlike with time sampling, the event to be recorded may occur a number of times during the observation. See Figure 6-6 for an example of event sampling.

For these reasons, event sampling is a favorite of classroom teachers. They can go about the business of teaching children until the event occurs. Then they can record the event quickly and efficiently. Prescribing the context within which the event occurs restores some of the quality often lost in time sampling. The only disadvantage is that the richness of detail of the narrative description is missing.

Rating Methods

Rating methods record either the presence or absence of a behavior or the degree to which a behavior is exhibited. The two most common forms are checklists and rating scales.

Checklists contain a great deal of information that can be recorded rapidly. A carefully planned checklist can tell a lot about one child or the entire class. The data are collected in a short period of time, usually about a week. Figure 6-7 is an example of an activity checklist. With data collected for a week, teachers have a broad picture of how these children spend their time and what activities interest them. At other times, yes/no lists are preferable.

Activity Checklist

Observer _____ Date_____ Time_____

Learning Center	Anna	Charlie	Leticia	Hiroko	Max	Josie	Totals
Indoors Science/Pets	1		1		1	1	4
Dramatic Play	1	1	1			1	4
Art	1		1				2
Blocks		1					1
Table Toys			1	1	1		3
Easels & Self Help				1			1
Music			1		1		2
Outdoors Sand/Water		1	1			1	3
Blocks				1	1		2
Wheel Toys		1			1		2
Climbers	1		1			1	3
Woodworking					1		1
Games	1						1
Totals	5	4	7	3	6	4	

FIGURE 6-7 An activity checklist. With data collected over the course of a week, teachers have a broad picture of how children spend their time at school and what activities interest them.

Checklists can vary in length and complexity depending on their functions. To develop one, teachers first determine the purpose of the observation. Next, they define what the children will do to demonstrate the behavior being observed. Finally, they design the actual checklist, one that is easy to use and simple to set aside when other duties must take precedence.

Although they are easy to record, checklists lack the richness of the more descriptive narrative. For instance, by looking at the checklist in Figure 6-7, teachers will know which activities children have chosen but cannot see how they played in each area, the time spent there, or whether and with whom they interacted. The advantages of checklists are that they can tally broad areas of information and

Yes/No Checklist

Motor Skills Observation (ages 2–4) Child _____

Date _____ Observer _____ Age _____

	Yes	No
Eating:		
1. Holds glass with one hand		
2. Pours from pitcher		
3. Spills little from spoon		
4. Selects food with pincer grasp		
Dressing:		
1. Unbuttons		
2. Puts shoes on		
3. Uses both hands together (such as holding jacket with one hand while zipping with the other)		
Fine Motor:		
1. Uses pincer grasp with pencil, brushes		
2. Draws straight line		
3. Copies circles		
4. Cuts at least 2" in line		
5. Makes designs and crude letters		
6. Builds tower of 6–9 blocks		
7. Turns pages singly		
Gross Motor:		
1. Descends/ascends steps with alternate feet		
2. Stands on one foot, unsupported		
3. Hops on two feet		
4. Catches ball, arms straight, elbows in front of body		
5. Operates tricycle		

FIGURE 6-8 A yes/no checklist gives specific information about an individual child's skills.

teachers can create one with relative ease. Checklists are often used in child evaluation, as in Figure 6-8.

Rating scales are like checklists, planned in advance to record something specific. They extend checklists by adding some quality to what is observed. The advantage is that more information is gathered. A potential problem is added because the observers' opinions are now required and could hamper objectivity.

Rating scales differ from checklists, as they "identify the degree to which a behavior is exhibited on a **continuum,** using numbers to rate the occurrence or strength of a characteristic (e.g., on a scale of 1–5)" (Bowers, 2008). For example, instead of simply recording which children are at circle time, a rating scale can measure attention using numbers or word phrases, such as in Figure 6-9. The result is a detailed description of (1) each child's behavior as each teacher sees it; (2) the group's overall attention level; and (3) an interesting cross-teacher comparison.

Modified Child Study Techniques

Because observation is the key method of studying young children in their natural settings, it makes good sense to develop many kinds of observational skills. Each can be tailored to fit the individual child, the particular group, the kind of staff, and the specific problem. Teachers who work in complex, creative classrooms have questions arise that need fast answers. Modified child study techniques can define the scope of the problem fairly quickly. Some of the techniques are shadow studies, experimental procedures, and the *methode clinique*.

The **shadow study** is a type of modified technique. It is similar to the diary description and focuses on one child at a time. An in-depth approach, the shadow study gives a detailed picture. Each teacher attempts to observe and record regularly the behavior of one particular child. The notes are then compared. Before starting a shadow study, give some form and organization to the notes, as illustrated in Figure 6-10.

The data in a shadow study are descriptive. In this, it shares the advantages of narratives. One of its disadvantages is that teachers may let other matters go while focusing on one child, and a shadow study can be quite time-consuming. Still, one interesting side effect often noted is how the behavior of the child being studied improves while the child is being observed. Disruptive behavior seems to diminish or appear less intense. It would appear that in the act of focusing on the child, teacher attention has somehow helped to alter the behavior. Somehow the child feels the impact of all this positive, caring attention and responds to it.

Two additional strategies are used to obtain information about a child. Because they involve some adult intervention, they do not consist strictly of observing and recording naturally occurring behavior. Still, they are very helpful techniques for teachers to understand and use.

Experimental procedures are those in which adult researchers closely control a situation and its variables. Researchers create a situation in which they can:

1. observe a particular behavior
2. make a hypothesis, or guess, about that behavior
3. test the hypothesis by conducting the experiment

For instance, an experimenter might wish to observe fine motor behavior in 7-year-olds to test the hypothesis that these children can significantly improve their fine motor skills in sewing if given specific instructions. Two groups of children are tested. One

Rating Scale: Circle Time

Rating: <u>Circle Time</u>   Child: _____   Dates: _____

NEVER ATTENDS (wiggles, distracts others, wanders away)

SELDOM ATTENDS (eyes wander, never follows fingerplays or songs, occasionally watches leader)

SOMETIMES ATTENDS (can be seen imitating hand gestures, appears to be watching leader about half the time, watches others imitating leader)

USUALLY ATTENDS (often follows leader, rarely leaves group, rarely needs redirection, occasionally volunteers, usually follows leader's gestures and imitations)

ALWAYS ATTENDS (regularly volunteers, enthusiastically enters into each activity, eagerly imitates leader, almost always tries new songs)

FIGURE 6-9 A rating scale measuring attention at group times requires data in terms of frequency, adding depth to the observation.

Shadow Study

Child's Name _____Jeff_____

Time	Setting (where)	Behavior/Response (what and how)
9:00	Arrives—cubby, removes wraps, etc.	"I can put on my own nametag" (enthusiastically). Uses thumb to push sharp end of pin, grins widely. Goes to teacher, "Did you see what I did?"
9:15	Blocks	Precise, elaborate work with small cubes on top of block structure, which he built with James. "Those are the dead ones," pointing to the purple cubes outside the structure. Cries and hits Kate when her elbow accidentally knocks tower off.
9:30	Wandering around room	Semidistant, slow pace. Stops at table where children are preparing snack. Does not make eye contact with teacher when invited to sit; Ali grabs J's shirt and tugs at it. "The teacher is talking to you!" J blinks, then sits and asks to help make snack. Stays 10 minutes.

© Cengage Learning

FIGURE 6-10 A shadow study will profile an individual child in a class and can be very helpful when communicating with families.

group is given an embroidery hoop, thread, and needle and asked to make 10 stitches. The other receives a demonstration of how to stitch and is then given the identical task. The embroidery created by both groups is then compared. Some previously agreed-on criteria are used to quantify the fine motor skill demonstrated by the two groups' work.

The major criteria for a scientific experiment may be applied to this procedure as follows:

- The experimenters can control all relevant aspects of the behavior. (In this case, the materials can be controlled, although previous experience with embroidering cannot.)
- Usually, only one variable at a time should be measured. (Only fine motor skill as it relates to embroidery is observed, not other skills such as language or information processing, or even fine motor proficiency in printing or drawing.)
- Children are assigned to the two groups in a random manner. (In other words, the groups are not divided by sex, age, or any other predetermined characteristics.)

Few teachers working directly with children will use the stringent criteria needed to undertake a true scientific experiment. However, it is useful to understand this process because much basic research conducted to inves-

tigate how children think, perceive, and behave utilizes these techniques.

The **methode clinique** is the final information-gathering technique that involves the adult directly with the child. This method is used in psychotherapy and in counseling settings, as the therapist asks probing questions. The master of this **clinical method** with children was Piaget, who would observe and question a child about a situation (see Chapter 4). Note how the adults wonder "what or why" and then insert their own actions to find out what they want to know in these examples:

- Three-month-old Jenna is lying in a crib looking at a mobile. Her hands are waving in the air. The adult wonders whether Jenna will reach out and grasp the mobile if it is moved close to her hands. Or will she bat at the toy? Move her hands away? The adult then tries it to see what will happen.
- A group of preschoolers are gathered around a water table. The teacher notices two cups, one deep and narrow, the other broad and shallow, and asks, "I wonder which one holds more, or if they are the same?" The children say what they think and why. Then, one of the children takes the two cups and pours the liquid from one into the other.

In both examples, the adult does more than simply observe and record what happens. With the infant, the adult questions what Jenna's responses might be and then watches for the answer. The preschool teacher intervenes in the children's natural play to explore a question systematically with them and then listens for and observes the answers. The clinical method is not strictly an observational method, but it is an informative technique that, when used carefully, can reveal much about children's abilities and knowledge.

Observation and its various methods are used extensively in early childhood programs and, increasingly, in elementary education to assess children. Figure 6-11 summarizes these systems. It is safe to say that whenever a teacher encounters a problem—be it a child's behavior, a period of the day, a set of materials, or a puzzling series of events—the first step toward a solution is systematic observation.

How to Observe and Record Effectively

Learning how to observe is a serious activity and requires a great deal of concentration. Some preparations can be made beforehand so that full attention is focused on the observation. Thinking through some of the possible problems helps the teacher get the most out of the experience.

Observing While Teaching

There are *many* effective ways to observe. Some teachers find certain times of the day easier than others. Many prefer to watch during free play, whereas others find it easier to watch individual children during directed teach-

Observation skills are honed when teachers have opportunities to work with a few children at a time.

ing times. Most teachers keep a pencil and paper handy to record observations throughout the day; others choose to record what they see after school is over for the day. Contemporary teachers often keep a digital camera nearby, and some have hand-held video cameras. The professional team that is committed to observation will find ways to support its implementation.

Creating opportunities for regular observations can be difficult. Centers are rarely staffed so well that one teacher can be free from classroom responsibilities for long periods of time. Some ask for parent volunteers to take over an activity while a teacher conducts an assessment. In one center, the snack was set up ahead of time to free one teacher to observe during group time. The environment can be arranged with activities that require little supervision when a teacher is interested in making some observations.

When children know they are being observed, they may feel self-conscious initially, asking pointed questions of the observer and changing their behavior as if they were on stage. When a teacher begins to write, some of the children will pay immediate attention.

"'What are you writing about?' asks 4-year-old Nina as I sit down at the edge of the block area. 'I'm writing about children playing,' I explain. 'You're writing about what I'm doing?' Nina asks. 'Yes, I am.' She's pleased. She goes back to building a careful enclosure with the long blocks" (Jones and Carter, 1991). When effective observation strategies are used and regular observations are done by familiar adults, children will soon ignore the observer and resume normal activity.

Teachers can improve their observation and recording skills outside the classroom as well. Taking an "Observational Skills" class is helpful; so is visiting other classes in pairs and comparing notes afterward. Staff meetings take on added dimension when teachers role play what they think they have seen and others ask for details.

The teacher who makes notes during class time has other considerations. Be ready to set aside your recording when necessary. Wear clothing with at least one good pocket. This ensures the paper and pencil are available when needed and the children's privacy is protected. Take care not to leave notes out on tables, shelves, or in cupboards for others to see. They should be kept confidential until added to the children's records. Some teachers find the "low-tech" materials of pen and notebook or 3 × 5 cards easiest to find, carry, use, and set aside. Others find a camera, tape recorder, and even a video camcorder helpful, although the expense, storage, and distracting nature of such equipment need to be considered.

Observational Techniques

Method	Observational Interval	Recording Techniques	Advantages	Disadvantages
1. Narratives				
Running Record	Continuous sequences	Use notebook and pencil, clipboard; can itemize activity or other ongoing behavior; can see growth patterns.	Rich in detail; maintains sequence of events; describes behavior as it occurs.	Open to observer bias; time-consuming. Sometimes need follow-up.
Diary description	Day to day	Same as running record.	Rich in detail; describes behavior after it occurs.	
Specimen descriptions	Continuous sequences	Same	Usually documents behavior within a time frame [ex 1 hour].	
Log/Journal	Regular, preferred daily or weekly	Usually has space for each child; often a summary of behavior.	Less structured than other narratives.	
"On-the-hoof" anecdotes	Sporadic	Ongoing during class time; using notepad and paper in hand.	Quick and easy to take; short-capture pertinent events/details.	Lack detail; need to be filled in at later time; can detract from teaching responsibilities.
2. Samplings				
Time sampling	Short and uniform time intervals	On-the-spot as time passes; prearranged recording sheets.	Easy to record; easy to analyze; relatively bias free.	Limited behaviors; loss of detail; loss of sequence and ecology of event.
Event sampling	For the duration of the event	Same as for time sampling.	Easy to record; easy to analyze; can maintain flow of class activity easily.	Limited behaviors; loss of detail; must wait for behavior to occur.
3. Rating methods				
Checklists	Regular or intermittent	Using prepared recording sheets; can be during or after class.	Easy to develop and use.	Lack of detail; tell little of the cause of behaviors.
Rating scales	Continuous behavior	Same as for checklists.	Easy to develop and use; can use for wide range of behaviors.	Ambiguity of terms; high observer bias.
4. Modified techniques				
Shadow study	Continuous behavior	Narrative-type recording; uses prepared recording sheets.	Rich in detail; focuses in-depth on individual.	Bias problem; can take away too much of a teacher's time and attention.
Experimental procedures	Short and uniform	May be checklists, prearranged recording sheets, audio or video tape.	Simple, clear, pure study, relatively bias-free.	Difficult, hard to isolate in the classroom.
Methode clinique/ clinical method	Any time	Usually notebook or tape recorder.	Relevant data; can be spontaneous, easy to use.	Adult has changed naturally occurring behavior.

FIGURE 6-11 A summary chart of the major observational techniques that the early childhood professional can use to record children's behavior.

Regardless of what teachers use, they must organize themselves for success:

- *Gather and prepare the materials ahead of time:* This may mean getting everyone aprons with large pockets or a set of cards or labeled spiral notebook.
- *Consider where you will observe:* Set up observation places (chairs, stations); in a well-equipped yard and room, you can plan strategically.
- *Plan when you will observe:* In a well-planned day, teachers can have the freedom to practice observing regularly during play time.
- *Prepare every adult to be an observer:* Give every teacher some regular opportunities to observe and reflect on children's play.

Respect the privacy of the children and their families at all times. Any information gathered as part of an observation is treated with strict confidentiality. Teachers and students are careful not to use children's names in casual conversation. They do not talk about children in front of other children or among themselves. It is the role of the adults to see that children's privacy is maintained. Carrying tales out of school is tempting but unprofessional.

Beginning to Observe

In some schools, observers are a normal part of the school routine. In colleges with laboratory facilities on campus, visitors and student observers are familiar figures. They have only to follow established guidelines for making an observation (see Figure 6-12).

Many times students are responsible for finding their own places to observe children. If so, the student calls ahead and schedules a time to observe that is convenient. Be specific about observation needs, the assignment, the ages of children desired, the amount of time needed, and the purpose of the observation.

If you are planning to observe in your own class, several steps are necessary for a professional observation and a believable recording.

- *Plan the observation.* Have a specific *goal* in mind, and even put that at the top of your recording sheet. Goals can be general ("Let's see what activities Ajit

Guidelines for Observing

1. Please sign in with the front office and obtain a visitor's badge. **Your badge must be worn and visible at all times while at the center.**
2. Inform the front office when you have completed your visit.
3. **Be unobtrusive.** Please find a spot that doesn't infringe on the children's space.
4. If you are with a small group or another person, **do not observe together;** consciously separate and space yourselves. Do not talk to other visitors during observation, please.
5. Respond to the children, but **please, do not initiate conversations with them.**
6. **If a child seems upset that you are near him/her, please remove yourself from the area.** If you receive direct requests from a child to leave, please respond that you realize that he said you are in **his** space and will move.
7. **Please do not interfere with the teaching/learning process** during your observation. Either ask when you check out in the front office or leave a note in the teacher's mailbox requesting a time to meet. Please understand that we welcome questions but cannot interrupt the program to answer them immediately.
8. **Walk around the periphery of the outdoor area or classrooms rather than through them.**
9. **When possible, do not stand. Please do not hover over children.** Sit, squat, or bend down at the knees so you are at the children's level.
10. **Taking photographs is not permitted.** In special classes, permission for photographs may be given by the Dean of Child Development and Education.

Thank you for your help and consideration in making your visit to the center a pleasant one for everyone involved.

FIGURE 6-12 Establishing guidelines for observers and visitors helps remind us of the importance of teaching as watching, not just telling. (Courtesy of De Anza College Child Development & Education Department.)

chooses today") or specific ("Watch for instances of quarreling in the sand area").

■ *Be unobtrusive.* The success of the observation depends on how inconspicuous the observer can be. Children are more natural if the observer blends into the scenery. By sitting back, one can observe the whole scene and record what is seen and heard, undisturbed and uninfluenced. This distancing sets up a climate for recording that aids the observer in concentrating on the children.

■ *Observe and record.* To be objective, be as specific and detailed as possible. Write only the behavior—the "raw data"—and save the analysis and your interpretation for later.

■ *Interpret your data.* Reread your notes (transcribing them into something legible if anyone else might need to read them) and make some conclusions.

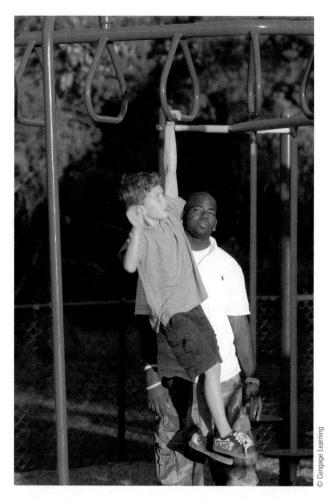

Learning to observe and record effectively takes time and practice. Knowing how to stay unobtrusive yet available allows children to continue their natural behavior without distraction and the teacher to ascertain noteworthy behavior.

Your observation was what happened; the interpretation is the place for your opinions and ideas of *why* it happened.

■ *Act on what you observed.* To implement your solutions, plan what you will do next, and then follow through with your ideas.

Wherever an observation is planned, it is critical to maintain **professional confidentiality.** If observing at another site, call ahead for an appointment. Talk about the purpose and format of your observation with both director and teacher. Finally, in any discussion of the observation, change the names of the children and school to protect those involved.

Assessment: Evaluating Children

How do we evaluate children? What do we look for? How do we document growth and difficulties? How do we communicate our findings to families and agencies?

An increased emphasis on child and program assessment is a result of the trend toward increasing **accountability.** Both No Child Left Behind legislation and accreditation criteria have raised the bar on assessment. How can early childhood educators make sure they are on the right track? These questions focus our attention on children's issues, assessment tools, and the evaluation process.

Why Evaluate?

Shepard, Kagan, and Wurtz (1998) outline four purposes of early childhood assessment:

■ The support of learning
■ Identification of special needs
■ Program evaluation and monitoring of trends
■ High-stakes accountability, defined as those assessments in which the outcome has major consequences for the child, teacher, or organization

Children are evaluated because teachers and parents want to know what the children are learning. Evaluations set the tone for a child's overall educational experience. Highlighting children's strengths builds a foundation from which to address their limitations or needs. The process of evaluating children attempts to answer several questions: Are children gaining appropriate skills and behaviors? In what activities does learning take place? What part of the program supports specific learning? Is

© Cengage Learning

the school philosophy being met? Are educational goals being met?

In assessing children, three goals stand out (Gullo, 2006):

1. To better understand their overall development
2. To monitor children's progress through the curriculum
3. To identify children who are at risk for failure or who may need special education services

In other words, evaluation processes can help teachers discover who children are, what they can (and cannot) do, and how we can help children grow and learn.

In evaluating children, teachers first decide *what it is they want to know about each child and why*. With an understanding of children in general, teachers then concentrate on individual children and their unique development. Goals for children stem from program objectives. For instance, if the school philosophy is, "Our program is designed to help children grow toward increasing physical, social, and intellectual competencies," an evaluation will measure children's progress in those three areas. One that claims to teach specific language skills will want to assess how speaking and listening are being accomplished.

Evaluations provide teachers with an opportunity to distance themselves from the daily contact with children and look at them in a more detached, professional way. Teachers can use the results to share their opinions and concerns about children with each other, with families, and with important agencies or specialists. For instance, an infant and toddler center might schedule parent conferences around a sequence of child evaluations: the first, a few weeks after the registration of the child; the second, six months after the child's admission into the program; and the third, just before the move up to an older age group (such as moving from the infant to the toddler class), which would include the parents and two teachers, the current and the receiving one. This concentrated effort expands everyone's vision of who and what the child can be, highlights patterns of the child's behavior, and helps in understanding the meaning of that behavior. It gives teachers the chance to chart growth and acknowledge progress and, in doing so, sets the child apart as an individual and unique human being. Evaluations are a reminder to all that they work with individuals and not just a group.

As with observations, evaluations contain varying degrees of subjectivity and opinion. For an evaluation to be reliable and valid, multiple sources of information should be used. Observing young children in action is

the key to early childhood assessment, and readers will notice that most of the child evaluation instruments described in this chapter are based on what children do spontaneously or in their familiar, natural settings. As Schweinhart (1993) notes, "the challenge of early childhood assessment is to apply the methods of the assessment field to the goals of the early childhood field." A proper evaluation of a child documents a child's growth over time (e.g., keeping a portfolio of the child's creations, dictations, and teacher observations-anecdotes of behavior or snips of conversations overheard). See the section on "Authentic Assessment" and the "Insights From the Field" feature in this chapter.

In general, evaluations are made to:

- Establish a baseline of information about each child by which to judge future progress
- Document children's learning
- Determine guidance and intervention
- Plan the curriculum
- Communicate with families
- Monitor program accountability and quality

Establish a Baseline

One purpose of evaluating children is to establish a starting point of their skills and behavior. This is the beginning of a collection over a period of time of important information on each child. Through this cumulative record, teachers learn a great deal about the children: whom they play with, how they spend their time, how they handle problems, what fears and stress they show. In other words, they learn a lot about how children live their lives.

A **baseline** is a picture of the status of each child—an overview of individual development. It shows where the child is in relation to the school's objectives because the child is being measured according to program expectations. Baseline data give a realistic picture of a child at that moment in time, but there is a presumption that the picture will change.

A Baseline Tool. The beginning of the school term is an obvious time to start collecting information. Records of a child are established in the context of the child's history and family background. Parents frequently submit this information with an application to the school. Teachers can gather the data by visiting the child at home or holding a parent conference and speaking directly with the parents about the child's development.

An entry-level assessment made during the first few weeks of school can be informative, particularly when

Entry-Level Assessment

1. Child's name ___Mariko Meade___ Teacher ___Kristin Franklin___
   Age ___3.0___ Sex ___F___
   Primary language ___Japanese___ Fluency in English? _____
   Any previous school experiences? ___none___
   Siblings/others in household ___sister Hiromi, 6 months___
   Family situation (one/two parents, other adults, etc.) ___Mother at home, father full-time outside home,___
   ___maternal grandmother, baby sister.___

2. Separation from parent:
   Smooth _____ Some anxiety _____ Mild difficulty _____ Unable to separate _____
   Did parent have trouble separating? ___mother/no; grandmother/yes; father/no___
   Comments: ___grandmother stays and has trouble leaving if M. protests___

3. How does child come to and leave from school?
   Parent ___grandma 2x/wk___ Car pool _____ Babysitter _____ Bus _____

4. Physical appearance [general health, expression, clothing, body posture]: *M. is carefully dressed, excellent health, cautious expression, opens up over morning and through week.*

5. Self-care [dressing, toileting, eating, toothbrushing, sleeping]: *M. dresses and toilets without assistance; little appetite, resists toothbrushing; still lays quietly but no sleeping yet.*
   Allergies/other health-related problems: ___none reported or observed___

6. Child's Interests: *Indoors—books, easel, art   Outdoors—swings, animals, sandbox*

   Group times (level of participation): *M. comes to circle, sits on my lap, watchful without any participation yet.*

7. Social-emotional development: *M. plays alone, seems happy, but has to be invited to any activity with other children; seems tense unless near me.*
   b.   Plays mostly with children of: *No play with other children yet.*
   c.   Moves into environment: *Hesitantly, but is getting around a little; tends to follow me.*
   d.   Special friends: *none yet.*
   e.   Does the child follow teachers? ___yes___ Anyone in particular? _____

8. Cognitive development: *follows directions, does not speak yet, points & nods.*

9. Physical development: *prefers R-hand; uses scissors & brushes well; have not yet observed climbing or running.*

10. Goals/points to remember: ___Does she have a security object to bring? What does she love to do at home___
    ___that we could have here? What Japanese terms should we learn & use? Schedule a home visit this month.___

FIGURE 6-13 Entry-level assessments collect baseline information. Once teachers and children have had some time together, these first impressions can be documented.

added to the child's family history. The evaluation itself should be done informally, with teachers collecting information as children engage naturally with materials and each other. A few notes jotted during the first month of school can serve as a beginning collection of pertinent data about the child. Many agencies ask for an initial assessment within the first 60 days of enrollment. Figure 6-13 outlines an entry-level assessment; others use the same form as needed all year.

Application. Teachers then use this information to understand children and their various levels of development. They can see children's strengths and weaknesses and where future growth is likely to occur. When the information is shared with families, they feel more relaxed about their child and even laugh when they recall those first few days of school. One must remember, however, that the entry assessment is only a first impression. Care must be taken to avoid creating a self-fulfilling prophesy by labeling children so that they become shaped into those beginning patterns. Again, teachers must be mindful of the cautions associated with all assessments as they document children's early behaviors. Still, so much happens in that short period of time; the rich information we gain from documenting this growth is invaluable.

Goals and Plans. Teachers use baseline data to set realistic goals for individual children. They tailor the curriculum to the needs and interests they have observed. An entry-level assessment is a vehicle for watching children's growth throughout the year. For instance, after setting a baseline of Mariko's language ability in English, teachers plan activities to increase her understanding and use of language. Then, they make periodic checks on her increased vocabulary as the school year progresses.

Document Children's Learning

Teachers use evaluations to document children's growth. Data collected provide evidence of children's growth or lack of progress. A careful evaluation of each child furnishes the teaching staff with the necessary foundation from which they can plan the next steps.

> Hita has mastered the brushes at the easel. Now we can encourage her to try the smaller brushes in table painting.
>
> Enrico has been asking how to spell simple words. Let's see that he gets some time away from the blocks to work at the writing center.
>
> All the 2-year-olds seem able to separate from their families and say good-bye comfortably now. How can we celebrate this progress with the group?

A Progress Tool. Figure 6-14 is a sample *midyear evaluation*. Criteria for each area of development are included to build a profile of the whole child. Teachers note the intervention and guidance steps they plan, where appropriate.

Many states, national programs such as Head Start, school districts, and individual programs are developing and using assessment tools to establish and

Assessments that include photos of children in action offer a snapshot of a child at a particular moment, which can serve as a baseline or as a mid-year evaluation.

A Tool for Monitoring Children's Progress

Check one of the evaluations below for each skill area; for those that need work, document with specific examples.

Developmental Area	Age Appropriate	Highly Skilled	Needs Work
Self-Management			
Personal care	*Can feed, dress, toilet self well*		
Making choices	*Prefers indoors to outside*		
Following routines	*Does fine in routines*		
Physical/Motor			
1. Fine Motor	*Uses easels—brushes good grasp, pens also*		
Art materials	*Likes blocks, table toys*		
Woodworking tools	*Hasn't chosen woodworking, but watches often*		
Manipulatives			
2. Gross Motor		*Very cautious, seems fearful*	
Ball handling		*Won't swing, slide, use climber*	
Balancing		*Wanders outdoors, sometimes does music*	
Jump/hop/skip		*Runs away when wheel toys are rolled down hill*	
Communication and Language			
Vocabulary		*Exceptionally strong*	
Articulation		*Converses with adults daily*	
Comprehension		*Responds to children but rarely initiates talk*	
English as a second language		*Outstanding at group time—lots of ideas*	
Converses with children		*Talks around fears, but fears seem to keep him from trying*	
Converses with adults			
Listens			
Expresses self (needs, ideas, feelings)			
Cognitive Development			
Sees cause and effect			
Processes and uses information			
Solves problems with:	*Dylan has so much information to share, and lots of interest in*		
objects	*problem-solving with indoor materials and interactions with teachers.*		
peers	*We wish he could extend these skills into work with children and*		
adults	*open up a bit more.*		
Premath (sequencing, measuring, numbers)			
Prereading concepts (size, colors, shapes, letters, position)			
Social-Emotional			
Independence/initiative			
Positive self-concept	*Does well on own, gets around*		
Recognizes/accepts own feelings	*Is comfortable and confident*		
Deals with frustration	*around adults*		*Seems hesitant/fearful outdoors*
Flexibility			*Is more solitary or onlooker; is*
Leadership			*this self-esteem or just fear?*
Initiates social contacts			*Don't know about leadership yet;*
Prosocial behaviors (friendly, sharing, inclusive, cooperative, empathic)			*have seen little because of lack*
Child–child interactions			*of interaction with children*
Child–adult interactions			

OVERALL STRENGTHS: GOALS

FIGURE 6-14 A midyear evaluation is a more detailed description of the child. It highlights areas of concern and progress.

monitor progress. There has been a reluctance in the early childhood field to use the word "standards," so these tools are often called "essential learning," "developmental guidelines," or "learning goals." One such tool, the California Desired Results Developmental Profile (DRDP), has profile forms for infant/toddler (birth through 36 months), preschool (age 3 to kindergarten), kindergarten through age 7, and 8 to 10 years. The DRDP describes four desired results for children; they are:

- Children are personally and socially competent.
- Children are effective learners.
- Children show physical and motor competence.
- Children are safe and healthy.

For each age group, the tool outlines several indicators for those results and describes growth along a continuum so that the phases children experience as they move toward accomplishing an objective can be documented. Many states have similar standards, and several national organizations have posted information about early learning standards from across the United States. (See "Helpful Websites" at the end of the chapter.)

Application. Information about a child will be used to assess growth and change. How often this happens can vary. Although many changes occur in rapid succession in these early years, it takes time for a child to integrate life experiences and for teachers to see them expressed as a permanent part of behavior. Evaluating too frequently does not reveal sufficient change to make it worthwhile and places an added burden on the teaching staff as well. Once the initial baseline data have been gathered, a progress evaluation approximately every three to six months is reasonable. The sample form in Figure 6-14 offers one such evaluation in progress.

Goals and Plans. Goals are established for children as a result of an assessment. These goals are changed as growth takes place. A good assessment tool monitors progress in each developmental area so that plans can be made to challenge the child physically, socially, emotionally, creatively, and intellectually.

At the same time, theory reminds us that the child develops as a whole, with each area of growth influencing and being influenced by what changes take place in other areas. Evaluations that document growth include information so that all teachers see the interrelationships among areas of development. By assessing growth in individual areas, teachers relate that development to the child's collective abilities. See what the teachers concluded as they went over his mid-year report:

Dylan's report shows he lacks dexterity in running and climbing and is quite strong in verbal and listening skills. This influences his development in the following areas:

Emotionally. He appears to lack self-confidence, and his self-esteem deteriorates the longer he feels inept at physical skills. He may even be afraid to master the art of climbing and running for fear he will fail.

Socially. Children tease Dylan because he often cannot keep up with them while playing outside. He often ends up playing alone or watching the other children in more active pursuits.

Intellectually. There is a lack of risk-taking in Dylan's whole approach to play. Because of his slow physical development he seems unlikely to challenge himself in other ways.

Goals: Focus on physical/motor skills. Help him talk about what he likes and dislikes about the outdoors and bring in picture books that depict characters persisting to master difficulties (such as *The Little Engine That Could*), using his language strength as a springboard for growth.

Determine Guidance and Intervention

A third purpose for evaluation is to help teachers determine guidance procedures. These are based on insights and perceptions brought into focus through the evaluation. This process serves as a primary tool on which guidance and planning are based. When teachers see a problem behavior or are concerned about a child, they plan for further assessment (see Chapter 7). If a developmental screening is done to assess if a child has a learning problem or needs special services, teachers will either refer the family to a proper specialist or agency or administer the screening themselves. Developmental screening tests will be discussed further in this chapter. Often the kinds of guidance and intervention required are more like those in the "What Do You Think?" feature on page 218.

A Guidance Tool. Evaluations help in behavior management. Once a need has been pinpointed, the teaching staff decides how to proceed. Individual problems are highlighted when teachers make a point of concentrating on the child's behavior. Figure 6-15 illustrates a form used to determine intervention. Used at a team meeting, this form demonstrates what steps are to be taken in addressing the concern directly. It also helps teachers clarify how to talk to parents in a concerned and supportive manner.

What Do YOU Think?

Meet Jody, age 5.

Observations:

- He uses scissors in a "hedge-clippers" fashion.
- He has an awkward grip when using a pencil.
- He finds it difficult to fit puzzle pieces together.
- He does not choose the woodworking table, manipulative table, or cooking project during free choice.

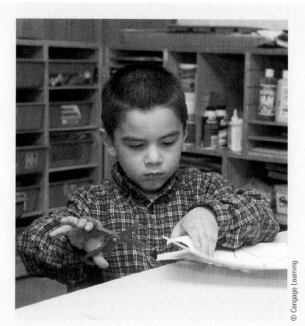

© Cengage Learning

Assessment: What would you do? Does he need intervention? How would you address this situation?

Results: The caregivers in his kindergarten after-school class were concerned about his fine motor skill development. A check with his parents revealed two important facts: Jody had trouble handling table utensils and could not button his sweater. They said there was no provision at home for him to pursue any fine motor activities. Knowing of Jody's interest in airplanes, the teachers used that to draw Jody into areas of the curriculum he did not ordinarily pursue. Small airplanes were added to the block corner, and airplane stencils were placed near the art table. A large mural of an airport was hung on the fence, and children were invited to paint on it. One day, children cut airplane pictures out of magazines and used them on a collage. Simple airplane puzzles were placed on the puzzle table. Felt shapes and small plastic airplanes in the water table helped draw Jody toward activities requiring fine motor skills. Jody's parents supplied him with a special art box at home, full of crayons, scissors, pens, water colors, and stencils. As his fine motor skills increased and refined, Jody became a more confident and happier child. By the end of three months, he was a regular participant in all areas of the school and seemed to be enjoying his newfound interest in art materials.

Application. The following case study and Figure 6-15 demonstrate how information from evaluations is used for guidance and intervention:

Trevor's parents report that he says he has no friends at school. At their staff meeting, the teachers make plans to suggest that Trevor's parents invite Ryan and Brooke to play with Trevor at home. Teachers have seen both children approach him, but he did not seem to know how to respond. At school, the teachers will give Trevor verbal cues when children make attempts to play with him.

Goals and Plans. An evaluation tool, such as the Child Guidance Form in Figure 6-15, helps teachers set goals for children. Narrowing the focus to include only those behaviors that concern the staff enables the staff to quickly review the needs of many children.

Plan Curriculum

Teachers plan the curriculum on the basis of children's evaluations. Translating the assessment to actual classroom practice is an important part of the teacher's role. A thorough evaluation helps teachers plan appropriate activities to meet children's needs. More importantly, observation itself drives curriculum development, particularly in the program models of Reggio Emilia, the Project Approach, and Emergent Curriculum (see Chapter 2). Figure 6-18 illustrates the connections between observation (listening to children's enthusiastic reports of a nearby construction project and their subsequent work in the block corner), curriculum development, and **documentation.** This documentation can be used in all six areas of child assessment discussed in this chapter, is the backbone of the curriculum development in Chapters 11 through 14, and is illustrated in Figure 6-16.

Planning Tools. All three of the previous evaluation tools can be used to plan curriculum. The entry-level assessment and midyear report can be summarized in a group chart. One such chart, made at the end of the first semester of a prekindergarten class, revealed this pattern:

> At least one-third of the class was having trouble listening at group time, as evidenced by the group chart that identified "Group Time" and "Language Listening Skills" as areas for growth for nearly half the children. The staff centered their attention on the group time content. It was concluded that a story made the group times too long; the children were restless throughout most of the reading. It was agreed to move story time to just before nap and shorten the group time temporarily.

Evaluation also applies to daily events, such as individual projects and the day as a whole. Chapter 10 discusses curriculum planning in further detail.

Application. Evaluation results assist teachers in seeing more clearly the strengths and abilities of each child in the class. Curriculum activities are then planned that will enhance growth. Also, areas of difficulty will be identified:

> Jolene has trouble mastering even the simplest puzzle. *Provide her with common shapes found in attribute blocks (small plastic shapes of varying color, thickness, size), and do some matching exercises with her.*
>
> The younger children in the class are reluctant to try the climbing structures designed by the older

Child Guidance Form

Problem [present in behavioral terms; limit to three]
Elizabeth has increased toilet accidents in the last 2 weeks.

Family History [ask family, include home, medical, changes]
Dad reports that she is wetting the bed at home, refuses to use toilet at night before bed.

Center History [child's relations to adults, children, materials, activities]
Higher incidence during midmorning snack, often at table or right afterwards.

Intervention [what has been tried with details; what has/not worked; child's strengths]
Teachers started to remind her to use toilet before washing hands for snack; she is resistant to suggestion.

Plans
1. In center: *check her comfort level—does she want privacy? teacher will walk her to bathroom or she can take a friend.*
2. With family: *parents will take her to toilet before bath, offer bedtime stories after she tries, will ask if she wants company/privacy, or take her teddy bear along.*
3. Date for reviewing results: *check-in 2 weeks.*

FIGURE 6-15 One purpose of evaluating children is to plan for behavior management. A good evaluation form will include how to follow through on plans made for intervention. (Adapted from McLaughlin & Sugarman, 1982.)

ones. *Build an obstacle course with the youngest children, beginning with very simple challenges and involving the children in the actual planning and building as well as rehearsing climbing techniques with them.*

There are practical connections to be made in learning to "read" the children and actual curriculum planning. Reflective work is critical for making curricular connections. (See "What Do You Think?")

Goals and Plans. Each of the previous case studies demonstrates how evaluation tools can be used to plan curriculum. By analyzing both group and individual skills through periodic assessment, teachers maintain a secure environment and challenging program.

Our Construction Project

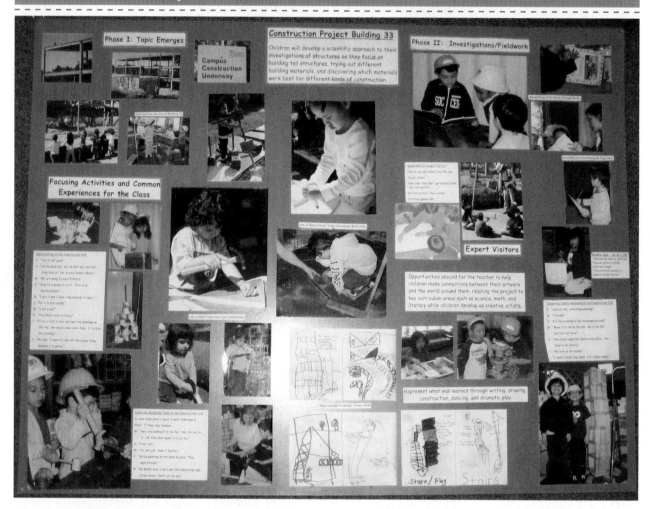

FIGURE 6-16 Documentation board. Thanks to the observational skills of teachers, a group of children were able to develop their interest and knowledge about building construction through curriculum development. Documentation panel by Maggie Lam and Kären Wiggins-Dowler (2006). Reprinted with permission from Mary Meta Lazarus Child Development Center, College of San Mateo.

Communicate with Families

Plans for evaluating children should include the means by which parents are to be informed of the results. Once the teachers have identified a child's needs and capabilities, parents are entitled to hear the conclusions. The teaching staff has an obligation to provide a realistic overview of the child's progress and alert the parents to any possible concerns. Using the child guidance form (see Figure 6-15), teachers define problem behavior for a child and work closely with the parents to reach a solution:

Yum-Tong refuses to let his mother leave. The teachers agree that there are two issues: (1) Y.-T.'s screaming and crying as his mother leaves and (2) his inability to focus on an activity while she attempts to go (though she stays as soon as he starts screaming). The family has told them that their other two children had separation problems as preschoolers. The previous school asked the parents to stay until the children stopped protesting, although the parents report that this took nearly six months and so was a hardship for them in their workplaces.

The teachers choose to intervene by asking Yum-Tong's mother to plan ahead with Y.-T., deciding before school how they will spend five minutes together each morning. After playing and helping him to settle in, she will then say good-bye and leave Y.-T. with Pete, his favorite teacher. Pete will be prepared to be with him at the departure and stay with him until he calms down. They also plan to have a conference date after two weeks of this intervention plan to follow through and review how it is working for everyone.

A Tool with Parents. Teachers and parents need to talk together, especially when problems are revealed by the evaluation. As parents and teachers share knowledge and insights, a more complete picture of the child emerges for both. Each can then assume a role in the resolution of the problem. The role of the teacher will be defined in the context of the parents' role, and the parents will be guided by the teacher's attitudes and actions.

Chapter 8 discusses the parent–teacher relationship and offers guidelines for effective parent–teacher conferences. The tool that works best is one that summarizes the school's concerns and solicits high parent involvement.

Application. Aside from identifying normal behavior problems, evaluations may raise questions concerning a child's physical development, hearing and visual acuity, or language problems. Recall that one purpose of assessment is to identify children who may need special education services (all ages), who may demonstrate issues of school readiness (pre-kindergartners), or who are at risk for academic failure (elementary-aged children). Potentially serious problems may emerge from the evaluation, and parents can be encouraged to seek further professional assessment or intervention. Evaluation tools can help parents target areas in which their child may need special help.

Goals and Plans. Because evaluation is an ongoing process, reevaluation and goal setting are done regularly. Communicating to parents both progress and new goals is critical for the feedback loop of an evaluation form to be effective, as shown in Chapter 5 on teacher evaluation.

Monitor Program Accountability and Quality

Evaluation results can help a program determine its quality and be accountable to others for its effectiveness. They can lead to changes in the overall program or in the school's philosophy. For example, a child care component might be added to the half-day program after learning that most children are enrolled in another child care situation after nursery school. Or an evaluation might conclude that there is too little emphasis on developing gross motor skills and coordination. To invite more active play, the administration might decide to remodel the play yard and purchase new equipment.

Child assessments can, therefore, be one measure of program quality. Other measures include evaluating the environment and schedule (see Chapter 9), the teaching staff (Chapter 5), and the curriculum (Chapters 11–14). The Accreditation process developed by NAEYC, based on the application of developmentally appropriate practices in programs, is a comprehensive program evaluation tool.

As regards assessment of children, early educators are reminded that, while evaluation is a central part of quality programs, the assessments must be ethical, appropriate, and valid. NAEYC and NAECS/SDE (2003) made specific, evidence-based recommendations concerning early childhood assessment. No matter what is used, the primary goal is to benefit children. Figure 6-17 lists the indicators of effective assessment practices. Specific points to emphasize are to use multiple sources of evidence and to use tools that help teachers make sound decisions about teaching and learning (Hyson, 2008).

Types of Assessments

With the increased accountability pressures, issues of assessment have arisen in both public schooling and early care programs. Regardless of agency or funding source, all early childhood programs must be knowledgeable about assessment: their purposes, tools, and complications. Whether you intend to improve children's learning, identify children with special needs, or account for your program, it is likely you will need to engage in some kind of child assessment.

Indicators of Effective Assessment Practices

- Ethical principles guide assessment practices.
- Assessment instruments are used for their intended purposes.
- Assessments are appropriate for the ages and other characteristics of children being assessed.
- Assessment instruments are in compliance with professional criteria for quality.
- What is assessed is developmentally and educationally significant.
- Assessment evidence is used to understand and improve learning.
- Assessment evidence is gathered from realistic settings and situations that reflect children's actual performance.
- Assessments use multiple sources of evidence gathered over time.
- Screening is always linked to follow-up.
- Use of individually administered, morn-referenced tests is limited.
- Staff and families are knowledgeable about assessment.

FIGURE 6-17 Principles of appropriate assessment in early childhood education. NAEYC & NAECS/SDE (2003, pp. 2–3).

Two Types of Assessments

"Generally there are two types of assessments: naturalistic assessments (sometimes referred to as informal or authentic) and standardized, norm-referenced assessments (sometimes referred to as formal)" (Maxwell and Clifford, 2004).

Naturalistic assessments include observations, note taking, self-assessments, parent interviews and surveys, samples of children's work, and teacher-designed forms (checklists, etc.). More **formal assessments** include standardized, **norm-referenced tests** and various "screening" instruments. The yearly tests taken in elementary and secondary school, using a #2 pencil, are an example of such procedures. "Standardized, norm-referenced assessments follow a standard set of administration rules so that each child theoretically experiences the assessment similarly (for example, each person administering the test gives the same instructions). Norm-referenced assessments permit a child's performance to be compared to those of other children his age" (Maxwell & Clifford,

2004). These are often used to identify special needs or to evaluate programs. As with the various observation methods, there are advantages and disadvantages to each type of assessment. Naturalistic types do not disrupt children, and a child has multiple opportunities to demonstrate mastery. They do not allow for easy comparison between children or in a group, and bias can affect the results. Standardized types do allow for comparisons and diminish some of the bias among many observers. Yet, they may not accurately reflect a child's skills due to administration outside the child's usual experience or setting. There are problems associated with testing and screening of young children (see the section "Testing and Screening" later in this chapter).

It is important to choose assessment tools and techniques that are appropriate for the group or the child under consideration. Informal observations can be made more systematic or comprehensive to gain more information about a specific problem. Formal, commercially developed instruments need to be used more carefully. There

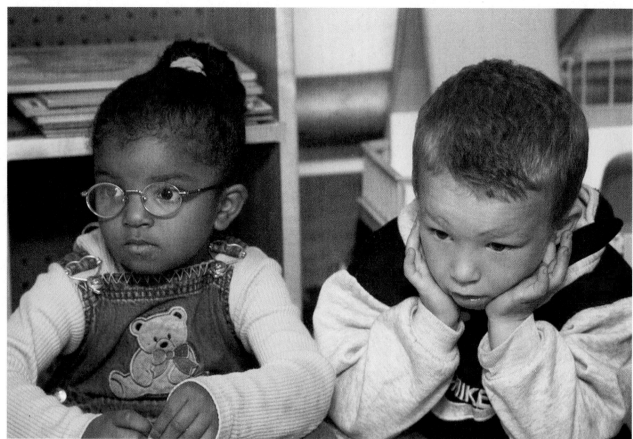

© Cengage Learning

Know the reasons for making an evaluation. Evaluations should avoid unfair comparisons, acknowledge individual differences and uniqueness, and not look at children in a comparative manner.

are several instruments that are widely used in the United States. The High/Scope Child Observation Record (COR), Work Sampling System (Meisels/Pearson), and Creative Curriculum's Developmental Continuum are three of the most well known. There are a wide variety of assessments to choose from; at the same time, many are not easily adaptable to individual programs or purposes, and many take considerable preparation and training.

"In choosing an appropriate assessment system, it is important to understand what a developmentally appropriate, valid, relative, and ethical assessment looks like. Some background research can provide this information" (Shillady, 2004), and the references at the end of the chapter can help. Before choosing any assessment tool or procedure, know the age group and the purpose as well as the children's cultures, languages, abilities, and disabilities. Assessing special populations is important but challenging, as the procedures need to account for cultural and linguistic differences (see helpful website CLAS).

Authentic Assessment: The Portfolio

The dictionary defines "authentic" as "of undisputed origin, genuine … made or done in a way that faithfully resembles an original" (*New Oxford American Dictionary*, 2005). For a child assessment to be authentic, it must try to capture who the child is, and what that child knows (or does not) and can (or cannot) do. Teachers must assess to know the child better in order to improve learning. How do we get there?

Many early childhood educators have embraced the idea that children's work samples in a portfolio form are an excellent way to document children's learning and faithfully capture the child's development. In light of the concerns you have read in this chapter about the mis-assessment of young children and the "test mania" that standardized tests in the primary grades have fomented, many professionals have looked for alternative assessment measures.

Portfolios can provide a "history of learning, a structured record of learner accomplishment… as well as a method for assessing progress" (Fenwich & Parsons, 2000). Although they take considerable planning, they help you collect children's work intentionally. You can evaluate children on their work and play as they are spontaneously, rather than with standardized tests or unnecessary screening.

There are several types of portfolios and plans for collecting material for them. Danielson and Abrutyn (1997) identify three types of portfolios:

1. Display portfolios—scrapbooks that collect items without teacher comments.

2. Showcase portfolios—the best pieces of the child's work.
3. Working portfolios—include selections of typical work along with teacher documentation to show the child's progress.

Gronlund (2008) recommends a working portfolio that combines work samples with teacher commentary. In our "Insights from the Field" article, Kären Wiggins-Dowler, an outstanding practitioner, describes this type of portfolio:

1. Make a portfolio plan. This includes a brief set of guidelines for collecting items for saving (see Figure 6-18). Since simple collection of work is not enough, here are some tips to expand upon collection (Pendowski, 2006):
   - Do not try to collect everything. Look for work samples that demonstrate your educational objectives and a child's progress over time on a goal.
   - Be organized when storing work samples. Ideas include pocket folders or even pizza boxes.
2. Collect children's work with purpose. Look for work in all developmental domains (Chapters 3 and 4), each interest area (Chapter 9), or other categories, such as those you are accountable for teaching. Many suggest you collect a piece of each child's work two or three times a year. Each child's individual portfolio may have completely different work samples from others in the program, but every portfolio will still show growth over time in every developmental area.
3. Add written comments to the work samples. The commentary "enhances the documentation by giving the information necessary to assess the process of learning that is going on. Teachers have told me that a picture may be worth a thousand words; but for assessment purposes, the words are essential, not the photo." At least, not the photo or drawing alone: Teacher commentary becomes a critical source of information to tell how the child did it, what it means, and how it shows growth or lack of it. Teacher observation and comments will document information for the teacher, the family, other specialists, or future teachers to use in a confidential and ethical manner.

Early Learning Standards

Standards, standards everywhere! … There are child outcome standards that define what young children should be learning. … What are the reasonable expectations that guide early educators in planning

Child Portfolio

- Identify the purpose of the portfolio (improving communication with families, connecting with other teachers or programs).
- Identify the types of items to be collected (artwork, photos of block or dramatic play, etc.).
- Specify who will collaborate to create the portfolio (teacher, other caregivers, the child, family).
- Set a timetable (for instance, the first set by November 15, second set by April 30).
- Establish any standards or tool you will use (for example, Desired Results or Child Outcomes).
- Have in writing when any portfolio conferences will take place and who will be there (teacher, family, child?).
- Identify procedure for maintaining confidentiality and for release of items.

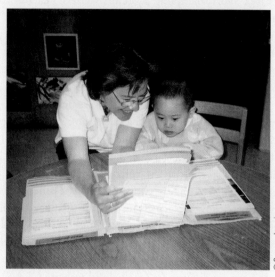

© Cengage Learning

FIGURE 6-18 Having a set of guidelines for developing and using portfolios keeps the process clear for all involved.

curriculum for preschool children and in assessing their progress in achieving these expectations? (Gronlund, 2006)

The standards movement in K–12 that began in the 1980s has arrived at the early childhood doorstep. More than half the states now have standards that describe results (see DRDP), outcomes, or learning expectations for children under kindergarten age, and Head Start has a framework for Child Outcomes. "The idea is to use standards to improve the odds that preschool programs will boost school readiness and lay a solid foundation for later achievement (Bodrova, Leong, & Shore, 2004). Yet the results are that more children are being denied entrance to a school system, being put in extra-year or pull-out programs, or being placed in kindergarten twice.

Using standards to clarify what children ought to learn and know how to do and to hold programs (and teachers) accountable is here to stay. **Early learning standards** are "statements that describe expectations for the learning and development of young children across the domains of: health and physical well-being; social and emotional well-being; approaches to learning; language development and symbol systems; and general knowledge about the world around them" (CCSSO, 2005).

The challenge is determining standards for children in the early years, since the ways children learn and what

they are learning is different from those in elementary school. "In early childhood, the development of foundational skills (skills that lay the foundation for later learning) is just as important as mastery of content matter" (Bodrova et al., 2004). It is essential that effective early learning standards (NAEYC & NAESC/SDE, 2003):

- emphasize significant developmentally appropriate content and outcomes
- are developed and reviewed through informed, inclusive processes
- gain their effectiveness through implementation and assessment practices that support all children's development in ethical, appropriate way
- require a foundation of support for early childhood programs, professionals, and families

There are benefits to early learning standards, as well as potential problems. These "reinforce the fact that there is an incredible potential for learning and growth in the infant, toddler, and preschool years and that there is value and importance in providing quality early childhood programs for children's long-term success in school and in life" (Gronlund, 2008). They can articulate both the sequence of typical development and set reasonable expectations for children at different ages. Learning standards are intended to set the bar for student achievement, and in the primary years, they can be crafted to apply brain and developmental research in their implementation (Schiller & Willis, 2008).

At the same time, standards can result in standardization, the notion that "one size fits all" about a vulnerable and tender population. The challenge is to implement standards that are developmentally appropriate and good for all children and that allow teachers to be creative and enthusiastic as they take good care of children Figure 6-19 details the pros and cons of early learning standards.

Testing and Screening

The practice of testing and **screening** for readiness, retention, and special needs has increased dramatically in the last decade. With the passage of Public Law 94-142 (Education for All Handicapped Children Act) and the early childhood amendment to the law (PL. 99-457), states now have the responsibility to establish specific procedures and policies to identify, evaluate, and provide services to all children with learning problems. Moreover, testing for admittance to kindergarten or promotion to first grade has become more common.

Ethical and appropriate principles state that early childhood educators shall not participate in practices that are "emotionally damaging, physically harmful, disrespectful, degrading, dangerous, exploitative, or intimidating to children" (NAEYC & NAECS/SDE, 2003). As mentioned previously, decisions about children must be based on multiple sources of information and not based on a single test score or single observation. One assessment could never tell all that is needed to know about a child or a group.

DAP

Early Learning Standards

Pros

- They can provide richness to our conversation about children's growth and learning.
- We can match standards to what we are already doing.
- They can be linked to primary standards so that we are indeed contributing to children's school readiness.
- They help us identity next steps and transitions.
- They are a strategy for professionalizing our field.
- They help us communicate across the grades, among ourselves, and with our public.
- They help us to have higher expectations for children.

Cons

- They lead to teaching to the standards only in a cookie-cutter curriculum.
- They bring a pressure of accountability with the risk of a push-down in curriculum and inappropriate expectations for younger children.
- Direct instruction is assumed as the only way that standards are addressed.
- Learning in self-directed, exploratory ways is not trusted.
- They contribute to a "we/they" mentality between preschool and elementary teachers.
- They take time for early educators to learn and work through, to figure out how to integrate into good practices.
- They result in testing and other inappropriate assessment methods being used.
- There is little money to support education and training of early educators in the standards and how best to use them.

FIGURE 6-19 There are both benefits and problems with early learning standards so teachers should use standards intentionally to inform their planning. (Adapted from Make Early Learning Standards Come Alive: Connecting Your Practice and Curriculum to State Guidelines, by Gaye Gronlund, pp. 4–5. Copyright © 2006 by Gaye Gronlund. Reprinted with permission from Redleaf Press, St. Paul, Minnesota, www.redleafpress.org.)

DAP   Decisions that have a major impact on children, such as enrollment or placement, are never made on the basis of results from a single developmental assessment or screening instrument/device but are based on multiple sources of relevant information, including that obtained from observations of and interactions with children by teachers and parents (and specialists, as needed).

Testing

Ironically, the last decade has also taught us that standardized tests fail to reflect adequately what children learn (National Commission on Testing and Public Policy, 1998). Indeed, "children know so much more than they are 'taught,' and what is tested may not be the important learning that the children have done" (Bergan & Feld, 1993). Howard Gardner, whose work on multiple intelligences is described in Chapters 4, 12, and 13, affirms:

> Over the past several decades the assumptions underlying the current testing edifice have been challenged by developmental, cognitive, and educational studies. There's a considerable body of scientific findings telling us that if we want to understand people's competence or knowledge about something, we should not examine them in an artificial way in an artificial setting. (1988)

Moreover, most formal testing engages only two (linguistic and logical mathematical) of the eight intelligences Gardner has identified. Such practices raise some practical and serious philosophical issues:

- Young children do not function well in common test situations, nor do the test results necessarily reflect children's true knowledge or skills.
- These practices (often based on inappropriate uses of readiness or screening tests) disregard the potential, documented long-term negative effects of retention on children's self-esteem and the fact that such practices disproportionately affect low-income and minority children. (National Center for Fair and Open Testing, 2006)
- Although the most needed and appropriate tests (teacher-made) are the hardest to create, the standardized ones are frequently misused and misunderstood by teachers and parents. (Meisels & Atkins-Burnett, 2005)
- Teachers are pressured into running programs that overemphasize the testing situation and test items.
- Most tests focus on cognitive and language skills; such a narrow focus ignores other areas of development.
- Special training to administer tests is imperative yet often overlooked, and standardized tests require specific protocols. (Klein & Estes, 2004)

The practice of standardized testing has caused early childhood curricula to become increasingly academic. Early childhood educators and parents are alarmed that:

> Many kindergartens are now structured, "watered-down" first grades, emphasizing workbooks and other paper-and-pencil activities that are inappropriate for 5-year-olds. The trend further trickles down to preschool and child care programs that feel that their mission is to get children "ready" for kindergarten. Too many school systems, expecting children to conform to an inappropriate curriculum and finding large numbers of "unready" children, react to the problem by raising the entrance age for kindergarten and/or labeling the children as failures. (NAEYC, 2003)

The implications of such testing further erode the curriculum when teachers, wanting their classes to do well on the test, alter activities to conform to what will be tested. They then begin teaching children to learn "right" answers rather than to engage in active, critical thinking. Rather than making teachers more accountable, "the overuse (and misuse) of standardized testing has led to the adoption of inappropriate teaching practices as well as admission and retention policies that are not in the best interests of individual children or the nation as a whole" (NAEYC & NAECS/SDE, 2003).

Teachers and schools can respond to the overuse and inappropriate use of tests. The National Association of Elementary School Principals now urges limited use of formal tests and retention. The Texas Board of Education has barred retention before first grade, and in New York State a coalition of groups is urging a ban on mass standardized testing of children before grade three.

Screening

Many kindergartens and some nursery schools use various kinds of screening tests before children begin school in the fall. The usual purpose of these evaluations is to determine readiness: that is, to verify that the child will be able to cope with and succeed in school. These tools are best devised with the individual child in mind. Their purposes are positive: to highlight the skills the child has and to identify the areas in which the child may need help in the next class.

Using valid screening tests to identify children who, because of the risk of possible learning problems or a handicapping condition, should proceed to a more intensive level of diagnostic assessment is an appropriate and necessary procedure. Note that screening tests are *not* diagnostic tools; a properly developed screening only indicates if more investigative work is needed. Such instruments are not achievement tests and are not meant to describe child learning outcomes:

> Developmental screening tests identify at an early point which children may have learning problems or

disabilities that could keep them from realizing their potential…By triggering in-depth assessment, screening instruments help teachers and other professionals decide who needs additional support for learning, rather than potentially being used to judge whether classrooms are meeting standards set from the outside. (Meisels & Atkins-Burnett, 2005)

Head Start programs use an "Ages & Stages Questionnaire," for instance, so parents/adult family members can inform teachers about children's behaviors that allow for more accurate child monitoring.

Perhaps most important is the reminder to all teachers that tests have no special magic. Assessment is more than testing. A standardized test, a homemade tool, or a screening instrument should be only one of several measures used to determine a child's skills, abilities, or readiness. Any test result should be part of a multitude of information, such as direct observation, parental report, and children's actual work.

Concerns about Assessment

Assessment is challenging! Of all the functions performed by teachers, probably none calls for more energy, time, and skill than evaluation. Anyone involved in evaluation should avoid:

- *Unfair comparisons.* Evaluations should be used to identify and understand the child involved, not to compare one with another in a competitive manner.
- *Bias.* Evaluations can label unfairly or prematurely the very people they are intended to help. Typecasting will not produce a useful assessment. Insufficient data and overemphasis on the results are two areas that need close monitoring. Evaluation tools should be free of language bias or other cultural bias. For instance, an evaluation of children should not include experiences unfamiliar to the cultural group being assessed.
- *Overemphasis on norms.* Most evaluation tools imply some level of normal behavior or performance, acceptable levels of interaction, or quantities of materials and space. People involved in an evaluation must remember to individualize the process rather than try to fit a child into the mold created by the assessment tool.
- *Interpretation.* There is sometimes a tendency to over interpret or misinterpret results. It must be clear what is being evaluated and how the information will be used. It is particularly important to be sensitive to the feelings of those being evaluated

when communicating the results of the assessment. Parents and teachers need to interpret evaluations clearly and carefully if they are to understand the findings and feel comfortable with them.

- *Too narrow of a perspective.* An evaluation tool may focus too much on one area and not enough on others. Moreover, no single occasion or instrument will tell teachers all they need to know about a child's abilities, a teacher's performance, or a program's effectiveness. It is essential that information be gathered in many ways and on several occasions. Sampling only children's skills as the single measure would lead to conclusions that were neither reliable nor valid. An imbalanced assessment gives an incomplete picture.
- *Too wide of a range.* An evaluation should be designed for a single level or age group and not cover too wide of a range. It is appropriate to measure a child's ability to print at age 6 but not at age 2. What is expected of the person or task should be taken into account and the evaluation method modified accordingly.
- *Too little or too much time.* The amount of time necessary to complete an evaluation must be weighed. The evaluation that is too lengthy loses its effectiveness in the time it takes. Time for interpretation and reflection must be included in the overall process.

Goals for children encompass all areas of development, and one measurement will not describe every area. Doing so also changes what happens in the program: "Teachers are very likely to shape their instruction to match a test's specific focus. This phenomenon, known as 'measurement-driven instruction,' [creates] a narrowing of the curriculum" (Meisels & Atkins-Burnett, 2005). Using a single yardstick to measure a child ignores the fact that young children do not always demonstrate what they know in a "testing" or single situation.

Some teachers conclude the year with a summary report. This evaluation serves as an overview of what a child has accomplished, what areas of strength are present, and what future growth might occur. These records are useful to parents as a summary of their child's learning experiences. Teachers may use them as references should they ever be consulted by another school about the child. Again, it is critical to assess a child in a sensitive and accepting manner, to keep the time period as brief as possible, and to communicate the results in the same tone. If this is not done, the child's self-esteem may be damaged and the family trust may be lost. The disadvantages of these tools parallel those of standardized tests.

Chapter 15 includes a discussion about the standards movement and the No Child Left Behind legislation. Above all, keep the testing to a minimum, thus guarding against "pulling up the plants to look at them before the roots take hold" (Cryan, 1986).

Using Observation and Assessment Information

Applying our observations to work in the classroom and with families and other professionals is a time-consuming, yet essential, aspect of teaching young children. Information gathered through direct observation and appropriate assessment reveals who children are, where their strengths and interests lie, and what challenges they have that need addressing in the program. Teachers use their observations to plan relevant space, materials, and curriculum for children. In addition, they adjust the environment and schedule based on what they have seen of the group in action. Finally, teachers adjust their interactions with children because of what they see.

Helping special populations and individuals is another way to use information gleaned from observation and assessment. Children with identified special needs will need an individualized plan for their educational experience, based on formal assessment and adjusted with accurate direct observation. Many children in early education and care may not have identified special needs but will require special handling. For instance, a child with a sensitive temperament may be repelled by ordinary cuddling; one adjusting to a new baby may need more teacher interaction for awhile; the children whose soccer team just won a game might be rambunctious that day. Observant teachers use what they see to good advantage.

There are four principles that guide our assessment practices in order for them to benefit young children, their families, and us as teaching professionals:

1. Standards should be in place that outline the important and developmentally appropriate outcomes we want for the children in our care.
2. Processes should be in place to develop and review the standards and our techniques for assessing children with them.
3. Assessment strategies must be ethical and appropriate for young children as they work and play in our settings.
4. Communication about both the standards and the observations and assessments we use must be in place that includes teachers, families, and relevant professionals.

Observation and assessment of children can be done appropriately and can tell us so much about children; we owe it to ourselves and the children we teach to use both to benefit all.

Insights *from the field*

The Portfolio: An "Unfolding" of the Child *by Kären Wiggins-Dowler, B.A.*

Early childhood portfolios are an excellent visual aid for showing the dispositions, strengths, and interests of a child as well as what universal skills and knowledge they have acquired under your care. They also serve as a history for each member of a shared community of learners. A portfolio organizes these samples into an integrated whole that offers parents and teachers a window into who the child is now and is becoming.

When you first think of portfolios, your initial reaction may be that it is too much work and that it adds one more responsibility to your already busy schedule. Instead, it can be a natural extension of your day and what you do with children. To have documentation become part of your regular day, keep clipboards, Post-it® notes, cameras, and tape recorders handy and ready to use. Every time a staff member points out an "a-ha" moment of a child's life, you can write it down immediately. Items to look for include:

1. art samples
2. cutting samples
3. dictated stories
4. invented writing
5. photographs of constructions
6. written samples
7. emergent play activities
8. written conversations during science and math activities
9. social interactions with peers and adults
10. photographs of children using motor and self-help skills

When children see adults engaged in data collection, they begin to take part. They take clipboards from the writing table to "write down important things." I had a 4-year-old child once who insisted I "support him." When I asked him to explain what he meant, he said, "Write down what I am doing: it's important."

Getting Started: What Works for Me

Recording what children say and how they interact can seem overwhelming. I use Post-it® notes as a convenient, quick way to capture revealing moments. I attach these to my lesson plans as they are easily transferred to individual portfolios. Photographs can also supplement written documentation.

During the beginning stages of developing portfolios, the gathered information tends to be just snapshots of moments out of time and context. Pictures look like scrapbook portraits and not examples of professional documentation. Do not despair; teachers who have limited experience in observation and assessment practices can begin with simplicity and convenience. These samples add to the total picture of a child's growth and should not be discredited.

Remember to keep your writing legible—rewriting your notes takes additional energy and time, which most teachers don't have. If English is not your first language, it is often easier to write in your primary language and translate later. If writing is difficult, use a tape recorder to document. A few lucky centers have video, although one must use it regularly enough so a taping is easy for you and so it doesn't become a dramatic play scene when the camera arrives. All samples and records need names of those involved, time, and date. As you become more proficient, your observation skills become more specific and the samples you choose are not just their best work but now are indicative of that child's developmental process.

Finally, I use a folding document with five separate sections for each developmental domain. Each labeled section has a cascading file of four to eight pages (depending of the length of stay in the program) and on each of these cascading pages are examples of developmental landmarks or unique attributes of the child. The most historical work samples and observations are located on the bottom page, with each overlap showing the child's progressive development. Then, on the top of each file is a developmental checklist or a summary of growth. Thus, the portfolio can be an excellent visual "unfolding" of the child. What results is the amazing image of each child as a competent learner who actively constructs knowledge within a social and cultural context. Parents are so excited when presented with this in-depth reflection of their child's history and learning!

Kären Wiggins-Dowler, B.A., is a head teacher at the Mary Meta Lazarus Children's Center of the College of San Mateo, California, and a State Mentor Teacher. She has a degree in Anthropology and Elementary Education from California State University, Hayward, and has done post-baccalaureate studies at San Francisco State University. She has also modified the portfolios to highlight the development of English proficiencies with a group of Korean ESL elementary school students.

SUMMARY

Systematic observation and recording of children's behavior are fundamental tools in understanding children. What children do and say and how they think and feel are revealed as they play and work. By learning to observe children's behavior, teachers become more aware of the children's skills, needs, and concerns.

The ability to observe is a skill in itself; teachers examine their own beliefs, influences, and attitudes to achieve a measure of objectivity. Recording the observations is another skill, one that requires facility with the written word and an understanding of the purpose for observing. To make a successful observation, teachers first decide what it is they want to find out about the child.

Key ingredients to successful observations include clear definitions of the behaviors to be observed and techniques for observing and recording them. These provide the tools for gaining a deeper understanding of individual children and the group. They also enhance knowledge about the interrelationships of developmental areas. Also, one gains insight into the dynamics of child behavior and what influences are brought to bear on it. Finally, observing children can give insight and greater understanding of self.

The general types of observational techniques explored in this chapter include narratives, time and event sampling, ratings such as checklists and scales, and the modified child study techniques of shadow studies, experimental procedures, and the clinical method. As teachers observe and record the behavior of young children, they are aware of professional guidelines that protect children. The guidelines help ensure accurate observation and help the observer respect the privacy of the individual or group.

Evaluating children involves assessing their growth in all of the developmental domains and over time. We evaluate children to establish a baseline and to document their learning. Evaluation helps us determine guidance and intervention, to plan curriculum, to communicate with families, and to monitor program accountability and quality.

Of all the functions performed by teachers, assessment is one of the most challenging. Two types of assessments are naturalistic and formal, and the authentic assessment tool of a child portfolio can include data from both types. Early learning standards are a new and complicated addition to the teacher's job of observation and assessment. Testing and screening, also used in many settings, can be inappropriate, costly, and can unduly affect teacher's curriculum and children's daily care and education. Many concerns arise as programs attempt to evaluate children, and there are several guidelines to follow in order to assess children appropriately.

KEY TERMS

assessment	running record	*methode clinique* (clinical method)
evaluation	diary descriptions	professional confidentiality
objectivity	specimen descriptions	accountability
bias	log/journal	baseline
authentic assessment	time sampling	documentation
individualized curriculum	event sampling	naturalistic assessments
connected knowledge	checklists	formal assessments
intervention	rating scales	norm-referenced test
accommodations	continuum	portfolio
norms	shadow study	early learning standards
narratives	experimental procedure	screening

REVIEW QUESTIONS

1. To see children through observations, teachers use several observational methods. List four and describe the advantages and disadvantages of each. Which would you prefer? Why? Which one(s) might best suit a beginning teacher? A parent? An experienced teacher? The director of the school?

2. In recording observations, teachers must be careful of bias. Poor observations usually contain inferences, over-generalizations, and/or opinions that cloud a complete, objective sampling of a child's behavior. Read the following segment and underline the language segments that contain such passages:

C is sitting on the rug with four friends and he is playing with cars and he starts whining about his car. He is just having a bad attitude about its not moving correctly. C is crying because he just got hit with the car. Let me tell you something about him. He is a big whiner about anything and he always wants it his way. Then he goes over to the book corner and is very quietly reading a book and he is happy by himself.

3. Put this chapter to the test. Match the behavior with the category it describes:

Category	Behavior
Children in general	Matthew cries when his grandma says goodbye.
Influences on behavior	Most 4-year-olds can pull up their pants on their own.
Understanding of self	To really know Celia, I'll have to observe her with scissors, at the climber, figuring out a problem, with her friends, in our small group time, when her mom leaves, and doing a painting.
Developmental relationships	I wonder why Mondays are so hard on Serena? Which weekends does she stay with her Dad?
Children as individuals	You know, I just overreact when I see children playing with their food.

4. Why and how can children's learning and skills be assessed? What are the reasons for assessing children's progress? Describe some of the problems with testing or screening of young children. How can you address these problems if you are required to administer a standardized test to your class?

5. How might a working portfolio help us understand a child?

6. How do we observe and record effectively? What do you consider to be the three most important guidelines to follow when observing young children? Why?

LEARNING ACTIVITIES

1. Observe a child for 10 minutes. Using language as your paintbrush, make a written picture of that child's physical appearance and movements. Compare the child's size, body build, facial features, and energy level with those of other children in the class. In narrative form, record as many of the body movements as you can, noting seemingly useless movements, failures, and partial successes, as well as final achievements.

2. Try a time sample of children's play in your classroom. Observe 10 children for one minute each during free-play times, and record the type(s) of social behavior they show. Using Parten's categories, your chart would look like this one. Compare your results with the impressions of the other teachers with whom you work. Did you come to any conclusions on how children develop socially?

Child/Age	Unoccupied	Solitary	Onlooker	Parallel	Associative	Cooperative
1.						
2.						
3.						
4.						
5.						
6.						
7.						
8.						
9.						
10.						
Totals						

3. If you can, try a shadow study on a child in your class. Choose a child you do not know much about, you have trouble working with, or who is exhibiting inappropriate behaviors. How did this study help you to see the class and school from that child's point of view?

4. Perceptions of a person's character are in the eyes of the beholder. These perceptions affect how teachers behave with children. What color are your glasses tinted? Divide a piece of paper in half, lengthwise. On one side, list some words to describe your feelings about childhood, school, teachers, children, authority, making friends, losing friends, hitting, and playing. On the other side, describe how these feelings may have influenced your teaching and helped create your own biases.

5. Does your own setting have an evaluation plan for child assessment? Analyze the goals of your plan and how the tools or implementation meet (or do not meet) those goals. Be sure to address the concerns about assessment.

6. Teachers have noticed that several children consistently interrupt at story time with seemingly irrelevant questions and constantly grab children seated nearby. What is happening—and why? What observational tools would you use to find out? What clues from individual behavior would you look for? How would you look at the group as a whole? What other information would you need?

HELPFUL WEBSITES

National Association for the Education of Young Children   **http: //www.naeyc.org**

Culturally and Lingustically Appropriate Services (CLAS) Early Childhood Research Institute
   http: //clas.uiuc.edu

Early Childhood Research Quarterly   **http: //www.elsevier.com/wps/find/**

Early Childhood Research Online   **http: //ecr.sagepub.com**

Early Childhood Education Assessment (ECEA) Consortium & Council of Chief State School Officers
   http: //www.ccsso.org

High/Scope   **http: //www.highscope.net**

National Center for Fair and Open Testing   **http: //www.fairtest.org**

National Institute for Early Education Research (NIEER)   **http: //www.nieer.org/standards/statelist.php**

Work Sampling System   **http: //www.worksamplingonline.com**

 Additional resources including the TeachSource Videos can be found on the premium website for this book. Go to **http://www.cengage.com/login** to register your access code.

REFERENCES

Bergan, J. R., & Feld, J. K. (1993). Developmental assessment: New directions. *Young Children 48(5)*, 41–47.

Bodrova, E., Leong, D., & Shore, R. (2004, March). Child outcome standards in pre-K programs: What are standards: What is needed to make them work? In *Preschool Policy Matters*. National Institute on Early Educational Research (NIEER), www.nieer.org. Issue 5.

Bowers, F.B. (2008, November/December). Developing a child assessment plan: An integral part of program quality. Beginnings Workshop: Assessment and Documentation, *Exchange*, 51-55.

California Department of Education. Desired results developmental profile—revised (2006). www.cde.ca.gov.

Cohen, D. H., Stern, V., & Balaban, N. (1997). *Observing and recording the behavior of young children* (4th Ed). New York: Teachers College Press.

Copple, C., & Bredekamp, S., Eds., (2009). *Developmentally appropriate practice in early childhood programs serving children from birth through age 8.* Washington, DC; National Association for the Education of Young Children.

Council of Chief State School Officers (CCSSO (2005). *The words we use: A glossary of terms for early childhood education standards and assessment.* Washington, DC: Early Childhood Education Assessment Consortium.

Curtis, D. (2008, November/December). Seeing children. Beginnings Workshop: Assessment and Documentation, *Exchange,* 37-42.

Curtis, D., & Carter, M. (2000) *The art of awareness: How observation can transform your teaching.* St. Paul, MN: Redleaf Press.

Cryan, J. R. (1986, May/June). Evaluation: Plague or promise? *Childhood Education,* 62 (5).

Danielson, C., & Abrutyn, L. (1997). *An introduction to using portfolios in the classroom.* Alexandria, VA: Association for Supervision and Curriculum Development.

Dawes, H. C. (1934). An analysis of two hundred quarrels of preschool children. *Child Development,* 5, 139-157.

Dowley, E. M. (not dated). Cues for observing children's behavior. Unpublished paper.

Feeney, S., Christensen, D., & Moravcik, E. (2008). *Who am I in the lives of children?* (8th Ed). Englewood Cliffs, NJ: Prentice Hall.

Fenwich, T., & Parsons, J. (2000). *The art of evaluation: A handbook for educators and trainers.* Clifton Park, NY: Thomson Delmar Learning.

Gardner, H. (1988, September/October) Alternatives to standardized testing. *Harvard Education Letter.*

Gonzalez-Mena, J. (2000). Focus Box: Understanding what we observe: A multicultural perspective. In A. Gordon & K. W Browne (Eds.). *Beginnings and beyond: Foundations in early childhood education* (5th Ed). Clifton Park, NY: Thomson Delmar Learning.

Gronlund, G. (2008). Creative and thoughtful strategies for implementing learning standards. *Young Children,* July, 10-13.

Gronlund, G. (2006). *Making early learning standards come alive.* St Paul, MN: Redleaf Press.

Gullo, D. F. (2006). Assessment in kindergarten. In D. F. Gullo (Ed.). *KToday: Teaching and learning in the kindergarten year.* Washington, DC: NAEYC, 138-147.

Hyson, M. (2008). *Enthusiastic and engaged learners: Approaches to learning in the early childhood classroom.* NY: Teachers College Press.

Irwin, D. M., & Bushnell, M. M. (1980). *Observational strategies for child study.* New York: Holt, Rinehart & Winston.

Jones, E., & Reynolds, G. (1992). *The play's the thing: Teachers' roles in children's play.* New York: Teachers College Press.

Jones, E.J., & Carter, M. (1991, January/February). The teacher as observer—Part 1, and Teacher as scribe and broadcaster: Using observation to communicate—Part 2. *Child Care Information Exchange,* 35-38.

Klein, A. S., & Estes, J. S. (2004, January/February). Using observation for performance assessment. *Early Childhood News.*

Lam, M., & Wiggins-Dowler, K. (2006). *Documentation panel: Our construction curriculum project.* San Mateo, CA: MML Children's Center, College of San Mateo, 2005-2006.

MacDonald, B. (2006, November/December) Observation, the path to documentation. Beginnings Workshop: Observation and Assessment, *Exchange,* 45-49.

Malaguzzi, L. (March, 1994) Your image of the child: Where teaching begins. *Exchange,* 52-56.

Maxwell, K. L., & Clifford, R. M. (2004). School readiness assessment in *Spotlight on Young Children and Assessment.* Washington, DC: NAEYC, 29-37.

McLaughlin, K., & Sugarman, S. (1982). Personal communications.

Meisels, S. J., & Atkins-Burnett, S. (2005). *Developmental screening in early childhood: A guide* (5th Ed). Washington, DC: National Association for the Education of Young Children.

National Association for the Education of Young Children (NAEYC) and the National Association of Early Childhood Specialists in State Departments of Education (NAECS/SDE). (2003). Position statement on early childhood curriculum, assessment, and program evaluation—building an effective, accountable system in programs for children birth through age 8. http: //www.naeyc.org/about/positions/pdf/CAPEexpand.pdf

National Center for Fair and Open Testing (NCFOT). Cambridge, MA: Fair Test, 2006.

New Oxford American Dictionary (2nd Ed). England: Oxford University Press, 2005.

Parten, M. B. (1932). Social participation among preschool children. *Journal of Abnormal and Social Psychology,* 27, 243-269.

Pendowski, J. L. (2006, Spring). Portfolios and their use in the early learning environment. *CAEYC Connections.*

Saxton, R. R. (1998, April). Personal communication.

Schiller, P., & Willis, C. A. (2008, July). Of primary interest: Using brain-based teaching strategies to create supportive early childhood environments that address learning standards. *Young Children*, 52-55.

Schweinhart, L. J. (1993, July). Observing young children in action: The key to early childhood assessment. *Young Children*, 45(5), 29-33.

Seefeldt, C., & Barbour, N. (1997). *Early childhood education: An introduction* (4th Ed). New York: MacMillan College Publishing.

Shepard, L. A., Kagan, S. L., & Wurtz, E. (Eds.) (1998). *Principles and recommendations for early childhood assessments*. Washington, DC: National Education Goals Panel.

Shillady, A. L. (2004) Choosing an appropriate assessment system. In *Spotlight on Young Children and Assessment*. Washington, DC: NAEYC, 54-59.

Special thanks to the following Early Childhood Education students for their observation samples: M. Duraliza, J. Gallero, C. Grupe, L. Hutton, C. Liner, C. Robinson, & M. Saldivar.

Guiding Children's Behavior

© Cengage Learning

PREVIEW QUESTIONS

- Why do children behave the way they do?
- What are the factors that affect children's behaviors?
- What is the difference between discipline and punishment?
- What are the most effective guidance techniques?
- What should the teacher do if school and home guidance techniques differ?

NAEYC CODE OF ETHICAL CONDUCT

These Core Values and sections from the NAEYC Code of Ethical Conduct are addressed in this chapter. As you read, note how the Core Values, Ideals, or Principles listed here apply to the topics in this chapter. (Reprinted with permission from the National Association for the Education of Young Children.)

Core Values: We have committed ourselves to helping children and adults achieve their full potential in the context of relationships that are based on trust, respect, and positive regard.

Section I:

I.1-4	To appreciate the special vulnerability of children
P-1.1	Not to participate in practices that are disrespectful, degrading, dangerous, exploitative, intimidating, emotionally damaging, or physically harmful.
I-2.4	To respect families' childrearing values and their rights to make decisions for their children.
P-3C.1	To utilize the education, training, experience, and expertise of staff members in decisions concerning children and programs.

The Guidance Triangle

Guidance is the ongoing process of helping children learn to control their basic impulses, express their feelings, channel their frustrations, and solve their problems. There are no quick fixes or strategies that apply to all circumstances. Positive guidance methods are created to fit a child, an adult (parent, teacher), and a situation. These three elements, when considered together, suggest the most appropriate guidance strategies. Figure 7-1 shows these three factors in relation to one another.

Throughout this chapter, the relationship between the child, the adult, and the situation will be reflected in guidance theory and practices.

Understanding Behavior

In the toddler class, 2-year-olds Shawnsey and Kim are playing in the dress-up area. Kim grabs at one of the many necklaces Shawnsey has draped around

The Guidance Triangle

In establishing effective guidance practices, adults take into consideration three important elements: the child, the adult, and the situation. For instance, a 2-year-old needing assistance is more likely to respond to the intervention of a familiar teacher than one who is substituting for the day.

Child

as an individual
- level of development
- unique style/temperament
- "whole child": physical, emotional, social, intellectual

as a member of
- a family
- a race/ethnic/cultural group
- the group of children in this class

Adult
- the role (teacher, parent, coach, advocate, friend)
- relationship to the child
- values, biases
- skills and guidance techniques

Situation
- the physical environment
- time of day
- who, what is involved
- what else is happening
- what is unique about it

FIGURE 7-1 The Guidance Triangle (From Ann Gordon & Kathryn Williams Browne, *Guiding Young Children in a Diverse Society*. Published by Allyn and Bacon, Boston, MA. Copyright © 1996 by Pearson Education. Reprinted with permission of the publisher.)

her neck. Startled, Shawnsey lets out a cry, grabs Kim's arm, and bites her.

Malcolm, a 5-year-old, rushes through the room, heading for the block area. For just a moment, he stands and watches Lorraine balancing blocks on top of one another in a tall column. With a swift wave of his arm, Malcolm topples the structure.

Mac, a 3½-year-old, is busy with a puzzle. When a teacher stops at the table to tell the children it is nearly time to clean up for snacks, Mac replies, "My daddy says that cleaning up is a girl's job and I don't have to do it." He throws the puzzle on the floor and dashes away from the teacher.

These are typical scenes in any early childhood center. No matter how plentiful the materials, how many or well trained the adults, or how good the program, conflicts are sure to occur. Helping children learn how to cope with their anger, their fears, their frustrations, and their **DAP** desires is one of the most challenging jobs for a teacher.

To teach children to respect themselves and each other is a complex and difficult task. It takes experience, skill, and practice. Look at the examples again. What do they say about children in general? What do they say about Shawnsey, Malcolm, and Mac? How should teachers respond to these children, and how does that response influence future behavior? (See "What Do You Think?" on spanking on page 240 and Figure 7-6 for discussing solutions to these types of situations.)

Theories

To guide children's behavior, a teacher must first understand it. This requires a background in child development, skills in observing, and an understanding about why children behave and misbehave.

There are several ways of explaining what people do and why. One idea is that people's behavior is mainly a result of heredity (nature). Another is that experience and environment shape behavior (nurture). A third theory suggests that children go through "stages" at certain times of their lives regardless of their genes or home background.

All sides have valid arguments in the nature/nurture debate. It is useful to remember that both heredity and experience affect behavior. Age and stage theory is also familiar. People speak of the "terrible 2s" or say that all 4-year-old girls are silly. There may be some truth to those generalities, but that does not excuse the inappro-

For guidance to be successful, a teacher must first understand children's behavior.

© Cengage Learning

priate behavior at the various developmental stages. Teachers and parents cannot ignore misbehavior (unless it is a specific guidance strategy) just because children are the "right" age or because of their home situations. That attitude implies adults are powerless to help children form new behavior patterns. Not true!

Adults can do something about children's behavior if they understand what is happening to the child. Where does appropriate behavior come from? Why do children misbehave?

Factors That Affect Behavior

Knowing what affects children's behavior and feelings helps adults understand and manage the misbehaving child. Teachers can anticipate problems instead of wait-

---

DAP Every culture has different ways of dealing with emotions, so early childhood educators will need to be aware of how they and the families respond to children's emotions.

ing for them to occur; preventive measures are part of guiding children's behavior. These factors combine aspects of both nature and nurture theories, as well as the theories of ages and stages of development. The three vignettes at the beginning of the chapter provide examples of all five factors, which are: (1) developmental; (2) environmental; (3) individual; (4) emotional and social; and (5) cultural.

1. *Developmental Factors.* Adults who work with children should be aware of developmental theory to know what type of behavior to expect of children at various ages. Developmental theory helps teachers anticipate what children will do so that they can maintain reasonable expectations. To see behavior as predictable and developmentally appropriate is to understand it more completely and guide it more effectively.

   The facts are that Shawnsey, Kim, Malcolm, and Mac have been in a group setting for more than three hours and it is nearly snack time. Teachers know that preschoolers cannot be expected to be in control of themselves over extended periods of time. Conflicts and disagreements happen in any group of children. Hungry children are often ineffective problem solvers; Mac might be more manageable after snack. It is also clear to the teacher that the toddlers do not have the language or social development skills to talk problems out with other children as do Malcolm and Mac.

2. *Environmental Factors.* Through the intentional use of the environment, the teacher indirectly influences behavior in the classroom. The goals for positive behavior should be reflected in the classroom setting. The physical environment should tell children clearly how to act in that space. Child-size furniture that fits the preschool body encourages sitting and working behavior. Room arrangements that avoid spaces that could be used encourage children to walk from place to place. Low, open shelves create an expectation that children will take materials out and put them away after use.

   Materials and equipment should be adequate and interesting to the age group. When children are occupied with stimulating and interesting age-appropriate materials, there are fewer opportunities for misbehavior. The materials can challenge children, overwhelm them, or bore them. If materials and equipment are suitable, children will feel more at ease with themselves and be more willing to accept adults' limits and controls. Adding materials and equipment can help prevent arguments over a favorite toy, create new and interesting challenges, and extend children's play ideas.   **DAP**

   > Shawnsey and Kim's teacher will want to add more necklaces to the dress-up area if there are not enough to outfit several children.

   Changing the environment when needed can help avert behavior problems. Removing attractive but breakable items reduces tears and conflicts. Some materials may prove to be too stimulating and may need to be removed for a while. Some activities may need to be limited to specific locations to control the level of activity and behavior. Look at Figure 7-2 to evaluate how the environment is related to your guidance philosophy and children's behavior. Chapter 9 contains a detailed discussion of many factors that should be considered when designing spaces for young children. Many of these environmental considerations directly influence children's behavior.

   The daily schedule and timing of events indirectly influence classroom behavior. When there are blocks of time to choose activities, children can proceed at their own pace without feeling hurried.

   > Mac, for instance, had just settled in at the puzzle table when the teacher told him that it was time to clean up. Uncooperative behavior is sometimes related to time pressures.

   Children feel free to work, move, and play and are able to accept the teacher's control when it is necessary. The physical needs of eating, sleeping, and toileting are met by careful scheduling so that children are able to play without concern for the necessities of life. Schedules that do not allow enough time for clean up and transitions produce a frantic climate.

3. *Individual Factors.* Teachers of young children soon learn the temperamental characteristics of each child in the class.   **DAP**

DAP Foster inclusion by choosing materials that reflect gender equity, varying abilities, and multiculturalism.
DAP Children's individual temperaments are a significant consideration in guiding their behavior.

Relationship of Family Patterns to Child's Behavior and Guidance Strategies

Time

____ Does the daily schedule provide enough time for unhurried play?

____ Are those periods that create tension—transitions from one activity to another—given enough time?

____ Is cleanup a leisurely process built in at the end of each activity, with children participating?

Program Planning and Curriculum

____ Is there enough to do so that children have choices and alternatives for play?

____ Is the curriculum challenging enough to prevent boredom and restlessness?

____ Are there activities to help children release tension? Do the activities allow for body movement, exploration, and manipulation of materials?

____ Are children included in developing the rules and setting guidelines? How is their inclusion demonstrated?

Organization and Order

____ If children are expected to put things away after use, are the cabinets low, open, and marked in some way?

____ Are the materials within easy reach of the children, promoting self-selection and independence?

____ Are there enough materials so that sharing does not become a problem?

____ Are the areas in which activities take place clearly defined so that children know what happens there?

____ Does the room arrangement avoid runways and areas with no exits?

____ Do children have their own private space?

____ Are children able to use all visible and accessible materials? Are there materials about which children are told "Don't touch"?

Personnel

____ Are there enough teachers to give adequate attention to the number of children in the class?

____ Are the group size and makeup balanced so that children have a variety of playmates?

____ Are the teachers experienced, and do they seem comfortable in setting limits and guiding children's behavior?

____ Do teachers use their attention to encourage behavior they want, and do they ignore what they want to discourage?

____ Do all adults consistently enforce the same rules?

FIGURE 7-2 Classroom checklist. By anticipating children's needs and growth patterns, teachers set up classrooms that foster constructive and purposeful behavior.

Hondi works and plays with great intensity; Norman is easily distracted. Tawana fears any change, whereas Enrique thrives on challenges. The consistent patterns of temperament that emerge help define each child's individual style. The teacher will want to support and comfort Kim at the same time she lets Shawnsey know that biting will not be tolerated. It is important to maintain a level of trust with Shawnsey so that she can help learn better ways to communicate her needs.

Research by Thomas and Chess (1977) has identified three types of temperament in babies: the easy child, the difficult child, and the slow-to-warm-up child. The traits used to classify these children were: activity level, regularity and rhythm of bodily routines, adaptability, physical sensitivity, intensity of reaction, ease of distraction, mood, and attention span. These differences were ob-

served in very young infants and seem to remain consistent as the child grows.

Research supports the concept of individual differences that are present from birth and the importance of acknowledging those differences. If parents and teachers come to know the nature of a child's temperament, they can accept that as part of the wholeness of that particular child. Guidance measures can be tailored to meet the unique needs of a slow-to-warm-up child, for instance, or a difficult child. Those strategies will need to be different from techniques used to discipline the easy child. Children's temperament also affects the way people deal with them. An easy child is easy to respond to; a slow-to-warm-up child may be harder to reach. Difficult children may tend to be blamed for things they did not do. Identifying traits can be useful as long as adults are careful not to label children unfairly or prematurely.

Malcolm, for instance, is enthusiastic and plunges into activities spontaneously, sometimes without looking ahead or surveying the wreckage he leaves behind. His teacher is aware that he can be personable and cooperative if he is given options and a chance to make decisions. As they talk together about Lorraine's blocks, the teacher offers Malcolm a choice: to talk with Lorraine to see if she would like to have him help rebuild the same structure or start a new one. Both Malcolm and the teacher find satisfaction in working together in ways that acknowledge and respect Malcolm's personal style.

4. *Emotional and Social Factors.* Some behavior problems stem from the child's attempt to express social and emotional needs. These include the need to feel loved and cared for, the need to be included, the desire to be considered important and valued, the desire to have friends, and the need to feel safe from harm. Young children are still working out ways to express these needs and feelings. Typically, because they are only just learning language and communication skills, it is often through nonverbal or indirect actions that children let us know what is bothering them. It is also important to provide children with models of language for resolving these conflicts. It is important

to let children know that we recognize they can be angry, jealous, or hurt. The supportive adult will help children find satisfying ways to cope with their social and emotional feelings.

Shawnsey is an only child of older parents and has little opportunity outside of school to interact with others her age. Malcolm comes from a big, boisterous family in which taking care of one's own desires and needs is instilled early on. Mac's parents are divorced and he is now living with his grandmother while his mother looks for work in another town. Their teachers understand their bids for attention and weigh each child's social and emotional history as they guide them toward positive behavior.

Other influences affect behavior. Weather seems to affect children. Wild, windy, rainy days seem to stimulate children into high and excitable behavior. Bright, sunny days also seem to influence a child's mood and temperament.

What Do YOU Think?

"Spanking may allow a parent to let off steam, but it doesn't teach a child the right way to behave. What's more, it is humiliating and emotionally harmful, and it can lead to physical injury. Worst of all, spanking teaches youngsters that violence is an acceptable way to communicate. The American Academy of Pediatrics strongly opposes hitting children" (American Academy of Pediatrics, 1997).

Spanking children is a controversial issue. Do you agree or disagree with the AAP? Why? Where in the Code of Ethical Conduct in Appendix A does it address this issue?

© Cengage Learning

Teachers are called upon to deal with a variety of emotional needs.

Problems that upset adults can make an impression on a child. A family crisis, a new baby, or a recent divorce has impact. Sharing a bedroom, visits from relatives, illness, television, videos or movies, siblings, nutrition, and health affect children's behavior. The longer teachers work with children, the more adept they become at seeing how these various factors shape the behavior of the individual children in their class. In Chapter 14, the young child's social and emotional growth is further explored.

5. *Cultural Factors.* Today's children are growing up in a country of unparalleled diversity. Many different cultures are converging and creating a nation of peoples, cultures, languages, and attitudes. Children and their teachers are living in a world of continual cross-cultural interactions, so the ability to communicate across cultures is a critical skill to have when guiding children's behavior. (See also discussions in Chapters 2, 5, 8, and 15.) A review of Erikson's and Vygotsky's theories in Chapter 4 and Bronfenbrenner's theory in Chapter 15 underscores the connection between culture and behavior.

Discipline is deeply embedded within the values and beliefs of the family. The family's culture shapes how they raise their children, and each family is unique in the way it interprets its cultural values. Child-rearing practices such as the timing of toilet training to physical punishment are culturally influenced. The messages children receive about their behavior should be consistent between school and home. Yet, conflict may be inevitable because the culturally influenced child-rearing practices of the family may be at odds with a teacher's ideas and expectations (Gordon & Browne, 1996).

In some cultures, children are encouraged to challenge adult opinions, whereas this would be considered disrespectful in other cultures. Each child must be valued as part of a family system, no matter the origin or structure, and the teacher's role is to support the child's sense of security and identity within the family. Children bring their unique individuality to the classroom, but they are also bearers of the context in which they are being raised: their family, culture, ethnicity, religion, socioeconomic status, and neighborhood. When we are aware of these influences, we are better able to match who the child is with the most effective guidance approach (Gordon & Browne, 1996).

In some families, a sense of community is valued over individualism, a concept that can create difficulty in the early childhood classroom unless it is understood and appreciated. Early childhood educators, for the most part, do not force children to share personal possessions before they seem ready to, and they encourage children to become autonomous at an early age. This is at odds with families in which cooperation and sharing are valued concepts, as is dependency on other family members. Teachers will need to become culturally sensitive to some of the long-held assumptions of teaching young children. The sections on "Self-Awareness" and "Attitudes and Biases" in Chapter 5 suggest ways in which teachers can address stereotypes and prejudices that may interfere with their effectiveness in guiding children's behavior.

Schools must be inviting and safe places in which families from all cultures can express their perceptions, concerns, and expectations about their children. Teachers will need to be flexible and nonjudgmental as they work with the cultural implications of children's behavior. Figure 7-3 shows how different family cultural patterns relate to a child's behavior and an appropriate guidance strategy. Kim (who was playing with Shawnsey) has a family culture that views the teacher as a respected authority figure and one who must be obeyed. This places Kim in an uncomfortable position if her teacher does not understand why Kim does not make activity choices easily and prefers to have the teacher tell her where to play and work each day. As teachers become familiar with the customs and beliefs of the families in the program, they will gain insights into children's behavior and understand the reasons for the way a child responds.

DAP

What Do YOU Think? Ask yourself: Do my classroom and teaching style reflect the patterns and relationships of one particular culture or many cultures?

DAP Culturally sensitive teaching strategies recognize the parent's perspective and the child's family experience.

Family Patterns and Children's Behavior

Family Culture	Child's Experience and Behavior	Guidance Strategy
Power Structure		
Democratic family—members share in decision making	Child is encouraged to negotiate and compromise.	Offer real choices; use problem-solving techniques.
One family member makes all of the decisions	Child is expected to obey, follow commands, and respect adult authority. Child may be unable to choose activities, look adults in the eye, or call them by name.	Don't insist on eye contact. Child may need help in selecting an activity. Work with the family members who make the decisions.
Values		
Strong, close-knit family	Child learns that the family comes first; the individual sacrifices for the family.	Recognize that family matters may take precedence over school.
Honor, dignity, and pride	Child's behavior reflects family honor; child is disciplined for rudeness or poor manners.	Share achievements with parents; help child learn manners; be sensitive when discussing child's behavior problems.
Expressing feelings is accepted	Child is allowed to cry, scream, throw temper tantrums.	Accept child's crying as you give comfort; stay with child until he is calm.
Issue of Discipline		
Clear, direct discipline	Child learns to respect authority and does what he is told to do; child may not take positive guidance strategies seriously or ignore them.	Use a sense of humor; make firm statements.
Discipline motivated toward inherent goodness	Child has freedom to explore consequences and is warned of possible embarrassment due to behavior.	Child may be passive if disciplined harshly. Use natural consequences; ask rather than demand.
Discipline motivated from inherent self-interest	Child is scolded, threatened, and controlled by promises.	Model desired behavior; use "if/then" statements: "If you finish eating, then you can play." Praise good manners and good behavior.

FIGURE 7-3 Sample of culturally diverse family patterns that affect guidance and discipline. Knowledge of culturally diverse family patterns and guidance strategies to parallel these child-rearing styles can allow you to begin a dialogue with the children you teach. (From *Roots and Wings* (Revised Edition), by Stacey York, pp. 66, 68, 69, 70. Copyright © 2003 by Stacey York. Adapted with permission from Redleaf Press, St. Paul, Minnesota, www.redleafpress.org.)

Guiding Young Children

The overall process of guidance is a common concern of parents and teachers and can be the basis for a strong partnership as they learn together why Dominick whines or Carrie dawdles or Cleo disrupts group time.

What Is Guidance?

Guidance is an ongoing system by which adults help children learn to manage their impulses, express feelings, channel frustrations, solve problems, and learn the difference between acceptable and unacceptable behavior (Browne & Gordon, 2009). The children we meet in early childhood programs are just learning how strong their emotions can be and what impact they have on their own behavior and on others. Behavior is the unspoken language through which children act out feelings and thoughts. Until they learn to express themselves vocally, they use a variety of behaviors to communicate. Using words (for instance, a resounding "No!" when someone takes a toy away) is slowly replacing biting, hitting, crying, and tantrums as a way to respond to frustration. Caring and respectful adults create a supportive atmosphere to help young children explore alternative behaviors, develop social skills, and learn to solve problems. This is called a positive approach to guidance.

Practice these examples of positive guidance:

- Tell children what it is you want them to do. Make directions and suggestions in positive statements, not in negative forms.
  "Walk around the edge of the grass, Hilla, so you won't get hit by the swing" instead of *"Don't get hit!"*
- Reinforce what children do right, what you like, and what you want to see repeated. This helps build the relationship on positive grounds.
  "Good job, Sammy. You worked hard on that puzzle."
- Give indirect suggestions or reminders, emphasizing what you want children to do. Help them refocus on the task without nagging or confrontation.
  "I know you are excited about the field trip, Mickey. Looks like you are almost finished putting on your jacket so we can go" instead of *"Hurry and button that jacket so we can go."*
- Use positive redirection whenever possible.
  "Let's get a basket for you to toss those balls in. That way you won't bother other children who are playing nearby."
- Use encouragement appropriately, focusing on helping children achieve success and understanding what it is you want them to learn.

"Harry, I notice you are being careful about where you put your feet as you climb that tree. It looks to me like you are finding good places to stand" communicates a supportive attitude and tells the child what he is doing well. Global praise, such as *"Great climbing, Harry. Good for you!"* may leave children wondering what exactly it is they have been praised for and omits the learning they can derive from the experience.

- Give reasons for your request. Let children know in simple, straightforward statements the reasons behind your request. Children are more likely to cooperate when they can understand the reason why.
  "Tom, if you move those chairs, then you and Dee will have more room to dance" instead of *"Move the chairs, Tom."*

Through daily experiences, children construct their moral and social world, and they need adult guidance. The concept of guide—one who leads, explains, and supports— is an important one (Gordon & Browne, 1996). A guide points out directions, answers questions, and helps you get where you want to go. This is what teachers do as they help children learn to balance impulse and outer controls.

A positive guidance approach requires the active participation of both child and adult in order to be successful. Adults help children learn appropriate behavior by serving as models of behavior. Good role models deliberately vary their teaching styles and strategies to accommodate different learning styles and cultural patterns.

Inductive Guidance

There are a number of guidance approaches woven throughout the chapter that have many similar components and fall under the definition of **inductive guidance.** The key elements of inductive guidance are:

1. Guidance is an interactive process that actively involves children, as well as adults.
2. Children are increasingly held responsible for their actions as they begin to understand the impact of their behavior on others.
3. Inductive guidance helps a child learn thinking and reasoning skills, which fosters self-control and the development of a conscience.
4. Children learn to reflect on their feelings and their actions.

These four elements of inductive guidance are supported when teachers provide choices for children, ask open-ended questions ("What would happen if you took her book?" "How do you think he would feel if you said you did not want to play with him?"), and communicate trust and confidence in children's ability to solve problems.

The inductive guidance principles are based on the theories of Erikson and Piaget but owe particular credit to Vygostsky, who placed children's learning in the context of social interactions. The zone of proximal distance (see Chapter 4), for instance, reinforces the reciprocal relationship between adults and children implied in most inductive guidance techniques. Thomas and Chess's (1977) "goodness of fit," in which the adult addresses the child's unique temperament in choosing guidance strategies, is reflected as well in inductive guidance. Family context also continues to be a priority when selecting appropriate guidance methods.

By integrating these principles into a positive guidance approach, teachers enlarge the child's capacity to become increasingly self-directed and self-reliant.

TeachSource Video ▶⏸

Watch the TeachSource Video Case entitled, "Elementary Classroom Management: Basic Strategies." After you study the video clip, view the artifacts, and read the teacher interviews and text, reflect upon the following questions:

1. Kindergarten teacher Amy spoke of building teamwork. What examples did you observe in this video case that supported teamwork as a way to promote positive behavior?

2. How do you think Amy's attitude toward behavior problems affects her relationship with the children in her class?

What Is Discipline?

Discipline is a part of the guidance strategies adults use to help children become responsible for their actions, learn self-control, and behave appropriately. **Discipline** stems from the word *disciple*, that is, a pupil, a follower, and a learner. This suggests two important concepts: that of following an example versus following rules and that of positive discipline. Discipline and guidance are similar in that effective discipline has the same foundation of thoughtful, nonpunitive methods that promote children's empathy and moral reasoning (Browne & Gordon, 2009).

What Is Punishment?

Punishment is a consequence for inappropriate behavior and a power assertive technique that relies on children's fears rather than the use of reason and understanding.

Punishment is too often a knee-jerk reaction by an adult and may be based on negative strategies such as threats, shaming, and spanking, which are damaging to children's self-esteem. To be effective, punishment should be related to the behavior and help children learn from the situation. For instance, when Georgia grabs a book from Ruthie, the teacher will want to help Georgia learn to negotiate for a turn rather than punish her with a time out. Georgia will learn new strategies for controlling her impulses. To maintain a positive approach to guidance, always avoid:

- Methods that will shame, frighten, or humiliate children.
- Physical abuse; physical punishment.
- Comparisons among children. Comparisons foster competitiveness and affect self-esteem.
- Carryovers from the incident. Once it is over, leave it behind; do not keep reminding children about it.
- Consequences that are too long, too punitive, or postponed. Children benefit most from immediate, short consequences.
- Making promises you cannot keep.
- Being overly helpful. Let children do as much as they can by themselves, including solving their own conflicts.
- Threatening children with the loss of your affection.

To some, the words discipline and punishment are synonymous. They are not as Figure 7-4 shows how these terms mean very different things.

Toward Self-Discipline

One of the major goals of a good guidance process is to help children achieve self-discipline. This happens only if adults lead in ways that support children's developing ability to control themselves. By gradually handing over to children the opportunity to govern their own actions, adults communicate trust. For young children with their emerging initiative, this is an important step to take. With added responsibility and trust comes an added dimension of self-respect and self-confidence. Such children feel capable and worthwhile.

Along with self-respect, the child must taste the freedom that comes with a lessening of adult controls. Children do not learn to handle freedom by being told what to do all the time. Only when they have an opportunity to test themselves and make some decisions on their own will they know their capabilities. Young children must learn this in safe places with adults who allow them as much freedom as they can responsibly handle.

An effective guidance approach is interactive. Adults and children both learn to change as they interact with one another toward a common goal. Figure 7-5 summarizes

Differences Between Positive Guidance and Punishment

Positive Guidance	Punishment
Emphasizes what the child should do	Emphasizes what the child should *not* do
Is an ongoing process	Is a one-time occurrence
Sets an example to follow	Insists on obedience
Leads to self-control	Undermines independence
Helps children change	Is an adult release
Is positive	Is negative
Accepts child's need to assert self	*Makes* children behave
Fosters child's ability to think	Thinks *for* the child
Bolsters self-esteem	Defeats self-esteem
Shapes behavior	Condemns misbehavior

FIGURE 7-4 Positive guidance encourages children's interaction and involvement; punishment is usually something that is done to a child.

Guidance: An Interactive Approach

Guidance is an interactive process in which both children and adults may learn. Everyone benefits from disciplinary practices that foster changes in attitudes and behaviors.

We Teach	Adults Learn to	Children Learn to
Values	Express	Internalize
Self-control	Maintain own	Practice
Respect	Give to child	Accord to others
Appropriate behavior	Model	Observe and imitate
Limits	Be clear and consistent	Accept consequences
Feelings	Accept own and child's	Identify and label
Problem solving	Offer meaningful choices	Make decisions
Self-esteem	Protect and enhance	Respect and appreciate self
Rule setting	Share power	Participate in creating behavior controls
Taking another's viewpoint	Be sympathetic and understanding	To be empathetic
Collaboration	Involve child in solutions	Problem-solve cooperatively

FIGURE 7-5 Guidance is an interactive process in which both children and adults may learn. Everyone benefits from disciplinary practices that foster changes in attitudes and behaviors. (From Ann Gordon & Kathryn Williams Browne, *Guiding Young Children in a Diverse Society.* Published by Allyn and Bacon, Boston, MA. Copyright © 1996 by Pearson Education. Reprinted with permission of the publisher.)

some of the ways children and adults can learn from a guidance and positive discipline philosophy.

Developmentally Appropriate Guidance

Each developmental stage has shared characteristics, modified, of course, by a child's individual rate of growth. It is as typical for 4-year-olds to test limits as it is for toddlers to have a strong sense of ownership about their possessions. To have a developmentally appropriate guidance approach, teachers take this knowledge and understanding of child development principles into consideration as they contemplate how best to respond to a child's behavior.

Identifying the behaviors that are typical to a specific age group provides a context in which to understand the child and behavior that can be seen as normal and predictable. Guidance based on a developmental approach will help a teacher to know that first and second graders have an ability to consider others' points of view, so they will choose problem-solving methods that will ask children to think of how their behavior affected others.

A developmentally appropriate approach also requires that the teacher consider what is known about the individual child, as well as what is typical for the age group. This ensures that the guidance techniques will match the capabilities of the child and that adult expectations will remain reasonable. You foster developmentally appropriate guidance when you:

- Allow plenty of time for children to respond. Give them an opportunity to decide their course of action.
- Review limits and rules periodically. Modify them as children's growth and maturation indicate. Change them as circumstances change; be flexible.
- Encourage children to talk things over. Be open to their point of view even if you cannot accept it. Let them know you are willing to listen to all sides of the conflict.
- Become aware of the climate in the room or yard. Anticipate the need for a change of pace or a different activity before children become bored or troublesome.
- Remember, it takes time and numerous opportunities for changes in behavior to occur. By using consistent positive guidance techniques, you will help children practice new behavior repeatedly.

Culturally Appropriate Guidance

An emerging issue, as our population becomes more and more diverse, has to do with cultural values and guidance. Teachers may be confronted by parents whose guidance practices are contrary to the school's philosophy. Pressure may be exerted on teachers to apply some of those same techniques at school that parents use at home. Teachers want to maintain the school's, as well as their own standards without communicating to the family that their values are wrong or have children feel that something about their home and family is diminished in the teacher's eyes. Gonzalez-Mena (2008) emphasizes the teacher's responsibility to learn cross-cultural communication when child-rearing practices are in conflict between home and school and suggests the following strategies:

- Accept that both viewpoints are equally valid.
- Work together to figure out a solution to the situation.
- Resist assigning meaning and values to the behavior of others on the basis of your own culture.
- Remember that your behavior does not necessarily convey your own meaning and values.
- Educate yourself about the different cultures represented in your classroom. Learn how and what is

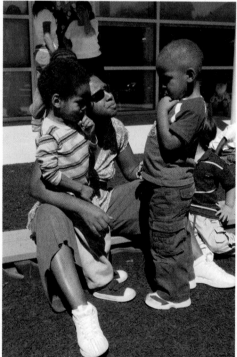

© Cengage Learning

Body height and position are important. Getting down to the child's eye level provides for greater impact and involvement.

communicated through facial gestures, touch, eye contact, physical closeness, and time concepts.

- Observe, ask, and talk about what the differences are; learn from the parents of the children in the classroom what you need to know about their culture.
- Maintain an open attitude that promotes respect and appreciation for each other's views.

Ethical issues involving culture-based differences are discussed in Chapter 5. The anti-bias curriculum, as described in Chapters 5 and 9, suggests some strategies as well. Also see "Child Development and Cultural Diversity" in Chapter 4. The NAEYC Code of Ethical Conduct (Appendix A) is a useful resource for ethical concerns when working with families from many cultures.

The Language of Guidance and Discipline

DAP Guidance has a language all its own. As teachers gain experience in handling problem behaviors, they learn to use that language. The result, in most cases, is **interdependence**: the more practiced teachers become in the language of guidance, the more comfortable they become in developing their own approach to guidance problems. Also, the more comfortable they are in that approach, the more effectively they use language to solve behavior problems.

The language and communication techniques in guidance are both spoken and unspoken. Teachers discover how potent the voice can be—what words will work best and when. They become aware of facial expressions and what a touch or a look will convey to children. How they use their body reflects a distinct attitude and approach to discipline. Through experience, new teachers will learn how to use these tools in ways that will work best for them and the children.

Voice

Some adults feel that when they are speaking to children they must assume a different voice from the one they normally use. Talk to children in the same way you talk to other people. Learn to control the volume and use good speech patterns for children to imitate. To be heard, get close enough to speak in a normal tone; get down to the child's level. Often, lowering volume and pitch is effective.

Words

The fewer the words, the better. Simple, clear statements, spoken once, will have more impact. The child will be able to focus on the real issues involved. A brief description of what happened, a word or two about what behavior is acceptable and what is not, and a suggestion for possible solutions are all that is necessary.

Choose words carefully. They should convey to the child exactly what is expected. "Richy, move the block closer to the truck so Sarah will not bump into it again" tells Richy in a positive, concrete way what he can do to protect his block building. If he had been told, "Richy, watch where you are building," he would not know what action to take to solve the problem.

Body Language

When working with small children, the teacher must be aware of body height and position. Sit, squat, or kneel—but get down to their level. It is difficult to communicate warmth, caring, and concern from two or three feet above a child's head, or by shouting from across the room.

Guidance is founded on a loving, caring relationship between child and adult. To help children gain control over their impulses and monitor their own behavior, teachers must establish a sense of trust and well being with children.

The way teachers use their body invites or rejects close relationship and familiarity. A child will find teachers more approachable if they are seated low, with arms available, rather than standing, with arms folded.

Making full use of the senses can soften the impact of words. A firm grip on the hand of a child who is hitting out, a gentle touch on the shoulder, tells children the adult is there to protect them from themselves and others. Eye contact is essential. Teachers learn to communicate the seriousness of a situation through eye and facial expressions. They also show reassurance, concern, sadness, and affection this way. Physical presence should convey to the child a message that the teacher is there, available, and interested.

Attitude

Attitude is part of the unspoken language of guiding children. Attitudes are derived from experience. You should examine the way you were disciplined and acknowledge your experiences and feelings about it, par-

---

DAP The language of discipline may differ from culture to culture. Gender differences, which may be cultural, may emerge, encouraging boys to "hit back" and girls to be more passive in solving conflicts.

ticularly assumptions you may have on how children behave depending on their race, gender, or culture.

Implications for Teaching

A teacher has *direct* and *indirect* influence on children's behavior. Some of the ways teachers deal directly with discipline are by what they say and what they do. Indirectly, a teacher's influence is felt just as strongly. Room arrangements and time schedules, attitudes, and behavior can work for or against good guidance practices. Teachers who are well grounded in the developmental process know that problem behaviors are normal and occur in every early childhood setting. They realize that growing children must have a safe, secure place in which to test themselves against the world.

A Behavior Model

The teacher as a **behavior model** is an important element in guidance. Children pattern their responses after adult behaviors. They are aware of how teachers respond to anger, frustration, and aggression; and how they solve problems and conflicts. Adults must be sure to model the desired behavior around the children they teach. To be successful models, teachers should be aware of their emotions and feelings; they do not want to compound a problem by their own reaction. Adults who express negative feelings to children must proceed carefully, stating their position clearly, honestly, and objectively in a low, calm voice:

- It bothers me when you call Roberto a dummy.
- You do not need to yell at me. I can hear you from right here. Tell me again in a quieter voice.
- I am serious about this—no biting.
- Sometimes I get angry when children try to hurt each other.
- It makes me sad to see all that food going to waste. Please put just enough on your plate so that you will eat it all.

Remember that children are frightened by strong feelings; do not overwhelm them with your own behavior.

Consistency

Being *consistent* is one of the key elements in good guidance practices. If adults want to develop mutual trust, the rules must be clear, fair, and enforced consistently and regularly. At the same time, children need to know what will happen if rules are not followed. Consequences, too, should be consistent.

Realistic Expectations

Teachers should have *realistic expectations* for children, neither too high nor too low. Sometimes they presume children have abilities and skills they do not yet possess, and this may cause children to respond in inappropriate ways. It can be helpful to rehearse with children how they are expected to act. Practice sessions are especially useful when introducing a new topic or plan.

> One teacher rehearsed the children for their first bus ride to go on a field trip. They practiced singing, looking out the windows, having snacks, and talking with friends. A large outline of a bus was drawn with chalk on the patio floor. The children pretended to board the bus, walk down the narrow aisle, find a seat, and remember to take big steps getting up and down the steps. When the field trip day arrived, children knew several appropriate ways of behaving while on the long bus trip.

Many times children are asked to do jobs that are too complicated for them. The young child who is just learning to put on a jacket is a good example. Children may not be able to accomplish the entire job at first; it is helpful to them if the task is broken down into smaller steps. Start out small: Let Gordie learn to zip up the jacket. Little by little, teach Gordie how to get his arms in the sleeves. Soon he will be doing the task by himself.

Effective guidance practice involves children as active participants. How would you help this child solve the problem of being excluded from play?

Actively Observe

As *active observers* in their classroom, teachers can learn a great deal about the effects of their guidance efforts. When teachers observe, they can time interventions or move into a situation before it becomes problematic. Observations can also be used to help children see how their actions impact others. Chapter 6 has many good observation forms for teachers to use.

Prevent Misbehavior

Preventing misbehavior is another part of the teacher's role. Effective guidance practices call for teachers to be alert to potential problems and situations before they result in children's inappropriate behavior. Even then, unpredictable situations occur: A child becomes tired in the middle of snack time; one of the teachers is called out of the room; rain forces an activity to move indoors; or a scheduled event gets postponed. At these trying and typical times, a teacher's full range of abilities is called into play. Ways to help children maintain positive behavior patterns in these situations include:

1. *Recognize and label the problem or situation.* Acknowledge the difficulties it presents to the children. Example: "You seem tired, Gus, and I know you had

to wait a long time for your snack. When you have finished your juice and cracker, put your head down on the table and rest for a minute."

2. *Ask children for their help.* Get them involved in working out the solutions. Example: "Mr. Gallo had to leave for a while. How can we continue with this math project when I need to help out in the writing area too? Who has an idea? What do you think would work?"

3. *Assign a job or a task to the children who are most likely to react to the crisis.* Example: "Lorraine and Paul, will you carry the special drums inside, please, while I help the others put the wagons away?"

4. *Always be prepared with a story to tell, songs to sing, guessing games to play, or exercises to do.* Help children pass the time in an appropriate way modeled by the teacher. Give a new focus. Example: "The fire truck hasn't arrived at school yet; we'll have to wait another five minutes. While we are waiting to go and see it, show me how firefighters climb ladders and slide down poles."

5. *Say what you would like to have happen.* Admit what you wish you could do to correct the situation. Example: "Oh, little Riko, I wish I could bring your mommy back right now but I can't. She has to go to work, but I will hold you until your crying stops."

These guidance practices apply equally to infants and toddlers, but there are some *special considerations* that teachers should remember. Infants cry—sometimes a great deal. It is their only means of communication. When they cry they should not be ignored or chastised, but comforted. It is helpful to talk to the baby, no matter how young, and begin to identify the steps you will take to ease the distress. "Fernando, you are crying and I don't know what's wrong. Let's take a look at your diaper; maybe a change will make you more comfortable. Perhaps you are teething; I know that can hurt. Maybe you are hungry; is it time for your bottle yet?" Those soothing words as a teacher changes diapers, rubs the baby's back, or cuddles and rocks ease this time of stress.

Toddlers, too, need adults to use words to express problem situations, and the preceding examples readily apply to working with this active and lively age group. One word of caution, however: Removing infants and toddlers from the group or confining them to a playpen or crib is not appropriate. Very young children do not understand that kind of isolation. To be effective, guidance should be helpful, not punitive.

The Guidance Continuum: Ten Essential Strategies

How do you decide which guidance strategy is the most appropriate for the situation? The following guidance methods are along a continuum that starts with the least intrusive, hands-off approach and moves to those that require greater intervention. They are valuable tools to help children become increasingly self-directed and self-reliant and to help teachers choose the most appropriate methods for the situation. Figure 7-6 illustrates how guidance techniques may be used to the best advantage.

Ignoring Behavior

When misbehavior is of a less serious nature—for instance, when a child whines constantly—it may be best to ignore it. This kind of behavior, although mildly annoying, is not harmful. To use the technique successfully, the adult chooses not to respond to the child in any way and may even become occupied elsewhere while the behavior persists. This method is based on the learning theory that negative reinforcement (the adult ignoring the child) will eventually cause the child to stop the undesirable behavior. At first, there might be an increase in the misbehavior as the child tests to see whether the adult will truly ignore the action. Once the child sees there is nothing to gain, the behavior disappears.

Active Listening and "I" Messages

Parents and teachers can learn the art of **active listening** to respond to a child's feelings as well as words. The adults listen carefully, trying to understand what the child is saying beyond the words being used. Then they reflect back in their own words what it is they think the child has said. The child has an opportunity to correct any misinterpretations. Further dialogue helps to clarify what the child meant. For example:

> Rita: I hate school!
> Teacher: Sounds as if you are really disappointed you didn't get a turn cooking today.
> Rita: I really wanted to help make pancakes.

"I" messages are an adult's way of reflecting back to children how their actions have affected others.

> Parent: When you scream indoors, it really hurts my ears.
> Parent: I feel sad when you tell me you don't like me.

"I" messages are honest, nonjudgmental statements that place no blame on the child but that state an observation of the behavior and its results.

The Guidance Continuum

Ignoring Behavior · Active Listening · Reinforcement · Redirection and Distraction · Giving Choices · Setting Limits · Active Problem Solving and Conflict Resolution · Natural and Logical Consequences · Time-Out · Physical Intervention

FIGURE 7-6 Follow the Guidance Continuum from left to right for the least intrusive to the most intervening strategies. (From Ann Gordon & Kathryn Williams Browne, *Guiding Young Children in a Diverse Society.* Published by Allyn and Bacon, Boston, MA. Copyright © 1996 by Pearson Education. Reprinted with permission of the publisher.)

Reinforcement

In Chapters 1 and 4, you met Pavlov, Watson, Thorndike, Skinner, and Bandura, who formulated behaviorist theory. Behavior modification is based on the premise that behavior is learned through experiences and can be changed by **reinforcement**. Reinforcement is the process in which a behavior is followed by a consequence that is likely to make the behavior repeated. If Jonah gets a smile from the teacher for saying, "Thank you," he is likely to say it again. A pleasant consequence is often called a reward, and unpleasant consequences are often called punishment (Berger, 2005). However, it is the effect of the consequence that really matters. If Angie is given an unpleasant consequence (such as being sent to her room for hitting her little brother), she may actually enjoy being isolated so that she can read books or watch videos in her room. In her case, the punishment is actually a reward.

Positive reinforcement is used to teach new and different behaviors to a child and to help the child maintain the change. Initially, the reinforcement (or reward) must be swift and consistently applied, as often as the behavior occurs. If the desired behavior is for Janie to always hang her coat on the hook, acknowledge the effort each time Janie hangs up her wraps. Once this is a well-established routine, the reinforcement (praise) becomes less intense.

Reinforcers, or rewards, must be individualized to meet the needs of the child and the situation. Social reinforcers, such as smiling, interest and attention, hugging, touching, and talking, are powerful tools with young children. Food, tokens, and money are sometimes used as reinforcers in home and school settings. The goal, however, is that inner satisfaction will become its own reward regardless of the type of reinforcer one might use initially. If that does not occur, then other positive guidance measures should be explored.

Parents and teachers often take for granted the positive, desirable behavior in children and may forget to acknowledge these behaviors frequently. Behavior modification helps to correct that oversight. Whenever adults focus on a negative aspect of a child's behavior and make an attempt to change it, they also look at the positive qualities the child possesses and reinforce them. This keeps a balanced perspective while working on a problem.

Behavior modification enables adults to invite children to be part of the process, giving them an active part in monitoring their own behavior. Children are capable of keeping a chart of how many times they finished their plate, made the bed, or fed the dog. This chart serves as a natural reinforcer.

Redirecting and Distraction

Sometimes the adult will want to change the activity in which the child is engaged to one that is more acceptable. If Pia and Elena are throwing books off the reading loft, the teacher will want to redirect them and may suggest throwing soft foam balls into a makeshift basket. This technique calls for the adult to make an accurate assessment of what the children really want to do. In this case, it appears they enjoy throwing from a height. Now the teacher can consider alternatives that permit the desired activity while changing the expression or form it takes: "It looks as if you two are enjoying dropping things from up there. Let's figure out a way you can do that so that books will not be damaged."

The substitute activity must be a valid one, acceptable to the adults and fulfilling to the children. In most cases, children are not being deliberately malicious or destructive. More than likely, they are expressing curiosity, imagination, and the need to explore. Positive redirection satisfies these needs in a way that enhances children's self-concept and self-control.

Distraction is similar to redirection and is used when the adult wants to focus the child's attention on an activity that may or may not relate to the previous behavior. Very young children, especially infants and toddlers, can easily be distracted from undesirable actions. Consider the example at the beginning of the chapter in which Kim grabs at one of the necklaces Shawnsey has. A quick-thinking teacher could present Kim with another attractive one. This method calls for well-timed intervention.

Giving Children Choices

Giving choices is a time-honored and popular method for helping children who are being resistant (Browne & Gordon, 2009). Choices help children practice self-reliance, self-direction, and self-discipline. "Seth, the cooking area is too crowded. It looks like there is plenty of room at the clay table or the writing table. Which one would you like to go to while you wait for a turn?"

You must give a choice only when you mean for children to make the choice and be prepared to accept the answer. "Some of the children are going in for music now. Would you like to join them?" This is a reasonable choice if there is another adult to supervise the outside.

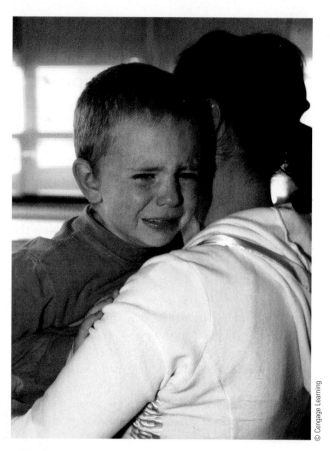

"I know you want to stay and play, but it is time to go home now. Do you want to get your jacket by yourself, or do you want me to help?" Choices allow children to gain some control over a stressful situation.

Suggest two choices when there is the possibility of resistance. This lets a child know you expect him or her to comply with the request but allows some decision making on their part. "It's time to go home now. Would you like to get your artwork before or after you put on your jacket?"

The choice must be valid and acknowledge children's growing ability to deal with responsibility and help them practice making reasonable choices. "It's rest time for everyone now. Do you want to pick out some books before or after you brush your teeth?"

Children should be aware of the consequences of the choices they are making. "If you choose the com-

puter now, you won't have time to finish your rain forest project." Helping children make reasonable choices gives them a foundation for decision making throughout their life.

Setting Limits

Limits are the boundaries we set to help children know what behavior is appropriate. Teachers generally have two reasons for setting limits: (1) to prevent children from injuring themselves or others; and (2) to prevent the destruction of property, materials, or equipment.

Limits are like fences; they are protective structures that help children feel secure. If children know where the fences are, they are free—and safe—to try out many behaviors.

Children may not like fences and may resist attempts to limit their behavior. A natural part of growing up is to stretch those limits and push those fences aside. Limits are self-protective when behavior goes out of bounds. Children are just beginning to exert that inner pressure (self-control) that will help them monitor their own actions. Until then, they need adults to help them learn when and how to apply self-restraint. Limits keep them from going too far.

Children can frighten themselves and others with anger, frustration, and fear. They need adults to stop them from doing physical or emotional harm to themselves or others.

Well-considered limits give the child freedom to try out, test, and explore avenues of self-expression in ways that will promote growth and protect budding autonomy.

Teachers must learn to set and maintain limits with confidence and authority. When setting limits:

- Set a limit appropriate to the situation. Example: "Andrew, get down from the table. You may finish your work either sitting in your chair or standing next to me. You may not stand on the table."
- Match the limit to the child's age, history, and emotional development. Example: "Sheila, you have interrupted the story too many times today. Find a place at the puzzle table until we are finished. Remember, I told you earlier that you would not be able to hear the end of the story if you yelled again."

DAP

DAP We help children live more successfully and productively when we teach them to become increasingly responsible for their own actions and behavior.

- See that all adults apply limits consistently. Example: "I know you want to bat the ball again, but both teachers have said it is Jordan's turn now."
- Reinforce the rules consistently. Example: "Judy, remember everyone walks inside. You can run later when you are outside."
- Follow through and support your words with actions. Example: "I cannot let you tear the books. Since this is the second page this morning, you will need to leave the book nook. I will walk with you while you look for another place to play."
- State limits simply, clearly, and directly. Example: "Roger, use your quiet voice indoors. When you are too loud, other people cannot hear one another."
- Respect and acknowledge the child's feelings. Example: "I know you want your Dad to stay, Megan. He has to go to work now, but I will stay with you while you feel sad."
- Act with authority, purpose, and confidence. Example: "Put the block down, Nick. I cannot let you hurt other people, and I will not let them hurt you."
- Maintain the limit and accept the consequences. Example: "I am sorry, Sarah. You will not be able to play here any longer because you keep calling Geneva 'fatty' and it hurts her feelings."
- Do not give in if the child threatens to fall apart or create a scene. Example: "I am sorry that makes you cry, Sarah, but I cannot let you make fun of one of your classmates. When you finish crying, we can talk about it some more."
- Involve children in creating the limits. Example: "We will be visiting our first grade reading buddies today. What are some of the rules we should follow when we are in their classroom?"

Active Problem Solving

Active problem solving engages children in confronting their differences and working together to solve their problems. The adult guides children toward solutions but does not solve problems for them. Posing open-ended questions, the adult helps keep the child focused so that they can suggest alternate solutions, for example:

"What could you do _____ ?
"How might she feel when _____ ?

"What might happen if _____ ?
"How can you _____ ?

All of the children's suggestions must be acknowledged seriously, even if they seem unreasonable. Young children may start the discussion by suggesting extreme solutions. In the case of Malcolm, for instance (see the second example at the beginning of this chapter), they might initially suggest: "Do not let Malcolm come to this school anymore." These suggestions will become tempered as other children respond; fair and reasonable solutions will eventually emerge: "Anyone who knocks over somebody else's blocks has to help them build it back up again."

Rather than assessing blame, teachers help children think through a number of alternatives, including the consequences of their suggestions: "If we close the block area, what will happen when you want to play with your favorite trucks this afternoon?" By assisting them in anticipating the results of what they suggest, teachers can help children understand how their behavior influences and affects others. This is an early lesson in a lifelong quest to become responsible for one's own behavior.

Conflict resolution should become part of the child's daily life. Teachers can help children solve disagreements nonviolently and explore alternative ways to reach their goals. Figure 7-7 outlines a process for active problem solving and conflict resolution (see also Figure 7-6). It is useful for resolving differences through group discussion, as noted earlier, or when one or more children become embroiled in conflict. By following such a process, children learn to respect others' opinions, to express their own feelings in appropriate ways, and to learn tolerance for doing things in a different way.

DAP

The process also suggests an important guidance principle: The adult role is to intervene as little as possible, allowing children the opportunity to come up with an acceptable solution.

When children help create a solution, they come away with a sense of commitment to it. This process also gives children a sense of power and control, a sense of independence, and a feeling of self-worth. Read Sue Warford's "Insights From the Field" article in Chapter 14 for a good example of active problem solving.

DAP Children should regard school as a caring community that fosters respect for and understands a variety of backgrounds and experiences.

The Six-Step Approach to Problem Solving

Scenario: Two children run outdoors to get the available wagon. They reach it simultaneously and start pulling on the handle, yelling, "Mine!" One child starts shoving the other child out of the way.

Step One: Approach (Initiate Mediation)

- Approach the conflict, signaling your awareness and availability.
- Get close enough to intervene if nessesary; stop aggressive behavior or neutralize the object of conflict by holding it yourself.

Step Two: Make a Statement

- *Describe the scene.*
- Reflect what the children have said.
- *Offer no judgments, values, solutions.*
  "It looks as if you both want the wagon."
  "I see you are yelling at each other."

Step Three: Ask Questions (Gather Data, Define the Problem)

- Don't direct questions toward pinpointing the blame.
- Draw out details; define problems.
- Help kids communicate versus slugging it out.
  "How did this happen?" "What do you want to tell her?" "How could you solve this problem?" "How could you use it without fighting?"

Step Four: Generate Alternative Solutions

- Give children the job of thinking and figuring it out.
- Suggestions may be offered by disputants or observers.

- Ask questions: "Who has an idea of how we could solve . . . ?"
  "You could take turns."
  "You could both use it together."
  "You could both do something else."
  "No one could use it."
- Common mistake: rushing to this stage; give it the time it deserves.

Step Five: Agree on Solution

- When both children accept a solution, rephrase it. ("So you both say that she will be the driver?")
- If any solution seems unsafe or grossly unfair, you must tell the children. ("It is too dangerous for you both to stand up and ride downhill together. What is another way you can agree?")

Step Six: Follow Through

- Monitor to make sure agreement is going according to plan. If the decision involves turn taking, you may need to be a clock-watcher.
- Tell the players and the group: "Looks as if you have solved your problem!"
- Use the power of language to:
  - Reinforce the solvability of the problem.
  - Note the ability of the players to do so.
  - Point out the positive environment to be successful.

FIGURE 7-7 Using these guidelines to help children solve problems, teachers listen more than talk, allow children the time to make mistakes and figure out solutions, and point out that diversity of viewpoints is natural, normal, and workable.

Natural and Logical Consequences

Natural consequences enhance children's ability to take responsibility for themselves. As implied, this approach lets children experience the natural consequences of their actions. Designed by Rudolf Dreikurs, it empha- sizes the opportunity children have to learn from the way their environment functions:

"If you do not eat your dinner, you might be hungry later."

"If you do not study your words, you might fail your spelling test."

"If you grab the book away from Ben, Ben may retaliate."

This method allows adults to define the situation for children without making judgments and lets children know what to expect. The consequences are a natural re- sult of the child's own actions.

Logical consequences, on the other hand, are a func- tion of what adults impose. For the adult, this means a commitment to follow through; consequences, once stated, must be enforced. It is important to give children an opportunity to choose their own course of action once they have some understanding of what is likely to happen. Nelson (2006) suggestions three criteria for using logical consequences: It must be related to the child's behavior; it must be respectful; and it must be reasonable. For example:

"If you bother Sally again, you will have to leave group time."

"If you take your favorite book to school, it might get lost."

"If you want dessert, you will have to eat your dinner."

Time Out

Removing a child from the play area is particularly appropriate when, owing to anger, hurt, or frustration, the child is out of control. Taking children away from the scene of intensity and emotion to allow them time to cool off and settle down is sometimes the only way to help them. The teacher is firm and consistent as the child is quietly removed from play. It is important that, if used, this technique be used with a positive attitude and approach, not as punishment.

Used appropriately, the time-out period is very much like that used in athletic events: a brief respite and a chance to stop all activity and regroup. There is no time-out chair. The teacher's role is to help the child talk about the incident—the feelings involved and the need for self-control—and to give the child an opportunity to gain self-control before resuming play. Children can monitor themselves and choose when they are ready to return to classroom activity. Noah, who persists in knocking down other children's block struc-

tures, might be told, "You may come back to the block area when you think you are ready to play without knocking over other children's work." Noah can then assume some responsibility for how he will behave and when he is ready to return to play.

Too often, time out is punitive. Children are pulled from an activity, pushed into a chair, and told to "watch how the other children are playing nicely," or "sit there until you can behave." There is no link made between the behavior and the consequences, so the child does not learn the strategy or skills he needs to change his behavior. One study notes that classrooms that used alternatives to time out were more likely to qualify as caring communities (Howes & Ritchie, 2002).

Time out is an invasive strategy and should be used judiciously. Adults can misuse it and leave the child with a sense of rejection.

Physical Intervention

There are times that a teacher must physically intervene to prevent children from injuring themselves, others, or property. Jude often gets out of control, and his playing becomes too rough. Today, Ramon pushed him away after telling him to stop. Jude retaliated by punching Ramon. The teacher intervened immediately, pulling Jude off Ramon and saying, "Stop! Stop hitting Ramon!" Jude raises his arms toward Ramon again, and the teacher puts her arms around him to hold his arms at his side. "I cannot let you hurt other children. Let's go over here and talk about this." The teacher gives Jude time to calm down before she talks with him.

Almost simultaneously, the teacher has assessed Ramon to see if he is hurt. If so, she calls another teacher over to provide comfort and assistance to him. There may be times when it is appropriate to talk with both boys together or deal with each of them separately. Once the sequence of events has been sorted out, the teacher can begin the conflict resolution process. Ideally, both boys would be able to participate in this discussion as they learn to solve problems without hitting and fighting.

For children who have a history of aggression, a more long-term approach is required that would include regular observations and assessments of the child. Outside professional advice may be necessary if the aggression persists.

What Do YOU Think? Is time out a useful strategy? Is it punishment, or can it be defined as guidance? Do you think children in "time out" are thinking about their behavior? What might they be thinking? How do you think children learn to gain self-control?

Guidance: An Interactive Approach

If This Is the Behavior	Try This	For Example
Whining	Ignore	Do and say nothing while whining persists. Pay attention to child when whining stops.
Playing cooperatively	Positive reinforcement	"You two are sure working hard on this garden! What a good team you make."
Refusing to cooperate	Provide a choice	"Reva, do you want to pick up the Legos off the floor or help Charlie empty the water table?"
Restlessness, inattentiveness	Change the activity	"This story seems long today; we'll finish it later. Let's play some music and dance now."
Daydreaming	Indirect suggestion	"As soon as you get your coat, Winona, we'll all be ready to go inside."
Arguing over the use of a toy	Active listening	"You really wanted to be the first one to play with the blue truck today, didn't you, Lief?"
Dawdling, late for snack	Natural consequences	"Sorry, Nate, the snacks have been put away. Maybe tomorrow you'll remember to come inside when the other children leave the yard."
Pushing, crowding, running inside	Change room arrangement	Create larger, more open spaces so children have greater freedom of movement and do not feel crowded together.
Unable to take turns, to wait	Review daily schedule, equipment	Buy duplicates of popular equipment. Allow enough time for free play so children won't feel anxious about getting a turn.
Boisterous play	Positive redirection	"You and Sergio seem to want to wrestle. Let's go set the mats out in the other room. If you wrestle here you disturb the children who are playing quietly."

FIGURE 7-8 Varieties of guidance techniques. The astute teacher selects from the options available and individualizes the responses.

Behavior That Is Challenging

Every teacher has experienced the child who disrupts the class, throws tantrums, hurts other children, and provides wear and tear on equipment, materials, and the adult's patience. Children with a high degree of energy and stress and a short attention span who are distractible and demanding are some of the children who challenge our skills in guiding their behavior. These children often do not respond to the usual guidance strategies. It takes a skillful teacher to work with children whose behaviors are often challenging, and it takes extra effort, patience, and perseverance.

The reasons for such behavior vary, as indicated earlier in the chapter when five factors that influence behavior were discussed. It is important to take these influences into consideration and understand the impact of children's development, environment, individuality, emotional and social growth, and culture on their ability to behave appropriately. Children who tend to act out frequently need extra support reassurance as they learn to live in a group and become responsible for their actions. That support and guidance comes in many forms:

DAP 1. *See and hear the uniqueness in each child.* Look at the five factors noted above, and assess their influence on the child who is causing disruption or behaving aggressively. What do you know about each of those influences on the child that challenges you? Be sure to note areas of strengths, as well as problems. Jake, for instance, tests every limit, disrupts class meetings and circle time, kicks the furniture, and yells at his classmates. However, Jake is a fast runner, climber, and jumper. He works puzzles that are difficult for most of his classmates and has a keen mind. So far, his teachers have been unable to create a trusting relationship with him.

DAP 2. *Build caring relationships with children and their families.* Respect for the individual child and family is where a relationship begins. Jake's teachers start with that premise and build a nurturing and responsive relationship from there. There may be a teacher on the team who is especially sensitive to children with more extreme behavior and offers to work with Jake and his family. She will find attributes in Jake that she likes and use them to develop his trust and to be a supportive presence to him and his family. Collaboration between home and school will foster Jake's self-confidence and improve his ability to change his behavior.

DAP 3. *Make observations.* Collect information about the individual child. When does Jake lose control? What leads up to his outburst? How long does it last? What cues does he give that he is becoming overwhelmed? Who usually intervenes and for how long? When is Jake's behavior appropriate? How is it acknowledged and by whom? Is Jake's behavior predictable?

4. *Modify the classroom and schedule.* Make legitimate opportunities for Jake to move about and use large muscles when inside. Are materials and curriculum challenging and age-appropriate? Do children select their own activities and make choices where they work and play for at least part of the day? Is there advanced warning when activities will conclude?

Challenging behaviors often occur during structured activities, such as group times or class meetings. What fits a teacher's agenda does not always fit a child's abilitites. Children lose interest and become restless, creating a recipe for frustration and outbursts. Does the schedule call for too many or too lengthy group meetings? How could meetings be modified to be flexibile in length and content? What behaviors or activities could be included that help children participate longer? What appropriate alternatives can children suggest if they need to leave the group?

5. *Teacher attention and language.* Take care of any injured party first; then use short, direct sentences, without judgment and without lecturing to the aggressor:

"Jake, that's not acceptable here."
"I cannot hear you when you are screaming."
Look at and speak to the child at eye level. Do not shame, ridicule, or use physical punishment. Give children the support they need to change rather than punish them. Talk with the child about alternatives to their inappropriate behavior:

"Next time, Jake, tell someone you are angry instead of hitting."
"What could you say to Corey instead of hitting him?"

Pay attention to disruptive, nonattentive, aggressive children when they are behaving appropriately:

"You look like you are trying to figure out where that puzzle piece goes. I know you are good at working puzzles and I am sure you will find it. There! You did it."

Follow through to help the child return to play, giving choices when possible. Find activities that require energy (clay, woodworking) or those that are more calming (water play, reading, painting), depending on what the child seems to need at the time.

Support the child's choice of activity with involvement and relevant comments, interests, and challenges:

"You can decide where you want to play now, Jake. There's room for you at the clay table. I'll help you get started if you like."
Later: "You look like you are having a good time with that clay, Jake. I bet you can squeeze it so hard it oozes out your fingers. Next time when you feel like hitting something, ask me to get the clay out."

With patience, positive interactions, and appropriate guidance practices, teachers will find creative and individual ways to help each child grow in social compentence and self-assurance.

DAP The most critical factor is to know each child as an individual.
DAP A full and equal partnership with families is marked by shared communication, respect, and mutual problem solving.
DAP A teacher who practices good observation skills may be able to prevent certain behaviors.

Insights *from the field*

Tantrums as a Teaching Tool: Ways to Help Children Learn

by Elizabeth Crary, M.S.

Marie doesn't want Stephanie to go home.
Josh wants the truck that Eli is playing with—right now!
David doesn't want his diaper changed, even though it stinks.

One of your jobs as a parent or teacher is to help children understand and deal with their feelings. There are several things you can do. During the tantrum you can acknowledge children's feelings and help them distinguish between feelings and behavior. Before the next tantrum, you can begin to teach children ways to deal with their feelings and the situation.

1. *Acknowledge children's feelings.* You can do that by helping children develop a "feeling" vocabulary and by validating their feelings.

   ■ Label children's feelings: "You're disappointed that we can't go to the park today."

   ■ Share your feelings: "I feel frustrated when I spill coffee on the floor."

   ■ Read books that discuss feelings, such as the *Let's Talk about Feelings* series.

   ■ Observe another's feelings: "I'll bet he's proud of the tower he built."

   Validate children's feelings. Many people have been trained to ignore or suppress their feelings. Girls are often taught that showing anger is unfeminine or not nice. Boys are taught not to cry. You can validate feelings by listening to the child and reflecting the feelings you hear. Listen without judging. Remain separate. Remember, a child's feelings belong to her or him. When you reflect the feeling ("You are mad that Stephanie has to go home now"), you are not attempting to solve the problem. Accepting the feeling is the first step toward dealing with it.

2. *Help children distinguish between feelings and actions.* All feelings are okay. Actions may or may not be okay de-

pending on the situation. For example, hitting a baseball is fine. Hitting a person is not acceptable. You can clarify the difference by saying, "It's okay to be mad, but I cannot let you hit Eli." You can also model the difference between feelings and action. You might say, "This morning someone cut me off on the road. I was so mad, I wanted to crash into them. Instead I ..."

3. *Teach children several ways to calm themselves down.* If telling children to "Use your words" worked for most kids, grown-ups would have little trouble with children's feelings. Children need a variety of ways to respond—auditory, physical, visual, creative, and self-nurturing. First children need to practice different responses when they are calm. Then when children are familiar with different ways to respond, you may ask them which they would like to try when they are upset.

   For example: "You're really angry. Do you want to feel mad right now or do you want to calm down?" If your child wants to change her feelings, you could say, "What could you do? Let's see, you could dance a mad dance, make a card to give to Stephanie, talk about this feeling, or look at your favorite book." After you've generated ideas, let the child choose what works for her.

4. *Offer tools to resolve situations that are hard for them.* If Josh wants the truck Eli has, teach him to ask, wait, or trade for it. If Sonja gets frustrated putting puzzles together, teach her how to take breaks or to breathe deeply so she does not get upset. You can use books such as *I Want It, I Can't Wait,* or *I Want to Play* to introduce options. Research has found that the more alternatives children have the better their social behavior.

Elizabeth Crary, M.S., teaches parent education independently and at North Seattle Community College, and has written many books and articles on guidance, including *Dealing with Disappointment* and *Love and Limits.*

SUMMARY

The early childhood educator provides opportunities for children to express their feelings in appropriate ways and to solve their social problems constructively. Young children are incapable of controlling their own impulses all the time, so caring adults are needed to guide them toward self-control. Teachers base their methods and guidance principles on an understanding of why children misbehave and what factors influence behavior.

Most guidance techniques begin by accepting the feelings the child expresses and verbalizing them. Then, the adult sets limits on what form the behavior may take, guiding the action as needed and following through to conclusion.

The most effective methods of guidance are clear, consistent, and fair rules that are enforced in consistent, humane ways. Children should be aware of the consequences if the rules are broken.

Good guidance practices emphasize the positive aspects of a child's behavior, not just the problem behaviors. Guidance measures have greater meaning to children if they are encouraged to take responsibility for their own actions and are part of the problem-solving process.

KEY TERMS

guidance	punishment	active listening
inductive guidance	interdependence	reinforcement
discipline	behavior model	positive reinforcement

REVIEW QUESTIONS

1. What developmental factors affect children's behavior? What environmental factors? How does a child's individual style affect behavior? What do developmental and learning theories (see Chapter 4) add to the discussion?

2. Why is it important to understand the child's family culture as you guide and direct behavior?

3. What is your own definition of discipline?

4. Why do teachers have to set limits on children's behavior? How does setting limits help the child?

5. Discuss in small groups the appropriate uses of time out. Describe those ways in which this technique can be harmful to young children.

6. How do teachers help children who have challenging behaviors?

LEARNING ACTIVITIES

1. Your 3-year-old daughter always interrupts when you talk on the telephone. She cries for you to play with her, hits her brothers, and crawls into cupboards. What is she doing and why? What is your reaction? How will you solve the problem?

2. List activities that channel aggressive feelings into acceptable ways to play. After each, note the emotion or feeling the specific activity might release. Example: Clay—anger, frustration.

3. Finish this sentence: "When I was 4 years old, the worst thing I ever did was …" How did the adults around you react? What would you do if you were the adult in charge? Discuss and compare responses with a classmate.

4. Children's literature helps us focus on guidance and behavior problems. Select a book from the following list. Define the problem behavior and the person creating the problem. Do you agree with the author's way of handling the situation? Suggest alternatives. When and with whom might you use this story?
Suggested books:
Peter's Chair by Ezra Jack Keats
Jamaica's Find by Juanita Havill
Momma, Do You Love Me? by Barbara M. Joosse
Tree of Cranes by Allen Say
Shy Charles by Rosemary Wells
Bread and Jam for Frances by Russell and Lillian Hoban
Where the Wild Things Are by Maurice Sendak

5. Observe a group of young children during play. See whether you can identify an example of a child who might be described as an easy child, a difficult child, and a slow-to-warm-up child. What guidance techniques do the teachers use with each child? Are they the same? If they are different, describe the differences. How successful are these techniques that are being used? What might you do differently?

6. How do you feel about spanking children? Were you spanked when you were a child? If so, what precipitated the spankings? Can you think of any other forms of behavior control that might have worked instead of spanking? Compare your thoughts and insights with those of another member of this class.

HELPFUL WEBSITES

Responsive Discipline   **http://www.ksu.edu/wwparent/courses/rd**

National Network for Child Care   **http://www.nncc.org/Guidance**

Urban Programs Resource Network   **http://www.urbanext.uiuc.edu**

Empowering People, Inc   **http://www.empowering.com**

 Additional resources including the TeachSource Videos can be found on the premium website for this book. Go to **http://www.cengage.com/login** to register your access code.

REFERENCES

American Academy of Pediatrics. (1997). *A guide to your child's symptoms.* Elk Grove Village, IL: Author.

Browne, K. W., & Gordon, A. M. (2009). *To teach well: An early childhood practicum guide.* Upper Saddle River, NJ: Pearson.

Gonzalez-Mena, J. (2008). *Multicultural issues in child care.* Menlo Park, CA: Mayfield.

Gordon, A., & Browne, K. W. (1996). *Guiding young children in a diverse society.* Boston: Allyn and Bacon.

Howes, C., & Ritchie, S. (2002). *A matter of trust: Connecting teachers and learners in the early childhood classroom.* New York: Teachers College Press.

Nelsen, J. (2006). *Positive discipline.* New York: Ballantine Books.

Thomas, A., & Chess, S. (1977). *Temperament and development.* New York: Brunner and Mazel.

Families and Teachers: Partners in Education

© Cengage Learning

PREVIEW QUESTIONS

- What is the history of the partnership between parents and schools?

- How do families and teachers contribute to the school–home partnership?

- What is a definition of family today?

- How can the home and school create a supportive separation process?

- What are some effective means of communicating with families?

NAEYC CODE OF ETHICAL CONDUCT

These Core Values and sections from the NAEYC Code of Ethical Conduct are addressed in this chapter. As you read, note how the Core Values, Ideals, or Principles listed here apply to the topics in this chapter. (Reprinted with permission from the National Association for the Education of Young Children.)

Core Values: We appreciate and support the close ties between the child and the family.

We recognize that children are best understood and supported in the context of their family, culture, community, and society.

Section I:
  P-1.3   We shall involve all of those with relevant knowledge (including staff and parents) in decisions concerning a child.

Section II:
  I-2.1   We shall develop relationships of mutual trust with families we serve.
  I-2.2   We acknowledge and build upon strengths and competencies as we support families in their task of nurturing children.
  I-2.3   We respect the dignity of each family and its culture, language, customs, and beliefs.

I-2.4   We respect families' childrearing values and their right to make decisions for their children.

I-2.5   We interpret each child's progress to parents within the framework of a developmental perspective and to help families understand and appreciate the value of developmentally appropriate early childhood practices.

I-2.6   We help family members improve their understanding of their children and to enhance their skills as parents.

A Historical Overview

Working with families can be one of the teacher's most satisfying responsibilities, or it can be one of the most frustrating. It is usually both. The potential is present for a dynamic partnership between the most important adults in a child's life. The common goal is obvious: nurturing the child. Each has knowledge, skills, and a sense of caring to bring to that relationship. Each has a need for the other. Partnerships usually begin with such a need. So, families and teachers become co-workers and colleagues in a joint effort to help the child develop fully.

Note: Throughout this chapter, the terms *parents* and *parenthood* are meant to include mothers and fathers, as well as other extended family members and caretakers who have the responsibility for raising a child.

Historical Precedent

There is a historical **precedent** for the partnership between families and teachers. Pestalozzi and Froebel, early 18th century educators, detailed many of their procedures for home use (as noted in Chapter 1). The involvement of the mother in the education of the child was considered important even then. When kindergartens were organized in the United States, classes for parents and for mothers' clubs were also started. The National Congress of Mothers evolved from that movement. Today, it is the National Parents and Teachers Association. This well-known organization is an integral part of most school systems and continues to promote a union between school and home, teachers and parents.

Decades of Change

During the 1930s, parent involvement in education was actively discouraged. Teachers were seen as experts who wanted to be left alone to do their job. In many cases, teachers felt they did little but remedy parental mistakes. That trend ended in the 1940s when the need for parent support and encouragement was recognized. Closer relationships between teachers and parents were established.

This view of a need for closer ties between teacher and families, now over 70 years old, stands today as a commonly accepted principle.

In training, teachers were exposed to curricula that would help them appreciate and use parents as co-workers in the child's development. By the 1960s, Head Start programs required parental involvement and set about developing parent education and parent training programs. A teacher's commitment to children included a commitment to the families of those children.

Parent involvement and education were largely ignored in the education reform movement of the 1990s. That omission was addressed as parents became empowered in the creation of **charter** and **magnet schools,** a mid-1990s phenomenon that created greater parent involvement in public schools.

Mutual Collaboration

Two particular changes, collaborating with parents and working within the family context, are significant in today's school programs. For much of the century just past, the early childhood "professionally driven parent education tradition" dominated the method of parent–teacher relationships, preceded by the "child-saver" approach that early childhood programs made up for deficient home environments (Powell & Diamond, 1995).

Demographic data reinforce the need for families and teachers of preschool children to become full and equal partners and set the stage for future school–family partnerships. Today's early childhood professional will need to be skilled in ways that will strengthen the family–school bond. Increasingly, ethnic, racial, and cultural diversity will affect relationships between families and schools. Further discussion of the parent support movement follows.

At no other level of education is the responsiveness to the needs of parents so high. Today, we are experiencing the change from serving only children to serving children and their families, and to deepening parent involvement. There is general agreement among early childhood teachers that such a relationship has always been a part of the early childhood educators' portfolio in ways that have not been understood or developed by teachers of other age groups.

Gestwicki (2007) suggests five attitudes a teacher must have to form successful partnerships with families:

1. A concept of professionalism that believes in sharing responsibility and power with parents
2. A strong sense of self based on clarifying one's own values

A true partnership happens when parents and teachers share their strengths with one another for the benefit of the children they care for and love.

3. A sense of humility that allows teachers to be approachable and have an open mind
4. A sense of compassion that recognizes the feelings families may have and the ability to be empathetic with them
5. A genuine respect for others so that they treat each family with dignity as they acknowledge the family's experience and knowledge

Strengthening the Partnership

What Families Contribute

Families have a unique contribution to make in the child's schooling. They have different knowledge about the child from what the teacher has. They know the child's history: physical, medical, social, and intellectual. They know the child as a member of a family and the role that child plays in the total family group, the extended family, and the community.

Families provide the context with which the teacher can view the whole child. As the teacher will soon learn, the family already knows what makes their children happy or sad or how they react to changes in routines.

Thus, families have a wealth of intimate knowledge about their children that the teacher is only just beginning to discover.

How Families Benefit

One of the greatest values of a strong parent program is the opportunity for families to meet each other. They find that they share similar problems and frustrations and that they can support one another in finding solutions.

DAP

Friendships based on mutual interests and concerns about their children can help them forge new relationships.

Through close home–school relationships, parents can find ways to become more effective as their children's first and most important teachers. They benefit from involvement in their children's education in many ways:

- They can observe modeling techniques that teachers find successful in dealing with children.
- They can learn what behaviors are appropriate at certain ages.
- By observing how their children relate to other adults and children, families can come to know them better as social beings.
- They may become more aware of school and community resources that are available to them and, in the person of the teacher, they now have access to a consultant who knows and understands their child and can help them when they need it.

Family members teach by word, by example, by all they do and say. Through closer home–school relationships, families can be helped to see that their everyday experiences with their children provide teachable moments, those spontaneous opportunities for educating children. Families feel supported in their roles when teachers:

- keep them informed about each stage of the child's development
- show them how to encourage language and thinking skills
- educate them to children's social needs at any given age
- provide lists of books and toys that encourage children's thinking and creative abilities
- make sure parents have copies of children's favorite songs, recipes that are popular at school, and information, in a bilingual format as needed, on how to teach health and safety habits at home

DAP Parents and teachers do not always agree. It is up to the early childhood professional to begin a dialogue for sharing perspectives and insights in a nonthreatening and supportive way.

10 Tips for Supporting Families

1. *Prepare families* for what they can expect from their child's school experience and what is expected of them. School policies and a yearly calendar should be clearly written and reviewed with the family when the child first enters school so that they will know what their responsibilities are and where the school can be of assistance to them.

2. *Support all families,* including those with differing opinions. Acknowledge their concerns and questions calmly. There is a greater chance to discuss differences and effect change if there are areas where teachers and families find agreement, so try to find some common ground. Differences of opinion should be discussed out of the child's hearing, and teachers should do nothing that would undermine the family in the eyes of the child.

3. *Respect the values of all families.* Social, cultural, and religious differences, various lifestyles, family make-up, child-rearing methods, and educational philosophies are reflected in every classroom. It is important that families feel accepted. Focus on the similarities among families and develop an anti-bias approach to teaching (see Chapters 2 and 9).

4. *Keep a professional distance.* The temptation to move into a social relationship with some families in your class is one that many teachers face. You are better able to maintain a more realistic, objective picture of the child if there is some detachment. The child and the family will probably benefit the most if a close relationship is postponed until the child moves on to another class.

5. *Ask, don't tell.* Collaboration begins with the concerns of the family. A teacher's role is one of helping families clarify their own goals for their children and identifying the trouble spots, then encourage and support the family as they work together to solve the problem. Families may feel overwhelmed or inadequate if they think they must abandon their child-rearing practices. The sensitive teacher will observe the situation and help the family move toward a reasonable solution.

6. *Contact families frequently.* Keep the lines of communication open and flowing between the school and the home. Know the family members by name. Take advantage of the daily contact as they bring their child to and from school. It may be brief and breezy, but it is a good way to stay in touch. Find ways to touch base with those families who do not come to school every day, by telephone, e-mail, note, or home visit.

7. *Help families support each other.* Any group of families represents a multitude of resources and common concerns. Each family member has accumulated experiences that might prove helpful to someone else. Introducing two families to each other with the suggestion that their children play together outside of school is a good way to start. Family meetings, work parties, and potluck dinners are methods for getting families involved with one another. The teacher's role can be that of providing the setting, encouraging attendance, and then letting it happen.

8. *Enhance the family's perception of their children.* Families want teachers who know and enjoy their child, and who are an advocate for their child. That means acknowledging the child's strengths and those personality traits that are particularly pleasing. Help the family recognize the joys of parenthood rather than focusing on the burdens.

9. *Focus on the family-child relationship.* Help families learn the "how-tos" of their relationship with their child rather than the "how-tos" of academic skills. Concentrate on the nature of family–child interactions—how they get along with each other and how they interact as a family. These issues are the heart and soul of family interactions, and teachers have a role to play in enhancing the quality of those relationships.

10. *Listen to families.* Hear them out. Learn to listen to them with a degree of understanding; try to hear it from their point of view. Listen to families without judging them or jumping to conclusions; this is the basis for open communication.

▌ **FIGURE 8-1** Ten tips to effective interactions with families.

Families need not teach a curriculum; they do need to use common, everyday routines and experiences to encourage children's total growth. The teaching staff has a strong role to play in helping them learn how to capitalize on those teachable moments.

A family-centered approach to school relationships supports the growth of the family as well as the child. When families have a meaningful partnership with their children's teachers, it raises their sense of importance and diminishes some of the isolation and anxiety of child rearing. By empowering families and allowing them to participate in decisions affecting their children's education, teachers can help families see themselves as part of the solution.

Guidelines for effective interactions and family support are outlined in Figure 8-1.

Family Cultural Influences

Families represent a wide range of cultural backgrounds, so it is important that their contributions be sought out, acknowledged, and used. All of the subtle communication styles that exist within various cultures can be blocks to good family–school relationships, or they can be the basis on which teachers and families connect with each other. This is one of the most pressing issues in teaching effectively today. Bradley and Kibera (2007) ex-plore four different characteristics of family culture to consider when working with families from diverse backgrounds.

Families whose linguistic and cultural backgrounds are different from the teacher need to share their perspectives so that issues relating to basic routines such as eating and sleeping may be understood in their cultural context. The same is true for a family's expectations about their child's experiences in the classroom. Only through forging such a partnership can families of diverse cultural backgrounds become true contributors to their children's education and care. Chapter 10 discusses Culturally Responsive Teaching on pages 349 and 350.

What Teachers Contribute to the Partnership

Teachers see the child in relation to normal milestones and appropriate behaviors. They notice how each child plays with other children in the group—what seems to challenge Mickey and when Ramon is likely to fall apart. Unlike families, teachers see individual children from a perspective that is balanced by the numerous other children they have taught. They observe how the child behaves with a variety of adults, sensing children's ability to

Cultural Dimensions of Families

Cultural Dimension	Questions for Reflection
Values and Beliefs	How is *family* defined? What roles do adults and children play? How does the family make sense of the child's behavioral difficulties? How does culture inform the family's view of appropriate and inappropriate ways of dealing with problem behavior and guidance? What is most important to the family?
Historical and Social Influences	What strengths and stressors does the family identify? What barriers do they experience?
Communication	What is the family's primary language? What support is required to enable communication? How are needs and wants expressed? How are unhappiness, dissatisfaction, or distress experienced or expressed?
Attitudes Toward Seeking Help	How does the family seek help and from whom? How do members view professionals, and how do professionals view them?

FIGURE 8-2 Exploring the cultural dimensions of families is part of an on-going process to develop greater cultural awareness. From "Closing the Gap: Culture and the Promotion of Inclusion in Child Care," by J. Bradley and P. Kibera, 2007 in D. Koralek (Ed.) *Spotlight on Young Children and Families*. Washington, DC: National Association for the Education of Young Children. Adapted with permission from the National Association of Young Children.

trust other adults through interactions with them at school. When families need help for themselves or for their child, teachers become resources. They work with the families to find psychologists, hearing and speech specialists, or other educational programs, if warranted.

Take a look at the excerpts from NAEYC's Code of Ethical Conduct at the beginning of this chapter to review ethical responsibilities to families. Note the ideals and principles stated in Section I, P-1.3, Section II, I-2.1 and 2.5. These three passages call for building mutual trust, communicating children's progress in developmentally appropriate terms, and the right of parents to participate in decisions that affect their child. Supporting and encouraging families is part of the teacher's role. Good teachers are sensitive to parent concerns and understand their needs, similar to those expressed by Libby Miles's "Insights From the Field" article at the end of this chapter.

Families want to learn the best ways to raise their children and to improve their child-rearing skills. There are numerous opportunities for the early childhood teacher to help families achieve these goals. Figure 8-3 cites a multitude of ways a school, center, or family child care home can become a family-friendly early childhood program.

What Children Gain

Children reap the rewards of parent involvement. Decades of research show the positive effects on achievement when children's families are involved in their edu-

---

A Checklist for Making Your School "Family Friendly"

_____ Hold an orientation for families at a convenient time.

_____ Provide a place for families to gather.

_____ Create a parent/family bulletin board.

_____ Give annual family awards for involvement.

_____ Create a family advisory committee.

_____ Allow families to help develop school policies and procedures.

_____ Schedule events on evenings and weekends.

_____ Provide child care for meetings.

_____ Establish a book or toy lending library.

_____ Make informal calls to families, especially to share a child's successes.

_____ Provide transportation for families who need it.

_____ Provide translators for families who need them.

_____ Send appropriate duplicate mailings to noncustodial parents.

_____ Survey families for issues of interest and need.

_____ Develop links to health and social support services.

_____ Provide resource and referral lists.

_____ Publish a school newsletter on a regular basis.

_____ Provide multilingual written communications as needed.

_____ Hire teachers with a strong commitment to supporting families and parents.

_____ Provide in-service training for teachers in working with families and parents.

_____ Hire teachers who are respectful of social, ethnic, and religious backgrounds of families.

_____ Hire staff that is reflective of the cultural background of students and families.

_____ Encourage regularly scheduled conferences between parents/family and teachers.

_____ Offer a variety of family support programs.

_____ Provide many opportunities for family members to volunteer.

_____ Provide frequent opportunities for parents/families to air their concerns.

_____ Encourage parents/families to ask questions, to visit, and to call.

_____ Encourage families to know what goes on in the classroom.

_____ Encourage families to report back on what works well.

_____ Encourage families to attend social events.

_____ Encourage teachers to make home visits.

FIGURE 8-3 A checklist for a family-oriented approach to meeting children's needs.

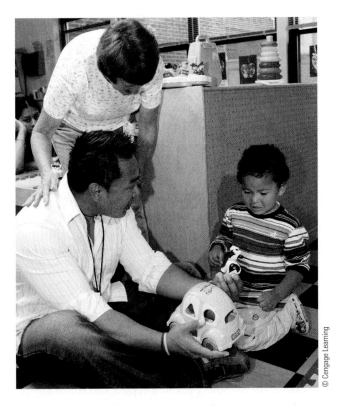

© Cengage Learning

A parent's participation in his or her child's school life can heighten the child's sense of belonging.

cation. The family is the primary source from which the child develops and grows and is needed to reinforce the learning, attitudes, and motivation if children are to succeed. Family visibility is especially important for low income and minority children; their family's presence can heighten a sense of belonging. Children gain when families are able to monitor their children's progress and reinforce the educational goals at home.

Families come to an early childhood program looking for teachers who know about children and who will help them in raising their own children. Children benefit when teachers respond to family concerns with caring and encouragement.

Becoming Full and Equal Partners

Families and schools are natural allies; together they claim the primary responsibility in educating and socializing children. They can and should be equal partners in that effort.

Family-Centered Support

Early childhood educators have long recognized the importance of providing families with child-rearing information and support to strengthen families to meet the challenges of parenting in the years ahead. The early childhood program is often the first time a family has the opportunity to collaborate in their child's education, so it is important that the experience be meaningful and effective.

Factors that support the need of a more family-centered approach are: increase in the divorce rate, the growing number of single-parent families, families in which both parents work, and increasing numbers of immigrant families. (See the following section, "Today's Families," and Chapter 15 for examples and discussion.) Powell (1998) notes that this family-centered approach serves as a modern-day version of the traditional extended family.

Long-held school perceptions of what constitutes a family may no longer correspond to the reality of today's definition of a family. Family support takes on new meaning when the differences in family styles are acknowledged and supported.

Powell (1989) has defined four components of a high quality family-centered program that promote the family's contribution to the child's education and growth as well as a more equal and consistent partnership. A good family-centered program is a collaborative effort and:

1. has goals, methods, and content that are responsive to family needs. These needs are reflected in the number, type, and kinds of opportunities it provides for families.
2. does not overshadow the needs of the child when strengthening social services and community support networks for the family. The common goal of the program is always what is in the best interest of the children.
3. must be tailored to the needs and characteristics of the specific family population, responding to cultural characteristics and values of ethnic populations.
4. allow for frequent discussion groups in which families are free to share their experiences and insights with one another. These conversations give families the freedom to accept what is useful and reject what they do not want to adopt for themselves.

Empowering parents to be change agents in their children's educational process creates greater commitment and involvement on the part of the families.

DAP

DAP Families feel valued when teachers listen to them and respect their opinions and share in the planning and decision making for their children.

TeachSource Video ▶❚❚

Watch the TeachSource Video Case entitled, "Communicating with Families: Best Practices in an Early Childhood Setting." After you study the video clip, view the artifacts, and read the teacher interviews and text, reflect upon the following questions:

1. A family-centered program acknowledges the critical influence of the family unit on the child's growth and development. What examples does teacher Mona Sanon talk about and model that strengthen the family-center relationship?

2. What lessons can be learned from the discussion Mona had with a father about his son's block building skills?

Public Recognition

A growing awareness of the need for a family-centered approach to parent education has been recognized by several government agencies. From its beginning in 1965, Head Start mandated parent involvement as necessary for the health and welfare of many young children. The Education of the Handicapped Amendments (P.L. 99-457) in 1986 required early intervention services aimed at the family, not just the child. P.L. 99-457 includes parents as members of a team of professionals who develop an individualized plan related to the child and family's needs. Two states, Minnesota and Missouri, have developed comprehensive, family-centered early childhood programs funded through local school districts.

Reggio Emilia: An Exemplary Partnership

One of the best examples of school–family partnerships that bears witness to Powell's criteria for high quality programs and a successful partnership are the schools of Reggio Emilia, Italy (see discussions in Chapters 1 and 10). There is strong and active family involvement at every level of school functioning. This is not surprising, since the schools were originally founded as parent cooperatives; part of the guiding philosophy continues to uphold a model of equal and extended partnership. Malaguzzi (Edwards, Gandini, & Forman, 1993) refers to this balanced responsibility of teachers, parents, and children as a "triad at the center of education," who, in turn, count on the rest of the community to provide a cultural context for children's learning.

School-based management in the schools of Reggio Emilia fosters meaningful participation of all families since the discussions and decisions are made by the teachers and parents within each school setting. No area seems the exclusive property of either parents or teachers. Curriculum planning, for instance, depends on the family's involvement, interest, and contribution.

Parents are the core of the individual school boards and on the city-wide school board as an integral part of the decision making. Frequent meetings inform family's of the school's program and bring them up to date on what their children are doing. Smaller groups of parents meet throughout the year with the teachers to talk about their children and the program; individual parent–teacher conferences, which either can request, are held to deal with specific concerns.

There are opportunities to be actively involved in the daily life of the school. Family members, teachers, and town residents build furnishings and maintain materials for the classrooms and the schoolyard and rearrange the space to accommodate program needs. In sessions with teachers and **pedagogistas,** parents learn various educational techniques necessary to the program, such as photography and puppet making, and they use these new skills in the classroom with their children. Using the whole town as a backdrop, families participate in many of the field trips to city landmarks or as small groups visiting a child's home. Recording and transcribing children's activities and projects are often a parent's responsibility (see Chapter 10).

The meaning of family is communicated to the children of Reggio Emilia throughout their school environment. In classroom dramatic play areas and in the school's own kitchen, there are displays of foods, materials, and utensils common to the region and found in the children's homes. Children are encouraged to bring special objects from home, and these are accorded special and beautifully arranged display space. Photographs of children and families abound. These elements are the vehicles used to ensure a rich flow of communication between the school and the homes of the children of Reggio Emilia.

The schools of Reggio Emilia seem to have a unique reciprocal relationship with the families they serve. Families have influence and help affect change; in turn, the schools influence and change families. Each becomes a stronger voice for what is in the best interest of the child.

Because half of the women with children younger than age six work outside the home, fathers often bring children to child care.

Courtesy of the author

Today's Families

There is little preparation for the job of a parent, and many parents feel inadequate in their role. Many families do not live around the corner from grandparents or other family members, so there is often no extended family to teach some of the traditional, time-honored child-rearing skills. There are few with whom parents can share their worries, frustrations, and concerns. Men, influenced by changing values and attitudes toward traditional sex roles, are taking an active part in raising their families. Fathers seem aware of the critical role they play in the child's life and are making appropriate changes to see that they have the time to be with their children.

What Is a Family?

The definition of today's families reflects the cultural changes in the United States over the last 50 years. The nuclear family, made up of a father, mother, and two children, has become blended, mixed, and extended. Look

around your neighborhood to see the variety of family units. Parents today may or may not be married to one another, may have the same sexual orientation, and may include foster parents and adoptive parents. Grandparents, aunts and uncles, and/or siblings may be the parental figures in a household. Two people can be defined as a family. So can those that include half- and step-siblings, close friends, and gays and lesbians (Browne & Gordon, 2009).

The term "parent" usually means a mother, father, or someone who is a legal guardian. That definition, too, has been stretched to accommodate the complexities of today's lifestyles. Browne & Gordon (2009) define parents as those individuals who are raising their own biological children, foster children, adopted children, and children of other family members and/or friends.

Understanding Parenthood

The role of a parent is ever-changing. Parents grow and develop along with their children. Parents have to adapt to the size of their family and the ages and stages of the each child. Every family has its own unique systems and patterns for raising their children. Two of them are worth exploring as you focus on working with parents and families.

Patterns of Child Rearing

Baumrind (1972) defined three types of parental styles: authoritative, authoritarian, and permissive. These styles differ in the ways parents accept the child and are involved in the child's life, their control of the child, and how much autonomy they grant (Berk, 2009). The most successful approach is *authoritative* parents who foster the highest levels of self-esteem, self-reliance, independence, and curiosity in children. They provide a warm, loving atmosphere with clear limits and high expectations. Authoritative parents are consistent in reinforcing rules and allow their children to make reasonable decisions appropriate to their age and experience.

In contrast, *authoritarian* child-rearing patterns reflect high control and demands combined with relatively low communication and nurturance. They rarely listen to the child's point of view. Authoritarian parents are strict; they expect and demand obedience and may lack warmth, and affection. They exert control through belittling, threats and criticisms and may resort to force. With *permissive* parents there is a high level of overindulgence or inattentiveness, warmth, and affection but little control. Clear standards and rules are not set, nor are they reinforced consistently. Permissive parents allow children to make decisions that are not appropriate for their age.

The positive effects of the authoritative parent model demonstrates that using reason over power, maintaining appropriate limits yet supporting appropriate autonomy, and encouraging give-and-take, create more successful children.

What makes a healthy and successful family? In Figure 8-4, Gonzalez-Mena (2002) lists some characteristics that promote strong families.

Stages of Parent Development

Just as children have various stages of development, parents, too, grow and change throughout the course of raising their children. The parent of one child has different knowledge and feelings than does a parent with three children. Older first-time parents' experiences differ from those of teenage parents. Galinsky (1987) defined six distinct phases that parents go through. (1) During pregnancy, they fantasize about their role as parents. (2) During the first two years of a child's life attachment is a key issue. They also reconcile their child-rearing fantasies with their actual experience. (3) Parents establish their authority style and family rules, (4) The values, knowledge, and skills they want for their children are the concerns for this stage. (5) Rules and authority are renegotiated during the teenage years as parents and children create new relationships with one another. (6) Another redefinition of roles occurs when children leave home and parents reflect on their relationships with their children. The role of the parent changes and adapts as they and their children grow.

As you work with families, it is helpful to look at what stage or stages through which parents might be going. Depending on the size of the family, they may be going through several stages at once. In some cases, boundaries are being readjusted, relationships are in flux, and issues of autonomy are being questioned all within the same time period. Each family will have different needs, concerns, and experiences depending upon the age of their children and their own stage of parent development. The early childhood professional's role is to support and understand the various forces within the family that affect their journey of parenthood.

Families with Diverse Needs

Parents are parents the world over and have mutual problems and pleasures as they go about bringing up their young. Their shared experiences create an automatic bond whenever they meet. There are some families who face additional challenges in child rearing and who may need added teacher support. These are:

- families of children with developmental delays and disabilities
- single-parent families
- adoptive and foster families
- parents who both work outside the home
- divorced families
- gay/lesbian families

Characteristics of Successful Families

1. There is a healthy attachment and involvement with each other. Family members have a deep sense of commitment to one another and give time and attention to the family.

2. There is mutual nurturing that supports appropriate independence and healthy interdependence on one another. All family members get their needs met.

3. Self-esteem is important for all family members. It is cultivated in all interactions.

4. Effective communication allows family members to express and respond to feelings, resolve conflicts, and problem-solve together. They have the coping skills to deal with daily stress.

5. A secure, safe environment protects all family members, allowing them to connect with the rest of society in healthy ways.

6. The importance of passing on the culture, values, and goals of the family is accomplished through modeling, discussion, teaching, problem solving, and communication.

FIGURE 8-4 Enhancing healthy and successful families creates a supportive atmosphere for children. (Gonzalez-Mena, J. (2002). *The child in the family and the community.* Upper Saddle River, NJ: Pearson Education.)

- homeless families
- teenage parent families
- grandparents raising grandchildren
- families who are raising children in a culture different from their own; families who do not speak English and whose child is in a setting in which English is not the predominant language
- multiracial families
- first-time older parents

Many of these family characteristics place parents in situations in which they do not have access to an extended family support system. Any one or combination of these situations can create added challenges to the family. For the most part, teachers can help these families by focusing on the many interests and concerns they share with other families. In some cases, additional support for the family is needed, such as:

- Help them locate community resources to address their needs.
- Connect them with other families who have similar circumstances.
- Assist them in exploring school settings for the future.
- See that they are included in all school functions.
- Learn about their special needs.
- Seek their help and advice.
- Help them establish contact with other families who may be willing to assist in translating, transporting, babysitting, and sharing friendship.

Supporting Single Parent Families

- 26 percent of all children live in families with only one parent
- 84 percent of single parents are women
- 16 percent of single parents are men
  (U.S. Census Bureau, 2007)

What Do YOU Think? Do you think all families are comfortable and welcome in the setting in which you work or observe? Are there families who have unique needs? Do you think those needs are being met? What are some stumbling blocks families might experience in this setting? What would you change?

Faced with the economic necessity to work, single parents must cope not only with raising children alone, but also with child care arrangements and costs. Particularly hard hit are women who head single-parent households. They are more likely than men to live below the poverty level, to never have married, not to have finished high school, and to be members of a minority population.

Single-parent families need the early childhood professional to be part of a support system for them and their children. Early childhood educators must be sensitive to the unique aspects of raising children alone. This means reexamining school policies and attitudes that ignore the needs of single parents. Over-burdened child care professionals, some of whom are single parents themselves, need to be flexible in exploring new avenues of home–school collaboration. They need to ask:

- What kind of involvement in a child's classroom is possible for a working single parent?
- How can I help families feel connected even if they are unable to be at the center?
- What is appropriate support for single parents?
- Am I judgmental about single parents? About single mothers?
- How do I help parents and children deal with the absent parent?
- What are some of the best strategies for helping children cope with the transitions when visiting one parent or the other?

These and other similar questions must become an agenda of staff meetings, in-services for teachers, and parent/family-group meetings.

Challenges of Immigrant Families

In 1970, 4.8% of the U.S. population was born outside of the United States.

In 2006, 13% of the U.S. population was born outside of the United States.

These immigrants come from:

Latin America	54 percent
Asia	27 percent
Europe	13 percent
Other regions	6 percent

These data from the U.S. Census Bureau (2007) highlight the extensive changes in immigration over a nearly 40-year period. This has affected school populations across the country. A comparison of school populations tells another story in the following chart:

In 1972, 22 percent of public school students were part of racial or ethnic minority groups:

> 6 percent were Hispanic
>
> 15 percent were black
>
> 1 percent were other minority groups.

In 2006, 43 percent of public school students were part of racial or ethnic minority groups:

> 20 percent were Hispanic
>
> 16 percent were Black
>
> 3.8 percent were Asian
>
> 7 percent were other minority groups (Planty et al, 2008).

These statistics affect our teaching as the future of school population in this century will be defined by the lack of minority or majority groups. The percentage of children who are Hispanic has increased faster than that of any other racial or ethnic group, increasing from 9 percent in 1980 to 21 percent in 2007. The largest growth will continue to occur among Hispanics, who are expected to reach 25 percent of the school-age population by 2020 (U. S. Census Bureau, 2008). These data, added to existing ethnic populations already present in the United States, challenge the early childhood teacher to a multicultural sensitivity not yet realized.

These data also challenge the profession to aggressively recruit and train early childhood professionals within these cultures. A willingness to learn various cultural norms and a knowledge of languages will be helpful for teachers to communicate with children and parents whose primary language is not English. Some studies suggest those teachers' stereotypes of social and racial subgroups influence their attitudes about a parent's ability and competence. Teachers will want to examine their own biases. See the appropriate sections in Chapters 5, 9, and 10 for discussion of teacher bias, anti-bias curricula, and anti-bias environments.

Miscommunication may be a problem when teaching a classroom of diverse children. When cultural perspectives of the family and the school differ markedly, teachers can easily misread a child's attitude and abilities because of different styles of languages and behaviors. Teachers may also use classroom practices that may be at odds with a child's cultural norms. For example, in some preschool settings, children are encouraged to call their teachers by the teacher's first name. This informal style of addressing authority figures may make some parents uncomfortable. How adults and children interact with children, the language they use, and the strategies they use to guide children's behavior are areas in which immigrant parents can help teachers learn some of the important cultural differences.

Valuing All Families with Diverse Needs

One of the most important things teachers can do when working with non-traditional families and families from cultures different from their own is to recognize that they share many of the same values and aspirations as other families and that there are commonalities among them. All parents want their children in environments that value and accept their family.

Depending on the family's situation, communication may be difficult. In many instances, non-traditional families and families from some other cultures may not want to divulge personal information. They may be influenced by previous negative experiences when they have talked about their lifestyle, values, or culture. In these cases, the early childhood educator must work hard to assure these families of confidentiality, stressing the concept that when we know more about a child's family situation, we are in a better position to support and help the child and the family.

Families will sense whether or not an early childhood environment is truly inclusive and supports and celebrates all varieties of families. The inclusive environment is explored further in Chapter 9. In Chapter 10, curriculum is viewed from an inclusive and culturally appropriate point of view. Dealing with attitudes and biases among staff members is discussed in Chapter 5 and Chapter 9. These are all important considerations for working with families with sensitive issues as we help their children achieve their potential. Eisenbud (2002) suggests some ways to create an environment that supports family diversity:

- Ask family members what names the child has for their caregivers, and use these names with the child.
- Create enrollment forms that allow for diverse answers other than "mother" or "father," that indicate the person who is legally responsible for the child and child custody arrangements.
- Find out what the child has been taught about his or her family situation and discuss with the family how you can support their position.
- If one or the other parent is absent, find out if and how that parent(s) is involved with the child's life.
- Be aware of any drug use/addiction related to the child's health and welfare.

- Treat all adults who care for the child, such as grandparents, guardians, caregivers, or adoptive parents, as the child's parents.
- Review the curriculum, books, and physical environment on a regular basis to ensure that all types of families are represented in the classroom.
- Adapt your conversations with children to reflect the diversity of families; for instance, "two mommies, step-brother, foster dad," etc.

Look around at the classroom where you are teaching and add other suggestions to strengthen all family units, no matter their make-up.

Francis Wardle's "Insights from the Field" column in Chapter 3 offers more specific ideas, especially for children of mixed heritage.

Separation: The Beginning of Trust

DAP   Each year, as school begins, a child enters a classroom and says good-bye to a loved one.

> This is a new experience for that child, no matter how long he or she might have been enrolled in school. Even children returning to the same classroom will find some changes. There may be a new room, new teachers, and new children along with some familiar faces, or the school, teacher, and children may all be strangers. Some children will have had previous group experience to draw on; others will never before have been a part of a group.

Each child will react differently, and it is difficult to predict how a child will respond: Paul clings to his dad's leg; Sherry bounces in and runs off to play, leaving her mother standing alone; Taryn clutches a stuffed dog as she enters with her grandmother, and the teacher interacts with Taryn for a few minutes before Taryn can let go of her grandmother's hand and say good-bye. Every child has a natural way of dealing with the anxieties of coming to school. Their behavior will be as varied as they are themselves.

The transition from home to school or child care setting is an important time for children and their families. Leaving familiar adults and learning to trust other adults is a major milestone in a child's life.

Helping Parents and Children Separate

The **separation process** is often as hard on the parent or family member as it may be on the child. Emotions run high as the time comes to say good-bye. Feelings of guilt, sadness, anger, and unhappiness may emerge among everyone as the parent/family member and child deal with the pain of separation. Adjustment is a gradual process; families need encouragement and guidance as their child moves toward independence. When families are reassured their child is acting normally and their own anxieties are common, they relax and begin to help the child feel more comfortable.

Listen carefully to their concerns and assess the kind of support that will be most reassuring to them. Assure the family that you are available by telephone, e-mail, or fax to help them through this transition. The key to the separation process is a trusting and respectful relationship between the teacher and the family.

Working Together

Parents and teachers must be especially clear with one another during the separation transition. Written school policies and procedures are helpful so that the teacher and family can go over the process step by step on an individual basis as each child enrolls or at a general parent meeting held before the opening of school.

In some settings, teachers arrange to make a home visit to each child enrolled in the class before school begins. This helps the teacher know more about students before they enter school and gives children a chance to become acquainted with a teacher on their home ground. Many early childhood programs offer an orientation period in which the child visits the school for a short time before the first day of school. Others schedule half of the class for an hour and the other half joins them later. Creating a smaller group size allows the teachers to have more individual time with a child and observe his or her interactions with others. This process may continue throughout the first week during which many separations are made. While this is a good model to follow, there are times and situations when family members do not have the time to help the child make the adjustment readily. Separations are particularly had on working parents who have a short period of time to leave the child at school and then get to work.

The teacher's role is to help the family and child be prepared for the first day and the first few weeks, encouraging the child to move out from the family member as they become more comfortable. Together, they assess the child's progress and make the decisions regarding the time of actual separation. The parent and teacher prepare children and tell them when it is time. The teacher supports the family member's exit and stands by the child, ready to give comfort, if needed. This is a time when a teacher needs to act with conviction. Families appreciate firmness and confidence at a time when their own feelings may be ambiguous. Teachers whose attitudes express a belief in what they are doing reassure children.

In Chapter 4, Figure 4-5 may be helpful as a reminder of how patterns of attachment affect the separation process. For most children, the separation process is a struggle between their natural desire to explore the world and their equally natural resistance to leaving what is "safe." It is during these years that children are learning to move about under their own power and to trust themselves. Coming to school can provide each child with the opportunity to grow, starting with the separation from their family. Through careful planning, close communication, and sensitivity to one another, families and teachers will assure the child mastery of this task.

Communicating with Families

Families can be an invaluable source of information, support, and affirmation to the teacher and to the school. There are many ways to meet the needs of both the parents and children with clear and sensitive communications.

Parent/Family Education and Involvement

Almost any contact between the teacher and the parent can be perceived as parent/family education. Teachers interpret children's behavior to their family, suggest alternative ways for dealing with problems, show them toys and games that are appropriate, hold workshops on parenting skills, mention books and articles of interest, and reinforce family interest and attention to their children's education. All of these activities are considered parent/family education. Some are planned; some are spontaneous.

The separation process will be successful if the parents and children know that teachers will be there when children need comfort and support.

Young children become intensely involved when parents participate in classroom activities.

Parent/family education happens frequently, whether in a meeting that focuses on positive discipline or in an informal chat about car seat safety. Many early childhood settings offer family support programs based on the needs of families and their children. Again, the Code of Ethical Conduct in Appendix A can be useful, especially the sections that outline the teacher's professional role to families.

Keeping in Touch

Five of the most common ways teachers can involve and inform families are:

1. *Classroom Newsletters.* provide a general idea of what the children are doing in class, any special events taking place, personal information about new babies, vacations, or other important events in the lives of the children. Be sure the newsletter is written in the language of the families in the class. See Figure 8-5 for an example.
2. *Bulletin Boards.* Posted where families can see them, these boards contain notices about parent/family meetings, guest speakers, community resources, child care, babysitting, clothing and furniture exchanges, and library story hours. Information regarding health programs, automobile and toy safety, and immunization clinics is also publicized. Post information on cultural events appropriate to the ethnic makeup of the school community.
3. *A Parent/Family Place.* Providing an area or room at the school set aside for family use can be an important step in letting families know they are wanted and needed. Some schools provide space for a parent/family lounge, complete with a library of resource books on child rearing. If there is no available space, set up a coffee bar in the office or hall. The smallest amount of space—even a countertop with magazines—is a start.
4. *Informal Contacts.* These are the easiest and most useful lines of communication with families. All it takes is a phone call, a note, an e-mail, or a brief talk on a daily basis. For families who have difficulty attending meetings or who do not accompany their child to and from school, teachers can send home a

The Importance of a Classroom Newsletter

Why	What
To Keep Families Informed	Next Thursday is our first nature walk around the school and the neighborhood. Make sure your child wears boots or waterproof shoes to keep feet dry while we explore. Join us on our walk, if you can.
For Insights into Learning	The nature walk is part of our science curriculum. We want the children to explore the out-of-doors to stimulate their natural curiosity and delight in their discoveries. Firsthand experiences with the texture of tree bark or birds' nests help a child create a base of knowledge on which to build their understanding of the natural world around them.
To Bring Learning Home	You might want to try this at home with the whole family. Walk around your neighborhood and look at what is growing. Take a bag or basket to collect leaves and other natural materials. The children can make a collage out of them when you return home. Comment as the children make discoveries: "I wonder what makes the leaves so green." "What do you think happens to that flower when it snows?" Open-ended questions such as these help children clarify their own thinking and learning.
To Keep Communication Flowing	Several questions about our guidance philosophy came up at the last family meeting. We are putting together an insert for next month's newsletter and we would like your help on one of the topics. How do you deal with bedtime issues (delaying tactics, such as one more story, another glass of water, etc.) in your home? What works for you? Talk with Mrs. Olga or Miss Leona if you want to participate.

FIGURE 8-5 Classroom newsletters enlarge a family's understanding of what their child is experiencing and extends the learning between home and school.

note along with a sample of artwork, or a story the child has dictated, or a photograph of the child with friends.

5. *Home Visits.* Depending on its purpose, a home visit can be used to enhance communications. The visit might be set up to focus only on the relationship between the teacher and the child. Or the visit might have a purely social function—a way for teachers to meet the whole family and for them to get acquainted with the teachers. In any event, the teacher can use this as a bridge to build a pleasant, casual beginning with this family.

Parent/Family–Teacher Conferences

Parent/family–teacher conferences are the backbone of any good family–school relationship. A conference is a mutually supportive link between the adults who are most concerned about a child and should be a regular part of the communication process in all early childhood programs.

Conferences are held for many reasons. The initial conference, when the child first enrolls in school, may focus on the child's development, daily habits, and interests, as well as the family's hopes and expectations. Further into the school year, the teacher will share observations and assessments of the child and work with the family to develop mutual goals that will be reinforced at home and at school. Individual conferences may be called at any time by the family or the teacher to express concerns, resolve conflicts, and problem-solve together.

Every occasion when families and teachers get together to talk about a child is a step toward building trusting relationships between home and school. A successful conference is the result of good planning and clear communications, such as:

- Be prepared and organized and have a clear purpose. Use a written format to maintain focus. Ask for other staff input and up-to-date examples. Ask parents to help set the agenda.
- Put the family at ease with a warm welcome and thanks for their time. Help them relax by stating

some of their child's strengths, citing examples. Compliment them on something you have noticed, either with their own child or when in the classroom with other children. Be sensitive to any cultural differences that may arise.

- Ask—don't tell. Begin with open-ended questions ("How is that new bedtime schedule working out?" or "Can you tell me more?"). Learn how to listen carefully to what is being said.
- Keep the focus on the child. Keep the conversation based on mutual concerns and how to help each other. Make a plan of action together and discuss ways to follow through and stay in touch.
- Write a brief report after the conference. Make a special note of the important issues that were discussed, solutions that were agreed on, and dates for checking progress. Many of the child assessment forms used in early education programs require teachers to keep these records along with information about child progress.
- Student and beginning teachers should find a good role model in a more experienced teacher who will act as a mentor. Ask that person to sit in on a conference with you and afterwards have them reflect on it with you. Learn from your experiences.

Maintaining Privacy and Confidentiality

The more involved families are in the workings of the school, the more important it is to establish guidelines for protecting the privacy of all the families enrolled. Family members who volunteer in the office, the classroom, or on a field trip must understand they cannot carry tales out of school about any of the children, the teachers, the administration, or other parents. The school must be clear about its expectations for ensuring such privacy and communicate policies to families. Family members who work on advisory boards, planning committees, or other activities that allow them access to the school office should be sensitive to the confidentiality issue and respect the privacy of every family enrolled in the school.

Insights *from the field*

It All Starts with the Stories *by Libby Miles, M.A., Ph.D.*

Early childhood practitioners shine in their relationships with the children, and this is as it should be—your work with the children is the heart of what you do. Likewise, most students in a course like this one know how to build good working relationships with their own teachers. Chances are, you are as comfortable in your relationships with children as you are with your professors. But where do parents fit in? Relations among students and parents are rarely well defined and can be tricky territory to navigate. Nonetheless, it is worth it to try. All it takes to get started are a few stories.

I have been fortunate as a parent to have experienced wonderful caregivers in three different types of settings:

1. As an infant, my daughter spent several days a week with a family child care provider.

2. As a toddler, my daughter was enrolled in a child care center owned and run by a national chain.

3. Now, as a full-fledged preschooler, Abra attends the lab school at the university where I teach.

In all three settings, I have been confident she was in good hands, that she was treated with respect and an affection for who she was at that stage of her life. In all three settings, I have learned—and admired—how sensitive caregivers connected with me as a parent. For you, as students of the field, I offer examples of some best practices culled from my three different child care experiences. Wonderful caregivers:

■ *Tell parents descriptive—not judgmental—stories about their children.* I hunger for stories about my daughter; I want to know what she does and who she becomes during those hours we are apart. I can't get enough stories and appreciate those teachers (or the students learning to be teachers) who begin by telling me something Abra did that day. For example, she ate her own banana one day as an infant. She made up new lyrics to "Twinkle, Twinkle" as a toddler. The next day, she enjoyed painting a "bear cave." (It looked like a large brown blob to me.) At preschool, she laboriously lined up every peg during a manipulative activity, even though it took her 25 minutes to do so. Last week, she worked with friends to construct an enormous rainbow from colored paper. Each story helps me fill in the ever-changing picture of who my child is and helps me understand who my child might become.

■ *Exude an energetic affection for the children.* The best caregivers really like the children with whom they work. They appreciate each for his or her strengths and challenges, and cheer through his or her struggles and successes. Their affection for the kids carries over into conversations with parents, often in the stories they choose to tell or the way they choose to tell them. I watch my daughter connect with the teachers who are open for hugs, with those who make their laps available for reading and cuddling, and with those who sparkle while she tells her elaborately thought-out plans.

■ *Ask me my name.* As much as I love being "Abra's mom," I am always impressed with the college students who make a point to ask me my name. For some reason, I feel less like someone who impedes or undermines their work and more like I'm working with them. As a result, I tend to feel more comfortable with those students and often follow up with stories of my own.

■ *Make connections with other parts of our lives.* They may say they saw us playing at the park or at a community concert. They may honk as they drive by us on campus or on the way to the grocery store. And, most importantly, they ask my daughter about everyday activities and listen attentively to her version of an event. They elicit her stories as well.

■ *Problem-solve with parents.* Bolstered by a rich bank of stories, a strong sense of affection for the child, and an understanding that there are real constraints outside the child care setting, the best teachers engage me in helping my daughter through her current struggles, whether it is where and when to use the toilet or how to encourage her to rest quietly, or supporting her to stand up for herself when another child convinces her she is frequently wrong. With a solid foundation, we can work on these challenges together.

As I look back now, I see it all starts with the stories. Everything builds from there. Teachers (and students learning to be teachers) who take the time to tell me stories about my daughter stand out from the crowd. Teachers who illustrate for me where my daughter is in her social, emotional, cognitive, and physical development enable me to make better choices about what we can do at home. These teachers watch her, like her, interact with her, and translate their insights into stories for me since I can't be there to do it myself. Then, when she and I are together, their stories infuse what we do, how we do it, and who we are together. Those teachers and their stories have given us quite a gift.

Libby Miles, M.A., Ph.D., is a professor of writing and rhetoric at the University of Rhode Island. A working mom, she has been enriched by her daughter's committed and thoughtful caregivers.

SUMMARY

The partnership in education between families and teacher has a long and varied history, with each partner recognizing the unique part he or she plays in the child's life. The value of sharing the information they have about the child highlights the separate but important functions of the family and the teachers. The definition of today's family is broad to include all of the people who care for and nurture young children in their homes. Today's teacher needs sensitivity to and understanding of the many ways children are being raised so that they provide sensitive and appropriate support to all.

The current practice is a family-centered approach. An equal partnership, based on mutual respect for the strengths that both families and teachers bring to the relationship, this approach requires a deepening of family involvement, particularly in the decision-making process.

One of the first and most intensive ways families and teachers work together is through the separation process that takes place when the child enters school. There are other basic skills teachers must have to work successfully with an increasingly diverse family population. Frequent and open communication, comfort with diversity, and planning for varied family education activities are but a few. Conferencing is a critical part of the parent/family–teacher partnership.

KEY TERMS

precedent
charter school
magnet school

pedagogista
separation process

REVIEW QUESTIONS

1. Describe the influence of early 18th century educators on the creation of school and family partnerships. How has parent and family involvement changed over the last century?

2. Describe three ways you would strengthen family–school partnerships. Cite the advantages for the (a) children, (b) family, and (c) teacher. Are there any disadvantages?

3. What is the definition of "family"?

4. What are some of the key elements in a successful parent–child separation? What is the role of the teacher?

5. What are five of the most effective ways to communicate with families?

LEARNING ACTIVITIES

1. Discuss the following in small groups, and then share your responses with the rest of your classmates. Finish the sentences:

   "For me, the most difficult part of being a parent today is or would be … ."

   "When I have children, I plan to (work/stay at home/do both) because … ."

   "As a single parent, I would … ."

   "When I have children, I will raise them (just as my parents raised me/the opposite of the way I was raised) because … ."

2. Look at the Patterns of Child-Rearing on page 269. Discuss the following with a classmate: Which style are you using or will you use with your own children? Why? Do you see these different styles in the parents and families in your classroom? Does it affect your relationship with the parents? If so, how?

3. Question on Stages of Parenthood: What are the six stages that parents go through as they raise their children? What are some of the factors that make each stage different?

4. Are there immigrant families in your school setting? How are these families supported or not supported by school practices and policies? What changes would you make?

5. The last step in conducting a successful parent/family conference suggests that you find a good role model. Look around at the teachers you know and select one. Discuss with her your own concerns and/or experiences with parent/family conferences.

6. As a teacher, how does the Code of Ethical Conduct in Appendix A influence your decision to report another teacher who uses harsh methods of behavior control and who yells at children when she is angry with them?

HELPFUL WEBSITES

National Association for the Education of Young Children　**http://www.naeyc.org**

Center for Immigration Studies　**http://www.cis.org**

Center for Social Organization of Schools　**http://www.csos.jhu.edu**

Especially for Parents　**http://www.ed.gov/parents**

National Coalition for Parent Involvement in Education　**http://www.ncpie.org**

Culturally and Linguistically Appropriate Services　**http://www.clas.uiuc.edu**

Zero to Three　**http://www.zerotothree.org**

Canadian Childcare Federation　**http://www.cfc.efc.ca**

Family Communications, Inc.　**http://www.misterrogers.org**

KidSource Online　**http://www.kidsource.com**

 Additional resources including the TeachSource Videos can be found on the premium website for this book. Go to **http://www.cengage.com/login** to register your access code.

REFERENCES

Baumrind, D. (1972). Socialization and instrumental competence in young children. In W. W. Hartrup (Ed.), *The young child: Review of research (Vol. 2)*. Washington, DC: National Association for the Education of Young Children.

Berk, L. (2009). *Child development*. Boston: Allyn and Bacon.

Bradley, J., & Kibera, P. (2007). Closing the gap: Culture and the promotion of inclusion in child care. In D. Koralek (Ed.) *Spotlight on young children and families*. Washington, DC: National Association for the Education of Young Chidren, 38-43.

Browne, K. W., & Gordon, A. M. (2009). *To teach well: An early childhood practicum guide*. Upper Saddle River, NJ: Pearson Education.

Galinsky, E. (1987). *Between generations*. Reading, MA: Addison-Wesley.

Gestwicki, C. (2007). *Home, school, and community relations*. Clifton Park, NY: Thomson Delmar Learning.

Gonzalez-Mena, J. (2002). *The child in the family and the community*. Upper Saddle River, NJ: Pearson Education.

Eisenbud, L. (2002, March). Working with non-traditional families. *Child Care Information Exchange*, 16-20.

Planty, M., Hussar, W., Snyder, T., Provasnik, S., Kena, G., Dinkes, R., KewalRamani, A., & Kemp, J. (2008). *The condition of education 2008* (NCES 2008-031). National Center for Education Statistics, Institute of Education Sciences, U. S. Department of Education, Washington, DC.

Powell, D. R. (1989). *Families and early childhood programs*. Washington, DC: National Association for the Education of Young Children.

Powell, D. R., & Diamond, K. E. (1995). Approaches to parent-teacher relationship in U.S. early childhood programs during the twentieth century. *Journal of Education 177*, 71-94.

U. S. Bureau of the Census (2008). *Population estimates and projections (2008)*. Washington, DC.

U.S. Bureau of the Census (2007). *Custodial mothers and fathers and their child support: 2005*. Washington, DC.

U.S. Bureau of the Census (2007). American Community Survey: Percent of people who are foreign born: 2007. *American Fact Finder*. Washington, DC.

U.S. Department of Labor (2005). *Working in the 21st century*. Washington, DC: Bureau of Labor Statistics.

Creating Environments

© Cengage Learning

PREVIEW QUESTIONS

- What does the term *environment* mean in early childhood education?

- What is a developmentally appropriate learning environment?

- What is involved in planning environments?

- How do teachers create a complete environment?

NAEYC CODE OF ETHICAL CONDUCT

These Core Values and sections from the NAEYC Code of Ethical Conduct are addressed in this chapter. As you read, note how the Core Values, Ideals, or Principles listed here apply to the topics in this chapter. (Reprinted with permission from the National Association for the Education of Young Children.)

Section I:
- I-1.5. To create and maintain safe and healthy settings that foster children's social, emotional, intellectual, and physical development and that respect their dignity and their contributions.
- P-1.4. For every child, we shall implement adaptations in teaching strategies, learning environment, and curriculum, consult with the family, and seek recommendations from appropriate specialists to maximize the potential of the child to benefit from the program.

Section III:
- P-3C.2. We shall provide staff members with safe and supportive working conditions that permit them to carry out their responsibilities.

What Is the Environment?

What does it mean to create an environment appropriate for young children? What makes up the environment? The environment is the stage on which children play out the themes of childhood: their interests, triumphs, problems, and concerns. An environment for children, therefore, includes all of the conditions that affect their surroundings and the people in it.

Each environment is unique. There is no such thing as a single model or ideal setting for all children. Each program has goals that reflect the values and priorities of its teachers, families, and communities. When growth goals and the setting mesh, the atmosphere encourages enthusiasm and engagement.

Definition

The **environment** is the sum total of the physical and human qualities that combine to create a space in which children and adults work and play together. Environment is the content teachers arrange; it is an atmosphere they create; it is a feeling they communicate. Environment is the total picture—from the traffic flow to the daily schedule, from the numbers of chairs at a table to the placement of the guinea pig cage. It is a means to an end. The choices teachers make concerning the **physical environment** (the equipment and materials, the room arrangement, the playground and the facilities available), the **temporal environment** (timing for transitions, routines, activities), and the **interpersonal environment**

The environment includes not only physical space and materials but also aspects of time and interpersonal relationships such as who plays together and how much time they need to engage deeply in the play.

(number and nature of teachers, ages and numbers of children, types and style of interactions among them) combine to support the program goals.

The environment speaks volumes to children, and their development is strongly influenced by settings and materials. Our ideas about the environment have been influenced by educators such as Montessori, Vygotsky, and Malaguzzi (see Chapters 1 and 4). As Wurm (2009) notes:

> Each of these educators has left their own influence: from child-sized furnishings, to the creation of social spaces for language development, and the importance of a stage for storytelling. These details, when woven together, have shown us both in theory and practice that schools for young children are spaces that attend to social interaction, problem solving, dramatic play, storytelling, fantasy, conflict and its resolution, and communication as a few of the vehicles for children to build their repertoire and further their understanding of the world.

Teachers arrange the environment to promote what they feel is best in children. Whether the environment is an adapted church basement, an elementary school classroom, or a space made especially for young children, it will be a powerful force in their lives. Beyond the families and staff, it is the child's third teacher. "The environment," say Dodge, Colker, and Heroman (2002), "is the curriculum's textbook." It is the canvas on which children and teachers create their work.

Characteristics of the Environment

All settings for the care and education of young children have similar basic environmental components and goals—meeting the needs of children—despite the fact that programs vary widely in the size of the group, age of children, length of day, program focus, and number of staff. Although physical environments vary on the surface, all high quality environments:

- convey a welcoming feeling
- give clear cues about what can be done in each area
- provide varied spaces that let children concentrate, as well as letting them experience lively group interactions and vigorous physical activity (Hyson, 2008)

Such variation on this common educational theme is one of the reasons why our field is so diverse and interesting. Caution must be exercised, however, to ensure a quality experience for all children. For instance, *size does matter*. Research conducted over 35 years ago (Prescott, Jones, & Kritschevsky, 1972) and corroborated more recently (Fowler, 1992) found that when a center gets too large, rules and routine guidance are emphasized, outdoor areas often have little variety, and children are often less enthusiastically involved and more often wandering. On the other extreme, too many of us know the problems associated with crowding and cramped conditions, little rooms that become institutions that

DAP dehumanize.

Group size is recognized as one of the most important indicators of quality child care (Howes, Phillips, & Whitebook, 1992; Bredekamp & Copple, 1997). The National Association for the Education of Young Children (NAEYC) continues its work with program accreditation of programs and developmentally appropriate practices (DAP); Figure 9-1 gives recommended standards for group size and adult–child ratios. Although there are endless variations in planning for children, certain common elements must be considered and principles used to create developmentally appropriate learning environments for young children.

Physical Plant

Before creating an environment for children, the early childhood teacher must analyze the physical plant. The building that is inviting and beautiful beckons children to enter; a space with color and light encourages children to play with both. Many settings use space designed for other purposes, such as a family home, a church basement, or an empty elementary school classroom. The size and shape of the designated space determine how to plan for safe and appropriate use.

To rescale the space, teachers shift from an adult perspective to a child's scale. Getting on one's knees provides a glimpse of the environment from the child's point of view; child space is measured from the floor and playground up. A child's stature determines what is available to and noticed by that child. For crawling infants, space consists primarily of the floor, whereas school-aged children can use and learn from the space up to about five feet, roughly their own height. It is this perspective that teachers must remember as they plan the physical space for children.

Resources

In planning the environment, the teacher must know what kinds of resources are available. Rarely do teachers have unlimited dollars: "This year we can only afford ..." determines many of the decisions made about the environment. Priority is usually given to teachers' salaries and benefits, equipment and materials for the school, and other related services (maintenance, office help, bus service). Despite budget constraints, teachers must beware of operating on too low of a materials budget. Lack of necessary materials can create increasingly passive, angry, and unhappy children out of sheer boredom. Only by knowing the extent of the fiscal boundaries and budget limits can a teacher plan a complete environment.

There are ways to stretch that budget, however. Good environmental principles do not depend on numerous or expensive equipment, materials, or buildings. A creative child-centered environment can happen in any setting, regardless of the lack of financial resources. Some equipment can be made, borrowed, or purchased secondhand. In church-based schools, annual rummage sales at the church provide a wealth of dress-up clothes, books, toys, and some appliances. Resource books are filled with ideas for recycling materials into usable equipment for young children. Parents and others can provide computer paper, wood scraps, or office supplies for dramatic play kits. Community sources, such as the public library storyteller or a senior citizens group, may be available for extended experiences for the children. Effective fund raising provides an added source of revenue in many schools and centers.

The human resources must also be identified. Adults do their best with children when their abilities, experience, and availability are matched with what is expected of them. Volunteers, for instance, will feel satisfied if their time is organized and spent in ways meaningful to them. A first-year teacher's resources are best expended in the classroom rather than on administrative projects. A master teacher is ready to be challenged in other ways, such as orienting parents or evaluating curriculum materials. When the entire community values its children, as in the case of Reggio Emilia, the school is a showcase, sending a strong message of how important children are in the life of its citizens. Just as we try to match children's developing skills to the tasks at hand, so, too, should we consider individual people as part of an environment's resources.

DAP Teachers arrange firsthand, meaningful experiences that are intellectually and creatively stimulating, invite exploration and investigation, and engage children's active, sustained involvement. They do this by providing a rich variety of materials, challenges, and ideas that are worthy of children's attention.

Teacher[a]–Child Ratios within Group Size

Age Group	Group Size									
	6	8	10	12	14	16	18	20	22	24
Infants										
Birth to 15 months[b]	1:3	1:4								
Toddlers/Twos (12–36 months)[b]										
12 to 28 months	1:3	1:4	1:4[c]	1:4						
21 to 36 months		1:4	1:5	1:6						
Preschool[b]										
2.5–3s (30–48 months)				1:6	1:7	1:8	1:9			
4-year-olds						1:8	1:9	1:10		
5-year-olds						1:8	1:9	1:10		
Kindergarten								1:10	1:11	1:12

NOTES: In a mixed-age preschool class of 2.5-year-olds to 5-year-olds, no more than two children between the ages of 30 months and 36 months may be enrolled. The ratios within group size for the predominant age group apply. If infants and toddlers are in a mixed-age group, the ratio for the youngest child applies.

Ratios are to be lowered when one or more children in the group need additional adult assistance to fully participate in the program (a) because of ability, language fluency, developmental age or stage, or other factors or (b) to meet other requirements of NAEYC Accreditation.

A group or classroom refers to the number of children who are assigned for most of the day to a teacher or a team of teaching staff and who occupy an individual classroom or well-defined space that prevents intermingling of children from different groups within a larger room or area.

Group sizes as stated are ceilings, regardless of the number of staff.

Ratios and group sizes are always assessed during on-site visits for NAEYC Accreditation. They are not a required criterion. However, experience suggests that programs that exceed the recommended number of children for each teaching staff member and total group sizes will find it much more difficult to meet each standard and achieve NAEYC Accreditation. The more these numbers are exceeded, the more difficult it will be to meet each standard.

[a] Includes teachers, assistant teachers, and teacher aides

[b] These age ranges purposely overlap. Programs may identify the age group being used for on-site assessment purposes for groups of children whose ages are included in multiple age groups.

[c] Group sizes for this age group would require an additional adult.

FIGURE 9-1 Group size and staff–child ratio are two aspects of the environment that affect the quality of children's experience. (*NAEYC Early Childhood Program Standards and Accreditation Criteria: The Mark of Quality in Early Childhood Education*, Table 2, p. 83. Reprinted with permission from the National Association for the Education of Young Children.)

Program Goals

The goals and objectives of the program are expressed directly in the arrangement of the environment. Harms (2005) names three general goals in designing environments: to plan soft and responsive settings that avoid behavior problems, to set up predictable environments that encourage independence, and to create a stimulating space for active learning. The physical space and materials should tell the children exactly what is going to happen and how they are to go about their work. In every program, consideration of what children are to accomplish puts goals and environments together.

The goals of an early childhood program will vary widely because early childhood settings contain such a wide range of age and experience. Some programs are housed in large centers, others in homes; children may attend all day or for part of the day and for educational, recreational, or even custodial reasons. The important point is that good environments for children must reflect clear and reasonable program goals. Once we know what we wish to do and why we want to do it, we can create space, timing, and an atmosphere in which to meet those goals.

Goals into Action

Creative teachers plan a program directed toward goals for each dimension (physical, temporal, and interpersonal) of the environment:

1. The room and yard are arranged to give maximum exposure to the materials and equipment they want children to use.
2. They take care to arrange the daily schedule in ways that provide the time blocks needed to teach content when and how they want to teach it.
3. They see that a warm relationship exists among the teachers and in their interactions with children.

With a clear idea of their program goals before arranging the environment, teachers make room/yard blueprints, daily schedules, and personal styles match what they believe. For example, if a program develops cognitive and fine motor skills, a space with games using prereading and writing materials should be prominent. Puzzles and table toys should have a central place in the classroom. Enough tables and chairs should be provided to accommodate all the children. Larger amounts of time should be made available for children to work on these activities every day, and teachers should be available to reinforce and encourage children as they play. Research shows that teachers who emphasize "learning goals" are more likely to have children who approach situations with mastery and goals in mind (Midgley, 2002).

When children walk into a center, the environment should communicate how they are to live and work in that setting. Children should receive clear messages about what they can and cannot do there as well as cues that tell them:

- where they are free to move to and where they cannot go.
- how they will be treated.
- who will be there with them.
- what materials and equipment they can use.
- how long they have to play.
- that they are safe there.
- what is expected of them.

Teachers communicate these messages in many ways. Figure 9-2 describes how teachers use the environment to tell children what is important there. For instance, when it is time to go outside, the doors are opened. If children need to stay off a piece of equipment, it is marked by dividers or a flag, and a teacher stationed nearby explains the instruction. Children know that they matter when they are welcomed each day, and they know their time is valued when teachers tell them how long they have to complete a project or play sequence and when that time is nearly up.

The teacher is the key element in creating the environment. It is not the facility alone that counts, as much as it is the teacher's understanding of all the environmental factors and how they are related to one another. Indicators of program quality, such as the adult–child ratio; the stability, education, and experience of the caregiver; and group size all contribute to an environment that meets its goals for children. Chapter 2 details these indicators, and Chapter 5 describes their place in teacher evaluation.

A room is just a room and a yard is just a yard until a teacher makes them environments for learning. The teachers themselves are the most responsive part of the environment; it is they who converse, hug, appreciate, give information, and see the individuality of each child. They are the ones who create the space, the time, and the atmosphere that will engage children's curiosity and involvement. Figure 9-2 summarizes these environmental goals.

Principles for Developing Appropriate Learning Environments

Because children live in the world of the senses, actions, and feelings, they are greatly influenced by their immediate surroundings. Therefore, we must pay attention to what is in their environment and what happens during their stay there. The following are 15 elements of developmentally appropriate learning environments:

1. *Create high-activity, low-stress, and brain-compatible environments.* Positive neurological changes occur when a child is engaged in a learning experience and the brain can shut down when a threat is perceived (Jensen, 1998). The environment calls into use many of children's senses, choices and some autonomy, and cooperative learning and so determines, to

Messages from the Environment

Children Need to ...	So the Environment Should...
Be treated as individuals, with unique strengths and developmental goals.	Have low teacher–child ratio for one-to-one interactions. Provide private as well as public spaces for group and solitary play. Place teachers and materials for ready access. Be staffed by teachers who set goals for each child based on observation and assessment. Have materials that match the developmental level of the group. Provide a balance of quiet and active times.
See themselves and their family culture represented positively and be exposed to cultural diversity in meaningful ways.	Include pictures, books, dolls, dramatic play materials, activities, and people that reflect many cultures and life experiences. Have teachers who understand and value home cultures and diverse family practices. Provide opportunities for various cultural habits, activities, and celebrations to occur.
Make choices and independent learning.	Be arranged with clearly marked available choices. Offer a variety of activity centers for exploration. Allow large blocks of time for child-initiated choices Provide an adequate number of trained teachers to support self-discovery.
Learn to be part of a group.	Be set up for group play—several chairs around tables, easels next to each other, more than one telephone and wagon. Regularly schedule small and large group times and encourage participation. Include trained staff who can create engaging group activities. Allow children to use each other as resources. Provide activities that emphasize cooperation and social interaction.
Become responsible for the setting.	Schedule cleanup times as part of the daily routine. Include teachers and children working together to restore order. Allow time for children to be instructed in the proper use of materials and care.
Be aware of the behavioral limits.	Ensure that teachers and the daily schedule reflect important rules of behavior. Have teachers who deal with behavior problems in a fair and consistent way. Allow plenty of time during transitions that reduces stress during changes. Be arranged to avoid runways and dead ends.
Be with adults who will supervise and facilitate play and encourage learning throughout the day.	Be set up before children arrive so teachers are free to greet them. Encourage teacher–child interactions through the use of small groups. Create a daily schedule that allows time for in-depth interactions.

FIGURE 9-2 The goals of the program are mirrored in the environment.

some degree, the functioning ability of children's brains (Rushton, 2001). Allowing small groups to form and focus on an activity stimulates learning without pressure or stress to perform or wait. "A developmentally appropriate learning environment is designed for individual children to be messy, noisy and quiet, alone and social, and active and still," says Greenman (2000). "It is designed to accommodate

much *stuff*—loose parts—the raw materials of discovery for active hands and minds."

The Academy of Neuroscience for Architecture is working to identify classroom design elements that encourage learning and describe design flaws that can cause or exacerbate problems. For example, "students with language or learning problems have more difficulty learning in rooms with excessive reverberation and noise. Lighting is also critical because it plays a role in alertness" (Nieer, 2006). *Physical attributes* such as acoustics, light, colors, and other stimuli may affect the brain.

2. *Build culturally responsive environments.* First and foremost, it is important that the environment reflects the cultures of the children in the classroom. The Euro-American cultural value of independence will be expressed in aspects of a self-help environment (later in this section). Values of group harmony and interdependence should also be included. If the teachers do not look like the children, and their spaces do not look like home, it is critical that the interpersonal and temporal aspects of their environment complement their home culture. (See Figure 9-3 and the Anti-Bias section of this chapter).

3. *Consider children's developmental levels.* Recognize that there are many things young children will not be able to do on their own, but allow them the chance to do all they can. Be developmentally aware—know what children in the class are capable of, at what point they are now in their development, and what the next step should be. Three-year-old Sophie can only zip her jacket now, so having dressing frames helps her put the zipper in the housing. "Kindergarten children thrive when they can work independently and cooperatively with a small group of peers" (Heroman & Copple, 2006). "Using centers to organize and manage the learning environment is a strategy attuned to who kindergarten children are and how they learn." (See Inclusive section of this chapter.)

4. *Give families ways to identify their children's space.* Label cubbies, storage bins, or baskets with names, a photo, or a familiar picture so that children can see where to put jackets, artwork, and other personal belongings.

5. *Provide access to enough toys and materials.* Help children imagine and live in alternative worlds, communities, and homes where things are different. Make sure that supplies are stored in such a way that adults do not have to hand them to children each time they will be used. Equipment placed at a child's height on open, low shelving permits children to proceed at their own pace and to select materials without depending on adults to serve them.

6. *Give opportunities for making choices.* Both indoors and out, children should be given an abundance of materials and a range of activities from which to choose so that they may decide how they will spend their time. Choosing to play with the hamster rather than in the block corner helps a child practice self-direction. Children should also be able to decide with whom they would like to play and with which teachers they would like to establish close relationships most of the time.

7. *See that children are responsible for caring for the environment.* Have a clean-up time in the daily schedule and allow children time to help restore the room and yard. Label shelves and cupboards with pictures or symbols of what is stored there so that children can readily find and return things. Outlining the specific shapes of the blocks that are stored on each shelf will help develop children's self-help skills. Outdoors, a clearly marked "parking lot" for wheel toys or bins for sand toys helps independence. An accessible drying rack with large clothespins tells children that they are expected to care for their own artwork.

8. *Involve children in planning and setting up the environment.* Let the children help decide what they want to learn. For instance, if a Sarita's cat has kittens, encourage a visit and then send a newsletter asking for other pets, arranging a field trip to a pet store, and organizing a dramatic play corner as a pet hospital or pet shop. Make the yard more interesting by encouraging the children to rearrange climbing boards and assist them in moving the pieces themselves. The class feast is made more exciting when the children themselves move all the tables together and plan the menu!

9. *Provide children with enough time.* One of the ways children learn is to repeat an activity over and over again. They explore, manipulate, experiment, and come to master puzzle, to shape a lump of clay, or how to brush their teeth. Large blocks of time in the daily schedule—especially for routines—let children proceed to learn at an unhurried pace. (See section on Temporal Environment further in the chapter.)

10. *Make expectations clear and consistent.* Both in the environment and in words, let them know what you want them to do. Putting on a clean-up song that lasts several minutes tells them in both verbal and nonverbal ways that the group knows they can do a job without pressure. Give clues that indicate how to proceed. For example, Isaac usually has someone dress him at home. In the toddler class, he sees the poster of a child dressing himself, and plays a

Culturally Responsive Environment

Overall Environment

1. In general, is the classroom hospitable?

2. What is on the walls?
   *If there is work done by children, does it all look alike? For example, are there teacher-made shapes that the children colored, or is the art *genuinely* done by the children?
   *Are all of the pictures for children and the art hung *at children's eye level*?
   *Are the pictures of people hanging on walls or bulletin boards representative of a multicultural community?
   *Even if pictures *do* represent a diverse population, are they stereotypic in any way? For example, is there an alphabet chart that uses "Indian" to symbolize the letter "I"?

3. Is there evidence of families in the environment?

Social Studies

1. Does the curriculum as a whole help the children increase their understanding and acceptance of attitudes, values, and lifestyles that are unfamiliar to them?

2. Are materials and games racially or sex-role stereotypic—for example, black people shooting dice or boys playing war games? Are women depicted only as caregivers while men do lots of exciting jobs?

Music and Games

1. Do the music experiences in the curriculum reinforce the children's affirmation of cultural diversity?

2. Are fingerplays, games, and songs from various cultural groups used in the classroom?

3. Are there many varieties of musical instruments, including ones made by children?

Dramatic Play

1. Is there a wide variety of clothes, including garments from various cultural groups?

2. Are the pictures and the props representative of a diversity of cultures?

3. Are the dolls representative of a broad variety of racial groups?
   *Are they just white dolls with changed skin color?

Blocks

1. Are the accessories representative of various cultural groups and family configurations?

2. Are the people block accessories stereotypic in terms of sex roles?

Language Arts

1. Does the classroom have a wide variety of age-appropriate and culturally diverse books and language-arts materials?

2. Are there stories about a variety of people from each of the following groups in the book corner?
   _____ Native-American cultures
   _____ Asian-American cultures
   _____ Black cultures
   _____ White ethnic cultures
   _____ Spanish-speaking cultures
   _____ Biracial or multiracial people
   _____ Family configurations, including biracial and multiracial families and gay and lesbian families

3. Are there any books that speak of people of diverse cultures in stereotypical or derogatory terms (e.g., describing Latinos as "lazy" or Japanese as always taking photographs)?

Cooking

1. Do the cooking experiences in the classroom encourage the children to experiment with foods other than those with which they are familiar?

2. Are the cooking experiences designed to give young children a general notion of the connections between cultural heritage and the process of preparing, cooking, and eating food?

FIGURE 9-3 A multicultural environment checklist provides questions for teachers to evaluate and monitor progress toward an anti-bias environment for children. (Adapted from Frances E. Kendall, *Diversity in the Classroom: New Approaches to the Education of Young Children.* New York: Teachers College Press. Copyright © 1995 by Teachers College Press, Columbia University. Reprinted with permission.)

dressing game in circle time: when the teacher prompts him—"If you pull up your underpants first, it will be easier to get your pants up"—and then gives feedback on what is working—"Good. You've got the back up. Now reach around the front."—he hears the teacher's confidence in his ability to finish the task.

Be sure staff expectations are consistent. The teaching team should set common goals for each child and reinforce them consistently. For instance, Janice will become confused if one teacher tells her to get her cot ready for nap and another teacher does it for her.

11. *Let children teach one another.* Encourage children to share the skills they have mastered with their peers. Actively seek out each child's way of doing things; support a diversity of approaches. Those who can tie shoes enjoy helping their friends with stubborn laces or slippery knots. Whether reading or telling stories to one another, or showing a friend a fast way to put on a jacket, children benefit from helping each other.

12. *Allow children to solve their own problems whenever possible.* In solving social or mechanical problems, young children can begin to find out for themselves what is or is not successful. See how far a child can go in discovering how to manipulate a pin so that it will close, or to work out with another child who will use the red paint first. A good teacher tries not to intervene too early and can let a child struggle sufficiently with a problem before stepping in to help.

13. *Accept children's efforts.* To support children in their quest for independence, the adult must be satisfied with children's efforts. Be ready to accept the way that Tom made his sandwich or that Shelley put her boots on the wrong feet.

14. *Make it safe to make a mistake.* Children learn from their own actions and their own experiences. Let them know it is perfectly acceptable, indeed inevitable, that they will at times make mistakes. Help them deal with the consequences of their mistakes. When Chelo spills her juice, she is encouraged to find a sponge and clean up the table. The teacher reinforces Chelo's efforts by commenting on her scrubbing ability and swift action.

15. *Give credit where it is due.* Provide feedback so that children will know when they have been successful. Compliment Chaz on the length of time he took sorting through the nails to find the one he wanted.

Tell Ellen she worked hard at opening her own juice box. Let children take pride in their own accomplishments.

A well-planned environment opens up infinite possibilities for children to achieve a feeling of self-satisfaction while they explore the boundaries of their own beings. Adults who work with children should remember to interact with children in ways that will help them grow toward independence. To perceive children as helpless is to rob them of the satisfaction of achievement (see Self-Help section of this chapter).

A final note: *Include beauty in your planning.* The environment in which children grow and learn should also be visually appealing and relaxing. There are so many assaults on our visual senses in schools: concrete, barred windows, heavy doors, tiny windows, clutter and chalkboards, to name a few. People become numbed to balance, shape, form, line, and color. While resources are limited, beauty does not need to be ignored. The environment is one of the few things that teachers can control and use to everyone's advantage.

The Anti-Bias Environment

Among the core values (see Code of Ethics in Appendix A) in any good early childhood program is the recognition of each child as unique, as deserving of respect, and as a part of a family. Each child has the right to achieve full potential and to develop a positive self-esteem. Each family deserves support for the unique role it plays. Part of the commitment of the early childhood teacher is to help children learn to value one another's uniqueness, the differences as well as the similarities. Teachers do this, in part, by expressing such inclusive attitudes. Early learning standards (Gronlund, 2006; NAEYC, 2002) should be flexible enough to encourage teachers to embed culturally relevant experiences in the curriculum. Adaptations to standards will then promote success for all.

The **anti-bias** curriculum, developed at Pacific Oaks College, encourages children and adults to:

- Explore the differences and similarities that make up our individual and group identities.
- Develop skills for identifying and countering the hurtful impact of bias on themselves and their peers. (Derman-Sparks & Edwards, 2010)

The physical and interpersonal environment can be used to help children see that culture consists of the various ways people do similar activities. This approach is different from the "tourist curriculum," which provides only superficial information that is often detached from the child's own life. It is also different from an approach that is based only on the interests of the class and gender, racial, and cultural groups represented therein. The anti-bias environment incorporates the positive aspects of a multicultural curriculum and uses some of the activities that highlight other cultures, but it provides a more inclusive, ongoing approach. This approach avoids patronizing or emphasizing trivial, isolated, exotic differences. There is an inherent feeling of fairness to self and others in the anti-bias approach, as children explore the many ways people do the basic human tasks of everyday life. Think of the diverse cultures expressed in how babies and things are carried from place to place in different parts of the world. How many ways do people eat? Cook? Shop for food?

A value common to all early childhood programs is expressed in this anti-bias curriculum: that every person matters, so diversity is valuable and peaceful, and just cooperation among all is possible. If unity is the completed puzzle, then diversity is the pieces of the puzzle. In this curriculum, the environment and the activities are derived from three sources: the children and their activities, the teachers' awareness of the developmental needs and learning styles of the group, and societal events. Teachers, of course, make general selections of what children are to learn and arrange the environment for learning to begin. Then, the environment, which includes the children themselves, begins to change. If children are especially interested in making things, perhaps the theme "All people live in homes" emerges, with activities that focus on how people build things, what they use the buildings for, and how they work to get something built.

Lessons about children's identity and budding attitudes concerning race, gender, disability, and age are learned early in life. With the prevalence of stereotyping in society, and the impact of bias on children's development (Cross, 1985; Gutierrez, 1982; Kutner, 1984), early childhood educators have a responsibility to find ways to prevent, even counter, the damage done by such stereotyping. Teachers do this by arranging an anti-bias physical environment, as well as creating an atmosphere of problem solving and learning in the day-to-day conflicts and interactions that arise naturally. Think about how teachers provide the materials and encourage an atmosphere of trust and time for conflict resolution in these examples:

A kindergarten teacher shows the children a magazine picture entitled "Brides of America." All of the women pictured are Caucasian. She asks, "What do you think of this picture?" Sophia responds, "That's

a silly picture. My mom was a bride, and she's Mexican." (Derman-Sparks & Edwards, 2010)

A toddler teacher sets up the water play table for washing babies. Choosing dolls that represent several racial and ethnic groups, she invites the children to soap and rinse them. One 2-year-old begins to wash the teacher's arm, then scrubs it hard. "Do you wonder if my color will wash off?" the teacher asks. The child nods, and several others look up. "Does it? Go ahead and try… See, a person's color is her own and stays with her. Try yours, too. That's one way people look different: we all have skin, and yet we each have our own color." (Gutierrez, personal communication, 1987)

The anti-bias approach to creating environment has its roots in the theories of Maslow, Piaget, and Erikson (see Chapter 4). Research data reveal that children begin to notice and construct classifications and evaluative categories very early; indeed, 2-year-olds begin to notice gender and racial differences and may even notice physical disabilities (Froschl, Rubin, & Sprung, 1984; Honig, 1983). Early childhood programs must develop a child's basic sense of trust and mastery so that children can learn to understand themselves and become tolerant and compassionate toward others (see Figure 9-3).

A Place at the Table

The anti-bias approach takes a broad view of a classroom, as a kind of "mini-society" in which children and adults work together to form a just world. There is a place for everyone at the table, no one is left out, and conflicts and problems are solved.

Further, injustices from the outside world are sometimes addressed. For instance, in one "anti-bias" video, a teacher helps children ticket parents' cars who improperly park in the class-made handicapped parking space (Derman-Sparks, 1989). An anti-bias classroom fosters:

- *Positive self-concept.* Curiosity and creativity stem from being able to affect the environment and what is in it. When Jamal says his baby's hair is fuzzy like his, his smile tells how good he feels about the similarity.
- *Awareness.* All people have interests and feelings, both about themselves and about others. Yoko notices that her classmate Julie runs and throws her arms around her dad, but she prefers a less demonstrative greeting.

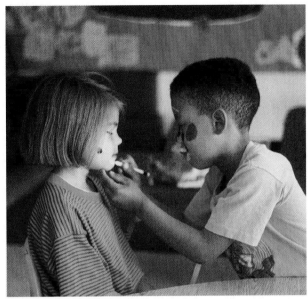

The anti-bias environment encourages girls and boys to play together, respecting differences and including others in new ways.

- *Respect for diversity.* This stems from the ability to classify similarities and differences and then to appreciate both. For example, when the children create self-portraits for their class books, some choose different colors of paper for drawing faces, but all of them use the same markers to draw in their features.
- *Skills in communication and problem-solving.* Learning how to express thoughts and feelings includes being able to hear others and finding peaceful ways to resolve conflicts. Jim and LaNell are quick to tell Eben he cannot play, but they find out that telling him he is "too little" does not work. He does not accept that simply being 3 years old is enough reason to leave him out, so they must either try to include him or make a claim for privacy.

As Elizabeth Jones (personal notes, 1984) states:

> The pluralistic view assumes that (1) people are different from each other and (2) differences are valuable; they add to the richness of everyone's experiences. The task of the worker with children, then, is to acknowledge and appreciate differences. The developmental view assumes that growth and learning are spontaneously motivated. The task of the teacher is to provide a supportive environment that frees each individual to grow and learn—to empower children so that they will assert their needs and develop thoughtful strategies for meeting them.

Self-Help Environment

A **self-help** environment has as one of its fundamental goals the development of children's own skills—fostering their mastery of basic abilities that will allow them to become responsible for their own personal care, their own learning, their own emotional controls, their own problem solving, and their own choices and decisions. A self-help environment gives children the feeling that they are capable, competent, and successful. It allows children to do for themselves, to meet the challenge of growing up. A self-help environment reflects the belief that autonomy and independence are the birthright of every child.

I Can Do It Myself

Nothing renders people more helpless than not being able to maintain their own needs or to take care of themselves in basic ways. Children are still in the process of learning about what they can and cannot do. They need many different kinds of experiences to help them learn the extent of their capabilities. Most of all, they need adults who understand their tremendous drive to become self-reliant, adults who will not only encourage their abilities and provide the time for them to practice skills, but adults who understand that it is the nature of the child to develop this way.

Self-concept is based on what we know about ourselves, which includes the ability to take care of our own needs. To care for oneself, to feel capable of learning, to solve problems, are all related to feelings of **self-esteem.** Self-esteem is the value we place on ourselves; how much we like or dislike who we are. Helping children achieve a positive self-concept and self-esteem is the most important part of teaching. The development of a strong sense of self-esteem is a lifelong process; its origins are in the early years.

A program designed to promote self-help skills uses every aspect of the environment, from the room arrangement to the attitudes of the teachers. Each activity is designed to foster self-reliance, thereby building self-esteem. A supermarket is a real-world example of an environment created for maximum self-reliance. Shelves are accessible and the products are clearly marked and attractively displayed.

That kind of thoughtful preparation can create spaces that say to children, "Do me. Master me. You are capable." Teachers want to communicate to children that they value self-help skills as much as they appreciate an art project or science experiment. The ultimate goal is for children to see self-reliance as valuable. If Claudia feels that learning to tie her shoes is worth doing just because of the pleasure it gives her to manipulate the strings, weave them through the holes, and bring them together in a knot, then that becomes her reward. She becomes capable of reinforcing herself.

The Inclusive Environment

In 1975, the Education for All Handicapped Children Act (P.L. 94-142) called for an end to segregation for disabled students from kindergarten through high school. This policy filtered down to preschools and child care centers, and in 1986, an amendment made to this bill (P.L. 99-457) mandated that preschoolers with special needs be placed in the **least restrictive environment.** The practice of placing children with disabilities in the same classroom as children without disabilities is called **mainstreaming.** A more comprehensive method is known as **full inclusion,** in which both typically developing children and children with diverse abilities are taught together by a teaching staff with expertise in both normal child development and special education (see Chapter 3). The Americans with Disabilities Act of 1990 prohibits child care centers from denying admission to a child simply because the child has a disability. Together, these federal laws form part of the rationale for early childhood centers to become more inclusive environments.

Children with diverse abilities need the same things in their environment as their more typically-developing peers. They need an environment that is safe, secure, and predictable and one that provides a balance of the familiar and novel, so that there are materials and activities that provide for their development. "When a child with disabilities has different developmental needs than other children of the same age, adaptations must be made" (Youcha & Wood, 1997). These may require either adding something to the environment that is not already there or using something in the environment in a different way. Our Code of Ethical Conduct supports the right of each child to play and learn in an inclusive environment that meets the needs of children with and without disabilities.

Environmental adaptations are changes that make the environment fit the child better, so they will vary with the children. Children with motor disabilities need different adaptations than those with hearing or language disabilities or with visual impairments. Physical changes may be necessary, modifications in the schedule may be recommended, or individualizing activities may be best. Parents will be the best source of information about the child; other readings or specialists can be further guides. Three key concepts are helpful to remember—access, usability, and maximizing learning:

1. Can the child get where s/he needs to be in the classroom to learn something?
2. Once the child is in that location, can s/he use the materials and equipment and participate in the activity as independently as possible to learn something?
3. Are the learning activities arranged and scheduled to meet the individual learning needs of the children, including the child with disabilities?

Figure 9-4 is an abbreviated checklist for adaptations to create an inclusive environment.

Come Together for a Child

Consider Andrew (Rogers, 1994), who at 5 years of age had a motor/muscle disability with some speech difficulties. His cognitive skills were very strong and his social skills very weak. Andrew's mother talked to everyone during class about Andrew's needs and fears. If he fell down, he had a hard time righting himself. He needed help sitting and standing. He was afraid of getting bumped because he could not catch himself before falling very hard and then could not get up. The children all agreed to be careful about **roughhousing** around him. *The setting for success was being created.*

Because Andrew did not have much control of his fine motor skills, the teachers provided him with painting

Checklist for an Inclusive Environment

Physical Environment:

Visual Environment

Questions to think about:
- How can we enhance or adapt the physical environment for children who have difficulty moving (or who move too much)?
- How do different children use their bodies or the space around them for learning?
- How can we capitalize on the physical environment for children who learn by moving?

Accessing the environment safely:
❑ Are doorway widths in compliance with local building codes?
❑ Ramps in addition to or instead of stairs?
❑ Low, wide stairs where possible (including playground equipment)?
❑ Hand rails on *both* sides of stairs?
❑ Easy handles on doors, drawers, etc.?
❑ Kids' chairs with armrests, "cubes" or footrest and/or seat strap?
   *When adapting seating, mobility, and/or motor activities for a specific child with physical disabilities, consult a physical therapist.

Learning through the environment:
❑ Are toys and equipment physically accessible?
- Glue magnets to backs of puzzle pieces and attribute blocks and use on a steel cookie tray.
- Attach large knobs or levers to toys with lids, movable parts.
- Attach tabs to book pages for easier turning.
- ☛An occupational therapist can provide specific suggestions for adapting materials and activities.

Questions to think about:
- How do different children use their vision for learning?
- How can we enhance the visual environment for a child with low or no vision?
- How can we capitalize on the visual environment for children who learn by seeing?

Accessing the environment safely:
❑ Are contrasting colors used on edges and when surfaces change (e.g., tile to carpet, beginning of stairs, etc.)?
❑ Can windows be shaded to avoid high glare?
- Also consider darker nonglossy floors and tabletops.
- Some children's behavior and learning may improve dramatically once a strong glare is eliminated.
❑ Is visual clutter avoided on walls, shelves, etc.?
- Visual clutter can interfere with learning, predictability, and safety.
❑ Is "spot lighting" (e.g., swing arm lamp) in a dimmer room available?
- Spot lamps help some children pay attention and work better on table tasks.
❑ Orientation and mobility specialists help children with visual impairments learn to navigate the environment.

Learning through the environment:
❑ Are large-print materials, textured materials, and auditory materials available (e.g., big books, sandpaper letters, books on tape)?

(continues)

FIGURE 9-4 When designing an inclusive environment, keep in mind that the environment needs to be safe and to help everyone participate, learn, and communicate. (Adapted from Haugen, K. [1997, March].)

❏ Is the daily schedule represented in words and pictures?
  • A Velcro schedule that allows children to post the schedule and then remove items as activities are completed can help children to stay focused and make the transition more easily from one activity to the next.
❏ Are children with low vision seated close to the center of activity and away from high glare? *Consult family about the need for "running commentary" for blink or low-vision child.

Auditory Environment

© Cengage Learning

Questions to think about:
• How do different children use their hearing for learning?
• How can we enhance the auditory environment for a child who is deaf, hearing impaired, or has poor auditory discrimination skills?
• How can we capitalize on the auditory environment for auditory learners?

Accessing the environment safely:
❏ Is there a way to eliminate or dampen background noise (using carpeting, closing windows and doors, etc.)?
  • Some kids are unable to do the automatic filtering out of background noises.
❏ Is "auditory competition" avoided?
  • Raising one's voice to compete with a roomful of noisy children is rarely as effective as using a "silent signal," for example, holding up a peace sign and encouraging children who notice to do the same until the room is full of quiet children holding up peace signs!
❏ Are nonauditory signals needed to alert a child with a hearing impairment?
  • Turning the lights on and off is a common strategy.

Learning through the environment:
❏ Are auditory messages paired with visual ones (e.g., simple sign language, flannel boards, picture schedules)?
❏ Are children with hearing impairments seated so they can see others' faces and actions?
  • Ask the child's parents what strategies are used at home and about the use of sign language.

Social Environment

© Cengage Learning

Questions to think about:
• How do different children use social cues for learning?
• How can we adapt the social environment for children with impulsive behavior, attention deficits, or other behavior problems?

(continues)

▌ **FIGURE 9-4** *(continued)*

- How can we capitalize on the social environment for children who learn by relating to others?

Accessing the environment safely:
- ❑ Is the schedule predictable? Are children informed of schedule changes?
- ❑ Does the schedule provide a range of activity levels (e.g., adequate opportunities for physical activity)?

Learning through the environment:
- ❑ Does the environment have a positive impact on self-esteem?
  - Allows all children to feel safe, invites participation, allows for independence?
- ❑ Do learning materials and toys include representations of all kinds of people, including children and adults with disabilities?
  - People with disabilities should be represented in active and leadership roles, not just as passive observers.

- ❑ Does the schedule include opportunities for a variety of groupings (pairs, small groups, whole class) as well as quiet time or time alone?
- ❑ Does the schedule provide both structured and open activity times?
  - Children who have difficulty with a particular type of activity may need extra support at those times.
  - ☛School psychologists and behavior specialists can help analyze misbehavior and modify the environment or schedule.

▌ **FIGURE 9-4** *(continued)*

and play-dough. They set up a crafts table; soon he was gluing pictures on paper, with or without order, and was very proud of his accomplishments. He even started using scissors on simple patterns. *The physical environment was responding to his needs.*

He was a wonderful puzzle builder, and the other children asked for his help often when they were stuck. It was wonderful to watch how they included him in many things. They accepted his differences right from the beginning and treated him just like all the rest—except they were careful when running and playing around him. His fear was apparent, and they respected it. *Thus, the interpersonal environment was emerging.*

There was a regular P.E. time each day in the big room where the group jumped rope, played "Simon Says," played "Red Light, Green Light," and ran obstacle courses. At first, Andrew sat on the sidelines and watched. He cheered and looked interested, so one teacher started asking him if he'd be my partner because she was a little afraid. At first he refused and told her to use someone else. The teacher kept asking but would drop it as soon as he gave his answer; then one day he said, "OK." The two of them ran and jumped over the snake (rope), and all the kids laughed. They hugged and that was the beginning. *When given the time that is needed (the temporal environment), the child triumphs.*

Planning for the Environment

Who Is in the Environment?

Many people live and work in the early childhood environment. Cooks, bus drivers, office personnel, and yard and building maintenance people are but a few. Each person has special demands on the environment to do the job they are hired to do.

Children, teachers, and families have the greatest influence on the early childhood environment; their needs are outlined in this section.

Children

Children's needs are met through the environment. The physical, social, emotional, and intellectual requirements of children suggest the type of building, the size of the furniture, the choice of equipment, the size and age range of the group, the number of teachers who lead and supervise, and the budget allocations. Guided by child development principles, teachers match the setting to the children who will learn and play there. The individuality of a particular group of children, of a school, and of its philosophy is expressed by the arrangement of the envi-

© Cengage Learning

Children develop a sense of self when they have their own space, labeled with a photo or other visual clue so that they can easily identify it as their own.

ronmental factors. First and foremost, though, are the questions: Who are the children who will use this space? What are their needs? How can those needs be met in this particular setting?

Teachers

What has been done to meet the needs of the teachers? Do they have an office? A teachers' room? A place to hold conferences? Where do they keep their personal belongings or the materials they bring to use at school? Do they have a place to park? All teachers need room to create curriculum materials, to evaluate their programs, to review other educational materials, and to meet with their peers. Research (Whitebook, 1996) indicates that the working environment of caregivers (including the general context of the setting, opportunities for professional development, status, and wages) are important predictors of the quality of care children receive. How well teachers are provided for helps to determine the atmosphere they will establish in their classrooms. Adult space indoors is described in more detail later in the chapter.

Families

The needs of parents and other adults in children's families will differ, depending on whom the program serves. Adults who bring their children to child care or school need adequate and safe parking facilities. In settings in which adults are free to stay, a reading room, resource library, or a comfortable place to talk with others is desir-

able. Those who participate in the class are welcomed by a teacher, shown a place to put their belongings, and given a name tag and appropriate directions.

There are many reasons families may need to contact the school or center. Are there ways to reach teachers and children in emergencies? How welcoming is the environment as they enter the building? The office? The classroom? What does the environment say about family involvement and interest?

The teacher can make the environment accessible and welcoming in several ways. Posting telephone numbers at which school authorities and teachers can be reached when the school is closed assures families that teachers are available whenever needed. A bulletin board for community notices and for family use can be put up along with mail pockets. Written communication can go between parents and teachers and among families. Working with families is vital to creating both an anti-bias and a self-help focus in children's education and care. Teaching from these perspectives is more likely to create positive changes in children's lives when families are included in the process. The center that offers parents both an authoritative teacher and other useful resources helps them feel that their children are important.

Health and Safety in the Environment

Regardless of how many children are in the setting and for how long, the first priority is to provide for their health and safety. Health, safety, and nutrition are closely related because the quality of one affects the quality of the others (Marotz, 2009). Therefore, programs for children must establish policies that provide for the protection, service, and education of child health and safety at all times. Government regulations and professional recommendations vary, but all establish some kind of standards to ensure good health and safety practices. Key documents are noted in the reference section of this chapter.

Keeping Children Healthy

Sanitation. When groups of people live in close quarters, proper sanitary conditions are imperative to prevent the spread of disease. For an early childhood center, the physical plant must have adequate washing and toileting facilities for both children and adults. The number and size of toilets and wash basins are usually prescribed by local health or other regulatory agencies. Children do not realize their role in spreading germs, especially as

On the left, towels are color coded in easily recognizable shapes in a Russian child care center. On the right, toothbrushes and towels are accessible so that children in the Reggio Emilia centers in Italy can help themselves.

their moist and warm hands touch and handle everything. Through gentle reminders and role modeling, teachers help children learn the habit of washing their hands at important times such as before snack and mealtimes.

Sanitation depends on frequent, systematic cleaning. The classrooms require daily cleaning, and equipment that is used regularly should be sanitized on a periodic basis. Nontoxic paint must be used in all circumstances, including on outdoor equipment, cribs, and for art activities with children. Classroom dress-up clothing, pillows, nap blankets, and cuddle toys all need regular laundering, either at school or at home.

The nature of preventive health care in educational settings has expanded in the last decade. Knowledge of how disease is spread and concern over infectious diseases such as hepatitis B and infection by the human immunodeficiency virus (HIV) have increased awareness of the kinds of practices teachers must engage in on a daily basis. These include hand washing (the number-one way to prevent unnecessary spread of germs) and an approach known as **universal infection control precautions.** All teachers should receive training in using universal health precautions with all children.

Because we cannot be guaranteed of the infectious state of an individual, it is very important to always follow universal safety procedures with all children. The steps that keep a barrier between persons and blood can apply to more than blood-borne infections. All programs should be equipped with sets of latex gloves and plastic bags to properly handle and dispose of anything with blood or fecal material. Because intact skin is a natural barrier against disease, it may not always be necessary or possible to use gloves, but it is essential that hands be washed immediately after any toileting activity. All areas for eating, diapering, and toileting must be cleaned and sanitized, using a water-diluted bleach solution after cleaning away visible soiling.

Temperature, Ventilation, and Lighting. Heating and ventilation should be comfortable for the activity level of the children and should change when weather conditions do. Adequate, nonglare lighting is a necessity. Studies indicate that uniform, fluorescent lighting may not be the best environment for children; therefore, a mixture of lighting, such as is in homes, is preferable (Alexander, 1995). Rooms should have some means of controlling light (shades, blinds). Cross-ventilation is necessary in all rooms where children eat, sleep, or play. Proper heating and insulation are important.

Communicable Disease. This is an important issue when dealing with young children in group care. Some people question the advisability of early group care on the grounds that it exposes children to too much illness. Others claim that such exposure at an early age helps children build up resistance and that they are actually stronger and healthier by the time they enter primary grades. In the largest U.S. study to date on children's health, the Environmental Protection Agency and Centers for Disease Control and Prevention concluded that, although infants and toddlers face a higher risk of colds and viruses, day care was not seen as increasing children's illnesses at older ages and not a risk overall (CDC, 1997).

Families should be notified when normal childhood diseases (such as chicken pox) or common problems (such as head lice) occur in the classroom. Infections of special concern to adults include chicken pox, hepatitis A, and cytomegalovirus (CMV). A handout that describes symptoms, dates of exposure, and incubation is helpful to families who can then help prevent the spread of infectious disease.

In group care, children can contract a fair number of colds and viruses, especially when they are eating and sleeping close to each other. Figure 9-5 summarizes the 10 most common health problems in school, with tips for dealing with them. The school and its staff have responsibility to ensure that good health standards are instituted and maintained to keep illness to a minimum.

Health Assessment and School Policies. Every early childhood center should establish clear health policies and make them known to families. A daily inspection of each child will help adults spot nasal discharge, inflamed eyes, and throat and skin conditions of a questionable nature. This daily check will screen out more serious cases of children too ill to remain at school and may be done by a teacher, nurse, or administrator. Educating families about the warning signs of illness will encourage sick children to be cared for at home.

It is very important for the school to inform families about what happens when children are refused admittance or become ill during the school day. Every school should provide a place for sick children where they can be isolated from others, kept under supervision, and be made comfortable until they are picked up. For their part, parents must arrange to have sick children cared for elsewhere if they are unable to take them home. School

Tips for Common Children's Health Problems

Condition	Tips
1. Allergies and asthma	Post a list of all children with chronic conditions; check ingredient lists on foods; watch what triggers reactions.
2. Scrapes and cuts	Reassure and sympathize with child; supervise child's washing with soaped pad and caring comments; use packs of ice or frozen peas in towel for swelling.
3. Bumps on the head	Notify parents of any loss of conciousness and watch for signs for two to three days.
4. Sand in eyes	Remind child "Do not rub!," have child wash hands and cover eyes with tissue; normal eye tearing will bring sand to inside corner of eye; remove with clean tissue.
5. Splinters	Clean area with alcohol and remove with tweezers or cover with adhesive strip and let parent remove.
6. Conjunctivitis	"Pinkeye" is highly contagious; watch for excess eye rubbing and red eyes; have child wash hands; isolate with washable toys until parent takes child home and gets treatment.
7. Head lice	Distressing but not dangerous; wash shared clothing, stuffed animals, bedding; vacuum rugs and furniture; remove hats, combs, and brushes from dramatic-play area; send notices home and inspect children's hair for two to three weeks.
8. Chicken pox	Isolate child until parents pick up; alert all parents about contagious period; watch for signs on all children for three weeks after exposure.
9. Strep throat	Send home notices; wash all equipment that might carry germs.
10. Lingering coughs	At onset, send child home until evaluated; frequent drinks will soothe; coughs may last up to two weeks; if longer, may suggest infection or allergy.

FIGURE 9-5 Tips for common children's health problems. (Adapted from Needlman, R., & Needlman, G. [1995].)

policies on these issues must be explicit and upheld consistently and compassionately for the sake of all the children.

Teachers must be sensitive to families' feelings and situations when sending a sick child home. This situation often produces guilt feelings in parents and work-related stress. Working families may need school assistance in locating alternatives for care of a sick child.

Most schools require, under state or local laws, a doctor's examination and permission to participate in an early childhood education program before a child can enter the program. This includes a record of immunizations and the child's general health. Parents, too, should submit a history of the child, highlighting eating, sleeping, and elimination habits. It is critical to note any dietary restrictions or allergies and then post them in the classrooms for a reminder.

Nutrition. What children eat is also important for proper health. Places where food is prepared and stored must be kept especially clean. The child who has regular, nutritious meals and snacks will likely be healthier and less susceptible to disease. Many children do not have the benefits of healthy meals and snacks. Some do not receive adequate food at home; others are used to sugar-laden treats and fast foods. Education about child nutrition is needed for families and teachers in all programs, regardless of social or economic status. Some centers establish food regulations in an attempt to ensure that nutritionally sound meals are served to children. Most schools attempt to provide a relaxed atmosphere at meal and snack time. Children are asked to sit and eat, sharing conversation as well as food. Because lifelong eating patterns are established early in life, teachers of young children have a responsibility to understand the critical role nutrition plays in the child's total development.

Clothing. The health and safety of children are affected by the clothing they wear. A simple way to be sure children stay healthy is to encourage them to dress properly for play and for varying weather conditions. Children need clothing in which they can be active—clothing that is not binding and is easy to remove and easy to clean. To promote a self-help environment, parents and teachers should provide clothes the children can manage themselves (elastic waistbands, Velcro™ ties, large zippers). Pants are a good choice for both boys and girls; long dresses can become a hazard when climbing, running, or going up and down stairs. The safest shoes for active play should have composition or rubber soles. Whenever possible, it helps to keep changes of clothes at school.

Children need clothing in which they can be active, playful, and messy!

Health of the Staff. A responsible early childhood center is one that supports and maintains a healthy staff. Teachers should be in good physical and mental health to be at their best with children. It is wise to check the health regulations and benefits of the individual center when employed there. Many states require annual chest X-rays and tuberculosis clearance as a condition of employment. Sick leave policies should be clearly stated in print. Early childhood education is an intense job involving close interpersonal contact. Most teachers work long hours, often with low wages and few health benefits, and with clients in various stages of health. Such working conditions produce fatigue and stress, which can lead to illness or other stress-related problems.

Guarding Children's Safety

Beyond the continual supervision of indoor and outdoor space, everything is planned with the children's safety in mind. Creating a hazard-free environment that still allows for risk and challenge for children takes careful observation and attention to detail. A quick walk around the room and yard will reveal potential problems. Sharp corners, loose rug edges, and gated stairwells are sample indoor items; fences and broken equipment in the playground, use of scissors/hammers, and appliances everywhere are just some of the examples. Figure 9-6 is a safety checklist for a typical early childhood setting.

Most importantly, there must be safety rules that are explained to children and upheld by adults. Outdoors is especially important because children are physically active. Approximately 200,000 children are sent to an emergency room every year as a result of a playground accident (Consumer Product Safety Commission, 2009). With an estimated 27 to 30 million children between 5 and 14 years of

Safety List for Indoor Environments

_____ Person monitoring children (at entrances, indoors, outdoors)

_____ First aid and emergency

    _____ Materials readily available to adults, out of children's reach, and regularly stocked and updated

    _____ Adults trained in first aid and CPR regularly and familiar with emergency routines

_____ Safety plugs on all outlets

_____ Cords

    _____ Electrical cords out of children's reach; avoid using extension cords

    _____ Curtain and window cords, window pulls and poles out of children's reach

_____ Floormat and carpet tacked down to avoid slippage

_____ Doors

    _____ Made to open and close slowly

    _____ All clear access, marked exits, and not blocked

_____ Cubbies and storage cabinets

    _____ Bolted to walls (or back-to-back together)

    _____ Any dangerous materials in locked area

_____ Toys

    _____ In good repair; no splinters or sharp, broken edges

    _____ Check for size with younger children (purchase safety-sizing gadget or estimate to keep at the size of a child's fist)

    _____ Check for peeling paint

_____ Plants and animals

    _____ Nonpoisonous plants _only_

    _____ Check animal cages regularly

    _____ Supervise animal handling carefully

    _____ Store animal food away from children's reach

_____ Adult materials

    _____ Keep adult purses, bags, and so on, away from children

    _____ Avoid having hot beverages around children

    _____ No smoking in children's areas

_____ Kitchen and storage

    _____ Children allowed in _only_ with adult supervision

    _____ Poisonous or hazardous materials stored in a locked area

FIGURE 9-6 Children's safety is of primary importance to teachers and caregivers. Careful evaluation and regular safety checks eliminate dangerous materials and conditions in children's spaces.

age participating in organized sports each year, safety issues are paramount for school-aged children. The adults serve as the link between children and sports and are the chief means of prevention of injuries and accidents. Figure 11-6 shows how to make playgrounds safe.

First Aid. Every school should establish procedures for dealing with children who are injured on the property. First aid and CPR training should be required of all teachers and made available as part of their in-service training. Teachers should know how to handle a child who is not breathing as well as treat bumps and bruises, minor cuts and abrasions, bleeding, splinters, bites and stings, seizures, sprains, broken bones, and minor burns. Each classroom should be equipped with two first aid kits. One is for use in the classroom and yard; the other should be suitable for taking on field trips. Each kit

should be readily available to adults, but out of children's reach, and supplies should be replenished regularly.

Emergency numbers to be posted near the telephone in each room include those of the ambulance squad, fire department, police, health department, nearest hospital, and a consulting physician (if any). All families enrolled at the school should be aware of center policy regarding injuries at school and should provide emergency information for each child: the name of their physician, how to locate the family, and who else might be responsible for the injured child if the parents cannot be reached. The school, in turn, must make sure they notify parents of any injuries the child has incurred during the school day.

Natural Disaster. Most adults are familiar with the most common disaster preparation: the fire drill. Most local fire regulations require that fire extinguishers are in working order and placed in all classrooms and the kitchen area. Fire exits, fire alarms, and fire escapes should be well-marked and functioning properly. Children and teachers should participate in fire drills regularly. Other natural disasters vary by geographical location; helping children prepare for earthquakes, tornadoes, hurricanes, floods, and snowstorms will include participating in drills for those disasters. Proper preparedness will include eliminating potential hazards (e.g., bolting down bookcases), establishing a coordinated response plan (a "Code Blue!" emergency plan should involve children, parents, all staff, and local emergency agencies), and, in some areas of the country, conducting regular earthquake and tornado drills. These experiences can reinforce in parents the need for establishing similar procedures at home.

Automobile Safety. Automobile safety is a related concern when considering potential hazards for preschool children. The use of approved car seats and restraints for children riding in automobiles has received national attention in recent years. Some states have passed legislation requiring the use of specific devices to ensure safer travel for young children. Whether or not they walk to school, children should also be aware of basic rules for crossing streets. The school parking lot can be a source of danger unless the school articulates policies to parents regarding the safety needs of children. There are potential risks when cars and children occupy the same space. Children should not be left unattended in parking lots.

Maintaining Children's Well-Being

The overall environment for children takes into consideration many factors. To provide for children's health and safety, teachers look at the physical environment carefully—its materials, the equipment, and their arrangement. Another factor in children's care and education is their well-being. Young children are growing up in a world threatened by violence abroad and at home, drug abuse, unresolved conflicts among adults, and constant bombardment of television and other media.

Since young children do not easily separate the home and school parts of their lives, early childhood educators learn about children's lives and family details readily. They are often at a loss as to what to do, either with information that a child shares or with the child's behavior in the program. Yet, a situation does not need to be a crisis to affect a child's well-being. As a rule of thumb, when you feel the child's physical or emotional development is in jeopardy, you have a responsibility to take further action.

Children's well-being can be threatened by a difficult situation at school, such as being bitten, left out, or ridiculed. They are also at risk for the myriad of crises from home—problems with family members, separation or divorce, violence, or substance abuse. Although much of our response will be with adults—families, community resources, professional supports—we are also responsible for trying to provide a psychologically safe and positive environment. By design (physical and temporal) and by responsiveness (interpersonal), teachers provide an environment that soothes and cares for young children.

Creating the Environment

The Physical Environment

Every educational setting is organized fundamentally around physical space. The building itself may be new and designed specifically for young children. In Reggio Emilia, for example, it is the environment that creates an atmosphere of discovery. As founder Louis Malaguzzi explains (Edwards et al., 1993):

> There is an entrance hall, which informs and documents, and which anticipates the form and organization of the school. This leads into the dining hall, with the kitchen well in view. The entrance hall leads into the central space, or piazza, the place of encounters, friendships, games, and other activities that complete those of the classrooms. The classrooms and utility rooms are placed at a distance from but connected with the center area. Each classroom is divided into two contiguous rooms…to allow children either to be with teachers or stay alone. … In addition to the classrooms, we have established the atelier, the school studio and laboratory, as a place for manipulating or experimenting.

More than likely, however, the space is a converted house or store, a parish hall, or an elementary classroom. Sometimes a program will share space with another group so that mobile furniture is moved daily or weekly. Family child care programs are housed in a private home; therefore, adaptations are made in the space both for the children and the family that lives there. There may be a large yard or none at all. Some playgrounds are on the roof of the building, or a park across the street may serve as the only available playground. (See the section on playgrounds in Chapter 11.)

Constraints also come in the form of weather conditions. Outside play—and therefore large-muscle equipment—may be unavailable during the winter, so room for active, vigorous play is needed inside during that time. Hot summer months can make some types of play difficult if there is little or no shade outdoors. Weather conditions must be considered when planning programs for children.

Early childhood programs have specific needs that must be met by the buildings they occupy. Although the choice of building is generally determined by what is available, at a minimum the setting should provide facilities for:

playing/working	food preparation
eating	washing/toileting
sleeping/resting	clothing and wraps
storage	office/work space

Ideally, the setting should have enough space to house these various activities separately. In practice, however, rooms are multipurpose, and more than one event takes place in the same space. A playroom doubles as an eating area because both require the use of tables and chairs. When a school room serves many functions (playing, eating, sleeping), convenient and adequate storage space is a necessity.

General Requirements

Ground floor classrooms are preferable for young children to ensure that they can enter and leave with relative ease and safety. For noise reduction, the walls and ceilings should be soundproofed. Carpeting, draperies, and other fireproof fabrics in the room will help absorb sound. Floors must be durable, sanitary, and easily cleaned. They should be free from drafts. Rugs should be vacuumed each day. Room size should be sufficient to allow for freedom of movement and the opportunity to play without interference. Some licensing agencies may suggest minimum room and yard size standards.

Many local and state agencies have regulations regarding the use of space for children in group care settings. The fire marshal, health department, and similar agencies must be consulted and their regulations observed. It is wise to consider their requirements when arranging space.

The National Academy of Early Childhood Programs (NAEYC, 2005) has developed guidelines for indoor and outdoor facilities that promote optimal growth. Besides floor and play space (minimum 35 [and recommended 50] square feet indoors and 75 square feet outdoors), the guidelines suggest how to arrange activity areas to accommodate children and what kinds of activities and materials are safe, clean, and attractive. This document, along with *Designs for Living and Learning* (Carter & Curtis, 2003), *The Creative Curriculum* (Dodge, Colker, & Heroman, 2002) and the Environmental Rating Scales from Harms and others (2005) are used extensively to develop this material. There are several key dimensions to any environment that are helpful to consider. If we are to offer children both balance and variety, these criteria need to be included in developing space both indoors and out. Figure 9-7 outlines these dimensions in detail.

Indoors

Interest Areas/Learning Centers. "An activity area has five defining attributes. Physical *location*, with visible *boundaries* indicating where it begins and ends, within which are placed *work and sitting surfaces*, and the *storage and display of materials* used to execute the activities for which the area is intended. An area, like a room, has a *mood* or personality distinguishing it from contiguous spaces" (Olds, 1989). Deciding what interest centers you want, reflective of program philosophy and children's interests, and what kind of space you will need is good preparation to making a basic floor plan and sketching in the interest centers.

As you consider transforming your early childhood environment, start with an assessment of the way your space is designed now. "First draw a simple floor plan of the room you are currently working in, one you are familiar with, or one you imagine using in a new job. As you sketch out the arrangements of the room, do not include a lot of detail… Put yourself in the shoes of the children who spend their days in your space" (Carter & Curtis, 2003).

> You will consider their ages and needs of the group, and make a list of "I can" and "I like to" statements as if *you* are those children. Now check your floor plan; if you had trouble finding any of the components in your room, make some changes.

Most programs will include basic areas for small group play, for flexibility, and for engagement. **Learning centers** are areas of the environment focused on different activities for different developmental experiences. For infants and toddlers, areas for movement and for sensory experiences will dominate; preschoolers will want more creative and manipulative choices; school-age children might include areas for academic stimulation or practice.

Key Environmental Dimensions

1. Softness/Hardness

   Soft: rugs, pillows, play-dough, finger paints, grass, sand, swings

   Hard: tile floor, wooden furniture, asphalt, cement

2. Open/Closed

   Open (no one right way to use it): sand and water, dress-up, collage materials, painting

   Closed (manipulated only one way to come out right): puzzles, many board games, most Montessori equipment

   In between: many manipulatives such as Legos®, Tinkertoys®, blocks, balls

3. Simple/Complex

   "Play equipment can differ in its holding power; i.e., the capacity to sustain attention . . . A simple unit has one manipulable aspect; a complex unit has two different kinds of materials combined; and a super unit has three different kinds of materials that go together."

   > *Simple:* swings, climbers, sand pile with no toys

   > *Complex:* dramatic play with only a kitchen

   > *Super:* climbers with slides and ropes, playhouse with kitchen, dress-up clothes, dolls, and/or play-dough; sand area with equipment and/or water

   As you add more features to a unit, you increase its complexity and the children's interest in it. To simple play-dough, add cookie cutters; then add toothpicks or a garlic press and it becomes a super unit.

4. Intrusion/Seclusion

   Intrusion: places where children can enter or go through easily; blocks, housekeeping, even the entire environment are often highly intrusive areas

   Seclusion: places where children can be alone or with only one child or adult; cubbies, a fort, or under a table become secret places

5. High Mobility/Low Mobility

   High: whole-body places and activities, outdoors, climbers, trike lanes, gym mats

   Low: sitting-still places and activities; puzzles and games, story and group times, nap time

   In-between: dramatic play, block corner, woodworking

FIGURE 9-7 Key dimensions when considering an early childhood environment. (Adapted from *Exchange Magazine*, E. Prescott, 1994.)

The teacher plays an important role in implementing the use of learning centers. They must be interesting, accurately reflect the goals for children, and take into consideration space, traffic flow, the number of people, and availability of equipment and materials. The teacher uses environmental cues to communicate to children what may happen there, and makes good use of the learning centers as places for observation and assessment (see Figure 9-8). Creating learning centers is a standard early childhood practice that has tremendous potential in school-age and primary settings.

Bathrooms. Bathrooms should be adjacent to the play and sleeping areas and easily reached from outdoors. Child-sized toilets and wash basins are preferable, but if unavailable, a step or platform may be built. In most settings for children under 5, the bathrooms are without doors, for ease of supervision. Toileting facilities for children should be light, airy, attractive, and large enough to serve several children at a time. An exhaust fan is desirable. Paper towel holders should be at child height and wastebaskets placed nearby.

All photos © Cengage Learning

Early childhood programs provide for children to play and work alone and together, with friends and teachers, indoors and out.

If diapering is part of the program, areas for this purpose should be clearly defined and close to hand washing facilities. Hand washing regulations for the staff should be posted, and an area should be provided for recording children's toileting and elimination patterns. Closed cans and germicidal spray must be used, and diapering materials should be plentiful and handy.

Room to Rest. Programs that provide nap and sleeping facilities require adequate storage space for cots and bedding. Movable screens, low enough for teacher supervision, allow for privacy and help reduce the noise level. Cots or cribs should be labeled with children's names and washed regularly. They should be placed consistently and in such a way that children feel familiar, cozy, and private—not in the center of the room or in rows. Teachers can develop a "nap map" that places children so they can get the rest or sleep they need while still feeling part of the group.

Food Service. "Good nutrition affects the health and well-being of individuals of all ages," states Marotz (2009). "Small children need nutrients for growth and energy...regardless of the guideline selected, the common factor necessary for good nutrition is the inclusion of a wide variety of foods." As early childhood classrooms have become more diverse and multicultural, routines and choices around food must take into consideration families' cultural practices and preferences.

Feeding young children and teaching toddlers and older children about good food choices can be a challenge throughout the early childhood span. In an infant program, storing formula and milk is a necessity. As toddlers assert their independence, they begin to make their preferences known. Care must be taken to offer a variety of foods at regular times, but avoid a battle of wills over what the child will eat. Preschoolers are influenced by a teacher who sets a good example of eating with balance and variety. School-aged children can understand nutri-

Environmental Components of the ECE Curriculum Framework

Infants, Toddlers & Twos

Routines

Hello/goodbye, diapering/toileting, eating

Sleeping/napping, getting dressed

Experiences

Playing with toys, imitating/pretending

Enjoying stories, connecting with music

Creating with art, tasting food, exploring

Sand and water, going outdoors

Partnering with Families

Plenty of display space

How Children Develop and Learn

The Learning Environment

The Family's Role

Blocks
Dramatic Play
Toys and Games
Art
Library
Discovery
Sand and Water
Music and Movement
Cooking
Computers
Outdoors

What Children Learn

The Teacher's Role

Theory and Research

School-Agers

Being with Friends

Quiet area for just talking, tables for being in groups, large area for whole group

Completing Homework

Place with lighting, computer access, teacher availability, away from noise

A Place for Everyone

Special place for either older [10+] or younger [K only]

FIGURE 9-8 Environmental features in the environment are set in a framework that helps build appropriate experiences for children in the early years. Components for Preschool. (From *The Creative Curriculum® for Preschool* (p. xiv), by D. T. Dodge, L. J. Colker, & C. Heroman, 2002, Washington, DC, Teaching Strategies, Inc. Copyright 2002 by Teaching Strategies, Inc. Reprinted with permission.)

tional concepts better but are more influenced by what their peers are eating.

Whether involved in a light snack or full meal program, the center must adhere to the most rigid standards of health protection and safety provisions. Every precaution must be taken to ensure maximum hygienic food service. Daily cleaning of equipment, counters, floors, and appliances is a necessity. Proper disinfecting of high chairs and tables requires 1/2 cup of bleach to one gallon of water; bottles of this solution can be stored away from children's reach yet handy for teachers.

Local school districts, Coordinated Community Child Care (4Cs), or affiliates of the NAEYC may be consulted for guidelines on serving nutritional foods and may even offer financial subsidies. For infant and toddler programs, space for recording feeding information must be designated, and enough high chairs or low tables must be provided to prevent an unreasonable wait for eating.

Each age has its unique food-service needs. Infants will need to be held or seated near an adult. Toddlers should not be fed popcorn, nuts, or raw carrots because of the hazard of choking. All children must be served food on disposable dishes or on dishes cleaned in a dishwasher with a sanitation cycle. Lunches brought from home by school-age and full-day children must be checked for spoilage. Information about eating patterns, proportions, and nutritional needs should be regularly shared with parents.

Adult Space. "Oh, for a real 'teacher's desk,'" the early childhood caregiver moans. "I'm lucky if I can find a place to stash my bag in the morning!" A common issue for ECE programs is to donate nearly all the available space to child use and materials storage. Yet, the personal and professional needs of adults deserve environmental support. Early education programs sometimes have an adult space in the director's area. An adult bathroom is also common. Elementary classrooms include a desk and a bookshelf for the teachers and a workroom or lounge for staff in the school office. However, in programs for children under age 5, even a desk can seem a hazard, taking up precious space for children.

Still, early childhood professionals deserve environmental support for their work. A safe place for their belongings, space for first aid/emergency materials and information for families, and an area for a special adult project goes a long way in respecting the teachers' lives in the classroom. We show our priorities by the space and time we give them.

Outside

"Children's access to outdoor play has evaporated like water in sunshine. It has happened so fast, along with everything else in this speed-ridden century, that we have not coped with it… Some of our deepest childhood joys—those of field and stream, rocks and vacant lots; of privacy, secrecy, and tiny things that creep across or poke out of the earth's surface" (Rivkin, 1995)—can be experienced out of doors, and nowhere else. Free and fresh air and open space to move about at will are often children's favorite spots in a program. Indeed, many a preschooler has been able to say goodbye easier when the great outdoors beckons.

The traditional playgrounds—typically on a flat, barren area with steel structures such as swings, climbers, a slide, perhaps a merry-go-round or seesaws, fixed in concrete and arranged—are poor places for children's play from both safety and developmental perspectives. Children as young as toddlers and through the primary years much prefer the adventure or creative playground, spaces that have a variety of fixed and movable equipment. Raw materials, such as sand, water, tires, spools, sawhorses, bowls, or pans, in combination with larger superstructures or open-air "houses" with some flexible parts, stimulate a wide variety of both social and cognitive play (including constructive, dramatic, and games play).

A wide porch or covered patio is ideal for rainy days or days when the sun is too severe. Many activities can be extended to the outside area with this type of protection. The physical plant should include adequate playground space adjacent to the building. A variety of playground surfaces makes for more interesting play and provides suitable covering for outdoor activities. Tanbark can be used in the swing area, cement for wheel toys, and grass for under climbers. Sand is used for play in a large area and also in a sensory table. No matter what the surface, the yard should be constructed with a good drainage system. Trees, bushes, and other plantings will allow for both sunshine and shade. Fences are *mandatory*. They must be durable, an appropriate height, with no opportunity for a child to gain a foothold. Because there are no mandatory standards for the manufacture of play equipment, adults who work with children must assume responsibility for playground design. Teachers can familiarize themselves with the literature, visit high quality playgrounds, and consult with child development specialists when selecting equipment. Given the importance that young children attach to the outdoors, teachers are well advised to concentrate their efforts in a similar fashion. Chapter 11 discusses playgrounds and safety in detail.

What Do YOU Think? Close your eyes. Think back to the places you like to play when you were a child. Was it outdoors? Was it a cozy spot near a loving adult? Did it involve other children? Sketch one of these places, adding a side column of sounds and smells. Can you help the children in your care have these delightful places?

Materials and Equipment

Selection of materials and equipment is based on a number of criteria. Most program budgets limit the amount of money available for such purchases. To make every dollar count, teachers select materials that:

- are age and developmentally appropriate.
- are related to program philosophy and curriculum.
- reflect quality design and workmanship.
- are durable.
- offer flexibility and versatility in their uses.
- have safety features (e.g., nontoxic paints, rounded corners).
- are aesthetically attractive and appealing to children (and adults).
- are easy to maintain and repair.
- reflect the cultural makeup of the group and the diversity of the culture overall.
- are nonsexist, nonstereotypical, and anti-bias.

Materials should be appropriate for a wide range of skills because children within the same age group develop at individual rates. "What makes good playthings? Simplicity of detail, versatile in use" (Community Products, 2008). Selecting equipment and toys to support development is important; because young children typically will try to play with everything in their environment, the selection of play materials involves many decisions. Many of the materials can be **open-ended;** that is, they can be used in their most basic form or they can be developed in a variety of ways. As with the environment (Figure 9-7), a key dimension is the simple/complex elements; unit blocks, clay, and Legos® are examples of materials that children can use in a simple fashion and, as skills develop, these materials can be manipulated in a more complex manner.

Toys and materials need to reflect the diversity of the class, the families, and the community:

- From a DAP perspective, materials need to appeal to individual interests and also respond to children's cultural and linguistic strengths. "The nature of the classroom atmosphere contributes greatly to children's success in learning English as a second language" (Elgas et al., 2002). Home-made materials and a variety of cultural artifacts help the environment feel familiar.
- From a self-help viewpoint, dressing frames and plenty of workable doll clothes will help children learn those self-care tasks.
- Children's books that demonstrate social values and attitudes that expand gender roles and family lifestyles show a value for an anti-bias environment.
- An inclusive viewpoint might include materials to highlight tactile, auditory, and olfactory experiences for children with visual impairments.
- Educational philosophy might determine materials, such as this Waldorf classroom kindergarten (Waldorf, 1995):

The feeling of warmth and security is largely created by using only natural materials—woods, cotton, wool—in the construction of the decor and toys. The curtains transmit a warm glow in the room. Ideally, the walls and floor of the room are of natural wood. In this warm environment are placed toys which the children can use to imitate and transform the activities that belong to everyday adult life. In one corner stands a wooden scale and baskets for children to pretend they are grocery shopping; a pile of timber stands ready to be constructed into a playhouse, a boat, or a train; a rocking horse invites a child to become a rider; homemade dolls lie in wooden cradles surrounded by wooden frames and cloths the children can use to create a pretend family and play house. Pinecones and flowers are artistically dispersed. Lovely watercolors adorn the walls. The effect of this beautiful arrangement of decorations and toys is the feeling of stepping out of the business and clutter of modern life into a sanctuary where one can breathe easily, relax, and play according to the impulses of one's heart.

Figure 9-9 is a list of basic materials that are then enhanced by individual and program interests.

Try to avoid toys that have limited play value. The organization "Teachers Resisting Unhealthy Children's Entertainment" (TRUCE, 2002) suggests that we steer away from toys that:

- make electronic technology the focus of play.
- lure girls into focusing on appearance.
- model violent and sexualized language or behavior.
- are linked to commercial products and advertisements.

Children are active learners, and their materials should provide them with ways to explore, manipulate, and become involved. Young children learn through all their senses, so the materials should be appealing to many of the senses. All children need opportunities for quiet, private time and space as well, with materials that parallel the balance of key environmental dimensions (Figure 9-10).

Organizing Space

There are many different ways to arrange and organize space in an early childhood setting; the final result expresses the diversity of the program. Most early childhood centers are arranged by **interest areas,** learning centers, or activity areas. The amount of space devoted to any one activity says a great deal about its value to the staff. For example, teachers at a child care center noticed the high interest in sociodramatic play with several new babies in children's families. They built up the housekeeping area, making sure there were at least six baby dolls, four telephones, and three doll buggies, and countless bottles, tippy cups and pretend baby food. As interests change, so do the room and yard—someone brings in a hamster and the discovery area blossoms, or family camping brings out tents around the grassy outdoor areas.

Basic Materials for ECE Environments

Basic Materials for Indoor Environments

Floors and Seating: Various surfaces (carpet, linoleum or tile, wood floor) kept clean and draft-free, comfortable seating (chairs at tables, rocking chair or sofa, carpet squares)

Areas: Art, blocks, dramatic play, toys and games, library, discovery/science, music and movement, cooking, media

Equipment:

Art: Easels, paints, watercolors; playdough, clay; pens, pencils, brushes; scissors, hole punch; glue, paste; collage materials; assorted paper

Blocks: Unit, hollow blocks; props (people & animal figures); accessories (signage, doll furniture)

Dramatic play: Mirrors; furniture; clothing; dolls, cooking utensils, pretend food items; purses and backpacks; expanded materials beyond house as needed

Toys and games: Puzzles, constructions toys, math toys, Montessori materials, cooperative games

Library/book nook: Picture books; flannel board and items; photos; writing center materials; listening post items

Discovery/science: Nature materials; pets; sensory materials; water/sand table; magnifying glasses and scales, etc.; textured materials or other 'theme/interest' related displays

Music and movement: CD/tape player and items; instruments, dancing scarves (may also be used in circletime)

Cooking: Food preparation materials (may also be used in discovery or art areas)

Media: Computers, tape/cd deck; TV

Infant-toddler: Limit materials and reduce number of interest areas; offer fewer choices in each area; substitute soft blocks and push/pull toys; have knobbed puzzles and stacking toys

School-age: Increase game area, vary units, add self-help in art and chapter books in library

Basic Materials for Outdoor Playgrounds/Yards

Grounds: Various surfaces (grass, asphalt, gravel/sand, tanbark), as much natural habitat as possible

Areas: Climbing place, sand/water space, wheel toy/riding place, games & dramatic play spot, building space, pet/garden area

Equipment: Climbing apparatus with ramps, slide, pole, ladder; swings (various types); house/quiet area; ramps and supports to build; tires, "loose parts"

- Sand and water toys
- Various wheel toys
- Large building blocks
- Dramatic-play props
- Balls and game materials
- Workbench and woodworking/clay materials

Infant-toddler: Have plenty of simple riding toys, eliminate woodworking, have apparatus correct size and simplicity and/or foam wedges

School-age: Increase game area, may eliminate number or kinds of wheel toys; substitute a stage, mural, boat, creek; increase "loose parts" for child-created forts

FIGURE 9-9 Basic Materials in an Early Childhood Program.

Room arrangement and choice of materials. Room arrangement and choice of materials play such an important role in children's educational experience. A developmentally appropriate room will invite children in and welcome them at their level, as seen in these four examples:

1. *Toddler Program.* Simplicity is a watchword in a toddler room. Notice how room arrangement changes with children's age ranges (Lowman & Ruhmann, 1998):
   - A large-motor zone is essential in a toddler room.
   - The dramatic-play zone is particularly conducive to pretend play.

- The messy zone is that area of the room where children are encouraged to "mess around" with a variety of fluid materials.

   Every toddler room needs a haven where children can unwind, kick back, chill out, sink in, and just relax. The quiet zone provides such a spot.

2. *Family Child Care.* Having a program in a home presents special challenges, both in the space and the mixed age ranges of children. Weinberger (2000) suggests that creating retreats, such as allowing children into a cabinet or behind the couch,

FIGURE 9-10 A preschool child care center needs clearly defined boundaries and obvious pathways so children can use the space independently.

allows moderate privacy while still insuring supervision.

3. *Preschool and Kindergarten.* Harms and others (2005) recommend these environmental areas for preschool and kindergarten:
   ■ space and furnishings
   ■ personal care routines
   ■ language-reasoning
   ■ activities (motor, cognitive, creative)
   ■ interaction (social, emotional)
   ■ program structure (schedules)
   ■ parents and staff (personal and professional needs)

4. *School-Age Programs.* After-School programs for children from kindergarten through third and sometimes fifth or sixth grade have special requirements, as those environments have an extensive range of physi-

cal size, interests, and developmental needs. The National School-Age Standards for Quality School-Age Care (NAA, 1998) recommends tables for projects and experiments, homework tables in a quiet corner, a place for snack and club meetings, art, blocks, house corner, and large group activity area.

The placement of the interest centers is important. Balance the number of noisy and quiet activities, both indoors and out. Some activities are noisier than others, so place the noisier centers together and cluster the quieter ones together. Quieter activities, such as puzzles, language games, and storytelling, take place in areas away from blocks, water play, or dramatic play, because the last three tend to kindle animated, active, and sometimes noisy behavior. Some programs create a kind of layered room—entry, quiet, messy, noisy.

Adult needs also should be met through proper organization. How can the teachers supervise all areas while ensuring cozy spots for children's privacy? Are the teachers deployed evenly throughout all the space? Is storage integrated so that equipment is located near the place where it will be used? Is the space arranged for cooperation and communication among the adults as well as the children? In other words, is this a workplace that is accepting, inviting, and challenging to all?

Figures 9-10 through 9-12 show sample indoor environments for the three major age groupings.

Playground Designs

Environments must be arranged so that there are enough play spaces for the number of children in the group. When the number of play opportunities in school settings—both indoors and out—is analyzed, areas and activities can be assigned a value (Prescott, Jones, & Kritschevsky, 1972). A simple area (swings, climbers) counts as one play space, a complex area (housekeeping/dramatic play) counts as four play spaces, and a super area (sand and water play combined) counts as eight play spaces. The value assigned an area generally coincides with the number of children who might be accommodated in that space. When the total for the space is figured, it is matched against the actual number of children in the group to see if there is a place for everyone to play.

Clearly defined boundaries and obvious pathways make it easy for children to live and work in the space. There should be enough space for larger groups to gather together as well as small groups. Figure 9-13 shows a playground suitable for 4- to 8-year-olds. See Chapter 11 for more information about outdoor play spaces.

In summary, the physical environment should be organized for children according to these criteria:

- *Availability.* Open, low shelving with visual cues for placement of toys, equipment aids in clean up and room set up.
- *Consistency in organization.* Neat, systematic, in logical order.
- *Compatibility.* Noisy activities are grouped away from quiet ones; art needs natural light when possible; water play near a bathroom or kitchen; messy projects done on washable floors.
- *Definition.* Clearly defined boundaries indicating available space and what is to take place; obvious pathways outlined in class and yard; ways to get in and out of an area without disrupting activity in progress; no dead ends or runways.
- *Spacing.* Interest areas with enough space to hold the children who will play there; one third to one half of the surface should remain uncovered; materials stored near space where they are used; storage and activity spaces have visual cues.
- *Communicability.* Tells children what to do instead of relying on adult to monitor activities; communicates to children what behavior is expected; arrangement suggests numbers of children, levels of activity.

The Temporal Environment

The second dimension of the environment to consider is the time and timing of a program. What happens, when it occurs, and how long it takes all affect both individual children and group functioning.

Daily Schedule: Time to Learn

The **daily schedule** defines the structure of each program. It creates the format for how children will experience the events of the day—in what order and for what length of time.

DAP

DAP Teachers organize the daily and weekly schedule to provide children with extended blocks of time in which to engage in sustained play, investigation, exploration, and interaction (with adults and peers).

FIGURE 9-11 A toddler environment has safety and accessibility in mind so children can be maximally involved with a minimum of distraction from others.

No two schedules are alike because each reflects the program it represents. The amount of time devoted to specific activities communicates clearly what value the school places on them. The amount of time given to certain aspects of the curriculum, the variety of events, and the level of flexibility tell children and adults what is important in this particular setting. Figure 9-14 and Chapter 10 expand on this issue of time.

In developing a schedule by which to function on a daily basis, teachers first decide what is important for children to learn, how that learning should take place, and how much time to allow in the daily program. If small group work and individual attention are program goals, enough time will have to be set aside to ensure their success. More time is needed to allow children several curriculum choices than if they had only one or two activities from which to select. Three-year-olds need more time for toileting activities than do 5-year-olds, who are considerably more self-sufficient.

The golden rule for child care is to treat children as we want them to treat us. The children in child care to-

FIGURE 9-12 A school-age center has learning centers to allow children to engage in peer connections and homework constructively.

day are the adults of tomorrow who will be taking care of us in our old age. Remembering that, it helps to think of how often children are asked to do and finish their tasks on others' schedules, to ask permission to do what they wish, or to participate in activities of someone else's choice. A children's program must be for children, on

their timetable as much as possible. Stonehouse (1990) offers five recommendations for scheduling:

1. Suitable choices are built in as much of the time as possible, avoiding the expectation that everyone should do the same thing at the same time. Flexibility makes for a more humane environment.

Fence

Toys

Sand

Slide

Grass

Boat

Trees and shrubs

Play
Structure

Tire
swing

Roller skate, scooter bike

Grassy
Knoll

Cement

Sand/water
table

Toys

Swings

Patio
Overhang

To classroom

Garden

Storage

Animals

Moveable
table,
woodworking
art, snack

Easels

Large Blocks

Fence

FIGURE 9-13 A playground/yard, suitable for ages four and older, will give children a sense of security and adventure, contact with nature, opportunities for social play, and freedom for active physical play. (Adapted from Themes, 1999.)

2. The need for a sensitive and flexible settling-in period is taken into account. This starts with respect for the client and the client's family and the recognition that different people cope with change and new experiences in different ways.

3. Meaningless and sometimes mindless activities that simply "fill up the day," "help pass the time," or that have no intrinsic value are avoided.

4. A healthy balance between an individual's need for autonomy, freedom, and independence on the one hand, and the need for rules that help us get along together on the other, is desired.

5. Staff balances the need for a routine, for the comfort and reassurance of the familiar, with the need for variety and novelty for change.

Daily Schedules

Half-Day Toddler Program

9:00–9:30	Greet children Inside activities • playdough and art/easel • home living • blocks and manipulatives • books
9:30	Door to outdoors opens
9:45–10:20	Outdoor play • large motor • social play
10:20	Music/movement outdoors
10:30	Snack/"Here We Are Together" song • washing hands • eating/pouring/cleanup
10:45–11:45	Outside
11:15	"Time to Put Our Toys Away" song • all encouraged to participate in cleanup
11:20	Closure (indoors) • parent–child together • story or flannel board

Full-Day Program for Preschoolers

7:00	Arrival, breakfast
7:30	Inside free play • arts/easels • table toys/games/blocks • dramatic-play center; house, grocery store, etc.
9:00	Cleanup
9:15	Group time: songs/fingerplays and small group choices
9:30	Choice time/small groups • discovery/math lab/science activity • cooking for morning or afternoon snack • language art/prereading choice
10:00	Snack (at outside tables/cloths on warm days) or snack center during free play
10:15	Outside free play • climbing, swinging; sand and water, wheel toys, group games
12:00	Handwash and lunch

12:45	Get ready: toileting, handwashing, toothbrushing, prepare beds
1:15	Bedtime story
1:30	Rest time
2:30	Outdoors for those awake
3:30	Cleanup outdoors and singing time
4:00	Snacktime
4:15	Learning centers; some outdoor/indoor choices, field trips, story teller
5:30	Cleanup and read books until going home

Half-Day Kindergarten Plan

8:15–8:30	Arrival Getting ready to start • checking in library books, lunch money, etc.
8:30	Newstelling • "anything you want to tell for news" • newsletter written weekly
9:00	Work assignment • write a story about your news or • make a page in your book (topic assigned) or • work in math lab
9:30–10:15	Choice of indoors (paints, blocks, computer, table toys) or second-grade tutors read books to children • when finished, play in loft or read books until recess
10:15	Snack
10:30	Recess
10:45	Language: chapter in novel read or other language activity
11:15	Dance or game or visitor
11:45	Ending: getting ready to leave • check out library books • gather art and other projects
12:00–1:30	For part of group each day Lunch, then: • field trips • writing lesson • math or science lab

FIGURE 9-14 Daily schedules reflect the children's needs and ages; the time and timing of the day show in the program's values and priorities.

The physical plant itself may dictate a portion of the daily schedule. If toilet facilities are not located adjacent to the classroom, then more time must be scheduled to travel to and from the bathrooms. If the building or space is shared with other groups, some portion of the program may be modified. For example, a program housed in church buildings may schedule field trips during the annual church rummage sale to free up the space for the church's use.

The daily schedule is important for everyone in the setting. Two important aspects of a schedule are routines and transitions.

Routines

The regular or habitual performance of an established procedure is a **routine.** Routines provide an important framework to a program. Each day, some events are repeated, providing continuity and a sense of order to the schedule. Routines are the pegs on which to hang the daily calendar. When should children eat? Sleep? Play? Be alone? Be together? These questions are answered by the placement of routines. The rest of the curriculum—art activities, field trips, woodworking—works around them. Routines in an early childhood environment setting include:

- self-care (eating, rest/sleeping, dressing, toileting)
- transitions between activities
- group times
- beginning and ending the day or session
- making choices
- task completion
- room clean up and yard restoration

Most routines are very personal and individual rituals in children's daily lives. Children bring to school a history firmly established around routines, one that is deeply embedded in their family and culture. Routines are reassuring to children, and they take pride in mastering them; they are also a highly emotional issue for some.

The self-care tasks—eating, sleeping, dressing, and toileting—can be difficult issues between adult and child, virtually from the moment of birth. Everyone can recall vivid memories associated with at least one routine. They seem to become battlegrounds on which children and adults often struggle. Many times this is where children choose to take their first stand on the road to independence.

The early childhood teacher must be able to deal with the issue of self-care routines in sensitive and understanding ways. Children adjust to routines when they are regularly scheduled in the daily program and when there are clear expectations.

Routines are an integral part of creating a good environment for children. All three environmental factors are influenced by routines:

1. *Physical.* Child-sized bathroom and eating facilities; storage of cots, blankets, and sleeping accessories; equipment for food storage and preparation.
2. *Temporal.* Amount of time in daily schedule for eating, resting, toileting, clean up.
3. *Interpersonal.* Attitudes toward body functions; willingness to plan for self-care tasks; interactions during activities and transitions; expectations of staff, parents, and children.

As teachers plan for children's basic needs, they are aware of the learning potential of ordinary, everyday routines. Figure 9-15 illustrates how self-care routines teach the young child important skills and habits. In the four curriculum chapters of this book (Chapters 11–14), there is specific planning for routines, transitions, and group times. It is these times that provide a sense of security for children. Beyond the planning for indoor and outdoor activities, careful teachers realize that helping children with the routines of daily living provides a solid underpinning so other learning can take place.

When the time sequence is clear to all, then everyone can go about the business of learning and teaching. Children are more secure in a place that has a consistent schedule; they can begin to anticipate the regularity of what comes next and count on it. In that way, they are then free to move, explore, and learn without hesitation. Children can freely involve themselves without fear of interruption. Adults, too, enjoy the predictability of a daily schedule. By knowing the sequence of events, they are then free to flex the timing when unforeseen circumstances arise.

It is the unforeseen that often does happen. Amidst the noise of children at work, the play is likely to be interrupted by a number of things that can affect the "best laid plans" of all teachers. For instance, Chad unexpectedly decides that he does not want Dad to go—just as the teacher was helping Shana onto the toilet for the first time. Or an argument breaks out in the block corner—at the moment a teacher was leaving with a group of children for the kitchen with several cookie sheets full of carefully constructed gingerbread people. Or a visitor comes in the door with a special group time activity—just as two children collide and bump heads.

Routines: Learning Opportunities in Self-Care

- Eating Teaches:

Health: Introduction to new and different foods, good nutritional habits

Social Skills: How to manage in a group eating situation, how to focus on eating and conversing; what is acceptable mealtime behavior and manners

Fine-Motor Skills: Pouring; handling spoons, forks; serving self, drinking, eating without spilling

Independence Skills: Finding and setting one's place, serving self, making choices, cleaning up at snack and lunch

Respect for Individual Differences: Likes and dislikes; choices of food; pace of eating

- Toothbrushing Teaches:

Health: How to keep teeth and tongue clean

Independence Skills: Self-awareness, perceptual-motor to use toothbrush in mouth.

- Resting/Sleeping Teaches:

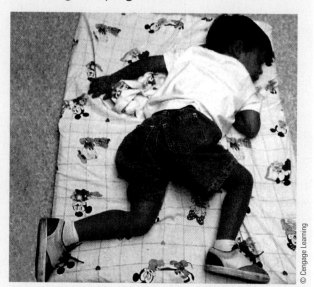

Health: Personal care skills; relaxation habits; internal balance; change of pace; alternating activity to allow body to rest

- Dressing Teaches:

Independence Skills: Self-awareness, how to get one's own area ready—blanket, cuddly, book

Respect for Individual Differences: Comparisons between clothes for girls and boys, younger and older, larger and smaller children, and children in and out of diapers or training pants

Self-esteem: Caring for one's own body; choosing one's own clothes

(continues)

FIGURE 9-15 Every routine can be used as a vehicle for learning within the environment.

Fine-Motor Skills: How to manage snaps, buttons, zippers; handling all garments; maneuvering in and out of a snowsuit or jacket; matching hands and feet with mittens and boots or shoes

- **Toileting/Handwashing Teaches:**

  Self-awareness: Body functions, learning the names and physical sensations that go with body functions

  Self-identity: Comparisons between girls and boys (sit versus stand)

  Self-esteem: Caring for one's own body without guilt, fear, shame

  Human sexuality: In a natural setting, promotes healthy attitudes toward the body and its functions, and that adults can be accepting, open, and reassuring about the body and its care

© Cengage Learning

▌ **FIGURE 9-15** *(continued)*

Transitions

Humans are known as a species for their adaptability. And yet we are resistant to change. For young children, too, change is difficult. Teachers and caregivers can make the necessary changes easier for children if they focus their attention on those times. Rather than trying to rush through quickly to get to the next event, provide enough **transition** time. Helping children anticipate, figure out, work through, and successfully manage the changes in their day guides them to maturity. Figure 9-16 offers some strategies that will make transition easier to handle and positive learning opportunities.

Good teachers prepare children for upcoming transitions, using a song or strumming of an instrument and the words, "Get ready to clean up soon." They are also prepared for children's perceptions of time, immediacy, and closure to collide with the schedule. Recall the unexpected chaos in the previous section on Routines. If Chad does not want his dad to go, perhaps getting Shana on the toilet will have to wait; or Dad can read him another story until Shana's "All done now!" has taken place. The gingerbread sheets can be held up momentarily so the quarrel can be resolved, or some of the "fighters" could be invited to be door-

openers and help to march the group to the kitchen. Perhaps another teacher could help the visitor begin with the rest of the class on the rug while you get ice for the bumped heads.

These examples all illustrate the common clash of "adult timetables and children's quest for engagement" (Ambery, 1997). Programs need to be designed to allow for both consistency and **flexibility.** Consistency brings security and closure, allowing for teacher authority and expertise to assert themselves; flexibility invites sensitivity to individuals and respectful agreements to be reached. As teachers work with schedules, they continually balance the needs of individuals with those of the group.

Developmentally Appropriate Schedules

Just as the arrangement of space should reflect the group of children within, so does the daily schedule allow for appropriate growth at the developmental level of the group. There are common factors to consider for all children in the early years, as well as some developmental distinctions at the various ages.

There are common elements in all schedules, whether they are designed for toddler groups or 5-year-olds,

Transition Times Made Easier

Questions for Planning

- Who is involved in the transition time (child, parents, teachers, other children, visitors, etc.)?
- What kind of activity has preceded the transition time and what will follow?
- What will the children be asked to do during transition?
- What will the teachers be doing during transition?
- How will the children be told or find out what to do *during* the transition?
- What do you know about child development and this particular child(ren) that can help with these questions?

Teaching Strategies

Arrival

- Greet each child with a smile, and welcome child and parent with what activities are available.
- Make name cards and/or an attendance sheet that child and parent can participate in as a starting point.
- Plan with parents, and alert the child, a simple and clear way for them to say goodbye and for the parents to leave (see Chapter 8 for details).

Cleanup Materials

- Give the children a five-minute "warning" to alert them to upcoming changes.
- Have a consistent and calm signal to start putting away toys.
- Use music as background and/or sing during cleanup.
- Consider having necklaces or cards of specific areas for children, or make teams.
- Construct the environment so that it is clear where things go and children can do the majority of it themselves.
- Occasionally thank the children publicly for cleaning up, noting individual efforts and specific chores done well.

Preparing Children to Attend

- Make a chart that shows the choices available.
- Sing a song or familiar fingerplay to get everyone's attention and participation.
- Ask the children to put on "elephant ears" (rabbit, etc.) or lock their lips and put the key in their pockets.

Ready to Rest/Nap Time

- Prepare the environment ahead of time to be restful—darkened room, soft blanket/cuddlies nearby, quiet music, teachers whispering and available to walk children to their places and stay with them.
- Read a story to the group in one place before they are to lie quietly, or split larger groups into small subgroups with a teacher reading to each.

Moving to Another Place/Building

- Gather the group and tell them exactly what will be happening.
- Ask for ideas of how to behave ("What will we need to remember? How can we stay safe and have fun together?") and reinforce with a few concrete rules.
- Have the children be a train, with adults as the engine and caboose, or a dragon with head and tail.
- Have the children choose a partner to stay with and hold hands.
- Ask preschoolers and early primary children to remember the "B" words ("beside or behind") in staying near adults.

Waiting for Others to Finish

- Prepare a part of the room for children to move to, such as a book corner or listening post, having an adult in that space with more than two children.
- Make an apron or hanging with several pockets filled with activity cards or small manipulatives for children to use alone.
- Plan a special table with folders or large envelopes with activities.
- Have a "waiting box" with special small items for these times only.

FIGURE 9-16 Transitions are a regular part of children's routines and should be learning times that are as well-planned as other parts of the day.

all-day or half-day programs. Sound child development principles provide the framework on which the daily schedule is structured. Individual programs then adapt these requirements to their own philosophy as they work out their own daily schedule. All schedules must:

- include time for routines (to eat, rest, wash, toilet) as well as time for transitions (what happens when there is a change from one activity to another) and **group times** (circle time to begin the day, song time for announcements, or story time as closure).
- alternate quiet and active play and work to help children pace themselves.
- provide opportunities for both inside and outside play.
- allow children to participate in structured activities as well as those of their own choosing.
- make it possible for children to work individually, in small groups, or in larger ones.
- gear the time to the age and developmental levels of the group.
- provide for flexibility so that children's interests can be maintained and emergencies met.
- have a beginning and an end (meet and greet to start, close and review to finish, anticipate tomorrow).
- involve the adults in planning and review (include a regular meeting time for more substantial discussion of children, long-range planning, and evaluation).
- include time for clean up and room restoration.
- incorporate the teachers' roles and assignments so that they will know their area of responsibility.
- be posted in an obvious place in the classroom for all to see.

All schedules have a great deal in common, but certain age-related differences can be seen. See Figure 9-14 as it illustrates several important differences in schedules for the various age groups:

- *More choices* are available to children as they grow.
  Example: Two-year-olds could be over stimulated by the selection of materials that is appropriate for school-aged children.
- *Transitions* can be handled differently in the various age groups.
  Example: Older children can move through some transitions as a group, such as changing from one activity area to another or going out with a specialist in pairs or even in a single file. This is difficult for younger children, who would push or wander away. For them, the door to the yard opens quietly, allowing children to go out slowly.

Example: A child care class of 3- and 4-year-olds is dismissed from song time to snack by the color of people's shirts, or the first letter of their names, rather than as one whole group.
- *The structure* of the day changes with age.
  Example: The balance of free play and teacher-directed activities shifts from relatively few directed activities for younger children to more for preschool. A kindergarten schedule provides more structure both in individual work projects and teacher-focused time. A first grade schedule has more whole-group teacher instruction times.
- *The content of group activities* changes with age.
  Example: A toddler circle time is simple, with a short finger play, flannel board or puppets story, and a goodbye song. Preschool group times include several songs, a dramatization of a favorite finger play, and a short story. By kindergarten, groups can last 15 to 20 minutes, with announcements and a weather board, children's "news telling," longer dramas, and even chapter stories.

Centers are very busy environments for children. So many things, so much learning, so much to do! Developmentally appropriate schedules will include a balance to the noise and busyness (Kielar, 1999):

- Reserve an area of your school or center for those who want to sit quietly.
- Make lunch time a time for peace and quiet.
- Wake up children from naps a little sooner than is needed to give them time to transition.
- Don't decorate every window with paintings.
- Change room displays often.

Finally, try not to over schedule or make too many small time segments. Just because young children have short attention spans for adult-centered activities and "teacher talk," they need longer periods of time to discover their interests and stay focused. We show respect for children when we put the temporal environment to work for them.

The Interpersonal Environment

A child responds to everything in school: the color of the room, the way the furniture is arranged, how much time there is to play, and how people treat one another. To the child, everything is a stimulus. The feeling in a room is as real as the blocks or the books. Thus, the interpersonal or social aspects of an early childhood setting are powerful components of the environment.

Defining the Tone

Children are the most important people in the setting; they should feel safe and comfortable. A warm, interpersonal environment invites children to participate and to learn. When children feel secure with one another and with the setting, they will be able to engage more fully in the total program.

Because it is understood that the single most important factor in determining the quality of a program is the teacher (see Chapter 5), it follows that teachers will be the key ingredient in determining the interpersonal "flavor" of a class. The first component of the National Academy's criteria for high quality early childhood programs is the interactions among the staff and children (see Chapter 10). The human component, the connections among the people in a center or home, makes all the difference to young children, for they are the barometers of interpersonal tension or openness and freedom. Families matter in the life of a program, especially in the early years. The way people feel about each other and how they express their feelings have an impact on children. Teachers have to see children within their family and social context, and to do so, they must invite families into the schooling process, as in these situations:

> You can't believe it; no matter how many times you tell Kai's grandfather that school starts at 9 a.m., he continues to bring him between 9:30 and 10 … until you find out that in China, old people are often late and people respect their habits. Now you may need to flex your schedule to allow for this late arrival and support this family custom.

> Elena's father speaks with such an accent you can hardly understand him. You would like to just avoid talking with him, but then you would connect only when there is a problem … and you discover that, in his Central American culture, "good parents" are those that ask for teacher's opinions. You need to overcome your own discomfort and converse more, asking him respectfully to repeat what he is saying a bit more slowly so you can understand.

> Every day Maryam brings her lunch, and it is so difficult to manage. These Iranian foods are not the same as the other children's, and the kindergartners tease each other about what they bring in their lunch boxes. You wonder if you should simply tell her auntie to send her with a sandwich … only you realize that every child wants familiar foods, and letting Maryam eat what her parents send should be coupled with teaching tolerance to the other children. Now you might use the lunch time situation to help everyone become curious and interested in new foods.

The interpersonal connection between families and teachers cannot be overstated. Good relationships create a positive mood and can bolster what happens to the child within the classroom and can provide a smooth transition between school and home. Learning is enhanced when parents and teachers come to communicate in supportive, nonthreatening ways.

Just how important is the interpersonal environment? Although most experts agree that the relationship between teacher and child is important, extensive research has only recently begun to document exactly how teacher–child interactions occur and how variations in such interactions might be related to behaviors or other results in children. "Researchers demonstrate a pattern of positive relationships between children's sensitive, involved interactions with teachers and children's enhanced development. The impacts of these types of interactions are likely to be seen in children's cognitive, socioemotional, and language development" (Kontos & Wilcox-Herzog, 1997). Such research confirms the findings of recent brain-based research and theories of Erikson, Bandura, and Vygotsky (see Chapter 4) and confirms our belief that how teachers interact with children is at the heart of early childhood education.

Young children develop best through close, affectionate relationships with people, to a great degree with adults. Although this is true for all young children, it is particularly important for children under 3 and those without facility in the dominant language spoken in the class. "The interpersonal aspect of environment is the central element affecting the quality of toddler play, more important than elaborateness of physical setting," declares Zeavin (1997). "Toddlers cannot talk about what is going on inside them. It is through their play that they externalize troubling feelings, work out emotional conflicts, and gain control of their world…Every issue is a relationship issue."

In a human and humane environment, people are respected, and the focus of the staff is on children's strengths and capabilities; limitations are seen as needs rather than liabilities. Children model their behavior on what they see others doing, so teachers engage children in interactions that include smiling, touching, listening, asking questions, and speaking on eye level. The language and tone of voice used are respectful and friendly, with children treated equally across lines of race, culture, language, ability, and gender. Staffs use positive guidance rather than punitive discipline techniques (see Chapter 7) and develop warm relationships with families (see Chapter 8). What teachers do—and how they do it—determines what learning takes place in the class and how each child feels about being there.

© Cengage Learning

The teacher's posture and facial expressions show respect for children and their learning pace and style.

A Quick Check

The attitudes and behaviors of teachers affect children's behaviors. Questions teachers can ask themselves as they evaluate the quality of the environment are:

- Is there a feeling of mutual respect between children and adults?
- Do teachers pick up on nonverbal and verbal expressions of both girls and boys? Of children with varying abilities? Of children of color?
- How do children treat one another?
- Do teachers model cooperative behavior with other adults and children? Do they show by example how to work through a disagreement or problem?
- Does the physical set up allow the teacher to focus on the children?
- Do housekeeping details keep teachers disconnected from children?
- Do teachers encourage children to use one another as resources?
- Do teachers take time to show children how to accomplish a task by themselves?
- Are girls complimented only on appearance and boys just for achievement? Are all children helped to appreciate similarities and differences?
- Do teachers use reasoning and follow-through?
- How and when do teachers interact with children?
- What are the teacher's posture and facial expression when involved in a problem situation?
- If I were a child, would I like to come to school here?

The answers to these questions provide teachers with a barometer of how well they are maintaining an atmosphere of positive social interaction. The most important thing to remember is that the way people feel about each other and how they express their feelings have an impact on children. Teachers must focus as much attention on the interpersonal part of the environment as they do on buying equipment or arranging the room. Chapter 10, on curriculum and play, and Chapter 14, on social and emotional skills, will emphasize the interpersonal aspects of the environment further.

TeachSource Video

Watch the TeachSource Video Case entitled "Oral and Literacy Related Activities in an Early Childhood Setting." After you study the video clip, view the artifacts, and read the teacher interviews and text, reflect upon the following questions:

1. How does preschool teacher Maranatha Falaise use the various centers in the environment to teach children the skills of anti-bias, self-help, and inclusive education described in the chapter?

2. Why are room/yard arrangement and intentional schedules important in ECE programs?

Insights *from the field*

Thinking about the Environment: Inspirations from the Reggio Approach *by Louise Cadwell, M.E., Ph.D.*

I have heard Carlina Rinaldi say, "The best environment for children is one in which you can find the highest possible quantity and quality of relationships." Reflecting on this idea while writing *Bringing Reggio Emilia Home* (1997), I wrote,

> *We interpret this to mean relationships between people— children, teachers, and parents; between people and materials and languages—words, numbers, pens, paper, clay, paint, wood; between people and ideas; between people and experience with the world in which they live.*

When I look back over the last 10 years of our work in St. Louis at The College School and the other two schools in the St. Louis–Reggio Collaborative, The St. Michael School and Clayton Schools' Family Center, I see continual evolution in our interpretation of Carlina's words in our work. For example, every year, every month, and in fact almost every day, we have changed our spaces in school, and they have consequently changed us. We have developed environments based on who we are as individuals, and "who we are" is inseparably connected to where we find ourselves in space and time and what is important to us. Otherwise, we could live anywhere and we could be anybody.

The school environments we have created are actually made up of parts of all of us and fragments of the world in which we live. For example:

- Children's words and ideas
- Teachers' and parents' words and ideas
- Fabric patches from 3-year-old Sam's baby blanket
- My mother's button collection
- Papers of every kind from every family, all sorted and displayed for use on an accessible shelf
- A miniature tea set from my colleague Jennifer's childhood

I love Loris Malaguzzi's image of thinking with children as being a little like a game of tossing a ball back and forth. A child or a group of children have an idea or are drawn to something. If we are listening, we notice. Then perhaps we want to play a game, so we "toss" them a twist, a provocation, a wide-open question about their idea. They respond with something marvelous that we did not anticipate, and the game continues. We don't know where the next idea will come from, but the game is fun and challenging for both child and adult, and we get better at playing it in many situations and scenarios.

The space can be like this as well. It is actually alive or dead depending on whether we are in a living, nourishing relationship with it or not. We make a change, the change alters the way we do things, and then new possibilities emerge. We are inspired to make another change, and so it goes. This is the way of an alive environment.

A basic, underlying principle that the educators in Reggio Emilia have incorporated into their schools, classrooms, piazzas, and dining rooms is: School needs to be comfortable, pleasant, orderly, inviting, and homelike. As children, teachers, and parents we have the right to spend our days in school surrounded by spaces that will enhance our lives, support our growth, and hold us in respectful ways. Little by little, we can examine the spaces that we have and shape them into more livable and amiable rooms.

As teachers in the St. Louis–Reggio Collaborative, we strive to look at our classrooms with critical and observant eyes as often as we can. We ask ourselves, "What needs care, repair, a new coat of paint, a sparkle of light, a splash of color? What areas of the room need to be enriched? What needs to be given away in order to make room for new life, energy, and new ideas? What aspects of ongoing experiences are unclear, left unexplained, or empty of meaning?"

One rule of thumb that guides us suggests that everything be out in the open so that we can see it and use it. On the high shelves, there are Lucite boxes of fabric, ribbons, twines, and raffias of all colors. On nearby shelves, you will find collections of clear folders of sparkly paper, patterned papers, handmade papers, white and cream colored paper curls. On the low shelves, transparent jars of shells, buttons, beads, wires, tiny pine cones, dried rose petals and sequins beckon. Children know where things are and can find them; so do the teachers and the parents. The abundance, diversity, order, and availability of materials seem to attract energy, ideas, connection, and possibility, all of which propel us in a positive direction.

Along with the evolution of our spaces, a deep respect for the complexity and order of our environments has developed. The children here used to dump blocks in piles. They used to empty little plastic boxes of sequins or mix things up to be a bit mischievous or to see what would happen. Some even used to draw on the walls or color on the tables on purpose. Now, this rarely happens. Why? The children know that the materials wait like treasures to be touched, explored, transformed, and composed. The children recognize the materials for their power to hold stories, inventions, and layered ideas. Now, the children teach each other to care and respect the many aspects of our complex environment.

We have established, slowly but surely, with children and parents, a culture of respect, appreciation, interaction, care, and love of the spaces in which we live. The way the materials are displayed and used parallels the way ideas flow and circulate, gathering energy, excitement, form, and shape whether among children or adults. This phenomenon generates an atmosphere that feels electric and alive. Many elements of our life in school overlap and intersect, setting in motion a complex network of relationships of all kinds.

Louise Cadwell, M.E., Ph.D., is coordinator of curriculum and professional development at The College School in St. Louis, Missouri, studio teacher/researcher with all three schools in the St. Louis–Reggio Collaborative: The College School, The St. Michael School, and Clayton Schools' Family Center. She returned to St. Louis after a one-year internship in the preschools of Reggio Emilia, Italy. She is the author of *Bringing Reggio Emilia Home: An Innovative Approach to Early Childhood Education* and *Bringing Learning to Life: The Reggio Approach to Early Childhood Education* and co-editor of *In the Spirit of the Studio: Learning from the Atelier of Reggio Emilia.*

SUMMARY

A good environment for young children is a combination of many factors. Teachers must consider the needs of the children, teachers, and families as well as the program goals and priorities.

The physical environment includes the buildings and yard, the equipment and materials, and the way the space is organized and used. The setting is organized to support the program's goals and must meet necessary health and safety standards.

The temporal environment is about the time and timing of the program. The daily schedule outlines the timetable of events. Time blocks are arranged around the daily routines of food, rest, and toileting. The schedule is balanced so that children alternate indoor and outdoor play, quiet and active play, and self-selected activities with teacher-directed learning.

It is the interpersonal relationships that set the tone in each environment. Good interactions between children and staff are characterized by warmth, personal respect, and responsiveness. The size of the group, the number of teachers per child, and the quality of relationships affect the interpersonal environment.

It is essential to have a clear idea of program goals before arranging the environment. The environment mirrors those goals in the way the room is arranged, teachers are deployed, and the time schedule is framed. In early childhood settings in which children's independence and self-reliance are valued, the environment is created to enhance the child's budding sense of autonomy. Anti-bias environments value individual differences in race, ethnicity, ability, and gender to help children develop positive identities. Inclusive environments help children and teachers alike see every child, regardless of ability, as competent and every place as adaptable for all. All environments reflect the goals through careful application of many factors.

Creating good environments for young children does not require great sums of money or newly designed buildings. In most settings, teachers can adapt general principles of environments to create challenging, safe, and effective group settings for children.

KEY TERMS

environment
physical environment
temporal environment
interpersonal environment
anti-bias
self-help
self-concept
self-esteem
least restrictive environment

mainstreaming
full inclusion
environmental adaptation
roughhousing
universal infection control
  precautions
learning centers
open-ended

interest areas
daily schedules
routines
transition
flexibility
group times

REVIEW QUESTIONS

1. Write a definition of environment in early education including the three aspects to consider when planning programs for young children.

2. What are the major principles in creating developmentally appropriate learning environments?

3. Who and what is involved in planning safe and healthy environments?

4. How do teacher create a high quality environment?

LEARNING ACTIVITIES

1. Hunch down on your knees and look at a classroom from the child's perspective. Describe what you see in terms of the principles of successful environments.

2. Examine a daily schedule from an early childhood center. What do you think are the program goals of the school? How can you tell? Compare this with a daily schedule of a family day care home. How are they alike? How are they different?

3. The following list names some common problems that can be remedied by changing the environment. List at least one solution for each problem.

   a. too many children crowding into one area

   b. overcrowded shelves

   c. grabbing or arguments over the same toy

   d. hoarding of materials

   e. lack of cooperation during clean up

   f. wheel toy collisions

   g. children crying when others' parents leave

4. Discuss three school health and safety policies that help keep illness and injury to a minimum. Interview a director or head teacher about their policies, how they explain the guidelines to parents, and how they handle problems that have arisen.

5. Visit an early childhood center. How are the interest areas defined? Name the centers of interest, and indicate which of them are for quiet play and which are for active play and work.

6. If possible, visit a program for children with special needs. If those children were to move to full-inclusion programs, what kinds of adaptations might be needed to provide an inclusive environment? For children with motor disabilities? With visual impairments?

7. Check a classroom for diversity. Using the following checklist (de Melendez & Ostertag, 1997), enter a checkmark whenever you find something in the classroom that complies with the element of diversity.

Checking the Classroom Environment for Diversity

ELEMENT OF DIVERSITY

	Culture	*Gender*	*Social class*	*[Dis]ability*	*Age*
Pictures/posters					
Books					
Housekeeping items					
Manipulatives					
Art materials					
Dramatic area					
Music					

Comments:

Things I need to change:

Things I need to add:

HELPFUL WEBSITES

American Alliance for Health, Physical Education, Recreation & Dance   http://www.aahperd.org

Canada Institute of Child Health   http://www.cich.ca

Centers for Disease Control and Prevention   http://www.cdc.gov

Children's Health   http://www.kidshealth.org

Consumer Product Safety Commission   http://www.cpsc.gov

National After School Association   http://naaweb.yourmembership.com

National Association of Child Development   http://www.nacd.org

National Institute on Out-of-School Time   http://www.niost.org

National Program for Playground Safety   http://www.uni.edu/playground

National Safety Council   http://www.nsc.org/index/

Teachers Resisting Unhealthy Children's Entertainment   http://www.truceteachers.org

Zero to Three   http://www.zerotothree.org

 Additional resources including the TeachSource Videos can be found on the premium website for this book. Go to **http://www.cengage.com/login** to register your access code.

REFERENCES

Alexander, N. P. (1995, September). Turning on the light: Thinking about lighting issues in child care. *Exchange.*

Ambery, M. E. (May, 1997). Time for Franklin. *Young Children, 52.*

Bredekamp, S., & Copple, C. (Eds.). (1997). *Developmentally appropriate practice in early childhood programs serving children from birth through age 8* (Rev). Washington, DC: National Association for the Education of Young Children.

Bredekamp, S., & Willer, B. (Eds.). (1996). *NAEYC accreditation: A decade of learning and the years ahead.* Washington, DC: National Association for the Education of Young Children.

Carter, M., & Curtis, D. (2003). *Designs for living and learning: Transforming early childhood environments.* St. Paul, MN: Redleaf Press.

Centers for Disease Control and Prevention. (1997). *The ABCs of safe and healthy child care.* Atlanta, GA: Author.

Community Products, LLC. (2008). *Children come first: Selecting equipment for early childhood education.* Rifton, NY.

Consumer Product Safety Commission. (2009). *Public playground safety checklist, CPSC Document #327.* Washington, DC: Author.

Cross, W. E. (1985). Black identity: Rediscovering the distinctions between personal identity and reference group orientations. In Spencer, Brookins, & Allen (Eds.), *Beginnings: The social and affective development of black children.* Hillsdale, NJ: Erlbaum.

de Melendez, R. W., & Ostertag, V. (1997). *Teaching young children in multicultural classrooms.* Clifton Park, NY: Thomson Delmar Learning.

Derman-Sparks, L., and Olson Edwards, J. (2010). *Anti-bias education for young children and ourselves.* Washington, DC: NAEYC.

Dodge, D. T., Colker, L. J., & Heroman, C. (2002). *The Creative Curriculum® for preschool* (4th Ed). Washington, DC: Teaching Strategies.

Edwards, C., Gandini, L., & Forman, G. (1993). *The hundred languages of children.* Norwood, NJ: Ablex Press.

Elgas, P. M., Prendeville, J., Moomaw, S., & Kretschmer, R. R. (2002). Early childhood classroom setup. *Child Care Information Exchange, 143,* 17–20.

Fowler, W. J. (1992). *What do we know about school size? What should we know?* Washington, DC: Office of Educational Research and Improvement.

Froschl, M., Rubin, E., & Sprung, B. (1984). *Including all of us: An early childhood curriculum about disabilities.* New York: Educational Equity Concepts.

Greenman, J. (2000). What is the setting? Places for childhood. In A. Gordon & K.W. Browne, *Beginnings and beyond* (5th Ed). Clifton Park, NY: Thomson Delmar Learning.

Greenman, J., & Prescott, H. E. (1994). *Caring spaces, learning places.* Redmond, WA: Exchange Press.

Gronlund, G. (2006). *Make early learning standards come alive.* Washington, DC: NAEYC.

Gutierrez, M. E. (1982). *Chicano parents' perceptions of their children's racial/cultural awareness.* Unpublished master's thesis, Pacific Oaks College, Pasadena, CA.

Harms, T., Clifford, R. M., & Cryer, D. (2005). *The early childhood (revised), family day care, infant/ toddler, and school age environmental rating scales.* New York: Teachers College Press.

Heroman, C., & Copple, C. (2006) Teaching in the kindergarten year. In D. F. Gullo (Ed.), *Teaching and learning in the kindergarten year.* Washington, DC: NAEYC, 59–72.

Honig, A. S. (1983). Sex role socialization in early childhood. *Young Children, 38*(6), 57–90.

Howes, C., Phillips, D., & Whitebook, M. (1992). Thresholds of quality: Implications for the social development of children in center-based care. *Child Development, 63*(4), 449–460.

Hyson, M. (2008) *Enthusiastic and engaged learners: Approaches to learning in the early childhood classroom.* NY: Teachers College Press.

Jensen, E. (1998). *Teaching with the brain in mind.* Alexandria, VA: Association for Supervision and Curriculum Development.

Jones, E. (1984). *Personal notes about pluralistic and developmental viewpoints.* Unpublished.

Kendall, F. (1996). *Diversity in the classroom* (2nd Ed). New York: Teachers College Press.

Lowman, L. H., & Ruhmann, L. H. (1998, May). Simply sensational spaces: A multi-"S" approach to toddler environments. *Young Children 53*(3), 11–17.

Marotz, L. (2009). *Health, safety, and nutrition for the young child* (7th Ed). Clifton Park, NY: Thomson Delmar Learning.

Midgley, C. (Ed.). (2002). *Goals, goal structures, and patterns of adaptive learning.* New Jersey: Erlbaum Publishers.

National After-School Association (NAA). (1998). National School-Age Care Alliance Standards for Quality School-Age Care. http://www.naaweb.org.

National Association for the Education of Young Children. (1995). *Keeping healthy: Parents, teachers, and children.* Washington, DC: Author.

National Association for the Education of Young Children. (2005). *Accreditation performance criteria.* Washington, DC: Author.

National Association for the Education of Young Children. (2005). *Position statement: Code of ethical conduct* (Appendix A is the entire text of the Code). Washington, DC: Author.

Needlman, R., & Needlman, G. (1995, November/ December). Ten most common health problems in school. *Scholastic Early Childhood Today.*

National Institute for Early Education Research. (December/January, 2006). Blueprint for new research: Classroom design and achievement. Volume 4, No. 1: 3.

New, R. (2000). The role of the environment in Reggio Emilia. In A. Gordon & K. W. Browne, *Beginnings and beyond* (5th Ed). Clifton Park, NY: Thomson Delmar Learning.

Olds, A. (1989). Psychological and physiological harmony in the child care center design. *Children's Environments Quarterly 6,* No. 4: 13.

Prescott, E., Jones, E., & Kritschevsky, S. (1972). *Group care as a child-rearing environment.* Washington, DC: National Association for the Education of Young Children.

Rivkin, M. S. (1995). *The great outdoors: Restoring children's right to play outdoors.* Washington, DC: NAEYC.

Rogers, C. (1994, Spring). *Mainstreaming: Special needs—Special experiences.* Unpublished paper.

Rushton, S. P. (2001, September). Applying brain research to create developmentally appropriate environments. *Young Children 56*(5), 76–82.

Standards for quality school-age care (1998). Charlestown, MA: National After School Association (NAA).

Stonehouse, A. (1990, November/December). The Golden Rule for child care. *Exchange.*

Teachers Resisting Unhealthy Children's Entertainment (TRUCE). (2001-2002). *Toys and toy trends to avoid.* West Somerville, MA: Author.

Waldorf School (author unknown). (1995, January). *What is a Waldorf kindergarten?* Los Altos, CA: Author.

Weinberger, N. (2000). Overcoming obstacles to create retreats in family child care. *Young Children 55*(5).

Whitebook, M. (1996). NAEYC accreditation as an indicator of quality: What research tells us. In S. Bredekamp and B. Willer (Eds.), *NAEYC* accreditation: A decade of learning and the years ahead. Washington, DC: National Association for the Education of Young Children.

Wurm, J. (2009). Working in the Reggio way. Redmond, WA: Redleaf Press.

Youcha, V., & Wood, K. (1997, March). Enhancing the environment for all children: Beginnings workshop. Exchange.

Zeavin, C. (1997, March). Toddlers at play: Environments at work. Young Children, 52(4), 72–77.

SECTION

4

What Is Being Taught?

© Cengage Learning

© Cengage Learning

Curriculum: Creating a Context for Learning and Play

PREVIEW QUESTIONS

- What is developmentally appropriate curriculum?
- What are the four basic factors in creating effective curriculum?
- Why is play a foundation for learning?
- What does curriculum planning involve?
- Why are written plans important and how are they developed?
- What are four effective curriculum models?

NAEYC CODE OF ETHICAL CONDUCT

These Core Values and sections from the NAEYC Code of Ethical Conduct are addressed in this chapter. As you read, note how the Core Values, Ideals, or Principles listed here apply to the topics in this chapter. (Reprinted with permission from the National Association for the Education of Young Children.)

I-1.2   To base program practices upon current knowledge in the field of child development and related disciplines and upon particular knowledge of each child.

1-1.3   To recognize and respect the uniqueness and potential of each child.

P-1.4   For every child we shall implement adaptations in teaching strategies, learning environments, and curricula, consult with the family, and seek recommendations from appropriate specialists to maximize the potential of the child to benefit from the program.

I-3B.1   To assist the program in providing the highest quality of service.

I.4.1   To provide the community with high quality (age and individually appropriate, and culturally and socially sensitive) education/care programs and services.

Developmentally Appropriate Curriculum

Ira, a 2-year-old, is more interested in the process of pouring milk (especially what happens after the cup is filled) than in eating and conversing at snack time. Kindergartners Bert and Leo become absorbed in watching a snail make its way across the sidewalk, ignoring for the moment the lesson on running relays. Each of these children are involved in the curriculum of an early childhood program.

What Is Curriculum?

In an early childhood setting, the curriculum consists of the art activity and language game; it is also the spontaneous investigation of liquids at snack time, the song that accompanies digging in the sand, and the teacher's explanation of why the hamster died. The **curriculum** is the planned and the unplanned and includes all of the activities as well as the subject matter, the interactions with people, and all of the experiences of the child's day.

Young children absorb everything going on about them. They do not discriminate between what is prepared and structured for them to learn and whatever else happens to them at school. It is *all* learning.

Creating a good curriculum for young children is not simply a matter of writing lessons plans. It is understanding the process of how children interact with people and materials to learn. It is the sum of a teacher's knowledge about children's needs, materials, and equipment and what happens when they meet.

Bredekamp and Rosegrant (1995) provide an all-inclusive definition:

> Curriculum is an organized framework that delineates the *content* that children are to learn, the *process* through which children achieve the identified curricular goals, what *teachers* do to help children achieve these goals, and the *context* in which teaching and learning occur.

- The *content* is what is being taught—the subject matter reflects the interests, needs, and experiences of the children, as well as what children should learn.
- The *process* is how and when learning takes place, the choice of activities and how they integrate with one another, and the time frame within the daily schedule or yearly calendar. The process enhances children's learning through a hands-on, exploratory approach with a variety of open-ended materials. Play is the medium for the process.
- The *teacher* is the person who creates the curriculum, planning and providing for activities and materials in relation to the age range of the group and observing and evaluating children's growth. Teachers are grounded in child development theory, have an understanding of how children learn, and are aware of the need to individualize to meet children's special needs.
- The *context* is why certain projects and activities are chosen, based on the program's philosophy and goals, the cultural backgrounds of the children, and their family and community values and influences.

Curriculum must also be relevant to the child. Head Start classes on Native American reservations will develop curricula that represent the history and traditions of the tribes the students represent. Relevant curriculum for a preschool in Seattle may include field trips to the Pike Street Market to see the recent salmon catch,

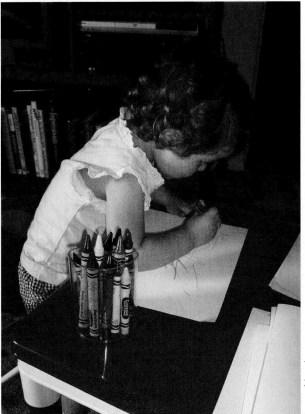

Children respond to curriculum materials that are inviting and accessible.

Courtesy of the author

whereas a transportation unit for inner city Boston children may include subway rides.

Developmentally Appropriate Curriculum

Appropriate early childhood curriculum is based on the theory, research, and experience of knowing how young children develop and learn. An infant curriculum meets the basic needs of young babies; a toddler curriculum considers the emerging independence and mobility of toddlers. Four-year-olds require different materials and teaching techniques, as do 5- or 8-year-olds. Each age level deserves special consideration when curriculum is being planned.

As noted in Chapter 2, developmentally appropriate programs, curricula, or practices are defined by NAEYC (Copple & Bredekamp, 2009) as having the following core considerations:

- What is known about child development and learning of a particular age group so that the curriculum has appropriate experiences and learning activities to help children achieve and to challenge them.
- What is known about each individual child, the individual rate of growth, and the unique learning style so that the curriculum will reflect their needs, interests, and preferences.
- What is known about the social and cultural context of each child so that the curriculum provides meaningful and relevant learning experiences that are respectful of the backgrounds of the children and families in the group.

A developmentally appropriate curriculum takes into account knowledge of child development theory, research, and practice. It includes various related disciplines, cultural values, parental desires and concerns, community context, individual children, teachers' knowledge and experience and is related to overall program goals.

The foundation for **developmentally appropriate practices** and curriculum content is historically rooted in John Dewey's vision that schools prepare students to think and reason in order to participate in a democratic society (see Chapter 1). Figure 10-1 lists recommendations jointly endorsed by the National Association for the Education of Young Children and the National Association of Early Childhood Specialists in State Departments of Education to ensure developmentally appropriate curriculum. It can be used as a checklist as you move through the next three chapters, which focus on curriculum.

Culturally Appropriate Curriculum

If meaningful learning is derived from a social and cultural context (as Vygotsky asserts), then a multicultural atmosphere must be created in which awareness and concern for true diversity (including ethnicity, gender, and abilities) permeate the program. This calls into question the familiar ways of doing things and requires new insights and ways of thinking about culture. Multicultural education is about "modifying the total school environment so that students from diverse ethnic and cultural groups will experience equal educational opportunities" (Banks, 1994).

Culturally appropriate curriculum is also developmentally appropriate curriculum. The challenge is to develop a curriculum that reflects the plurality of contemporary American society in general and the individual classroom, in particular, and present it in sensitive, relevant ways. Creating a truly multicultural classroom calls into question the familiar ways of doing things and provides new insights and ways of thinking about culture. Banks (2006) describes this approach as **transformative curriculum.**

The goal of transformative curriculum is to help teachers develop critical thinking skills so that they question some of the opinions and images of people and cultures that are represented in the Eurocentric curriculum that dominates American schools. A transformative curriculum helps a teacher view events and situations from different perspectives. This approach, for instance, would encourage teachers to look at Christopher Columbus from the perspective of a Native American Indian before creating a curriculum about Thanksgiving, the Pilgrim, or Native Americans. Transformation curriculum is a way to help develop more positive attitudes toward all racial, ethnic, and cultural groups.

The common practice in many early childhood programs of cooking ethnic foods or celebrating ethnic or

DAP

DAP There is no "recipe" for developmentally appropriate practice; rather, sound practice is related to individual children, families, and the community in which one teaches.

Recommendations for Effective Curriculum

NAEYC and the National Association of Early Childhood Specialists in State Departments of Education recommend implementing curriculum that is thoughtfully planned, challenging, engaging, developmentally appropriate, culturally and linguistically responsive, comprehensive, and likely to promote positive outcomes for all young children. The indicators of effectiveness for developing curriculum are:

- *Children are active and engaged.* Children of all ages and abilities can become interested and engaged, develop positive attitudes toward learning, and be supported in their feelings of security, emotional competence, and links to family and community.
- *Goals are clear and shared by all.* Curriculum goals are clearly defined, shared, and understood by program administrators, teachers, and families. The curriculum, activities, and teaching strategies are designed to help achieve the goals in a unified, coherent way.
- *Curriculum is evidence-based.* The curriculum is based on evidence that is developmentally, culturally, and linguistically relevant for each group of children and is organized around principles of child development and learning.
- *Valued content is learned through investigation, play, and focused, intentional teaching.* Children learn by exploring, thinking about, and inquiring about all sorts of things that are connected to later learning. Teaching strategies are tailored to children's ages, developmental capabilities, language and culture, and abilities or disabilities.
- *Curriculum builds on prior learning and experience.* The content and implementation builds on children's prior individual, age-related, and cultural learning, is inclusive of all children, and is supportive of the knowledge learned at home and in the community. The curriculum supports children whose home language is not English by building a base for later learning.
- *Curriculum is comprehensive.* All developmental domains are included in the curriculum, such as physical well-being and motor development, social and emotional development, language development, and cognition and general knowledge. Subject matter areas are included, such as science, mathematics, language, literacy, social studies, and the arts.
- *Professional standards validate the curriculum's subject-matter content.* Curriculum meets the standards of relevant professional organizations (for instance, The American Alliance for Health, Physical Education, Recreation and Dance, The National Council of Teachers of English, The National Science Teachers Association) and are reviewed so they fit together coherently.
- *Curriculum is likely to benefit children.* Research indicates that the curriculum, if implemented as intended, will likely have beneficial effects. These benefits include a wide range of outcomes.

FIGURE 10-1 NAEYC & NAECS/SDE (National Association of Early Childhood Specialists in State Departments of Education). 2003. *Early Childhood Curriculum, Assessment, and Program Evaluation: Building an Effective Accountable System in Programs for Children Birth through Age 8.* National Association for the Education of Young Children.

cultural holidays as isolated experience often trivializes or stereotypes groups of people. Folk tales, songs, food, and dress are symbols and expressions of a culture, not the culture itself. For children to gain any meaningful knowledge, the content must contribute to a fuller understanding of human diversity, not just a special occasion topic. Including diverse food, music, and clothing are important artifacts in the curriculum only when they expand a concept of diversity and serve as a link to discuss other aspects of a culture. For instance, songs and dances could lead to a discussion of what games children play in different cultures.

Transformative education and curriculum planning helps us reach out to understand another culture's point of view. Through that experience, curriculum can become more culturally sensitive and appropriate for all. The principles of the Anti-Bias environment that you learned about in Chapter 9 apply equally to developing curriculum that reflects today's diversity. Figure 10-2 highlights the differences between creating curriculum from a Eurocentric or dominant culture point of view and from a transformative curriculum approach.

Inclusive Curriculum

Inclusive curriculum reflects an awareness of and sensitivity to diversity in all areas of a child's life: cultural, social, language, religion, gender, and capabilities. The inclusion of children with any and all varieties of disabilities and those who reflect various cultural backgrounds has been built into the chapters of this text.

Cultural sensitivity is described in terms of developmentally appropriate practices in Chapter 3 and in defining the young child later on in that chapter. Chapter 7 includes cultural influences on children's behavior and various patterns of family behavior, and Vygotsky's theory that development and knowledge are culturally specific is discussed in Chapters 4 and 13.

Chapter 3 describes how a child with disabilities is included in the early childhood program. In Chapter 9, you will find suggestions for creating inclusive environments, with a checklist on pages 293–295; in Chapter 12, there are ideas for inclusion in physical activities. Throughout the text, there are references and examples of inclusion.

Characteristics of a Multicultural Classroom

Common Practices of Dominant Culture	For a Multicultural Approach
Focuses on isolated aspects of the histories and cultures of ethnic groups	Describes the history and cultures of ethnic groups holistically
Trivializes the histories and cultures of ethnic groups	Describes the cultures of ethnic groups as dynamic wholes
Presents events, issues, and concepts primarily from Anglocentric and mainstream perspectives	Presents events, issues, concepts from the perspectives of diverse racial and ethnic groups
Is Eurocentric—shows the development of the United States primarily as an extension of Europe into the Americas	Is multidimensional and geocultural—shows how many peoples and cultures came to the United States from many parts of the world, including Asia and Africa, and the important roles they played in the development of U.S. society
Content about ethnic groups is an appendage to regular curriculum	Content about ethnic groups is an integral part of regular curriculum
Ethnic minority cultures are described as deprived or dysfunctional	Ethnic minority cultures are described as different from mainstream Anglo culture but as rich and functional
Focuses on ethnic heroes, holidays, and factual information	Focuses on concepts, generalizations, and theories
Emphasizes the mastery of knowledge and cognitive outcomes	Emphasizes knowledge formation and decision making
Encourages acceptance of existing ethnic, class, and racial stratification	Focuses on social criticism and social change

FIGURE 10-2 A comparison of two different approaches to multicultural curriculum, one from a Eurocentric point of view, the other from a culturally sensitive perspective. (From James A. Banks, *Cultural Diversity and Education: Foundations, Curriculum, and Teaching* 5th ed., p. 238. Published by Allyn & Bacon, Boston, MA. Reprinted by permission of the author.)

Arce (2000) describes "authentic inclusion" as an approach that builds upon and integrates multicultural and anti-bias strategies for a sensitive and culturally affirming program. Multiculturalism becomes a part of a whole area of inclusiveness, so that all children feel and see how they are included.

The curriculum philosophy becomes a crucial element in an inclusive environment. How are differences in children accommodated in the curriculum? The curriculum should be flexible and provide a variety of learning activities and opportunities for a wide range of skills and abilities all at one time. It needs to be a curriculum in which children can participate at their developmental level, yet be challenged enough to help them learn.

The basic premise in this text is that children with disabilities, children from immigrant families, children from families whose first language is not English, girls and boys, and young children from all cultures need the same elements in a learning environment. Quality early childhood education programs operate under the same sound principles, no matter what characteristics define the children who attend these programs. Adaptations are made to fit the capacities of each individual child as needed.

Effective Curriculum: Four Basic Factors

Effective curriculum consists of any number of factors. Four important features are curriculum that is (1) integrated; (2) emergent; (3) based on multiples intelligences; and (4) bears in mind differences in learning styles. With these in mind, the curriculum becomes more flexible and suited to all children in the class.

Integrated Curriculum

Do you remember back in Chapter 3 the discussion about the whole child? The developmental concept that growth is related is a significant point made in Figure 3-1. That drawing shows how one area of development affects and is affected by the others. As young children learn, the social, emotional, cognitive, creative, and physical areas of development work together to help children find meaning in and mastery of their world.

It is useful to think of integrated curriculum in the same way. Integrated curriculum coordinates many subject areas, such as math, science, reading, writing, and social studies, and utilizes a holistic approach to learning. It is curriculum that depends upon the individual differences in children, blending hands-on learning with the acquisition of skills. An integrated curriculum makes it possible for teachers to include skill development activities in context, not in isolation, weaving across many subject areas throughout the day. For instance, tracing square shapes in the Writing Center and cutting out squares with scissors can expand the concept of a square. A book about shapes shows squares in many configurations to make a picture; and in the Block Center, fences and building are constructed in square shapes. In this way, each activity center supports the concept of squares in different ways. See Figure 10-3

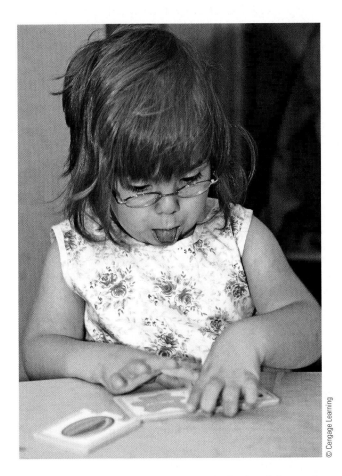

Developmentally appropriate materials fit the abilities of all children.

© Cengage Learning

Integrating Math Throughout the Curriculum

In music: Singing *Five Little Pumpkins*

In routines: Waiting for a turn because "too many" are brushing teeth already

In books: *Inch by Inch* by Lionni, *Millions of Cats* by Gag

In block play: Observing and using the fractions and wholes that make up a set of unit blocks

In physical development: Playing hopscotch

In cooking: Measuring and counting items in the recipe

In dramatic play: Noting there are only four hoses but five firefighters

In science: Counting the number of rainy/sunny/snowy days; recording temperatures (thermometers); time (clocks and calendars); and seasons (charts)

In art: Numbers: learning one-to-one correspondence by counting brushes, crayons, Magic Markers®, and colors

FIGURE 10-3 Young children learn best from an integrated approach to curriculum. Mathematical concepts are reflected throughout the classroom in a variety of activities.

for a good example of applying mathematical concepts in an integrated way.

Integrated curriculum means that subject matter is not taught as separate and unique topics, such as math, science, art, and language. Instead, they are all planned components of the total curriculum. The subject areas cut across the learning activity and reinforce concepts in meaningful ways as children engage in their work and play. If this sounds familiar, go back to Chapter 1 and read about John Dewey's philosophy of education. The concept has been used in curriculum development for many years. The guidelines for developmentally appropriate curriculum found in Figure 10-1 contain many of the characteristics of an integrated curriculum.

It is easy to see how an integrated curriculum works. Experiencing a concept in a variety of contexts is a natural rather than a contrived way for children to learn. Unit blocks, a staple in most early childhood programs, are a good example of how much learning potential is available in one activity. While playing with blocks, children learn about many concepts:

- *Science:* weight, gravity, balance, stability, height, inclines, ramps, interaction of forces
- *Mathematics:* classification, order, number, fractions, depth, width, height, length, fractions, size relationships, volume, area, measurement, shape, size, space, mapping
- *Social Studies:* symbolic representation, mapping, grids, patterns, people and their work
- *Art:* patterns, symmetry, balance, design, texture, creativity, drawing
- *Language:* making comparisons, recognition of shapes and sizes, labeling, giving directions, communicating ideas and needs, writing and drawing plans, using books as resources.

They also experience growth in:

- *Physical Development:* eye-hand coordination, clean up, hand manipulation, fine motor, visual perception
- *Social Development:* cooperation, sharing, clean up, conflict resolution, negotiation, respect for the work of others
- *Cognitive:* planning, naming, differentiation of sizes, shapes, inductive thinking, discovery.
(Adapted from Hirsch, 1974)

It is easy to see why one teacher has called block play "the perfect curriculum: It has everything children need to learn!"

An integrated curriculum provides numerous advantages (Gestwicki, 2007), Miller (1996), and Arce (2000) and:

- reflects the natural way children develop at their own rate and not in all areas of growth at the same time.
- allows for a wide range of abilities within a classroom age range of one year as well as within a mixed-age group.
- accommodates individualization as children meet a variety of materials and experiences at their own unique development levels.
- maximizes the effect of rates of learning, different styles of learning, and multiple intelligences.
- provides for learning to take place within the context of meaningful activity.
- requires large blocks of time so learning can be more in-depth.
- promotes self-motivation and extension of learning.

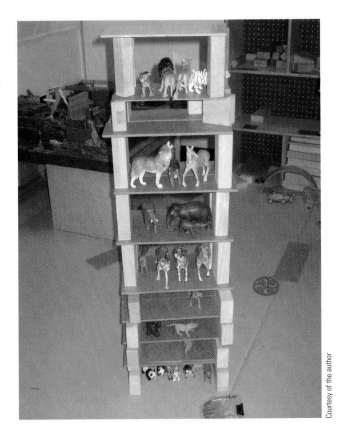

Courtesy of the author

What math and science concepts did the 4-year-olds use while creating this block building?

- blends hands-on learning with skill acquisition.
- lends itself to both a theme and project approach to curriculum planning.

Emergent Curriculum

Emergent curriculum is just what it says: curriculum that emerges—comes from or slowly evolves—out of the child's experiences and interests. The emphasis is on children's interests, their involvement in their learning, and their ability to make constructive choices. Teachers set up materials and equipment in the room and the yard, sometimes planning a few activities each day that will capture children's attention. For the most part, teachers then watch and evaluate what children do and support and extend what use children make of their experiences.

The curriculum begins with the children rather than with the teacher, who observes what children do, how they play, and what captures their interest and imagination. The point is to deepen and extend children's learning as they discover meaning and understanding in their play. The following example shows how emergent curriculum can be developed by following the children's lead.

Taking Cues from Children

A lively group time discussion one day in the 4-year-old classes involved a new bridge that was being built near the school. The teachers had noticed that the block area had sat unused during the week so they added books on bridges, paper, crayons, and scissors to the shelves near the blocks, and put up pictures of different kinds of bridges. These additions drew children to the block area where they built bridges, made paper bridges, and counted the number of different kinds of bridges that were in the books nearby. Further conversations between the children and the teachers led to a woodworking project to create wooden bridges. Songs and poems about bridges became a routine part of circle time. Outdoors, the sand pit became a waterway with bridges and was soon followed by projects with boats and other water transportation. The curriculum content in this example is apparent, but an end product is not the focus. It is an example of integrated curriculum as well as emergent curriculum because the process children go through in creating knowledge through the extension of bridge play fosters new insights and learning. The focus is always on the child, not on the activity.

This practice of taking cues from children—noting what they play with, what they avoid, what they change—is one of the components of emergent curriculum and stems from the belief that in order to be a meaningful learning experience, the curriculum should come out of the daily life in the classroom. Based on the principles of Erikson, Piaget, and Vygotsky, emergent curriculum assumes that children are active, curious, powerful learners, capable of taking the initiative and constructing their knowledge through experience. Children are encouraged to use whatever style of learning is most natural to them (Gardner, 1983), making use of the variety of materials in their own way. A materials-rich environment in which play is valued forms the foundation for the curriculum. For example,

- Anton, a first grader, noticed how dark the sky was as he and his classmates waited for the school bus to take him home. His teacher responded that the days were shorter in winter so there was less daylight. The children began to ask questions about how this happened. The next morning many of the Activity Centers had materials for exploring light/dark; charts for tracking the changes of light to dark; and a new outdoor thermometer. Over the next few months, children were immersed in the seasonal changes that occurred outside their windows.
- Four new babies were born to families with children in the 3-year-old class. The dramatic play area teemed

with dolls, blankets, bottles, and baby beds. As the children talked about their new siblings, the teachers posed questions about the care and feeding of a newborn and how different it is from what the 3-year-olds ate. Children were asked to bring in pictures of themselves as babies and created a collage that was hung on the wall near the dramatic play area. During music, the children moved like babies and outside the wagons became baby carriages. As long as their interest held, the curriculum was deepened and extended.

In each instance, the curriculum followed the children's curiosity and became more complex in order to maintain their interests and learning potential. The teacher's role was to be a co-creator with the children to ensure that learning goals and objectives were met.

Planning emergent curriculum requires good observation and listening skills and the ability to interpret children's play. Webbing, which is discussed later in the chapter, is a good way to clarify with children what they know and what ideas they have for further exploration. Webbing also helps integrate the activity to include all learning domains.

Collaboration and Mutual Learning

The emergent curriculum calls for collaboration on the part of the teachers with children and on the part of children with other children and with adults who offer **DAP** suggestions and ideas.

The accent is on mutual learning for both children and adults. For example, when the first grade class took a subway to the museum, this prompted a great many questions about subways and how they work. Because of the children's interest and the teacher's awareness of their developmental and educational needs, a project emerged and was developed over the next few weeks. It required the teachers to learn more about what the students wanted to know about subways, as well as to learn more about the topic so they could facilitate the children's learning and define the goals and objectives. The children helped plan the project. They asked questions, investigated, researched, explored, and, with the teacher's support and encouragement, formed small groups and completed assigned tasks. Books became an important resource, as did people. The teacher, knowing what the children needed and were ready to learn, guided the discussion to ensure that educational goals would be met.

For emergent curriculum to be successful, teachers have a responsibility to listen and observe carefully as children generate new ideas and then respond to what they hear and see that children have learned. Many observations methods were described in Chapter 6 and are appropriate ways to help teachers find ways and materials to advance and deepen what children learn. While emergent curriculum calls for collaboration and negotiation between children and teachers, it is the teacher who knows what is necessary for children's education and development and sets the goals for learning.

Sources for Curriculum Ideas

Children are only one of many sources of curriculum possibilities. A number of other sources feed into emergent curriculum, as noted by Jones (1994):

- Teachers' and parents' interests and skills
- Developmental tasks of the age group
- The physical and natural environment as well as people and things
- Curriculum resource books
- Family and cultural influences
- Serendipity or the unexpected
- Daily issues of living together, problem solving, conflict resolution, routines
- Values expressed by the school philosophy, the families, and the community

Emergent curriculum seems to capture the spontaneous nature of children's play and blend it with the necessary planning and organization. In the discussion of curricular models that follows in this chapter, you will see that emergent curriculum has many applications.

Multiple Intelligences

In Chapter 4, you read about Gardner's theory of multiple intelligences (MI). According to this theory, children are capable of at least eight distinct categories of intelligence. That is, they have many different ways of knowing or of being "smart." Refresh your memory by reviewing Chapter 4, page 126–128. The potential for developing the various intelligences is based on the child's experience, culture, and motivation. The following is a summary of this theory (adapted from Armstrong, 2000 and The New City School, 1994). The eight MI categories with examples are:

1. *Linguistic Intelligence.* Sensitivity to the sounds, structure, meanings, and functions of words and language.

DAP When children work collaboratively, they help each other succeed as well as to negotiate and solve problems together.

Linguistic intelligence.

Example: Children who enjoy word games, understand jokes, puns, and riddles, and enjoy the sounds and rhythms of language. They have a good vocabulary, spell easily, memorize readily, and are good storytellers.

Examples: Adults such as Maya Angelou, Amy Tan, Martin Luther King, Jr.

2. *Logical-Mathematical.* Sensitivity to and capacity to discern logical or numerical patterns; ability to handle long chains of reasoning.

Example: Children who notice and use numbers, patterns, and shapes and explore the relationships in them; they have a systematic approach to problem solving and organize their thoughts well. They think conceptually and are able to move easily from the concrete to the abstract. They like puzzles and computer games.

Logical-mathematical intelligence.

Spatial intelligence.

Examples: Adults such as Stephen Hawking, Madame Marie Curie, Bill Gates

3. *Spatial.* Capacity to perceive the visual-spatial world accurately and to perform transformations on one's initial perceptions.

Example: Children who like to draw, build, design, and create things. They enjoy patterns and geometry in math as well as maps and charts. They think in three-dimensional terms and enjoy color as well as design. They love videos and photos.

Examples: Adults such as I. M. Pei, Maria Martinez, Frank Lloyd Wright

4. *Bodily-Kinesthetic.* Ability to control one's body movements and to handle objects skillfully.

Example: Children who are agile, coordinated, have good body control and who take in information

Bodily-kinesthetic intelligence.

Musical intelligence.

Interpersonal intelligence.

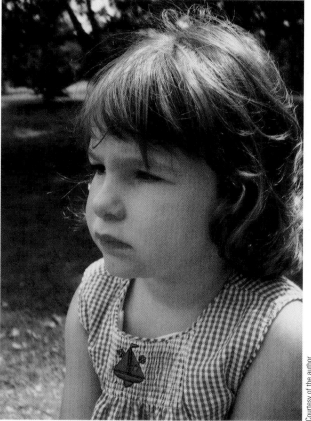

Intrapersonal intelligence.

through bodily sensations. They are hands-on learners with good motor skills. They like to touch things, run, and use body language.

Examples: Adults such as Jackie Joyner-Kersee, Marcel Marceau, Kristi Yamaguchi

5. *Musical.* Ability to produce and appreciate rhythm, pitch, and timbre; appreciation of the forms of musical expressiveness.

Example: Children who like to sing, dance, hum, play instruments, and move their bodies when music is playing. They remember melodies, are able to keep and imitate a beat, make up their own songs, and notice background and environmental sounds. They enjoy listening and differentiating patterns in sounds and are sensitive to melody and tone.

Examples: Adults such as Stevie Wonder, Carrie Underwood, and Yo-Yo Ma

6. *Interpersonal.* Capacity to discern and respond to the moods, temperaments, motivations, and desires of other people.

Example: Children who have a lot of friends, who like to talk, who prefer group problem solving, and can mediate conflicts; who like to hear someone else's point of view; who volunteer to help when others need it.

Naturalist intelligence.

Examples: Adults such as Marion Wright Edelman, Mother Teresa

7. *Intrapersonal.* Access to one's own feelings and the ability to discriminate among one's emotions; knowledge of one's own strengths and weaknesses.

Example: Children who pursue personal interests and set goals; who identify and label feelings; are insightful, sensitive, reflective, intuitive; who may daydream and are comfortable being alone. They know their own strengths and weaknesses.

Examples: Adults such as Sigmund Freud, the Buddha, Maria Montessori

8. *Naturalist.* Expertise in distinguishing among members of a species; recognizing the existence of other neighboring species; and charting out the relations, formally or informally, among several species.

Example: Children who enjoy all the features of the outdoor world. They recognize and classify plants, animals, rocks, clouds, and other natural formations; they garden and like to have animals at home and school to care for. They enjoy zoos, aquariums, and places where the natural world is on display and can be studied.

Examples: Adults such as John Muir, Jane Goodall, George Washington Carver

In a group of preschoolers, it is easy to notice the different strengths children have in the eight MI categories. Some children excel at puzzles and manipulative games while others are busy dictating stories, building a boatyard with blocks, or holding the guinea pig. There are children who cannot be still for very long and need to be actively and physically involved in play and work for much of the day. We all have the capacities for the eight categories of MI, but we are not equally proficient in all of them.

MI theory is based on Gardner's belief that general intelligence is too narrowly defined and suggests that intelligence has more to do with the capacity to solve problems and engage in a wide variety of culturally valued activities (Berk, 2009).

Through a wide variety of meaningful learning experiences, children's strengths (and primary intelligences) can be assessed, and curriculum can be developed that fosters new knowledge and thinking. Jmel is strong in spatial intelligence, and that can serve as a context for other learning in different intelligence categories. Her intrapersonal and linguistic intelligences can be encouraged through activities that include her telling or writing stories about something she drew and what it means to her. Bodily-kinesthetic and music abilities can emerge through dancing and moving the body through space in different ways. This allows Jmel to experience and reinforce her own strengths and increase her strengths in other areas as well.

The relationship of curriculum based on MI to integrated curriculum is fairly clear from the example of Jmel and from Figure 10-4. If children have different ways of knowing, they should experience a concept, lesson, or subject matter in a variety of ways. As teachers and caregivers expand their own thinking about children's abilities, they can vary what and how they teach and teach to many intelligences instead of just one, many developmental areas instead of just one. An integrated MI curriculum makes it possible to involve many intelligences in a wide range of activities and enable more children to succeed by drawing on their own capacities to learn. The lesson plan in Figure 10-4 is a good example of planning curriculum with an MI emphasis.

Gardner (Woolfolk, 2001) has written about the good uses of MI theory when it is applied to teaching. "Schools should cultivate those skills and capabilities that are valued in the community and the broader society," he says, and, "At the heart of the MI perspective—in theory and in practice—[is] taking human difference seriously." In both comments, Gardner affirms criteria for DAP.

Multiple Intelligences are also discussed in Chapter 4 and Chapter 12.

Learning Styles

Some people like going to lectures to learn about a new culture or country. Others prefer to watch a travelogue. Still others get the most out of traveling to that country and living among its people, eating the food, absorbing the atmosphere. Each of these is a legitimate method of learning and processing information, and each indicates

Sounds of the City

MI Context: Students from diverse communities need to develop an awareness and appreciation for the unique nature of the urban environment.

Learner Outcomes: Student will recognize the sounds of the city.

Procedure

1. Elicit from students the sounds that are unique to an urban area and list these sounds on chart paper. Show pictures of different urban settings to enhance the activity. Some sounds that might be included in this list are airplanes, traffic, emergency sirens, and street vendors.

2. Have students record city sounds on their empty playground if the school is located in an urban area. For homework, they could record city sounds from their neighborhoods or from the television.

3. Instruct the students to create a rhythm chant based on the sound word list created earlier, and use the taped examples to enhance the mood of the chants. Percussion instruments may be used to accompany portions of the chants. Students perform their musical numbers for the class.

Materials

Pictures of city scenes, tape recorders, cassette tapes, percussion instruments, chart paper, markers

Assessment/Reflection

Are the students able to identify urban sounds? How are the sounds the students collected from the various locations the same and different? What generalizations are the students able to make from this information?

MI Extensions

Interpersonal: Help the students develop an awareness of how these city sounds affect their relationships with others.

Intrapersonal: How do city sounds affect moods?

Bodily-Kinesthetic: Use movement to complement the compositions.

Linguistic: Read *Apt. 3* by Ezra Jack Keats. List all the sounds that are heard within the story and who made those sounds. Use the sound hints to determine who lives on each floor.

Logical-Mathematical: Collect data on the number of times specific sounds can be heard within a community. Interview people and graph their reactions to these sounds. Propose a hypothesis as to how the frequency of sounds might affect the lives of the people they interviewed.

Spatial: Create cityscape murals that capture the city and its sounds.

A practical guide created by the faculty of The New City School © 1994

FIGURE 10-4 Planning curriculum around multiple intelligences. (From *Celebrating multiple intelligences: Teaching for success* (paper) by the faculty of the New City School. Copyright © New City School. Reprinted by permission.)

the preferred style of that particular person. In Chapter 3, the discussion was about **learning styles** related to differences in children's behavior. In this chapter, we will focus on how basic learning styles affect curriculum planning.

Sensory Styles Three basic sensory styles were mentioned in Chapter 3 and they follow here with examples (Schirrmacher, 2002). These are the preferred mode of each child but not the only method by which the child can integrate knowledge.

1. *The Visual Learner.* These are children who prefer pictures to words; photos, charts, and graphs provide the necessary clues; they like to represent their learning by reading, writing, and drawing; the finished product is important.

2. *The Auditory Learner.* These are children who listen to others to learn and speak and discuss what they are learning. They are good at following directions in the appropriate sequence from one task to another.

3. *The Tactile-Kinesthetic Learner.* These children are active, full-body learners; they need hands-on activity and learn by doing, not listening or sitting still.

These modalities are the favored ways children learn through the use of their five senses. It seems clear that an integrated, emergent curriculum would be easily adaptable to all three learning modes. In fact, most early childhood experiences are heavily weighted toward the development of the five senses that provide many opportunities for children to learn through their preferred style.

Field Dependent/Independent Learning Style One of the most useful aspects of this model of learning styles (Witkin, Moore, Goodenough, & Cox, 1977) is that it seems to be found in all cultures throughout the world.

The two facets of this model, with examples (McNeely, 1997; Ramirez & Casteñada, 1974), are:

Field Dependent Learning Style (FD). These children are able to grasp broad distinctions among concepts, and they see relationships through a social context, working with others to achieve a common goal. They learn best through material that is related to their own experiences. FD learners are more person-oriented in their play and engage in social interactions sometimes for the sake of the interaction itself. They often use social conflict to make a social contact. They learn concepts through watching others, and their learning is reinforced by rewards such as verbal praise, helping the teacher, and showing the task to others. They de-

pend on authority, seek guidance and demonstration from teachers, and need to have the performance objectives of the curriculum carefully explained.

Field Independent Learning Style (FI). These children look at things analytically, imposing their own structure to the task, and learn things for their own sake. They prefer self-defined goals and reinforcements and are motivated through competition, their own values, and are more assertive than FD learners. FI learners prefer to work independently, and rarely seek physical contact with teachers; they are more idea-oriented than people-oriented. They like to try out new tasks without help. These children like the details of concepts because they find meaning in the various parts. They focus on the materials and their uses; social interactions are not as important to them.

Figure 10-5 suggests some curriculum approaches that work well for these two learning styles.

A Teacher Provides Opportunities for:

Field Dependent Children to:	Field Independent Children to:
• Engage in global thinking	• Engage in analytical thinking
• Follow a given structure	• Generate own structure
• Be extremely directed	• Be internally directed
• Attend to social information	• Be inattentive to social information
• Resolve conflict	• Think things through philosophically
• Be social	• Be distant in social relations
• Work with others	• Work alone
• Have friends	• Have acquaintances
• Work with a provided hypothesis	• Generate own hypothesis
• Work with facts	• Work with concepts
• Use others' decisions	• Use own decisions
• Be sensitive to others	• Be insensitive to others
• Use stress for learning	• Ignore external stress for learning

FIGURE 10-5 A teacher must make use of learning styles for Field Dependence/ Independence. (Adapted from Sharon L. McNeely, Ph.D. [1997], *Observing students and teachers through objective strategies.* Published by Allyn & Bacon, Boston, MA.)

Play-Based Curriculum: The Foundation for Learning

In Chapter 4, you learned about the value and process of children's play. You may want to review that section for a clear understanding of why play-based curriculum enhances children's potential for learning, and is, in fact, the foundation for learning.

The vast knowledge of human development and behavior comes from researchers who spent countless hours observing and recording children playing. As noted by many, from Froebel to Vygotsky to Gardner, children need meaningful materials and activities in order to learn. They need to be physically as well as mentally and emotionally involved in what and how they learn, and they need to play. Through the use of activity centers, a variety of play opportunities are available throughout the school day (see Figure 10-6).

The Teacher's Role in Play

Classroom teachers learn about children by listening to and observing spontaneous play activity and planning curriculum that encourages play. They discover each child's individual personality, learning style, and preferred mode of play.

Interest and Understanding

Genuine interest is one way teachers show their approval of the play process. Creating a safe environment in which children feel physically and emotionally secure is another. To establish play as an important part of the curriculum, teachers must *understand, appreciate, and value* play experiences for young children; *focus* on the process of learning rather than on the process of teaching; and *reflect* on their observations in order to know what activities, concepts, or learning should be encouraged or extended.

Frost (1996) reminds us of the excellent advice from one of the most able contributors to the field of human development:

> Erikson advises that play has a very personal meaning for each individual. Perhaps the best thing that we as adults can do to discover this meaning is to go out and play; to reflect upon our own childhood play; to once again look at play through the eyes of the child.

Supporting Play

One of the most difficult tasks teachers face is knowing when to join children at play and when to remain outside the activity. They must ask themselves whether their presence will support what is happening or whether it will inhibit the play. Sometimes teachers are tempted to correct children's misconceptions during play:

> Abby and Salina, deeply involved in their grocery store drama, are making change incorrectly. A teacher must judge whether to explain the difference between nickels and quarters at that time or to create an opportunity at a later date. Teachers must be aware of what happens if they interrupt the flow of play and how they influence the direction it takes. If Abby and Salina begin to talk about their coins, showing an interest in learning how to compute their change, the teacher can move into the discussion without seeming to interfere.

Many adults enjoy playing with the children in their class; others feel more comfortable as active observers. But every teaching situation will demand the teacher's involvement at some level. The hesitant child may need help entering a play situation; children may become too embroiled in an argument to settle it alone; play may become inappropriate, exploitative, or dominated by a particular child.

Vygotsky gives us other reasons to be involved with children as they play, particularly in relation to the interpersonal nature of teaching (see Chapter 4). The belief that learning is interpersonal and collaborative is exemplified by the teachers of Reggio Emilia (see Chapters 2 and 5), who guide and support children's learning by engaging in play and knowing what strategy will best help an individual child reach the next level of skill (*zone of proximal development*). The Reggio Emilia approach to curriculum (discussed at the end of this chapter under "Curriculum Models") finds an appropriate and appealing blend of Vygotsky's concern for individual exploration and assisted discovery.

The teacher's role in facilitating play is about balance: how to allow children the space and time to create their own play while still taking advantage of the teachable moments in which further learning is enhanced. Use the following guidelines to maintain a good balance:

- Guide the play, but do not direct or dominate the situation or overwhelm children by participation.
- Capitalize on the children's thoughts and ideas; do not enforce a point of view on them.
- Model play when necessary; show children how a specific character might act, how to ask for a turn, how to hold a hammer.

Play-Based Curriculum: Enhancing Children's Learning

Cognitive/Language

Distinguishes between reality and fantasy
Encourages creative thought and curiosity
Allows for problem solving
Encourages thinking, planning
Develops memory, perceptual skills, and concept formation
Learns to try on other roles
Acquires knowledge and integrates learning
Learns communication skills
Develops listening and oral language skills

Creative

Fosters use of imagination and make-believe
Encourages flexible thinking and problem solving
Provides opportunity to act upon original ideas
Supports taking risks
Learns to use senses to explore
Re-creates images in buildings and art media
Sharpens observational skills
Provides variety of experiences
Learns to express self in art, music, and dance
Develops abilities to create images and use symbols
Acquires other perspectives

Social

Tries on other personalities, roles
Learns cooperation and taking turns
Learns to lead, follow
Builds a repertoire of social language
Learns to verbalize needs
Reflects own culture, heritage, values
Learns society's rules and group responsibility
Shows respect for others' property, rights
Teaches an awareness of others
Learns how to join a group
Builds awareness of self as member of a group
Gives sense of identification
Promotes self-image, self-esteem
Experiences joy, fun

Physical

Releases energy
Builds fine- and gross-motor skills
Gains control over body

Provides challenges
Requires active use of body
Allows for repetition and practice
Refines eye–hand coordination
Develops self-awareness
Encourages health and fitness

© Cengage Learning

Emotional

Develops self-confidence and self-esteem
Learns to take a different viewpoint
Resolves inner fears, conflicts
Builds trust in self and others
Reveals child's personality
Encourages autonomy
Learns to take risks
Acts out anger, hostility, frustration, joy
Gains self-control
Becomes competent in several areas
Takes initiative

▌ **FIGURE 10-6** Play is the cornerstone of learning.

- Ask questions; clarify with the children what is happening.
- Help children start, end, and begin again.
- Give verbal cues to enable children to follow through on an idea.
- Focus children's attention on one another; encourage them to interact with each other.
- Interpret children's behavior aloud when necessary.
- Help children verbalize their feelings as they work through conflicts.
- Expand the play potential by making statements and asking questions that lead to discovery and exploration.

TeachSource Video

Watch the TeachSource Video Case entitled, "Curriculum Planning: Implementing Developmentally Appropriate Practice in an Early Childhood Setting." After you study the video clip, view the artifacts, and read the teacher interviews and text, reflect upon the following questions:

1. "Play is the child's work," according to one teacher in this case. How is that ideal implemented throughout the program?

2. How did the teaching staff at this preschool center demonstrate that they value meeting the needs of individual children?

Setting the Stage for Play

Teachers set the stage for learning through play by developing curriculum that includes many forms of play, some of which is spontaneous, some of which is guided and/or directed by the teacher. The environment (physical, temporal, and interpersonal) is a key element in reinforcing a play-based curriculum.

Structuring the Environment

To structure the environment for play, teachers include uninterrupted time blocks in the daily schedule (at least 45 minutes to an hour) for free play time. This allows children to explore many avenues of the curriculum free from time constraints. It is frustrating to young children to have their play cut off just as they are getting deeply involved.

Established routines in the schedule add to the framework of a day planned for play. The raw materials of play—toys, games, and equipment—are changed pe-

riodically so that new ones may be introduced for further challenge:

- In choosing materials, teachers select dress-up clothes and accessories that appeal to all children's needs, interests, and emotions.
- Props are required for a variety of roles: men, women, babies, doctors, nurses, grocers, mail carriers, teachers, and firefighters.
- Hats for many occupations help a child establish the role of an airline pilot, tractor driver, construction worker, police officer, or baseball player.
- Large purses are used for carrying mail and babies' diapers; they also double as a briefcase or luggage.
- Simple jackets or capes transform a child for many roles.

Props that represent aspects of the child's daily life are important; children need many opportunities to act out their life stories.

For younger children, teachers make sure there are duplicates of popular materials. Group play is more likely to occur with three telephones, four carriages, eight hats, and five wagons. Social interaction is enhanced when three space shuttle drivers can be at the controls.

Materials that are open-ended further enlarge play. These are materials that will expand the children's learning opportunities because they can be used in more than one way. Blocks, a staple of the early childhood curriculum, are a case in point. Children explore and manipulate blocks in many ways. The youngest children carry and stack blocks and also enjoy wheeling them around in wagons or trucks. They also enjoy the repetitious action of making small columns of blocks. Older preschoolers build multistoried structures as part of their dramatic play—offices, firehouses, and garages.

Classroom Activity Centers

The **activity centers** in most early childhood programs consist of:

Indoors	*Outdoors*
Creative arts	Climbing equipment
Blocks	Swings
Table toys	Sand/mud/water
Manipulatives	Wheel toys
Science/discovery	Woodworking
Dramatic play	Hollow blocks
Language arts/books	Music
Math	Nature/science
Music	Organized games

All of these centers offer activities and materials for children to choose from during free play time—the greatest portion of their school day. (See typical daily schedules in Chapter 2.) Paints are in the easel trays, puzzles on the tables, dress-up clothes and props in the housekeeping/dramatic play center, blocks and accessories in the block corner, and books and tapes in the language area. Teachers plan the resources and materials and place them so that children readily see the alternatives available to them. Some of these activities might be teacher-directed: cooking snacks in the housekeeping area. For the most part, however, these activities will be self-initiating and child-directed. At all times, the emphasis will be on providing a child-centered curriculum.

Whatever the activity center, it needs attention and planning. Wherever children are present, learning and playing will take place. Because each play space will make a contribution to children's experiences, teachers should develop appropriate curriculum for that learning area.

Go back and review what Chapter 9 describes as the important principles in creating environments that reflect curriculum goals, and see Chapter 2 for daily schedules.

Planning for Skills Acquisition

Just as focusing on the activity or learning centers can develop curriculum, so, too, can an early childhood program be planned around the skill levels of the children in the class. The next three chapters provide a more in-depth identification of the types of skills that children need to learn.

The first decision teachers must make concerns what particular skill they wish to help children develop. The skill can be in the area of physical, cognitive, language, creative, social, or emotional development.

The nature of the individual class and the program philosophy will help teachers establish priorities for these skills. Teachers then select the activities and materials that will enhance the development of any one or more of those particular skills. Figure 10-7 shows how the cognitive skill of classification can be implemented in the classroom, making it the focus of the entire curriculum.

The next three chapters provide a more in-depth identification of the types of skills that children need to learn.

DAP

Planning Curriculum

The aim of the curriculum is to help children acquire the skills and behaviors that will promote their optimal growth physically, socially, emotionally, and intellectually. Teachers consider a number of factors in developing a curriculum to provide maximum learning opportunities. Among these are the *educational philosophy and goals* of the program. A family day-care provider plans activities for a few children in an intimate setting while the kindergarten teacher arranges small working groups so that the large group will not seem overwhelming. The activities should support the goals of the program and result in the accomplishment of those goals.

Factors That Enhance Maximum Learning

1. Probably the single most important determinant the teacher must consider is *the children themselves.* Their ages, developmental levels, individuality, and learning styles are barometers of what will be a successful and stimulating curriculum.
2. The *number* of children in the class will affect the teacher's planning as will the number of teachers, aides, and volunteers who help out in the classroom.
3. The *ethnic and cultural backgrounds* of the children must be taken into consideration. Teachers need to plan curriculum experiences that draw on children's

---

DAP The power of play in the young child's life drives a play-based curriculum that includes many opportunities for social, physical, and intellectual development.

Developing Classification Skills through Integrated Curriculum

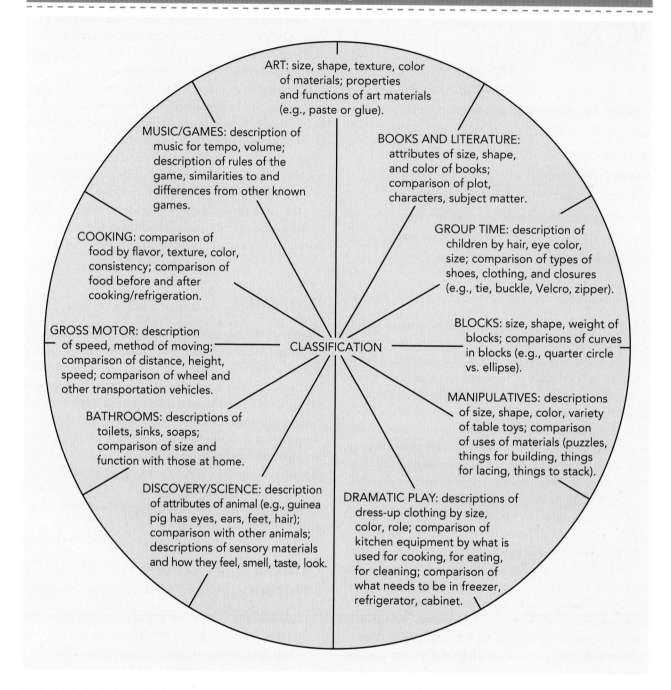

FIGURE 10-7 Curriculum can be developed with a focus on a particular skill. Classification skills can be enhanced throughout the curriculum and in activity centers. **Note:** This is a graphic way to demonstrate an integrated curriculum, not an example of a format for how to write curriculum plans.

knowledge and experience but that also extend their thinking.

4. Effective curriculum planning stems from *a knowledge of young children*. Teachers ask themselves what concepts children should learn and how they will teach those concepts; what does the child already know, and how can the teacher build on that? What is the most effective way to teach a particular concept to this group of children? In many ways, teachers start at the end: They look at what they want the child to accom-

plish or to learn as a result of this experience and then plan the curriculum to lead toward those results.

5. Planning for a *broad range of developmental skills and interests* is a key factor in creating a classroom curriculum. Because the abilities of children even of the same age vary, activities must be open-ended and flexible enough to be used by a number of children with varieties of skills. Remember, too, that some children may not be interested in formal or organized art projects or science experiences. These children may learn more easily through self-selected play: by wearing a space helmet and fantasizing a trip to the moon, by building with blocks for long periods, or by running and climbing out of doors.

6. The developmental word pictures of children from birth through age 8 found in Chapter 3 can be useful in determining *what kinds of activities appeal* to young children. All activities—especially those that are planned and formal—should be conducted in an *atmosphere of play* that offers the children options in choosing what they need to learn.

A **prerequisite** for planning is the *availability of people and material resources* and ways to use them. The strengths of the teaching staff, adequate supplies and equipment and enough adults to supervise the activities are taken into consideration.

7. The *amount of time* available in the daily schedule and *the amount of space* in the room or yard affect a teacher's planning. Finger painting requires time for children to get involved, proximity to water for clean up, and an area in which to store wet paintings. All of these elements must be considered in the planning process.

Culturally Responsive Teaching

Positive attitudes toward self and others emerge when children know they are valued for their individuality and appreciated as members of a family and a culture. The school environment can reflect this in a number of ways. Figure 10-8 lists ways in which an early childhood program can use culturally diverse materials on a daily basis to foster the relationship between home culture and school.

Banks (2006) identifies five important characteristics of the effective teacher in a multicultural society. They are teachers who:

1. Will seek pedagogical knowledge of the characteristics of students from diverse ethnic, racial, cultural, and social class groups; of prejudice and prejudice reduction theory and research; and of teaching strategies and techniques.

2. Have reflected upon and clarified an understanding of their own cultural heritage and experience and have knowledge of how it relates to and interacts with the experiences of other ethnic and cultural groups.

3. Have reflected upon their own attitude toward different racial, ethnic, cultural, and social-class groups.

4. Have the skills to make effective instructional decisions and reduce prejudice and intergroup conflict.

5. Will devise a range of teaching strategies and activities that will facilitate the achievement of students from diverse racial, ethnic, cultural, and social class groups.

Children with special needs are often able to use most of the curriculum materials typically found in early childhood classrooms. They, too, need their life mirrored in the school setting with dolls, books, and play accessories that signify acceptance and belonging.

Throughout this text, especially in Chapters 2, 5, and the upcoming chapters, cultural sensitivity on the part of teachers and curriculum goal is emphasized. Woolfolk (2001) suggests the following guidelines for culturally relevant teaching. They provide an accurate summary of many of the points found elsewhere in this book:

- Experiment with different group arrangements to encourage social harmony and cooperation. Provide a range of ways for children to learn material to accommodate a wide range of learning styles.

Use direct teaching methods for important information that everyone should know, such as telling children how to take care of materials, acceptable ways to disagree, and how to get the teacher's attention.

Learn the meaning of different behaviors of your students; find out how they feel when they are praised or corrected; talk with family members to discover the meaning of gestures, expressions, or other responses that are unfamiliar to you.

Emphasize meaning in teaching; that is, make sure students understand the concept by using examples from everyday experiences.

Get to know the customs, traditions, and values of your students; analyze different traditions for common themes; attend community fairs and festivals.

Help students detect racist and sexist messages, analyze the curriculum for biases, and help children discuss ways that their communication with each other may be biased. Discuss expressions of prejudice.

A sound curriculum is the **linchpin** of a quality program for children. Curriculum planning and develop-

Play Materials to Enhance Cultural Diversity and Inclusivity

Curriculum Area	Materials and Equipment
Music	Rainstick (Chile), marimba (Zulu), balaphon (West Africa), ankle bells (Native American), maracas (Latin America), Den-den (Japan), Shakeree (Nigeria), drums (many cultures), ocarina (Peru), songs of many cultures
Literature	Books on family life of many cultures, stories of children from far and near, legends and folktales from many countries, stories with common childhood themes from many lands, favorite books in several languages, wordless books, sign language, Braille books
Blocks and accessories	Variety of accessories depicting many ethnic people, aging people, community workers of both sexes in nonstereotyped roles and with various disabilities; Russian nesting dolls, Pueblo storytellers[1], animals from around the world
Art	Paints, crayons, markers, and construction paper in variety of skin-tone colors, child-size mirrors
Dramatic play	Anatomically correct dolls representing many ethnic groups; doll accessories, including glasses, wheelchairs, crutches, walkers, leg braces, and hearing aids; doll clothes, including cultural costumes and dress-up clothing from many cultures; cooking utensils, such as a wok, tortilla press, cutlery, chopsticks
Games	Language lotto, dreidel game, lotto of faces of people from around the world, black-history playing cards, world globe
Outdoors	Elevated sand and water tables and ramps for wheelchair access, lowered basketball hoops, sensory-rich materials
Classrooms	Carp banners (Japan), paper cuttings from Mexico and China, photographs and magazine pictures of daily life from many cultures, artwork by artists from a variety of ethnic backgrounds, pictures of children from many ethnic backgrounds and cultures

FIGURE 10-8 A child's family and culture can be brought into the classroom through a variety of curriculum materials; so, too, can children with disabilities feel included.

ment is a creative act, one that is rewarding for teachers. Figure 10-9 highlights some of a teacher's thoughts in the planning process. In the next four chapters, curriculum implementations will be explored from another perspective, that of the major areas of development in the child's growth. In Chapter 11, the focus will be on how curriculum affects the growing body. Chapter 12 will emphasize the curricular role in developing the mind, and Chapters 13 and 14 will explore the curricular issues surrounding social and emotional growth.

Integrating Learning Standards

Curriculum planning may be affected by a set of standards mandated by the state. Over 75 percent of the states in the United States (Copple & Bredekamp, 2009)

have developed some sort of explicit learning expectations for children to meet at various age and grade levels, often termed "outcomes" or "desired results." At the federal level, there is the Head Start Child Outcomes Framework and the content standards that other national organizations have created for math, science, and literacy. **Standards** describe the kinds of learning that should take place and often, but not always, includes most areas of developmental domains.

Gronlund (2006) notes some of the benefits of such standardization. When linked to primary grade standards, early childhood standards may enhance school readiness. Standards help to define the foundational skills for learning and help teachers identify the next steps in their learning. To the public, they could reinforce the potential for learning in very young children

How Teachers Plan Curriculum

Sets specific objectives

Integrates curriculum

Allows children meaningful choices

Uses environment as co-teacher

Knows what is worthwhile to teach

Uses people and materials as resources

Knows each child's capabilities

Expresses school philosophy and goals

Invites families and diverse cultures into curriculum

Balances child-initiated and teacher-directed learning

Plans activities

Uses play and active learning

Recognizes and accommodates individual differences

Uses knowledge about individual children's learning styles and intelligences

▌ **FIGURE 10-9** The effective teacher's role in creating curriculum. (Photo © Cengage Learning.)

and the importance of quality early childhood programs. Standards also provide a vehicle for demonstrating the breadth of learning that takes place in the early years and, if used with thought and planning, they can work hand in hand with developmentally appropriate practices.

Many early childhood professionals have concerns over the potential misuse of these standards. They may foster "teaching to the test" rather than a more developmental approach to teaching and cause pressure on the child through inappropriate expectations. They may promote testing and other assessment methods inappropriate for young children as noted earlier in Chapter 6. Too often, standards do not address all of the developmental domains but focus only on literacy and/or math and science. Bowman (2006) reminds us that children's sociocultural experiences are a significant part of their learning and that standards need to recognize this when determining what children should know and be able to do. Frost and others (2008) warn against depriving children from recess and play because of the national em-

phasis on high stakes testing and the belief that play is less important than academics.

A joint position paper by NAEYC and the National Association of Early Childhood Specialists in State Departments of Education (NAECS/SDE) (2002) cited four essential features that early learning standards should include: significant, developmentally appropriate content and outcomes; informed, inclusive processes to develop and review the standards; implementation and assessment strategies that are ethical and appropriate for young children; and strong support for early childhood programs, professionals, and families. By following these guidelines, standards could contribute to more positive outcomes for all children.

Today's teachers will need to learn more about their own state's requirements and reflect with other early childhood professionals on the tension between meeting the standards and remaining true to developmentally appropriate practices. Figure 10-10 is an example of how a developmentally appropriate curriculum includes learning standards.

Standard	Activity	Demonstrates Mastery
Personal and social competence: Identifies self by categories of gender, age, or social group.	1. Graph children's ages. 2. Make an "All about Me" book. 3. Create self-portraits with dictation.	1. Says correct age and shows correct number of fingers. 2-3. Says, "I'm a girl," "I'm 4 years old," or "I'm Vietnamese."
Effective learner: Completes increasingly complex puzzles.	Play with knob-puzzles, puzzles with and without frames, and floor puzzles.	Uses puzzles with interlocking pieces without the help of frames.
Physical and motor competence: Manipulates two or more objects at the same time.	String beads; play with Legos or Duplos; practice buttoning, zipping, lacing cards, and cutting paper.	Two hands manipulate object at the same time to complete task successfully.

FIGURE 10-10 Early learning standards are beneficial when they can be linked to developmentally appropriate curriculum and have clear goals and outcomes. (Source: Adapted from Kim Yuen, San Mateo County Office of Education, San Mateo, CA. Taken from Browne & Gordon's *To Teach Well: An Early Childhood Practicum Guide.* Upper Saddle River, NJ: Pearson Learning, 2009.)

Setting Goals

The process of developing curriculum begins with setting goals and then choosing the most pressing ones for attention. The following five steps are guidelines to setting and achieving curriculum goals:

1. *Set goals.* Decide what it is you want children to learn. What do you want them to know about themselves? About others? About the world? State goals clearly, preferably in behavioral terms so results can be measured.
2. *Establish priorities.* Make a list of three to five goals or objectives you consider most important. State the reasons for your choices; your own values and educational priorities will emerge more clearly.
3. *Know the resources.* A rich, successful, and creative curriculum relies on a vast number of resources. To create a health clinic in the dramatic play area, for instance, you might need the following resources:
   - *Materials.* Props, such as stethoscopes, X-ray machines, tongue depressors, adhesive strips, medical gowns, and masks.
   - *People.* Parents and/or community people in the health care professions to visit the class.
   - *Community.* Field trips to a nearby clinic, hospital, dentist's office.

4. *Plan ahead.* Set aside a regular time to meet for curriculum planning. This may be on a weekly, monthly, or seasonal basis. Discuss the curriculum activities as well as the daily routines in order to integrate the two.
5. *Evaluate.* Reflect on the outcome of your planning. Consider what worked and what did not, why it was successful or not. Look at the part of the experience that did not work as well as you would have liked. How can it be improved? What can you change about it? An evaluation should be immediate, precise, and supportive. Teachers need feedback about their planning and implementing skills. The needs of children are best served when the curriculum is refined and improved. Figure 10-11 is a useful example of how to evaluate an activity.

Teacher-Directed Learning

When is teacher-directed learning appropriate? Arce (2000) notes that this is a good teaching strategy when materials are complex or the concept is unknown to the children. Teaching certain skills, such as writing or cutting with scissors, requires teacher guidance. The continuum that is shown in Figure 10-12 suggests a broad range of

Evaluating Classroom Activity

Activity _____

How many children participated?_____   Did any avoid the activity? ____

How involved did children become? Very _____ Briefly _____ Watched only _____

What were children's reactions? Describe what they said and did. _____
_____
_____
_____
_____

What did you do to attract children? To maintain their interest? _____
_____
_____

How would you rate the success of this activity? Poor _____ Adequate _____ Good _____ Great _____
Why? _____
What skills/abilities were needed? Did the children exhibit the skills? _____
_____
_____

What parts of the activity were most successful? Why? _____
_____
_____

Describe any difficulty you encountered. Give reasons and tell how you would handle it if it happened again.
_____
_____
_____

If you did this activity again, what would you change? _____
_____

In light of your evaluation, what would you plan for a follow-up activity? _____
_____
_____

How did this activity compare with your goals and expectations? _____
_____
_____

FIGURE 10-11 Evaluating daily activities lets teachers use assessment as a curriculum planning tool. Although not every activity will need this scrutiny on a daily basis, careful planning and evaluation create effective classrooms. (Originally adapted from Vassar College Nursery school. From *Beginning Essentials in Early Childhood Education*. Fig. 10.18, p. 393. Copyright © 2007 Wadsworth, a part of Cengage Learning, Inc. Reprinted by permission. www.cengage.com/permissions.)

teaching behaviors, including teacher demonstration and directive teaching. Schirrmacher (2002) makes the point that all methods on the continuum are "valid at certain times for certain children and certain activities." Helm and Katz (2001) observe that teachers using the project approach often use teacher-directed instruction for teaching certain skills and concepts while keeping a high degree of child choice and initiative in the project themselves.

DAP

DAP Children benefit from selecting their own activities and play options as well as from more structured activities that teachers present.

A Continuum of Teacher Behavior

Nondirective			Mediating				Directive
Acknowledge	Model	Facilitate	Support	Scaffold	Co-construct	Demonstrate	Direct
Give attention and positive encouragement to keep a child engaged in an activity	Display for children a skill or desirable way of behaving in the classroom, through actions only or with cues, prompts, or other forms of coaching	Offer short-term assistance to help a child achieve the next level of functioning (as an adult does in holding the back of a bicycle while a child pedals)	Provide a fixed form of assistance, such as a bicycle's training wheels, to help a child achieve the next level of functioning	Set up challenges or assist children to work "on the edge" of their current competence	Learn or work collaboratively with children on a problem or task, such as building a model or block structure	Actively display a behavior or engage in an activity while children observe the outcome	Provide specific directions for children's behavior within narrowly defined dimensions of error

FIGURE 10-12 A continuum of teaching behavior. (From S. Bredekamp & T. Rosegrant, eds., *Reaching Potentials: Appropriate Curriculum and Assessment for Young Children,* vol. 2, Figure 2, p. 21, 1995. Reprinted with permission from the National Association for the Education of Young Children.)

Group Times

There are certain times within the daily routine when teachers call children together. The size of the group is determined in part by how many teachers there are and how they want to present various learning experiences. The reverse is also true. Various types of learning experiences best lend themselves to small or large group discussions. In using the project approach, for instance, small group work seems to provide the best format for developing ideas and listening to one another's opinions. A presentation by a visiting parent or expert on the project theme would be more appropriate for the large group. Smaller groups could then form to discuss in greater detail the ideas presented.

Large group times are used for a variety of reasons. Teachers may use them as opportunities to bring the entire class together to:

- Provide transitions in the daily schedule.
- Bring in a special guest or presentation.
- Introduce new ideas and materials.
- Sing, dance, and do finger plays.
- Read stories.
- Plan activities with children.
- Review the day's events.
- Initiate group problem solving.

Small groups, on the other hand, are opportunities for teachers and children to have a closer and more personal experience. This setting provides the teachers with ample opportunities to:

- Help children practice a specific skill, such as cutting with scissors.
- Encourage children in their social interactions with one another.
- Enjoy conversations with children.
- Teach a new game to a few children at a time.
- Closely observe each child's growth and development.
- Hold discussions regarding their project work, and move the project along.
- Explore topics in depth.

© Cengage Learning

Group times are more meaningful when children's home language is used for story time. One teacher reads the book in English, the other reads it in Spanish.

- Eat a meal or have a snack with children and encourage the social process.
- Provide close supervision for some experiences, such as cooking.

What is common to all group times is the occasion for teachers to encourage listening and speaking skills; provide an arena in which children share thoughts and ideas with one another; and introduce any number of cognitive and social activities. Teachers must make the determination about which type of group best suits the experience.

Written Plans for Creating Curriculum

A written plan is an organized agenda, an outline to follow, a framework for the curriculum. It may include a list of activities, goals for children's learning experiences, the process or method of instruction, the teacher's responsibilities, the time of day, and other special notations. A plan may be developed for a day, a week, a month, or a specific unit or theme. Figure 10-13 illustrates a weekly curriculum. The four chapters that follow also contain many examples of written plans.

Advantages of Written Plans

Setting lesson plans to paper has many advantages. Doing so helps teachers focus on the nature of the children they teach—their interests, their needs, their capabilities and their potential. A written plan encourages thorough, in-depth planning of curriculum in a logical progression, provides a direction, and helps teachers clarify thoughts and articulate a rationale for what they do. Team teaching is more stimulating when teachers plan together, sharing their ideas and resources; everyone knows what is happening; in case of absences, a substitute teacher can carry out the plans. Changes can easily be made to allow for flexibility, adaptation, and on-the-spot decisions.

When plans are written down, it is easy to see what resources are needed and to have the time to prepare materials. Written plans serve as a communication tool for the teaching staff, for parents, and for the governing agency, and provide a concrete format from which evaluation and assessment can be made.

Planning by Objectives

Another approach to curriculum development requires more formal, organized planning. Comprehensive lesson plans are developed, sometimes for the whole year, and usually include objectives, the stated concepts that children will learn through this experience. These are commonly called behavioral objectives. The lesson plans include specific, stated, observable behaviors that children will be able to demonstrate to show that the teaching objective has been met. In other words, a behavioral objective states clearly what children will actually do (e.g., be able to hold scissors properly; grasp a pencil between thumb and first two fingers). If the behavioral objective is to improve fine motor skills, the lesson plan includes activities and events that foster children's use of their fine motor skills. Several objectives may apply to a given activity. It is then important to order the objectives so that the purposes of the lesson remain in focus. To plan successfully, the teacher needs to know developmental and behavioral theory (Chapter 4), to have good observational strategies (Chapter 6), and to possess tools to assess whether the objective has been accomplished (Chapter 6).

One example of using behavioral objectives is Figure 10-10, which shows the use of behavioral objectives when meeting learning standards. A more developed plan found in early childhood classrooms would include activities for the full range of curriculum areas, such as art, motor activities, and dramatic play, for each of the objectives. Important factors in developing curriculum objectives are how much knowledge and understanding children have, what children are interested in, and what standards are mandated by the individual state for the specific age group.

Elements of Written Plans

A clearly written lesson plan serves as a curriculum map that guides the daily experiences and agendas. It should reflect the program's goals and priorities as well as the teachers' objectives for each student, such as what skills the activity fosters. The activities themselves should provide for first-hand learning experiences that promote discovery through active exploration of materials. A written lesson plan is a good way to demonstrate how well the curriculum is integrated, inclusive, and culturally sensitive.

The plan should present a balance to the day in which activity and play alternate with opportunities for quiet times, including the time spent outdoors. Large and small group times that are teacher-directed are included, as well as blocks of time in which children select their own activities. The plan should also note when and where teachers are able to work individually with children. Many written lesson plans also include any changes that need to be made to the environment or schedule.

Figure 10-13 demonstrates many of the key elements for a weekly lesson plans. Figure 10-14 shows a written

THE CREATIVECURRICULUM®
FOR INFANTS, TODDLERS & TWOS

Teacher(s):	LaToya
Group:	Twos
Week of:	November 4–8

Group Planning Form

Changes to the Environment:

Bring baskets outside for leaves gathered on the playground.
Add easel to the playground.
Introduce magnifying glasses.

Changes to Routines and Schedule:

Remind children during outdoor play to use the bathroom.

Family Involvement:

Ask for volunteers to go on a walking trip around the neighborhood.

Special Experiences I Plan to Offer This Week					
	Monday	**Tuesday**	**Wednesday**	**Thursday**	**Friday**
Indoor Experiences	Music & Movement: move like leaves Read Red Leaf, Yellow Leaf and discuss leaves on playground	Read Red Leaf, Yellow Leaf and discuss the colors of the leaves on the playground	Read A Simple Brown Leaf Use magnifying glasses to look at leaves at the sensory table	Read A Tree Is Nice Use magnifying glasses to look at leaves at the sensory table	Prepare for the walking trip
Outdoor Experiences	Collecting leaves on the playground	Easel Painting	Easel Painting Raking leaves	Raking leaves	Walking trip around the neighborhood to look at and collect leaves

FIGURE 10-13 From *The Creative Curriculum® for Infants, Toddlers, & Twos*, 2nd ed. (p. 103), by D.T. Dodge, S. Rudick, and K. Berke, 2006, Washington, DC: Teaching Strategies, Inc. Copyright 2006 by Teaching Strategies, Inc. Reprinted with permission.

FIGURE 10-14 The most effective curriculum grows out of the child's needs and experiences. (From *The Creative Curriculum® for Infants, Toddlers, & Twos*, 2nd ed. (p. 97), by D.T. Dodge, S. Rudick, and K. Berke, 2006, Washington, DC: Teaching Strategies, Inc. Copyright 2006 by Teaching Strategies, Inc. Reprinted with permission.)

plan for a curriculum that individualizes a child's specific needs and experiences.

Webbing

Webbing is the process through which teachers develop a diagram based on a particular topic or theme, highlighting key ideas and concepts (Katz and Chard, 2000). Ideas generated from brain-storming sessions flesh out the topic with many subheadings and lists of curriculum possibilities Webbing is a planning tool that provides depth to a topic and creates a map of possible activities and projects. A web may be organized around a theme (water), into curriculum areas (language arts, music), or around program goals (problem solving, cooperation). By their very nature, webs foster an integrated curriculum approach and help teachers extend children's learning and experiences.

Creating a web can be fun as it allows teachers to use their imaginations and calls into play their knowledge, resources, and experience. Katz and Chard (2000) suggest the following process to develop a web about the fall season:

1. *Brainstorming.* Using small slips of paper, teachers write down theme or topic ideas that the children suggest—each idea on a separate piece of paper. For the topic "Things that happen in fall and winter," for instance, the slips would contain ideas such as "cut jack-o-lanterns" or "rake leaves."
2. *Grouping.* The slips of paper are organized into groups of similar ideas, and, on a colored piece of paper, a heading is given to each group. "Canning and preserv-

ing" and "seasonal recipes" fall under the heading of "Cooking." Subgroups can be created, if necessary.

3. *Sharing*. Teachers can share their ideas with one another, rearranging the headings and subheadings as they share skills, resources, and information with one another.

4. *Drawing*. The ideas can be transferred to a piece of paper, placing the topic or theme in the center and drawing lines radiating out to the headings (group time, manipulatives, dramatic play). This creates a visual record of the relationships between and among the ideas and becomes what Workman and Anziano (1993) call "a living, growing resource."

Jones and Nimmo (1994) emphasize the organic nature of a web. First created as a response to children's ideas, it creates a picture in which ideas emerge and connect in any number of ways. It is, of course, a tentative plan, for what happens next depends on the children's responses. The web creates a flexible plan that can be altered and adapted as teachers observe children and evaluate their interests.

Figure 10-15 is an example of children and teachers working together on a curriculum web that grew out of the children's involvement with play animals. The project that evolved is featured in the photos on page 362.

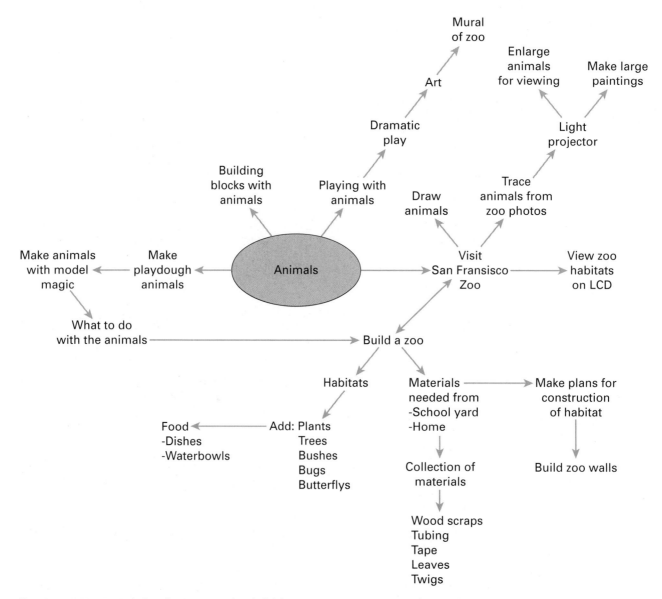

FIGURE 10-15 Web for elementary school children. (Tracy Pierce, Geo-Kids, Menlo Park, CA. Used by Permission.)

Themes

A traditional method of developing curriculum is to focus on a broad, general topic or theme, also known as a unit. Though used interchangeably, themes are generally a smaller part of a unit, allowing for a more specific focus. For example, a unit on the body may have "What I can do with my hands" as one theme. This mode of planning is used in many early childhood and elementary settings. Focusing on themes, however, can and should be much more than an in-depth study of a topic and should be integrated into the whole curriculum.

A thematic approach can utilize many of the attributes of an integrated curriculum:

- Children can help choose and plan themes, thereby constructing their own learning.
- Activities can be chosen to reflect the curriculum goals.
- The emphasis is on active learning.
- The most appropriate themes are those that have a meaningful connection to children's lives.

- Many subject areas can be integrated in the different activities.
- The program lends itself to flexibility, teacher permitting.
- It provides for an in-depth study of a topic.
- It can support the use of multiple learning styles through different media.
- It adds coherence and depth to the curriculum.
- It has the potential for good multicultural curriculum emphasis.

Figure 10-16 is an example of a theme on the five senses for toddlers.

Gestwicki (2007) cites some disadvantages of using a traditional theme approach to curriculum. It can be restricted and narrow and too adult-directed, not allowing for children's curiosity and initiative. There is a danger of creating an artificial unit that has no relevancy to the children's experiences or interests. Teachers may find it hard to deviate from the curriculum plan and not be flexible enough to extend the topic further. When too rigidly applied, themes can isolate the experience into a particu-

Curriculum through Play for the One-and-a-Half-Year-Old

Sensory Stimulation

Objective: To help toddlers begin to explore and understand the five senses.

	Activity	Small-Group Focus	Optional Activities
Monday	Soap painting	Guessing game: textures. Distinguish soft from hard using familiar objects.	Play hide-and-seek with two or three
Tuesday	Water table play	Guessing game: smells. Identify familiar scents in jars.	Blow bubbles.
Wednesday	Fingerpainting	Guessing game: weights. Distinguish heavy/not heavy using familiar objects such as book or doll.	Take walk to collect collage materials of different textures.
Thursday	Making collages of textures collected day before	Guessing game: shapes. Using puzzles of shapes and shape-sorting boxes.	Have a parade of sounds from many musical instruments.
Friday	Play dough	Food fest of finger foods: Try different textures, sizes, shapes, and flavors	Make foot or hand prints on large mural paper.

FIGURE 10-16 Example of teacher-directed activities to help toddlers explore their sensory skills.

lar subject or concept and miss the opportunities to broaden the learning potential. At its worst, a theme can be recycled every year without regard for the different group of children and their needs and interests.

Holiday Themes or Not?

An inappropriate use of themes is to limit them to specific times of the year, such as Thanksgiving or Valentine's Day, or to celebrate holidays. Themes are not just for special occasions since they tend to isolate and narrowly define the topic.

Some holiday themes may not be appropriate to every family represented by the group. One teacher decided that making Easter baskets on Good Friday (a religious day for many Christians) was offensive to those who practiced Christianity and was uncomfortable for the non-Christians in the class. The practice was dropped throughout the school in the name of cultural and religious sensitivity.

Some schools have adopted policies that do not permit celebrating holidays as part of the school curriculum. Holidays do provoke a particularly sensitive time for celebrating. There are many who believe that celebrating holidays from around the world brings a sense of multiculturalism to the curriculum. York (2003) suggests that when done with thought and care, holidays can be an important addition to the curriculum. To ensure the most positive outcomes, according to York, all holidays are celebrated with equal importance; only those that have importance to the children and families in the class are observed; parents are enlisted to help; the celebration takes place within the context of the daily life of people and families; and sensitivity to the children and families who do not celebrate a particular holiday is observed.

Others might say this is a tourist approach to cultural diversity or that it is a quick visit to another culture without follow-up and depth of exploration. Too often in early childhood programs, holiday curriculum units are the only expression of cultural diversity. According to Derman-Sparks & Edwards (2010), there are no meaningful developmental reasons for the strong emphasis on celebrating holidays in most early childhood programs today. She further argues that this overuse of holiday themes actually interferes with a developmentally appropriate curriculum because too many foods or songs are used, bypassing the opportunity for children to learn about common areas of life. It seems that holiday themes paint a flat picture of a cultural or religious event without taking into account how people in those cultures live, work, sleep, or play in ways that are familiar or similar to other cultures.

What Do YOU Think? Should celebrating holidays be part of an early childhood curriculum? Justify your response with personal examples from your childhood, your teaching experiences, and your understanding of development. Debate your answer with a classmate who has a different opinion.

Life-Oriented Themes

Themes that are of great interest to young children are those that directly concern them. The body as a theme suggests many avenues for development: body parts may be emphasized; exploration using the senses may be stressed; measuring and weighing children may be used to demonstrate growth of the body. Another subject to which children readily respond is that of home and family. Animals, especially pets, are appealing to young children and can lead into further curriculum areas of wild animals, prehistoric animals, and so on.

The more in touch with children the teachers are, the more their classroom themes should reflect the children's interests and abilities. Children who live in Silicon Valley in California, in Houston, Texas, or in Central Florida may have a local interest in computers and space shuttles. The urban child of New York, Detroit, or Washington, DC, will relate more readily to themes about subways, taxis, and tall buildings. Children's interests often focus on, but are not necessarily limited to, what they have experienced. By choosing themes that coincide with children's daily lives, teachers promote connected and relevant learning. Take another look at Figures 10-4 and 10-8 from this perspective.

Some themes in an early childhood setting can address children's own issues. All young children share similar fears and curiosity about the world they do not know but imagine so vividly. The cues children give, particularly about their concerns, suggest to the observant teacher some important themes of childhood. During Halloween, for example, it can be helpful and reassuring to children if the theme of masks is developed. Select some masks that have a function, such as hospital masks, ski masks, safety glasses, sunglasses, snorkel masks, or wrestling and football helmets. Children can try them on and become comfortable with the way their appearance changes. They can laugh with friends as they look in the mirror to see how a mask changes the appearance but does not change the person.

Themes can be inclusive, integrated, and appropriate. It takes a teacher with a child-centered approach to respond to children's innate excitement and curiosity about learning.

The Project Approach

Much of what you have just learned about emergent and thematic curriculum as an integrated approach applies equally to projects. As you read ahead, keep in mind what you have learned about the advantages of an integrated curriculum (page 335), how to take cues from children as explained in the discussion on emergent curriculum (page 337), the concept of children and teachers collaborating (page 338), and the sources for curriculum ideas found on page 338. A **project approach** embodies these characteristics as well. On the continuum of teacher-directed versus child-directed learning, a project requires the greatest amount of child involvement.

Projects are the epitome of an integrated curriculum, embracing all of the key characteristics of integrated learning and allowing for the incorporation of a wide range of subject areas. Katz (1994) defines the "project approach" as:

> ...an in-depth investigation of a topic worth learning more about...usually undertaken by a small group of children within a class...the whole class... or even an individual child. The key feature...is that it is a research effort deliberately focused on finding answers to questions about a topic posed either by the children...or the teacher.

A recent revival of this curriculum approach used in progressive schools (see Dewey, Chapter 1) is worth noting here. Based on the belief that "children's minds should be engaged in ways that deepen their understanding of their own experiences and environment" (Katz & Chard, 2000), the project approach consists of exploring a theme or topic (such as babies, dinosaurs, riding the school bus) over a period of days or weeks.

Preplanning by the children and teachers is the first step: They observe, question, estimate, experiment, and research items and events related to the topic. Together, they make dramatic play and display materials they need. Children work in small groups throughout the process and have the opportunity to make numerous choices about their level of participation. The teacher often records the activity on tapes and with photographs. Proj-

ect work has different levels of complexity, so it meets the needs of children of different ages and abilities.

In the small town of Reggio Emilia in northern Italy, a similar approach to curriculum has received worldwide attention. The project approach is used in even greater depth as it permeates the entire curriculum and school environment. It will be discussed later in this chapter.

Projects emerge from children's own interests, teacher observations of children's needs and interests, and parents' suggestions. The topics reflect the local culture of the children. In fact, Chard (1998) suggests that since life experiences and interests of the teacher and of the children are so strongly reflected in the project itself, it is a singular occurrence relevant only to that group. Another group may adopt the same topic, but it will not be a duplicate process due to the individual nature of the children and teacher planning the project.

This approach to teaching and learning easily lends itself to an inclusive classroom and curriculum, responding to diverse points of view as well as diverse cultures. Projects created by the children of Reggio Emilia, for instance, will differ from those of American children due to many cultural influences—in particular, the children's ability to argue their point and defend their ideas to others as the project emerges. In the Italian culture, this is a natural part of discourse and is usual in the beginning of conversation between people; in American mainstream culture, it is usual when two people "agree to disagree" for the conversation to end.

The planning process is crucial to the success of the project approach as is the underlying philosophy that children can be co-constructors of their own education. This approach has much in common with the approaches of both Dewey and Neill's *Summerhill* (see Chapter 1). The teacher helps children explore what they already know about the topic, what they might need to know, and how they can represent that knowledge through various media, reinforcing Vygotsky's theory that interaction and direct teaching are important aspects of intellectual development. Teachers pose questions for children that lead them to suggest a hypothesis: What might happen if you do that? What do you think you could do to make that work? Children are encouraged to evaluate their own work and learn to defend and explain their creations to others. Figure 10-5 on page 343 exemplifies this process.

The following is a summary of the process involved in a project approach as outlined by Chard (1998), Katz and Chard (2000), and Helm and Katz (2001). There are three phases to a project approach:

1. *Representation.* Children express and communicate their ideas. Through the use of drawing, writing, construction, dramatic play, maps, and diagrams,

Playing with animals in classroom

Making animals from Model Magic

Making animals from Model Magic

Using their animals with blocks

Visiting the zoo

Drawing plans for building the zoo

Drawing plans for building the zoo

Building the zoo

Making the zoo habitat

The zoo

Photos courtesy of Tracy Pierce and Michele McMath

This project evolved from the web shown in Figure 10-15 and took several months to accomplish. We thank the children at Geo-Kids in Menlo Park, CA, and photographers Tracy Pierce and Michele McMath.

children share their experience and knowledge. Representation documents what children are learning.

2. *Fieldwork.* Investigations take place outside the classroom, through events, objects, places, and people so that children build on their own knowledge through direct experiences.

3. *Investigation.* Using a variety of resources, children explore and research the topic. This includes fieldwork as well as closely analyzing, sketching, and discussing what they find.

4. *Display.* Exhibits of children's work on the project serve as a source of information and provide an opportunity to share their work and ideas with others. As the project progresses, the children are kept up to date on their progress by displays of their work.

Play-Based Curriculum Models

Five distinct models demonstrate curriculum that embrace the five guidelines for developmentally appropriate practice: creating a caring community, teaching to enhance development and learning, planning curriculum to achieve important goals, assessing children's development and learning, and establishing reciprocal relationships with families. Each model is unique with its own strengths and characteristics and each is play and development integrated.

High/Scope: Cognitively Oriented Model

The High/Scope curriculum stresses active learning through a variety of learning centers with plenty of materials and developmentally appropriate activities. The schedule includes extended periods of free play time and guidelines for teacher's intervention in play activities (Frost, et al, 2008). Active problem solving is encouraged as children plan, with teacher's assistance, what they will do each day, carry out their plan, and review what they have done. Appropriately, this is known as the "plan-do-review" process. Teachers use small groups to encourage, question, support, and extend children's learning while emphasizing communication skills.

There is a balance between child-initiated experiences and teacher-planned instructional activities. Teachers use observational techniques to focus on children and to understand children's play. Teachers are responsible for planning curriculum organized around key experi-

ences that reinforce and extend the learning activities the children select for themselves. These key experiences form the basis of the curriculum and include creative representation, language and literacy, initiative and social relations, movement, music, classification, seriation, number, space, and time (Hohmann & Weikart, 2002).

Children with special needs are integrated readily into High/Scope programs and with a curriculum developed especially for K–3 grades and early adolescents. High/Scope extends its active learning philosophy into further school years.

High/Scope's approach to children's learning is deeply rooted in Piagetian theory and supports Vygotsky's theory of social interaction and cognition: Children learn when interacting with the people and materials in their environment. The schools of Reggio Emilia share core elements of the High/Scope philosophy. Both philosophies stress the importance of children's constructing their knowledge from activities that interest them; team teaching is an important concept, to allow the children access to adult support; and the process of planning, acting, recording, and reassessing is one that both approaches use to foster critical thinking skills.

To document children's growth using a portfolio system (see Chapter 6), the High/Scope program uses the following categories (Schweinhart, 1993; Brewer, 1995):

- *Initiative:* Expressing choices, engaging in complex play.
- *Creative representation:* Making, building, pretending.
- *Social relations:* Relating to children and adults, making friends.
- *Music and movement:* Exhibiting body coordination, following a musical beat.
- *Language and literacy:* Showing interest in reading, beginning reading, beginning writing.
- *Logic and mathematics:* Sorting, counting objects, describing time sequences.

Teachers evaluate these abilities as they observe children's use of key experiences and plan the curriculum accordingly.

Bank Street: Developmental-Interaction Model

Bank Street was founded by Lucy Sprague Mitchell (see Chapter 1), and its roots reflect the thinking of Freud, Dewey, Erikson, Vygotsky, and Piaget, among others.

There is a clear connection between education and psychology in its approach (Mitchell and David, 1992). It is a developmental approach because child development principles influence the curriculum planning, and it is an interactive model because of the connections made between children, adults, and the greater environment. The interaction between cognitive and socio-emotional development is a key element as well, underscoring the connections between thinking and emotions (Mitchell & David, 1992).

The Bank Street model originated the play-based approach used in many early childhood settings today through the use of interest centers, water and sand play, blocks, puzzles, painting, and small and large group play. Teachers use play to enhance children's cognitive and language skills through frequent conversations and interactions (Frost, et al, 2008).

Children are seen as active learners who learn by interacting with and transforming the world about them. Play is the primary vehicle for encouraging involvement between and among children, adults, and materials. The teacher's primary role is to observe and respond to activities initiated by the children. Classrooms are organized into learning centers, in which children can work individually or in groups.

The Bank Street model exemplifies an integrated curriculum. It is rooted in social studies (Mitchell & David, 1992) so that children learn about the world in which they live through concrete, first-hand experiences. Mitchell and David emphasize that the school is an active community connected to the social world of which it is a part and that "the school shares the responsibility with children's families and with other neighborhood institutions." Units and themes are used to focus the curriculum. There is freedom of movement and choice and easy access to materials (Epstein, Schweinhart, & McAdoo, 1996).

A teacher's knowledge and understanding of child development principles is crucial to this approach. Educational goals are set in terms of developmental processes and include the development of competence, a sense of autonomy and individuality, social relatedness and connectedness, creativity, and an integration of different ways of experiencing the world.

The Schools of Reggio Emilia

Respect for children's investigative powers and for their ability to think, plan, criticize, collaborate, and learn from all they do is the hallmark of the Reggio Emilia approach and is an excellent example of an integrated and emerging approach to learning. This collection of schools in Italy, with separate programs for infants to 3-year-olds and 3- to 6-year-olds, has commanded worldwide attention for its philosophy and practices. "Nowhere else in the world," states Gardner (in the classic work of Edwards, Gandini, & Forman, 1993), "is there such a seamless and symbiotic relationship between a school's progressive philosophy and its practices." The curriculum takes the project approach to its highest levels.

Influenced by Dewey's progressive education movement, the philosophies and practices of Reggio Emilia owe a great deal as well to Piaget's constructivist theory, Vygotsky's belief in social discourse as a method of learning, and Gardner's theory of multiple intelligences (see Chapters 1, 4, and 13). Children are actively engaged in long-term projects that they initiate, design, and carry out with the support of the teacher. Art is the primary medium for learning.

Some of the key components of the Reggio Emilia approach are: a materials-rich environment that is aesthetically appealing; a community-based attitude involving the entire city; a family support system; and a commitment to process.

These elements are manifested in the program through astonishingly beautiful school settings, replete with the work of children and evidence of their projects elegantly displayed throughout; by support realized through a large portion of the city's budget; through small groups of children who stay together for a three-year period with the same teacher; and through intentionally bringing the children's culture into school life.

Play, in the Reggio Emilia classroom, is focused on children's ability to represent their experiences through the arts. As such, play is more collaborative with several

The Reggio approach: order and beauty.

Reggio Emilia: a materials-rich environment.

children working on one project while another group is working elsewhere. "Working" in this context is playing; art is the form that play often takes in this model. The teacher's role is more involved than in other models as the philosophy of Reggio Emilia is to work with children and assist them with their activities.

Cadwell (1997) identifies eight fundamentals of the Reggio Emilia approach. Each has implications for creating a curriculum that is fully integrated and one that emerges from children's interests and ideas. These eight essential points are:

1. *The child as protagonist.* All children are strong and capable and have the potential and preparation to construct their learning. They are protagonists (i.e., central characters) with teachers and parents in the educational process.
2. *The child as collaborator.* There is an emphasis on working in small groups. This stems from the belief that we are social beings and form ourselves through interactions with people and things.
3. *The child as communicator.* Symbolic representation, through dance, art, painting, sculpting, building, dramatic play, music, and words help children discover and communicate what they know and what they question. Teachers support the use of these "many languages" to help children make their thinking visible.
4. *The environment as third teacher.* Every corner of the environment has an identity and purpose and en-

courages encounters, communication, and relationships. There is order and beauty in the design of the equipment, the space, and the materials.
5. *The teacher as partner, nurturer, and guide.* Teachers listen and observe children closely in order to facilitate and guide their process of open-ended discovery. They ask questions to find out about children's ideas and theories and then provide the opportunities for their learning.
6. *The teacher as researcher.* Teachers work in pairs and collaborate with other members of the staff, engaging in continuous discussion and interpretation of their work and the work of the children. This provides ongoing staff development and deeper exploration of theoretical foundations. Teachers see themselves as researchers who prepare and document their work. They consider children researchers as well.
7. *The documentation as communication.* Thoughtful care is given to ways in which the thinking of children is presented. Teachers make transcripts of children's dialogue, take series of photographs of their projects, and arrange them in panels that hang throughout the school or in books. This documentation is a way to communicate to the rest of the school what the children's work is about, to help parents become aware of their children's work, to assist teachers in evaluating children's work, and to show children that their work is valued.
8. *The parents as partner.* Parent participation is considered essential, and parents discuss their ideas and skills with the teachers. This underscores the collegiality and collaboration between home and school and ensures a curriculum that represents the diversity of the children and their families.

The teacher's role is unique: two coequal teachers work with a class of 25 children. There is no head teacher or director of the school. The teachers are supported by a **pedigogista,** a person trained in early childhood education who meets with the teachers weekly. Also on the staff of every school is an **atelierista,** a person trained in the arts who teaches techniques and skills the children learn for their projects.

The process of the activity is highly respected as the way to plan and work together. Teachers and children—collaborators—listen to one another, and many points of view are encouraged. Debate and discussion are key elements in the process of deciding what project to do and how to go about it. The attitude that a child is a natural researcher as well as an able learner and communicator has molded the organization and structure of the schools.

The schools of Reggio Emilia are worth knowing about just for the strong and powerful view they hold of the child and the concept of teacher and student learning from one another. There are a growing number of American models as well.

Cadwell (1997), who has assisted two schools in St. Louis to adopt the Reggio Emilia approach pictured on these pages, offers a hopeful challenge: "We can learn from the Reggio educators to look at children differently, to expect more of them and of ourselves, and to offer them many more possibilities for full development."

Waldorf Schools

The Waldorf curriculum, shaped by Rudolf Steiner in 1919 (see Chapter 1), emphasizes the development of the whole child through "the head, heart, and hands." Based on the belief that young children learn primarily through observation, imitation, and experience, the curriculum provides a rich environment for children to explore and role models who provide appealing activities. Waldorf schools are play-based: A hallmark of the curriculum is learning through play, and large periods of time are devoted to creative play. Steiner agreed with Froebel and others that education should begin where the learner is: Whatever the child brings to the educational experience is to be worked with, not against. Academics are de-emphasized in the early years of schooling. Looping is common in the elementary school years as the teacher stays with the class for up to eight years. Other defining features (WECAN, 2005) of a Waldorf curriculum include:

- *Strong rhythmic elements based on the cycles of life and nature:* A daily rhythm of play, work, circle time, outdoor play, ending with a nature or folk tale creates a consistent pattern for each session. The weekly rhythm evolves from activities, with one day for baking, another for crafts, and another for painting, and so on. Seasonal activities, such as planting bulbs, harvesting produce, or gathering leaves, stress nature's impact on our lives.
- *Environments that nourish the senses:* The walls of the classrooms are usually painted with soft watercolors, curtains may be made from plant-dyed fabrics, and tables and chairs are made of solid wood. The materials used are natural and real; the surroundings are simple and calming.
- *Extensive use of natural materials:* Wood, cotton, and wool are used throughout the classroom. Most of the toys are handcrafted from these natural materials, encouraging children to use their imagination. A piece of wood becomes a ticket to ride the train, which is made from chairs and pieces of wood. It may also become a telephone, a piece of food, or animal in a barn made of similar materials. The Waldorf philosophy suggests that other, more "finished" toys limit the power of fantasy, imagination, and creativity that is natural in a young child.
- *Play as an imitation of life:* The curriculum fosters skills that imitate the work of adults. Children participate in activities focused on the home— cooking and baking, cleaning, washing and sewing, gardening and building. Engaging in meaningful life activities are seen as preparation for later academic challenges.
- *Enhancement of a sense of reverence and wonder:* Children's natural sense of awe and wonder is fostered and deepened, primarily through activities, stories and festivals that celebrate the cycles of the seasons. In the fall, the classroom may be decorated with corn stalks and sheaves of grain; the seasonal table will be draped with beautiful fabrics in fall colors and hold gourds, pumpkins, acorns, and leaves. When parents join them for a harvest festival, songs of thankfulness and praise are sung before the feast begins. Each season this is repeated in order to expand the child's sense of reverence for life.

A Waldorf curriculum has much to offer, especially to those who put a premium on the use of imagination and an appreciation for the natural world. Learning is noncompetitive with no grades or set textbooks. There are many elements in the Waldorf Method that are common to the Montessori Method and to the Reggio Emilia Schools.

Montessori Schools

In Chapter 1, Maria Montessori was discussed in relation to the history of early childhood education. What follows here is an explanation of the Montessori Method as a curriculum model for young children.

Montessori's approach to learning has had a continuing influence in education since those early years. Of her work, three features stand out: (1) adapting school work to the individual rather than molding the child to fit the curriculum; (2) insisting on freedom for children in selection of materials and choice of activities; and (3) training of the senses and on practical life issues.

Montessori programs may not be play-based in the way the four previous models are, but they are certainly child-centered and child-based in philosophy and practice. Montessori held that the choices children make during free activity time is work that others might rightly identify as play. Montessori programs have art activities as well as music, movement, and some group games. Fantasy play, a staple in other early childhood settings, is not part of the Montessori curriculum. Instead, the Practical Life area, where children learn personal care and care of the environment, is the closest Montessori comes to dramatic play. In the Practical Life area, children imitate adult activities, such as pouring and food preparation, but with real glasses, pitchers, and utensils readily available to them.

The Program

A common misunderstanding is that all schools with the Montessori name are the same. They are not. There are many variations and types of Montessori schools throughout the United States, reflecting an infinite variety of interpretations of the Montessori Method. Within the Montessori movement itself, there are at least two factions claiming to be the voice of the true Montessori approach to education.

Although, the most common form of Montessori program is one in which 3- to 5-year-olds are grouped together, there are a growing number of schools for 6- to 9-year-olds and even 9- to 12-year-olds. Teacher education programs now prepare Montessori teachers to work with infants and toddlers as well as high school students.

The most striking feature of the Montessori classroom is its materials. Many are made of wood and designed to stress the philosophy of learning through the senses. Color, texture, and quality of craftsmanship of the materials appeal to the hand as well as the eye; they demand to be touched. "Smooth" and "oval" take on new meaning as a child runs a finger around Montessori-designed puzzle shapes.

Montessori materials have other unique characteristics besides their tactile appeal. They are self-correcting; that is, they fit together or work in only one way so that children will know immediately whether they are successful. The Montessori curriculum presents the materials in a sequence, from simplest to most difficult. Many of the learning tasks have a series of steps and must be learned in a prescribed order. Whether sponging a table clean or using the number rods, the child is taught the precise order in which to use the materials. Montessori developed curriculum materials and tasks that are related to real life. Practical Life activities range from cleaning tasks (hands, tables) to dressing tasks (lacing, buttoning, or tying garment closures).

In a Montessori classroom, children work by themselves at their own pace. They are free to choose the materials with which they want to "work"—the word used to describe their activity. Children must accomplish one task before starting another one, including the replacing of the materials on the shelf for someone else to use.

The prepared environment in a Montessori program has child-sized furniture and equipment—one of Froebel's ideas that Montessori used. Materials are set out on low shelves, in an orderly fashion, to encourage children's independent use. Only one set of any materials—their shape, form, and the way they are presented for children to use—are the vehicles for learning.

The teacher in the Montessori setting has a prescribed role, one of observing the children. Teachers become familiar with skills and developmental levels, and then match the children to the appropriate material or task. There is little teacher intervention beyond giving clear directions for how to use the materials. Group instruction is not common; learning is an individual experience.

Program Changes

Many changes have taken place in Montessori practices over the years, and today's best Montessori programs are those that are true to philosophical traditions of the Montessori Method but constantly make small changes and adjustments. Many Montessori schools are adding curriculum areas of art, dramatic play, gross motor development, and computers. There is also greater teacher flexibility to promote social interaction.

For years, Montessori was separated from the mainstream of American education. Today that has changed, with over 100 public school districts offering Montessori programs in their elementary schools and with the increased interaction between Montessorians and other early childhood professionals.

Maria Montessori has found her way into nearly every early education program in existence today. Whether labeled so or not, much of the material and equipment as well as many of the teaching techniques in use today originated with this dynamic woman nearly 100 years ago. She is firmly established in early childhood history and its future. The Montessori Method should be weighed in light of contemporary knowledge and should be tailored to meet the needs of vigorous, eager, often needy children of the 21st century.

Insights *from the field*

Making a Difference in Young Children's Lives *by Marjorie Kostelnik, Ph.D.*

Nurturing children's development and learning throughout the early years is an exciting and awesome responsibility. As an early childhood educator, you will constantly be faced with situations in which you must make judgments about how to support and guide the children in your care. On any given day, you may wonder:

- Should I insist that all children play together and that everyone be "friends?"
- What should I do to help a child who has difficulty cutting with scissors?
- When is it reasonable to expect children to begin recognizing the letters in their names?
- What are sensible expectations when it comes to children following rules?
- How can I help children develop empathy and respect for all kinds of people?

How you answer questions like these and the actions you take can be more or less helpful to children. Your actions could enhance children's feelings of self-worth or detract from them. Your responses could increase children's interpersonal abilities or leave children at a loss about how to interact effectively. You could either promote or inhibit children's developing literacy, numeracy, or motor skills. Although there is not just *one* right answer for any of these situations, the things you say and do will make a real difference in children's lives.

What resources are available to help you frame the most effective responses? Your past experiences with children, advice or models provided by colleagues, and your intuitive feelings about what is best all contribute to your knowledge base. However, it is not sufficient to guide your actions professionally. Your personal qualities and experiences must be supplemented by theory and research regarding how children develop and learn. This knowledge extends beyond what you have absorbed from encountering the five, 10, or even 100 children with whom you have interacted so far. It encompasses the accumulated wisdom of our profession that goes back further than any of us have been alive. Such knowledge includes terms, facts, principles, and concepts that will help you understand how and why children think and behave as they do. It will also provide evidence-based insights into potentially useful intervention techniques. Ultimately, this combination of personal, conceptual, and research-based understandings will help you make the transition to bona fide early childhood professional.

As part of your professional education you will become familiar with common sequences of development and what char-

acterizes typical development in various domains (cognitive, emotional, language, social, physical) at different ages. This knowledge helps determine reasonable expectations for children, so you can plan educational activities that are age appropriate. You will also learn how rates of development vary from child to child. This will sensitize you to the wide range of abilities represented among the youngsters in your group and help you create activities that are best suited to children's individual needs.

Likewise, there are theories and research describing how young children learn. For instance, as you become more familiar with children's learning styles and the role of play in children's learning, you will be able to create educational environments that suit how children learn best. Finding out what researchers think about teaching by example, the use of rewards and consequences, and different ways to coach children in the learning process will give you much to think about regarding your interactions in the early childhood setting. In addition, becoming more aware of research that describes how children's families and cultural contexts impact the educational process will help you develop approaches that are socially and culturally relevant.

Some of the professional knowledge base seems logical, but some is counterintuitive. For example, common sense might tell you that praising children when they do something well is a good strategy for increasing positive behaviors in the future. Yet, researchers have found that certain kinds of praise actually interfere with children's learning and make it less likely that they will repeat desired actions.

Finally, you need to put these learnings into practice. You need to gather both time-honored curriculum and innovative ways to organize the environment and the daily schedule. You must work to plan activities that help all children learn in every domain. While professionals in the field have attempted to catalogue such practices in a variety of documents, you will have to do more than memorize or copy them. There is more than one way to think about things; there are contradictory ideas to consider; different contexts will demand different approaches. In the end, you have to make your own judgments about how to interpret and respond to children in a variety of circumstances. And that will help you define what is being taught to young children.

Marjorie Kostelnik, Ph.D., has been an early childhood educator for 30 years. Currently, she is Dean of the College of Education and Human Sciences at the University of Nebraska. Most recently, she and her coauthors have written *Guiding Children's Social Development* (5th ed.), Delmar Publishing, and *Developmentally Appropriate Curriculum: Best Practices in Early Childhood Education*, Merrill/Prentice Hall.

SUMMARY

Curriculum encompasses the planned and unplanned events children experience in group settings. Curriculum can include whatever happens to a child while in school or day care, or it can be a syllabus with detailed lesson plans. Today's teachers and caregivers ensure that children are exposed to developmentally appropriate, inclusive, and culturally appropriate curriculum.

Developing curriculum includes setting goals, establishing priorities, knowing what resources are available, planning ahead, and then evaluating the process. As teachers develop their curriculum plans, they may focus on the classroom activity or learning centers and the skills of the children. All three lend themselves to a basis for curriculum planning, and all are important vehicles for creative and effective curriculum for young children. State mandated learning standards now influence curriculum development in the early childhood and elementary years. Although standards have the potential to improve teaching and learning, they carry the risk that inappropriate teaching and testing will take the place of developmentally appropriate practices.

Integrated curriculum provides opportunities for children of diverse skills and abilities to learn through the same experience. Emergent curriculum takes its cues from the children's interests, and the teacher helps them to explore their ideas in more depth. An extension of this is the project approach, which may last for weeks and months. There are many ways of learning, and the multiple intelligence theory helps teachers understand how to create curriculum that covers a broad range of abilities and interests. Various curriculum models demonstrate the application of curriculum development theory to practical use.

Play is the way curriculum is expressed in the early childhood setting. Teachers, aware of play as a foundation for learning, provide an atmosphere that supports the play process. They provide a setting in which play is recognized as the curriculum of the child, the primary process through which children learn. Curriculum comes alive as children discover and take pleasure in learning.

Teachers demonstrate their appreciation of diversity by carefully selecting materials and planning experiences that are culturally responsive and inclusive and provide opportunities for learning in large and small groups.

KEY TERMS

curriculum	emergent curriculum	standards
developmentally appropriate practice (DAP)	learning styles	webbing
	activity centers	project approach
culturally appropriate curriculum	prerequisite	pedigogista
transformative curriculum	linchpin	atelierista
inclusive curriculum		

REVIEW QUESTIONS

1. Define developmentally appropriate curriculum for early childhood programs. What three core considerations determine whether a curriculum is DAP?

2. Name four factors that influence effective curriculum.

3. Why is play considered a foundation for learning?

4. What is the teacher's role in curriculum planning?

5. What are the key elements of written lesson plans?

6. Describe five play-based curriculum models that are developmentally appropriate. Include the elements that foster development through play.

LEARNING ACTIVITIES

1. Create a curriculum web with several classmates following the process described on pages 357 and 358.

2. Develop a project for (a) 3-year-olds in a half-day nursery school; (b) 6-year-olds in an after-school extended-day program; and (c) a family day care home. Use a nonholiday theme.

3. Observe teachers as children play. What is the difference in the play when (1) a teacher interacts with children in their play and (2) a teacher intervenes? What happens to the play immediately after teacher contact is made? How long does the play last? What is your conclusion?

4. Use Gardner's Multiple Intelligences to determine your own ways of knowing. How has this style affected your abilities as a student?

5. Use Figure 10-14 to plan an activity for (1) toddlers; (2) 4-year-olds; and (3) first graders.

6. What materials do you find in early childhood classrooms that enhance cultural diversity? What would you add? Take away? Why?

HELPFUL WEBSITES

High/Scope   **http://www.highscope.org**

NAEYC   **http://www.naeyc.org**

The Creative Curriculum®   **http://www.TeachingStrategies.com**

Anti-Defamation League   **http://www.adl.org**

Reggio Emilia   **http://www.reggiochildren.org**

 Additional resources including the TeachSource Videos can be found on the premium website for this book. Go to **http://www.cengage.com/login** to register your access code.

REFERENCES

Arce, E. (2000). *Curriculum for young children: An introduction.* Clifton Park, NY: Thomson Delmar Learning.

Armstrong, T. (2000). *Multiple intelligences in the classroom.* Alexandria, VA: Association for Supervision and Curriculum Development.

Banks, J. (2006). *Cultural diversity and education: Foundations, curriculum and teaching.* Boston: Allyn & Bacon.

Banks, J. A. (1994). *Multiethnic education: Theory and practice.* Boston: Allyn & Bacon.

Berk, L. E. (2009). *Child development.* Boston: Allyn & Bacon.

Bowman, B. T. (2006, September). Standards at the Heart of the Education Equity. *Young Children* 61(5), 42–48.

Bredekamp, S., & Rosegrant, T. (Eds.) (1995). *Reaching potential: Transforming early childhood curriculum and assessment* (Vol. 2). Washington, DC: National Association for the Education of Young Children.

Brewer, J. (1995). *Introduction to early childhood education.* Boston: Allyn & Bacon.

Cadwell, L. (1997). *Bringing Reggio Emilia home.* New York: Teachers College Press.

Chard, S. (1998). *Practical guide to the project approach.* New York: Scholastic.

Copple, C., & Bredekamp, S. (Eds.) (2009). *Developmentally appropriate practice in early childhood programs serving children from birth through age 8.* Washington, DC: National Association for the Education of Young Children.

Derman-Sparks, L., & Edwards, J. O., (2010) *Anit-bias education for young children and ourselves.* Washington, DC: National Association for the Education of Young Children.

Edwards, C., Gandini, L., & Forman, G. (1993). *The hundred languages of children: The Reggio Emilia approach to early childhood education.* Norwood, NJ: Ablex.

Epstein, A. S., Schweinhart, L. J., & McAdoo, L. (1996). *Models of early childhood education.* Ypslanti, MI: High/Scope Press.

Frost, J. L., Wortham, S. C., & Refifel, S. (2008). *Play and child development.* Upper Saddle River, NJ: Pearson Education, Inc.

Frost, J. L. (1996). *Play and playscapes.* Clifton Park, NY: Thomson Delmar Learning.

Gardner, H. (1983). *Frames of mind: The theory of multiple intelligences.* New York: Basic Books.

Gardner, H. (1998). Reflections on multiple intelligences: Myths and messages. In A. Woolfolk (Ed.), *Readings in Education Psychology.* Boston: Allyn & Bacon.

Gestwicki, C. (2007). *Developmentally appropriate practice: Curriculum and development in early education.* Clifton Park, NY: Thomson Delmar Learning.

Gronlund, G. (2006). *Making early learning standards come alive: Connecting your practice and curriculum to state guidelines.* St. Paul, MN: Redleaf Press.

Helm, J. H., & Katz, L. (2001). *Young investigators: The project approach in the early years.* New York: Teachers College Press.

Hirsch, E. S. (Ed.). (1974). *The block book.* Washington, DC: National Association for the Education of Young Children.

Hohmann, N., & Weikart, D. P. (2002). *Educating young children: Active learning practices for preschool and childcare programs.* Ypslanti, MI: High/Scope Press.

Jones, E. (1994). An emergent curriculum expert offers this afterthought. *Young Children, 54,* 16.

Jones, E., & Nimmo, J. (1994). *Emergent curriculum.* Washington, DC: National Association for the Education of Young Children.

Katz, L. G. (1994). *The project approach.* Champaign, IL: ERIC Clearinghouse on Elementary and Early Childhood Education.

Katz, L., & Chard, S. (2000). *Engaging children's minds: The project approach.* Norwood, NJ: Ablex.

McNeely, S. L. (1997). *Observing students and teachers through objective strategies.* Boston: Allyn & Bacon.

Miller, R. (1996). *The developmentally appropriate inclusive classroom.* Clifton Park, NY: Thomson Delmar Learning.

Mitchell, A., & David, J. (Eds.). (1992). *Explorations with young children.* Mt. Ranier, MD: Gryphon House.

National Association for the Education of Young Children (NAEYC) & National Association of Early Childhood Specialists in State Departments of Education (NAECS/SDE). (2002). Position Paper: Early Learning Standards: Creating the Conditions for Success. Retrieved from NAEYC website (http://www.naeyc.org) March, 2009.

New City School. (1994). *Celebrating multiple intelligences: Teaching for success.* St. Louis, MO: The New City School.

Ramirez, M., & Casteñada, A. (1974). *Cultural democracy, bicognitive development, and education.* New York: Academic Press.

Schirrmacher, R. (2008). *Art and creative development for young children.* Clifton Park, NY: Thomson Delmar Learning.

Schweinhart, L. J. (1993, July). Observing young children in action: The key to early childhood assessment. *Young children,* 29–33.

WECAN (Waldorf Early Childhood Association of North America). (2005). *The Waldorf kindergarten: The world of the young child.*

Witkin, H., Moore, C., Goodenough, D., & Cox, P. (1977). Field dependent and field independent cognitive styles and their educational implications. *Review of Educational Research, 47,* 1–64.

Woolfolk, A. (2001). *Educational psychology.* Boston: Allyn & Bacon.

Workman, S., & Anziano, M. C. (1993, January). Curriculum webs: Weaving connections from children to teachers. *Young Children,* 4–9.

York, S. (2003). *Roots and wings: Affirming culture in early childhood programs.* St. Paul, MN: Redleaf Press.

© Cengage Learning

Planning for the Body: Physical/Motor Development

PREVIEW QUESTIONS

- What are the physical and motor skills children learn in an early childhood setting?

- What do teachers consider when planning for physical/ motor development?

- How is physical/motor development integrated into the curriculum?

- Why is outdoor play important?

NAEYC CODE OF ETHICAL CONDUCT

These Core Values and sections from the NAEYC Code of Ethical Conduct are addressed in this chapter. As you read, note how the Core Values, Ideals, or Principles listed here apply to the topics in this chapter. (Reprinted with permission from the National Association for the Education of Young Children.)

Core Values: We have committed ourselves to basing our work with children on knowledge of child development.

Section I:
  1-1.5   To create and maintain safe and healthy settings.
  1.1.7   To ensure that children with disabilities have access to support and resources.

Learning through Movement

One of the first things you notice about young children is their energy and movement. Teachers often characterize children through their movements. "Trina never walks … she runs!" Pregnant mothers are aware of fetal motions and often assign personality traits to their children by these movements. "This baby is so active I think it must be in training for the Olympics." Infants show the extent of their full-bodied, random movements when they cry, roll over, and reach for a crib mobile.

In the Beginning

Basic motor skills develop in the early childhood years and form the foundation for movement and motor proficiency. If children do not develop them during the early years, these skills often remain unlearned.

A child's first few years of life are an astounding time of physical growth and acquisition of motor skills. The many milestones, such as rolling over, sitting up alone, crawling, walking, and running, are reinforced daily by parents and caregivers. This reinforcement strengthens the network of synapses, and they become a permanent part of the brain. By adolescence, the brain is beginning to rid itself of excess synapses. Those that have been activated and experienced most often are the ones that will survive (Shore, 1997). This research makes a strong case for activities and experiences, which foster physical growth and motor skills in young children. Greenman

Children are the picture of movement, spending the greatest portion of their day in physical activity.

Courtesy of the author

says, "Movement is as necessary to their learning as air and light" (2000).

Physical growth and motor development are partly determined by a child's genetic make-up. Equally important are environmental factors, such as nourishment, health, safety, stimulation, opportunity, practice, encouragement, and instruction. The crucial interplay of heredity and environment guides the child's progress through life.

Learning Is Integrated

Motor abilities affect other areas of development. Research reinforces the notion that physical and motor development is integrated with a child's cognitive development. Factors that affect children's physical growth, such as poverty and malnutrition, can affect their ability to learn.

This relationship between movement and learning continues throughout life (Jensen, 1998). Complex movements such as dancing or throwing a ball engage areas of the brain used for problem solving, planning, and sequencing new things to do. This mind–body integration can be seen in other areas of development as well:

Tim is reluctant to climb outside. He is frightened when he—or anyone else—is up in a tree or on a climber. Because he cannot risk using his body in space, he stops himself from playing with anyone who invites him to try these activities. Tim's lack of gross-motor development is affecting his social skills.

Samantha loves to draw and cut. She chooses the art area every day she attends the 2-year-old class. Not only are her fine-motor skills well developed for her age; she takes great pride in her creations. Her motor skills enhance her self-confidence in school. In turn, she receives praise and attention from others as she communicates with both adults and children through her work.

Program Needs

The greatest portion of the young child's day is spent in physical activity. Quality early childhood programs recognize this, providing for a full range of physical and motor experiences, planned and spontaneous. Indoors, children use puzzles, scissors, and dressing frames as they practice fine-motor skills. They dance with scarves and streamers to music. Perceptual-motor development, as with body awareness, occurs when children learn songs and games ("Head and Shoulders, Knees and Toes" or "Mother May I Take Two Giant Steps?") or while finger painting. Outdoors, gross-motor skills are refined by the use of climbers, swings, hopscotch, and ring-toss.

Movement Exploration Enhances Children's Ability to

- Solve problems.
- Exercise divergent thinking.
- Respond at their individual age and developmental level.
- Learn to cooperate with others.
- Become more aware of others' viewpoints and ideas.
- Share, take turns.
- Be self-expressive.
- Be creative.
- Gain confidence.
- Develop strong muscles.
- Refine motor skills.

Children need time as well as equipment and activities to practice their skills. The value teachers place on physical and motor development is directly related to the time allotted in the daily schedule for children to pursue them.

For years, early childhood programs have made an outdoor environment available to children, assuming a great need for physical activity and that children will find ways to fill that need themselves. However, many school outdoor areas contain few challenges, perhaps only a blacktop for bouncing balls and a small metal climber for hanging and climbing. Moreover, American children are exposed to a value system in which physical/motor fitness is not always a high priority. Children are often encouraged toward sedentary activities at an early age, such as watching television, videos, and playing computer games.

Physical/motor development is the central focus of the needs and interests of young children; it should play a central role in planning the curriculum.

Physical Growth/Motor Development

Children do not need encouragement to participate in physical activity. They need the opportunity, time, and support of their teachers to learn the fundamental fine and gross-motor skills necessary for a healthy, active life. Physical activity should be an important part of children's everyday life.

Physical Growth

The average preschooler grows 2 ½ inches and gains five to seven pounds each year (Santrock, 2008), so understanding physical development is important to teachers and parents. For example:

- New behavior is made possible through physical change: A toddler can be toilet trained once anal sphincter muscles develop.
- Growth determines the child's experiences: Observe the new vistas that open up when children learn to climb.
- Growth changes the way people respond to the child: The mobility of crawlers and toddlers leads to more restrictions from parents, and teachers choose materials that are more challenging and complex.
- Self-concepts are profoundly related to physical development: An obese first grader avoids the running and chasing games during recess.

Development follows a directional and sequential pattern, even with children who are physically or mentally disabled. Variations in growth patterns are influenced by environment and genetic make-up. Large muscles develop before smaller ones—one reason why most preschoolers are more proficient at running than at cutting with scissors. Growth also starts at the center of the body and moves outward. Watch a toddler walk using whole-leg action and compare that with a 5-year-old whose knees and ankles are involved in a more developed response. Children also tend to develop in a head-to-toe pattern. Infants move their eyes, head, and hands long before they learn to creep or crawl. It is important to remember, however, that growth does not occur in a smooth and unbroken pattern.

By the age of 5, a child's brain is almost adult size and continues to mature into adolescence. As the brain matures between the ages of 2 and 6, children gain greater impulse control, speed, and coordination of arms and legs. Eye-hand coordination is complete around the age of 4 years (Berger, 2005).

When looking at these growth patterns and brain development, parents and teachers must keep in mind the wide individual differences in the rates at which children grow and in the timing of each change. As a general rule, the pattern within individuals is consistent; that is, a child who is early, average, or late in one aspect of

Growth Patterns of the Young Child

Age	Weight	Height	Proportion	Teeth
Newborn	7 lb.	20 in.	Head = 1/4 of length	None
Infancy (up to 18 months)	Gains 15 lb. (now 20–25 lb.)	Adds 8 in. (now 28–29 in.)	About the same	6
Toddler (18 mo. to 2½ years)	Gains 5 lb. (now 28–30 lb.)	Adds another inch or two (now 29–33 in.)	Legs = 34% of body	20
Preschool (2½– 5 years)	About 5 lb./yr. (now 30–40 lb.)	Add 14–15 in. from birth; at age 2 = half of adult height (now 35–40 in.)	Head growth slows; legs at age 5 = 44% of body	20
Early-middle childhood (5–8 years)	Doubles before adolescence (age 6 = 45–50 lb.)	Adds 9–10 in. (age 6 = 44–48 in.)	Continues to move slowly toward adult proportions	Begins to lose baby teeth; replaced by permanent teeth (age 6 = 20–24 teeth)

FIGURE 11-1 An overview of growth shows how rapid physical growth is in childhood.

physical development will be so in all aspects of growth. Figure 11-1 shows the range of dramatic changes in growth for children up to age 8.

See also Chapter 3 for an overview of developmental norms.

Gender Differences

There are gender differences in growth patterns. Boys have a larger proportion of muscle tissue than girls, are more physically active and participate in more rough-and-tumble play than girls. Girls have more fat tissue than boys and are smaller and lighter until puberty (Santrock, 2008). Girls mature earlier than boys, and their growth is more regular and predictable. In motor skills, preschool girls have an edge in fine-motor skills, such as writing and drawing, and gross-motor skills, such as hopping and skipping. By age 5, boys can jump slightly farther, run slightly faster, and throw a ball about 5 feet farther than girls. These gender differences remain small until adolescence (Berk, 2002).

During middle childhood, motor development becomes smoother, more controlled, and coordinated. In gross-motor skills, boys usually outperform girls through speed, strength, and agility. Fine-motor skills increase as hands become steadier and more precise in both boys and girls (Santrock, 2008).

Ethnic Variations

There is some indication that physical development differs among ethnic groups. We need to be aware of the possibilities in the way children grow, but be careful not to stereotype them. African-American infants and toddlers seem to walk earlier and as a group are taller than Euro-Americans. Asian children also seem to develop physically earlier than Euro-American babies but are smaller and shorter overall (Bee & Boyd, 2009). Some researchers suggest that because African-American children have longer limbs, they have better leverage, which accounts for their superior performance in running and jumping (Berk, 2002). In the United States, children of African descent tend to be the tallest, followed by Europeans, Asians, and Latinos (Berger, 2005). Health and nutrition are factors that influence growth, and their effect is evident in the smaller size and weight of children in underdeveloped and/or poor nations.

Including Children with Special Needs

Every classroom is likely to have children who have special needs that must be met. It has already been established (see Chapters 3 and 9) that inclusion of children with special needs in early childhood programs is not only appropriate but is mandated by law. Physical education is the only subject area cited in the definition of an "appropriate education" in Public Law 94-42 (Gallahue, 2003), providing an opportunity for children to grow and develop through movement and physical activities.

Children with physical, cognitive, emotional, or learning disabilities are faced with a variety of challenges, many of which may be met by adapting the environment and planning for activities that help children function within their range of abilities. "The Inclusive Environment" and Figure 9-4 in Chapter 9 offer a number of ways for teachers and caregivers to individualize the setting for a variety of needs. In Chapter 3, many types of disabilities are discussed.

There are a number of teaching strategies that can enhance the participation of children with special needs in regular classroom activities in Figure 11-2. These brief examples make it clear that including children with special needs takes some careful thought about what kinds of movement experiences and physical development activities are within their abilities. Many of the suggestions are appropriate for all children, reminding us that the needs and interests of all children are essentially the same.

Adapting the environment and planning activities that help children function within their range of abilities is an important responsibility of the teacher. To plan physical activity for children with special needs, a teacher needs to:

- Evaluate the child's physical and motor development, focusing on the child's capabilities and needs. *Kareena is a 4-year-old girl who is blind, with age-appropriate motor skills except when she is in a new environment. She has a hesitant and unsteady gait as she learns furniture placement and activity area layout. Kareena is at ease with the teachers and is willing to approach other children, some of whom seem uncomfortable with her. She is generally cheerful and has a strong sense of herself and her abilities.*

- Set appropriate goals. *Involve Kareena in more group activities that promote social relationships. Pair her with a child who is sighted but whose own physical development needs are similar. Playing with peers supports learning and a growing sense of competence.*

    In this way both children can build confidence and friendships. Utilize outside play for balancing activities,

obstacle courses, and music and movement with scarves. Involve other children to help Kareena move from one activity to another and support her by modeling conversations that aid her in becoming oriented to materials and equipment: "There are a lot of fish in the water table, Kareena. Let's see if you can find the shark. Renee and Leo, can you tell Kareena what other fish and toys are in the water and who else is playing here?"

Teaching Strategies for Children with Special Needs

1. *For Children with Learning Disabilities*
   Help children gain a better understanding of their body, the space it occupies, and how it can move.

   Structure personalized activities that work within the child's present level of abilities.

   Progress from simple to more complex activities in small increments.

   Make frequent use of rhythmic activities, stressing the rhythmical elements to movement.

2. *For Children Who Are Visually Impaired*
   Use many auditory cues to help children gain a sense of space and distance.

   Include strenuous, big-muscle activities.

   Modify activities that require quick directional changes.

3. *For Children with Cognitive Disabilities*
   Stress gross-motor activities.

   Focus on fundamental stability, locomotor, and manipulative skills.

   Allow children to repeat their successes to enjoy the accomplishment.

   Avoid activities in which participants are eliminated from the game.

FIGURE 11-2 Many physical activities are appropriate for all children and encourage those with special needs to take an active part in the daily program. (From Gallahue, D. L. (2003) *Developmental physical education for today's children.* Madison, WI: Brown and Benchmark.)

DAP Children of varying abilities enjoy difficult tasks and challenges that give them an opportunity to experiment, learn, and make progress.

- Consider what modifications need to be made to materials and equipment that individually support children's wide range of capabilities. Use multisensory toys and objects when possible. *The balance beam may need to be wider or possibly placed on the ground for Kareena's first attempts. Add textured materials (cotton balls, velvet, rubber, and plastic objects) to the obstacle course and other equipment that will help direct Kareena as she moves. A wind chime hanging near the beginning of the obstacle course and balls with bells or other noisemakers inside will also guide her. Simplify activities by starting with what Kareena can do. For instance, kick a ball that is stationary before kicking a moving ball.*
- Make space modifications as necessary. *Check to see if walkways are clear and if equipment is readily accessible. Be consistent in storing classroom materials and equipment. Move equipment closer to where children can easily reach it. Equip riding toys with bells or beepers. Create physical boundaries, if necessary, and purchase equipment that is specifically designed for an individual child's disability.*
- Evaluate children, materials, and activities on a regular basis. *When Kareena masters the balance beam on the ground, how high might you move it for her next attempt? Is the obstacle course too challenging and, if*

so, how does it need to be modified? Does Kareena seem to enjoy these outside activities and is she growing in her social relationships?

Motor Development

Motor development "is the process of change in motor behavior brought about by interaction between heredity and environment" (Gallahue, 2003). It is a lifelong process of continuous change based on the interaction of (1) maturation (i.e., the genetically controlled rate of growth); (2) prior experiences; and (3) new motor activities. Like physical growth, motor development is a sequence of stages that is universal but still allows for individual differences. Each stage is different from, yet grows out of, the preceding level. Figure 11-3 charts motor development through the early years.

Any discussion of motor development should include reference to bodily-kinesthetic intelligence, part of Gardner's multiple intelligence theory (see Chapters 4, 10, and 12). Bodily-kinesthetic intelligence occurs when children use their bodies to help them process information and communicate their understanding of school. For instance, children who learn best through bodily-kinesthetic intelligence need active manipulation of materials. Drama, creative movement, dance,

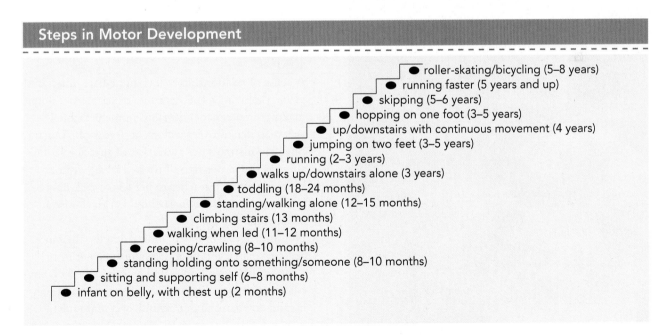

Steps in Motor Development

- roller-skating/bicycling (5–8 years)
- running faster (5 years and up)
- skipping (5–6 years)
- hopping on one foot (3–5 years)
- up/downstairs with continuous movement (4 years)
- jumping on two feet (3–5 years)
- running (2–3 years)
- walks up/downstairs alone (3 years)
- toddling (18–24 months)
- standing/walking alone (12–15 months)
- climbing stairs (13 months)
- walking when led (11–12 months)
- creeping/crawling (8–10 months)
- standing holding onto something/someone (8–10 months)
- sitting and supporting self (6–8 months)
- infant on belly, with chest up (2 months)

FIGURE 11-3 Motor development follows a developmental sequence. (Adapted from Allen, K. E., & Marotz, L. (2007). *Developmental profiles: Prebirth through eight.* Clifton Park, NY: Thomson Delmar Learning.)

manipulatives, games, and exercises, both indoors and outdoors, benefit the bodily-kinesthetic learner (New City School, 1994).

Gross-Motor Development

Gross-motor activity involves movements of the entire body or large parts of the body. Using various large muscle groups, children try to creep, crawl, roll, bounce, throw, or hop. Activities that include balance, agility, coordination, flexibility, strength, speed, and endurance foster gross-motor development.

Fine-Motor Development

Fine-motor activity uses the small muscles of the body and its extremities (the hands and feet). Such movement requires dexterity, precision, and manipulative skill. Grasping, reaching, holding, banging, pushing, spinning, and turning are all activities that refine these skills.

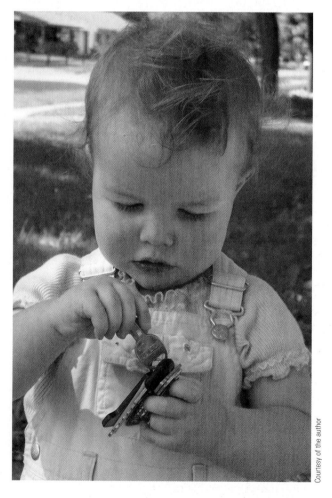

Courtesy of the author

Fine-motor activity requires using the small muscles of the body with dexterity and precision.

Perceptual-Motor Development

Perceptual-motor development is a process in which the child develops the skill and ability to take in and interpret information from the environment and respond to it with movement. Children obtain data and impressions primarily through their senses. How often have you seen babies mimic a parent's or caregiver's mouth movements—taking in visually the various expressions, then physically responding in kind?

In a sense, every moment is perceptual-motor activity because the body and mind must work together to complete all motor tasks. The perceptual task is to process information; the motor response activates what is received in a physical way although perceptual and motor abilities do not necessarily develop at the same time or the same rate (Gallahue, 2003). The complex nature of perceptual-motor development can be seen when examining the three basic categories of spatial, temporal, and sensory awareness, which also include perceptual-motor concepts of body and directional, visual, and auditory awareness.

Spatial Awareness

For children, **spatial** awareness means a sense of body awareness and the body's relationship to space, as well as a knowledge of what the body parts can do.

- For the toddler, concepts of spatial relationships are developed through motor activity: dropping objects from a high chair or forcing a large stuffed animal into a small box. Their definition of space is related to the action and movement involved in specific activities.
- A sense of relationship to less immediate things and places (knowing a specific route to school and home, making simple maps) develops in the preschool years. To illustrate, let us look at 3-year-old Tamara. She demonstrates her awareness of spatial relationships as she moves herself up to a table (without bumping into it), reaches to her left to pick up a ball of clay, and turns around behind her to choose a rolling pin.
- Not until ages 6 to 8 do children develop the more abstract spatial ability of distinguishing left from right on their own bodies and on others' bodies. Specifically, directional awareness refers to left and right, up and down, front and behind, over and under.

Temporal Awareness

Temporal awareness is the child's inner clock, a time structure that lets the child coordinate body parts. Dancing to a rhythmic beat, speeding up, and slowing down develops this kind of skill. It is also a force that helps children predict time. For instance, 7-year-olds Luis and Aref ask if it is time to clean up as they finish their game of soccer. The after-school center has sports time for about an hour before getting ready for snack; the children have an inner sense of time that parallels their knowledge of the daily schedule.

Sensory Awareness

Sensory awareness refers to use of the senses. It is another way the body gives the mind information. Vision is the dominant sense for young children. Visual awareness is the ability to mimic demonstrated movements and to discriminate faces, emotions, sizes, shapes, and colors. It is the ability in 3-month-old babies to recognize their mothers. Auditory awareness includes the ability to understand and carry out verbal directions and to discriminate among a variety of sounds ("Is this loud? fast? soft?" "Is that Josie or Dominick who called you?"). Auditory skills help children process information about language. From infancy, children seem to be able to combine visual and auditory awareness. Further sensory awareness develops through touch. Babies seem to put everything in their mouth to learn. When 4-year-old Stephanie picks up each object at the display table, she is using her sense of touch to discover size, shape, and volume.

DAP

Physical/Motor Skills in Early Childhood

Types of Movement

Physical/motor skills involve three basic types of movement: locomotor, nonlocomotor, and manipulative abilities:

1. *Locomotor* abilities involve a change of location of the body (Gallahue, 1996) and include the skills of walking, running, leaping, jumping, climbing, hopping, skipping, galloping, sliding, and riding a tricycle.
2. *Nonlocomotor* abilities (sometimes referred to as balancing or stabilizing) are any movements that require some degree of balancing (Gallahue, 2003). These skills are turning, twisting, pushing, bending, stretching, pulling, swinging, rolling, dodging, and balancing.

3. *Manipulative* abilities include the operation and control of limited and precise movements of the small muscles, especially those in the hands and feet. Manipulative skills include throwing, catching, reaching, bouncing, striking, kicking (gross-motor manipulation) and holding, grasping, cutting, and sewing (fine-motor manipulation).

These three basic movements are necessarily combined when children are active in physical play:

With doll buggy:	Holding onto buggy— Manipulative
	Pushing buggy— Nonlocomotor
	Walking with buggy— Locomotor
Playing ball:	Bending down for the ball— Nonlocomotor
	Throwing the ball— Manipulative
	Running to base— Locomotor
Jumping rope:	Holding and turning the rope— Manipulative
	Jumping—Locomotor
	Balancing self after jump— Nonlocomotor
Breaking a piñata:	Holding the bat— Manipulative
	Swinging the bat— Nonlocomotor
	Running to get the prize— Locomotor

Figure 11-4 shows age appropriate toys and games that foster the development of the three types of basic motor skills.

Learning Motor Skills

Children must use their bodies to learn motor skills. They acquire these skills by making comparisons between their past experience and new actions. Such comparisons use memory and experience. Physical movement activities require full involvement of the mind and body.

DAP Physical abilities and cognitive growth are intricately connected.

How to Foster Basic Motor Skills

Type of Motor Skill	Infants 0 to 1½ Years	Toddlers 1½ to 3 Years	Preschoolers 3 to 5 Years	Early School 6 to 8 Years
Locomotor: Walking Running Jumping Hopping Skipping Leaping Climbing Galloping Sliding	Safe areas to explore body movements Balls to roll Hanging jumpseats Walkers on wheels Simple obstacle course	Walker wagons Pull/push toys Dancing Wide balance board Toddler gym—stairs and slide "Ring around the Rosey"	Hippity-hop balls Sled Beginning skis Trampoline Roller skates Jump rope Balance beam Climber Dancing	Jump rope Roller skates Ice skates Climbing rope Tumbling mats Hopscotch
Nonlocomotor: Pushing Pulling Bending Balancing Stretching Rolling turning Twisting	Large, safe areas for exploration Parent/caregiver play: holding, pushing arms, legs, sturdy push toys Soft obstacle course of pillows	Pounding board Simple, low rocking horse Ride-on toys Toddler-type swing Large Legos® Sturdy doll buggy Wagon Fabric tunnels Blocks Cars, trucks to push	Shopping cart/doll carriage Wheelbarrow Pedal toys, trike Rakes, shovels Slide Swing Punching bag	Scooter Two-wheel bike Sled, toboggan Exercise mat Acrobatics Diving mask for swimming Doorway gym bar
Manipulative: Grasping Throwing Catching Kicking Receiving/moving objects Bouncing	Mobile attached to crib—kicking feet moves it Rattles, teething rings Crib activity board Soft foam blocks Snap beads Floating bath toys	Variety of balls Stacking, nesting toys Activity box—on floor Shape sorters Large, fat crayons Large pegs and board Water/sand table	Crayons, markers Clay, dough Bowling games Puzzles Woodworking tools Balls Lacing board Water/sand table	Baseball glove/bat Ring toss game Full-size balls Oversize bat Frisbee "Miss Mary Mack"

FIGURE 11-4 Toys and games help develop specific motor skills in young children.

Memory and Experience

Memory plays an important part in learning motor movements because children need to recall what they just did to make corrections or refinements. The ball that does not reach the basket is tossed farther on the next shot. To get the puzzle piece to fit, a child remembers other ways to manipulate the pieces. A long-term memory of movement is one that may go unrehearsed for long periods of time. The experience of swimming, for example, may be recalled only in the summer.

The experiences children have and the ability to recall those experiences are necessary to the process of gaining motor skill. Rehearsal is as important to the young child as it is every day children repeat and practice specific movements over and over as they play and work.

Practicing Basic Skills

A child's typical day, at home or at school, provides numerous opportunities to practice motor skills. Through play, the child can practice fine-motor skills such as:

- Holding a paintbrush, scissors, or rattle.
- Tiptoeing to music.
- Grasping a bottle, a hand, a toy.
- Threading a bead or a wide needle.

To learn a motor skill, children must combine memory with experience, taking advantage of opportunities to try something new, and practice what has already been learned.

© Cengage Learning

The child can also practice gross-motor skills such as:

- Pumping on a swing.
- Climbing a tree.
- Digging a garden.
- Balancing on a board, on one foot.

Through self-help activities the child can practice fine-motor skills such as:

- Buttoning a coat or doll's clothes.
- Brushing teeth, hair.
- Turning a faucet handle or doorknob.
- Feeding self with utensils.

Gross-motor practice includes:

- Moving a nap cot or table.
- Kicking covers off.
- Walking, holding onto furniture.
- Climbing up stairs or on a climber.

Children learning motor skills need experience in basic skills; they must learn simple skills before combining them into complex activities. Children must have time to try, refine, and try again.

TeachSource Video

Watch the TeachSource Video entitled, "Two–Five Years: Fine Motor Development for Early Childhood." After you study the video clip, reflect on the following questions:

1. What activities did you see that lay the foundation for writing?

2. Compare and contrast the video clip's fine-motor activities with those described in the text.

Feedback

Children modify and improve their motor skills as they receive information about their movements, both **intrinsic** (the paintbrush makes marks when it is pushed across the paper) and **extrinsic** ("I notice that your legs are very far apart as you try to somersault; how about holding them together as you roll next time?").

A Range of Developmental Levels

Any group of young children will have various levels of motor growth and physical development. An individual child may have different abilities and skills in gross-, fine-, and perceptual-motor areas; activities should be offered on several developmental levels. Play materials and equipment, such as balls, climbers, and ladders, should accommodate a variety of skill levels, particularly if children with physical disabilities are in the class. Climbing boards put on several levels and puzzles ranging from 6 to 60 pieces are two examples of how teachers can meet the need for success and challenge.

Role of the Teacher

Considerations

As teachers plan programs for physical/motor development, they reflect on several important issues. One often overlooked area is that of gross-motor development as an everyday occurrence. Teachers sometimes take for granted children's progress as they walk up and down stairs, climb on and off platforms and benches, and dance with abandon. Favorite rainy day activities such as moving around like Tyrannosaurus

Rex or spinning like a top are exercises in physical/motor development using gross-motor skills. Remember that the normal classroom setting can promote physical development every day through established routines and curriculum.

Childhood Obesity

The frequency of children who are overweight and childhood obesity has increased alarmingly. According to the National Center for Health Statistics (NCHS, 2006), the prevalence of childhood obesity among children ages 2 to 5 has increased from 5 percent in 1980 to 13.9 percent in 2004. Health risks include heart disease, high blood pressure, diabetes, depression, and low self-esteem. Part of the problem is that children are less active on a daily basis than in previous generations.

While there are many factors influencing obesity, such as socioeconomic status, family eating habits, heredity, and television viewing, a key factor seems to be whether or not one of the parents is obese (Berk, 2002). The American Obesity Association (2008) notes that if one parent is obese, the child is three times as likely to be obese in adulthood; if both parents are obese, the risk is 10 times more likely that the child will be an obese adult.

The dramatic increase in childhood obesity only serves to underscore the need for regular physical exercise in programs for young children. Sanders (2002) suggests structuring physical activity into the schedule to help children maximize their movement experiences.

Children do not learn by play alone. Organized movement experiences provide certain skill development that unstructured play cannot.

The National Association for Sport and Physical Education (NASPE) and the Council on Physical Education for Children (COPEC, 2000) established developmentally appropriate guidelines for preschool-age children (see Figure 11-5).

Sex-Role Stereotyping

Is motor behavior different for boys and girls? If so, why? Research indicates that there are differences between girls and boys in these areas. For example, behavioral differences in motor development are apparent in early life: 1-year-old girls already spend more time in fine-motor tasks, while baby boys are more engaged in gross-motor activity. Around the age of 2, children begin to identify people by their gender. Preschoolers often characterize many toys, articles of clothing, occupations, and behaviors with one sex or the other (Huston, 1993; Picariello, Greenberg, & Pillemer, 1990). Girls of this age increasingly seek out other girls to play with in quieter pursuits, whereas boys seem to prefer more active, aggressive play (Bennenson, 1993; Maccoby & Jacklin, 1987).

Why does this happen? Probably some sex differences are the result of genetics. At the same time, **sex-role stereotyping** expectations profoundly affect the motor and physical development of young children. This is the crucial issue for teachers, for their attitudes can ei-

---

Developmentally Appropriate Practices for Preschool Movement Programs

1. Toddlers should participate in at least 30 minutes a day of structured play and one to several hours a day of unstructured physical activity. Preschoolers should participate in at least one hour of daily structured physical activity.
2. Preschoolers should not be sedentary for more than one hour at a time and be engaged in unstructured physical activity whenever possible.
3. Basic movement skills should be the building blocks for more complex movement abilities.
4. Indoor and outdoor environments should exceed recommended safety standards for performing large-muscle, gross-motor activities.
5. Teachers and caregivers should understand the importance of physical activity and integrate movement programs as part of the daily educational program.
6. Teachers serve as facilitators, encouraging children to explore and discover a range of movement possibilities.

FIGURE 11-5 From *Appropriate Practices in Movement Programs for Young Children, Ages 3–5*. The Council on Physical Education for Children (Reston, VA: A position statement of the National Association for Sport and Physical Education/NASPE, 2000, pages 8–9, 11, 15, 17) and Sanders, S. W. (2002), *Active for life: Developmentally appropriate movement programs for young children*. Washington, DC: The National Association for the Education of Young Children).

ther encourage or discourage children from developing to their fullest potential. Teachers must acknowledge the differences that exist, and then ask themselves:

- What messages do I give children about physical activity? Do I value it for myself? For children? Do I value physical expression for girls as well as boys?
- Do I emphasize sports as a way to have fun? A way to be healthy? Do I praise only the "winner"?
- Can I provide male and female role models for physical activities using parents, grandparents, older siblings, staff, visitors, and guests?
- Do I encourage children to wear clothing that allows them the freedom to run, climb, or tumble? What do I do when girls arrive in long dresses and party shoes? (Be sensitive to family and cultural influences about appropriate clothing.) What should I wear?
- Are all physical/motor activities made equally available and attractive to boys and girls? What should I do if some children dominate these activities, while others never choose them?
- How do I actively engage all children in every form of physical activity? Do I let them know I think it is important?

Pica (2004) notes that children between the ages of 6 and 8 usually play with others of the same sex. She further suggests that this growing gender awareness can be addressed by assigning play partners of the opposite sex for certain games or suggesting that all children take on the roles of people in various occupations (firefighters, police officers, hairdressers, dancers) regardless of gender. By working and playing together, children learn to appreciate not only their own ideas and ways of doing things, but also those of others. See Chapter 15 for further discussion on gender-related issues.

What Do YOU Think? Are you physically active? Do you participate in a sport or exercise on a regular basis? What would you do to create opportunities for all children to be physically active for some part of each school day? List some examples that would be especially appropriate indoors.

A Safe and Challenging Environment

First and foremost, teachers ensure the safety of the children. To maintain a safe physical environment, they see to it that materials and equipment are in usable condition and that overall traffic patterns are free of hazards. For example, to make a gymnastic activity safe, teachers would provide mats and make sure that only one child is tumbling at a time.

Psychological safety requires an even finer sensitivity on the part of the teaching staff. Fear is a learned response, and teachers must be careful not to discourage children from using their full range of abilities, creating overly anxious and fearful children. The new teacher is often concerned about children's safety, particularly when they are climbing. It helps to remember that children generally climb to heights that are comfortable for them; in other words, they set their own limits.

Picking children up and placing them on equipment, often at their own request, is questionable. If teachers comply with children's wishes to be lifted and set somewhere high, they are placing those children in situations outside of their natural limits. The children may see this as saying, "You are incapable of climbing up there yourself," or "It is too dangerous for you to try that alone." Also, this does not allow children to gain experience in basic skills first, but puts them in a situation that calls for skills more complex than they have at the time. This denies the child the opportunity to practice those skills and increase their capabilities. When they must seek solutions to getting up, out, in, or down, they learn to handle realistically their current level of physical and motor development. Teachers lend encouragement and confidence to children by saying, "I cannot put you up there, but I will help you try." Making playgrounds safe is a good way to promote physical growth and sets the stage for learning through motor development as shown in Figure 11-6.

Playground Enrichment

The playground is the natural arena for optimal physical development and the ideal environment to promote physical fitness. On the playground, all motor skills are called into play. Outdoor activities should challenge children to use a wide range of motor skills and provide for a wide range of differences among their abilities:

Carmine grabs a scarf and begins to dance, *twirling* and *whirling, hopping* and *bending* in time to the mu-

Making Playgrounds Safe

Safety in the yard means:
- Enough room for the number and age of children who will use it.
- Adequate empty space.
- Availability of both hard and soft surfaces.
- Soft surfaces under any equipment from which a child might fall.
- Shady areas alternating with sunny spots.
- No standing water—good drainage.
- No poisonous or thorny plants, or litter or debris.
- Areas of play clearly defined and differentiated from one another.
- Sand area protected at night from animals.
- Fences high enough and in good repair.
- Gates secure with latches out of children's reach.

Equipment is:
- Well maintained—no exposed nails, screws, sharp edges, chipped paint.
- Chosen with children's ages in mind in regard to height and complexity.
- Stable and securely anchored.
- Repaired immediately or removed if damaged.
- Varied to allow for wide range of skills.

- Not crowded.
- Smooth where children's hands are likely to be placed.
- Checked frequently.
- Placed appropriately: sides facing north, swings away from other structures and busy areas.
- Scaled to age level: steps and other openings are 4 inches or less apart or 8 to 10 inches apart.
- Modified for age levels: swings have soft seats.

Teachers:
- Reinforce safe practices.
- Wear appropriate outdoor clothing.
- Check frequently where children are playing.
- Involve children in safety checks of yard, equipment, and grounds.
- Provide continual, adequate supervision.
- Avoid congregating to talk.
- Get involved with children.
- Provide enough activities and challenges.
- Watch for sun exposure, especially with toddlers.
- Assist children when they want to rearrange movable equipment.

FIGURE 11-6 Before children are allowed to use a playground, teachers should use a checklist such as this to ensure that safety standards are met. A safe playground stimulates physical development, social interaction, and full exploration of the materials and environment.

sic. Following the teacher's lead, Carmine *balances* on his toes and *waves* his scarf high over his head. Tina *walks* to the climber, *grasps* the highest rung she can reach, *pulls* herself up by *lifting* one leg and then the other until she *stretches* vertically full-length along the climber bars. Satisfied, she *pushes* off with her feet and *jumps* backward to the ground. She *bends* her knees as she lands, *balances* herself to an upright position, and *runs* off.

Ramon *toddles* over to *pick up* the large red ball. Momentarily overwhelmed by its size, he *falls* backward to *sit on* the grass. As a teacher approaches him, he *rolls the* ball toward her. She *throws* it back to him and Ramon imitates her movements. Soon they are involved in *kicking* and *tossing* the ball to each other.

Using both small and large muscles, children gain control over their bodies as they run and play. The play-

ground provides open space where full-bodied action takes place, providing many opportunities to develop balance and coordination.

Physical skills, however, are not the only benefit of outdoor play. Social and cognitive skills are enhanced as well. On the playground, children must negotiate turns with the wagons, ask for a push on the swing, and wait in line going up the slide. Some of the most intricate and involved dramatic play takes place outdoors. Problems get solved when two tricycles collide. Science experiences are all around—finding a bird's nest or planting a garden. "There are indeed advantages of the outdoors that cannot readily be provided indoors" (Frost, et al, 2008).

On the playground, no one says "Be quiet!" or "Quit wriggling!" It is a place of motion and space, filled with the special sensations found only outdoors.

When creating and maintaining a challenging environment, teachers consider both variety and level of

Playground equipment should be challenging, and it should provide a variety of movement experiences and a significant amount of physical activity.

challenge. A choice of surfaces encourages a variety of movements, and while cement may be appropriate for transportation toys, tanbark and rubber mats are better for climbing, hanging, and dropping.

Varying the equipment also stimulates motor activity. Equipment that is mobile allows for greater range of uses and allows children to manipulate their own environment. By creating their own physical challenges with wooden crates, children make platforms, caves, and houses to crawl in, over, and through. Another way to provide variety is to focus on the less developed skills, such as catching and throwing, rolling, latching, snapping, or zipping.

When children are encouraged to discover their own physical potential, they learn to solve problems of movement defined by the limits of their own abilities rather than by performance. This kind of learning encourages self-confidence as children find success through their own challenges.

A Child's Self-Concept

The image of physical self is an important part of self-concept. How people feel about themselves is rooted in the way they feel about their bodies and what they can or cannot do with them. Attitudes about the body and its abilities directly affect the types of activities children will try. Studies show that skill in games appears to be tied to peer group acceptance (Gallahue, 2003). Psychologists and teachers often notice a link between learning problems and clumsiness. Skilled early childhood educators carefully observe children, document their observations, and make referrals if a child needs an individual assessment.

Physical activity, then, contributes to a child's self-concept. With practice comes a sense of competence. Children can learn to relax as they gain experience in physical activities, and thus reduce the stress of anticipating failure. Competence breeds self-confidence and a willingness to try greater challenges. As children try new activities, they learn more about themselves. And physical activity increases awareness of what fun it is to move—to run through a field or pump a swing just for the sheer joy of it!

Teachers support positive self-concept through physical and motor development in several ways. They let children discover their own physical limits, rather than warning or stopping them from trying out an activity for themselves:

- *"I'm stuck!"* A child shouts across the yard. Rather than rushing to lift the child down, the teacher walks over to the child and replies, "Where can you put your foot next?" "How can you find a way to get across that branch?"
- *"I'm afraid!"* The teacher stands close to the child who is climbing and responds to the fear. "I will stand close to the climbing ropes so you will feel safe."
- *"Look what I can do!"* Teachers reinforce children who try something new. "Greg, it's good to see you cutting out that pumpkin all by yourself."
- *"I tried."* Teachers congratulate efforts for the achievement they really are. "Your hands reached the top this time, Shannon. I bet you are feeling proud of yourself."
- *"I can't do it."* Children who stand on the side lines observing others may need some encouragement from the teacher to take the first step in mastering the climbing frame or slide. "Here is a good place for you to put your foot, Arturo. I will hold on to your hand until you ask me to let go."

It is often not so much what teachers say to children that influences their feelings about themselves as it is the way in which children are treated. Children value them-

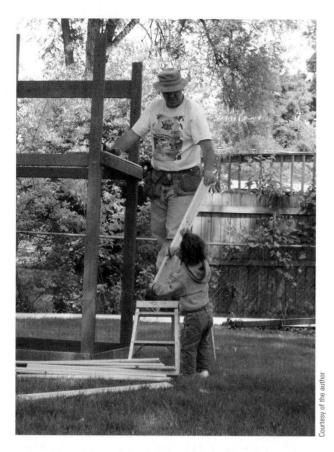

Courtesy of the author

Adults support children's self-confidence when they let them help with physical work and activity.

selves to the degree they are valued by others. The ways in which teachers show how they feel about children actually builds their self-confidence and sense of self-worth. Children create a picture of themselves from the words, attitudes, body language, and judgment of those around them.

Games that promote competition may affect a child's self-concept. Rae Pica's **"Insights from the Field"** article at the end of the chapter raises questions about the use of competitive rather than cooperative games with young children.

Encouraging Physical Play

The vital role of physical activity is best fulfilled when teachers:

- Create time in the daily schedule for periods of physical activity, preferably, but not limited to, outdoors.
- Actively participate while supervising and encouraging all children to become involved in strenuous activity.

- Set goals for children's motor development and physical fitness.
- Use a variety of activities on a daily basis, including science, art, and music, to stimulate physical development.
- Select age-appropriate equipment and materials, providing a variety of props to enhance their use.
- Give children opportunities to repeat, practice, and refine the skills they learn.

When children develop their physical and motor skills under this kind of encouragement, their confidence and sense of competence grow. This sense of personal worth is at the core of their being.

Observing children while they play outdoors allows teachers an opportunity to assess potential problems in motor development. The checklist in Figure 11-7 indicates some areas to observe.

Curriculum Planning for Physical/Motor Development

Teachers plan activities that promote physical/motor skills in the areas of gross-motor, fine-motor, and perceptual-motor development. They look at the envi-

Check Whether Child

- ❑ 1. Has trouble holding or maintaining balance
- ❑ 2. Appears to have difficulty balancing and moves awkwardly
- ❑ 3. Cannot carry self well in motion
- ❑ 4. Appears generally awkward in activities requiring coordination
- ❑ 5. Has difficulty making changes in movement
- ❑ 6. Has difficulty performing combinations of simple movements
- ❑ 7. Has difficulty in gauging space with respect to own body; bumps and collides with objects and other children
- ❑ 8. Tends to fall often
- ❑ 9. Has poor eye–hand coordination
- ❑ 10. Has difficulty handling the simple tools of physical activity (beanbags, balls, other objects that require visual–motor coordination

FIGURE 11-7 A checklist of possible problems in physical/motor development serves as a guideline when devising a developmentally specific profile for spotting problems.

ronment, both indoors and out, to see that all three areas of physical growth are encouraged.

In the Classroom Setting

When thinking of physical/motor development in the classroom, teachers tend to focus on the fine-motor (or small-muscle) tasks for the classroom and on gross-motor (or large-muscle) tasks for the outdoor play space. The indoor area lends itself more readily to activities with less movement, and the outdoor area encourages whole-body play. Yet children can have a wider variety of activities if teachers remember that both gross-motor and fine-motor projects can happen everywhere in the environment.

DAP

Indoor Areas. Indoors, the art area is stocked with pens, crayons, scissors, and hole punches that develop the fine-motor skills:

1. Add large brushes or rollers to the easel, or plan finger painting, and the art area now includes gross-motor development.
2. When children use templates to trace both inside and outside spaces, they practice perceptual-motor skill.
3. In the science area, getting "just a pinch" of fish food is a fine-motor activity; cleaning out the turtle house requires larger muscles to move rocks and sand.
4. Perceptual-motor development occurs as children use pitchers to fill the fish tank or turtle tub and learn about water levels.
5. At the manipulative table, when a child puts a peg into a pegboard, fine-motor skills are used.
6. Removing puzzles from a shelf and carrying them to a table brings in gross-motor skills. Add nuts and bolts, and the child's perceptual-motor skills are called into play.
7. The block area has endless possibilities, from lifting and carrying (gross-motor), to balancing and stacking (fine-motor), to building a space so that an animal or car will fit through (perceptual-motor).
8. The language and library areas are places for turning pages or looking at words and pictures (fine-motor). They also involve taking books off shelves and replacing them and trying out the movements and activities read about in books. For instance, Tana Hoban's *Is It Hard? Is It Easy?* encourages

children to act out the scenes pictured in the story, all gross-motor tasks. With a listening post nearby, children listen for the "beep" and coordinate what they hear (perceptual) with turning the pages (motor).

Outdoor Areas. Outdoors, children develop motor skills of all kinds.

1. In the sand, children dig, a gross-motor activity. As they judge how big a hole is, or how much water will fill it, they are practicing and improving their perceptual-motor skills. Turning on a faucet, planting seeds, and making mud pies are for fine-motor development.
2. Wheel toys offer children opportunities in all motor areas.
3. Pushing someone in a wagon develops arm and leg strength—gross-motor development.
4. Guiding tricycles and carts on a path and around obstacles requires perceptual-motor skill.
5. Trying to "repair" or "paint" a wheel toy with tools or with large brushes, tying wagons together, or weaving streamers through the spokes of a bicycle all use fine-motor skills.

By looking at the classroom and yard with one eye to physical and motor development, teachers can plan activities that support growth in all skill areas.

The outdoor area has great potential for developing gross-motor skills (climbing, bending, sliding), fine-motor skills (grasping, reaching, holding), and perceptual-motor skills (eye–hand coordination, directionality, tempo).

Transitions and Group Times. Every part of the daily schedule can be planned to use all physical/motor skills. For instance:

1. Getting in and out of coats and snowsuits is a large muscle activity. Children learn perceptual-motor skills as they try to get their arms in the correct sleeves.
2. Buttoning, zipping, and tying are fine-motor activities.
3. As children get ready for group time, often a difficult transition, they might practice drawing faces in the air or making their bodies into the shapes of letters, both perceptual-motor tasks.
4. Group times also include activities for motor development, such as stretching, dancing, jumping, as well as working puzzles, pounding clay, and writing stories.
5. When there are balloons, scarves, or a parachute at music time, children practice gross-motor skills.
6. Finger plays at group time are a fine-motor task. Activities for developing the senses of hearing and sight are two areas of sensory growth that can be utilized as content for group times.

Focus on Skills

The physical/motor skills include those that use large and small muscles and that coordinate perception and motor response. Teachers planning activities for children can focus on any one of these as a basis for curriculum planning.

Eye-Hand Coordination. Developing stitchery skills uses the perceptual-motor skill of *eye–hand coordination*. A series of activities can be planned to help children learn these skills.

1. It begins in infancy, when the baby first begins to manipulate and examine an object, learns to grasp with thumb and forefinger (pincer grasp), and shows a hand preference.
2. Stringing large wooden beads is a first step and leads to using pieces of straw and punched paper, with somewhat smaller holes. Macaroni can be strung on shoelaces or on stiff string, and then onto yarn, which is softer and more challenging.
3. Sewing cards made by punching holes in polystyrene trays can be introduced as the next activity. Large, plastic needles can be used with the lacing cards or with the trays; large embroidery needles with big eyes can be used for stitching yarn onto burlap.
4. Children may be ready to use embroidery hoops with which they can make a design on burlap first

and then stitch over the outlines. Buttons can be sewn on burlap or other fabric. Popcorn or packing material can be strung using a needle.

5. A final project might be to make a group wall hanging, with squares of children's stitchery sewn together. Simple backpacks and coin purses might be made with the children sewing most of it themselves.

Walking on a Balance Beam. Look again at Kareena's story on page 376 for the process teachers use to help Kareena and others with a wide variety of capabilities learn how to use a balance beam.

Figure 11-4 on page 380 lists age-appropriate equipment that fosters the development of motor skills.

Use of Themes

When teachers plan activities, they often have a theme or unit as their focus. Themes can be used to encourage physical and motor involvement. A unit of "Outer Space" involves ample opportunity to involve all the motor skills.

- Gross-motor skills are used in jumping around on the moon, taking a space walk, getting in and out of the rocket ship, and building a spaceship with large blocks.
- Fine-motor skills are needed to manipulate knobs on the instrument panel, to draw maps of the stars, or to write out a countdown on a chalkboard.
- Perceptual-motor skills are needed to work out how to get ready for a trip to Mars, what happens on the trip, and when and how to get back to Earth.
- Use the sample forms in Chapter 10 to develop an outer space unit as well as other appropriate themes to encourage motor skills.

Once teachers realize which physical/motor skills the children possess and what the group is ready to learn, they can plan activities around a classroom unit.

Parents can be a good source of ideas for ensuring that themes and activities reflect the various cultures within the classroom. Figure 11-8 lists many activities that are culturally related.

Curriculum planning for motor and movement skills requires teachers to know principles of physical growth and motor development. They then can use this knowledge to plan activities that encourage children to master their own movements and to learn other skills through movement. In the early childhood setting, curriculum can be planned by concentrating on activity areas, focusing on a specific motor skill, or using a classroom theme.

Appreciating Cultural Diversity through Motor Development

For Indoor and Outdoor Play

Activity	Motor Skill Practice	Culture
Lion or dragon dance	Gross-motor	Chinese (New Year)
Making and flying carp kites	Fine- and gross-motor	Japanese
Dodgeball	Gross-motor	Euro-American
Chinese jump rope	Gross-motor	Chinese
Breaking the piñata	Gross-motor	Latino
Spinning like a dreidel	Gross-motor	Jewish (Hannukah)
Origami art	Fine-motor	Japanese

Activity	Motor Skill Practice	Culture
Weaving	Fine-motor	Native American
Country/Western dance step	Gross-motor	Euro-American
Make mariachi instruments	Fine-motor	Latino
Dancing to mariachi band music	Gross-motor	Latino
Hokey pokey	Gross-motor	Euro-American
Make and twirl a grager	Fine-motor	Jewish (Purim)
Cooking; stir-fry rice	Fine-motor	Chinese
Making fry bread	Fine-motor	Native American
Kick the can	Gross-motor	Euro-American
Making and beating drums	Fine-motor	Native American

FIGURE 11-8 A variety of activities that reflect many cultures can be integrated into the curriculum for motor and physical development. **Note:** These activities are, at best, an approximation of traditional cultural expressions and not authentic presentations, yet they can enlarge the child's world view through physical play.

Insights *from the field*

Is Competition Developmentally Appropriate? *By Rae Pica*

The subject of competition is one that provokes some pretty strong feelings in the United States. The prevailing belief is that competition is good for us and that being competitive is human nature. But is it human nature or is it learned behavior?

The research shows that, given a choice, most preschoolers prefer cooperative to competitive activities. This would seem to indicate that competitive behavior is not a natural inclination. Also, in a *New York Times* essay, Nicholas Kristof told a hilarious story about trying to teach the traditional game of musical chairs to a group of 5-year-old Japanese children who kept politely stepping out of the way so their peers could sit in the chairs! This would seem to indicate that competitive behavior is taught in some societies—and not taught in others.

It's no wonder the research has determined that competition fosters such antisocial behaviors as aggression and cheating. In case you don't recall from your own childhood (or you were always the one winner among many losers), being eliminated feels terrible, as does feeling like a loser. And those other kids you're playing with? For the duration of the game, they're not your friends; they're what are standing in your way. Children only have to play an elimination game once to know that, if they're not going to be labeled losers, they have to do whatever it takes to win. And we've all seen what that can mean: punching, poking, kicking, scratching, screaming, and shoving.

When the important adults in their lives consistently place children in situations where winning is the ultimate goal—where the winners are considered heroes and the losers "losers"—winning is what children come to value. They learn that only the end result (the product) counts—not enjoyment of the game (the process). This, in turn, places more emphasis on extrinsic, rather than intrinsic, reward. Yes, winning feels good when everyone around you is making a big deal out of it. But does that feeling last? What happens when the possibility of being "number one" becomes the only reason for doing something? And what about the children who aren't winning?

Consistently playing cooperative, rather than competitive, games with the children lets them know you value the process. It lets them know you value collaboration. Moreover, when children participate in games like Footsie Rolls (which requires partners to perform log rolls with the soles of their feet together) or Body Balance (which requires a group to work together to maintain a steady balance through a series of challenges), they come to realize how good it feels to work and be together. In place of the punching, poking, and kicking, there is problem solving, encouragement, and a whole lot of laughter. As a result, they want to experience more of it!

Musical chairs actually has a great deal to offer children—in all three developmental domains—but only when the children have the opportunity to continue playing! With a simple modification—challenging the players to find a way to *share* the remaining chairs—the children develop listening skills, learn to discriminate between sound and silence, and learn to solve problems (the cognitive domain). Because no one is eliminated, they experience feelings of belonging. They're also developing their cooperative skills (the social/emotional domain). And the activity gives them a chance to get their blood flowing, while also offering practice with stopping and starting (the physical domain).

Dare I say it? Winning isn't everything—particularly in early childhood. Because I consider it more important for children to grow up to be self-assured, character-driven adults—who also happen to have positive feelings about physical activity—I prefer that the children participate in games and activities without competition, elimination, or humiliation.

I believe that, because we've been entrusted with the education of the whole child, we should regard the activities we present in light of what they offer children cognitively, socially, emotionally, and physically. I believe we should select games and physical activities just as we select the other parts of the curriculum—based on whether they are developmentally appropriate.

Rae Pica is a children's movement consultant and the author of 15 books, including *Experiences in Movement, Moving & Learning across the Curriculum,* and *Great Games for Young Children.* For more ideas and activities, visit www.movingandlearning.com.

SUMMARY

Children are in motion virtually from conception and develop their abilities to move their bodies as they grow. Young children spend most of the day in physical activity; therefore, the development of physical and motor skills must take a high priority in early childhood programs. Physical growth, which pertains to the body, is for teachers an issue of fitness and health. They need to have an overview of growth to help children develop functional and flexible bodies. Motor development means learning to move with control and efficiency. Development involves maturation and experience. Teachers must know the sequence of development and what part they play in providing physical and motor experiences for the young child.

Muscular development can be categorized as gross-motor, fine-motor, and perceptual-motor. Gross-motor movements use the entire body or large parts of it, such as the legs for running or the arms and torso for throwing. Fine-motor movements, such as manipulating objects, are those that use smaller muscles and that require precision and dexterity. Perceptual-motor movements are those that combine what is perceived with a body movement. Spatial, temporal, and sensory awareness all play an important part in the development of perceptual-motor skills.

In the early childhood years, children need exposure to many motor activities. They need a chance to practice, to get feedback, and to have a broad range of experiences of variety and challenge. Because children acquire motor skills through short- and long-term memory, rehearsal plays an important role as well.

When planning curriculum, teachers must have an awareness of sex-role stereotyping and must consider safety as well as challenge. A child's self-concept is linked with the concept of physical self and skill, so teachers must keep in mind which behaviors should be encouraged and which behaviors may indicate potential problems. As they plan activities for children, teachers use classroom and yard areas, focus on a specific skill, or use a theme to develop curriculum for physical/motor skills.

KEY TERMS

gross motor	spatial	intrinsic
fine motor	temporal	extrinsic
perceptual-motor development	sensory	sex-role stereotyping

REVIEW QUESTIONS

1. What factors influence motor development in young children?

2. What physical/motor skills are appropriate for young children to develop?

3. How can the teacher of young children support motor development in classroom areas?

4. How can the teacher support acquisition of specific motor skills in young children with special needs?

5. Have you observed gender differences in the physical development of young children? If so, what implications are there for teachers planning motor activities?

6. How would you explain the importance of outdoor play to a parent?

LEARNING ACTIVITIES

1. Map the classroom in which you are currently working. List at least one activity in each area that develops physical motor skills. Add one more activity of your own that widens such development.

2. In what ways does a school program you know reinforce sex-role stereotyping in motor activities? What could be done to change this?

3. Try to develop the theme of "at the beach" or "camping" in your setting in such a way that physical/motor skills are used. Be sure to include gross-motor, fine-motor, and perceptual-motor activities. List at least six other themes around which you could build a similar curriculum.

HELPFUL WEBSITES

American Academy of Pediatrics   **http://aappolicy.aappublications.org/**

National Program for Playground Safety   **http://www.uni.edu/playground**

National Association for Sports & Physical Education   **http://www.aahperd.org/naspe**

 Additional resources including the TeachSource Videos can be found on the premium website for this book. Go to **http://www.cengage.com/login** to register your access code.

REFERENCES

Allen, K. E., & Marotz, L. (2003). *Development profiles: Rebirth through 8.* Clifton Park, NY: Thomson Delmar Learning.

American Academy of Pediatrics Policy Statement (2003, August). *Pediatrics Vol. 112, No. 2,* 240–243.

Bee, H., & Boyd, D. (2009). *The developing child.* Menlo Park, CA: Addison-Wesley.

Bennenson, J. F. (1993). Greater preference among females than males for dyadic interaction in early childhood. *Child Development, 64,* 544–555.

Berger, K. S. (2006). *The developing person.* New York: Worth Publishers.

Berk, L. E. (2002). *Infants and children.* Boston: Allyn & Bacon.

COPEC (Council on Physical Education for Children). (2000). *Appropriate practices in movement programs for young children ages 3–5: A position statement of the National Association for Sport and Physical Education.* Reston, VA: NASPE.

Frost, J. L., Wortham, S. C., & Reifel, S. (2008). *Play and child development.* Upper Saddle River, NJ: Pearson Education, Inc.

Gallahue, D. L. (2003). *Developmental physical education for today's children.* Madison, WI: Brown and Benchmark.

Greenman, J. (2000). Guest editorial: Places for childhoods. In A. M. Gordon & K. W. Browne, *Beginnings and beyond: Foundations in early childhood education.* Clifton Park, NY: Thomson Delmar Learning.

Huston, A. C. (1993). Sex typing. In E. M. Heatherington (Ed.), *Handbook of child psychology* (Vol. 4, 387–467, Socialization, personality, and social development). New York: Wiley.

Jensen, E. (1998). *Teaching with the brain in mind.* Alexandria, VA: Association for Supervision and Curriculum Development.

Maccoby, E. E., & Jacklin, C. N. (1987). Gender segregation in childhood. In E. H. Reese (Ed.), *Advances in child development and behavior* (Vol. 20, 239–287). New York: Academic Press.

National Center for Health Statistics. (2006). *Prevalence of overweight among children and adolescents: United States, 2003-2004.* Hyattsville, MD: U. S. Department of Health and Human Services, Centers for Disease Control and Prevention.

New City School, Inc. (1994). *Celebrating multiple intelligences: Teaching for success.* St. Louis, MO.

Pica, R. (2004). *Experiences in movement: Birth to age 8.* Clifton Park, NY: Thomson Delmar Learning.

Picariello, M. L., Greenberg, D. N., & Pillemer, D. B. (1990). Children's sex-related stereotyping of colors. *Child Development, 61,* 1453–1460.

Sanders, S. W. (2002). *Active for life: Developmentally appropriate movement programs for young children.* Washington, DC: National Association for the Education of Young Children.

Santrock, J. W. (2008). *Children.* Boston: McGraw-Hill.

Shore, R. (1997). *Rethinking the brain: New insights into early development.* New York: Families and Work Institute.

© Cengage Learning

Planning for the Mind: Cognitive Development

PREVIEW QUESTIONS

- What is cognition?
- What perspectives aid in understanding the development of cognition?
- What are the cognitive skills of early childhood?
- How can the teacher support cognitive development?
- How might computers be used with young children?

NAEYC CODE OF ETHICAL CONDUCT

These Core Values and sections from the NAEYC Code of Ethical Conduct are addressed in this chapter. As you read, note how the Core Values, Ideals, or Principles listed here apply to the topics in this chapter. (Reprinted with permission from the National Association for the Education of Young Children.)

Core Values: We have committed ourselves to basing our work with children on knowledge of child development.

Section I:
Ethical Responsibilities to Children—Ideals and Principles:
I-1.5. To create and maintain safe and healthy settings that foster children's social, emotional, intellectual, and physical development and that respect their dignity and their contributions.
P-1.4. For every child we shall implement adaptations in teaching strategies, learning environment, and curricula, consult with the family, and seek recommendations from appropriate specialists to maximize the potential of the child to benefit from the program.

Learning through Cognitive Experiences

Ah, to be a child again! The world is a place of wonder and promise. There are worlds and people to discover, explore, and understand. Childhood is a time:

- *Of self* … a baby plays with his hands and feet for hours and rolls over just for the sake of doing it.
- *Of things everywhere* … a toddler invades the kitchen cabinets to see what treasures can be found.
- *Of people* … a preschooler learns the teachers' names and then makes a first "friend."
- *Of faraway places* … a kindergartner packs for the first "sleepover."

The amount of learning that takes place in early childhood is staggering. How do children manage to absorb the sheer quantity of information and experience they accumulate in their first few years of life?

Every child accompanies this mighty feat by thinking. Early theories about cognition were based on the idea that intelligence was a general capacity or potential that can be measured by standardized tests (such as IQ tests) and, therefore, that cognition could be developed by a specific, rather narrow, set of teaching techniques. During the last half of the 20th century, however, new ideas began to emerge. All of the recent theories revolve around the same fascinating question: What accounts for the remarkable changes in thinking, language, and problem solving in young children? The theories of Piaget and Vygotsky (see Chapter 4) have become an important part of early childhood educational philosophy. Recent research on the brain and information pro-

cessing and the theories of Gardner have broadened our notions of thinking and intelligence.

Cognition is the mental process or faculty that children use to acquire knowledge. To think is to be able to acquire and apply knowledge. By using conscious thought and memory, children think about themselves, the world, and others. Educating the thinking child is a critical function of parents and teachers. Curriculum in the early years must address the thinking, or cognitive, skills.

The relationship between cognition and language is important. Typically, we find out what children think by listening to them talk or asking them to tell us what they know. Cognition *can* occur without the language to express it. For example, an infant's laughter during a game of peek-a-boo indicates the child's knowledge that the hidden face will reappear. Conversely, the use of language can occur without cognition (i.e., without knowing the meaning). A child's counting from 1 to 20 ("…11, 13, 17, 19, 20!") is a case in point. At the same time, language and thought are intertwined. The growing child communicates through meaningful language. Children get their needs met better when they can name them. Their thoughts are expressed more clearly to adults when they are put in words, and feelings can be mediated through language. Cognition and language generally become more interdependent as development progresses. Children expand their knowledge base through language. They listen, question, tell. The child with good language skills can thus apply them to widen the horizons of knowledge.

Cognition is related not only to the developing mind but also to all areas of the child's growth. Young thinkers are at work no matter what they are doing. For example, physical/motor development is also a cognitive process. Learning to roller skate involves skinned knees and learning to balance (motor tasks), along with analyzing, predicting, generalizing, evaluating, and practicing the art of locomotion on wheels (cognitive skills). When trying to enter into group play (a social task), children will think of strategies for how to get started (cognitive skill).

This chapter explores in depth the framework for planning curriculum for the mind. Chapters 3 and 4 describe cognitive development in early childhood. This chapter applies cognitive development principles to curriculum planning by elaborating on the development of cognition in the early years, on the skills acquired by children from birth to age 8, on the role of the teacher, and on specific curriculum content.

For the purposes of clarity, cognition and language will be separated into two chapters. Both cognitive and language development are nurtured through a rich environment of meaningful print (see Chapter 13) and intel-

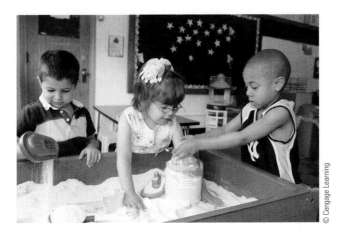

© Cengage Learning

As children investigate the world of people and places, they ask themselves and others what they want to know.

lectual content stimulated by curiosity and inquiry. Teachers must remember that these work together. Planned programs for early childhood will be more successful if that link is recognized.

The Development of Cognition: Multiple Perspectives

An Eclectic Point of View

In trying to enhance cognitive development, early childhood educators draw on developmental and learning theories and their direct experiences with children. By combining theoretical and practical viewpoints, teachers take a blended, or eclectic, perspective on the development of the thinking process. They work with children to encourage their ability to formulate ideas and to think rationally and logically. Regardless of theoretical viewpoint, the early childhood professional works toward helping children acquire skills that will lead to the development of:

Concepts: Labeling or naming an idea, moving from the specific to the abstract.

Example: "What is a grape?"

Relationships: What is the association between two or more things? How are they similar or different? What are their functions, characteristics?

"What colors of grapes are there?" "Do all of them have seeds?" "What sizes do you see? Taste alike?"

Generalizations: Drawing conclusions from concepts, grouping things and finding common elements.

"Are grapes a fruit or meat?" "How do grapes grow?"

The primary viewpoints that inform teachers in planning curriculum for cognitive development in early childhood are cognitive, multiple intelligences, sociocultural theories, and brain-based research.

A Piagetian Perspective

Developmental psychology, particularly through the works of Jean Piaget, has provided a deeper understanding of cognitive development. Piaget's view of cognition

is twofold. First, learning is a process of discovery, of finding out what one needs to know to solve a particular problem. Second, knowledge results from active thought, from making mental connections among objects, from constructing a meaningful reality for understanding.

For Piaget, knowledge is an interpretation of reality that the learner actively and internally constructs by interacting with it. Piaget divided knowledge into three types: physical, logical mathematical, and social.

1. *Physical knowledge* is what children learn through external sensory experiences. Watching leaves blow in the wind, grabbing a ball, and sniffing a fresh slice of bread are all instances of children learning about different physical objects and how they feel, taste, smell, move, and so on. The basic cognitive process involved in the development of physical knowledge is **discrimination.** For example, by touching magnets to paper clips, puzzles, and paper dolls, children learn firsthand about magnetism. They learn to discriminate between those objects that "stick" to the magnet and those that do not.

2. *Logical mathematical knowledge* derives from coordinating physical actions into some kind of order, or logic. This is not to be confused with formal mathematics; rather it is the kind of mathematical thinking children use in making connections about what they see, such as an infant's lifting the blanket to find a hidden toy. The logic of the young child is seen in the coordination of actions to make an **inference.** Think back to the magnets example. If a child deliberately takes a magnet to the metal drawer pulls and metal climbing bars, we can see the logical knowledge used: the child has made the inference that it is the metal things that "stick" on the magnet.

3. *Social knowledge* comes from our culture—the rules of the game, the right vocabulary, the moral codes. It includes learning vocabulary and being taught or told things, as well as knowledge about the social aspects of life. Value-laden and often arbitrary, it can rarely be constructed logically but is learned through life. With the aforementioned magnets, social knowledge would need to be used to decide who gets to play with the magnets, or when it is somebody else's turn.

In developing cognitive curriculum, teachers plan experiences that enhance those types of knowledge. They can teach using different forms of knowledge. **Rote knowledge** is information given with no particular meaning to the learner—that which could be learned meaningfully but is not. A teacher talking about magnets or telling children what attracts or repels gives children rote knowledge. **Meaningful knowledge** is what children learn gradually and within the context of what they already know and want to find out—like the example of letting the children handle the magnets themselves if they choose, and answering their questions as they arise. Both telling (rote) and asking or allowing (meaningful) can be useful; the question for the children is the balance between the two in everyday educational encounters.

As you may recall from Chapter 4, a special topic of Piaget's theory of cognitive development was constructivist theory. In applying this theory to curriculum, the constructivist classrooms likely look like this (adapted from Roberts & Spitz, 1998):

- *Choice.* It is crucial to practice life in a democracy and to learn to evaluate choices and decisions from a variety of materials or activities, so children can focus on formulating their own real questions and learn how to find genuine answers.
- *Play.* Through play experiences, children will develop their own thinking because it will allow for self-selection and create situations in which children must exchange views and solve problems.
- *Materials and Activities.* Concepts will be developed through interactions and experimentation with real objects, materials, and people and thus will need an environment that provides materials both appropriate and interesting as well as many activities that stimulate interaction with peers.
- *Time.* Each day will allow long blocks of uninterrupted time for child-initiated activities.
- *Teacher.* The teacher's role is to facilitate and to impart information and social knowledge, along with providing an emotionally safe and intellectually stimulating environment.
- *Curriculum Content.* The content arises from the issues of the students' real lives, their interests, family, and events so that learning is in the context of meaning for each child.

Vygotsky, Thinking, and Culture

Focusing on how our values and beliefs affect what we transmit to the next generation, Vygotsky's sociocultural theory (see Chapter 4) shows that much of children's development and knowledge is culturally specific. This understanding of the role of social interaction in thinking has spawned a new understanding of group differences and the role of social experience and language in shaping our human capabilities (Bowman,

2007; Rogoff, 2003). The most salient sources of knowledge are family members, the media, and school. The psychological tools children need to learn higher mental functions, such as symbolic thought, memory, attention, and reasoning, need the mediation of someone who knows the tools of that particular society. "With a growing population of people of color, speaking a variety of different languages, belonging to many religious groups and ethnic and national communities, the question is not can all children learn, but how to teach them" (Bowman, 2007).

Vygotsky adds an important element to our understanding of thinking. If knowledge is connected to what a culture values, then learning must be done in a collaborative style. Teachers and parents must have some agreement about what is important to teach children. The best way of teaching is a kind of assisted learning that allows for scaffolding, a natural learning technique known as *apprenticeship*. An older child or adult serves as a guide who is responsive to what the child is ready to learn. There are three implications of this theory for curriculum:

1. Mixed-age groupings so that young children can learn from older children and the more advanced ones have opportunities to help others. Indeed, the most effective strategy for preventing early reading failure is one-to-one tutoring.
2. Play is a valuable way for children to work with the symbols and other higher forms of thinking. With other people alongside, the child practices what is to be expected and valued in society.
3. The teacher can be both observer and participant. For instance, if a child builds with blocks, the adult might sketch the building and then encourage a joint effort to make a map or use measurement tools.

Gardner's Multiple Intelligences

Research into cognition documents that children possess different kinds of minds and therefore understand, learn, remember, and perform in different ways. Most experts agree that **intelligence** is complex and that traditional tests do not measure the entire host of skills or abilities involved.

"Gardner's theory is a dream come true for teachers," says Nelson (1995), "because it means many intelligences can be nurtured. And with that in mind, I [can] reinvent my curriculum and the way I teach it so that it meets the needs of a wider range." Multiple intelligences theory acknowledges that people learn and use knowledge in different ways. In practice, it is a systematic approach to basic skills. *Project Spectrum* was founded to develop an innovative approach to curriculum and assessment in the preschool and early primary years. "The work was based on the conviction that each child exhibits a distinctive profile of different abilities, or spectrum of intelligences. The power of these intelligences is not fixed, but can be enhanced by educational opportunity and an environment rich in stimulating materials and activities" (Chen, et al., 1998).

Because MI is neither a curriculum nor a model of pedagogy, there are many ways that the intelligences can be brought into the classroom. The overall framework involves four steps:

1. Introduce children to a range of learning areas
2. Identify each child's strengths
3. Nurture those strengths
4. Bridge their strengths to other subject areas

A relatively easy start is to create the various learning centers that correspond to the different intelligences:

> Students who need to learn counting, one-to-one correspondence, or math facts can do so, for example, through centers which tap into their spatial talents: students draw items—or group already-drawn images—to capture the math concepts. Students might go to a bodily-kinesthetic center to snap fingers or jump as they count by twos. Or perhaps students listen to music, clapping hands to catch the rhythm and beat of the numbers. (Hoerr, 2004)

This does not mean that teachers must develop every activity to all eight intelligences! Rather, teachers learn about each individual child and then tailor their curriculum to build on their children's strengths. Figure 12-1 gives examples of how an MI approach can build a bridge between children's curiosity and the school curriculum.

Brain-Based Research

"The human brain is the most fascinatingly organized three pounds of matter on this planet" (Schiller, 2008). The only unfinished organ at birth, it continues to grow throughout the life cycle. The principal task of the brain in early childhood is the connection of brain cells, as a child's brain is two-and-a-half times as active as an adult's. "Cognitive science unites psychology, computer science, and neuroscience to produce research and insights about the science of children's minds" (Gopnik, 1999). During the first three years of life, an infant's brain creates an estimated one trillion synapses. Providing quality experiences and relationships will create lasting effects on how the brain gets wired.

As noted in Chapter 4, a child is born with a billion cells (neurons) not yet connected in a meaningful way. Over the next few years, the brain forms trillions of networks (synapses), many more than a child will ever need.

The MI Approach: Sample Early Learning Activities

Learning Center	Sample Activity	Intelligence Area
Mechanics/construction	Making wire designs	Spatial
Science	Tools for biologists	Naturalistic
Music	Sound cylinders match-up	Musical
Movement	Statue game	Body-kinesthetic
Math	Weights and measures	Logical
Social understanding	Making silhouettes	Interpersonal
Language	"Reporting the news"	Linguistic
Visual arts	Making an art portfolio	Intrapersonal

FIGURE 12-1 Same activities from Project Spectrum (Chen, Isberg, & Krechevsky, 1998), based on a year-long research project aimed at improving performance of at-risk first graders in a Boston-area public school.

As they multiply and connect, a sophisticated network of neural pathways is created. Research on the brain development of young children (see Chapter 4) has important implications for curriculum. Indications are strong that children's brains need to be stimulated for the network of connections to grow and be protected from deletion. "Brain connections that have been reinforced by repeated experience tend to remain while those that are not are discarded" (Galinsky, 1997). We need to develop curriculum that brings children to interesting places and brings interesting things to children (see Figure 12-2).

In general, teachers of children can keep these ideas in mind:

- *Birth to age 4.* Provide for healthy sensory stimulation. This means all the senses need to be included in a child's exploration of the world. Very young children should live in an enriched environment—

visual, auditory, language, and so on, because "there are circuits that are responsible for emotional and social functioning (not just perception and motor action) that come 'on line' during the first years of life" (Siegel, 1999).

- *Age 4 to 8.* The brain is eagerly searching for stimulation; it is most flexible, or plastic, early in life to accommodate a wide range of environments and interactions, but its capacity for change decreases with age (NSC, 2008). Programs from preschool through fifth grade must be richly stimulating with activities that reward the brain's appetite for meaning. Give children plenty of opportunities to use stories, explore ideas, and master tasks rather than use worksheets or other repetitive tasks that kill enthusiasm for learning.

- *All ages.* Develop curriculum that provides for children's well-being. Emotions affect memory and

Brain-Based Research: Influences on Cognitive Curriculum

Brain Research Findings

The brain is strongly run by patterns rather than facts. Children learn best with curriculum developed around themes, integrated learning, and whole experiences. The key to our intelligence is the recognition of patterns and relationships.

Stress and threat affect the brain in many ways. Emotions run the brain, and bad emotions reduce the capacity for memory and understanding, as well as reducing higher-order thinking skills. Good emotions create excitement and love of learning.

The brain runs better when food intake is steady. Insulin levels stay more even, cortisol levels are lower, and glucose tolerance is better. Diet activates memory; children need diets rich in proteins (meats, nuts, cheese), omega-3 fatty acids, and selenium and boron (leafy green vegetables), as well as enough restful sleep so the brain can reorganize itself.

All learning is mind–body. A child's physical state, posture, and breathing affect learning. Our brain is designed for cycles and rhythms. Practice makes permanent, and memory is kept more accurate when information is revisited.

Curriculum Implications

Conclusion: Develop meaningful themes for activity planning. Uninteresting or abstract pieces of information (e.g., drilling young children on alphabet letters) will not provide understanding. Plan some kinds of "immersion experiences" that encourage children to go deeply into their play and work.

Conclusion: Make a positive, personal connection with each child, and avoid threats by loss of approval, hurried schedules, or implying children are helpless or bad. A secure environment counteracts the problems that may occur when the stress regulation mechanisms are triggered too often. Good emotions enhance memory.

Conclusion: Snacks are good! Regular snack times may lead to better cognitive functioning, *fewer* discipline problems, and an enhanced sense of well-being.

Conclusion: Keep track of and teach to children's bodily functions and body states and how long they are expected to sit or nap. Plan a daily schedule with both variety and balance, and work in regular routines and productive rituals.

FIGURE 12-2 Teachers must translate new findings into appropriate curriculum.

brain function. When a person feels content, the brain releases endorphins that enhance memory skills (Jensen, 2005) and undue stress short circuits these skills. Exercise and positive social contacts, such as hugging, music, and the supportive comments of friends create opportunities for collaboration and cooperation.

In summary, research from cognitive developmental psychology and brain research supports curriculum development that is engaging and that encourages exploration. The biological evidence strongly suggests that there are sequences in children's thinking, that there are at least multiple expressions of intelligence, and that the context of learning affects what children know.

Cognitive Skills

The actual skills children acquire as they learn to think are considerable. A basic skill is defined by two fundamental qualities:

- A skill is basic if it is **transcurricular:** that is, if the child can use it in a variety of situations and activities throughout the school day. For example, children who can express feelings and opinions clearly—who can let adults know when they are having difficulties with a particular task or social situation—have acquired a skill that is useful anywhere.
- A skill is also basic if it has **dynamic** consequences: that is, if it leads to other worthwhile responses. For instance, children who are articulate tend to elicit more verbal responses from adults. Consequently, they are exposed to more verbal stimulation, which in turn strengthens their verbal abilities, and so on. Thus, having this skill leads to major dynamic consequences in a favorable direction, whereas not having the skill leads to dynamic consequences in an unfavorable direction.

Most skills fall into the nine categories that follow. The list, though long, is comprehensive; what children learn in the thinking realm of their development will fall into one of these categories. The teacher plans activities for all cognitive skills to ensure challenging children's thinking.

Skills of Inquiry

Young children are curious, watching the world carefully. Through exploration and examination, they increase their attention span. Inquisitive children begin to organize what they see, analyzing and identifying confusions or obstacles for themselves. All the senses function at birth, and both *sensation* and *perception* are used to make sense of the world.

> Cognition is one step beyond perception. It occurs when a person actually thinks about what he or she has perceived. Thus, there is a sequence, from sensation to perception to cognition. A baby's sense organs must function if this chain of comprehension is to begin. No wonder the parts of the cortex dedicated to the senses develop rapidly: this is what allows all other developments to occur. (Berger, 2006)

Thus, the skills of inquiry include the development of *attention span* and *memory*. According to Chouinard (2007), children need to take an active role in questioning and information gathering. They cannot just sit passively while the adults do all the work; they remember information better when they are actively involved. The child asks questions, listens, gets ideas, and makes suggestions. They interpret what others communicate, seeking assistance from other people and materials.

Piaget called these skills of **inquiry;** several of Gardner's intelligences would also be included, as would Vygotsky's notion of cultural ways of learning. Organizing and finding patterns, reasoning, and problem solving are also inquiry skills. As children examine alternatives, they choose a course of action, revising their plans as needed. The National Education Standards of Kindergarten–Grade 4 have been translated into early childhood and concentrate on an inquiry-based approach. This means we develop this skill by helping children build on what they already know in order to construct new knowledge.

Young children thrill in making educated guesses, then checking their hypotheses by experimenting and taking risks. As Drew and others (2008) describe it:

> Constructive play involves building and making things no one has seen before. As young children fiddle with, sort, and arrange materials, ideas and imagination begin to flow. Questions arise naturally. They wonder: What will happen if I put this here? How tall will it go? Where did the bubble come from? In this way, constructive play serves to focus the minds of children through their fingertips and leads them to invent and discover new possibilities, to fulfill their sense of purpose.

These basic skills of inquiry are the foundation for thinking; as such, they are far more important to develop than are rote letter or numeral recognition.

Knowledge of the Physical World

How do children learn about the physical world? First, they use objects, spending plenty of time exploring, manipulating, choosing, and using toys and natural materials. Babies search for something to suck; they begin to grasp objects and let them go. Toddlers will pick up and throw things or drop objects from a highchair to see what happens. Children observe reactions, discover relationships, and try to predict what will happen. Six-year-olds with balloons and water explore how to fill, roll, throw, and burst the balloons. This knowledge is part of Gardner's logical mathematical intelligence, for knowledge of the physical world is essential to making order of it. We have learned that participation in an environment filled with interesting sights, sounds, and people enriches a child's schemes of thought and action (Lally, 1998).

As they learn the properties of objects, children gain a better understanding of the concept of cause and effect. Experience with the physical world gives children a base for comparing and contrasting, key skills for mathematical classification and scientific thinking.

Knowledge of the Social World

DAP Relationships are primary to development. Early experience significantly influences social and emotional brain function, and "toxic stress damages developing brain architecture, which can lead to life-long problems in learning, behavior, and physical and mental health" (NSC, 2008). Learning about others is hard work because the social world is not concrete and is often illogical. The child needs an awareness of self before developing an awareness of others and how to interact socially. To Gardner, this kind of knowledge requires both intrapersonal (access to one's own feelings and a range of emotions) and interpersonal (the ability to notice others, making distinctions among individuals, particularly their moods and motivations) intelligence. Attachment relationships are important in the unfolding of the emotional and social development of the child: "it is not a matter of overwhelming enrichment or excessive sensory stimulation that is needed during this time, but one of attunement between adult and child" (Siegel, 1999).

Infants begin by distinguishing friends from strangers. Toddlers learn to use "mine" and then to use others'

Being able to explore actual materials and objects encourages children to assimilate and use new knowledge.

names as well. The next step is to expand their knowledge of roles to include those of family, school, and the community. Four- and 5-year-olds are provided with daily opportunities to cooperate, to help, and to negotiate with others about their needs and wishes. According to Vygotsky, preschoolers learn appropriate actions by playing with older children. Also, make-believe is a major means through which children extend their cognitive skills.

In the best of circumstances, children are encouraged to notice both similarities and differences in people and then are led to develop tolerance for both. School-aged children seek small group teamwork and moments of private time with a close friend. In learning rules for social living, children learn appropriate conduct for various situations—indoors or out, happy or sad, at the grocery store or at the dinner table.

Classification

Knowledge of the physical world teaches children to have different responses to different objects. **Classification** is the ability to group like objects in sets by a specific characteristic. During their first year, infants use their senses to sort and classify their many experiences. As toddlers, they initially classify by sorting groups of completely different objects, using a logic that only the child understands. During the preschool years, they begin to sort objects using consistent criteria. Once they develop language proficiency, they can name and classify objects. Gradually, and with help from adults who stimulate describing and manipulating, they learn that objects have more than one attribute and can be classified in more than one class.

To clarify this process, consider how 2-year-old Tisa learns to classify:

> What can Tisa do to her stuffed bear and the family dog? What can she do with one and not the other? Which are her toys? Which are Rover's? Which ones have fur? What is different about them?

Tisa learns the attributes of the objects by exploring, learning the class names of "toy" and "pet." Tisa makes collections, sorting by similarity those that are Rover's toys and those that are her own. She uses class relationships to understand that both animals have fur, but she can tug on only one animal's ears without encountering a problem.

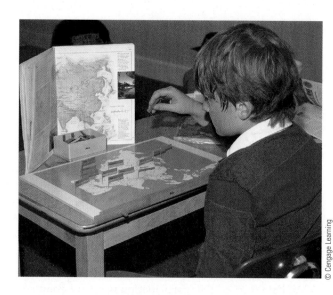

Cognition in action! The concepts of the world come to life through Montessori materials.

Seriation

Seriation is "the ability to put an object or group of objects in a logical series based on a property of those objects" (Geist, 2001). Many of the sensorial and practical life materials designed by Montessori were developed to make clear to children exactly what seriation is and how it can be learned. These toys distinguish grades of intensity by size, color, weight, number. Children build pyramid towers, fit nesting blocks together, and use the counting rods. By noting differences, often through trial and error, children learn seriation systematically. For instance, the pyramid tower is ordered from largest piece to smallest as it is built. Boxes are nested, one inside the other, by their graduated size or volume. The counting rods can be put into a staircase array, the units building on each other from one to 10. Children can arrange several things in order and fit one ordered set of objects to another. Gardner's category of musical intelligence requires seriation, as well as the skill of inquiry ("How do I make noise? Rhythm? Musical song?") and a knowledge of the social world ("How can we make music together? A real band?").

Numbers

Understanding the concept of number means learning about quantity: understanding amount, degree, and position. Mathematical knowledge is an emergent understanding of concepts. Once infants develop an understanding of object permanence (that an object exists

whether or not it can be seen), they are ready to learn about quantity. Toddlers compare objects, for example, by stacking rings on a stick, sorting by groups (large versus small, hard versus soft), and noticing what is "more."

Preschool children can learn songs, chants, and finger plays that include numbers ("One Potato, Two Potato" or "Five Speckled Frogs"). Once children comprehend numbers, they are ready to use mathematical terms and forms of expression. For instance, after singing about the frog that jumped into the pool in the song "Five Speckled Frogs," Chantel can begin to understand that four is "one less than" five.

But a knowledge of numbers is neither complete nor meaningful unless children have direct experience with materials and objects. "Quantification is the basis for formal mathematics, and is a synthesis of order, the basic understanding that objects are counted in a specific sequence and each object is counted only once" (Geist, 2001). Learning about quantity also means comparing amounts (as when children work with table toys, blocks, sensory materials, and the like) and arranging two sets of objects in one-to-one correspondence ("Each person needs one and only one napkin for snack, Tyler"). Children can also count objects and begin computation ("Parvin, you have three shovels. Here is one more; now how many do you have?"). As with language and prereading skills, children who grow up in poverty tend to enter school already lagging behind their middle class peers in key math knowledge, so teachers "can help build on their natural predisposition through instruction, games, and hands-on activities that focus on five major areas of mathematics: numbers and operation, algebra, geometry, measurement, and data analysis and collection" (Lense, 2008). The importance of math learning in the primary grades and children's potential to learn math have implications for teaching primary grade math. The early years are especially important for math development, as knowledge in math is predictive of both math achievement and later reading success as well (Sarama & Clements, 2009).

Symbols

A symbol stands for something else; it is not what it appears to be! Young children have to think hard and long to symbolize. It is a task of some skill to imitate or use one object to represent something else. They begin by using their bodies. Infants and toddlers love to play peek-a-boo, reacting to "Boo!" with full-bodied excitement. Pretend play is the hallmark of using symbols. Preschoolers revel in playing favorite characters. Primary school children make up plays and puppet shows.

Make-believe helps in the process of symbolizing, as does making sounds to represent objects ("Choo-choo" is a train, for example). Using and making two- and three-dimensional models are other ways children symbolize, when they transfer what they see to the easel or to the clay table. Children are also symbolizing when they dress up in costumes and uniforms. The Reggio Emilia approach (see Chapters 2, 9, and 10) encourages children to use a variety of media to express their thinking and deepen their understanding.

Teachers add to the symbolizing process when they use descriptive words. Description games encourage children to do the same. For example, "It is round and red and you eat it. What is it?" (An apple!) After all these skills have been mastered, children are ready for written symbols when they can use the written word to label, take dictation, or write notes. Using Gardner's and Vygotsky's ways of thinking, educational environments for school-age children might take the form of discovery centers, a kind of museum, in which apprentice groups with children of different ages would help children with numerical and computer skills (see "Computers in the Classroom" and "Insights from the Field" at the end of this chapter).

Spatial Relationships

Spatial relationships develop early. Infants visually track what they see, trying to reach and grasp. As they experience one object's position in relation to another, they begin to have a mental picture of spatial relationships. Toddlers find this out as they learn to steer themselves around tables and seat themselves on the potty. The concept of "close" (the chair) and "far away" (the quesadilla cooling on the counter) give clues to length and distance ("How far do I have to reach to get one?"). As spatial skills develop, children learn to fit things together and take them apart. They rearrange and shape objects. They observe and describe things from different spatial viewpoints. This perspective is learned only through experience. The child under age 5 needs to describe and then try out the notion that what one sees from the side of the hill is not what can be seen from the top.

Adults help children learn such skills by letting them locate things at home, in the classroom, in the department store. Cognitive theories of Piaget and Gardner suggest that body and kinesthetic knowledge are used in this type of activity. In Reggio Emilia, for instance, mirrors are placed around corners, found at the school entrance, and embedded in the floors, giving children a sense of self in space in a number of ways. Teachers encourage children to represent such spatial relationships in their drawings, with pictures, and in photographs.

When considering intellectual development, teachers should keep in mind that, to children, education is exploration. Let children use their imagination to use materials in new and different ways.

Time

Understanding time is a complicated affair because time is composed of at least three dimensions: time as the present, time as a continuum, and time as a sequence of events. Children must learn each of these to fully understand the concept of time. In some settings, children learn to stop and start an activity on a signal (when the teacher strikes a chord on the piano for clean-up time). They try to move their bodies at different speeds, indoors and out. Older children begin to observe that clocks and calendars are used to mark the passage of time. Specifically, children come to know the sequencing of events in time: which comes first, next, last. Having an order of events through a consistent daily schedule helps children learn this aspect of time. They also benefit from anticipating future events and making the appropriate preparations. Planning a course of action and completing that plan give meaning to the idea of time.

What children learn intellectually in the early years is massive in quantity and quality. Yet young children are ready—eager, in fact—to engage themselves with the world around them to acquire these cognitive skills. Figure 12-3 gives examples of activities that address the nine cognitive skills. By remaining aware of how much is to be learned, educators keep a realistic—and humble—appreciation for the "work" of children.

TeachSource Video ▶❙❙

Watch the TeachSource Video Case entitled "Communicating with Families: Best Practices in an Early Childhood Setting." After you study the video clip, view the artifacts, and read the teacher interviews and text, reflect upon the following questions:

1. How does preschool teacher Mona Sanon provide experiences with blocks to develop the nine cognitive skills?

2. How can children's thinking be developed at school and home through play, language, and sharing experiences?

Cognitive Skills into the Curriculum

Cognitive Skill	Sample Activity	Age
Inquiry: senses, perception, attention, memory	Playing with water: what can you find out?	Toddler, Preschool
Knowledge of the physical world	Take an outdoor sound walk	Toddler, Preschool
Knowledge of the social world	Make a Wheel of Feelings; read Aliki's *Feelings* book	Preschool, School-Age
Classification	Collections: put together, identify describe, and classify a nature collection	Preschool, School-Age
Seriation	Yeast grows: see which expands most, with flour, sugar, salt, juice	School-Age
Numbers	Play "fives" game with playing cards numbered 1–4	School-Age
Symbols	Making shapes: bodies and shape cards	Preschool, School-Age
Spatial relationships	Geoboards	Preschool, School-Age
Time	Play "Stop & Go" with music	Preschool, School-Age

▌ FIGURE 12-3 Every cognitive skill has a place in planning curriculum.

Role of the Teacher

Considerations

When considering children's intellectual development, teachers should keep the following in mind:

- *Education is exploration.* The process of education is more than its products. Teachers enhance learning by allowing children to interact with the environment. The teacher is a source of information and support rather than one who gives answers or commands. A project approach (see Chapter 10), based on the belief that children's minds should be engaged in ways that deepen their understanding of their own experiences and environment, may be used. Consisting of exploring a theme or topic (such as shadows, houses, building a table) over a period of weeks, this approach reflects Dewey's progressive education and the British Open Schools (see Chapter 1) and is implemented regularly in the Reggio Emilia schools. The goal is to have children ask their own questions and create their own challenges.
- *Children do not think like adults.* Children think and perceive in their own ways, as Piaget believed. They think in sensory and concrete terms and come to conclusions based on what they see and touch.
- *Children's thinking is legitimate and should be valued.* Their thought processes and perceptions are as valid as those of adults. Teachers support those processes by asking questions to stimulate further thought and by providing materials for exploration.
- *The language of the teacher should support cognitive development.* Throughout their interactions with children, teachers help children use words, terms, and concepts correctly:

> Mariko: (at water table): I need that suckup.
> Teacher: The baster really does suck up water, doesn't it?

- Their *questions* are open-ended to help children *think* and often leave the child with something to ponder:

> Teacher: I wonder why the turtle's head went back in its shell when you put your finger close?
> Teacher: If you want to play with José, how can you let him know?
> Teacher: What do we need from the woodworking shelf to make a spaceship?

What Do YOU Think?

"Back to basics" is a phrase commonly heard in conjunction with academic and cognitive curriculum. Its intention is to focus attention on what is fundamental to be learned, and often refers to intellectual skills. Fondly known as the 3Rs—reading, 'riting, and 'rithmetic—these skills are often taught by whole-group telling and by drill-and-skill repetition.

But what should early childhood professionals be doing? Surely, the 3Rs cannot be taught as such in programs for children under age 5, and a program of only direct instruction has been criticized by developmental advocates. How do we teach "before the basics"?

Bev Bos has been teaching and demonstrating just this notion for over 30 years. She suggests giving one's curriculum a "child-centeredness test." See how your cognitive curriculum holds up (Bos, 1983):

- Does this activity help the child's sense of identity?
- Is the activity open-ended—that is, can the child change this material?
- Does this activity allow the child to create?
- Does this activity provide a framework for the child to cooperate with others while retaining a sense of self?
- Is the activity fun? Will it inspire laughter and a love of learning?

The teacher must match the child's cognitive capacity with the instruction. Child-centered, self-initiated learning (see Chapter 10) is a great motivator, so observing children's intensity with materials and asking questions to extend their thinking is recommended. Use conversation, document children's thinking, use drawing, and incorporate problem solving.

The teacher must consider, include, and plan for children with learning disabilities and other varied learning "styles." Each type of learning disability (see Chapter 3) has its own description and treatment. Teachers must develop a wide range of techniques to address such disabilities. After the identification and assessment phases, teachers and families need to work with specialists and devise options (an individualized education plan, or IEP) that include the child and establish reasonable learning goals.

Figure 12-4 shows further how teachers' use of language helps children think and develop cognitive skills as part of their early childhood experience.

Teacher's Role in Developing Cognitive Skills

Skill	Teachers Can
Inquiry	• Ask questions so children make statements about their conversations. *Example:* "What do you notice about the guinea pig?" • Try to be more specific if such questions seem overwhelming or if they elicit little response. *Example:* "What sounds do you hear? What can you find out by touching her?" • Ask how children arrived at their answers. *Example:* "How did you know that the marble wouldn't roll up the ramp?"
Social knowledge	• Try not to respond to unstated needs. *Example:* "Do you want something? Can I help you?" • Help children define what they want or need, so that they learn how to ask for it. *Example:* Marie: "I wonder who is going to tie my shoes?" Teacher: "So do I. When you want someone to tie your shoe, you can say, 'Would you tie my shoe?'" Marie: "Would you tie my shoe?" Teacher: "I'd be glad to."
Classification	• Ask questions that will help children focus on objects and see differences and details. *Example:* While cooking, ask "Which things on the table do we put in the bowl?" "What are made of plastic?" "Which go in the oven?" "What on the table is used for measuring? How do you know?" "Now look carefully—what do you see on the measuring cup?" "What do those little red lines mean?"
Spatial relationships	• Ask for the precise location of an object the child asks for or is interested in: *Example:* "Where did you say you saw the bird's nest?" "You can find another stapler in the cabinet underneath the fish tank."
Concept of time	• Use accurate time sequences with children. *Example:* Teacher: "Just a minute." Milo: "Is this a real minute or a 'wait a minute'?" Teacher: "You're right. I'm with Phoebe now. I'll help you next."

FIGURE 12-4 Teachers' use of language affects how children develop cognitive skills. The more children are allowed and encouraged to think for themselves, the more their cognitive skills will develop.

Curriculum Planning for Cognitive Development

In the Early Childhood Setting

Teachers can plan cognitive curriculum for their children by considering the class setting, both indoors and out, throughout the daily schedule. Each activity center can be used to encourage intellectual development with a variety of curriculum materials and methods (see High/Scope in Chapter 2). The environment and methods required to help children think include challenging situations, enriching materials, and supportive adults. Most children under age 3 have a limited attention span and can be over stimulated unless the environment is kept simple. Three-to 5-year-olds can absorb more information and finer detail as they have more developed motor and perceptual skills. Older preschoolers and kindergartners learn best trying to solve real problems, and the child in primary school still benefits from discovery-oriented, "learn by doing" situations. Figure 12-5 shows how one activity (which can be done with nearly all ages) contributes to the development of children's thought processes.

Teachers can create what Jensen (1998) calls high activity, low stress, brain-compatible learning environments. An optimal environment will have several learning centers for the children to choose from so that the brain is stimulated to be attentive, to absorb new information, and to store this information in long-term memory. Teachers should aim to create a balance between meaningful experiences and optimal stimulation of the brain in their classrooms. "Such an environment offers children experiences with real-life, hands-on, theme-based activities oriented to solving problems, such as children counting out play money when shopping at the store in the dramatic play center" (Rushton, 2001).

Indoor Areas

The indoor environments described in Chapter 9 include the basic ingredients of a stimulating cognitive environment. The indoor areas might have some of the following materials and activities:

- *Art.* Include a "help yourself" shelf for child-chosen projects. A variety of paper, drawing implements, and tools encourages children to re-create their own reality, using representational art forms that show how children see the physical and social worlds.
- *Blocks.* Have paper models of each block shape on storage shelves to help children with classification by shape and size. Be sure you put a priority on having enough unit blocks (a 600+ piece set for a preschool class of 16) and provide enough space (40–80 square feet per group) with a firm carpet that supports balancing towers and controls noise. Accessories, such as animals and homemade trees and lakes, help children symbolize. As they experiment with blocks, they learn about physical laws and reality and have experiences in cooperative learning and living, all of which are cognitive tasks. Counting blocks, which builds on one-to-one correspondence rather than rote memorization, contributes to genuine understanding. Building structures with young children inspires them as young mathematicians and scientists (Chalufour & Worth, 2004).
- *Discovery/science.* Rotate a display of "touch me" materials. This gives children firsthand experience with plants, seeds, animals, magnets, sea shells, foods, and so on. Have a "Fix It" or "Take Apart Shop" with nonworking appliances and radios, equipped with plenty of screwdrivers, pliers, and containers for small parts. School-age children can find out which plants grow in saltwater or freshwater by setting up plants in each environment and watching daily ("Today something has changed!" wrote a 7-year-old. "The duckweed is not really green anymore. A second root is hanging"). If you can, have a computer available with developmentally appropriate software.
- *Dramatic play.* Stock this area with materials for role playing, puppet making, and acting out adult activities. Have anatomically correct boy and girl dolls of a variety of races and some with disabilities. Include clothing for all types of work, equipment for carrying things, and babies that reflect the homes of all the children in the group but also extend the play to include new ways of dressing, eating, and playing. When several pre-kindergarten children got haircuts, the class developed a "Hairy Heads" theme, transforming this area into a hair salon with brushes, barrettes, and wigs. The dolls got plenty of shampoos that month!
- *Language/library.* Choose books that focus on both the physical and social worlds. Children's interests in numbers, symbols, and time can also be extended by selecting literature that reflects their level of understanding. Look for the message in children's books and choose good stories that reflect diversity, such as *Helping Out* (Ancona) and *George the Babysitter* (Hughes). Be sure to listen to the group's interests, and make a point to place books that respond to those interests in the library.

Cooking as a Cognitive Activity

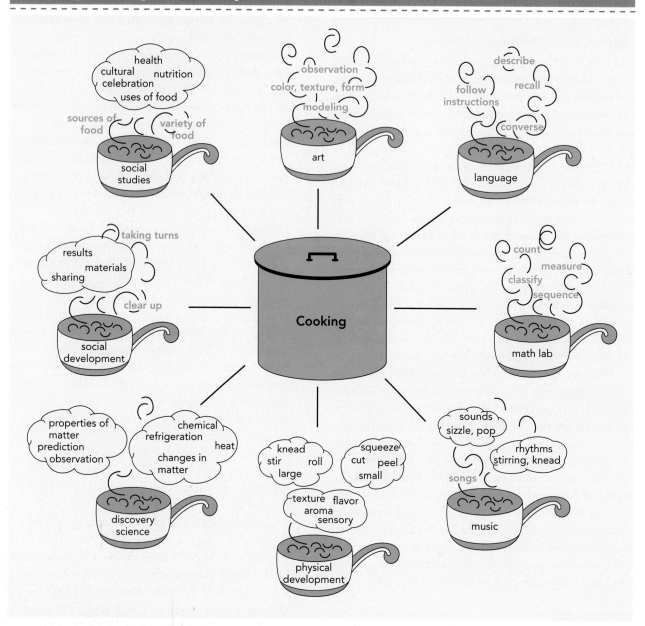

FIGURE 12-5 Each activity, such as cooking, can enhance cognitive development throughout the curriculum. A trip to the market can be an experience in classification and calculation.

■ *Manipulatives (table toys).* The manipulatives area is an ideal place for materials that encourage cognitive development; highlight this area with both favorites (Legos® or Crystal Climbers®) and new items (Construx® or sewing cards). Counting cubes aid in classification and seriation, whereas puzzles or nesting blocks focus on spatial relationships. Information processing theory emphasizes the importance of ex-

periences that develop children's working memory and familiarity. Manipulative materials and games give children hands-on experiences with counting, sorting, and organizing that are both meaningful and socially natural. Homemade lotto games or puzzles with the children's photos encourage self-esteem and group identity as well as cognitive and motor development.

Outdoor Areas

The outdoor area provides opportunities for children to plan and organize their own thoughts. Offer your yard as a place for discovery. "A kinder garden needn't be manicured or tamed. Shrubs and viney tangles are secret hideouts. Fallow beds are places where worms, roots, and rocks can be explored. Vegetables sometimes ignored at dinner are trailside snacks. Pests are pets" (Ross, 2000).

Toddlers can classify what they find as they look for balls, sand buckets, and toy trucks hidden around the yard. Preschoolers in the sand pit predict how water will affect the sand, using their growing knowledge of the physical world. Children learn to classify water table and wheel toys and learn seriation when they select sand buckets by size. Counting shovels to see that there are enough to go around, building with large, hollow blocks, and watching the seasonal changes are all cognitive skills children gain as they play outside.

Physical and logical mathematical activities are easily incorporated into the curriculum outdoors. Piaget's *methode clinique* (see Chapter 4) inspires experimenting and reasoning: "I wonder why?" or "What would happen if…?" are common teacher inquiries. The water table outdoors could have a large block of ice, a variety of materials such as wood, cotton balls, straws, and cardboard, or containers of colored water and eyedroppers. Balancing activities might mean hollow blocks, milk cartons, or beanbags (or all three). A hillside or long plank can become a site for predicting and trying out rolling, using different sizes of balls or even bodies.

Routines, Transitions, and Groups

Groups, transitions, and routines are more structured times and all play a part in developing children's knowledge of the social world. As children learn to conduct themselves in school, they learn:

- To enter a room and start to play (transition).
- To take care of their own belongings and those of their school (routines).
- To concentrate on an activity with others around (group times).
- To interact with others while at the same time paying attention to a leader or task (group times).
- To end an activity, an interaction, a school day (transition).

Teachers plan environments, activities, and grouping of children to give the class experience in all these cognitive challenges. Look back at Figures 9-15 and 9-16 about routines and transitions in a daily schedule. Teachers use signs, their own words, and helpful tips that illuminate for children what is happening, what is expected of them, and how they can express themselves in all three of these daily segments.

Moreover, many routine activities offer wonderful opportunities for cognitive learning. For example, consider the snack table. Incorporating math concepts into snack time will engender enthusiasm and skill development. Whether as a part of free choice time or a time period on its own, snack time becomes "think time" as children:

- Fill out and use menu cards.
- Learn the concept of sets ("*Everyone* needs five of *everything,* huh?").
- Work with the concept of uniform units ("Are the ham and cheese pieces the same?").
- Understand the concepts of equal, less, and more.
- Learn how to count "wet stuff" and to count by the spoonful or handful.
- See geometry and fractions at work (circles for raisins, triangles for sandwiches, "Break the graham cracker in pieces for everyone … fair!").

Focus on Skills

How can teachers help children develop specific cognitive skills? After observing the children carefully, teachers identify a particular skill and then list those processes, concepts, and vocabulary involved. For instance, the skill of inquiry can be encouraged in every part of the curriculum by asking questions. Teachers model curiosity by observing and asking questions about what they see and what children may be thinking. This stimulates children to look, wonder, and interact:

Teacher: I wonder which piece of wood you will choose to glue on your board next.

Teacher: What part do you want to play in our grocery store?

Teacher: How can we find out how long your road of blocks is?

Figure 12-6 offers key questions to ask children that stimulate their thinking.

The processes of mathematical literacy involve using representation, performing manipulations, making sense in math reasoning, and problem solving. For instance, help children as they use markers to "stand for" people or animals or dolls in place of real babies—this representational thinking is a hallmark of the preschool period, and fantasy play can help in mathematical thinking if the teacher makes children aware. Using manipulatives can

Questions to Help Children THINK

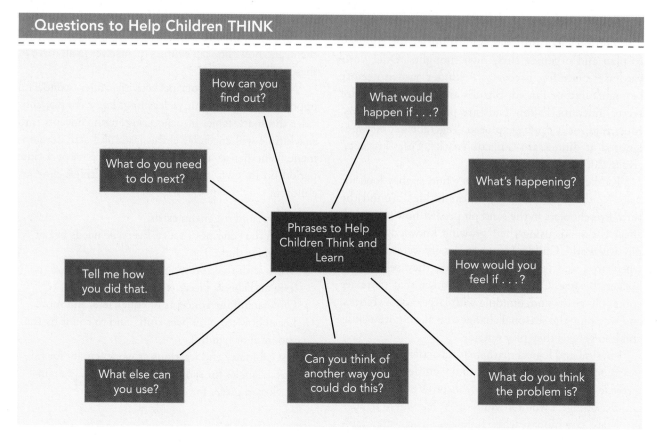

FIGURE 12-6 Teachers encourage children's thinking when they ask questions. Posted in the classroom or given to students and parents, this chart serves as a reminder that to TEACH is to ASK more often than to TELL.

help children add and subtract, and will make such operations understandable. Guessing games can be a fun way to elicit reasoning when the teacher asks "How did you know that?" once the child has made a guess. Remember that children have limited knowledge and need to be encouraged to keep guessing, while you stimulate them to offer, justify, and question their ideas. Developing math games based on children's literature (Cutler, et al, 2005) is an inviting way to provide math experiences, so try using Ormerod's *Joe Can Count* or McMillan's *Eating Fractions* with a small group and have circle time follow through.

Problem solving is mentioned often in early childhood education circles, in social and artistic contexts as well as for cognitive development. For this to be successful, two issues must be addressed: problem posing and making investigations (National Council of Teachers of Mathematics, 2000). Problem posing is difficult for many children, and they will need guidance so that the problem is clear before the group or individual launches

into looking for a solution. Investigations are "authentic problem solving situations in which children work as mathematicians and have opportunities to develop mathematical power" (Diezmann & Yelland, 2000). When children see that it is all right to ask "Why?" they feel encouraged to ask questions. Brainstorming is a technique that helps children get ideas and use resources to find out how many ways there are to make a kite or build a castle.

Outdoors, inquisitive children explore their environment. Children ask questions: "Can we turn on the water? What if we bury all the toy bears in the gravel? Could we use the ladder to see over the fence? Let's all hide from the teacher!" The way teachers handle inquiries from children about what they want to do sends a message that supports—or discourages—this cognitive skill. When there is no harm in asking (though the answer may be "No"), children are encouraged to develop further the skill of inquiry. Figure 12-7 illustrates exactly how the cognitive skills of reasoning and problem solv-

Problem Solving: An Intellectual Pursuit

The Concepts:
    Selecting a course of action
    Making educated guesses
    Making and revising a plan
    Risking and evaluating the results

The Vocabulary:
    Guess
    Plan
    Problem
    Solution/solve
    What? why? how?

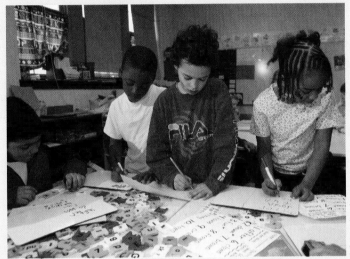

© Cengage Learning

The Process:

Activity area	Process question
Art	How many ways can you use the brush (pen, squirt bottle) to make a mark on the paper? Why is it dripping? How can you stop it when you're ready?
Bathrooms/cubbies	You found Paul's sweater. . . . How can you find where it goes? Where did the water come from? How can you clean it up?
Blocks	What makes the tower of blocks fall over? How can a block be used to connect two others?
Cooking	How do we mix these ingredients together? What will happen when it is put in the oven?
Discovery/science	Why did the magnet pick up the nail and not the pen? What is the difference between the rabbit and the guinea pig? How are they alike?
Dramatic play	Who will be the dad? What happens when these other children want to play? How can you get to wear the costume you want?
Language/library	What happens next in the story? Why do you think so? Why did the child feel unhappy at first? Then what happened?
Large group	Why can't you see/hear the leader? What can you do about feeling too crowded? What can you do when your friend keeps whispering to you during storytime?
Gross-motor	How do you jump rope? What do you use to pump yourself on a swing? How will you find a ball?
Manipulatives	How do you figure out what puzzle piece fits? Do you see a pattern on the peg board? What is it?
Sensory	How do you get the water from the large pitcher to the small cup? How will you get the wet sand through the funnel?

FIGURE 12-7 Problem solving is a cognitive skill that involves problem posing and making investigations.

ing could serve as the basis for curriculum development around the entire classroom.

Use of Themes

DAP   A specific theme can be chosen for cognitive development. Themes that bubble up from the children's interests will engage their thinking more than those imposed by the teachers. Units based on things in the physical world (season changes, pets, the garden), on unexpected or current events (a new load of sand, a community fair,

road work nearby), or on the special interests of the children (sharing the African masks, swimsuits, or dinosaurs) are all appealing. Current events must be chosen carefully because young children may have only passing knowledge or interest in most of them. Meaningful events might be a space shuttle mission or a solar eclipse. More likely, the event will be a local one, such as the discovery of ants on the playground or someone's new baby. Figure 12-8 shows an investigation of rocks and sand.

Rocks and Sand: An Inquiry-Based Project in Cognitive Curriculum

A Topic Emerges

Kindergarten cubbies and pockets have collections of rocks and pebbles in them.

We Investigate It

- Make a rock vocabulary list [boulders, crystals, fossils].
- Take a rock walk.
- Display our findings with a table and poster.
- Make rock gift store with jobs.
- Set up a trading game with rules.
- Take photos for documentation boards and newsletters.
- Have a rock show and invite families.

Reflecting on the Journey

- Ask questions that invite constructive input and validate prior knowledge. [What do you know about rocks?]
- Ask open-ended questions [What do you notice? What might happen if...?]
- Encourage children to wait a few seconds before giving an answer to allow time for thinking. [Close your eyes & think before you say your idea.]
- Repeat or paraphrase what the children say without praising or criticizing. [Joe thinks sand comes from rocks, and Andrea says it is dirt from the ocean. What do you think?]

© Cengage Learning

FIGURE 12-8 An inquiry-based project uses the discovery method engages the children in scientific thinking and is related directly to their own thinking. (Adapted from Ogu & Schmidt, 2009.)

DAP   Compared with preschoolers and kindergarteners, school-age children are more logical and flexible in their thinking, have more knowledge of the world, have improved memory, and can better sustain their attention. No matter what the subject area, teachers should keep learning concrete, relevant to children's everyday lives, and connected to previously learned material.

The critical point is to have a meaningful theme for children; rehashing the same old themes year after year may be easy for adults but can crowd out other interests of each unique group. The Project Approach (see Chapter 10) describes the use of themes in curriculum, making it accessible so that the children can interact and "own" it. Infants and toddlers will have less need for a theme; curriculum ideas for them concentrate on cognitive stimulation at their particular level of development.

Computers in the Classroom

A computer can be as nonthreatening as a watercolor brush. In the hands of a child, it can be a tool for experiencing the world. Early childhood classrooms are arranged so that children learn about the world directly by piling blocks, molding sand and clay, and bouncing a ball. Through these experiences, children gradually form concepts about how the world works and how they can affect it. As children touch the keys of a computer, they are challenged to explore and discover in ways never before possible.

There are two reasons why every classroom or child care center should have a computer—children love them, and they can provide a positive learning experience for every child, even the most difficult or contrary. Many professionals are skeptical of computers and other screen media. They worry that children will become passive for long periods of time, unwilling and unable to disengage and become involved in physical and social play. Indeed, specialists such as Elkind (1998) and Haugland (1999) do not recommend computer use for children under age 3, maintaining that children at those ages need to be learning through their bodies and motor manipulation of objects. NAEYC has published a position statement on Technology and Young Children for Ages 3–8 (2005): "Computers will have the most positive impact when they provide concrete experiences; children have free access; children and teachers learn together; peer tutoring is encouraged; and children control the learning experience."

Discovery-oriented experiences with computers enhance children's learning, especially in stimulating their cognitive thought processes. Unlike a teacher or playmate, computers and screen games can wait patiently for a child in a nonjudgmental way, do not tease or exclude, and often can adjust to children's diverse abilities and styles. Children design and control places and things of their own choosing, such as a house, the seashore, or a

Using the computers in a classroom can individualize a program and offer social experience.

face. Then, they create events that challenge them to think through the consequences of their actions. Moreover, computer programs can be *process highlighters* for children; the program can speed up or detail hidden processes and cause-and-effect relationships that are more difficult to observe, such as a plant growing, a face changing expression on command, or a dance put together with a special sequence of steps.

Technology use is especially meaningful in primary classrooms. "Appropriate use of technology [includes] documenting events in the classroom using digital still or video cameras, creating multimedia electronic portfolios that document children's learning, using informational software or websites to find the answers to questions that come up in the course of ongoing learning, or working with children to create multimedia slide shows to present to families during open house or parent events" (Murphy, DePasquale, & McNamara, 2003). School-age programs can create a website, make newsletters, and build interesting curriculum webs.

To integrate computers and take advantage of what they can offer children, educators should select developmental software, select appropriate websites, integrate using the computer as a resource into the program, and select the actual computers and support items.

Developmentally Appropriate Software

Along with blocks and paints, the computer can become an expressive medium that encourages skills in a variety of ways. It is important that the computer be used in addition to other concrete experiences, not instead of them.

For instance, children need to have real materials on the art and manipulatives tables; only then is it meaningful to manipulate images of those same kinds of materials at the computer table. Children need to have many experiences with *concrete* items such as paint, crayons, and markers. They are then ready to try their creative hand at computer graphics.

To use computers appropriately in the classroom, teachers must first be *comfortable* with the computer themselves.

1. Put the computer area in a quiet spot of the classroom (such as in or near the library/ listening spot), against a wall to minimize damage to the equipment or cords.
2. To introduce the computer, show small groups of children the basic care and handling of the computer.
3. The computer can be one of many choices offered during free play, or it can be a more limited choice with a waiting list.
4. Interaction between children can be encouraged by including space for two or more at the computer; assigning turns to a pair or small group of children, particularly if the computer seems to be dominated by a few; and watching to ensure that no one becomes "stuck" at the computer or any other area.

It is in the area of **software** that teachers of young children have many choices. These choices must be carefully made. Not every program intended for children is developmentally appropriate, and teachers must pay thoughtful attention to the program and to what they know about their own group of children. Teachers must know what to look for and how to choose programs that will be useful and appropriate for the specific age of the group. Haugland and Shade (1990) suggest 10 criteria for evaluating computer programs. Computer software should:

1. Be age appropriate.
2. Allow children to control it (children setting the pace and being active participants).
3. Include clear instructions.
4. Have expanding complexity.
5. Support independent exploration.
6. Be "process oriented" (having the software program be so engaging that the product of using it is secondary).
7. Include real world representation.
8. Have high quality technical features (colorful, uncluttered, and realistic).
9. Provide trial-and-error opportunities.
10. Have visible transformations (the ability to affect the software, for example, by transposing objects).

Selecting software can become easier by using a rating system (Haugland, 1997). The website, Children and Computers (http://childrenandcomputers.com), can help with software recommendations.

Websites

Many centers will use a computer simply with software; others, particularly those with primary-age children, may be interested in using the Internet. The Internet has been less researched than software, and its potential is untapped. There are a variety of learning opportunities using the Internet; however the sheer volume of Internet sites is overwhelming, and there has been no screening.

There are four types of children's websites:

1. *Information.* Information sites are great reference resources; for instance, the National Zoo from the Smithsonian (http://nationalzoo.si.edu) would be a wonderful introduction or follow up to a field trip.
2. *Communication.* These sites connect children to experts to answer questions on projects, such as "Ask an Astronaut" (http://coolcosmos.ipac.caltech.edu) for an Outer Space theme.
3. *Interaction.* These work like software programs, only more slowly. The program "Name-Jumping" asks children to jump around a floor-sized keyboard.
4. *Publication.* These sites can post children's work, such as Kid Pub® (http://www.kidpub.com).

In addition, there are many online resources on technology as a learning tool; while many websites change, a few that have stood the test of time include the Center for Media Literacy (www.medialit.org), Children and Computers (www.childrenandcomputers.com), Common Sense Media (www.CommonSenseMedia.org), and NAEYC's Beyond the Journal (www.journal.naeyc.org).

Integrating the Computer into Learning

Specific methods have been devised for teaching young children to work successfully with computers. For instance, a child must be able to maneuver a joystick or mouse, find the keys on the keyboard, or even insert a disk into the computer correctly. Because very young children cannot read, they will need help getting started. Teachers must be able to help children learn by setting up their classrooms with a computer positioned in a safe yet accessible place, structuring activities and the daily schedule to give children plenty of time to manipulate the machinery and programs, and choosing specific hardware and software that work with the class.

One of the most exciting aspects of computers in the classroom is their ability to support other learning. Teachers who use the computer effectively as an educational tool integrate their program goals to use the computer with individual children. To maximize the benefit computers can give children, teachers should attend to three components: access, availability, and home collaboration. In the classroom, be sure the computer is open regularly, enough so that the issue of crowding or frantic behavior around access is eliminated. Pay close attention to who is using the computer: by the time children are age 10, boys spend more time at computers than do girls.

Although this difference is not significant at preschool age, teachers need to ensure that girls get access and that selected software is not catering to males only. Recognize that many of your families may not have a computer at home, yet computer use can be helpful to all children. Jackson (2006) found that a group of underperforming children whose families were provided with a computer and free Internet access had higher scores on standardized reading tests after six months and higher grade point averages nearly one and a half years after the start of the study than those who used one less (Jackson in Packard, 2007). Regardless of your family population, be sure to communicate to parents about computer use and learning, and be ready to offer ideas, when appropriate, about quality software, supervision, and using the Internet.

Insights
from the field

How Does Technology in the Early Childhood Classroom Relate to Children's Learning? *by Arleen Prairie, M.Ed.*

In most early childhood classrooms, the computer center is where children freely choose to explore selected children's software. This is a worthwhile activity for children to realize their skills in using software. Yet the possibilities for learning go far beyond the limits of the classroom when teachers use technology to create opportunities to examine and explore ideas, find information, and communicate ideas. Along with the children, teachers can access software programs designed for classroom use, the digital camera and PhotoSuite, the Internet, and e-mail.

Just imagine …

With technology, teachers, along with the children, can find more information and view pictures on practically any topic through accessing the Internet: When a small group of children found a strange-looking tiny insect on the classroom wall, the teacher heard the children's attempt to label it. "It's a-a-a ant," "A frog 'cause it has back legs." "I know. It's an ugly spider." Mr. Ed had no idea what it was. They put the strange creature in a collection jar for the afternoon. With children excitedly looking on, Mr. Ed downloaded photos and a large diagram of an ant, a frog, a spider, and an insect. They compared the pictures and the creature. They discussed the body parts and counted legs. "You found out it was an insect. Let's search the Internet some more."

With technology a group of children can generate ideas and develop plans: While developing the new topic about the study of earthworms, the group listed what they knew about earthworms as the teacher entered them on computer using a computer program. To add to the list, one child announced. "They have eyes." Several children agreed. Others did not. The group posed several questions they could explore to determine whether worms have eyes. This started a lengthy investigation over several days, looking at them through the magnifying glass, looking at diagrams, taking close-up photos and enlarging them using PhotoShop, and asking the worms if they see their reflection in the mirror they held up to it.

With technology, teachers can communicate the ideas and learning of children with parents: When the children returned from their short trip to visit "their class tree" in De-

cember, Renee was particularly concerned about what she called "our dead tree." When Ms. Jonel, her teacher, sent a photo of the tree from this short trip via e-mail to parents, she also suggested that parents and children together look at trees around their house. She added a note to Renee's mother about her daughter's comment. Later that evening, Renee's mother viewed the e-mail and the photo with her daughter. Together they looked out the window at trees and bushes nearby. Renee noted the difference between the green of the "growing trees" (evergreens) and "dead trees." Outside they found dead leaves and small branches from "dead" and "alive" trees. Back inside, Renee looked at, smelled, and bent the deciduous branch. Later Renee thought aloud, "Maybe it's sleeping in the cold."

"Rather than being merely an enrichment or add-on to the curriculum, technology has taken a central place in early childhood programs" (NAEYC, 2003). Teachers develop the knowledge and skills to use technology as a teaching tool. In this way, they show children how to use both the computer and other learning tools to discover more about their world.

References

National Association for the Education of Young Children. (2003). NAEYC standards for early childhood professional preparation: Initial licensure programs. In M. Hyson (Ed.), *Preparing early childhood professionals: NAEYC's standards for programs* (17–64). Washington DC: Author.

Prairie, A. P. (2005). *Inquiry into math, science, and technology for teaching young children.* Clifton Park, NY: Thomson Delmar Learning.

Arleen Pratt Prairie, professor emeritus, taught Child Development in the City Colleges of Chicago for 25 years. In her teaching, she focused on preschool education, infant and toddler care, and brain development in the early years. She developed a series of videos in Infant and Toddler Care, and also worked with the production of the video course, The Developing Child, of which she recently revised 12 of this series. Prairie earned a B.S. in Child Development from Iowa State University and a M.Ed. in Early Childhood Education from Erikson Institute. She resides in Chicago where she enjoys her two grandchildren and her love of sailing.

SUMMARY

Cognition is the ability to learn, remember, and think abstractly. Children's cognitive development is related to learning in all other skill areas. Early childhood educators see cognitive development from an eclectic point of view and draw heavily from the works of Jean Piaget.

Cognitive skills in the early years can be put into several categories. The teacher's role is to understand how cognition develops in children and to put that knowledge to work in the classroom. While creating curriculum, teachers keep certain attitudes and ideas in mind. Then they set about planning for their programs.

The methods of developing children's cognition skills are as varied and creative as the teachers—and children—can be. By focusing on the class setting, a specific skill, or a theme, teachers help children acquire and use the skills of thinking to understand themselves and the world around them. Special consideration should be made when considering computers in the classroom.

KEY TERMS

cognition
physical knowledge
discrimination
logical mathematical knowledge
inference

social knowledge
rote knowledge
meaningful knowledge
intelligence
transcurricular

dynamic
inquiry
classification
seriation
software

REVIEW QUESTIONS

1. Write a working definition of cognition, including the connections between language and thought.

2. List at least three theories that offer a perspective on cognition and describe their contributions.

3. Match the cognitive skill with the appropriate activity.

inquiry	being aware of others
physical world	learning to locate things
social knowledge	pretending to be a puppet
classification	asking questions
seriation	sequencing events
numbers	using nesting blocks
symbols	expressing amounts
spatial relationships	sorting objects
time	manipulating materials

4. How does the teacher's use of language affect how children develop cognitive skills? Give several examples of what discourages such growth; counter that with how what a teacher says encourages skills.

5. Name three considerations when planning for computer use in a classroom.

6. What is an activity in each environmental area that stimulates cognitive development?

LEARNING ACTIVITIES

1. Look at the program in which you now teach, or recall your own first classrooms. Find at least one example of rote knowledge, social knowledge, and meaningful knowledge.

2. Take one cognitive skill and trace how it could be developed in each curriculum area of an early education setting.

3. Observe block play at your school. Make a chart as in Figure 12-3 that describes the learning processes involved.

4. Make a list of the classroom areas. Beside each, name one activity that would foster cognitive development and one that calls for language skills.

5. One theme often used in early childhood programs is that of the changing seasons. How can that theme develop language and thinking skills in younger preschoolers? Kindergarteners?

6. Consider the use of a computer in the following programs, and then answer the questions below:

   - toddler child care program

   - preschool half-day program

   - kindergarten

   - after-school primary program

   Is a computer appropriate in each of them? Why and how? What guidelines, if any would be needed in each setting? What would be the adult's role in each?

HELPFUL WEBSITES

Center for Media Literacy   **http://www.medialit.org**

Children and Computers   **http://www.childrenandcomputers.com**

Common Sense Media   **http://www.CommonSenseMedia.org**

I Am Your Child   **http://www.iamyourchild.org**

National Association for the Education of Young Children   **http://www.naeyc.org**

Beyond the Journal (NAEYC)   **http://www.journal.naeyc.org**

National Child Care Information Center of the U.S. Dept. of Health and Human Services   **http://www.nccic.org**

National Scientific Council on the Developing Child   **http://www.developingchild.harvard.edu/**

SuperKids® Educational Software Review   **http://www.superkids.com**

Zero to Three   **http://www.zerotothree.org**

 Additional resources including the TeachSource Videos can be found on the premium website for this book. Go to **http://www.cengage.com/login** to register your access code.

REFERENCES

Berger, K. S. (2006). *The developing person through adolescence* (7th Ed). New York: Worth Publishers.

Bos, B. (1983). *Before the basics*. Roseville, CA: Turn the Page Press.

Bowman, B. (2007, May/June). The effects of culture on thinking. *Exchange*.

Buckleitner, W. (1995, January). Getting started with computers and children. *Exchange*.

Chalufour, I., & Worth, K. (2004). *Building structures with young children.* St. Paul, MN: Redleaf Press.

Chen, J. Q., Isberg, E., & Krechevsky, M. (1998). *Project Spectrum: Early learning activities.* New York: Teachers College Press.

Chouinard, M. N. (2007). Children's questions: A mechanism for cognitive development. Serial no. 296. *Monographs of the Society for Research in Child Development, 73* (1).

Cutler, K. M., Gilkerson, D., Parrott, S., & Bowne, M. T. (2005, Spring). Developing math games based on children's literature. *Connections.*

Diezmann, C., & Yelland, N. J. (2000). Developing mathematical literacy in the early childhood years. In N. J. Yelland (Ed.), *Promoting meaningful learning.* Washington, DC: NAEYC.

Drew, W., Christie, J., Johnson, J. E., Meckley, A. M., & Nell, M. L. (2008, July). Constructive play: A value-added strategy for meeting early learning standards. *Young Children 66*(4).

Elkind, D. (1998). Computers for infants and young children. *Child Care Information Exchange* (123), 44–46.

Galinsky, E. (1997, Winter). New research on the brain development of young children. *CAEYC Connections.*

Geist, E. (2003). Infants and toddlers exploring mathematics. In D. Koralek (Ed.), *Spotlight on young children and math.* Washington, DC: NAEYC.

Gopnik, A., Meltzoff, A. N., & Kuhl, P. K. (1999). *The scientist in the crib.* New York: HarperCollins.

Haugland, S. W. (1997). *The developmental scale for software.* Cape Girardeau, MO: K.I.D.S. & Computers.

Haugland, S. W. (1999, November). What role should technology play in young children's learning? *Young Children, 54.*

Haugland, S. W., & Shade, D. D. (1990). *Developmental evaluations of software for young children.* Clifton Park, NY: Thomson Delmar Learning.

Hoerr, T. (2004). MI: A way for all students to succeed. In A. Gordon & K. Browne, *Beginnings and Beyond* (6th Ed). Clifton Park, NY: Thomson Delmar Learning.

Jensen, E. (1998). *Teaching with the brain in mind.* Alexandria, VA: Association for Supervision and Curriculum Development.

Lally, J. R. (1998, May). Brain research, infant learning, and child care curriculum. *Child Care Information Exchange, 121.*

Lense, S. (December, 2008). *Preschool curriculum: What's in it for children and teachers.* New York: Albert Shanker Institute, American Federation of Teachers.

Milken, E., & Hart, P. D. (1999). Public opinion poll, 1998. Available online at http://www.milkenexchange.org/publications.

Murphy, K. K., DePasquale, R., & McNamara, E. (2003, November). Meaningful connections: Using technology in primary classrooms. In *Beyond the Journal: Young Children on the Web.*

NAEYC. (2005). Position statement on technology and young children ages 3 through 8. Washington, DC: Author.

National Council of Teachers of Mathematics. (2000). *Principles and standards for school mathematics.* Reston, VA: NCTM.

National Scientific Council on the Developing Child. (2008). *In brief: The science of early childhood development.* Cambridge, MA: Author.

Nelson, K. (1995, July/August). Nurturing Kids: Seven ways of being smart. *Instructor.*

Ogu, U., & Schmidt, S.R. (2009). Investigating rocks and sand: Addressing multiple learning styles through an inquiry-based approach. *Young Children 64* (2), 12–18. www.journal.naeyc.org/btj/200903.

Packard, E. (2007). It's fun but does it make you smarter? In E. Junn & C. Boyatzis (Eds.). *Annual Editions: Child Growth and Development,* 09/10, 16e. New York: McGraw Hill.

Roberts, J. M., & Spitz, G. (1998). What does a constructivist class look like? Unpublished paper developed with the Advisory Board of "Under Construction," Monterey, CA.

Rogoff, B. (2003). *The cultural nature of human development.* New York: Oxford University Press.

Ross, M. E. (2000, March). Science their way. *Young Children, 55.*

Schiller, P., & Willis, C. (2008, July). Using brain-based teaching strategies to create supportive early childhood environments that address learning standards. *Young Children, 63,* 4.

Schiller, P. (2001, July). Brain research and its implications for early childhood programs. *Child Care Information Exchange, 140.*

Shore, R. (1997). *Rethinking the brain: New insights in early development.* New York: HarperCollins.

Siegel, D. L. (1999, November). Relationships and the developing mind. *Child Care Information Exchange, 130.*

Sarama, J., & Clements, D. H. (2009, March). Teaching math in the primary grades: The learning trajectories approach. In *Beyond the Journal, Young Children on the Web.*

Planning for the Mind: Language Development

© Cengage Learning

PREVIEW QUESTIONS

- How do children learn through language experiences?
- How does language develop in the early years?
- What language skills are developed in an early childhood setting?
- What is the teacher's role in language development in young children?
- How does the teacher include early literacy and children's literature in a program?

NAEYC CODE OF ETHICAL CONDUCT

These Core Values and sections from the NAEYC Code of Ethical Conduct are addressed in this chapter. As you read, note how the Core Values, Ideals, or Principles listed here apply to the topics in this chapter. (Reprinted with permission from the National Association for the Education of Young Children.)

Core Values: We have committed ourselves to basing our work with children on knowledge of child development.

Section I:
- I-1.5.   To create and maintain safe and healthy settings that foster children's social, emotional, intellectual, and physical development and that respect their dignity and their contributions.
- P-1.4.   For every child, we shall implement adaptations in teaching strategies, learning environment, and curricula, consult with the family, and seek recommendations from appropriate specialists to maximize the potential of the child to benefit from the program.

Section II:
- I-2.3   To respect the dignity of each family and its culture, language, customs, and beliefs.

Learning through Language Experiences

Alexis: Laleña, will you help me full this pitcher up?

Laleña: No, because my ponytail is keeping me in bothers.

Veronique: Hey, come here! I accidentally dropped a piece of bread and the birds yummed it right up!

Abhi: I know that's what the tooth fairy did to my tooth.

Marty: I'm going to keep all my baby teeth in a jar and the next time a baby comes along I'll give him my baby teeth.

Language is the aspect of human behavior that involves the use of sounds in meaningful patterns. This includes the corresponding symbols that are used to form, ex-press, and communicate thoughts and feelings. Any system of signs used for communication is language. For the developing child, language is the ability to express oneself. Language is both **receptive** (listening, understanding, and responding) and **expressive** (articulation, vocabulary, grammar, and graphic language). In other words, as illustrated above, language is meaningful, enjoyable communication.

Language and thought are closely related. Thoughts are produced when people internalize what they experience, and language is how they express or describe it. Language shapes the way thoughts are produced and stored.

"Language is a logical and analytical tool in thinking" (Vygotsky, 1962). Farmers who work the land develop tools to till the soil and language to describe their work. The child who comes to the bazaar with her mother learns the language of bargaining better than one who is in a shopping cart in a grocery store. Tribes who are snowbound develop tools to deal with the ice and

Research tells us that language experiences during preschool and kindergarten are reflected in later literacy success.

© Cengage Learning

language to describe the many kinds of water conditions. Language and thought are tools to make sense of and interact with the world.

A baby may not start life with language, yet he or she always communicates. Crying, laughing, smiling, and wiggling are body language to express and transmit information. Some communication is nonsymbolic (gestures or pointing), and some is symbolic (words). A child progresses naturally from nonsymbolic communication (pointing at the window to mean go *outside*) to symbolic communication, when the child says "out go" or "me go out." "Spoken language is by far the most common form of symbolic language" (Willis, 1998). The growing child learns to use meaningful language to communicate thoughts; thus, language and thought are intertwined.

Language is also related to other areas of development. Children learn to offer an idea as well as use language as a prop to get social play started. They use language to develop emotionally, as they learn to label, describe, question, and demand when they tell each other how they feel and what they want. Anyone who has heard a child talk himself down from a tree knows how language can be a great help in using physical skills.

Language Development

Language seems to be an innate characteristic of humankind. Wherever people live together, language of some form develops. Languages worldwide vary remarkably in their sounds, words, and grammatical structure. Nonetheless, young children around the world acquire language.

What Research Tells Us

Research into language development and expression reveals several interesting characteristics. First, *the language of children is different from adult language*. Children's language deals with the present and is egocentric, taking into account only the child's own knowledge. There appears to be a lack of awareness on the child's part of language form. Preschool children do show awareness of language structure (for instance, "feets" to mark the plural form) but do not seem to know the parts of speech. In other words, children use language to communicate but seem to have no understanding of language as an entity itself.

Second, language *is not learned simply by imitating adult speech*. Child language is not garbled adult language, but rather is unique to the child's age and linguistic level. Gardner lists language ability as one form of cognition (linguistic intelligence), and most language development theorists agree that there seems to be an innate human tendency toward language (Chomsky, 1993). Children are not just trying to imitate others and making mistakes but are trying to come to terms with language themselves. A child will try out theories about language in attempts to understand its patterns. In language, as in so many areas of cognition, children are involved as active participants in their own learning. The use of speech is not merely imitative but productive and creative.

Third, *experiences help build language*. The more experiences a child has, the more she has to talk about; thus, vocabulary is built on firsthand life. "The size of a child's vocabulary is strongly correlated with how much a child is talked to, cuddled, and interacted with. Recent research shows that at 20 months of age children who have mothers who frequently talk to them average 131 more words than children of less talkative mothers" (Willis 1998).

Fourth, *the language experiences during the first five years are reflected in later literary success*. High quality programs can reduce the degree of delay for high risk children in communicative skills, and personal interactions in a stimulating environment increase children's communication effectiveness (Isbell and Phillips, 2001). Three dimensions of children's experiences that relate to later literary success (Dickenson & Tabors, 2002) are: exposure to *varied* vocabulary; opportunities to be part of conversations that use **extended discourse;** and *home* and *classroom environments* that are cognitively and linguistically stimulating. The level of language and literary skills that young children acquire provide a strong base for their later years; indeed "the scores that the kindergartners achieved on the measures were highly predictive of their scores on reading comprehension and receptive vocabulary in fourth and in seventh grade" (Dickenson & Tabors, 2002).

Finally, *language development is a process of experience and maturation*. Teachers must be aware of children's diverse language skills and challenges, particularly in the areas of bilingualism, speech or language disorders, and dialects, all of which are addressed in this chapter. Just as in the development of cognitive skills, there are stages of language growth that follow a specific sequence. There are also variations in timing that are important to remember.

Stages of Language Development

Children follow a six step sequence in language development. Except in cases of deafness or trauma, this sequence seems *invariable* regardless of what language is being learned.

1. *Infant's Response to Language.* Babies begin by attending to speech, changes in sound, rhythm, and intonation. These are the **precursors** of speech, and young infants are especially sensitive to some sound differences. Infants need to hear speech, and plenty of it, to develop the foundations of sound.

2. *Vocalization.* By 3 to 4 months of age, infants begin cooing and babbling. Babbling increases with age and seems to peak around 9 to 12 months. This is a matter of physical maturation, not just experience; children who are deaf or hearing impaired do it at the same time as those whose hearing is normal. Furthermore, similar vocalization patterns are seen among different languages.

3. *Word Development.* The child must first separate the noises heard into speech and nonspeech. The speech noises must be further separated into words and the sounds that form them. The growing infant starts to shift from practice to playing with sounds. The end result is planned, controlled speech.

   Children begin playing with sounds around 10 to 15 months of age. From this point, the development of speech is determined as much by control of motor movements as by the ability to match sounds with objects.

   Most children can understand and respond to a number of words before they can produce any. Their first words include names of objects and events in their world (people, food, toys, animals). Then the child begins to overextend words, perhaps using "doggy" to refer to all animals. Finally, single words can be used as sentences: "Bye-bye" can refer to someone leaving, a meal the child thinks is finished, the child's going away, a door closing.

4. *Sentences.* Children's sentences usually begin with two words, describing an action ("Me go"), a possession ("My ball"), or a location ("Baby outside"). These sentences get expanded by adding adjectives ("My big ball"), changing the verb tense ("Me jumped down"), or using negatives ("No go outside"). Children learn grammar not by being taught the rules but as they listen to others' speech and put together the regularities they hear.

Child language, although not identical to that of adults, does draw on language heard to build a language base. Children incorporate and imitate what they hear to refine their own language structures.

5. *Elaboration.* Vocabulary begins to increase at an amazing rate. Sentences get longer, and communication begins to work into social interaction. In the hospital corner of a nursery school, this conversation takes place:

   Chip: I'm a nurse.
   Brooke: I'm going to try to get some patients for you.
   Megan: Do I need an operation?
   Chip: Yeah, if you don't want to be sick anymore.

6. *Graphic Representation.* By late preschool and kindergarten, reading and writing emerge as children become aware of language as an entity itself and of the written word as a way of documenting what is spoken. Awareness of print and emerging literacy are the outgrowth of this last stage of development.

In fact, alphabet knowledge and **phonemic awareness** are predictors of early reading success (Wasik, 2001). Children who learn to read well and most easily in first grade are those with prior knowledge of the alphabet and the understanding of the sounds that letters represent. Within the guidelines of developmentally appropriate practice, the teaching focus must be on creating meaningful experiences and will be addressed in the section on "Early Literacy" later in this chapter.

As children create a linguistic representation of their cognitive understanding, they see the potential of language reading and writing as a tool for communicating. Known as *literate thinking*, this is the hallmark of the last early childhood developmental stage in language development. Later sections on "Reading and Writing" and "Children's literature" address this area. Figure 13-1 is a sample of a child's developing language skills.

Dual Language Learning

Children who begin formal schooling ready to learn are more likely to succeed in meeting the academic and social challenges they encounter. In 1994, the U.S. Congress passed the "Goals 2000: Educate America Act" that stated all children in America should start school ready to learn (see Chapter 15). A major challenge facing the education system in the United States and other countries is the increased number of students in public schools who speak English as their second language

Language Skills: Ages and Stages

Stage	Age (approx.)	Sample
1. Response	0–6 months	Smiles, gazes when hearing voices
2. Vocalization	6–10 months	Babbles all types of sounds, creating babble-sentences Uses vocal signals other than crying to get help
3. Word development	10–18 months	Mama, Dada, Doggie Bye-bye, No-no
4. Sentences	18 months–3 years	Me want chok-quit (I want chocolate) She goed in the gark (She went in the dark)
5. Elaboration	3 to 5 or 6 years	You're my best Mommy, you can hold my turtle at bet-bis (breakfast) (Cough) That was just a sneeze in my mouth
6. Graphic representation	5 plus to 8 years	

▌ FIGURE 13-1 Children's language skills develop with both age and experience.

(NCELA, 2007a). In the United States, "the majority of these children are born in the United States and thus from a very young age are acquiring both the language of their family as well as the language of the larger community. These very young children are **dual language learners [DLLs]**" (NCELA, 2008).

These learners may not have had access to those early learning experiences that prepare children for learning in school. They may not have had quality preschool experiences, may live in poverty, have parents with low levels of education, and have not had access to health care services. Research on instruction indicates that young DLLs:

- Benefit from instructional techniques that work to include them in classroom social interactions and recognize the value of their home language
- Require sufficient time (4 to 6 years) to become proficient in their second language
- Benefit from explicit vocabulary instruction
- Can transfer literacy skills from their first language and retain the benefits of first language literacy through eighth grade measures of reading proficiency (NCELA, 2008)

Schools, communities, and families can work together to get children ready to succeed in education. Children who are age 3 to 5 are still in the process of acquiring their first language, even as they are also acquiring their second. At the same time, DLLs are diverse in their linguistic backgrounds:

> They may differ in terms of the amount of English that their parents speak (from very little English at all to fluent English). Their parents may also differ in terms of the extent that they speak one or more languages in the home. In some families, parents may speak one language at home and another at work. In other families, parents may speak two languages interchangeably. Family members may come from different language backgrounds, so a child may speak English to a parent but Spanish to a grandparent living in the home. Dual language learners arrive at school with language backgrounds and skills which are substantially different from monolingual English speakers. (NCELA, 2008)

The sections that follow address some of these issues. The strategies for dealing with bilingualism and dialect

DAP

DAP   Teachers attend to the particular language needs of English language learners and children who are behind in vocabulary and other aspects of language learning. They engage the child more frequently in sustained conversations and make extra efforts to help them comprehend.

Providing books that are in tune with all children's cultures and language backgrounds expands everyone's world.

differences overlap with those of developmentally appropriate practices for helping all children acquire language skills.

Bilingualism

In early childhood terms, **bilingualism** (or multilingualism) is the ability of a person to communicate in a language other than their native language with a degree of fluency. Baker (2004) explains:

> There is not just one dimension of language. We can examine people's proficiency in two languages in their *listening (understanding), speaking, reading and writing* skills. Calling someone *bilingual* is therefore an *umbrella* term. Underneath the umbrella rest many different skill levels in two languages. Being bilingual is not just about proficiency in two languages. There is a *difference* between *ability* and *use* of language. … In practice, a person may be bilingual, although ability in one language is lacking (but improving steadily).

A bilingual child must learn to comprehend and produce aspects of each language and to develop two systems of communication. This is a lengthy and complicated process of getting used to a new culture and a new language before feeling comfortable enough to use it in a classroom.

Second language learning occurs in two general ways. **Simultaneous acquisition** happens if a child is exposed to two languages from birth. These bilingual children tend to lag behind in vocabulary development in the early years, often mixing sounds or words. By 4 or 5 years of age, however, most children have separated the languages successfully.

The second pattern is known as **successive acquisition.** This occurs as a child with one language now enters the world of a second language, as when children with one home language enter a school that uses another language. A common pattern among immigrants and many children in the United States, this learning seems to favor younger children in their accent and grammar, but there is no evidence that younger children are any more successful with vocabulary and syntax.

With more bilingual/bicultural children in early childhood classrooms, it helps to understand how children learn a second language and how to apply this research in practical ways. Since language is a key to every child's success, teachers must understand the myths and truths relating to bilingualism (Figure 13-2). Research shows that the process of learning a second language in childhood depends, in part, on the individual child (NCELA, 2007a, 2008). Cognitive, social, and linguistic skills are all at work in acquiring a second language. Moreover, the child's culture, unique temperament, and learning style play a part as well. For instance, Tjarko is of Swiss-German ancestry, so is it any wonder he pronounces an English "v" like an "f," as in "Can I *haff* one of those?" Sachiko, who has moved from Japan within the year, complains, "My *neck* hurts when I drink," and disagrees that it is a sore throat since "neck" is the word she knows.

First and second language acquisitions are similar in many ways. Language acquisition is a natural process. However, children need to be exposed to language in meaningful ways. A particularly important point for all early educators to understand is the effect of a new language on a child in the classroom and at home. First, children of linguistically and culturally diverse backgrounds may face isolation at school. In an English-speaking school, for instance, the child who does not yet understand or speak English may find it difficult to interact appropriately with children and teachers. Lack of a mutual language can result in the child being treated as nearly invisible or like a baby by other children, or as less intelligent or capable by teachers:

> They are caught in what I call the double-bind of second language learning: To learn a new language, you have to be socially accepted by those who speak the language; but to be socially accepted, you have to be able to speak the new language. (Tabors, 1998)

Myths and Truths about Bilingualism

Myths	Truths
Children who are exposed to more than one language get confused.	Young children have the brain capacity and the neural flexibility for learning two or more languages without becoming confused.
Bilingual achildren are slower than monolingual children in developing speech.	There is no evidence regarding a later age in developing speech for bilingual children.
Mixing languages or "code switching" is a sign of the child being confused.	"Code switching" is a normal part of bilingual language development and a common communication strategy for bilingual children and adults.
Home language interferes with children's ability to learn English.	Home language does *not* interfere with the ability to learn English. In fact, a strong foundation in the home language positively impacts the learning of a second language.
Children can learn a second language very quickly.	It takes *two* years for children to incorporate a conversational level in a second language, and *five to seven* years to achieve an academic level (e.g., school-related skills, language of text).

FIGURE 13-2 Myths and truths related to bilingualism. (Developed by the Early Childhood Language Development Institute, a project of San Mateo County Office of Education, Redwood City, California. June 2005. Reprinted by permission of the author, Soodie Ansari.)

Moreover, children acquiring language in an English-dominant classroom often begin to isolate themselves from their families. They may refuse to use their home language anymore, as it is difficult to use both, and English may have greater status in the children's eyes. Families sometimes promote this, as they wish their children to learn English. However, if they themselves do not speak English, they become unable to communicate at length with their children. The lack of a mutual language then grows at home, creating problems of family cohesiveness and harmony.

Teachers need guidance in educating second language learners. Support for second language acquisition includes environmental organization, language techniques, classroom activities, and family contact (see Figure 13-3). The following recommendations serve as guidelines for teachers of children who are acquiring a second language:

1. *Understand how children learn a second language.* There is a developmental sequence of second language acquisition. First, children may continue to speak their home language with both those who speak it and those that do not. Next, children begin to understand that others do not understand their language and give up using it, substituting nonverbal behavior that may appear less mature. Allowing them to watch and listen and also interpreting and inviting children into play will help. Third, children begin to break out of the nonverbal period with a combination of telegraphic and formulaic language. One-word phrases such as "no, yes, mine, hey" all telegraph meaning, as do catch-words such as "ok, lookit, I dunno" that are used as formulas for communicating. Finally, productive use of the new language appears:

> She describes an activity ("I do an ice cream"), an idea ("I got a big"), or a need ("I want a play dough"). Because she is no longer using memorized phrases, it may seem that her language ability has actually decreased because there will be many more mistakes. (Tabors, 1998)

The perceptive teacher will see that it is a positive step in a cumulative process.

2. *Make a plan for the use of the two languages.* Try to have bilingual staff or at least one teacher who specializes in each language. The children are then exposed to models in both the home language and

Checklist for Language-Friendly Classroom Practices

1. Help children make sense of language.
   ____ What is their "language dictionary"?
   ____ What can their family experts tell you?

2. Provide comprehensible input.
   ____ What information talk can you provide in the moment?
   ____ What multisensory experiences can you plan?

3. Be prepared for the "silent period."
   ____ How do they communicate when they aren't speaking?
   ____ What sign of progress and learning do you see?
   ____ In what ways is the child able to communicate?

4. Be sensitive to the affective filter.
   ____ How can you tell when the child is in emotional discomfort?
   ____ When do you invite participation?

5. Create a connection.
   ____ What is your morning greeting?
   ____ What is the predictable schedule?
   ____ When does the child need your support?

6. Build a community of acceptance.
   ____ Does the environment reflect the child's life?
   ____ How is the child's home language validated?
   ____ Have you helped the child find buddies?
   ____ How have you worked with the family?

7. Examine teacher behaviors.
   ____ When/how are teachers helpful and encouraging?
   ____ When/how have teachers ignored or been unhelpful?

FIGURE 13-3 A checklist for teachers to examine their own daily practices with children who are acquiring a second language (with help from Soodie Ansari, 2005).

English. Many programs in communities in which the children and educators have the same first language background use the children's home language while learning English in a naturalistic setting. They may start a year with the language of the children and gradually use more English until the languages are equal.

3. *Accept individual differences.* Take note of both the style and the time frame of language learning. Children bring a range of individual differences to learning a second language. Motivation to learn, exposure to the dominant language, the age of the child in relationship to the group, and temperament can all affect language acquisition. Do not insist that a child speak, but do invite and try to include the child in classroom activities. Assume developmental equivalence: that is, that the children, although different, are normal. For example, Maria Elena just will not come and sit at group time. Allow her to watch from a distance and believe that she is learning, rather than be worried or irritated that she is not with the group yet.

4. *Support children's attempts to communicate.* Encouraging children's communication bids rather than correcting them will help children try to learn. Recognize developmentally equivalent patterns. For instance, Kidah may not say the word "car" but can show it to you when you ask. Receptive language precedes expressive language.

5. *Maintain an additive philosophy.* Recognize that children are acquiring more and new language skills, not simply replacing their primary linguistic skills. Asking Giau and his family about their words, foods, and customs allows teachers to use a style and content that are familiar to the Vietnamese, thus smoothing the transition and adding onto an already rich base of knowledge.

6. *Provide a stimulating, active, and diverse environment.* Give many opportunities for language in meaningful social interactions and responsive experiences with all children:

   > Two aspects of classroom organization can help second language learning children. The first is to have a set routine for activities so that children can catch on and get into the flow of events… The second is to provide safe havens in the classroom [so that] children can spend some time away from the communicatively demanding activities and develop competency in other skill areas besides language. (Tabors, 1998)

Make use of story time, increasing the amount of time when you tell or read aloud stories; the predictable plot and repetitive language help children follow along and understand. Choose chants, finger plays, and songs for the same reasons. Allow children to "assume a new identity—second language learners are often willing to speak when they can use another identity (puppets, masks, costumes)" (Chesler, 2002).

7. *Use informal observations to guide the planning of activities.* Provide spontaneous interactions for speakers of other languages. Teachers will need to expand the types of observations used for assessment to see a child's physical, cognitive, or emotional abilities in language-free situations. Additionally, a home visit observation may help to learn how a child is doing in first language development. Also, only by actively watching will a teacher find special moments in a classroom to help a child be accepted and join in. Seeing a group of girls building a zoo, a teacher gives a basket of wild animals to Midori. Walking with her to the block corner, she offers to stock the zoo and then helps all the girls make animal signs in Japanese and English. Thus, Midori enters the play in a positive and strong way.

8. *Find out about the family.* Establish ties between home and school. School learning is most likely to occur when family values reinforce school expectations. Parents and teachers do not have to do the same things, but they must have a mutual understanding and respect for each other and goals for children. For example, Honwyma's parents and his teacher talk together about what of the Hopi language and culture can be brought into the classroom. When there are differences between the Hopi patterns and those of the school, teachers will try to accommodate.

9. *Provide an accepting classroom climate.* It must value culturally and linguistically diverse young children. Teachers must come to grips with their own cultural ethnocentricity and learn about the languages, dialects, and cultures beyond their own. It is critical to value all ways of achieving developmental milestones, not just those of the teacher's culture or educational experience.

The challenge to young children and their teachers is enormous. With informed, open-minded teaching, children can learn a second language without undue stress and alienation. As of this date we can conclude that:

- Children can and do learn two languages at an early age, though the process and time vary with the individual child.
- Two languages can be learned at the same time in a parallel manner. The depth of knowledge of one language may be different from that of the other, or the two may develop equally.

- The acquisition of languages may mean a "mixing" of the two, as heard in children's speech when they use words or a sentence structure of both languages.
- Learning two languages does not hurt the acquisition of either language in the long run.

Dialect Differences

Teachers may encounter differences in the way words are pronounced or grammar is used, even among English-speaking children. These differences reflect a **dialect,** or variation of speech patterns within a language. When we travel to New York, for example, our ear is attuned to the unique pronunciation of "goyl" (girl), and when we move north we hear "habah" (harbor). Southern speakers are easy to identify with elongated vowel sounds such as "Haiiiii, yaaw'll!" In addition to regional dialects, there are also social dialects that are shared by people of the same cultural group or social class.

Italian, Russian, and numerous other languages have regional and social dialects. Linguists, the scholars who study languages, argue that there is no such thing as a good or a bad language. Each language and dialect is a legitimate system of speech rules that governs communication in that language. Some dialects, however, are not viewed favorably within the larger society and often carry a social or economic stigma. In the United States, the dialect that has received the most attention and controversy is **Ebonics,** or Black English.

The unique linguistic characteristics of African-American children have been studied for decades. The name "Ebonics" is made up of the words ebony and phonics. "It has a West African base with English vocabulary superimposed on top," says Hoover (1997). "It's based on the grammar of West African languages." Thus, you might hear a child using Black English say "I been done knowed how to read!" while in the book corner.

The debate over the significance of Ebonics was thrust into the public spotlight in 1997 when the Oakland, California, school district voted to view Ebonics as a separate language and adopt it to help improve student learning. Critics cite educators who claim the dialect will interfere with reading achievement, whereas supporters insist that the real barrier to academic success is teachers' low expectations of dialect speakers. The National Head Start Association has spoken out against Ebonics, emphasizing that all children must be taught to use language in ways to increase their power, not to segregate.

Often cited in the argument is the concern for how nonstandard speakers will fare in adult society. Negative views of Black English or any nonstandard dialect are of concern to parents who want better opportunities for their children. The early childhood educator would be prudent to develop the goal of "communicative competence" (Cazden, 1996) or "language power" (Saxton, 1998) for all students. This goal would strive to empower each child to be a comfortable and capable speaker in any situation demanding "standard" English or the language of his own "speech community."

Language Skills

Teachers translate language development theory into practice as they work with children. Language skills in the early childhood setting include articulation, receptive language, expressive language, graphic language, and enjoyment. Children's conversations, their ways of talking, some children's lack of expressive language, and their ways of asking questions all offer glimpses into children's language skills.

Articulation

Articulation is how children actually say the sounds and words. Children's ability to produce sound is a critical link in their connecting the sounds to form speech. Mispronunciation is common and normal, especially in children under 5 years of age. The preschool teacher can expect to hear "Thally" for Sally, "wope" for rope, and "buh-sketty" for spaghetti. Children who repeat sounds, syllables, or words in preschool are not stutterers; 85 percent of 2- to 6-year-olds hesitate and repeat when talking. As children talk, teachers listen for their ability to hear and reproduce sounds in daily conversation. Can they hear and produce sounds that differ widely, such as "sit" and "blocks?" Can they produce sounds that differ in small ways, such as in "man" and "mat?"

How adults respond to disfluencies can help a child through this normal stage of language development. Chesler (2002) suggests:

- Pay attention to the child when she talks to you. Do not rush her.
- Do not demand speech when a child is upset or feels stressed.
- Do not put children on exhibition by asking them to recite or talk when they do not want to.
- Avoid interrupting a child when she is talking; avoid completing a sentence for her.

- Statements like "slow down" or "think before you talk" draw attention to his speech and usually cue the child that there is something wrong with the way he talks.
- Do make an example of your speech by talking slowly, smoothly, and distinctly.

Receptive Language

Receptive language is what children acquire when they learn to listen and understand. It is what they hear. With this skill, children are able to understand directions, to answer a question, and to follow a sequence of events. They can understand relationships and begin to predict the outcome of their behavior and that of others. They develop some mental pictures as they listen.

Children begin early and can become experts in reacting to words, voice, emphasis, and inflection. How many times does the child understand by the way the words are spoken?

"You finally *finished* your lunch." (Hooray for you!)
"You *finally* finished your lunch?" (You slow poke.)

Children learn to listen for enjoyment, for the way the wind sounds in the trees, the rhythm of storytelling, or the sound of the car as it brings Mom or Dad home.

Expressive Language

Expressive language in the early years means the process and steps involved in expressing ideas, feelings, and intentions in language. This includes words, grammar, and elaboration.

Words

Expressive language is the spoken word. Children's first words are of what is most important to them (Mama, Da-Da). Adults help children extend their knowledge and vocabulary by using the names of objects and words of action (walk, run, jump) and feelings (happy, sad, mad). By describing objects in greater and greater detail, teachers give children new words that increase their skills. Children are then ready to learn that some words have more than one meaning (the word "orange," for example, is both a color and a fruit) and that different words can have the same meaning (such as "ship" and "boat" as similar objects, or "muñeca" and "doll" as the same word in different languages).

Grammar

Basic grammatical structure is learned as children generalize what they hear. They listen to adult speech patterns and use these patterns to organize their own language. It helps to hear simple sentences at a young age, with the words in the correct order. Next, children can grasp past tense as well as present, plural nouns along with the singular. Finally, the use of more complex structures is understood (prepositions, comparatives, various conjugations of verbs).

Elaboration of Language

Elaboration of language takes many, many forms. It is the act of expanding the language. Through description, narration, explanation, and communication, adults elaborate their own speech to encourage children to do the same. For instance, communication for children includes talking to themselves and others.

Verbalize a process aloud.	"I'm trying to get the plant out of its pot, but when I turn it upside down it doesn't fall out."
Give and follow directions.	"It's time to make a choice for cleanup. You find something and I'll watch you."
Ask and answer questions.	"How do you feel when she says she won't play? What can you say? Do?"
Stick to the subject.	"I know you want to go play kickball, but first let's solve the problem of the wagon."
Use speech to get involved.	"What a great house you built. How do you get inside?"

Graphic Language

"Talk written down" is the essence of graphic language. The child now learns that there is a way to record, copy, and send to another person one's thoughts. Learning to put language into a symbolic form is the gist of the reading and writing process. Children learn about print when they are read to regularly, when they see adults reading and writing, and when they are surrounded with a print-rich environment. Because words and letters are simply "lines and dots and scribbles" to young children, the teacher and parent must demonstrate how meaningful graphic language can be. Moreover, the translation of talk into print is a cognitive task (that of symbols, see previous section), so children's intellectual development as well as their language abilities are at play when learning about the printed word. See later section on "Children and Writing."

Enjoyment

To encourage language is to promote enjoyment in using it. As teachers converse with children, parents, and other adults, they model for children how useful and fun language can be. Knowing the power and pleasures of language gives children the motivation for the harder work of learning to read and write.

Children learn to enjoy language by participating in group discussion and being encouraged to ask questions. Reading and listening to stories and poems every day are essential parts of any program. The program should also include children's literature and stories children dictate or write themselves.

Word play and rhyming are fun as well as educational. Group language games are useful, such as asking the question, "Did you ever see a bat with a hat? A bun

Teachers and children can share intimate moments when they enjoy using language together.

having fun? A bee with…?" and letting the children add the rest. Begin a song, for instance, "Do You Know the Muffin Man?" and add the children's names. Whatever contributes to the enjoyment of language supports its growth, from varying voice and tone to fit the situation (in storytelling, dramatic play, and ordinary activity periods) to spontaneous rhyming songs.

Role of the Teacher

Considerations

When considering how to work with young children in language development, teachers should keep several things in mind:

1. *Children need an "envelope of language."* "Babies already read; think about how they read you," says Miller (2001). Start with creating a language-rich environment. Magda Gerber encourages people to be a play-by-play announcer, providing language labels for everything the child does and touches. When you expose children to quality literature every day, be sure there is an emotional response to reading that conveys that it is a warm and pleasant thing to do and they are learning how books work.

2. *Children must use language to learn it.* Adults often spend much of their time with children talking—to, at, for, or about them. "Be careful not to dominate when talking with children. Lean toward more child than adult talk" (Epstein, 2009).

   Children's conversations with each other are important in learning the basics of how to take turns and keep to one topic and of saying what they mean, getting their ideas and themselves heard and accepted. Time with peers and adults, in both structured (group times) and nonstructured (free play) situations, allows children to practice and refine language skills. Children as young as age 2 can engage in *talk time,* as described here:

   > Our talk time program has three governing rules: only one person at a time may speak; everyone gets a turn to choose a subject; and we don't leave the talk time table until everyone has had a turn and the activity is officially over. (Selman, 2001)

   Talk time cannot be used to correct children's language or ideas and yet is a useful way to help delayed talkers.

3. *The most verbal children tend to monopolize language interactions.* Research shows that teachers

Children can use story time as "talk time" as well as for engaged listening.

interact verbally with the children who are most skilled verbally. Seek out and support language development in those with fewer skills, generally by drawing them out individually through (a) reading the unspoken (body) language that communicates their ideas, needs, and feelings and (b) helping them express verbally those ideas, needs, and feelings.

4. *Adults should know the individual child.* Consistency in adult–child relationships may be as important for language as for effective development during the early years. If so, teachers must have a meaningful relationship with each child. This includes knowing the parents and how they communicate with their child.

5. *Home languages are to be invited into the program.* "The explanations for home language are several fold," writes Chang (1993). "First, when centers do not use the home language, they reinforce existing societal messages that a child's language is lower in status than the dominant language, English…Language and culture are closely related since the language of an ethnic group is usually the vehicle through which the community transmits to its young its customs and beliefs…The development of a child's primary language skills is integral to helping a child succeed academically and to eventually develop skills in English."

6. *Dialect differences expand your speech community.* Dialects are as much a part of children's culture and identity as is their home language. Providers may

mistakenly see children speaking their own dialect as less capable, or even delayed. We need to not make the assumption that different means "less than."

7. *Some children may have speech and language disorders.* Early detection of and intervention for speech and language disorders is possible without the teacher being a speech therapist. With a basic knowledge of typical speech development and signposts of speech and language problems, the perceptive teacher can alert families and recommend specialist assessment and input. Once a child with a disability comes into a program with specific learning objectives, the staff needs to plan how to address those needs in the curriculum and with the children. "For children with learning challenges, adult communicative input can often make or break the child's chances for optimizing learning potential" (Klein, Cook, & Richardson-Gibbs, 2001). They suggest the following strategies:

   a. Follow the child's lead.

   b. Use progressive matching (also known as expansion: modeling language just slightly more complex than the child's current capability).

   c. Use labels and specific descriptors.

   d. Repeat key words and phrases.

   e. Use appropriate pacing.

   f. Give children ample time to respond.

   g. Create the need to communicate.

See Figure 13-4 for a checklist for supporting language development in children with communication and language disorders.

8. *The language of the teacher influences the classroom.* What teachers say—and how they say it—is important. Moreover, it is often what they do not say that communicates the most to children in their struggle to gain mastery of the language. Teachers provide a rich environment and a high quality of interaction with the child that encourages all language skills:

- *Articulation.* Reinforce clear speech by letting them practice frequently.
  Alter your speech to use a higher pitch, short utterances, and repeating the child's language attempts.
- *Receptive language.* See the strategies for developing receptive learning in Figure 13-5.

A Readiness Checklist

Ask yourself these questions, then complete the checklist.

	Ready	Not
Is information presented in multiple formats? Use pictures, picture schedules, symbols, and words to communicate with children.	❏	❏
Do teachers supplement spoken words with eye contact and gestures?	❏	❏
Do teachers modify their language to reflect the developmental levels of the children they are speaking to? For example, use shorter sentences when talking with 3-year-olds and longer ones with 5-year-olds.	❏	❏
Do teachers frequently check to make sure children understand what was said? Look for signs such as eye contact and gestures; consider asking children to repeat back what they heard.	❏	❏
Do teachers encourage children to "use their words" and then model appropriate language?	❏	❏
Does the classroom library include a variety and range of books suitable for different ages and developmental levels?	❏	❏
Do teachers read books with children one-on-one in addition to reading aloud to a group?	❏	❏
Do teachers encourage children who use language to ask for materials and join in activities?	❏	❏
Do adults have frequent conversations with children on topics of interest to the children?	❏	❏

FIGURE 13-4 A checklist for getting your program ready for children with communication and language disorders. (Watson & McCathren, 2009, adapted with permission.)

Helping Children with Receptive Language

1. *Give clear directions.* "Please go and sit on the rug next to the chairs," instead of "Go sit over there."
2. *Let children ask questions.* Give them acceptable answers. For example, repeat a phrase from the child's last sentence that asks the child to try again: "You want what?" or "You ate what?" Or cast the question back to a child by changing the phrase "Where did you put it?" into "You put it where?"
3. *Give instructions in a sequence.* "Put your lunch on your desk, then wash your hands. Then you are ready to go to lunch." It often helps to ask the children what they think they are to do: "How do you get ready for lunch? What comes first? Next?"
4. *Try to understand what the child means, regardless of the actual language.* Look for the purpose and intent beyond what the child may have said. This is particularly important with toddlers, non-English speakers, and newcomers.
5. *Ask children to state their thoughts out loud.* "Tell me what you think is going to happen to the eggs in the incubator. Why do you think some might hatch and some might not?"
6. *Use literature, poetry, and your own descriptions.* Give children an idea of how words can be used to paint verbal and mental pictures. Ask questions about children's own images and dreams. To older children read aloud from books without pictures.

FIGURE 13-5 Teachers do more than insist "Listen to me" to encourage receptive language.

■ *Expressive language.* Use short, concise sentences to frame or highlight a word. For example, if a child says, "Look!" you might reply, "Is it a butterfly or a bee?"

a. Have them describe their own actions or thoughts in words.

Michelle: I have something to show you.
Teacher: Can you give us some clues?
Michelle: It's not a record and it's not a book, and you can't play with it.
Teacher: Can you hold it in your hand?
Michelle: No, silly, it's a kiss!

b. Make a statement describing the child's behavior or actions.

c. Encourage listening and repeat one child's words to another.
"Bahrain, did you hear what Joanna said about the sand truck?"

d. Help children stick to the subject.
"Stevie, now we're talking about our field trip to the track. You can tell us about your new dog next."

■ *Graphic language.* This can be developed in hundreds of ways. What is now called "emer-

gent, or early literacy" is a broad view of reading and writing as developing, or emerging, out of language development as a whole. Rather than a simple set of skills, early literacy involves a set of attitudes, behaviors, and understandings related to written language. See the section "Early Literacy" at the end of this chapter.

What Do YOU Think? What is your home language? What do you remember of your first schooling experiences and language? Was it easy to speak up? How did you interact with your teacher and with other children when using language? What can you remember about learning to read? Was it easy or difficult? Can you recall reading aloud to others? How do these memories inform your educational practices?

Curriculum Planning for Language Development

Teachers who plan curriculum for language skills, just as for cognitive development, focus on the class setting, specific skills, and themes. They organize the environment and activities to help children acquire linguistic skills of their own (NAEYC, 2005).

In the Early Childhood Setting

Indoors. Teachers arrange space so that children will practice speaking and listening and, in programs for older children, reading and writing. Indoor areas can be arranged to enhance language development as follows:

Art

- Have signs and pictures that show where things are kept.
- Ask children to describe the materials they use.

Blocks

- Ask children to give each other directions for where blocks go and what they are used for.
- Label block shelves with shapes and words.
- Sketch children's structures and then write their verbal descriptions.

Cooking

- Label utensils.
- Describe actions (pour, measure, stir).
- Use recipe cards with both pictures and words.

© Cengage Learning

Small groups are language-intensive activities that call for teachers to provide material and experiences in everyone's home language.

Discovery/Science

- Label all materials.
- Ask questions about what is displayed.
- Encourage children's displays, with their dictated words nearby.
- Graph growth and changes of plants, animals, children, and experiments.

Dramatic Play

- Provide a variety of equipment for a diversity of gender play, including male and female clothes.
- Set up spaces in addition to a "house/kitchen," such as a "reader's theater" in which children choose a story to act out and eventually write their own scripts.
- Offer cooking and eating utensils, objects, and tools that reflect cultural and linguistic diversity, such as a tortilla press and molcajete in the kitchen and different kinds of combs and brushes for the dolls, beginning with the cultures of the children in your program and then adding other groups.
- Have plenty of child-sized mirrors.

Language/Library

- Label the bookshelf, cassette player, and computer in children's languages.
- Help children make their own books that involve description (My family is …), narration (It is winter when …), and recall (Yesterday I …).
- Have children "write" notes, lists, or letters to one another, the teachers, and their families.
- Develop a writing center with a typewriter, office supplies, etc. (see Figure 13-12).

Manipulatives

- Recognize this area as a place for self-communication, as children talk and sing to themselves while they work.
- Explain similarities and differences of materials and structures.

Outdoors. Outdoors, motor skills can be described and pointed out by teachers and children, as both use words of action and of feeling. For example, what actions does it take to get a wagon up the hill? How does a child's face feel when swinging up high? How do people sit? move? carry things? (see Figure 13-6)

Routines, Transitions, and Groups

Transitions and routines are more manageable if the children understand what is happening and exactly what they are to do. Teacher language helps talk children

© Cengage Learning

A language-rich environment includes a welcoming spot for books and reading.

Environmental Elements that Promote Acceptance

Classroom posters, signs, bulletin boards
a. Hello, Buenos Dias, Ciao, Jambo . . . in as many languages as you have or want to learn.

Children as ambassadors
a. Every new child gets a "buddy for the day" for as long as they want.
b. The small group builds a "talkalot kit" for a new child to take home, a collection of materials that they can talk/show/add to at home.

Reading, math, science materials
a. Plenty of books and signage in several languages.
b. For older children, a "writer's briefcase" filled with stationery items such as paper, blank books, pens or crayons, envelopes, paper clips and brads, scissors and stapler, stickers; children check it out overnight, and their creation is shared at school.
c. A preschool alternative is "My Sleepover," a favorite toy, such as Curious George, takes turns going home in a bag with a journal. Families write or listen to their children's adventures with George, to be read in school.

Music, dance, and activities
a. Families bring in music or teach songs and dances to the teachers and children.
b. Teachers bring in materials that honor diverse cultures, teach songs in more than one language, and incorporate both in daily activities.

FIGURE 13-6 Teachers consider environmental elements to promote a sense of acceptance and belonging.

through the process so that they can internalize what they are asked to do. Arrival is an easy time to reinforce name recognition. Mark cubbies with names and photos:

> Each day, encourage children to find their own cubby. Point out their printed name. It is also helpful to point out other children's names and to notice the differences. "Oh look, here's Robert's name. His starts with an R just like yours. And here is Ann's. Her name starts with an A. Her name is very short." (Klein, Cook, & Richardson-Gibbs, 2001)

Children's belongings should also be labeled. These steps take a little time to make but can increase children's awareness of print.

A chart that shows in pictures and written language the steps children are to take from lunch to nap is invaluable, and children will refer to it daily. *Pillow Talk* is another ritual one Head Start class began to ensure that children have regular and predictable one-on-one conversations with a teacher:

> Once children are settled on their cots, Nancy sits on the floor next to a child. Her prompt "Do you have anything you want to talk about today?" initiates the conversation. Most children are eager to share a personal statement about themselves or their families...Nancy closes the conversation with a warm and affectionate gesture, such as a light pat on the shoulder. The final step in the routine is to tell the child that it is time to be very quiet and take her nap, accompanied with the message, "I'll see you when you wake up." (Soundy & Stout, 2002)

Finally, a teacher can write a note to "Please save" for the child who does not have time to finish a project, or they can write children's dictated notes to parents.

Group times, with finger plays, songs, and stories, are language-intensive activities. Children's articulation skills are strengthened, as is receptive language through listening to others. Group times are also opportunities for children to express themselves. When children discuss daily news and important events, brainstorm ideas about a subject, or report on what they did earlier in the day, they gain experience in listening and speaking. Children can also dramatize familiar stories and finger plays. Snack tables at one preschool began to exchange notes ("Dear Teacher Adrienne's Table: What are you doing? What are you eating?"), passing notes to each other's groups, including the sign language two children used ("How do you sign banana? What's the sign for graham crackers?").

Using visual aids or name cards gives children experience in graphic language. These might include having felt letters for the song "B-I-N-G-O," numbers for the finger play "One, Two, Buckle My Shoe," or name cards for the activity "I'm Thinking of Someone…" Children enjoy the cadence and rhythm of language spoken or chanted.

Focus on Skills

Recall that language skills are the ability to articulate, to learn vocabulary and put words together into complete sentences, and to understand when others speak. It also refers to the pragmatics, the appropriate and effective use of language in social communication. Speech skills refer to the ability to produce sounds (**phonemes**) that make words and articulate those sounds in meaningful, understandable ways (Klein, Cook, & Richardson-Gibbs, 2001).

Teachers can plan curriculum based on any one of the skills:

- To increase speech, vocabulary, and awareness of other languages, get a familiar book such as *The Very Hungry Caterpillar* (Carle) from the Children's Braille Book Club and also make name cards in Braille for every child.
- To encourage receptive listening skills, have children bring a favorite item from home or choose something from the class or yard and hide it in a "guessing bag." Children take turns looking into the bag and describing their item until others guess it. They can then pull it out and talk about it with the group.
- To emphasize expressive language, teachers allow children to express themselves by practicing words and grammatical structure and by elaborating on their own expressions. Outdoors, 4-year-old Hadar describes her actions: "Teacher, look at me! I'm taller than you!" The teacher responds, "You climbed up the ladder to the top of the tunnel. Now, when you stand up, your head is above mine."
- For developing graphic language, consider activities that extend the age range experiences of the children. For example, a kindergarten class makes a group story about "The Mystery of Space." Then, they separate into small groups with second grade helpers to write their own books in story form, complete with illustrations.

Themes

How could an emerging project or theme for curriculum planning be used to develop language skills? One unit with universal appeal is "Babies," charted in Figure 13-7.

Theme: Babies

Art: Limit art materials to just what toddlers and infants can use.

Cooking: Make baby food.

Discovery/science: Display baby materials, then bring in baby animals.

Dramatic play area: "The baby corner" with dolls, cribs, diapers.

Manipulatives: Bring in several infant and toddler toys.

Gross-motor/games: Make a "crawling route," an obstacle course that requires crawling *only*.

Field trip/guest: A parent brings a baby to school to dress, bathe, feed.

Large group time: Sing lullabies ("Rock-a-Bye-Baby")

Small/large group: Children discuss "What can babies do?"

Joshua: Babies sleep in cribs. They wear diapers. Babies can't talk.

Becky: They sometimes suck their thumbs. Babies cry when they are hungry.

Dennis: Babies go pee in their diapers.

Stevie: Babies sit in highchairs. Babies eat baby food that looks like squashed bananas.

Corey: Babies sleep in a bassinette. Then they crawl and bite your finger.

FIGURE 13-7 Teachers plan a unit to promote the skills they are focusing on in the class. A "babies" theme brings out the expert in all children and encourages language.

Other units that elicit an extensive use of language are:

1. *Harvest.* Activity: Ask children (2 + years) to bring food from home for a "feast corner." Make a display of food from a harvest feast in the past or change the housekeeping corner into a "feast for all" area.

   Group time: Begin a group story using the sentence "I am thankful for …"
   Special project: Plan a feast, with the children creating the menu and preparing both the food and the table for their families at the school.

2. *Friends.* Activity: Choose a favorite book (3 + years) to introduce the topic; the *Story Stretchers* book series (Raines & Canady, 1989) has several suggestions, such as *Heine's Friends.*

   Group time: Talk with the children about the kinds of things friends like to do together. Make a list; then read the book. Later, select children to act out the animal parts. Do not worry about reading lines; keep it imaginative!
   Special project: Put a flannel board in the library corner with characters and props from the book. Encourage the children to tell the story from the perspective of the various animals and then the farmer.

3. *The Earth Is Our Home.* Activity: Have the group (5 + years) make a large circle in a shade of blue, sketching the continents. Provide brown, green, and blue paint in pie tins and let children make a hand print on the ocean or land. Next, have the children bring from home the names of the countries of their family's ancestry. Help them locate those areas and attach their names to those parts of the world.

   Group time: Sing "The Earth Is Our Home" (Greg and Steve) and "One Light, One Sun" (Raffi). Read *Just a Dream* (Van Allsburg) and *Where the Forest Meets the Sea* (J. Baker).
   Special project: Help make a class recycling area or compost heap. Take a field trip to recycle the materials, or visit a garden that uses compost. Young children can learn about endangered species through Burningham's *Hey! Get Off Our Train;* older children can do research on an animal and make its natural habitat in a shoebox.

Although preschool and school-age children are challenged by specific themes, curriculum for infants and toddlers does not usually need this kind of focus. Curriculum for younger children should emerge naturally from their developmental level and interests. A gentle, supportive environment with adults who listen and respond to sounds made can be expanded on themes of favorite stories or activities.

Early Literacy

The ability to read and write does not just happen when children reach a certain age. Their readiness for graphic language must be nurtured. A child's language proficiency will determine readiness for reading. Research shows that gaps at kindergarten end up being consistent with those in later grades (Cannon & Karoly, 2007). Many entering kindergarteners (20 percent in California, for instance) have no familiarity with basic reading skills, including not knowing how to read words left to right or top to bottom or how to recognize letters of the alphabet. Successful readers see a relationship between spoken language and the written word. They are aware that sounds are how language is put together. So, teachers plan activities that make connections between what is said and what is written.

With the emphasis on early reading, the growth of early learning standards, and legislation such as No Child Left Behind (see Chapter 15), teachers feel pressured to bring direct instruction into their early education programs. It is important to emphasize that early literacy is not equivalent to early direct instruction. Yet much must go on in the early years for a child to be ready to read in primary school.

How exactly do infants (and adults) strive to make sense of everything they encounter in the world? They read it. Reading is the most natural activity in the world…We read the weather, the state of the tides, people's feelings and intentions, stock market trends, animal tracks, maps, signals, signs, symbols, hands, tea leaves, the law, music, mathematics, minds, body language, between the lines, and above all we read faces. "Reading," when employed to refer to interpretation of a piece of writing, is just a special use of the term. We have been reading—interpreting experience—constantly since birth and we continue to do so. (Smith, 2004)

Language-rich interactions and relationships with peers and challenging, well-planned curricula offer depth, focus, choice, engagement, investigation, and representation. Actively promoting concept and skill development can be achieved only in connection to young children's interests and abilities. Figure 13-8 describes some of these strategies.

There is an important role for teachers of young children in the early stages of reading and writing. Teachers can influence positive attitudes toward reading and writing. They encourage children to talk and converse with others about what they see and do; this gives them

Essential Early Literacy Teaching Strategies

Rich teacher talk	Engage in conversation, use rare words, extend their comments.
Storybook reading	Read aloud once or twice a day.
Phonemic awareness activities	Play games or sing songs that involve rhyme, alliteration, match sounds.
Alphabet activities	Use magnetic letters, alphabet blocks and puzzles, alphabet charts and books.
Support for emergent reading	Provide a well-designed book center, repeat reading children's favorites, have functional and play-related print.
Support for emergent writing	Encourage scribble writing, invented spelling, provide a well-stocked writing center and play-related writing materials.
Shared book experience	Read Big Books, draw attention to basic concepts of print such as left-to-right and top-to-bottom, cover and title page.
Integrated, content-focused activities	Investigate topics of children's interest, helping children gather data and record it, engage in dramatic play, use emergent writing to record what they learn.

FIGURE 13-8 The pressure of early reading instruction can be relieved by encouraging early forms of reading and writing that also give play a prominent role (Roskos, Christie, & Richgels, 2003).

increasing experience in using and attaching experiences to words. Taking the time to write down what children say and then reading it back gives a sense of importance to children's language and their ability to express themselves. Organizing the environment to support literary development and learning to teach toward reading in developmentally appropriate ways are all part of building an early literacy curriculum. In these ways, teachers can help children get involved with print in natural and unpressured ways.

Children and Reading

The role of the adult is one of engaging children with print in ways that make sense to them. By creating an environment that provides rich opportunities to use the printed word, teachers help motivate children toward reading. High quality preschool is a powerful force in building language and cognitive skills. Research shows that children who attend quality Pre-K score higher on school readiness measures at kindergarten entry (Karoly, et al, 2008). Early literacy experiences are the first step in closing the achievement gap.

But what are developmentally appropriate early literacy experiences? Adults and even children often have a stereotypical concept of reading. They think the ability to read is only the literal translation of signs and symbols on a printed page (called **decoding**). Learning to read is also attaching experiences and knowledge to words and understanding the use of the written word in daily life. In fact, learning to read is a complex process that includes both language and literary competencies. Building upon these skills takes time and has tremendous individual variation; thus, it is known as emergent literacy.

Emergent Literacy

Emergent literacy involves the "skills, knowledge, and attitudes that are developmental precursors to conventional forms of reading and writing. These skills are the building blocks for learning to read and write. Interventions in preschool should focus on emergent literacy skills since very young children are not yet engaged in conventional literacy" (Shanahan, 2005). The processes involved in helping children with emerging literacy include beginning literacy awareness and involvement before kindergarten, using reading and writing concurrently and in an interrelated manner, interacting with the written word in everyday activities, and using it to interact with the world. Literacy development is part of the total communication process that includes listening, speaking, reading, and writing.

The International Reading Association (IRA, 2006) declares that most children pass through five stages of early literacy development:

1. Awareness and exploration
2. Experimenting with reading and writing
3. Early reading and writing
4. Transitional reading and writing
5. Conventional reading and writing.

Teachers can help children succeed as they travel these stages. First, help them learn that print is a form of language. Read them books filled with magic, messages, and mystery (prereading). Next, be sure they hear stories, poems, chants, and songs many times. Programs such as *Raising a Reader* and other take-home book bag preliteracy programs help children and families access books in an enjoyable, consistent way. Look in "Helpful Websites" for several resources. Third, help them rehearse by chanting, singing, resaying, and "reading along" as we read to them (prereading). Fourth, observe as they learn to recognize words (see Figure 13-9). They read and know the text and begin to use some phonics to discover which words say what (beginning reading). Finally, children start to read more and more on their own or with a friend. Now the task is to make them better readers (reading).

Adults encourage children's writing by taking their attempts seriously.

© Cengage Learning

A Language Experience Chart

When is your birthday?
- Where is your name?
- How many children have birthdays in April? February? December?
- How many children have birthdays on the 10th? the 2nd? At the end of the month?

JAN.	FEB.	MAR.	APRIL	MAY	JUNE	JULY	AUG.	SEPT.	OCT.	NOV.	DEC.
13 Ann	1 José	3 Leon	2 Mrs. K.	16 Brian	11 Katie	5 Mr. W.	2 Carrie	8 Jim	21 Chris	7 Nick	13 Keesha
19 Bill	3 Mary	7 Kirk	10 Peter	27 Adele		9 Panya		29 Danny	30 Jay		25 Carol
26 Judy	6 Sue	15 Roberto	11 Jon			12 Kevin					30 Mrs. M.
24 Tom	11 Andy		18 Jill								
	19 Sean		23 Libby								
			30 Mia								

FIGURE 13-9 A language experience chart involves children through the subject matter and the way in which information is displayed.

Starting Out Right (1999) outlines the findings of a major report of the National Research Council entitled "Preventing Reading Difficulties in Young Children" (1998). It divides the reading process into two stages in the early years.

1. *Growing up to read* (birth to 4 years old). Falling in love with words and using everyday narrative are followed by first attempts: pretending to read, learning about print, and nourishing the mind with high quality books. Toward the end of this period, children know that alphabet letters are a special category of visual graphics and may recognize some. They pay attention to separate and repeating sounds in language, show an interest in books and reading, and display reading (signs in the local environment) and writing attempts (name on a birthday card; taking orders in a pretend restaurant).

2. *Becoming real readers* (kindergarten through third grade). To become real readers, children need well-integrated instruction that focuses on three core elements: (1) identifying words using sound spelling correspondence and sight word recognition; (2) using previous knowledge, vocabulary, and comprehension strategies to read for meaning; and (3) reading with fluency.

- During kindergarten, children should gain a solid familiarity with the structure and uses of print, be familiar with sound-by-sound and word-by-word analysis of language, and have an interest in the types of language and knowledge that books can bring them.
- First grade makes a transition from emergent to "real" reading. Children continue phonemic awareness, letter knowledge, and print awareness

to help with writing attempts and fluent reading. Spelling becomes a focus during the year, starting with **invented spelling** and growing into a sensitivity to conventional spelling. Literacy activities are done voluntarily, such as choosing stories to read or writing a note to a friend.

- Second and third grades help children build automatic word recognition, spelling skills, and reading fluency. Comprehension improves, along with recall of facts and participation in creative responses to texts, and children move toward producing a variety of written work. "Learning to read" is now shifting toward "reading to learn."

Whole Language or Phonics?

The concept of **whole language** has many familiar and exciting elements from the early childhood tradition. An approach that was popular in the early 1980s but has suffered in the early 21st century as direct instruction has dominated, whole language (Cruikshank, 1993):

> …is different in both theory and practice from the traditional basal [direct instruction] approach. Because it is child-centered rather than teacher-dominated, curriculum activities arise from children's current interests, needs, and developmental levels. Making connections is emphasized, and it is through meaningful integrative themes that students acquire knowledge and skills. Children are also encouraged to share ideas and work with others, as socialization is valued. Evaluation focuses on the child's growth over time, and both pupil port-

folios and anecdotal reporting are common assessment tools.

Goodman (1986) offers key principles of the whole language approach:

- Whole language is a way of viewing language, learning, and people (children, teachers, parents) in a *holistic, integrated* way. All the language arts are related to each other. For instance, a teacher might read a story to the children and then ask them to make up their own endings. The class would be *listening* (to the story), *speaking* (telling their ideas), *writing* (trying their hand at spelling and handwriting), and *reading* (their creations to a friend or the class at the end of the lesson).

- *Meaningful* content is when children use language in a purposeful way, developing naturally through a need to communicate. The young child who is read stories and engaged in conversations from infancy is then led smoothly to reading and writing as another extension of language use.

- Whole language encourages this extension of *function into form*; that is, children's own mastery of oral language and unique interests are drawn on in teaching the "rules" of sounds, letters, and words. See Figure 13-10 for the elements of whole language.

Critics of whole language argue that this approach leaves out teaching the decoding skills, which a traditional phonics approach emphasizes. Phonics is a means of teaching reading that makes associations between letters and sounds. But even before teaching formal read-

Early Literacy Comes to the Classroom

1. Have a cozy library corner, giving children lots of time to explore and read all kinds of books.
2. Make a writing corner with different kinds of supplies, using this area to develop grouptime activities (children's stories), meaningful themes (post office), and connected learning (writing and sending letters).
3. Take field trips, pointing out print as they find it (street signs, store shelves, bumper stickers) and writing about it afterward.
4. Use large charts for poems, fingerplays, and songs as well as for listing choices available and for group dictation.
5. Plan activities that incorporate print: read recipes for cooking projects, make menus for lunch and snack, follow directions in using a new manipulative toy, write sales tickets for dramatic play units, bring books into science displays.
6. Use written notes regularly, sending a regular newspaper home that the children have written or dictated, writing notes to other team teachers that children deliver, encouraging children to send notes to each other.

FIGURE 13-10 Whole language in the primary classroom means integrating graphic language activities in a natural, meaningful way.

ing, teachers can help children develop phonological and phonemic awareness—a sensitivity to the sound structure of the language. Children who can detect and manipulate sounds in speech are beginners in the decoding process. The ability to discern syllables is an important part of learning to understand how sounds translate into individual and combinations of letters.

Noticing and manipulating the sounds of a spoken language are related to later success in reading and spelling. "In English—and many other languages—the written language is predominantly a record of the sounds of the spoken language. With a few exceptions, the English language is written out by sound" (Yopp & Yopp, 2009). Therefore, children must be able to grasp the sounds of speech if they are to understand how to use a written system that records those sounds.

Current knowledge concludes that, to learn, primary children benefit from both specific phonics instruction and a rich background in literature (such as being read stories). This approach blends early phonics instruction in the teaching of reading while at the same time stressing the importance of balance (see Figure 13-11). In addition, it must be repeated that children under 5 years of age are not ready for an onslaught of conventional, direct instruction methods. There is a lack of agreement in the field over what count as *emergent literacy skills*, and more research is needed along with more refined understanding of the skills involved. Learning graphic language is a cre-

Activities for Phonemic Awareness

Phonemic Awareness Includes	Teachers
1. Oral vocabulary	1. Encourage talking, learning new words and phrases, singing, finger plays, and remembering and reflecting verbally.
2. Auditory discrimination (the ability to detect sound differences)	2. Create sound discrimination boxes in the science area, a "listen-to-the-sound" walk, guessing games with musical instruments, and activities that teach letter sounds by using the children's names.
3. Phonological awareness	3. Help children play with individual sounds, both larger and smaller as well as different types of manipulations. The song "Old MacDonald" has 5 sounds (E-I-E-I-O), and playing with "apples/bapples/dapples" focuses attention on sounds.
4. Syllable awareness	4. Encourage children to listen and segment words into syllables, such as playing word games (me-mama-granpapa each have a different number of sounds: You want a drink of wa...*ter*, let's fix a sand...*wich*).
5. Onset-rime awareness	5. A more complex skill, onsets are the consonant sounds that precede a vowel in a syllable (d is the onset in dog, fr in frog) and rimes are a vowel plus any sound that follows it (og is the rime for dog and frog), so games that play with each "end" of a word help children hear the sounds.
6. Phoneme awareness	6. The smallest unit of speech are phonemes, which vary widely among languages; English has about 44, Spanish closer to 24 (Yopp & Yopp, 2009). Besides extending children's natural play with sounds, read aloud books, poetry, and songs that play with sounds, and play games such as "I Spy" that focus on a sound (I spy something that begins with /sh/...shoes!)

FIGURE 13-11 Children gain early literacy skills through activities for phonemic awareness.

DAP Teachers understand the typical trajectory of phonological skill development for preschool children—rhyming, alliteration, syllable segmenting, onset/rhyme blending, and segmenting. Teachers add challenges to learning experiences as children make progress along the skills continuum.

ative process that involves both an *art* (literature, rhyming songs, and invented spelling) and a *science* (the nuts and bolts of decoding). It is the teacher's job to be the master craftsperson in helping children put the two together.

Children and Writing

Children learn about words in print much the same as they learn about reading and other aspects of language: that is, by seeing it used and having plenty of opportunities to use it themselves. Writing can be as natural for children as walking and talking. "What is written language? For a child, print is just another facet of the world, not yet comprehended, perhaps, but not different from all the complex sights, sounds, smells, tastes, and textures in the environment—not especially mysterious or intimidating" (Smith, 2004). Children's **emergent writing** begins when they first take a pencil in hand and start to scribble. Later, they can write a story by drawing pictures or by dictating the words and having someone else write them down.

A Print-Rich Environment

Labels, lists, signs, and charts can make print a meaningful part of the classroom environment. Often, children are involved in making the signs to indicate where things go and what things are. Using the languages of the group expands this "literate room," as do helper charts, daily schedules, and even attendance charts. Road signs can be made for the block corner, recipe cards for cooking. "Do not touch" may be written for an unfinished project, as can "Inside voices here" for the library corner. For specific literary practice, Schickedanz (1999) suggests labeled picture cards for rhyming games, alphabet puzzles, magnetic letters, and scrabble games, as well as opportunities for children to give dictation, write grocery lists, and compose letters to friends and family.

Writing materials can be available throughout the room and yard. Paper and pencils come in handy in the dramatic play area. Menus, shopping lists, prescriptions, and money are but a few uses children will find for writing equipment. The block corner may need traffic signs; the computer, a waiting list. Outdoors, pictures can label the location of the vegetables in the garden; markers indicate where children have hidden "treasures" or where the dead bird is buried.

The early childhood classroom heightens an interest in writing through a writing center (see Figure 13-12). It can be part of a language area or a self-help art center. Wherever it is located, this center will include a variety of things to write with, to write on, and "writing helpers."

Children write with pencils (fat and thin, with and without erasers), colored pencils, narrow and wide marking pens, and crayons. They enjoy having many kinds of paper products, including computer paper, old calendars, data-punch cards, and colored paper. Children also enjoy simple books, a few blank pages stapled together. Carbon paper, dittos, and lined paper will add variety. "Writing helpers" might be a picture dictionary, a set of alphabet letters, a print set, an alphabet chart, a chalkboard, or a magnetic letter board. All of these serve to help children practice writing skills.

Emergent Writing

Children's first attempts at writing will likely include drawing or scribbling. Because drawing helps children plan and organize their thoughts (and, thus, their text), teachers encourage children to tell them about their stories and can ask for a child's help in "reading" these writings. As children begin to work with words themselves, adults can help them sound out words or spell words for them. Spelling development is similar to learning to speak: Adults support the efforts, do not correct the

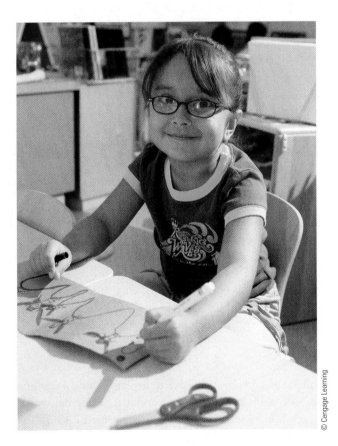

A literate classroom includes plenty of opportunities for experiences with writing.

Suggested Writing Center Materials

- Alphabet board
- Alphabet stamps
- Binders—yarn, string, "twist ties," to bind homemade books
- Book-binding machine (used by adults to bind special books)
- Cardboard—cereal/cracker boxes provide cardboard for covers
- Clipboards
- Collage materials—magazines, wall paper, and wrapping papers
- Colored pencils
- Crayons
- Envelopes (local card store will sometimes donate leftovers)
- Fabric
- Laminate (factories will sometimes donate end rolls)
- Magnetic letters
- Markers
- Mini books (½- and ¼-size sheets of paper, about 4–5, stapled. Another recommendation: ½ sheets of lined paper, about 30 pages for longer works.
- Name cards (children's names)
- Notebooks, notepads, stationary, odd-shaped/colored papers (printshops will sometimes donate these)
- Office-style rubber stamps and ink pads
- Old cards, invitations, and business cards
- Old date books and calendars
- Paper crimping tool (roll a piece of paper through and it comes out corrugated—found at a rubber stamping or craft store)
- Paper punches (with large button that can be easily pushed by children)
- Recycled paper (different sizes)
- Rulers
- Scissors
- Stamps: wildlife and other nonpostage stamps. (Homemade stamps can be made by painting the backs of pictures with "lick'em, stick'em"—one part strawberry gelatin and one part water. Apply to shiny magazine pictures, dry and then they can be licked and used as stamps.)
- Stapler (kindergarten)
- Stencil shapes
- Stickers
- Word wall (words and their corresponding pictures—whenever the children need to know how to write a new word, it goes up there.)

FIGURE 13-12 A writing center needs plenty of materials to stimulate graphic language development (Chesler, 1998).

mistakes, and allow children to invent their own spelling of words. Picture dictionaries and lists of popular words help children use resources for writing. Figure 13-13 is a sample of invented spelling in a kindergarten.

The *language experience* approach involves taking dictation, writing down and reading back to children their own spoken language. It is important to use the child's exact words so they can make the connection between their speech and the letters on the page. This is true for group stories, for children's self-made books, or for descriptions of their own paintings. A useful technique in taking dictation is to say the words while writ-

Invented Spelling

I ZMTMCGO TOTHE
BECH

I HVA BNE RABT

tS SAPFR WAL

I H V A DAL

I GOT AN YOO PE ROY
GLARSIS AT ASHOPK OOLD
FOR EYES

UAW Z RPT WT HO=M
DNDS NH EH HND

FIGURE 13-13 Early writing usually involves children's attempts at words of their own invention. Invented spelling can be treated with respect for the efforts and as a foundation for successful writing experiences. (Courtesy of Kim Saxe. Reprinted with permission.)

ing them, allowing the child to watch the letters and words being formed. When the content is read back, the child has a sense of completion.

In her book *Teacher*, Sylvia Ashton-Warner describes one technique for introducing printed language to young children. A kindergarten teacher who believed strongly in children's innate creativity and curiosity, Ashton-

Warner developed a system of *organic reading* in which the students themselves build a key vocabulary of words they wish to learn to read and write. This method was effective for her classes of native Maori children in New Zealand, for whom the British basal readers held little meaning. Ashton-Warner's personal, culturally relevant teaching works well because it flows naturally from the child's own life and interests. Figure 13-14 is an example of these kinds of language experiences in classrooms of 3-, 5-, and 6-year-olds.

Story maps help children see the parts and sequencing of the writing process. Depicted as a body, the head serves as the beginning (with facial features called "topic," "characters," and "setting"), the body as the middle, and the legs as the end ("Finally…"). A primary child can write in the various parts of the story and read it from the map or continue to elaborate with full sentences in a more traditional manner. In these ways, teachers help raise awareness of the use and enjoyment of the printed word.

Many teachers use a combination of key words, journals, and phonics along with holistic strategies such as DEAR (Drop Everything and Read), huddle groups (you choose who to work with), book bragging time (either in large or small groups), and BEAR/SST (sustained silent reading with a timer, usually done in grades one through three) as they teach reading in developmentally appropriate ways (Bobys, 2000; Reisner, 2001).   DAP

The Language Experience Approach

1. Start with a leading sentence.

If I were an instrument . . .
Michelle: I would be a piano with strings and lots of sparklies on top. And you could play me even if you were blind.
Janette: I would be a drum. I would be hit and I wouldn't be happy because they would make me hurt.
Dennis: I would be a violin. Someone would play me with a bow and I would make a beautiful sound.

2. Take dictation on topics and pictures of their making.

"On Our Halloween Nights"
Ehsan: There was a witch and skeleton and ghost in my room on Halloween night.
Lionel: Costume night. A cow jumping over the moon. The little rabbit sleeping.
Martine: There was a big pumpkin and a big bat and a bear and a pirate. There was a jack-o-lantern and the light glowed.
Andrew: There was a smiley monster and Aka-Zam!
Luke: We went to my church for hot dogs and cider.

3. Ask for stories of their own.

Once upon a time there's a boy named Timothy and he punched all the bad guys dead. And he was very strong and he can punch anything down. And he can do anything he likes to. And he makes all the things at winter. And he was so strong he could break out anything else. And he had to do very hard work all day long and all day night. And he had to sleep but he couldn't. And he had a very small house and cup. And then he did everything he want to all day long. The End. Tim (signed)

4. Make a group book (including illustrations).

All By Myself (our version of the book by Mercer Mayer)
"I can put on my overalls all by myself." (Stephanie)
"I can brush my hair all by myself." (Lindsey)
"I can make pictures all by myself." (Jessica)
"I can buckle my jeans all by myself." (Megan)
"I can make a drill truck with the blocks all by myself." (Lionel)
"I can jump in the pool all by myself." (Andrew)

FIGURE 13-14 The language experience approach takes many creative forms in a classroom. (Special thanks to Gay Spitz for example 1 and to Ann Zondor and Lynne Conly Hoffman and the children of the Children's Center of the Stanford Community for several of the examples in 2 and 4.)

DAP Teachers plan activities that give children a motivation to engage in writing ("How about we write a menu for your restaurant?"). They focus on capturing children's ideas, recording their dictated words in charts, stories, or messages to parents or others, and then reading the dictation back (using their finger to indicate the words so the child can follow along).

Children's Literature

Children's books bring us back to ourselves, young and new in the world. Our bones may lengthen and our skin stretch, but we are the same soul in the making…Children's books are such powerful transformers because they speak, in the words of the Quakers, to one's condition, often unrecognized at the time, and remain as maps for the future…In children's books, we preserve the wild rose, the song of the robin, the budding leaf. In secret gardens we know the same stab of joy, at whatever age of reading, in the thorny paradise around us. (Lundin, 1991)

Literature does indeed have an important place in the curriculum today. Through the use of good books, teachers can help children broaden their interests and concepts. Books that are primarily used for transmitting information expand the child's knowledge base. Thoughtful books that draw on children's everyday experiences widen their understanding of themselves and others. For instance, children can learn to see things in a variety of ways. Five different books will describe and illustrate the behavior of cats in five different ways. Exposure to *Millions of Cats* (Gag), *Angus and the Cats* (Flack), and *The Cat in the Hat* (Dr. Seuss), as well as to the cats portrayed in *Peter Rabbit* (Potter) or *Frog Went A-Courtin'* (Langstaff), will enlarge the child's concepts of cats. Different cultures are also represented in any number of children's books, teaching a greater awareness of all of humankind (see Figure 13-15 and "Insights from the Field" at the chapter's end).

Teachers have an opportunity to encourage divergent thinking through the use of children's literature. Children gain more than facts from books; they learn all manner of things, providing they can interpret the story rather than just hear the individual words. Quizzing children about whether the dinosaur was a meat- or plant-eater will bring about responses that are predictable and pat, but comprehension does not have to be joyless."Would a brontosaurus fit in your living room?" will get children to think about *Danny and the Dinosaur* (Hoff) or Kent's *There's No Such Thing as a Dragon* or Most's *If the Dinosaurs Came Back* in new ways that get them involved in the story.

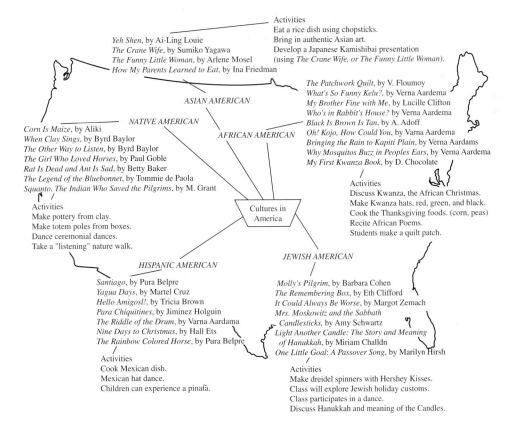

FIGURE 13-15 Using multicultural literature helps each child get connected with books and expands all children's outlooks (courtesy of de Melendez & Ostertag, 1997).

Selection of books is important (see Figure 13-16). The wise teacher will choose books that invite participation. Everyone can "roar a terrible roar, gnash their terrible teeth, and show their terrible claws" during a rendition of *Where the Wild Things Are* (Sendak). Meaning for children lies more in action than in words. When Andrea was struggling to find the words to describe a large amount, Mitra began to recite: "Hundreds of cats, thousands of cats, millions and billions and trillions of cats!" (Gag's *Millions of Cats*). As Trelease (1982) states, "If our first problem is not reading enough to children, our second problem is stopping too soon." Whether age 1 or 10, children need and thrive on being read aloud to regularly. Teachers could ask for no better activity to promote good listening habits than a wealth of good children's books.

Creating a Rich Literary Environment

The newspaper comics of yesterday are far outdistanced by the television and video games of today. How can teachers give children experiences in literature in the face of such competition?

Selecting and Reading Children's Books

Before reading:
Look at the cover.
Talk about pictures and text.
Activate prior knowledge.
Ask for personal connections.
Set a purpose.

THE LITTLE ENGINE

During reading:
Make predictions.
Pause and reflect.
Create mental images.
Summarize.
Read it again, pointing to words and pausing.

After reading:
Make connections.
Create reenactments.
Perform retellings.

1. ____ Could I read this book enthusiastically?

2. ____ Are the contents of the book appropriate for the children?

   ____ Is it age appropriate?

   ____ Is it suitable for the individual child(ren)?

   ____ What are the cultures and languages of the group?

3. ____ Is this book biased?

   ____ Are illustrations stereotyped or showing tokenism?

   ____ What is the story line: What is the standard for success; how are problems presented and resolved; what is the role of women, people of color, or the heroes?

4. ____ Is the book written with an understanding of my group's age characteristics?

5. ____ Is the author's style enjoyable?

   ____ Can the children understand the sequence?

   ____ Is there repetition of words or actions?

   ____ Does it end in a satisfying way?

   ____ Are there humorous parts?

6. ____ Does it have educational value?

FIGURE 13-16 Selecting books for children involves careful study (derived from Owocki, 2001, Machado, 1999, & Derman-Sparks & Olsen Edwards, 2010.)

The field of children's literature is rich in its variety, including both great classic stories and those of present day situations and concerns. Fiction and informational books, children's magazines, and poetry add balance to the literary curriculum. Every classroom should contain representative works from each of these areas and should:

- *Provide plenty of time for using books and other materials.* Children need time to browse, to flip through a book at their own pace, and to let their thoughts wander as they reflect on the story line. They also enjoy retelling the tale to others. Be sure to plan enough time to read to children every day.
- *Make a space that is quiet and comfortable.* In addition to soft pillows or seats, locate the reading area where there is privacy. Crashing blocks and messy finger painting will intrude on the book reader. A place to sprawl or cuddle up with a friend is preferable.
- *Have plenty of books and supporting materials.* The language arts center might contain a listening post, with headsets for a CD or tape player. Perhaps there is even a place where books can be created, a place supplied with paper and crayons. There may even be an old typewriter, puppet stage, or flannel board nearby so that stories can be created in new ways.
- *Display children's literary creations.* The efforts of children's stories and bookmaking should be honored by establishing a place in the room where they can be seen and read. Children then see how adults value the process of literary creation and the final product.
- *Model how to care for a book and keep classroom books in good repair.* Children can come to realize that a book is like a good friend and should be given the same kind of care and consideration.
- *Foster children's reading at home.* This is one of the important contributions a teacher can make to the reading process. Family literacy programs are developing for all families to gain skills in English; check your local community for availability. Families whose home language is not English face enormous challenges when encouraging reading; research supports development of the home language as a foundation for learning other languages (Kirmani, 2007), so programs should attempt to offer *book bags* to families with books in their home language as well as plenty of picture books that allow parents to "read" the pictures with their children (Teachout & Bright, 2007). Attitudes about reading are communicated to children from the important people in their lives. Posting the local library hours, establishing a lending library, and providing parents with lists of favorites will reinforce the child's interest in literature. Figure 13-17 gives parents ideas of helping children at home.

- *Use books around the room.* Do not confine them to just the book corner or the book shelf. Demonstrate their adaptability to all curriculum areas by displaying a variety of books in the activity centers. Ask children to help you retell or emphasize parts of a story (see the storytelling section), and ask them questions informally afterward: "How many bowls of porridge were on the kitchen table? Which one did Goldilocks like best? How did you know?" Figure 13-18 shows how books can enhance play and learning throughout the school room.

Extending Literary Experiences

Good literature comes in many forms and can be presented in a variety of ways. A creative teacher uses books and literature to develop other curriculum materials. Translating words from a book into an activity helps a child remember them. Books and stories can be adapted to the flannel board, storytelling, dramatizations, puppets, book games, and audiovisual resources.

12 Things Parents Can Do to Help Their Preschooler Become a Reader

1. Have daily conversations with your child.
2. Keep lots of printed materials and writing materials in your home.
3. Set up a reading and writing space for your child.
4. Let your child see you read and write.
5. Read with your child every day.
6. Call your child's attention to reading and writing in everyday activities.
7. Make a message board.
8. Encourage your child to read.
9. Display your child's writing.
10. Make a bank or file of words your child likes to write.
11. Go to the library with your child.
12. Use television and technology wisely.

FIGURE 13-17 Teachers foster reading at home by offering families practical ideas (Epstein, 2002).

Literature Across the Curriculum

Living Together: Reflecting Diversity

Knots on a Counting Rope (Martin, Jr., & Archambault)
The Big Orange Splot (Pinkwater)
Mei Li (Handforth)
Gilberto and the Wind (Ets)

Creating Art

Black Is Brown Is Tan (Adoff)
Start with a Dot (Roberts)
Little Blue and Little Yellow (Lionni)

Building Blocks

Changes Changes (Hutchins)
The Big Builders (Dreany)
Who Built the Bridge? (Bate)

Dramatic Play: On Our Heads!

Martin's Hats (Blos)
Caps for Sale (Slobodkina)
Hats Hats Hats (Morris)

Families

When You Were a Baby (Jonas)
All Kinds of Families (Simon)
Whose Mouse Are You? (Kraus)

Discovery/Science: Grow, Growing, Growest!

Growing Vegetable Soup (Ehlert)
The Carrot Seed (Krauss)
From Seed to Pear (Migutsch)

ABC, Just Like Me!

K Is for Kiss Goodnight: A Bedtime Alphabet (Sardegna)
A to Zen (Wells)
Grandmother's Alphabet (Shaw)

Math Lab: 1,2,3, Count with Me!

How Much Is a Million? (Schwartz)
Roll Over! A Counting Song (Peek)
Ten, Nine, Eight (Bang)

Making Music

Hush Little Baby (Aliki)
Ben's Trumpet (Isadora)
One Wide River to Cross (Emberley)

Having Friends

Friends (Heine)
George and Martha (Marshall)
Frog and Toad Are Friends (Lobel)

Books for Zero to Threes

Goodnight Moon (Brown)
Brown Bear, Brown Bear (Martin, Jr.)
Duerme Bien, Pequeno Oso (Buchholz)

Books for Early Primary

Charlotte's Web (White)
How Many Days to America? (Bunting)
Ramona (Cleary)

FIGURE 13-18 When literature is a natural part of the environment, children learn to appreciate and use it.

Storytelling

Storytelling is as old as humanity. The first time a human being returned to the cave with an adventure to tell, the story was born. Storytelling is the means by which cultural heritage is passed down from one generation to another. Children's involvement with a story that is being told is almost instantaneous. The storyteller is the medium through which a story comes to life, adding a unique flavor through voice, choice of words, body language, and pacing.

"The experience of hearing a story told is more personal and connected to the reader," states Isbell (2002). "Storytelling promotes expressive language development—in oral and written forms—and presents new vocabulary and complex language in a powerful form that inspires children to emulate the model they have joy telling the story and communicate their enthusiasm to children.

Dramatizing Stories

Acting out characters from a favorite story has universal appeal. Young preschoolers are introduced to this activity as they act out the motions to finger plays and songs. The "Eensy Weensy Spider" and its accompanying motions is the precursor for dramatization. Story reenactment helps children learn to work together so that their social development is enhanced, as is the cognitive ability to engage in collective representation. As an extension of Steiner's theories, Waldorf kindergartens include fairy and morality tales. "Fairy tales are told to the children on successive days for up to two weeks, culminating in the tale as a puppet show offered to the children by the teacher or as a play with costumes acted out by the children with the teacher narrating" (Waldorf Staff, 1994). Whether the child is an observer, walk-on, mime, or actor, the learning is real in each step of the continuum.

Stories such as *Caps for Sale* (Slobodkina) and *Swimmy* (Lionni), as well as fairy tales, are popular choices for reenactment by 4- and 5-year-olds. They need plenty of time to rehearse, and simple props help them focus on their role. A red scarf helps Jeannada become *Little Red Riding Hood*; an old pair of sunglasses transforms Joaquin into a character from *Goggles* (Keats).

Older children may choose to write (or dictate) parts or scripts; it is appropriate for 6-to 8-year-olds to have their playmates act out original stories. Once the "right" story has been chosen, the teacher helps the children to retell the story together, set the stage, and let the play begin.

Puppet Shows

Puppet shows can involve a large number of children as participants and audience. Children of all ages enjoy watching and putting on a puppet show. Because puppets are people to young children, they become confidants and special friends. Children will confide in and protect a puppet, engaging in a dialogue with one or more puppets that is often revealing of the child's inner struggles and concerns. Teachers can support their efforts by helping them to take turns, suggesting questions and dialogue to them, and involving the audience. The project of puppet making can be quite elaborate and very engaging for older children.

© Cengage Learning

Acting out characters from a favorite story is culturally relevant and has universal appeal.

experienced." The oral tradition is strong in many cultures, and the telling of the tale is memorable.

Instead of focusing on a book page, the teacher involves the children directly, with expressions and gestures that draw in the children. Repetition and questions get the children so involved they feel that they have created the story. Young readers will want to find the book, and young writers will want to draw and retell the story or create their own.

Teachers can use any familiar story, be it *The Three Little Pigs* or *Madeline*. Props can be added to draw attention to the story. Flannel board adaptations of stories are helpful; they give the storyteller a sense of security and a method for remembering the story. Children can be involved in the action by placing the characters on the felt board at the appropriate time. Puppets or an assortment of hats can be used as props. Good storytellers en-

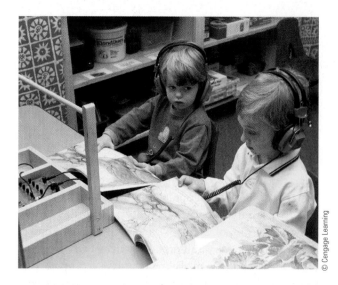

A listening post can provide additional interest in books and stories.

Book Games

Book games are a good way to extend the literary experience. Buy two copies of an inexpensive book with readable pictures, such as *The Carrot Seed* (Krauss). Tear out the pages, and cover each page with clear plastic. Children must then read the pictures to put the book into proper sequence. A book of rhymes, such as *Did You Ever See?* (Einsel), lends itself to rhyming games. Children can act out the rhymes from the story line or match rhyming phrasing from cards the teacher has made.

Audiovisual Resources

Audio files and videos enlarge the child's experience with books. The auditory and the visual media reinforce one another. Putting in a "listening post" so that a few children can listen to a story with headphones adds interest to stories. Music brings literature alive; besides tapping into the musical aspect of intelligence, it appeals to all children to move and express themselves and, thus, enjoy literature and books even more. The pictures can show children new aspects of the words; sometimes the music or the voices bring the book to life. Often both happen. Hundreds of children's stories—classics and modern day—have been translated to these media. Be judicious with videos, so that the images from the children's imaginations do not get erased by the dominance of the visual movie pictures.

Books are no substitute for living, but they can add immeasurably to its richness. When life is absorbing, books can enhance our sense of its significance. When life is difficult, they can give a momentary relief from trouble, afford a new insight into our problems or those of others, or provide the rest and refreshment we need. Books have always been a source of information, comfort, and pleasure for people who know how to use them. This is as true for children as for adults (Arbuthnot & Sutherland, 1972).

Welcoming English Language Learners to the World of Language and Literacy *by Wilma Robles de Meléndez, Ph.D.*

With a continuous high rate of immigration, cultural and linguistic diversity is already a pattern that characterizes early childhood education where an increasing number of young English language learners (ELL) are commonly found in preschool and primary classrooms around the country. Working with ELLs calls for teachers to be mindful and sensitive about the child's needs as they encounter a new context. Getting a sense that one belongs and that you are part of the group is an important factor that influences individual achievement. It is important to consider that some may come from settings with different cultural behaviors and that, in addition, they may have limited or no exposure to English. Coming into a classroom where social behaviors differ from those they know and where interactions are in a language different from theirs could be a challenging and, to an extent, a frightening experience. How to address these needs begins with the careful planning and organization of the environment. Environments are a powerful teaching and learning element that communicate ideas and expectations. They also help to validate the child's first language and heritage. Literally, environments "speak" to the child, a reason why at all times they should say, "This is your classroom." Successful environments for ELL children are characterized by having welcoming messages, meaningful content, and high child-appropriate expectations. Careful planning is the key to creating contexts that meet the needs of young children who are learning English.

A first step in planning a welcoming environment for young ELLs, as well as all children, is to think about the messages and impressions that the classroom communicates. Ask yourself if what hangs on the walls, what is displayed, and the materials offer a welcoming feeling for culturally and linguistically different children. Check the charts, bulletin board, and signs and see if they include postings in languages other than English and especially those reflective of the children's first languages. This would already communicate to the child "your language is valued!" For the ELL child, it also means finding something familiar, which is reassuring, helping her to feel a part of the setting. Visual impressions are compelling communicators of ideas, too, so take time to examine the images and illustrations posted. Check if these are representative of children and families from diverse backgrounds. Also, be sure to provide images that are inclusive of different social groups. You want to make everyone feel welcome!

Best practices remind us about the importance of making learning meaningful to the young ELL child. Effective environments for ELL should foster opportunities to connect experiences with what they know, which is another key step in creating a well-planned context. Take time to examine the themes that are explored in your classrooms. See if these relate to the children's experiences and backgrounds. Meaningful connections happen when the context includes opportunities such as listening and reading stories with themes and characters representative of the children's backgrounds. This supports their culture and language and provides experiences familiar to the child where opportunities abound to activate and link prior knowledge with what is learned in the classroom. Use of realia such as coins or tools and manipulatives carefully linked to what is explored also contributes to connecting concepts and content in meaningful ways.

Environments are also characterized for communicating expectations, another essential step in planning a supporting context for ELL children. Interactions with children and peers, use of materials, and nonverbal exchanges all communicate expectations in different ways to the young English language learner. Classroom contexts for children who are learning English should communicate and encourage them to participate in experiences fostering the sense "Yes, I can!" While building their linguistic proficiency, they should also explore rich and challenging content. Take time to reflect on the expectations that you hold for the young ELL child. Remember, knowledge about the individual needs and progress level guides the planning and selection of content that should match the child's learning level. Maintaining equitable expectations requires early educators to balance activities while setting up engaging and challenging experiences.

While these three aspects—environment, content, expectations—are essential, the key to a welcoming context is a sensitive and caring early childhood educator who will find that working with young ELL children is another exciting experience that calls for attention to meeting the child's linguistic needs.

Wilma Robles de Meléndez, Ph.D., is program professor of early childhood education at the Fischler School of Education and Human Services of Nova Southeastern University (FL) where she teaches and coordinates the graduate program in early childhood education and early literacy. Her research interests include research in services for young children with cultural and linguistically diverse backgrounds, multicultural education, social studies for young children, and early literacy development. She is the author of *Teaching Young Children in Multicultural Classrooms* (2007) and of the Lee y serás' Child Care Providers Conversations Series (2005), a national Latino early literacy initiative.

SUMMARY

Planning for language development is a huge part of a teacher's curriculum work. Language and thought are intertwined, and recent research on brain development and early literacy both indicate the importance of the early years in language acquisition and literacy skills. Children follow a sequence of language development. Language skills in early childhood include articulation, receptive and expressive language, graphic representative, and enjoyment.

The teacher's role requires an understanding of several considerations. Knowing language development and the role of home language is critical. Keeping individual children in mind and watching for dominance by the most verbal children helps. The teacher also needs an understanding of bilingualism and dialect differences and a working knowledge of speech and language disorders. The language of the teacher—both spoken and nonverbal—will influence children's use of language in a program.

Special topics emerge in language curriculum. Early literacy involves children in reading and writing experiences. Children and books belong together. Good literature gives insight into how to play peek-a-boo, escape a hungry lion, make a friend, and be brave. The early years should lay a foundation in literature upon which children can build throughout their lives.

KEY TERMS

receptive language
expressive language
extended discourse
precursors
phonemic awareness
dual language learners
bilingualism

simultaneous acquisition
successive acquisition
dialect
Ebonics
articulation
elaboration

phonemes
decoding
emergent literacy
invented spelling
whole language
emergent writing

REVIEW QUESTIONS

1. What are the stages of language development?

2. Describe dual language learning and how teachers help children who are English language learners.

3. List the five language skills and one way early education can help their development.

4. The teacher has several roles in language development; name at least three with an example of how to implement the consideration.

5. Describe three curriculum activities for language development. Simplify them for infants/toddlers/2s and elaborate for the primary-aged youngsters.

6. Name the two major steps in the development of children's reading, and how they can be encouraged in a program.

7. What is a "print-rich environment"? Give at least three examples that encourage children's writing.

8. How does one select good children's books?

LEARNING ACTIVITIES

1. Observe the children in your care. Identify the stages of language development of three children. Give concrete examples that validate your assessment.

2. Choose a child in your care whose primary language is not English. How is that child processing language? What are you doing to foster the child's emerging English skills? How is that child's first language being supported in your program? What can you do to involve the family?

3. Teaching reading readiness involves trying to develop oral language and listening skills. What could a teacher of toddlers plan for each? A kindergarten teacher?

4. Describe three ways children's books and literature can be extended in the curriculum.

5. Select four or five books from a bibliography of multicultural children's books. What themes are addressed? How does the vocabulary or speech style of the story characters teach children about diversity?

HELPFUL WEBSITES

American Library Association   **http://www.ala.org**

Braille Institute   **http://www.brailleinstitute.org**

Children's Book Council   **http://www.cbcbooks.org**

Early Childhood Research Institute on Culturally and Linguistically Appropriate Services   **http://clas.uiuc.edu/links.html**

National Association for Bilingual Education   **http://www.nabe.org**

National Association for Multicultural Education   **http://www.nameorg.org**

National Association for the Education of Young Children   **http://www.naeyc.org**

National Black Child Development Institute   **http://www.nbcdi.org**

National Center for Family Literacy   **http://www.famlit.org**

National Task Force on Early Childhood for Hispanics   **http://www.ecehispanic.org/about.html**

Raising a Reader Early Literacy Program   **http://www.raisingareader.org**

Reading Is Fundamental   **http://www.rif.org**

 Additional resources including the TeachSource Videos can be found on the premium website for this book. Go to **http://www.cengage.com/login** to register your access code.

REFERENCES

Ansari, S. (2005). *English Language Development Institute.* Redwood City, CA: San Mateo County Office of Education.

Baker, C. (2004). A *parents' and teachers' guide to bilingualism* (2nd Ed). Clevedon, England: Multilingual Matters Ltd.

Cannon, J. S., & Karoly, L. A. (2007). *Who is ahead and who is behind: Gaps in school readiness and student achievement in the early grades.* Santa Monica, CA: RAND Corporation.

Cazden, C. B. (1996, March). Communicative competence, 1966-1996. Paper presented at the annual meeting of the American Association for Applied Linguistics (ERIC No. ED 399764), Chicago, IL.

Chang, H. (1993). *Affirming children's roots: Cultural and linguistic diversity in early care and education.* Oakland, CA: California Tomorrow.

Chesler, P. (2002). Bilingualism: Literacy development and activities for the young child. Unpublished.

Chomsky, N. (1993). *Language and thought.* Wakefield, RI: Moyer Bell.

Derman-Sparks, L., & Olsen Edwards, J. (2010). *Anti-bias education for young children and ourselves.* Washington, DC: NAEYC.

Dickenson, D. K., & Tabors, P. O. (2002, March). Fostering language and literacy in classrooms and homes. *Young Children, 57*(2).

Epstein, A. (2009, January/February). Think before you (inter)act: What it means to be an intentional teacher. *Exchange.*

Hoover, M. (1997, March/April). Ebonics insider. *Stanford Magazine.*

International Reading Association (2006). Position statement: Literacy development in the preschool years. Retrieved from www.reading.org

Isbell, R. T. (2002, March). Telling and retelling stories: Learning language and literacy. *Young Children, 57*(2).

Isbell, R., & Phillips, L. (2001, Spring/Summer). Oral language development in learning centers. *Play, Policy, and Practice Connections* VI (1).

Karoly, L., Ghosh-Dastidar, B., Zellman, G., Perlman, M., & Fernyhough, L. (2008). *Prepared to learn: The nature and quality of early care and education for preschool-age children in California.* Santa Monica, CA: RAND Corporation.

Klein, M. D., Cook, R. E., & Richardson-Gibbs, A. M. (2001). *Strategies for including children with special needs in early childhood settings.* Clifton Park, NY: Thomson Delmar Learning.

Miller, K. (2001, September/October). Caring for the little ones: When do you teach them to read? *Child Care Information Exchange* (141).

NAEYC (2005). *Position statement on responding to linguistic and cultural diversity: Recommendations for effective early childhood education.* Washington, DC: Author.

National Clearinghouse for English Language Acquisition (NCELA) (2007a). The growing numbers of limited numbers of English proficient students: 1995/96–2005/06. Washington, DC: Author. Retrieved from www.ncela.gwu.edu

NCELA (2008). Dual language learners in the early years: Getting ready to succeed at school. Washington, DC: Author. Retrieved from www.ncela.gwu.edu.

Saxton, R. R. (1998, July). Different dialects. Personal communication.

Selman, R. (2001, May). Talk time: Programming communicative interaction into the toddler day. *Young Children, 56*(3).

Soundy, C. S., & Stout, N. L. (2002, March). Pillow talk: Fostering the emotional and language needs of young learners. *Young Children, 57*(2).

Tabors, P. O. (1998, November). What early childhood educators need to know: Developing effective programs for linguistically and culturally diverse children and families. *Young Children, 53*(6).

Vygotsky, L. S. (1962). *Thought and language.* New York: MIT Press and John Wiley and Sons.

Wasik, Barbara, A. (2001, January). Teaching the alphabet to young children. *Young Children, 56*(1).

Watson, A., & McCathren, R. (2009, March). Including children with special needs: Are you and your early childhood program ready? *Young Children, 64* (2).

Willis, C. (1998, May/June). Language development: A key to lifelong learning. *Child Care Information Exchange,* 121.

Special Topics: Early Literacy and Children's Literature

Arbuthnot, M. H., & Sutherland, Z. (1972). *Children and books* (4th Ed). London: Scott Foresman.

Bobys, A. R. (2000, July). What does emerging literacy look like? *Young Children, 55*(4).

Cruikshank, S. (1993). Whole language: A developmentally appropriate alternative. In A. Gordon, & K. B. Browne (Eds.), *Beginnings and beyond* (3rd Ed). Clifton Park, NY: Thomson Delmar Learning.

de Melendez, W. R., & Ostertag, V. (1997). *Teaching young children in multicultural classrooms.* Clifton Park, NY: Thomson Delmar Learning.

Derman-Sparks, L., & the ABC Task Force (1989). *The anti-bias curriculum.* Washington, DC: NAEYC.

Goodman, K. (1986). *What's whole in whole language.* Portsmouth, NH: Heinmann Educational Books.

International Reading Association and NAEYC (1998, July). Learning to read and write: Developmentally appropriate practice for young children. *Young Children, 53*(4).

Kirmani, M. H. (2007, November). Empowering culturally and linguistically diverse children and families. *Young Children, 62*(6).

Lundin, A. (1991, Summer). Secret gardens: The literature of childhood. *Childhood Education, 67*(4).

Machado, J. M. (1999). *Early childhood experiences in language arts.* Clifton Park, NY: Thomson Delmar Learning.

National Research Council. (1998). *Prevention of reading difficulties in young children.* Washington, DC: National Academy Press.

Owocki, G. (2001). *Make way for literacy.* Clifton Park, NY: Thomson Delmar Learning.

Raines, S. C., & Canady, R. J. (1989). *Story stretchers.* Mt. Rainier, WA: Gryphon House.

Ramirez, G., Jr., & Ramirez, J. L. (1994). *Multiethnic children's literature.* Clifton Park, NY: Thomson Delmar Learning.

Reisner, T. (2001, March). Learning to teach reading in a developmentally appropriate kindergarten. *Young Children, 56*(2).

Roskos, K. A., Christie, J. F., & Richgels, D. J. (2003). The essentials of early literacy instruction. In D. Koralek (Ed.), *Spotlight on young children and language.* Washington, DC: NAEYC.

Schickedanz, J. (1999). *Much more than the ABCs: The early stages of reading and writing.* Washington, DC: NAEYC.

Shanahan, T. (2005, February 14–16). What the national early literacy panel tells us about early literacy. IRA-NICHD Conference on Early Childhood Literacy Research. Washington, DC.

Smith, F. (2004). *Understanding reading—the psycholinguistics of reading and writing* (6th Ed). NJ: Lawrence Erlbaum Associates.

Teachout, C., & Bright, A. (2007, July). Reading the pictures: a missing piece of the literacy puzzle. *Young Children, 62*(4).

Trelease, J. (1982). *The read-aloud handbook.* New York: Penguin Books.

Waldorf Staff of Los Altos, CA (1994). *Understanding the Waldorf curriculum.* Pamphlet for parents.

Watson, A., & McCathren, R. (2009). Including children with special needs: Are you and your early childhood program ready? *Young Children* 64(2): 20–26. Retrieved from www.journal.naeyc.org/btj/200903.

Yopp, H. K., & Yopp, R. H. (2009, January). Phonological awareness is child's play. *Young Children, 64*(1).

© Cengage Learning

Planning for Heart and Soul: Psychosocial Development

PREVIEW QUESTIONS

- How do children learn through psychosocial experiences?
- What are emotional growth and skills?
- What is social growth in the early years?
- How is creativity developed?
- How can teachers address spiritual growth?
- How can art help children's psychosocial development?

NAEYC CODE OF ETHICAL CONDUCT

These Core Values and sections from the NAEYC Code of Ethical Conduct are addressed in this chapter. As you read, note how the Core Values, Ideals, or Principles listed here apply to the topics in this chapter. (Reprinted with permission from the National Association for the Education of Young Children.)

Core Values: We have committed ourselves to helping children and adults reach their full potential in the context of relationships that are based on trust, respect, and mutual regard.

Section I:
- I-1.5. To create and maintain safe and healthy settings that foster children's social, emotional, intellectual, and physical development and that respect their dignity and their contributions.
- P-1.4. For every child, we shall implement adaptations in teaching strategies, learning environment, and curricula, consult with the family, and seek recommendations from appropriate specialists to maximize the potential of the child to benefit from the program.

Section II:
- I-2.3 To respect the dignity of each family and its culture, language, customs, and beliefs.

Learning through Psychosocial Experiences

The heart and soul of any good program for young children is a commitment to help children as they struggle with (1) the reality of emotions, (2) the awareness of the need for social skills, (3) the creative urge, and (4) acknowledgment of the spirit. Together, these four areas comprise the psychosocial, or affective, side of development. Closely related to the child's self-concept and self-esteem, affective growth takes place in the context of personal identity. "Identity is tied to culture. In the critical early years, children begin to develop a sense of self as families hand down beliefs, attitudes, and behaviors" (Nakahata, 2001). It is primarily through psychosocial experiences that children learn who they are; only then can they see themselves successfully in relation to others. "K-12 standards have often focused on academic subject matter rather than including other domains…Because research has emphasized how powerfully early social and emotional competence predicts school readiness and later success, and because good early environments help build this competence, this domain should be given explicit attention in early learning standards" (NAEYC, 2002).

Each section of this chapter—emotional, social, creative, and spiritual growth—is explored individually to give a greater understanding of its importance to the developing child. An overview of development is followed by a discussion of the skills children learn in the preschool years. The crucial role of the teacher is emphasized next, followed by curriculum planning to reinforce each area.

The Psychosocial Domain

The first thing one notices on entering an early childhood classroom is the children at play. A quick survey of the area shows who is playing together, whether there is crying or fighting, and how happy or sad the children look. This overview gives an immediate sense of the emotional, social, and creative climate in that early childhood setting.

- *Emotional.* Toddler Abier giggles as she runs her hands across the water table, then cries after she splashes soapsuds in her eyes and needs to be comforted.
- *Social.* Preschooler Danny wants his favorite red wagon, so Pat, the student teacher, helps him negotiate a turn with Christa.

- *Creative.* Kindergartners Fabio, Erika, and Benjy work steadily to build a tall, intricate block structure. When it is finished, the three children stand back and marvel at their creation.
- *Spiritual.* The children see a nest being built in the backyard of Teresa's family childcare home. "How do the birds know how to make the nest?" wonder the children. They make daily checks and then hear the peeping sound of the newly hatched baby birds. "It's magic!" whispers Neefara, and the children sit quietly and reverently every time they see the mother return.

Together, these factors—emotional mood, social dynamics, creative, and spiritual tone—define the overall atmosphere in which children play and work.

The components of well-being are woven together in the developing child. Children who are sensitive to their own feelings and moods are able to begin understanding other people and, thus, become more socially effective and successful. Children with experience in many creative endeavors have the self-confidence that comes from having an outlet for self-expression. Children who are spiritually curious are likely to ask questions such as "How did the little seed do that?" when gardening, or they want to write a letter to their dead pet to make sure all is at peace.

The **psychosocial domain** is the third area of human development. It includes the development of emotions, of temperament, and social skills. Areas of self-concept and self-esteem are also in this realm. "Family, friends, the community, the culture, and the larger society are particularly central to the psychosocial domain. For example, cultural differences in appropriate sex roles or in family structures are part of this domain" (Berger, 2007). The domain is sometimes labeled **affective** as it deals with feelings, or *socio-emotional*, as the social and emotional areas are key components. The division into the three domains makes it easier to study, but development is holistic, not piecemeal, as seen in the following segment.

These four areas are also linked to other aspects of the child's growth. Below are four examples of how the developmental domains connect:

- *Creative/Physical.* Physical skills can define and limit children's creative abilities. Two-year-old Andrea, whose physical skills do not yet include balancing objects, plays with blocks by piling them on top of one another, filling her wagon with blocks, and dumping them or lugging them from place to place.

■ *Social/Cognitive.* It is hard for 5-year-old Karena to share her best friend Luther with other children. Her intellectual abilities do not yet allow her to consider more than one idea at a time, so she cannot understand that Luther can be her friend and Dana's at the same time.

■ *Emotional/Language.* Tyler is upset with his teacher's refusal to let him go outdoors during story time. "I hate you!" he screams, "and you aren't the boss of me!" Children learn to label and express their emotions through words.

■ *Spiritual/Creative.* The children make their daily trek to the henhouse as soon as outside time begins. They first gasp as they discover a raccoon has pried open the wire and killed their pet. After all the queries about what happened, Ellie speaks up, "I want to make a picture for Henny-Penny to take with her." The group paints a multicolored mural, for which each one dictates ideas. "I am sad you died," says Ellie. "But don't worry, you will rise again!" A child's spiritual notions are allowed to express themselves in creative ways.

It is difficult to measure the child's growth in these areas; it is easier to determine a child's progress in physical, cognitive, and language development. After all, a child counts or does not count, is either 40 inches tall or is not, and speaks in full sentences or in short phrases. Affective expressions are more subtle and subjective. Talbot may feel rejected and sad if no one greets him as he enters the playhouse. He may mistake the children's busy-ness as an act of exclusion. In reality, the children did not even notice he was there. Teachers can play a critical role in helping children express their inner selves and feelings.

Traditionally, early childhood educators have concerned themselves with children's well-being, knowing that in the early years the foundations must be laid for children to understand themselves and others. Social growth, creative expression, and experience with a wide range of emotional behaviors also help children develop a strong self-concept with positive self-esteem.

Building self-image is complex, multidimensional, and ever-changing. It affects everything we do and is affected by everything we do. Crucial to children's self-image is how children interpret the response of the environment to their actions. And much of a self-image is based on the way society views the child. Teachers play an important role as they provide an essential ingredient of self-image: the quality of human interactions.

Building self-image is complex, multidimensional, and ever-changing.

Courtesy of Chris and Stephanie Kelly

A Sense of Self

Children need to have several key experiences in the early years in order to develop and consolidate a sense of self (see Figure 14-1). "Kindness and hostility go hand in hand as children exercise their growing abilities to understand and affect the feelings of others" (Curry & Johnson, 1990). At the same time, the early years include formative experiences that shape a child in terms of moral worth, wrestling with good/nice and bad/mean. The curriculum can foster the development of the whole child. This will mean including the children's and their families' lives and incorporating multicultural and anti-bias elements (see Chapters 9 and 10).

Transformative education recognizes that all of us are socialized to take our place in society. Our sense of self is influenced by prevailing social values, and our social skills are shaped by social practices. The social realities of sexism, racism, classism, ethnocentrism, and heterosexism shape children's self-identity and the formation of prejudice and discriminatory behavior. Transformative education fosters a positive and knowledgeable self-identity by strengthening children's connections to their

Growing a Sense of Self

Age	Growth Focus	Help Children with . . .
Infants	Relationship	Attachment
Toddlers	Awareness	Self-regulation
Twos	Curiosity	Interactions with others
Preschool	Self-concept	Testing and evaluating self
	Authority	Testing their limits in play, making friends
Kindergarten	Self-in-the-world	Feeling effective
Primary	Competence	Managing failure/mistakes, finding their strengths

FIGURE 14-1 Children's emotional and social growth is an ongoing challenge as they enter new settings in their expanding world.

families, cultural communities, and geographic communities. (York, 1998)

A psychosocial curriculum that prepares children to be active and involved and promotes social action and problem solving helps children develop into involved citizens with a positive self-identity. In a curriculum for infants and toddlers, the emphasis is on relationships. In preschool, it is part of the traditional emphasis on social and emotional development. For school-age programs, it is often known as character education.

Affirming Identity

As children experience messages from others and through their own perceptions, they construct an understanding of race, ethnicity, gender, and ability. This will shape their self-image and, by extension, their relationships to others. *Starting Small* (1997) suggests activities to assist in promoting children's identity, which are incorporated in the theme/project in Figures 14-1 and 14-7.

Self-Esteem

An individual's sense of personal worth and an acceptance of whom one is helps them make judgments about themselves as they confront the world. To the extent that children feel worthy and capable, they are ready to suc-

ceed. If children disapprove of themselves, they may feel like failures and expect to do poorly.

Self-esteem develops as a reflection of experiences. The way people respond to you gives you some indication of your importance or value. Newborn infants have no concept of self and no past experience to judge their own worth. A young child who has positive experiences with others will more likely have a higher sense of self-esteem than one who has felt unloved or unnoticed.

There appear to be four components of self-esteem:

1. A sense of one's own identity.
2. A sense of one's uniqueness.
3. A sense of self (power).
4. A sense of belonging (connectedness).

Early in life, self-esteem is tied to family, friends, and other important people, such as teachers. Figure 14-2 shows how curriculum can develop each of these characteristics. Planning for children's success builds self-esteem. It includes the following four components, which we call the "Four I's":

- *I*. When children enter the classroom, the message they receive is "I am important and this is my place." The physical environment, the daily schedule, and the curriculum are designed to give all children permission to express themselves. This gives children a sense of identity and uniqueness.
- *Initiative*. Children are encouraged to initiate their own learning, to make contact with others, to take action, and to make choices. Power is important to young children; they want to know how to take (and when to let go) of control, and how to use power to get what they want and need.
- *Independence*. Self-management tasks of dressing, eating, and toileting are given an important place in the curriculum. Children are assisted in taking care of their own belongings and in developing independent judgment about events and activities. Every culture and group has its own intricate rules about when and how to be independent, and an early childhood group can give them experience.
- *Interaction*. Social interaction has a high priority in the program. The room and yard are busy places, with children moving about and talking among themselves and with adults. Conflicts are accepted as a natural consequence of social life. In the spirit of John Dewey (Chapter 1), democratic group living encourages children to interact. In respect for cultures that value collaboration and group harmony, such interaction fosters a consciousness of interde-

Curriculum for Psychosocial Development

Emotional Skill Development

Self Esteem

1. *Identity:* "Look at what I can do, the noise I can make, the weight I can pick up and move!"

2. *Connectedness:* "I can make the same snakes as you; we can all make cakes."

3. *Uniqueness:* "I'm pouring mine; you're dripping yours; and she is squeezing her stuff out her fingers!"

4. *Power:* "I can make this water go anywhere I want; look out for the tidal waves!"

Deal with Feelings

1. *Identification* (to notice and label): "Does it feel very smooth, slippery, slidy? Is it soft and soothing?"

2. *Mastery* (to accept): "She took your baker's dough and that made you angry. You can tell her you don't like it when she grabs what you are using."

3. *Expressing* (to express appropriately):

   Child: "Tami has all the big pitchers."

   Teacher: "How can you let her know you want one?"

   Child: "And she splashed me two times!"

   Teacher: "If you feel too crowded, you need to tell her so."

4. *Feelings* (to deal with others): "Whee! Yuk! Mmm! Ha!"

Curriculum: Activity (Use of Sense)

- Use rocks of various sizes with balances, so that children can touch and hear when they move things around.

- A malleable material such as play dough can be used first alone, then with tools.

- Make "oobleck," a mixture of cornstarch and water, in separate tubs for each child. Children can manipulate it in their own ways.

- Water play offers the child choices: pour into any of several containers, fill or empty the jug, use a funnel or a baster to squirt the water, make waves or splash hands.

- When fingerpainting, the teacher can describe what it appears the child is feeling. Children can identify their feelings as the teacher describes them while they use the materials.

- Whether the sensory material is clay, soapy water, or fine sand, the issues of ownership and use of materials arise. Then, teachers reflect children's feelings and help them take responsibility for their own feelings.

- As children begin to use the sensory materials, they need to communicate to others. Usually the issues are about wanting more material and personal space.

- When children share in a sensory activity, such as a feeling walking through tubs of small pebbles, sand, and soapsuds, they have the delightful experience of enjoying their own feelings with another.

FIGURE 14-2 A psychosocial curriculum offers sensorimotor opportunities to deal with materials in a nonstructured way. Because children relax with open-ended activities, they will often share their feelings as they use sensory materials in a comfortable atmosphere.

pendence. The need for relationships with other people is crucial, and interaction gives children a sense of connectedness.

A positive sense of self is critical for young children. Research (Marshall, 1989) shows that low self-image is correlated with poor mental health, poor academic achievement, and delinquency. In contrast, a positive self-concept is correlated with good mental health, academic achievement, and good behavior. Children with a positive self-image are ready to meet life's challenges. They will have the self-confidence to deal with the reality of emotions, the changing nature of social interaction, the joys of creativity, and serenity of spirituality.

Emotional Growth

The Development of Emotions

Emotions are the feelings a person has—joy and sorrow, love and hate, confidence and fear, loneliness and belonging, anger and contentment, frustration and satisfaction. They are responses to events, people, and circumstances. Feelings are an outgrowth of what a person perceives is happening. Emotionally healthy people learn to give expression to their feelings in appropriate ways. They do not allow their feelings to overshadow the rest of their behavior. The optimal time to learn these skills is in the early years.

Research in brain development (Pool, 1997; Goleman, 1995; Chapters 4 and 12) has identified key areas of the brain involved in emotional expression and development. An area in the limbic section of our brains is the control center of our emotions. Two almond-shaped organs behind our eyes, called the amygdala, are in constant communication with the rest of the brain (for thinking and perceiving).

The emotional brain scans everything happening to us from moment to moment to see if something that happened in the past that made us sad or angry is like what is happening now. If so, the amygdala calls an alarm to declare an emergency and to mobilize in a split second to act. And it can do so, in brain time, more rapidly than the thinking brain takes to figure out what is going on, which is why people can get into a rage and do something very inappropriate that they wished they had not. It is called an "emotional hijacking" (Goleman, 1995).

Children experience this constantly, and educators must help children develop dimensions of **emotional intelligence:** self-awareness, handling emotions generally, motivation, empathy, and social skills. These grow over time, with maturation and experience both at work. In infancy, there are first only two identifiable emotions: contentment and distress. Infants respond in agitated emotion whether wet, hungry, hurt, or bored. Gradually, the expression of the emotion becomes more refined and varies with the situation. Curiosity and anger begin to appear. A toddler's cry of frustration is different from the cry of discomfort or hunger. As children get older, their emotional expressions change as they gain control over some of their feelings and learn new ways to express them. "New emotions appear toward the end of the second year: pride, shame, embarrassment, and even guilt. Because these emotions require an awareness of other people, they emerge from the family setting, which is itself influenced by the culture" (Berger, 2007).

These strong external forces include parents, family members, teachers, and friends as social influence. They help the young child learn socially acceptable behavior, and can mediate aggressive or withdrawing behavior. Much of what children learn is by example (see Chapter 4). Therefore, children learn more from adult models than from simply being told how to behave and feel. In the preschool years, emotional regulation is a key challenge, which can lead to competence within every culture and domain (Matsumoto, 2004). The emotional foundation of the first five years is carried forth into school-age, as a friend, the peer group, and validation from adults help build resilience and coping skills for dealing with stress.

Emotional Skills in Early Childhood

The emotional skills children learn in their early years are substantial. Research shows that some emotions—interest, disgust, distress, to name a few—are observable in the newborn, and it is posited that all the **basic emotions** are present within the first few weeks of life. These include happiness, interest, surprise, fear, anger, sadness, and disgust. The more **complex emotions** of shame, guilt, envy, and pride emerge later, once children have had the social experiences of observing these emotions in others or have been in situations that might evoke such feelings. These expressions have been observed in a wide range of cultural and ethnic groups.

In early childhood, children learn to respond to new situations and to react and connect with a teacher, both very emotional experiences. Good teachers stimulate an emotional response to themselves and the curriculum that is a balance between interest and overwhelming fear. Creating the "right" emotional conditions is a primary way to gain access to a child's capacity for learning. Young children are not yet limited by **social mores** and standards of conduct that prevent them from sincere and truthful self-expression. Teachers observe children and learn how youngsters feel about facing their own feelings, the feelings of others, and the range of skills categorized as emotional growth.

Ability to Deal with Feelings

Dealing with feelings involves four steps. Each builds on the other so that they follow a developmental sequence; the learning that takes place at one level affects the development of what follows. Figures 14-2 and 14-4 describe how the early childhood classroom and teacher help children deal effectively with their feelings.

To Notice and Label Feelings. This ability is the first step and corresponds to Goleman's "self-awareness" dimension. The sobbing 1- or 2-year-old may have many reasons for feeling distress. As parents recognize the cries of hunger, hurt, and fear, they name these feelings. The child will learn to notice what the feeling is and recognize it. Teachers know how to "read" children's faces and body language to give them the words for and ways to express those feelings (see Figure 14-3). Chapter 6 has suggestions for becoming a skillful observer. For instance, we can help young children produce a label for their feeling of anger or sadness by teaching them that they are having a feeling and that they can use a word to describe their angry feelings. We can ask them to "Use your words" only

Learning to "Read" Feelings

Feeling	Behavioral Definition
1. Fear	Pale face, alert eyes, tense mouth, rigid body.
2. Surprise	Wide eyes, eyebrows uplifted, involuntary cry or scream, quick intake of breath.
3. Anger	Red face, eyes staring, face taut, fists and jaw clenched, voice harsh or yelling, large gestures.
4. Joy	Smiling face, shining eyes, free and easy body movements, laughing.
5. Pride	Head held high, smiling face, jaunty walk or strut, tendency to announce or point out.
6. Embarrassment	Red face, glazed and downcast eyes, tight mouth, tense body, small and jerky movements, soft voice.
7. Sadness	Unsmiling face, downturned mouth, glazed and teary eyes, crying or rubbing eyes, limp body, slow or small movements, soft and trembly voice.
8. Anxiety	Puckered brow, pale face, tight mouth, whiny voice, jerky movements, lack of or difficulty in concentration.
9. Curiosity	Raised brow, shining eyes, perhaps tense body in absorption of the object of curiosity; often hand movements to touch and pick up object; sometimes mouth agape.

FIGURE 14-3 As we observe children's behavior, we understand how their feelings are expressed. Expressions of fear, anger, sadness, disgust, and happiness are universal, and learning to read faces and body stance is essential to guiding emotional development.

after we have helped them learn and find those specific words.

Toddlers and 2-year-olds can be taught simple words for sad, mad, and glad. Preschoolers are quite verbal and curious about language and ready to learn words that describe a wider range of feelings. They can learn "lonely," "scared," "silly," "sad," and "happy." Labeling what one feels inside is a critical skill to learn. It is a healthy first grader who can say, "I have tried to cut this string three times and the scissors aren't working. I am frustrated. I need some help!"

To Accept Feeling. Teachers recognize that children are capable of strong feelings. Children can feel overwhelmed by the very strength and intensity of a feeling, be it one of anger or of love. As children come to accept feelings, they learn how to handle the depth of the feeling and not let it overpower them. The changing nature of feelings is also part of accepting the feeling. It can be a source of comfort and relief for young children to discover that the strong emotion they experience now will pass. Adults who work with young children help them work through those feelings safely.

For instance, 3-year-old Carlos feels sad as his mother prepares to leave. His teacher walks them to the door, then bends down and puts an arm around him as his mother waves good-bye. Acknowledging that he is sad, the teacher stays with Carlos, reminding him that his mother will return and that the teacher will take care of him while he is at school. Because the child is allowed to feel the sadness that is natural in leave-taking, the tense feelings are over in a few minutes. The teacher smiles and encourages Carlos to find something fun to do. Once he has recovered his composure, the teacher can point out that he's "okay now," and Carlos can feel proud for having lived through and grown from saying good-bye. Acknowledgment of the feeling and his ability to accept it help give Carlos the confidence to move on.

To Express Feelings in an Appropriate Way. Expressing feelings appropriately is a two-part process. First, children must feel free to express their feelings; second, they must learn ways of expression that are suitable to their age and to the situation. Many beginning teachers are uncomfortable because children express themselves so strongly (and often aggressively). Yet the child who is passive and unable to express feelings freely should be of equal concern and should be encouraged in self-expression.

When teachers create a safe emotional climate, they can effectively help children learn to understand and

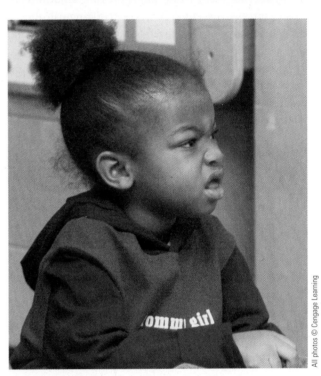

All photos © Cengage Learning

Young children feel their emotions strongly. Learning to read faces and body stance is essential to guiding emotional development and for children to be successful socially.

express themselves. "Adults who most effectively socialize … convey a simple, firm, consistent message, [for example,] acknowledging a child's right to feel anger while prohibiting expression of anger in destructive or hurtful ways" (Marion, 2006). Knowing how to handle upsetting feelings or impulses is the root of emotional intelligence. "I can see you are upset about Joaquin taking the zoo animal," you might say, "But I cannot let you hit him—and I will not let him hit you, either."

Encouragement to act out every emotion is not appropriate, for instance, for African-American children. "Living under oppressive conditions mandates learning

to handle oppression in ways … [such as] to learn where to express feelings and who it is safe to let know your feelings," says Cooper (1992). "Their reluctance to engage should be respected, not viewed as a challenge."

As children grow, they acquire the modes of expression that are developmentally appropriate for their age. Babies and toddlers without language cry to express their feelings; thus, this type of crying calls for the same kind of immediate response given to other forms of communication in later years. Two-year-olds express their displeasure by pushes and shoves; 4-year-olds use their verbal power and argue. By age 6 or 7, children learn to tell others—clearly and with reasons—what they are feeling. The ability to express feelings is intact, but the methods of expression change as children grow. Expression of feelings also has a cultural dimension. Some cultures are open in their display of emotions, whereas others are reserved.

To Deal with the Feelings of Others. Dealing with the feelings of others is the culminating step in the development of emotional skills. Feelings are the spark of life in people: the flash of anger, the "ah-hah" of discovery, the thrill of accomplishment, the hug of excitement. Because recognizing and expressing emotions are closely interwoven, children who can distinguish among different emotions and have some experience in taking the perspective of others by observing their feelings develop empathy. With increasing social awareness and decreasing egocentrism (see Chapter 4), two other emotions emerge: empathy, a true understanding of the feelings of another; and antipathy, intense dislike of other people. Toddlers may cry or gather near the

teacher when a playmate is hurt or sad; preschoolers smile at another's laughter; and kindergartners imagine themselves vividly in another's predicament during a story. Like the complex emotions discussed earlier, empathy requires cognitive abilities, such as seeing oneself as separate from other people (see Erikson, Chapter 4) and also as connected in some way to others (see Vygotsky, Chapter 4).

Older children, who are better able to put themselves in another's place (see Piaget, Chapter 4) and who understand a wider range of emotions, can respond to others in distress. Conducting class meetings to help children "Talk It Out" (see Figure 14-11) guides children through a process that builds problem solving, compassion, and community. Empathy is affected by early experience and needs nurturing to grow. Helping children to tolerate and appreciate how different people express their emotions leads to understanding and cooperation.

Ability to Handle Change

It is remarkable that, as one of the most adaptable species on the planet, we humans resist change so much. Even as our brains are programmed to find pattern and sameness, it is change that is inevitable. The very act of being born is a change, marking the beginning of a life in which stress is part of the act of developmental achievement. Witness the toddler's numerous falls toward walking, the separation of parent and child at the nursery school doorway, the concentration and frustrations of the 6-year-old on roller skates. A measure of **positive stress** encourages a child to strive and achieve, to find out and discover.

Stress can arise from several factors—both internal (severe colic) or external (moving to a new home). Some stresses are acute in a child's life, such as a hospitalization, whereas others are chronic, such as living in an alcoholic household. Inadequate housing, poverty, and war are ecological stressors (see Chapter 15). Family changes—the birth of a sibling, death or loss of a close family member, marriage problems, and divorce—are sources of stress on a personal level. Inept parenting practices that neglect or abuse children are especially troublesome as they hurt children and provide them with poor role models for learning how to cope with stress.

Helping children find a haven and creative interests also helps develop a protective buffer against difficulties in school or home. Perhaps the single most important intervention is you, the teacher, who is a confidant or a positive role model. Figure 14-4 lists the stages of stress and teacher strategies.

© Cengage Learning

Children learn to appreciate and understand feelings as their feelings are accepted by teachers who can show them how to deal with feelings and changes.

Coping with Stress: The Teacher Helps

Stage	Behavior	The Teacher Helps
Alarm	Feels arousal, fear, confusion. Has swift mood changes.	Notices when child is stressed (sees changes in behavior). Listens. Offers words for child's feelings. Offers age-appropriate explanations. Is accepting of unpredictable behavior. Reassures child of teacher's constant availability. Alerts parents and others of child's state. Takes preventive actions to lessen other stressful events.
Appraisal	Attempts to understand the problem.	Listens. Offers age-appropriate explanations. Helps child see situation more positively. May make a simple list of the problem. Reassures that the problem *will* be solved. Alerts other adults to the importance of child's work.
Search	Looks for coping strategy. Selects from what is at hand.	Listens. Asks for the child's ideas. Helps child list possible solutions. Tells parents and others of child's solutions. Demonstrates self-control and coping skills him/herself. Encourages and enhances child's self-esteem.
Implementation	Tries out a coping strategy. Applies a solution to the problem.	Listens. Observes child's implementing a solution. Gives supportive feedback about relative success or failure of the plan. Helps child refine or revise strategy as needed. Encourages child's efforts.

FIGURE 14-4 Stages of and strategies for coping with stress: the teacher is observant of the child throughout, makes regular time to talk individually, and encourages the child to use art, books, and class members as supports.

Teachers can help children accept change in several ways:

- Anticipate changes that are likely to occur and identify the process for children. "Junko, your mother will be leaving soon. We will go looking for that favorite puzzle after you say good-bye to her."
- Notify children of changes in the daily routine. "We will not be having snacks inside today; let's use the patio table instead."
- Model acceptance of unanticipated changes. When children are informed that change is anticipated, accepted, and not necessarily disrupting, they become more relaxed about handling the unpredictable.
- Be a resource for helping children cope in ways that are appropriate to the child and the situation at hand. "It's okay to cry when you are sad or scared,

Akbar. It is hard to figure out what to do when they say they do not want to play."

Ability to Exercise Judgment

The ability to exercise judgment is an important skill, for it helps children to make decisions and figure out what to do in new situations. On entering a program, a child faces many decisions: Where shall I play? Who shall I play with? Who will I turn to for help when I need it? Judgment is selecting what to do, when to do it, with whom to do it, and when to stop.

Making choices is an essential part of decision making. Children are bombarded with choices in America—too many choices, some people say. Some children must decide about issues that, in other times, only adults handled. But children have difficulty discriminating between

© Cengage Learning

Enjoying one's self includes being aware of one's power and learning to use it well, making important things happen without harming self or others.

big choices and little choices. Every choice is a big one for most children. Learning to make good choices takes thought, guidance, and lots of practice.

There is no easy way to teach children how to make decisions because each situation must be dealt with on an individual basis. The judgment a child exercises in choosing a friend to play with today may have other factors to consider tomorrow. Instead, teachers help children base their decisions on the best judgment they are capable of in each instance. One way to encourage decision making is to provide opportunities for choice (see "Focus on Skills" for specific suggestions).

Another aspect of judgment is a child's **self-regulation.** Research suggests that children can develop the capacity to plan and guide themselves. In contrast to self-control, in which we teach children to respond to an external rule, children's self-regulation is a combination of the cognitive and emotional realms.

> During the early childhood years, there is a great increase in self-regulation …[T]his increase is a "central and significant" developmental hallmark of the early childhood period. During these years, the child makes tremendous progress towards regulating emotional responses and is increasingly able to

comply with external requests, control behavior in familiar settings, control attention, and engage in self-directed thinking and problem-solving self-regulation. (Bronson, 2000)

The teacher can encourage this process by serving as a Vygotsky-like mediator, making children participants in their own learning (thinking), and by supporting children's focus on self-competence (emotional). As they mature, children are able to sort out what judgments might be made here, what factors need to be considered there.

Enjoying One's Self and One's Power

Teachers want children to feel powerful—to know that they can master their lives and feel confident in their own abilities. This feeling of power is particularly important in the early years, when so much of what a child can see is out of reach, both literally and figuratively.

Responsibility and limits, however, go hand in hand with power. The child who is strong enough to hit someone has to learn not to use that strength unnecessarily. The child who shouts with glee also finds out that noise is unacceptable indoors. By holding children responsible for their own actions, teachers can help children enjoy their power and accept its limitations.

One kind of fantasy play most teachers encounter is that of **superheroes.** Common to children as young as 2, superhero play is exciting and rowdy, usually active and loud, playacting of heroic roles that give children powers they lack in everyday life. Superhero play attracts children who are (Hoffman 2004):

- *Investigating power and autonomy*
- *Balancing the desire for power with the need for friendship*
- *Testing physical limits*
- *Exploring feelings*
- *Answering big questions about the world, such as*
  - *What is right and what is wrong, good, and bad?*
  - *What is fair and what is unfair?*
  - *What is life and what is death?*
  - *What is a boy and what is a girl?*
  - *What is real and what is fantasy?*

Imaginary companions often join superheroes, although they just as often accompany children on their own. This second type of fantasy play sometimes concerns adults. Piaget believed that they reflected immature thinking of the preoperational stage and should disappear by the time a child began elementary school (Chapter 4). More recent research by Carlson and Taylor (2005) suggests

Superhero Play: Exercising Power Responsibly

- Help children recognize humane characteristics of superheroes.
- Discuss real heroes and heroines.
- Talk about the pretend world of acting.
- Limit the place and time for superhero play.
- Explore related concepts.
- Help children de-escalate rough-and-tumble play.
- Make it clear that aggression is unacceptable.
- Give children control over their lives.
- Praise children's attempts at mastery.

FIGURE 14-5 Superhero play is a special type of dramatic play that calls for special handling.

that imaginary friends offer companionship and entertainment, and can help children through difficult times.

> [T]he creation of an imaginary companion is healthy and relatively common…[C]hildren with imaginary companions appear to be less shy, more able to focus their attention, and to have advanced social understanding when compared with other children…The bottom line is that although imaginary companions and other fantasies have sometimes been interpreted as signs of emotional disturbance, a break with reality, or even the emergence of multiple personalities, they are really just a variation on the theme of all pretend play.

Children need guidance to learn how to express themselves appropriately and exercise their growing powers responsibly. Fantasy play is an important component of children's cognitive and emotional development. Teachers can help children learn to appreciate and enjoy themselves. Each time a child is acknowledged, a teacher fosters that sense of uniqueness: "Carrie, you have a great sense of humor!" "Eric, your power bracelets are helping to collect all the trash here." "Freddie, I love the way you and your 'dog-friend Dan' sing so clearly." Saying it aloud reinforces in children the feeling that they are enjoyable to themselves and to others.

Resilience

Resilience is the ability to bounce back or recover from adversity. "Resiliency is not a fixed attribute; rather, it is

a set of protective mechanism that modifies a person's response to risk situations" (Breslin, 2005). Research indicates that resilient children are more successful in dealing with stressors than those who are not (Ginsburg, 2006). No one stressor inevitably causes great harm, yet any stress can be staggering, and cumulative stress can overwhelm.

A number of factors have been identified that constrain children's abilities to adapt. "For individuals, these factors include low intelligence, difficulty in emotional self-regulation, poor health, and low frustration tolerance" (Bowman, 2005). Losing a primary relationship such as through divorce or deportation, homelessness, abuse, and exposure to violence in the neighborhood are also contributing factors.

At the same time, some children who experience terrible circumstances or individual factors become happy, healthy adults. Nurturing children's capacity to develop resiliency is not simple, but teachers can help by knowing the protective mechanisms that promote resiliency. These include:

- *The child's personality and behavior:* help a child find his strengths and sense of humor
- *The family attributes:* find someone or something that reflects the child's capacity to succeed and meet high expectations
- *The social environment:* use your relationship to identify the child's competences and develop self-confidence

Resilient children have hope, and good self-esteem. Both of these are under the influence of the teacher and curriculum.

Role of the Teacher

Considerations

The first step in helping children develop healthy emotional growth is for adults to acquire good patterns themselves. For instance, are you a person who labels others? What happens when a child is difficult or does not meet your expectations? Looking inside, stepping back to think about what we are feeling, is helpful. Coming up with a positive label for every child may also help teachers deal better with the emotions and behavior of the children in their care.

Another step is to develop and use a "feeling" vocabulary. Words of an emotional nature can be used to label and identify feelings as teachers talk with young children. There are many ways to develop a list of words related to emotions. Identify some of the feelings children

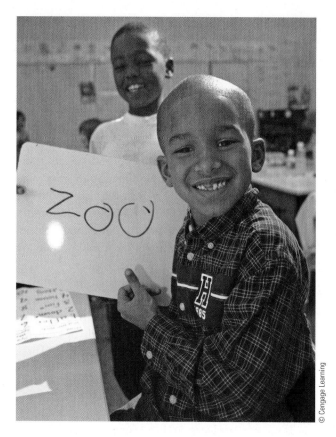

Observing children's feelings, such as the joy and pride in this child's face, helps teachers understand the children they teach.

© Cengage Learning

express; then describe how the children look and act when experiencing those emotions. This practice helps to build a vocabulary and an understanding of children's emotional expressions (see Figure 14-3).

Making the classroom a comfortable place for children is the third step to a healthy emotional climate. Teachers can also become more attuned to the emotional climate in the classroom by knowing when and how feelings are expressed. "Caring as total presence is a matter of attitude. Sometimes doing 'less' is doing 'more'" (Rofrano, 2002), particularly in curriculum for young children. To gain insights, teachers might ask themselves:

- What causes children in the class to become excited? Frightened? Calm? Loud? How does this knowledge guide curriculum planning? How can it help a teacher handle an unplanned event or change in the schedule?
- How do I anticipate children's emotional behavior? How do I follow through?
- What can teachers do to handle children's emotional outbursts and crises?

- What happens to the rest of the class when one teacher is occupied in an emotional incident with one or more children?
- What do I do when a child shows emotion? How do I feel when a child displays emotion?
- What types of emotions are most common with the young child?

In the early childhood setting, teachers help children come to grips with their strong feelings by discussing those feelings openly. They take the time to help children find names for feelings, to speak of their own feelings, and to begin to be aware of the feelings of others (see Figure 14-6).

When teachers perceive that children are ready to talk about their feelings, small group discussions or individual conversations can be helpful. Good books that touch on sensitive issues (being excluded, being blamed, caring for others) offer possibilities for teachers and children to talk about feelings. Games, joking, and teasing can help children to feel relaxed and to explore feelings in an accepting way. Classroom problems (not sharing materials, pushing on the climbers) offer topics for discussion.

The ability to express emotions verbally gives children the power to deal with them without resorting to inappropriate behavior. **Social referencing** involves "relying on another person's emotional reaction to form one's own appraisal of an uncertain situation" (Berk, 1999). Making use of others' emotional cues can help infants to deal with stranger anxiety, toddlers to calm themselves after saying good-bye, preschoolers to avoid overreacting to a fall, and school-aged children to begin to recognize that people can feel more than one emotion at a time. The teacher who runs to the rescue after a minor spill can engender "learned helplessness" and cause children to be overly dependent on others. Conversely, the teacher who fails to respond to children when they express emotions may give children the message that others' distress is to be ignored.

When adults show an understanding of feelings, children come to believe that adults are able to help them with their emotions, and the children become more at ease *with* their own feelings. When something painful happens to a child, adults can express what the child is feeling—"It really hurts to bend your knees now that you have scraped them" or "You look so sad now that Gabi is playing with someone else." Children then become familiar with ways to express how they feel in a variety of emotional situations.

Adults can also help children become aware of the emotional states of others. "Look! Paul is crying. Let's

The Teacher's Role in Children's Anger Management

1. Create a safe emotional climate . . . by having clear, firm, and flexible boundaries.
2. Model responsible anger management . . . by acknowledging when you are upset.
3. Help children develop self-regulatory skills . . . by giving children age- and skill-appropriate responsibilities and encouraging problem-solving with support.
4. Encourage children to label feelings of anger . . . start with "mad" and expand to include "upset, annoyed, irritated, furious, steamed," etc.
5. Encourage children to talk about anger-arousing interactions . . . by talking about situations when they aren't happening. "I felt mad when . . . " can start a lively conversation; cards with realistic scenarios can do the same, as can puppets.
6. Use appropriate books and stories about anger to help children understand and manage anger . . . see Figure14-7.
7. Communicate with parents. . . . Introduce the books or puppets, let them borrow them overnight. Tell them what you do in your program, and ask what they do.

© Cengage Learning

FIGURE 14-6 When children come to grips with their strong feelings, their emotional growth is encouraged (categories from Marion, 2003).

go over and see if we can comfort him." Teachers can encourage children to help care for each other's hurts and needs. A child can ease the pain of a friend by sitting nearby as a wound is cleansed or by giving a hug when an achievement is made. Teachers must be sure to allow children to express their concern and to help them learn ways to respond to the emotional needs of others.

Curriculum Planning for Emotional Growth

In the Early Childhood Setting. Teachers set up their classrooms and yards to promote emotional growth. Materials and activities enhance self-esteem and self-expression. How activities are presented and carried out is also a factor. In the class setting, the *how* is as critical as the *what* in curriculum planning for emotional development. Refer to Figure 14-8 to see how curriculum can be developed to encourage emotional growth.

Select materials that enhance self-expression. Indoors, children's inner thoughts and feelings are best expressed through:

- *The Arts.* Clay or dough lets children vent feelings, because it can be pounded, pinched, poked, slapped,

and manipulated. Finger painting and painting on broad surfaces with large brushes encourage a freedom of movement that permits children to express themselves fully.

- *Blocks/Manipulatives.* Vary the materials regularly to help children adjust to change and to allow them to exercise judgment about playing with different materials. A variety of props—motor vehicles, animals, people, furniture—gives children the opportunity to reenact what they see of the world.

- *Discovery/Science.* Often, science projects are geared toward cognitive and language development. They need not always be; some activities can focus on feelings. Caring for pets, for instance, brings out feelings of nurturing and protectiveness. Making "feeling clocks" can emphasize emotions. Blank clock faces are used as a base upon which children draw or paste pictures of people showing various emotional states. Display these at children's eye level so they can be changed frequently.

- *Dramatic Play.* Home-life materials give children the props they need to express how they see their own world of family, parents, and siblings. Through play, the child who is afraid of being left with a sitter may become the parent leaving the child-doll at home and then returning; the child who is afraid of the doctor can sometimes be seen gleefully giving shots to all the stuffed animals. Mirrors, telephones, and dress-up clothes encourage children to try out their emotional interests on themselves as well as each other.

- *Language/Library.* Stories and books in which characters and situations reflect a wide range of emotions are readily available (see Figure 13-20 and Figure 14-7 for some suggested titles). Children enjoy looking at photographs of people and guessing what the person in the photo is feeling. This activity encourages children to find words that label feelings; their responses can be recorded and posted nearby. Once children seem at ease in using feelings words, the discussion can continue when the teacher poses the question "Why do you think this person is sad/happy/angry?"

- *Music/Movement.* Music of all kinds encourages self-expression and permits an endless variety of movement and feelings to be shown openly and freely. Children can be introduced to classical, ethnic, jazz, or rock music while dancing with scarves or streamers or marching with rhythm sticks, as well as singing and dancing to children's recordings. Because musical knowledge is the earliest of human intellectual competencies (see Chapter 12), music can be part of the curriculum for children as young as toddlers. Pounding on drums and dancing both relieve tension in a socially acceptable manner. More structured activities, such as showing children how to use musical instruments, must be balanced by plenty of freedom for individual musical expression.

Outdoors, the environment itself encourages self-expression. Whether in the sand or on a swing, children seem to open up emotionally as they relax in the physical freedom the out-of-doors fosters. Outdoor games are usually highly emotionally charged. Running, chasing, and the dramatic play of superheroes provide emotional release for children.

The outdoor area is an ideal place for large, noisy, and messy activities. It is ideal for tracing body outlines, for instance. These life-size portraits of each child reinforce self-concepts and encourage a feeling of pride in one's self. Woodworking is an outdoor activity that allows children to vent anger and tension. Nails will not be hurt no matter how hard they are pounded; there is satisfac-

tion in sawing a piece of wood into two pieces. Music offers numerous opportunities for self-expression. Children can dance with scarves or streamers, march through the yard with drums pounding, imitate "The Wild Things" (of Sendak's picture book), make a maypole around the tree, and create a dragon for a parade. A rich musical repertoire of band instruments, phonograph records, tapes, and voices can stimulate children to pretend to be elephants, tigers, and dinosaurs, as well as circus performers and ballet artists. Even a simple project such as water painting becomes an avenue for self-expression as children use paint brushes and buckets of water on trees, cement, and buildings, giving them all a fresh coat of "paint."

Routines, Transitions, and Groups.   Routines, transitions, and group times have one thing in common: change. Because they all involve shifts from one kind of activity to another, there is a sense of uncertainty and they are emotionally charged. Children's behavior in these times is most likely to be unfocused. Here, you will find the wandering and chasing, even oppositional or withdrawn behavior.

Teachers help children best by creating an atmosphere of trust and clarity. Giving children ideas of what to do ("Each of you can sponge a table now," or "You can sit on my lap while your dad leaves today") helps each child feel a sense of confidence in managing through a routine or transition. Specific suggestions for group behavior, including those generated by the class itself, inspire success.

Finally, changes require teachers to be alert and flexible. As family caregiver McCormick (1993) affirms:

> Flexibility is the cornerstone of successful home child care, and an essential building block in provider/child relationships. Flexibility allows me to adapt to parents' changing schedules, children's changing sleep patterns, and even to alter the day's activities with the changing weather. By remaining flexible, especially to the children's needs, I have built a deep, personal relationship with each of the children I care for. I find ways to adapt to their schedules as much as possible instead of [always] forcing them into a [rigid] routine of the center.

Acknowledging a child's right to strong emotions and understanding a child's reactions to changes in these daily activities help children become comfortable and competent. Figure 14-7 outlines how specific materials and activities can be developed for emotional growth.

Curriculum for Emotional Skill Development

Indoor Activities

Art: Reflect children's expressions and see how they are feeling.

- "You look as if you are enjoying yourself."
- "Your face tells me that was funny (disappointing, etc.) to you."

Blocks: Be there/be aware/ask them how it feels when:

- You make a structure by yourself.
- It falls down.
- Someone knocks it over (accidentally or on purpose).
- Someone laughs.

Discovery/Science:

- Use the words "curious" and "proud" to describe what children do as they experiment with materials.
- Use computer program "Choices, Choices."

Dramatic Play: Give children freedom, variety, and reflection.

- Have books that reflect a variety of feelings and ways to deal with them, such as:
  Anger: *When Sophie Gets Angry—Really, Really Angry* (Bang); *The Grouchy Ladybug* (Carle); *My Name Is Not Dummy* (Crary)
  Fear: *There's a Nightmare in My Closet* (Mayer); *Storm in the Night* (Stolz)
  Self-Esteem: *The Growing Story* (Krauss); *Ruby* (Glen); *Things I Like* (Browne); *Amazing Grace* (Hoffman)
  Loss: *The Maggie B* (Keats); *Amos and Boris* (Steig)
  Change: *Changes, Changes* (Hutchins); *Sam Is My Half-Brother* (Boyd)
  Friendship: *Two Is a Team* (Bemelman); *That's What Friends Are For* (Kidd); *Big Al* (Clements)
  Security: *One Step, Two* (Zolotow); *The Bundle Book* (Zolotow); *Rise and Shine, Mariko-chan* (Tomioka)
  Choice: *Best Enemies* (Leverich); *Did You Carry the Flag Today, Charly?* (Claudill)
- Include books on themes, particularly when a child or group is dealing with an emotional issue:
  Death: *Death and Dying* (Stein); *The Dead Bird* (Brown); *Nana Upstairs, Nana Downstairs* (dePaoli)
  Divorce: *Two Places to Sleep* (Schuchman)
  Doctor/Dentist: *Curious George Goes to the Hospital* (Rey); *Your Turn, Doctor* (Robinson & Perez); *My Doctor* (Harlow)
  Moving: *Mitchell Is Moving* (Sharmat); *Jamie* (Zolotow); *The Leaving Morning* (Johnson)
  New Baby/Adoption: *Baby Sister for Frances* (Hoban); *I Want to Tell You about My Baby* (Banish); *Peter's Chair* (Keats); *The Chosen Baby* (Wasson)
  Nightmares: *Where the Wild Things Are* (Sendak); *In the Night Kitchen* (Sendak); *There's a Nightmare in My Closet* (Mayer)
  Spending the night: *Ira Sleeps Over* (Waber)
- When reading stories, stop and ask how a particular character is feeling.
- Tie in children's lives to books. For example, have children bring a special object or toy to share. A warm cuddly can be tied into the stories of *Goodnight Moon* (Brown) or *Teddy Bear's Picnic* (Kennedy).

Outdoor Activities

Movement:

- "How would you walk if you were glad?" (sad, mad, worried, giggly?)
- "A Tiger Hunt" (this game is known by many names). Go on a "hunt" with children, using their bodies to describe such movements as opening/shutting a gate, swishing through tall grass, climbing a tree, swimming in water, going through mud, looking in a cave, running home so that the "tiger" doesn't catch us.

(continues)

FIGURE 14-7 Whether 2 years old or in grade two, children learn about their feelings when teachers plan programs that encourage self-expression.

Music:

- Choose music that differs in tone and type. Ask children how each makes them feel, then have them show you with their bodies.
- Write songs or chants about feelings.

Routines, Transitions, Groups

Routines:

Respect children's feelings of anticipation.

- Have a chart of daily activities.
- Discuss upcoming field trips or visitors ahead of time when possible.

When possible, let the children take responsibility for known sequences.

- Set their own snack table.
- Get flowers for the table.
- Help clean a place for the next children.

Transitions:

When unexpected changes occur, discuss them with individuals and the group.

- "Andy isn't here today. He has a sore throat, so he is staying home. Esther will be the teacher in his group today."

Provide time for self-help *without unnecessary hurry.*

- Put on their own name tag.
- Wash and dry their own hands.
- Dress themselves—jacket for outdoors, shoes after nap, and so on.
- Take care of their rest items—blanket and stuffed toy in a labeled pillowcase, books back in a basket or bookshelf, and soon.

Group Times:

Use children's faces as a focus.

- Practice facial expressions with mirrors.
- Call out feelings, having them show you on their faces.
- Sing "If You're Happy and You Know It,..." with a variety of feelings. Ask children what situations have them feel each.
- Show photographs of children's faces; ask the group to tell you how that person is feeling, why, and so on.

Try idea completions.

- "I feel glad when..." (also mad, bad, sad, safe, excited, scared, silly) • "I like school when..." (also don't like, also my friend, mom, it) • "I wish...", • "The best thing I can do..."

Use situations to elicit feelings.

- "Here's a picture of a family. What are they doing? How does each person feel?"
- "I'm going to cover part of the picture of the face to see if you can guess what expression it's going to be."
- "These cards show situations the teachers have seen happen. As I read them think: 'How do I feel? What can I say? What can I do?'"

▌ **FIGURE 14-7** *(continued)*

Focus on Skills. Emotional development is a lifelong process that requires experience with one's own feelings. To help children learn to express and control their emotions, teachers consider each child's emotional skills. The goals teachers set for children will determine which emotional skills will be the focus: Maggie has difficulty with changes in the routine; Caroline never cries, no matter how she hurts; and Clyde screams when he is frustrated.

Making choices is a skill with an emotional focus. To help children make choices and decisions, focus on a step-by-step process:

1. Help children define the situation by turning it into a question. ("What can we do to fix up our playground?")
2. Make a list of options or alternatives. ("Plant flowers, get more bikes, add more sand toys.")
3. Ask the children to think of what might happen for each option. ("Flowers would look pretty, but we would have to water them.")
4. Make a choice. ("This is the key point!")
5. Check later to see how the choice turned out. ("Look how nice the yard is!" or "Darn, when we forgot to water, they died.")

Storytelling can be therapeutic and help children with issues of compliance, anger management, and fears. Caregivers can give children the opportunity to identify their fears and problems and come to resolution in satisfying ways (Cook, 2001). Be sure to elaborate and even let children add details along the way:

1. Introduce the main character. "Once upon a time there was a girl named Ning …"
2. Tell about the problem. "One day Ning ran away from school because …"
3. Talk to a wise person. "Ning's auntie knew just about everything, so …"
4. Try out a new approach. "So Ning decided she would try …"
5. Summarize the lesson. "Now Ning felt better. She told her friend …"

"Persona dolls" (Derman-Sparks, et al., 1989) encourage language involvement. Each doll has his/her story that can reflect the composition of the class and can offer experiences that extend the children's learning. All dolls are introduced with their own lives, and a teacher introduces each one and tells its story. Children ask questions, which expands the story. The teacher can tell a story that

arises from the everyday interactions in class, "hot topics" that parents are talking about or occur in the news, things the teacher decides are important to think and talk about, or stories based on history.

Themes. Themes can be useful when developing curriculum for emotional growth. One school-age program developed the theme of "Hurt and Healing" (Bowling & Rogers, 2001). The group brainstormed and came up with throwing water baggies at targets, kicking stacks of boxes, stomping on egg cartons, pounding anger out into clay, and throwing colored water at a painting. Dramatic play included acting out scared reactions; stories were dictated, pictures drawn, games made up. Figure 14-8 uses the theme "Who Am I?" to help with self-concept and self-expression.

Social Growth

Social development is the process through which children learn what behavior is acceptable and expected. A set of standards is imposed on the child at birth that reflects the values of the family and the society in which the child lives. Social growth refers to what happens with the child and others. Theorists from Freud and Piaget to Bandura and Gardner (see Chapters 4 and 12) acknowledge the relationship between social competence and learning. Indeed, enhancing social intelligence builds a set of skills that may be among the most essential for life success of many kinds.

The Development of Social Competence

Social development begins at birth. Within the first few months of life, the infant smiles, coos, and plays in response to a human voice, face, or physical contact (see "Attachment," Chapter 4). Young children are influenced from birth by a deliberate attempt on the part of adults to guide them in ways that society expects. Parents attempt to transmit behavior patterns that are characteristic of their culture, religion, gender, educational, and ethnic backgrounds. Teachers assist by incorporating some family rituals and traditions into the program.

Children imitate what they see; they adapt social expectations to their own personality. "Cooperation, generosity, loyalty, and honesty are not inborn. They must be

Theme: Who Am I?

1. *Art:* Body outlines
   Facial expressions pictures—variations (a) provide handheld mirrors, (b) give a blank face and let them draw in the features, (c) self-portraits: make them throughout the year, using "people colors," (d) cut out faces in magazine for collage
   Face painting
   Fingerprinting (hand and foot)

2. *Blocks:* People, furniture, structures people live in
   Pictures of same

3. *Cooking:* Share ethnic dishes (tortillas, pasta, things you like to cook at home)

4. *Discovery/Science:* Height/weight charts
   Drawing around hands and feet and comparing sizes
   Doing body outlines of a large group of children, each with a different color, and comparing sizes
   Mapping—charting where people live, charts of phone numbers, put out a globe
   Weather—make connections to types of homes

5. *Dramatic Play:* Lots of mirrors
   A variety of dress-up play for taking on a variety of roles and seeing how they feel

6. *Language/Library:* Have children write books about themselves—variations: (a) use *Is This You?* (Krauss) as model (b) loose-leaf binder of their own books they can add to themselves, (c) "Where I Live" as title, (d) families
   Books on children and families with diverse backgrounds (*Corduroy* [Freedman] lives in an apt.)
   Where animals live
   Feelings about where children live

7. *Manipulatives:* Puzzles with body parts, with people and clothing
   Self-help skills with dressing frames
   Encourage children to build a structure that things could live in (e.g., using Lincoln Logs).

8. *Sand and Water Play:* Bubble-blowing
   Using your bodies to build—digging with hands and feet, encouraging sensory exploration
   Use body parts to help you (e.g., using your foot on the shovel).

9. *Swinging/Climbing:* Both of these activities use body parts; teachers help the children become aware of how they do physical activity.

10. *Games:* Rolling the barrel, rolling yourself   Hide and Seek, Tag
    Mother May I?   Dramatic play games with family members
    Guessing games: Make "Who am I?" snapshots of the backs of children's heads or their hands. Use a shoe from each child, having them all tuck their feet under them.

11. *Large Block-Building:* Making house-like structures
    Using vehicles that need your body's force to move

12. *Woodworking:* Using body parts
    Make a map board of school, neighborhood, a city

13. *Routines:* Self-help: Awareness of what you can do by yourself by definition of "Who Am I?" tasks; teachers use verbal and musical reinforcement

14. *Transitions:* Use physical characteristics of children for transitions—"Everyone who has brown eyes/freckles/blue jeans can go outside."

15. *Group times:* "Head and shoulders"
    Description games—describe someone and guess who it is as a game "I'm thinking of someone" or with song "Mary Has a Red Dress"
    "Little Tommy (Tina) Tiddlemouse," voice recognition
    "Good morning little Teddy Bear," with bear going around circle and saying names

16. *Snack time/bedtime:* Mark places with names and pictures, such as beds or placemats
    Try to coordinate the name tag, bed, or placemat with symbol on cubby

FIGURE 14-8 A child's school experience is strongly related to how emotional events are handled.

passed on to the child by older people, [whether] they are parents, other adults, or older youngsters" (Kostelnik, 2005). There are many cultural variations in how people relate to each other, what and when to eat, how to dress, what feelings are to be expressed, how to think about time and personal space, how and who to touch, and how to respond to personal events.

This process—called **socialization**—includes learning appropriate behavior in a number of different settings. Children learn very early to discriminate between the expectations in different environments. At school, free exploration of play materials is encouraged, but in a church pew it is not. Grocery stores, circuses, libraries, and Grandma's home call for a repertoire of fitting behaviors. Children's understanding of others is critical for their social growth. Very young children show awareness of what other people feel, as infants pay special attention to emotional expressions of adults. Toddlers can ascertain if someone is happy, sad, or angry, and can try to comfort someone in distress. Three-year-olds know that if someone gets what he wants, he will be happy, and if not, he will be sad. Older preschoolers begin to understand that what they (or others) believe may turn out to be false. By kindergarten, one can see that children understand that others may think and feel differently than they do.

DAP

> Research suggests that children who understand others' minds at an early age may be more able to get along well with others and that parents and teachers can support the development of this understanding by encouraging pretend play and discussing mental states with them from storybooks or real-life encounters. (Lillard & Curenton, 1999)

In general, the socialization process in a school setting revolves around a child's relationships with the other people in it. During this time of their lives, children work out a separate set of relationships with their teachers, those adults other than their parents. They establish different relationships with adults than they do with other children, and, most important, they learn to interact with other children.

Through socialization, the customary roles that boys and girls play are also transmitted. Children come to understand how teachers, mommies, daddies, grandparents, males, and females are expected to act. Early childhood professionals need to be aware of the difference between a child's gender identity development and a child's sex role development. One needs to be able to communicate the difference to parents and to be aware of how different cultures may have differing notions about sex role development.

Children also learn social attitudes at an early age. They learn to enjoy being with people and participating in social activities. At the same time, young children can also develop attitudes of bias, and it is in these early years that prejudicial behavior often begins. How the teachers respond to negative comments, unfair acts, exclusivity based on race, gender, or ability is crucial in combating these negative attitudes. Favorable attitudes toward people and a strong desire to be part of the social world interacting with others are established in the early years.

Another important facet of socialization involves the development of a sense of community. A program's emotional climate and teacher's behavior contribute not only to children's sense of personal safety and belonging but also to the value of relationships that are sustained by communication. Teachers who strive for community awareness and bonding are adhering to an anti-bias philosophy (see Chapter 9) that promotes empathic interaction with people from diverse backgrounds and standing up for self and others in the face of bias.

Social Competence

Social competence involves the skills and personal knowledge children develop to deal with the challenges and opportunities they face in life with others. Katz and McClennan (1997) add, "They generally focus on an individual's ability to initiate and maintain satisfying, reciprocal relationships with peers." Our definition includes relationships with all other people, including family, teachers, caregivers, peers, and the community at large. Through their social interactions, children learn a sense of personal identity, adopt family and cultural values, acquire interpersonal skills, and learn how to "live in the world."

There are several components to social competence. These are:

- *Emotional regulation.* The ability to regulate emotions (see earlier in this chapter).
- *Social knowledge and understanding.* Knowledge of enough language and norms to interact successfully; understanding the reactions of others and their feelings (empathy).

DAP Caregivers recognize that toddlers constantly test limits and express opposition ("No!") as part of developing a health sense of self as an autonomous individual. In the preschool years, teachers model and encourage calm, patient behavior and facilitate children's development of self-regulation by supporting them in thinking ahead, planning their activities, and thinking about and using strategies to solve social problems.

- *Social skills.* Social approach patterns, attention to others, exchange of information, handling aggression.
- *Social dispositions.* Habits or characteristic ways of responding to experiences.

The elements of social competence are illustrated in Figure 14-9.

Why is social competence important? Such children are happier than their less competent peers. Children's social relations have been linked to academic achievement. Lack of social competence has been linked to rejection by peers, poor self-esteem, and poor academic performance (Kostelnik, et al, 2005). It is now widely accepted that young children who do not frequently interact with peers are at risk for a host of later socio-emotional difficulties (Coplan & Armer, 2007; Rubin, Bukowski, & Parker, 2006).

Social Development

All areas of children's development play a part in learning social skills:

- Having the confidence to try joining a group calls upon emotional skills.
- Remembering children's names or how a game works is a cognitive task.
- "Using your words" to express an idea or feeling requires language.
- Having the ability to play, chase, or walk in high heels for a dress-up game requires certain physical dexterity.

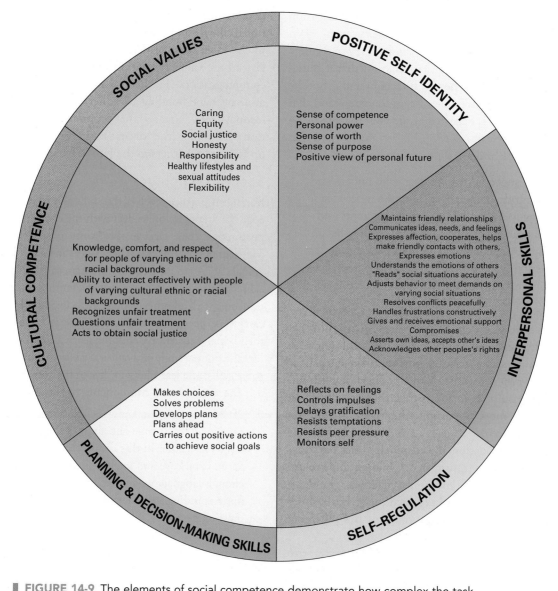

FIGURE 14-9 The elements of social competence demonstrate how complex the task of developing socially is for young children. (Adapted from Kostelnik et al, 2005.)

There are many variations that arise in social situations. For instance, children can sustain complex play without much language, and games can be adapted to include children with a variety of physical skills. Understanding the principle of interrelated development, however, helps teachers appreciate the process of social learning and recognize opportunities to guide their social development.

In the early years, children mature socially in discernible developmental stages. From birth to age 3, children's interest in others begins with a mutual gazing and social smile in the early months (birth through 8 months), continues with an exploration of others as well as some anxious behavior around strangers in the crawler and walker stages (8 to 18 months), and develops into an enjoyment of peers and adults along with an awareness of others' rights and feelings as a toddler and 2-year-old (18 months to 3 years).

In the preschool years, children learn to control their aggressive impulses, think about others besides themselves, and resist doing what they should not. This learning translates into four basic expectations. They will:

1. Show interest in others.
2. Learn right from wrong.
3. Learn to get along with others.
4. Learn a role for themselves that takes into consideration their own unique self-gender, race, ethnicity, and abilities.

Children of the primary years (5 to 8 years) show an increased interest in peers and social competence, and group rules become important. The development of a social conscience and of fairness rounds out the primary grade developmental milestones.

Children learn social skills in several predictable ways. First, the brain is wired to look for patterns. When an infant smiles and is met with a reciprocal smile, a pattern of responsiveness and attachment begins. The preschooler who grabs for toys and usually gets to keep them at home will be surprised (and unhappy) when the pattern is broken at the center and the toy is returned to the one who was using it. As a result of their experiences, children form ideas about how the social world works. They are active learners who will observe and experiment, learning firsthand what happens when they try something. In-the-moment, on-the-spot lessons will greatly help children learn socially.

Sarda wants to play in the block corner, but stands hesitantly as four boys shout and vroom the cars around. "Do you want to play here?" inquires the observant

teacher. When she nods, the teacher helps her move in and the two begin building. Soon, the boys notice and come to see a garage being built, so they drive their cars over. The teacher slowly steps aside. Sarda has experienced one way to get started.

Next, children have multiple ways of learning. Since teachers often do not know each child's ways of learning, it is best to try a variety of approaches when teaching social skills. Talking helps some (linguistic), others learn better by seeing patterns (logical mathematical), and many learn by modeling (see example just given). Rehearsing how to do or say the words helps the kinesthetic learner.

Finally, it is through play (Chapters 4 and 10) that children learn much of their social repertoires. Dramatizations, role playing, and dramatic play provide opportunities to act out many roles and help children deal with some of the demands placed on them. In play, the child experiments with options: finding out what it feels like to be the boss, to be the baby, to behave in ways that might otherwise be unacceptable. Carla was the oldest of three children and had many "big girl" expectations placed on her within the family setting. At school, Carla enjoyed being the baby, acting out a helpless infant role whenever she could. Under the guise of play, children, like Carla, rehearse for life without suffering the real life consequences. Figure 14-10 traces the route of social development from infancy through the primary years.

Common Social Challenges

Children of each age in early childhood experience a range of social difficulties (see Chapters 3, 4, and 7). For instance, toddlers develop many forms of testing behavior, including saying "No" to adult rules and other restraints. Grabbing, biting, and hitting are common forms of aggression and self-expression. Some of this occurs in preschoolers, as well as other forms of self-determination. There are problems children encounter when responding to emotions, both theirs and those of others. Peer status and friendship loom large in primary school, when loneliness and exclusion, teasing and bullying all occur (Gordon & Browne, 1996).

Teasing and bullying can become disruptive in groups and programs. Teachers need to be clear about what bullying is, and how to respond to it early. "Bullying is repeated, systematic efforts to inflict harm on someone who is unable or unlikely to defend himself or herself" (Berger, 2007). Children who are exposed repeatedly and over time to negative actions (words, physical contact, making faces, gesturing, or intentional exclusions

Social Development Timeline

Infant–Toddler	Preschooler	Primary Child
Response to Other's Distress		
Reacts emotionally by experiencing what the other seems to feel.	Begins to make adjustments that reflect the realization that the other person is different and separate from self.	Takes other's personality into account and shows concern for other's general condition.
Peer Interaction		
• First encounters mutual inspection • First social contacts • (18 months) Growth in sensitivity to peer play • (2 years) Able to direct social acts to two children at once (beginning of social interaction)	• Adjustment in behavior to fit age and behavior of other • (More than 3 years) Friendship as momentary • (3–5 years) Beginning of friendship as constant	• Friend as someone who will do what you want • Beginning of friend as one who embodies admirable, constant characteristics
Social Roles		
• (10–20 days) Imitation of adults • (3 months) Gurgles in response to others • (6 months) Social games based on imitation • (18 months) Differentiation between reality and pretend play • (2 years) Makes doll do something as if it were alive	• (3 years) Makes a doll carry out several roles or activities • (4–5 years) Acts out a social role in dramatic play and integrates that role with others (mom and baby)	• (6 years) Integrates one role with two complementary roles: doctor, nurse, and sick person • (8 years) Growing understanding that roles can influence behavior (doctor whose daughter is a patient)

FIGURE 14-10 A timetable of social development for the ages of infancy through the primary years. (Special thanks to Gay Spitz. Reprinted by permission.)

from a group) on the part of one or more others can develop low self-esteem and may become withdrawn or be rejected by their peers. Not every rejected child becomes a bully victim, and not every child who excludes or teases another becomes a bully. But the antisocial behavior results in difficulties for both sides: "Over time, the social costs to both bullies and victims include impaired social understanding and problems with human relationships in adulthood" (Berger, 2007).

Although bullying is more serious and noticeable late in childhood and adolescence, its roots are in early childhood. Teachers must take notice and do a better job of dealing with the behaviors. Preschool and school-age programs can also implement conflict resolution programs that teach children how to express themselves and listen to others in socially intense situations (Gordon & Browne, 1997; Porro, 1996). Systematic work with children to teach them these social competence skills helps them deal with what might be called the "garden variety"

conflicts—issues of property, territory, and power such as teasing, put-downs, hitting, not sharing, and who is the boss. Figure 14-11 is a sample chart used in such programs, preschool through elementary school.

Peer Relationships. For the young child, social development means the steady movement away from the *egocentric* position of self (and parents) as central points toward a more **sociocentric** viewpoint that involves others—both adults and, especially, children. During the early years, the child learns to socialize outside the family; social contacts outside the home reinforce the enjoyment of social activities and prepare the child for future group activity.

Peer interactions, that is, associations with friends of the same age group, become important to the child once infancy and early toddlerhood are past. Through peer interactions, children can identify with models who are like themselves and can learn from each other's

Talk It Out: Conflict Resolution

1.   Stop. Cool off.

2.   Talk and listen.

3.   Think of ways to solve the problem.

4.   Choose the idea you both like. ☺☺

FIGURE 14-11 A "Talk It Out" poster helps teachers mediate conflicts and teach children resolution skills. (From *Talk It Out: Conflict Resolution in the Elementary Classroom,* Copyright © 1996 by Barbara Porro. Reprinted with permission from ASCD. The Association for Supervision and Curriculum Development is a worldwide community of educators advocating sound policies and sharing best practices to achieve the success of each learner. To learn more, visit ASCD at www.ascd.org.)

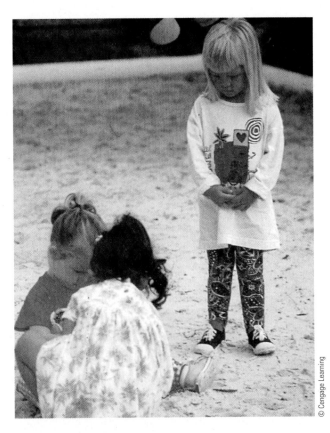

© Cengage Learning

Rejection is a common form of social behavior in young children. In the early years, children need to deal with the feelings that arise when they are told, "You can't play with us."

behavior. Friends provide models for imitation, for comparison, and for confirmation of themselves, and they are a source of support.

Playing with other children begins with solitary and parallel play at around age 2, in which two or more children are in the same area with each other but do not initiate social interaction. By the ages of 3 and 4, more interaction takes place. There are conversations and conflicts as well as cooperation in playing together (see Chapters 4 and 10).

There are stages in children's friendships. In the early years, friendship starts at an **undifferentiated** level, in which children are egocentric and a friend is more of the moment. This gives way to a **unilateral** level; a good friend does what the child wants the friend to do. Toward the end of early childhood, friendship becomes more **reciprocal,** involving some give-and-take in a kind of two-way cooperation. Listen to these children trying out their friendship:

Chris: I'll be the teacher, you be the kid.
Suzanne: NO! I want to be the teacher, too.

Chris: No! No! You can't be the teacher, too, 'cause then there'd be no kids.
Suzanne: OK. Next time, I get to be the teacher.
Chris: Maybe! OK, everybody go wash your hands for snack time. Suzanne, you can pass out your very nutritious snack to everybody.
Suzanne: Superfasmic, I'm the boss of snack.

A peer group is important for a number of reasons. Social development is enhanced because a child learns to conform to established social standards outside of his home setting. The expectations of the larger society are reinforced. To become autonomous, the child must also learn to achieve independence from the family, especially parents. Young children must also come to understand themselves as part of society. Self-concept is enlarged by a group of peers as they see how others respond to them and treat them.

Making and keeping friends are essential to children's positive social development, so important that children without friends by the primary years are considered at

© Cengage Learning

Peer relationships are a source of pleasure and support. As social understanding develops, children shift from a preoccupation with themselves to an awareness of the thoughts and feelings of their friends.

risk for overall school success. Developing friendships is more than teaching general interpersonal skills and is especially important for children with special needs. Facilitating friendship development in inclusive classrooms requires teacher awareness and interaction as well as careful environmental and schedule planning.

Social Skills in Early Childhood

Social skills are strategies children learn that enable them to behave appropriately in many environments. They help children learn to initiate or manage social interaction in a variety of settings and with a number of people. **Social cognition** is the application of thinking to personal and social behavior; it is giving meaning to social experience. For example, Nadia wants to play with Paul, a very popular 4-year-old. She remembers Paul's interest in the rope swing and challenges him to swing higher than she did. He responds enthusiastically and the friendship begins.

Social cognition requires children to interpret events and make decisions, to consider the impact of their behavior on others, and to consider the cause as well as the consequence of an action. Cognitive skills are necessary when we ask children to seek alternative solutions to social problems: "How else could you ask him for a turn, Pete?" These are all social cognition skills, and they serve as the basis for the acquisition of other skills.

Social Intelligence

Building on Gardner's multiple intelligences theory (see Chapters 4 and 12), Daniel Goleman outlined five dimensions of emotional intelligence (see previous section). The fifth element of emotional intelligence is social skills. Teachers who can help children handle their emotions (self-regulation) and learn to "read" other people's feelings by their body language or tone of voice (empathy) can then lead children to gain social skills. As mentioned earlier in this chapter, children who bully can be taught better social skills, and the early childhood setting is just the place to do so. Paley (1992) has written extensively about the social climate of classrooms:

> "Are you my friend?" the little ones ask in nursery school, not knowing. The responses are also questions. If yes, then what? And if I push you away, how does that feel?
> By kindergarten, however, a structure begins to be revealed … certain children will have the right to limit the social experiences of their classmates…
> Long after hitting and name-calling have been outlawed by the teachers, a more damaging phenomenon is allowed to take root, spreading like a weed from grade to grade.

With more social intelligence than most, Paley as kindergarten teacher decided to post a sign outside her door one year. "You can't say you can't play" turns the class upside down and requires both adults and children to learn new ways to interact.

Social skills can be viewed in different ways. The *Four Hows* is one set of categories for such a complex array of skills:

1. *How to approach.* Getting and being included.
2. *How to interact.* Sharing, cooperating.
3. *How to deal with difference.* Including others, helping, bullying, and teasing.
4. *How to manage conflict.* Handling aggression, problem solving.

Another is to realize that there is a skill set learned in every kind of interaction.

Skills Learned with Adults

In their relationship with adults, children learn:

- They can stay at school without parents.
- They can enjoy adults other than parents and respond to new adults.
- Adults will help in times of trouble or need.
- Adults will help them learn social protocol.
- Adults will keep children from being hurt and from hurting others.
- Adults will help children learn about ethnic differences and similarities, disabilities, gender identity, and language diversity.
- Adults will resist bias and stereotyping and teach children to actively do the same.
- Adults will not always take a side or solve the problem.
- Adults will work with them to solve problems.
- Adults believe that every child has a right to a satisfying social experience at school.

Skills Learned with Peers

In their relationship with other children, children learn:

- There are different approaches to others; some work, some do not.
- Interactive skills and how to sustain the relationship.
- How to solve conflicts in ways other than retreat or force.
- How to share materials, equipment, other children, friends, teachers, and ideas.
- How to achieve mutually satisfying play.
- Self-defense and how to assert their rights in socially acceptable ways.
- How to take turns and how to communicate desires.
- How to negotiate.
- How to be helpful to peers with tasks, information, and by modeling behavior.
- How to anticipate and avoid problems.
- Realistic expectations of how other children behave and respond toward them.
- Ways to deal with socially awkward situations and with socially difficult situations and children.
- How to make, be, share, and lose a friend.

Skills Learned in a Group

In groups, children learn:

- How to take part as a member and not as an individual.
- That there are activities that promote group association (stories, music).

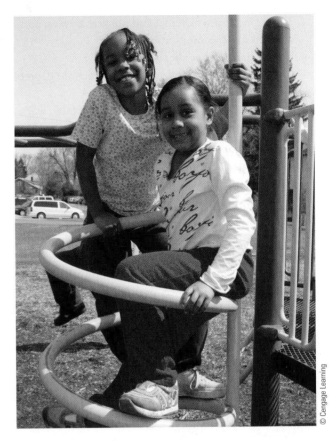

Friendship: "The more we get together, the happier we'll be!"

- A group identity (center room class, Mrs. T's group, 4-year-old group).
- To follow a daily schedule and pattern.
- To adapt to school routines.
- School rules and expectations.
- Interaction and participatory skills: how to enter and exit from play.
- To respect the rights, feelings, and property of others.
- To become socially active, especially in the face of unfair or biased behavior and situations.
- How to work together as a group, during clean-up time, in preparation for an event, etc.
- How to deal with delay of gratification: how to wait.

Skills Learned as an Individual

As individuals, children learn:

- To take responsibility for self-help, self-care.
- To initiate their own activities and to make choices.
- To work alone, close to other children.
- To notice unfairness and injustice and learn how to handle them.
- To negotiate.
- To cope with rejection, hurt feelings, disappointment.

- To communicate in verbal and nonverbal ways, and when to use communication skills.
- To test limits other people set.
- Their own personal style of peer interaction: degree, intensity, frequency, quality.
- To express strong feelings in socially acceptable ways.
- To manage social freedom.

Specific skills within these four areas include the social and moral aspects of nurturance, kindness, and sharing. As children get older, these skills become more specific: telling the truth, taking turns, keeping promises, respecting others' rights, having tolerance, and following rules.

Another social skill that has taken hold is that of **social action.** In an anti-bias curriculum (see Chapter 9), children can learn how to take social action to make unfair things fair. For instance, preschoolers discover that their adhesive strips are labeled "flesh-colored" but match the skin of only a few children; they take photos and send them to the company (Derman-Sparks & Olsen Edwards, 2010). Promoting activism may not always bring successful results, but the activity and the model are powerful learning experiences.

Role of the Teacher

A major role for the early childhood teacher is to see that children have enjoyable social contacts and to help motivate children toward a desire to be with others. The early childhood setting affords children numerous learning opportunities for social development.

The teacher has an important role to play as children learn the give-and-take of social interaction. In the role of social organizer, the teacher creates a physical and interpersonal environment that promotes the development of children's social skills.

Considerations

Plan and Arrange a Social Environment. Child-initiated activities, self-care, and group responsibilities are stimulated by the use of low, open shelves and furniture scaled to size. Group activities, toys, materials, and placement of furniture should be structured in ways that allow children to play alone or with someone. Establishing a **coaching** environment helps children in their "interacting with others, more often one-on-one than in larger groups, with an emphasis on process rather than product" (Bos, 1990). The placement of two telephones, three wagons, and eight firefighter hats fosters child–child interactions. Cooperation, which implies a mutually recognized goal, is an outgrowth of coaching (see Figure 14-15). Children will often act together in a spontaneous way; then get

Cooperation: "I'll help you, then you'll help me."

organized toward a planned end when they decide to build a single tower together. The teacher must also allow enough time in the daily schedule for children to get thoroughly involved in playing with one another.

Help Children Develop Trust. Trusting in themselves, their peers, and their teachers, is a part of learning about social relationships. Teachers enhance children's social knowledge as they gradually improve their sense of trust. General recommendations are:

1. *Help children recognize their own needs.* Notice children who need to clarify their wishes; ask uninvolved children with whom they would like to play; help arguing children say how they feel and what they want.
2. *Increase children's awareness of their social goals and the goals of others.* Teachers can aid children by helping them recognize their choices; they can also mediate so that others can express themselves.
3. *Help children develop effective social skills.* Provide a model for listening, for choosing another place to play, or for going along with another's ideas; help children find ways to stand their ground and also accommodate and learn to use conflict resolution,

cooperation, coping, and helping skills (see Chapter 7 and this chapter's Insights).

4. *Teach children to recognize others' emotions and intentions.* Children become flooded with their own strong feelings and are not likely to notice someone else's emotions in the heat of the moment; teachers can help children see another's face or hear a tone of voice, thus beginning to "read" another person.

5. *Reflect with children on how their behavior affects others by pointing out what is predictable in their interactions.* Young children do not always "connect the dots" between their behavior and others' reactions. When a teacher makes a statement without disapproval, the child can then understand the effects of her or his behavior on others: "Wow! When you use that loud voice, I see the kids looking scared, and then they tell you not to play here."

6. *Highlight children's success by helping them learn to monitor their own behavior.* It can help children to see their successful social encounters as well as the strategies that did not work. "When you asked them if you could play, they said, 'No!' But then you went and got shovels for everyone and that worked!"

7. *Avoid telling children who their "friends" are.* Early childhood teachers encourage children to learn about friendship; however, "legislating friendship" often backfires. Telling children "We're all friends here" or "Friends share their things with everyone" denies the distinction between positive, friendly experiences and friendship. "Classmate" and "friend" are not the same word.

8. *Develop a set of strategies to help the socially awkward and troubled in your class.* Although each child is unique, there are certain situations that arise time and again in an early childhood classroom. Children who are socially inept often do not use nonverbal language effectively and are "out-of-sync" because they miss the signs.

9. *Do not stay uninvolved or ignore teasing and bullying.* A lack of response can signal all children that it is okay to engage in these behaviors and acceptable to fall victim to it. Talk about it; read books such as *Rosie's Story* (Gogoll) or *Oliver Button Is a Sissy* (de Paola); make an experience chart ("I Feel (Un)Welcome When …"); and help the class with fair rules. In noncompetitive games, children learn to help each other rather than trying to win or gain power over others. Finally, foster friendships between girls and boys and actively counter gender bias.

10. *Work to provide a caring community in your class.* "In order for children to have the confidence to take the risks inherent in learning…they must experience a consistently accepting, inclusive and predictable atmosphere in the classroom" (Maniates & Heath, 1998). Brain research (see Chapter 4) confirms this point, and an anti-bias approach (see Chapters 3 and 9) supports the development of social action as an extension of "making right" the classroom and beyond.

11. *Invite parents and families into the process of children's socialization.* Both teachers and families share in the responsibility of helping children develop social skills; neither one can do it alone. There are many ways to make your program family friendly; see Chapter 8 for suggestions.

Facilitate Children's Interactions and Interpret Their Behavior. To help young children understand each other and to pave the way for continued cooperation, the teacher reports and reflects on what is happening. In the classroom setting, during an active, free play period, the teacher might:

Reflect the Action:	*Say:*
Call attention to the effect one child's behavior is having on another.	"Randy, when you scream like that, other children become frightened and are afraid to play with you."
Show approval and reinforce positive social behavior.	"I like the way you carefully stepped over their block building, Dannetta."
Support a child in asserting her rights.	"Chrystal is hanging on to the doll because she isn't finished playing yet, Wilbur."
Support a child's desire to be independent.	"I know you want to help, Keyetta, but Sammy is trying to put his coat on by himself."
Acknowledge and help children establish contact with others.	"Omar would like to play, too. That's why he brought you another bucket of water. Is there a place where he can help?"
Reflect back to a child the depth of his feelings and what form those feelings might take.	"I know George made you very angry when he took your sponge, but I can't let you throw water at him. What can you tell him? What words can you use to say you didn't like what he did?"

Adult responses to children's play are particularly critical in supporting positive social development. The teacher has a powerful, emotional role in children's lives at school. When children make judgments in error, coming to false conclusions about children on the basis of race, gender, native language, or ability, the teacher must intervene, for silence signals tacit approval. This is perhaps the most dynamic and challenging part of teachers' jobs, the heart of the profession. "Facilitation is fundamental to helping children achieve greater social competence. You engage in facilitation when you demonstrate empathy, warmth, respect, and authenticity in your interpersonal relations with children" (Kostelnik, et al., 2005).

As illustrated in Chapter 7, the social problems in early childhood range from possession of toys, to hitting others, to keeping promises. How a teacher helps children identify and resolve their own conflicts is often more important than the specific problem or solution. Teaching strategies that facilitate social competence are listed in Figure 14-12.

Curriculum Planning for Social Growth

Social curriculum happens everywhere in an early childhood program. One of the goals of a psychosocial curriculum is:

> ...to help the young child move from her or his sheltered family unit into a much more complex environment. ...The curriculum should develop the

knowledge and perspective which is commensurate with the kind of world in which we live, a world that ... is composed of an unlimited variety of outlooks, backgrounds, and standard of living. [Early education programs] can be a step in socializing the child, in helping the child change from an egocentric, ethnocentric person to one who understands and is sympathetic to people of considerable diversity. (Kendall, 1996)

In the Early Childhood Setting. Teaching social behavior in most classrooms usually occurs in response to spontaneous situations. The teacher's direct involvement in children's social interactions is the most frequent method used. Occasionally, teachers will approach the acquisition of social skills in a more formalized way through planned curriculum activities. The way the environment is arranged has a profound effect on social interaction among children.

Most indoor activities are planned and set up to encourage participation by more than one child at a time. Arrange the space into learning centers that provide for coactivity, with clear physical boundaries and ways to get around (see Chapter 9). Remember, the environment is one of the teachers.

- *The Arts.* At the art table, children will share collage materials and paste that have been placed in the center of the table. When easels are placed side by

---

Social Competence: The Teacher's Role

Do

- Respect individual timetables and feelings.
- Establish authority and credibility.
- Express expectations simply and directly.
- Redefine children's characters in positive terms.
- Encourage impulsive control.
- Appeal to children's good sense.
- Invoke ground rules.
- Mix it up: Arrange things to get one child next to another.
- Move it: people, toys, you.

Question everything you do: Could I open this up for more than one child?

Don't

- Make implied comparisons.
- Issue empty threats.
- Hover.
- Make teacher–child interaction be all about misbehavior.
- Motivate children by indirect disapproval.
- Lose your sense of humor.
- Allow a rigid curriculum to narrow possibilities for social interaction.

FIGURE 14-12 The Dos and Don'ts of facilitating social competence (adapted from Bos [1990] and Katz & McClelland [1997]).

side, conversation occurs spontaneously among children. A small table, placed between the easels, on which a tray of paint cups is placed, also encourages children's interactions. If there is only one of each color, the children will have to negotiate with one another for the color they want to use.

- *Blocks/Manipulatives.* A large space for block cabinets gives children a visual cue that there is plenty of room for more than one child. Puzzle tables set with three or four puzzles also tell children that social interaction is expected. Many times, children will talk, play, and plan with one another as they share a large bin full of Legos® or plastic building towers. A floor puzzle always requires a group: some to put the picture together, others to watch and make suggestions. As children build with blocks next to one another, they soon share comments about their work; many times this sharing leads to a mutual effort on a single building.

- *Discovery/Science.* Many science projects can be arranged to involve more than one child. A display of magnets with a tray of assorted objects can become the focus of several children as they decide which objects will be attracted to the magnets. Cooking together, weighing and measuring one another, and caring for classroom pets can be times when teachers reinforce social skills.

- *Dramatic Play.* This area more than any other seems to draw children into contact with one another. Provide an assortment of family life accessories—dress-up clothes, kitchen equipment and utensils—and children have little trouble getting involved. A shoe needs to be tied or a dress zipped. Someone must come eat the delicious meal just cooked or put the baby to bed. A medical theme in this classroom area also enhances children's social skills. They learn to take each other's temperature, listen to heartbeats, and plan operations, all of which require more than one person. Sociodramatic play can provide curriculum integration in the primary grades as well.

- *Language/Library.* Children enjoy reading books and stories to one another, whether or not they know the words. Favorite books are often shared by two children who enjoy turning the pages and talking over the story together. Lotto games encourage children to become aware of one another, to look at each person's card in order to identify who has the picture to match. Name songs and games, especially early in the year, help children learn to call each other by name.

- *Music Movement.* Build in regular times for music and movement activities. The entire group can participate in familiar songs; a sense of community is built by everyone's participation. Activities during the free choice times usually involve smaller numbers, in which group members can challenge one another to new ways to dance with scarves or use the tumbling mat. Finally, one-to-one experiences encourage new friendships as the intimacy of a shared musical experience brings two children or a teacher and child together. Preschoolers can dance their way to social competence and success (Colker, 2007). Sharing music and dance from home is an ideal way to incorporate children's individual cultures into the classroom. Translate a simple song into another language; teach the children the song, working in the language that is "home base" for most of the children, then reteach it. Words and phrases made familiar by melody are remembered and made valuable.

Outdoors, children need a space to run, a place to yell, a place where adults are not hovering and directing each activity. The pretend play of boys, in particular, is usually richer than inside, and many of the rough-and-tumble activities prohibited indoors are safe here. It may be more difficult to observe children, and directions are often harder to give with distance. The outdoor environment can be structured in ways to support group play:

- *Painting or Drawing.* Painting on murals or drawing chalk designs on the cement are art activities that promote social interaction.

- *Planning and Planting a Garden.* Planning and planting a garden is a long-range project that involves many children. Decisions must be made by the group about what to plant, where to locate the garden, how to prepare the soil, and what the shared responsibilities of caring for the garden will be.

- *Gross Motor Activities.* Most gross motor activities stimulate group interactions. Seesaws, jump ropes, and hide-and-seek require at least two people to participate. A-frames, boards, and boxes, as well as other movable equipment, need the cooperative effort of several children in order to be rearranged. Sand play, when accompanied by water, shovels, and other accessories, draws a number of children together to create rivers, dams, and floods. Ball games and relay races also encourage social relationships.

Routines, Transitions, and Groups. Routines and transitions are often social experiences, as they provide children with an opportunity for support and peer interaction. For instance, the routine of nap preparation can be structured with a "buddy" system so that older children are paired with the younger ones to set up the cots, choose a cuddly or books, and get tucked in. A clean-up time transition can be made fun and successful if children can wear a necklace to depict the job or area. Children with similar clean-up cards get a sense of teamwork when putting an activity area back in order (see Figure 14-13).

As a directed learning experience, small group times afford an opportunity to focus on social skills in a more structured way. Small groups provide a setting for children and teachers to participate in more relaxed, uninterrupted dialogue. The intimacy of the small group sets the stage for many social interactions.

Group time discussions, such as circle time in preschool and class meetings for school-age children, can focus on problems that children can solve. Too many children crowding the water table, a child's fear of fire drills, or the noise level on a rainy day are subjects children will talk about in small groups. The most relevant situations are ones that occur naturally in the course of a program. Another curriculum idea is to make "Situation Cards" of these and other common incidents. For instance, teachers can create illustrated cards that pose situations such as:

- You tell your friends to "stop it" when they take part of the toy you are using, but they do it again.
- You open your lunch and your mom or dad has packed your favorite foods.
- You come down the slide and your teacher calls "Hooray for you!"
- You promise your friend you will play with him at recess, but then someone else you like asks you to play with her.

The teacher then guides a discussion around the questions "How do you feel? What can you say? What can you do?" This activity can be simplified or elaborated depending on the individuals and group involved.

Figure 14-14 shows a sequentially planned curriculum that fosters the development of social skills in small group settings.

Focus on Skills. Social development for the preschool child includes gaining an awareness of the larger community in which the child lives. The early childhood curriculum contains elements of what is often in the later grades called *social studies*. Visits from police offi-cers, mail carriers, firefighters, and other community helpers are common in many programs. Try to invite men and women in nontraditional jobs to visit and talk about or demonstrate their work. Be sure to include skills that are important to each child's culture and family. Introducing children to a diverse range of creative adults—men and women from a variety of cultural backgrounds—helps children explore the world outside of their own experience.

Sharing. Learning to share involves using or enjoying something in common with others. Although sharing may seem simple to adults, it is not a skill that is learned overnight, nor is it easy to orchestrate in young children. When the dominant culture is one of individual competition, acquisition, and ownership, children get particular messages that can make teaching "sharing" difficult.

What does sharing mean to you? To a young child:

- giving up one's possessions   OR taking turns?
- holding onto a power position   OR bringing in more power?
- losing what you have   OR dividing everything equally?
- defining who I am   OR being the me who can give?
- losing the thread of the play   OR adding to the play?

What Do YOU Think?

Thus, sharing makes more sense over time. In the classroom, teachers can help by:

- Understanding that it is normal not to want to share and to have trouble doing so.
- Explaining in simple terms what they want the child to do.
- Making sure that children "get back" what they have shared so that taking turns really works.
- Being an example of sharing because "Do as I do" is more powerful than "Do it because I told you to."
- Giving children experience of there being enough.
- Letting the children experience ownership, too, and the good feeling that an act of generosity brings.

The Kindness Jar

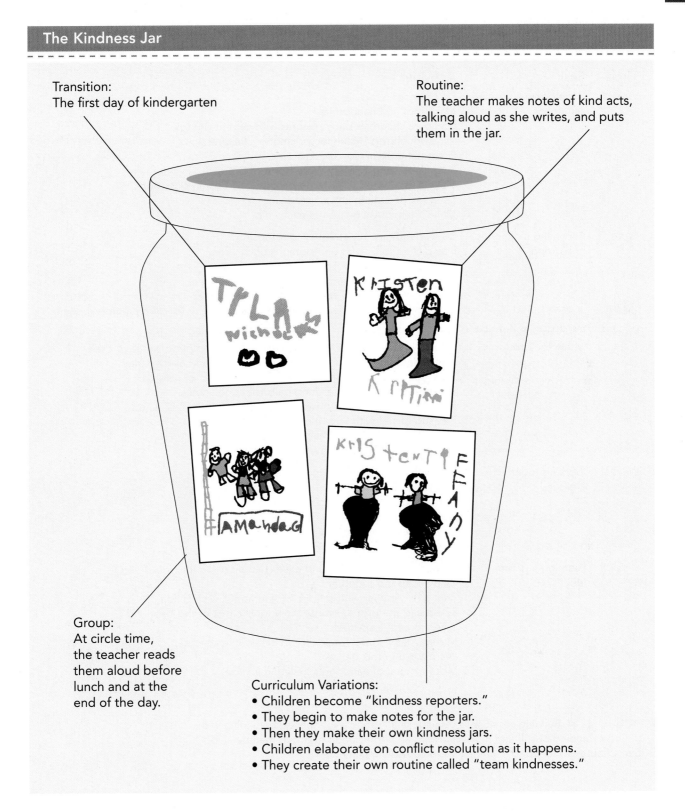

Transition:
The first day of kindergarten

Routine:
The teacher makes notes of kind acts, talking aloud as she writes, and puts them in the jar.

Group:
At circle time, the teacher reads them aloud before lunch and at the end of the day.

Curriculum Variations:
• Children become "kindness reporters."
• They begin to make notes for the jar.
• Then they make their own kindness jars.
• Children elaborate on conflict resolution as it happens.
• They create their own routine called "team kindnesses."

▍ **FIGURE 14-13** Kindness in a jar. (Adapted, by permission, from P. Whitin, 2001.)

Curriculum for Social Skill Development

Time	Skill	Activities
Week 1	Developing a positive self-image	Do thumbprint art.
		Make foot and handprints.
		Compare children's baby pictures with current photos.
		Play with mirrors: Make faces, emotional expressions.
		Dress felt dolls in clothing.
		Sing name songs: "Mary Wore Her Red Dress."
		Make a list: "What I like to do best is . . . " Post in classroom.
		Do a self-portrait in any art medium.
		Make a silhouette picture of each child.
Week 2	Becoming a member of a group	Take attendance together: Who is missing?
		Play picture lotto with photographs of children.
		Play "Farmer in the Dell."
		Share a favorite toy from home with older children.
		Tape record children's voices, guess who they are.
		Have a "friendly feast": Each child brings a favorite food from home to share.
Week 3	Forming a friendship within the group	Provide one puzzle (toy, game, book) for every two children.
		Take a "buddy walk": Return and tell a story together of what you saw.
		Play "telephone talk": Pretend to invite your friend over to play.
		Play "copy cat": imitate your friend's laugh, walk, cry, words.
		Practice throwing and catching balls with one another.
		Form letter together with two children's bodies: A, T, C, K, etc.
		Play tug-of-war with your friend.
		Build a house out of blocks together.
		Make "mirror images" movements with your friend.
Week 4	Working together as a group	Play with a parachute; keep the ball bouncing.
		Make snacks for the rest of the class.
		Plan and plant a garden.
		Make a mural together to decorate the hallways.
		Play "Follow the Leader."
		Sing a round: "Row, Row, Row Your Boat."
Week 5	Learning a group identity	Make a map of the town and have children place their house on it.
		Take a field trip together.
		Print a newspaper with articles by and about each child.
		Select and perform a favorite story for the rest of the class.
		Take a group snapshot.
		Make a "family tree" of photos of children in group.
		Learn a group folk dance.
		Make a mural of handprints joined in a circle.

FIGURE 14-14 Building social skills through small-group experiences, beginning with an understanding of self and moving toward an appreciation of group membership. (See Chapter 10 for specific guidelines to curriculum planning.)

Toddlers and the 2-year-olds are rarely ready to share on their own. Grabbing what they want makes sense to them, and sharing a toy or space may feel like giving it up forever. Preschoolers share more readily because of the experiences they have had in "getting it back," and because of the fuss they have seen occur when they do not share. School-age children become aware that some children feel the same as they do and that others may have needs and wishes different from their own.

Cooperating. Learning how to cooperate with others is one primary social skill in which young children need plenty of practice. Toddlers and 2-year-olds can begin to see the benefits of cooperation as they become more aware of others' feelings and wishes, and as teachers help all children get what they want through taking turns, dividing materials, looking for another item when it is in demand. Three- to 5-year-olds become more cooperative as they learn more self-help skills (motor development) and can express themselves (language development) as well as remember guidelines and understand reasons for prosocial behavior (cognitive development). School-age children develop an emotional sense of psychosocial competence (see Erikson, Chapter 4).

Structured activities that promote cooperation (see Figure 14-15) help children become aware of and learn

A Curriculum of Cooperation

Language
Plan and perform a favorite story.
Choose a story at the listening post together.
Learn "I love you" in sign language.
Copy someone's motions, dance, block patterns.
Put on a puppet show.
Develop a "What Can I Share?" chart.
Discuss how new toys, equipment will be shared
so everyone gets a turn.

Science
Care for classroom pets.
Have group cooking projects.
Plan and plant a garden.

Music
Sing together each day.
Have a rhythm band.
Dance in groups of two or three.
Dance with a parachute.

Environment
Schedule cleanup daily.
Have two children share cubbies.
Bring snacks from home to share.
Set tables for two or more children.
Use large bins to store some materials; children
will need to share contents.

COOPERATION

Social Studies
Make a group gift for a hospital, rest home.
Create an art display for the local library.
Make cookies to sell at the school fair.
Run errands for teachers, each other.
Develop dramatic play themes of: shoe stores,
hospital, doctors, ecology.
Collect and sort recycling materials.
Take a field trip to the town dump for recycling.
Write a "protest letter" about an inferior product.

Outdoors
Push someone on a swing.
Pull a friend in a wagon.
Make bird feeders.
Set up a bowling alley with bowler and pin setters.
Make an obstacle course.
Use seesaws.
Play group jump rope.
Play "Follow the Leader."

Art
Trace each other's bodies on paper.
Share paste and collage materials.
Share paints.
Make a mural.
Make litter bags.
Create a wall hanging: fabric, crayons and
sheets; each child draws part.
Create a class quilt: each child sews a square;
teacher puts it together.

Games
Play Simon Says.
Play board games:
Winnie-The-Pooh
and Candy Land.
Play Lotto.
Play Bingo.

FIGURE 14-15 The social skill of cooperation can be fostered throughout the curriculum. (How to plan a lesson and build a unit are discussed in Chapter 11.)

to work with others and to see viewpoints other than their own. Although most children spontaneously interact in free play periods (thus learning social skills in the process), some children need the structure of a more teacher-directed group activity to promote social development. Moreover, children's friendships can be expanded by the guided affiliation determined by a teacher and a project.

Successful implementation of cooperative learning activities in both older preschoolers and early elementary children usually needs a clear focus of project or activity (such as eating a snack, writing a newsletter, building a model, or catching a hamster on the loose). The group size and, often, members are determined by the teacher, who also needs to make the expectations for group behavior known. The teacher then monitors the interaction, providing assistance, clarification, or problem solving as needed. Evaluation is based on observation, and the group is rewarded for its success.

Being Included. Young children get involved in a variety of interpersonal situations that are beyond their capacities to handle with grace. An overly aggressive child, one who withdraws or stays apart from social opportunities, someone who chronically interrupts or disrupts the play, and children who deliberately leave another out all may end up becoming rejected by their peers. These socially awkward or troubled children need special help to learn the strategies for being included that all children

have to learn.

Developing a conflict resolution curriculum will help all children learn the communication and coping skills necessary for being included. Children who learn good observation and body language skills can then be helped to participate successfully in situations that require prosocial behaviors. In addition, children will need guidance and practice in deciding how to include others whose appearance, interests, age, or behavior differs from their own (Paley, 1992). Research has shown long-term positive effects of such conflict resolution training. When elementary children were taught impulse control, how to get what they wanted without aggression, and how to recognize others' feelings, along with teacher training and family management skills, the children were in better mental health and higher educational and economic achievement than a control group 15 years later (Hawkins, et al, 2008). Chapter 7 has additional suggestions.

Research findings on guided reading indicate that books and reading can change attitudes as well as shape as child's character (Sawyer & Comer, 1996). For instance, use books that help inform children about disabilities; *I'm the Big Sister Now* (Emmert) helps school-aged children learn about multiple handicaps. At the same time, there is a body of books known as "inclusionary literature, where the intent is not to inform, [but rather] a person with a disability is included in story much like a person might be a neighbor, a classmate, or a friend" (Blaska & Lynch, 1998). Examples include *Lester's Dog* (Hesse) and *Mama Zoom* (Cowen-Fletcher).

What Do YOU Think?

"Nobody likes to think about it, even though we know it is not okay to hurt a person with words, or things, or with the way we behave. So when some kids in my class started picking on Ray when the teachers were busy and just couldn't see, nobody knew what to do." Thus begins Becky R. McCain's picture book entitled *Nobody Knew What To Do*. What do you think? Do you advise children to "fight back?" Do you shrug off "tattling" about these incidents? How do you think bullying can be prevented? Dealt with when it happens?

Helping. One area of social development that is sometimes not emphasized in an individualistic society or classroom is that of helping others. Developmentally appropriate programs emphasize cooperation and find that children spontaneously offer help and sympathy to those in need. Snack time is a natural setting for practicing helping others in both words ("Please pass the fruit"; "No, gracias") and deeds (handing someone the pitcher or a sponge). Remember to sit face-to-face, rather than hover behind. Teachers who stand behind often fall into the trap of withholding food while eliciting rote words, rather than genuine or spontaneous positive social inter-

DAP Teachers model positive interaction with others and encourage prosocial behavior. All children in the class are provided opportunities to get to know and work with each other, and friendships are encouraged. Teachers actively involve children in conflict resolution.

Helping: "I'll help clean up."

action. Full-day programs can encourage children to help each other prepare and put away nap items. Curriculum can be developed from the classroom ("What can we do when someone's sad to say good-bye to Mom?") and the larger world ("Some children have noticed a lot of trash in the park next door") to enhance children's helping skills.

Themes. A popular theme that lends itself to social growth is that of friendship. One second grade teacher started an intergenerational program she calls "Forever Friends." Early in the year, Ms. Power introduces her class to a group of residents of a retirement center.

> The elders visit the school throughout the year, participating first-hand in the students' studies and activities. They share oral histories, favorite memories and stories, and introduce the children to their talents and hobbies, such as photography, playing musical instruments, and collecting coins and model trains. There are discussions about what each group thinks about age issues ("What is old?") and take an attitude survey. They visit museums together, the children invite the elders to an art show of their paintings, and there is a musical review at the end of the year, including a song "Forever Friends," which the teacher wrote (Holland, 2000).

Figure 14-16 illustrates how a unit on friendship can be developed for a setting with children as young as 3 and as old as third grade. Other themes can be generated from the children:

"Make It Fair"	Not enough raisins in the cereal, complained a kindergartner, sparking a class letter-writing campaign.
"The Girl No One Wanted to Play With"	Preschoolers rejecting another, so they wrote, made costumes, and performed a play.
"Saving the World"	Third-graders put on a sale to buy rainforest acreage.

Creative Growth

It's OK to try something you don't know.
It's OK to make mistakes.
It's OK to take your time.
It's OK to find your own pace.
It's OK to bungle—so next time you are free to succeed.
It's OK to risk looking foolish.
It's OK to be original and different.
It's OK to wait until you are ready.
It's OK to experiment (safely).
It's OK to question "shoulds."
It is special to be you. You are unique.
It is necessary to make a mess (which you need to be willing to clean up!).

Permissions by Christina Lopez-Morgan (2002) opens our discussion of creativity, to give the tone for what creativity is and how it develops.

In this section, we will discuss the development of creativity and creative skills, then look at the role of the teacher and creative curriculum.

The Development of Creativity

Creativity is the ability to have new ideas, to be original and imaginative, and to make new adaptations on old ideas. Inventors, composers, and designers are creative people, as are those who paint and dance, write speeches, or create curriculum for children. Thinking in a different way and changing a way of learning or seeing something are all creative acts.

Creative thinking is a cognitive process, expressed by children in all developmental areas. Picture the two

Theme: Friendship

Everyone has a name and likes to have it used.

Friendship songs, using children's names.

Having friends is fun.

Make a friendship ring: Each child traces own hands on mural making a circle.

Friends enjoy doing things together.

Go on a scavenger hunt with a friend.

Adults can be your friends.

Teacher helps child solve conflict or gives comfort when child is hurt.

Each person is something special and unique.

Make a "friend puppet" with paper plates and tongue depressor handles. Child decorates it with felt pieces and yarn to look like a friend.

Friends are different; they do not all look the same.

Children respond to "Tell me about your friend Alice. She . . . " (Child describes a friend as teacher writes the words.)

Friends will help you.

Form a relay team and have a race.

You can show someone you want to be friends.

Write a letter to a friend; invite a friend over to play.

To have a friend is to be a friend.

Children respond to: "A friend is someone who ..." (They describe their impressions while teacher writes down their words.)

Friends enjoy doing things for one another.

Children respond to "Being a friend with someone means ..." (Teacher writes down children's dictation.)

Everyone can have a friend.

Teacher reads stories about friendships: *Will I Have a Friend?* (Cohen), *Corduroy* (Freeman), *Play with Me* (Ets), *Little Bear's Friend* (Minarik), *A Letter to Amy* (Keats), *Hold My Hand* (Zolotow), *Jessica* (Henkes), *Harry & Willie & Carrothead* (Caseley).

Animals and pets can be your friends.

Children have an opportunity to bring small house pets to school to share with rest of class.

FIGURE 14-16 A friendship unit can encourage children to express positive emotions while they use their cognitive, language, and motor skills to enhance their social development. (Photo © Cengage Learning)

major ways of thinking as vertical and lateral. Vertical thinking involves learning more about something and tends to lead toward an answer. It is also known as **convergent thinking,** used when asked, "What shape is this block?" Lateral thinking is a process used to find the creative solution or unusual idea. Such **divergent thinking** tends to broaden the field of answers, as when responding to "how many different ways can you surprise your mother?"

Creativity engages certain parts of the brain. The left hemisphere controls the right side of the body and controls such operations as concrete thinking, systematic planning, language, and mathematical skills, what we might call the more rational and cognitive parts of thinking. It is the right brain that engages in more spontaneous ideas and thinks in nonverbal, intuitive ways. Of course, we need both sides to engage to develop, but clearly, the right side is the creative information processor.

The roots of creativity reach into infancy, for it is every individual's unique and creative process to explore and understand the world. Infants' creativity is seen in their efforts to touch and move. Toddlers begin to scribble, build, and move for the pure physical sensation of movement. Young preschoolers create as they try for more control, such as scribbling with purpose or bobbing and jumping to music. Older preschoolers enjoy their budding mastery. Their drawings take on some basic forms, and they repeat movements deliberately while making a dance. As they grow, 5- to 8-year-olds communicate to the world through artistic and expressive creation. With advanced motor control and hand–eye coordination, their drawings are representational and pictorial, their dramatic play more cohesive.

Creativity is a process; as such, it is hard to define. As one becomes involved in creative activity, the process and the product merge.

> It is probably best to think of creativity as a continual process for which the best preparation is creativity itself... [T]here is real joy in discovery—which not only is its own reward, but provides the urge for continuing exploration and discovery. (Lowenfeld & Brittain, 1975)

The young child is open to experience, exploring materials with curiosity and eagerness. For young children, developing the senses is part of acquiring creative skills. Children are also quick to question, wonder, and see things that do not quite match. In the early years, it is delightful to watch confident children elaborate in their creative expression with increasing detail and using more complex forms.

Creative Skills

There are characteristics common to creative people. For the teacher interested in fostering creative growth in children, these are the skills they should help children learn.

Flexibility and Fluency

Flexibility and **fluency** are dual skills that allow for creative responses. Flexibility is the capacity to shift from one idea to another; fluency is the ability to produce many ideas. "How many ways can you move from one side of the room to another?" is a question likely to produce many different ideas, one example of fluency. Children who must think of another way to share the wagons when taking turns does not work learn flexibility.

Sensitivity

Creativity involves a high degree of sensitivity to one's self and one's mental images. Creative people, from an early age, seem to be aware of the world around them:

how things smell, feel, and taste. They are sensitive to mood, texture, and how they feel about someone or something. Creative people notice details; how a pine cone is attached to the branch is a detail the creative person does not overlook.

A special aspect of this skill is sensitivity to beauty. Also known as **aesthetics,** this sensitivity to what is beautiful is emphasized in some programs (such as Reggio Emilia) and some cultures (such as tokonoma, an alcove dedicated to display, in Japanese homes). Teachers can ask the families of children in their care about special places, objects, and rituals that celebrate beauty and help children acquire an aesthetic interest in their environment.

Children have an awareness of and a value for their natural environment and what is aesthetically pleasing. Creative children take delight and satisfaction in making images come to life. Their creative response is in the way they paint a picture, dance with streamers, or find a solution to a problem. Figure 14-17 shows how a 5½-year-old's sensitivity to perspective and detail comes out through a drawing.

Courtesy of the city of Reggio Emilia, Italy

Creativity is the ability to be original and imaginative, to soar above the commonplace.

Seeing in New Ways: Creativity in Action

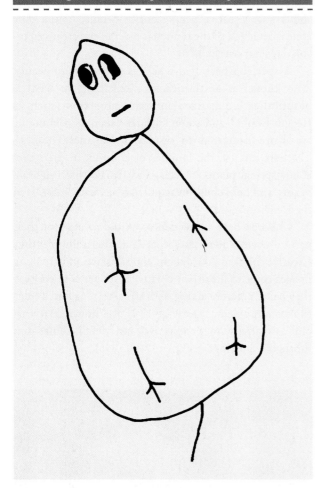

FIGURE 14-17 Sensitivity to one's own mental images, such as perceiving direction and movement, are part of creativity in the young child. A 5½-year-old sketched how a pet rat looked from below after picking it up often and watching it run on its exercise wheel.

Use of Imagination/Originality

Imagination is a natural part of the creative process. Children use their imagination to develop their creativity in several ways:

- *Role Playing.* In taking on another role, children combine their knowledge of the real world with their internal images. The child becomes a new character and that role comes to life.
- *Image Making.* When children create a rainbow with a hose or with paints, they are adding something of their own to their understanding of that visual image. In dance, children use their imagination as they pretend to be objects or feelings, images brought to life.

- *Constructing.* In building and constructing activities, children seem to be re-creating an image they have about tall buildings, garages, or farms. In the process of construction, however, children do not intend that the end product resemble the building itself. Their imagination allows them to experiment with size, shape, and relationships.

A Willingness to Take Risks/Elaboration

People who are willing to break the ordinary mental set and push the boundaries in defining and using ordinary objects, materials, and ideas are creative people. They take risks. Openness to thinking differently or seeing things differently is essential to creativity.

When children create, they are revealing themselves. Art, for instance, is a form of cultural communication, one of the basic language skills children need to participate in a multicultural democracy (Schirrmacher & Fox, 2009). Increasing opportunities for creative expression allows for nonverbal response and success without directions. It encourages children (and families) to share themselves in enjoyable ways. It is, therefore, a good way to teach about cultures and learn about each other in a relaxed, accepting atmosphere.

Self-esteem is a factor in risk-taking because people who are tied to what others think of them are more likely to conform rather than follow their own intuitive and creative impulses. People usually do not like to make mistakes or be ridiculed; therefore, they avoid taking risks.

A teacher concerned about creative growth in children realizes that it will surface if allowed and encouraged. When a child is relaxed and not anxious about being judged by others, creativity will more likely be expressed. With support, children can be encouraged to risk themselves.

Using Self as a Resource

Creative people who are aware of themselves and confident in their abilities draw on their own perceptions, questions, and feelings. They know they are their own richest source of inspiration. Those who excel in creative productivity have a great deal of respect for themselves, and they use the self as a resource.

Experience

Children need experience to gain skills in using materials creatively. They must learn how to hold a paint brush before they can paint a picture; once they know how to paint, they can be creative in what they paint. Teachers of young children sometimes overlook the fact that chil-

Courtesy of the city of Reggio Emilia, Italy

When children have a chance to create, with permission to use an abundance of materials, the results are creative.

dren need competence with the tools to be creative with them. A little sensitive, individual demonstration on proper use of a watercolor brush, sandpaper, or ink roller can expand a child's ability to create and eliminate needless frustration and disappointment. The teachers of Reggio Emilia, for instance, demonstrate how to use the tools so that the children can then make outstanding creations. Anecdotes from highly accomplished people in creative endeavors (pianists, mathematicians, Olympic swimmers) highlight the value of long-term systematic instruction in a sort of apprenticeship with inspiring teachers as well as parents who are committed to assist. As teachers we can see how Vygotsky's theory applies in the arts and can provide the initial palette of creative activities so that children can dabble and become experienced. When the skill of the medium is mastered, the child is ready to create.

Role of the Teacher

Teachers affect the creative process for children in several distinct ways. How they set up the environment, the choices and kinds of activities they provide, and the types of interactions they have with the children during creative activities all stimulate or discourage the creative process (Lopez-Morgan, 2002).

Considerations

To encourage creative development, follow these eight tips:

1. *Provide continuous availability, abundance, and variety of materials,* as is done in Reggio Emilia (see Chapter 2).
2. *Give children regular creative opportunities to experience and the skill necessary to be creative.* Children need frequent occasions to be creative to function in a highly creative manner. When children have a chance to create, their skills in perceiving the world are enhanced.
3. *Encourage divergent thinking.* Do not interfere. Once you have presented the materials, try to forget how you intended them to be used. When there are no "right" or "wrong" answers, children are free to create. Avoid models, making things for children to copy. It insults children and can make them feel inadequate in the face of something you can do so much better.
4. *Help foster conversation on issues and seeking solutions to problems:*

   Teacher: How do you think we could share the swings?

   David: The kids who give me a turn can come to my birthday party.

   Sabrina: No. We will have to make a waiting list.

   Xenia: Only girls can use the swings. The boys can have all the cars.

   Frederico: Buy a new swing set.
5. *Talk with young children about what they create.* Whether it is their artwork, table toy creations, or dramatic play sequences, talk helps creativity considerably. Rather than approach children's work with compliments, judgments, or even questions, Schirrmacher and Fox (2009) recommend that you:

   - Allow children to go about their artistic discoveries without your comparing, correcting, or projecting yourself into their art.
   - Shift from searching for representation in children's art to a focus on the abstract, design qualities.
   - Use reflective dialogue.
   - Smile, pause, and say nothing at first.

DAP

DAP Teachers do not provide a model that they expect children to copy. However, they demonstrate new techniques or uses of the materials to expand children's options. Teachers display children's art, as well as the work of artists, in the classroom and elsewhere in the program setting. Children have opportunities to experience music, art, and dance in the community.

6. *Allow children to take the lead in their own creative works from start to finish.* Adults do not need to take over at any point, particularly at the end with questions ("What is it?") or praise ("I like it!"). If a child seems to want more response, comment on the color ("What a lot of blue you used"), texture ("I see wiggly lines all down one side"), or the child's efforts ("You really worked on this painting, huh?").

7. *Integrate creativity and learning in the classroom.* Early childhood theorists from Dewey and Piaget to Montessori and Malaguzzi (see Chapter 1) have advocated multisensory learning through experimentation and discovery. (See "Art" later in this chapter.)

8. *Teacher timing and attitudes stimulate creativity.* Do not delay; children want to see immediate results and act on their ideas now. Teacher timing and attitudes are important in stimulating creative development. Give plenty of time for a dramatic theme to develop, to pursue the props needed, or to find the players and audience. "It is here that initial attitudes are established … and school can be a fun place where the individual's contribution is welcome and where changes can be sought and made" (Lowenfeld & Brittain, 1975).

Children need plenty of time and a relaxed atmosphere to be creative. They need encouragement and respect for the process and products of their creative nature. The teacher's attitude tells the children that what they do is important and that how they do it makes a difference. Rather than expecting a predetermined right answer, the teacher encourages creativity by valuing the answers the children give even when they appear unusual or illogical.

Note: The Reggio Emilia approach to curriculum (see Chapters 2 and 10) emphasizes children's creative and cognitive expressions. They have a special art teacher (atelierista) who operates an art studio within the school. The studio is stocked with art materials, and children work alongside this teacher. While most groups will not have this arrangement, the idea of children talking and learning with a more experienced adult can help them excel in creating.

Curriculum Planning for Creative Growth

The early childhood curriculum offers many rich avenues for self-expression and creativity. Beyond art and music, there is the ability to think and question, to find more than one answer to a problem. Blocks, climbing equipment, and social relationships offer risk-taking opportunities. Children use themselves as resources as they play outdoor games, experiment with science projects, and

participate in dramatic play. Taruna exhibits many creative traits as she attempts to enter into play with two other children. She first asks if she can play, and when met with rejection, she demands to be one of the mommies. Taruna finally offers her doll as a prop and is accepted into the group. Her persistence is exceeded only by her creative problem solving.

In the Early Childhood Setting. Teachers create the atmosphere and the environment for creative endeavors. "Studies show that teachers plan areas for discussions, walls for displays, centers for activities, and areas for supplies. In the organization of these classroom areas by teachers and their use by children, the spaces and artifacts take on meaning and influence learning" (Taunton & Colbert, 2000).

Open-ended materials provide a continuing challenge as children use them repeatedly in new and different ways. Clay, play dough, paints, crayons and pens, blocks, water, sand and other sensory materials, and movable outdoor equipment are good examples of open-ended materials that stimulate creativity. Particularly in the area of creative art, it is important to avoid projects that masquerade as creative activities, such as duplicated, photocopied, or mimeographed sheets, cut-and-paste activities, tracing patterns, coloring book pages, dot-to-dot books, and any art "project" that is based on a model for children to copy or imitate. Children are motivated to try new ways to use materials when a project is flexible and challenging.

Indoors, every classroom has a potential for creative activity.

■ *The Arts.* A wide variety of materials and opportunities to choose how they will be used is the basis of the creative process. An open table with a shelf of

© Cengage Learning

Offer many materials to create an open-ended art center.

simple, familiar materials that can be combined in many ways will lead to inventiveness. Two-year-olds like crayons, paste, and colored paper pieces; 3- to 5-year-olds will enjoy the addition of markers, string, hole punches and scissors, and tape. Older children can manage staplers, rulers, and protractors. Plenty of paper, such as recycled computer paper and cardboard, rounds out an open-ended, self-help art shelf. More organized art activities can also be offered, particularly for the preschool child, as long as the focus is on the child's process, rather than an end product or model. As they approach the primary years, children become interested in what their creations look like and then are ready for practical help and advice on getting started.

- *Blocks/Manipulatives.* Children use their imagination when blocks become castles, tunnels, corrals, and swamps. These areas encourage creativity when children have enough materials of one kind to "really" make something; one long block is just not enough for a road. Also, creations have a sense of permanence when they are noted and kept. Sketching or photographing a block structure, attaching signs (including taking dictation) for the day, even rethinking clean up periodically shows how valuable these creations are.
- *Discovery/Science.* Building geoboards or making tangrams and cube art all blend math and art. Art activities can lead children to discover scientific principles, such as color mixing, dissolving powder paint in water, and having water available with clay. Natural materials can be used for rubbings, mobiles, and prints. Collecting materials during a "litter walk" makes interesting and informative collages.
- *Dramatic Play.* The dramatic arts offer opportunities for children to express themselves. Every "unit" in the dramatic play corner brings out children's own interpretations of their world, whether it is a house, shoe store, market, or a camp out, dinosaur cave, or space shuttle. Favorite books and stories can be acted out in the dramatic play area. Start with a simple nursery rhyme, and move to short stories with a few characters, simple plots, and manageable speaking lines (Schirrmacher & Fox, 2009).
- *Language/Library.* Besides a variety of books and children's literary experiences (see Chapter 13), the book nook can be a place for teachers to ask open-ended questions for fun and pondering. "What if you were a twin? What would you wear or eat? Where would you live?" is a social creation; "If I were a hat, I would …" is a physical one.

Outdoors, creativity happens. Large, hollow blocks can become a stairway, and wagons and carts become fire engines, buses, doll carriages, moving vans, or trucks. Dancing with ribbons, making a banner for a parade, and rearranging equipment to make a tumbling or obstacle course all combine children's motor skills with music for creative growth. Sand, water, and mud provide a place for children to dig, haul, manipulate, and control in any number of ways.

Routines, Transitions, and Groups. Teachers can apply their own creativity to many routine situations. Children looking for a lost mitten organize a "hunt." Pretending to be vacuum cleaners, dump trucks, or robots gets the blocks picked up faster. Saying good-bye can be an exercise in creativity; the child can say, "See you later, alligator," and the adults (parents and teacher) can make up a silly response. Another day, the child and parent can reverse roles.

Creative "thinking games" can be part of any transition time. Since teachers are looking for unusual responses, children will stay engaged and the game stays fresh over time:

- "What would happen if…" is the prompt; provide endings such as "refrigerators ate food? bath tubs could talk? you could be invisible?"
- "Just Suppose" asks children to come up with endings to such short stories as "You found a magic flying carpet. Where would you go? What would happen?" or "You could be any animal."
- "Make It Better" uses a prop. The teacher brings a stuffed animal, race car, or other familiar toy. Pass it around carefully, and then ask, "How could we make it a better toy? What could we do to make it more fun to play with?"

Creativity does not respond well to the clock. These three issues—routines, transitions, and groups—must be handled so as not to interrupt children too often. "Children's own sense of time and their personal rhythms are considered in planning and carrying out activities and projects" (Gandini in Gillespie, 2000).

Children's creative expression in groups is enhanced through music. Music is a universal language that develops every aspect of psychosocial development. It allows the expression of emotions and provides the opportunity to take roles as well as a delightful time to create with movement.

There is a kind of developmental sequence in the creative expression of music:

- The very young child is receptive to music, responding by listening, singing, and making noise with instruments.

- Preschoolers move to rhythmic music, often singing spontaneously in play and responding to repeated songs or repetitious phrasing. Their interest in musical instruments precedes their skill, and they often need instruments to be introduced and their proper use demonstrated.
- Older preschoolers and school-age children are more accurate in matching their pitch and tempo to the group or played music.

Music can set the tone at nap time, signal that a clean-up task is at hand, summon children to a group, and offer cultural experiences that are meaningful and enjoyable. For instance, New Year is often a noisy time; it can be celebrated by making ankle bells and doing a Sri Lankan dance or making a West Indian Conga line. In Waldorf schools, music is quite important. Children are engaged daily in eurhythmic exercises (developed by Steiner, see Chapter 1). Taught by a specialist, it is a kind of creative form that translates music and speech into movement. (See Figure 14-18.)

Focus on Skills. The wide range of skills necessary for creative development can be supported throughout the early childhood program. The creative thinker is one who finds many ways to solve a problem, approach a situation, use materials, and interact with others. The teacher's role is one of supporting imaginative use of equipment and using a multisensory approach to deepen learning.

Music and Movement: Stages and Activities

Stage of Musical Development	Appropriate Music/Movement Activity
2-year-olds	
Use their bodies in response to music	Bounce to music with different tempos
Can learn short, simple songs	Repetitive songs like "Itsy-Bitsy Spider" or "If You're Happy and You Know It"
Enjoy experimenting with sounds	Pound on milk cartons, oatmeal boxes
	Make shakers with gravel in shampoo bottles
3-year-olds	
Can recognize and sing parts of tunes	Select songs that include their names, such as "Do You Know the Muffin Man?"
Walk, run, jump to music	Use Ella Jenkin's recordings or try "Going on a Bear Hunt"
Make up their own songs	Start "Old MacDonald" and let them make their own additions; dance with scarves or use shakers to sing along with a child
4-year-olds	
Can grasp basic musical concepts like tempo, volume, pitch	Be a flying car, trees swaying in the wind, sing "Big, Bigger, Biggest" with variations
Love silly songs	Change "Where Is Thumbkin" to "Where Is Fi-fo" and improvise with their ideas
Prefer "active" listening	Accompany music with instruments, "Green Grass Grew All Around" with action
5- to 6-year olds	
Enjoy singing and moving with a group	Use a parachute to music
Enjoy call-and-response songs	Try "Did You Feed My Cow?"
Have fairly established musical preferences	Be sure to ask the group and use them in selecting music activities
7- and 8-year olds	
Are learning to read lyrics	Use large word charts
Enjoy musical duets with friends	Do partner games
	Children pick instruments in pairs

FIGURE 14-18 Creative experiences in music and movement engage the whole child and offer children integrated experiences throughout the curriculum (adapted from Schirrmacher & Fox, 2009).

Themes. As teachers plan curriculum around a theme, they keep in mind what creative skills can be developed. Figure 14-19 charts the theme of "Green and Growing Things" and can bring out the child's creative nature as well as social responsibility by promoting ecological responsibility through the arts and nurturing an environmental and social ethic.

Creative themes can also revolve around other psychosocial issues.

One teacher brought to her second grade class an activity from an acting workshop known as the "Emotion Map." After leading a discussion about imaginative maps (*The Hobbit, Harry Potter*), she listed their suggestions ("Slump Swamp," "Guilt Garage," "Boring Boulevard," "Bridge of Joy"). Rolling out a piece of paper on the floor, they began to sketch and talk. Once the map was made and elaborately decorated, the students used it to plot how they felt daily using a Post-it® they had drawn of themselves. New ideas cropped up: Children wanted "emotion maps" made into books for journaling and to plan for performances about different emotions.

Theme: Green and Growing Things

Outdoor Activities

1. Plant a garden in a corner of the yard, in an old barrel, or in a box flat on a table. Children learn through experimentation why some things grow and others don't. Make space for a compost heap.
2. Add wheelbarrows to the transportation toys.
3. Take a field trip to a farm, at planting time if possible, or a garden center.
4. Add gardening tools to the sand area. With proper supervision, children can see how trowels, hand claws, rakes, and shovels can be used to create new patterns in the sand and mud.
5. Plan group games that emphasize green and growing things. Older children could run wheelbarrow races, using one child as the wheelbarrow and another as a driver.
6. Play "musical vegetables" with large cards or chalk drawings. Dance with gourds, coconut instruments, sugar cane rhythm sticks.
7. Have children select a potted plant (have older children pick a partner), then have them draw, paint, or collage what they see. Let children look, talk and compare, then make another creation.

Indoor Activities

1. Leaf rubbings, printing with surplus apples, onions, carrots, potatoes, lemons, oranges, and celery, and painting with pine boughs are ways children can create art with green and growing things; make cornhusk dolls, avocado seed porcupines.
2. Book accessories might include blue felt forms for lakes, hay for corrals and barns.
3. In the manipulative area, match a photo of familiar plants with a sample of the plant. Add sorting trays with various kinds of seeds to count, feel, mix, and match. Match pictures of eggs, bacon, milk, and cheese with other animals from which they come.
4. In the science area, grow alfalfa sprouts and mung beans. Let children mix them in salads and feed to classroom pets. As the sprouts grow, children can chart the growth. This activity can lead to charting their own development, comparing it with when they were infants.
5. The dramatic play center can be transformed into a grocery store to emphasize the food we buy to eat, how it helps us, and why good nutrition is important. Other dramatic play units are a florist shop or nursery, stocked with garden gloves, seed packets, peat pots, and sun hats.
6. The language area can be stocked with books about how plants, baby animals, and children grow. In small groups, children can respond to "When I plant a seed . . . " or "When I was a baby I . . . Now I . . . " to stimulate creative expression.
7. Songs and fingerplays help focus on green and growing things, children's growth, and animals. "The Green Grass Grows All Around" can be sketched by a teacher so that children will have visual cues to each successive verse. A favorite fingerplay, "Way Up in the Apple Tree," can be adapted to a number of fruits and vegetables.

FIGURE 14-19 Creativity around the classroom. Creativity and problem solving may stem from the same source. Real-life experiences, such as planning and building a garden, expand to provide creative thinking and logic in the classroom.

A preschool teaching team noticed the children's interest in shoes. They helped the children brainstorm what they knew about shoes and what they wanted to learn and do about them. The group built a shoe store, created a song and game called "Whose shoe are you?" and made elaborate "houses" out of old, donated adult shoes modeled after "I Know an Old Woman Who Lived in a Shoe." The project lasted nearly a month!

Spiritual Development

Spiritual development is rarely discussed in early childhood or developmental texts. In the United States, where the separation of church and state is mandated, the public classroom has avoided involvement in things spiritual or religious. Private schools are not under such legal restraints, and many (see Chapter 2) actively support or are sponsored by religious organizations. Still, the spiritual side of formal schooling is usually left to religious institutions and families.

Issues to Consider

Often adults tend to see children as not particularly spiritual. Without higher reasoning and abstract thinking skills, young children are seen as not able to have a spiritual life. Moreover, many think of spirituality solely in terms of religion, and "this focus on the 'religious' end of spirituality may be developmentally 'off target'" (Dillon, 2000). By seeing children as faulty thinkers (since they cannot articulate or conceptualize like adults) or by focusing only on organized religion and its ways of explanation, we may overwhelm or overlook children's spiritual experiences.

Some of the earliest contributors to the field have mentioned spiritual development. Froebel saw the child as having an innate spiritual capacity. Education was meant to build on the living core of the child's intrinsic spiritual capacity. Steiner developed the three spiritual dimensions of selfhood and felt that children of all levels of development were capable of spiritual experience. Montessori (Wolf, 2000) wrote:

> If education recognizes the intrinsic value of the child's personality and provides an environment suited to spiritual growth, we have the revelation of an entirely new child whose astonishing characteristics can eventually contribute to the betterment of the world.

It would appear that "profound levels of spiritual reality are accessible even to the youngest human being. ... These experiences typically involve unity, joy, mystery" (Dillon, 2000). Take, for instance, the children's awe as they see a banana slug inching its way up a redwood tree; or the wonder in their eyes at the many colors of autumn maple leaves; their gasp when they find a dead bird, or the sheer joy and outstretched arms (and tongues!) to catch snowflakes.

Saxton (2004) reminds us of the religious or spiritual influence on a child's cultural identity. Robert Coles (1990) conducted an inquiry of the spiritual life of children in the United States, Central and South America, Europe, the Middle East, and Africa. He concluded that children are "seekers, as young pilgrims well aware that life is a finite journey and as anxious to make sense of it as those of us who are farther along in the time allotted us."

Spiritual development in an early childhood program includes the child's deep experience with self and the world, with the mysterious and invisible, and with the joy and pain that real life offers. It can also be expressed through the emotional and social curriculum. Early childhood programs address general spiritual development in these four ways:

1. *Teaching about right and wrong.* Caring adults contribute to children's moral education by encouraging integrity. In their book *Moral Classrooms, Moral Children* (1994), DeVries and Zan assert:

   > Interpersonal conflict can provide the context in which children become conscious of others as having feelings, ideas, and desires... Piaget stated that conflict is the most influential factor in the acquisition of new knowledge structures. Conflict may thus be viewed as a source of progress in development.

   Children then learn issues of "right and wrong" in a caring setting, balancing their own wishes with those of others. "It is possible to train and habituate the young with respect, generosity of spirit, and intellectual curiosity. ... When the habit of justice becomes second nature, it inspires the habit of compassion—the habit of real sensitivity to the pain or suffering of others" (Delattre, 1990).

2. *Matters of death.* "For children ... death has a powerful and continuing meaning" (Coles, 1990). Whether it be a class pet, an accident or injury to a classmate or family member, even a teacher's absence due to illness, children's curiosity about death

is inevitable. For instance, a kindergarten pet rabbit died; the janitor had found it dead the night before. The group talked, asked questions, drew and painted pictures, made books and signs, and asked for stories and reassurance. "Had the teachers taken over, much of this rich experience would have been lost. … The children had different needs and different ways of expressing and processing those needs" (Sandstrom, 1999).

3. *Peace education.* "Peace education curricula generally include instruction in conflict resolution; global awareness; and social and ecological responsibility" (Johnson, 1998). Teaching respect and tolerance has become an educational focus of the peace movement and is certainly appropriate for the early childhood classroom. See "Insights from the Field" at the end of the chapter about the Peace Table in action written by Sue Worford.

4. *Love of nature.* One way to connect with children spiritually is through a love of nature and appreciation of the environment. Give children the firsthand experiences of a seed sprouting a plant, a live animal to care for, a running stream to play in, and a sunset to watch, and they will get closer to their spiritual side.

The Teacher's Role

Teachers are often unsure of their role in spiritual development. Juggling what is appropriate and lawful with what is respectful of diverse family values and affiliations is difficult. A teacher's own identity and beliefs must be considered (Saxton, 2004). "One of the most helpful things we can do for ourselves and our children is to keep in mind the difference between nurturing spiritual growth and passing on a religion" (Fitzpatrick, 1991). As Elkind (1992) explains:

> Spirituality can be used in either a narrow sense or a broad one. In the narrow sense, spirituality is often used to indicate a particular set of religious beliefs… Spirituality, however, can also be used in a much broader sense. Individuals who, in their everyday lives, exemplify the highest of human qualities such as love, forgiveness, and generosity might also be said to be spiritual. It is spirituality in the broad, nondenominational sense that I believe can be fostered by educational practice.

Families provide a vital ingredient in the development of children's spirituality. Working with families around spiritual issues is a delicate matter. Making clear your distinction between religion and spirituality helps parents see your priorities. Emphasize that you are thinking about the adults they may become and that you are trying to give them a kind of framework to face the state of the world as it is becoming.

A child's spiritual growth can be measured in terms of his/her ability to trust, to give love willingly, and accept self and others. Families may disagree with the teaching of some of those concepts, but the dialogue will be useful. In the end, teachers usually find that there is more agreement about these kinds of ideas than they expected. Once made clear, parents often have questions themselves about how to promote family spirituality.

Whether at home or in the classroom, spiritual nurturing does not happen according to schedule and does not entail a sense of teaching in the formal sense. "Spiritual nurturing can never be reduced to a set of techniques or a routine curriculum. It can only flow freely from the teacher's own inner essence and from his or her belief that each child is truly a spiritual being" (Wolf, 2000). Teachers and families have something to share— a way of setting the environment and the tone that opens up the process of self-knowledge, morality and relationship with others, and a reverence for life and spiritual experience.

Children as a Spiritual Resource

Children as a spiritual resource are active participants in their own experience and learning. As the teacher plans, he or she must also be prepared to listen and sit back. "Interactions with children present us adults with the opportunity to regain a sense of connectedness, spontaneity, emotional sensitivity, philosophical wonder and mystery, and attentiveness to value that we have long since left behind" (Dillon, 2000). Time to wonder, to be in awe, and to reflect need to happen and be in place in a program. A hurried or overscheduled program is unlikely to provide such times.

The basic curriculum of the early childhood program is to provide every child with repeated experiences of being loved, accepted, and understood, of finding people trustworthy and dependable, and of discovering the world to be a place that loves him/her and cares for him/her deeply. Spirituality is concerned with directly experiencing life via intuition and feeling. Early childhood educators can set the stage for these experiences in many ways. Figure 14-20 provides several suggestions.

What Do YOU Think? Can teachers remain spiritually neutral? Are there topics that are best left unmentioned or undeveloped in an early childhood program? How will you help children develop their spiritual sense? How do you involve families?

Spiritual expression in educational programs is new for many educators. Saxton and McMurrian (2002) suggest teachers ask themselves:

1. To what extent are you aware of the religious/spiritual diversity of students in your classroom?
2. Have students asked questions or made comments about religious or spiritual topics?
3. What is the source(s) of your information and support concerning the handling of religious/spiritual expression in the classroom?

4. Have you observed instances of religious bias in the classroom? Religious tolerance?

Questions such as these help teachers probe their feelings and attitudes about spiritual development and its expression in a classroom.

Art

"Just as the spirit of the artist is in the things the artist makes, the spirit of the child is in the things the child makes. True education helps children discover and revel in that spirit" (Feinberg, 2003). Art touches the whole child.

Whether the sweeping motion of a brush onto an easel, pounding the fist into clay, or rhythmic scissoring, art is a physical activity. Art may be an individual experience, but in the early childhood classroom, it is a social one as well. Children learn how to interact with others when sharing materials, taking turns, and exchanging ideas with others. Emotionally, children express their inner selves and work through feelings, both positive and negative, in their artwork. Indeed, art therapy has a long

---

Nurturing Spiritual Growth

Quiet Corner
Set aside a corner space or alcove, perhaps behind a shelf that holds the fish tank. Place a small table and chair where a child can sit alone, gaze at the water or out the window.

A Kindness Plant
Put a live plant next to a basket of artificial flowers. Each time a child receives a kindness, they put a flower in the plant.

The Peace Rose
Keep a lively silk rose in a vase within children's reach. Whenever two children have a quarrel, one of them, or a third child, collects the peace rose. Each child holds the rose while talking: Once they reach solution or simply get over it, together they put their hands on the stem of the rose and say, "We declare peace."

Guided Meditation
Have the children sit or lie down quietly and close their eyes. Lead them through a reflection, asking each child to think about his or her heart—the place where love lives.

The Garden
Plant seeds together, ask how things grow and how could a seed do that. Check as they sprout. Plant a button, a seed, and a penny—and see the power of the seed.

I Spy
Play the game of "I Spy" with the children you have observed helping others. "I spy someone who helped Danny clean up the paint he spilled."

The Universe Star
Make a star in your classroom. Taking turns, each child carries the star home, waits for a clear night, and goes outside at dark with a parent to look at the night sky. When the child brings back the star, take time as a class to talk about the wonder and size of the universe.

A Silence Game
At a time when the children are engaged and behaving well, give them a new challenge. Ask them to stop all talking and sit perfectly still for several minutes. Each time you initiate this activity, lengthen the time. When the time is up, children will report what they heard.

▌ **FIGURE 14-20** Aline Wolf (2000) offers several curriculum ideas for nurturing the spirit.

The spirit of the children is in the things they make.

history in helping therapists understand children. Art reflects what the child knows; planning and organizing, revising and finishing are all cognitive tasks. Moreover, early childhood professionals can encourage children to talk about their processes and making art a language activity as well. Finally, children's artistic creations may be similar in their development (see next section), but are unique expressions of each child's creativity.

Rhoda Kellogg (1969) described the developmental stages of art after having analyzed literally millions of piece of children's art from around the world over a 20-year period. Briefly, they are:

- *Placement stage:* Scribble, ages 2–3
- *Shape stage:* Vague shapes, ages 2–4; actual shapes, ages 3–5
- *Design stage:* Combined shapes, ages 3–5; mandalas and suns, ages 3–5
- *Pictorial stage:* People, ages 4–5; beginning recognizable art, ages 4–6; later recognizable art, ages 5–7

Figure 14-21 illustrates these stages.

The process of creating art follows a predictable four-step pattern, although there are as many variations on the theme as there are children and art experiences.

1. *Preparation.* Gathering materials and ideas to begin.
2. *Incubation.* Letting ideas "cook" and develop.
3. *Illumination.* The "a-ha" moment when everything gels; the "light bulb."
4. *Verification.* When exhilaration has passed and only time will confirm the effort.

When Howard Gardner began his studies of intelligence (see Chapters 4 and 12), he became intrigued with artis-

tic capacity. Project Zero is a program that has studied intelligence, the arts, and education for the last 30 years (Gardner, 1993) and has identified four key ideas about art education:

1. In the early childhood years, production of art ought to be central. Children need to work directly with the materials.
2. The visual arts ought to be introduced by someone who can think visually or spatially. An ECE team ought to be diverse enough to have someone with this intelligence on board.
3. Whenever possible, artistic learning should be organized around meaningful projects. Both the project approach and emergent curriculum address this (Chapter 10).
4. Artistic learning must entail emotional reflection and personal discovery along with a set of skills. Integration of development is encouraged.

Stages of Children's Art

1. Scribbling:

2. Drawing a single shape:

3. Combining single shapes into designs:

4. Drawing mandalas, mandaloids, and sun figures:

5. Drawing a human figure with limbs and torso:

FIGURE 14-21 Children's art follows a sequence of stages (From *Art and Creative Development for Young Children* (4th Ed.) by Schirrmacher. © 2002. Reprinted with permission of Delmar Learning, a division of Thomson Learning: www.thomsonrights.com.)

Taken together, these observations help teachers create developmentally appropriate art activities. If you work with infants or toddlers, be sure to help children explore materials and places with all their senses, and expect scribbling by 15 to 20 months. Young preschoolers will work in manipulating tools and materials, discovering what can be done and needing lots of repetition. Do not expect much concern about the final product. By 4 to 6 years of age, children's art becomes more symbolic and planned; more detailed work with forms and shapes may be seen. Children become interested in what they are doing and how it turns out.

Giving art its place in early childhood curriculum will require space, time, and attention. An art center (Schirrmacher & Fox, 2009) is:

1. An artist's studio.
2. Conveniently located and easily accessible.

Adapting Art for Children with Special Needs

____ **Visual:**

Verbally describe materials and how they might be used.

Provide a tray that outlines the visual boundaries.

Offer bright paint to contrast with paper.

Go slowly and encourage children to manipulate the items as you talk.

____ **Auditory:**

Model the process, facing the child and using gestures for emphasis.

Use sign language as needed.

____ **Physical:**

Make sure there is a clear path to the art center.

Provide adaptive art tools such as chunky crayons or large markers.

Provide double ambidextrous scissors so you can help, or a cutting wheel.

Velcro can be attached to marking instruments or paintbrushes.

Use contact paper for collage or glue sticks instead of bottles.

____ **Attention-deficit and/or behavioral:**

Provide children with their own materials and workspace, minimizing waiting and crowding.

Offer materials like play dough to express feelings and energy.

Limit children to few choices rather than overwhelming them with everything in the art center.

FIGURE 14-22 The value of art activities for children with special needs cannot be overemphasized.

3. Well-stocked with developmentally appropriate materials.
4. Orderly and organized.
5. A place with rules and limits.

See Chapter 9 for more details on space. Basic categories of art materials should include tools for mark making; papers in a variety of shapes/sizes/textures; modeling and molding materials, such as play dough/clay; items for cutting fastening and attaching, such as scissors and string; items for painting; and collage items. Figure 14-22 gives some suggestions for adapting art for children with special needs.

Merely labeling an activity art is no guarantee that the activity will have artistic merit. Some activities masquerade as creative and should be avoided. As Schirrmacher (2009) states:

> Crafts are often given as holiday gifts. Most parents would be delighted to receive a paperweight or pencil holder constructed by their child. Although it is important to please parents, it is equally important to meet the creative needs of children. Providing for child input, planning, decision making, and creative processing guarantees that each finished product will be as unique and individual as the child who produced it.

Taking the time to talk with families about children's art and creativity will help them appreciate the unique nature of children's creations.

Insights *from the field*

The Peace Table in Action *by Sue Warford, M.Ed.*

How can early childhood educators support children's development of a peaceful approach to conflict resolution? How can we help children in choosing peaceful solutions to interpersonal problems? How can the social emotional environment be structured in such a way that children's first impulse is to reconcile their differences and generate a solution to problems where everyone is satisfied? How can we support children's development of nurturing, tolerant, accepting, mutually empowering approaches to conflict? Do we expect to eradicate conflict from children's lives? No, that would be completely unrealistic and would eliminate many wonderful opportunities for children's growth in their ability to be peacemakers. Watch what happens with 4-year-olds Rose and Lydia ...

Rose: Lydia, I was using that doll.

Lydia: But Rose, you weren't holding it. It was in the crib.

Teacher: It sounds like there is a problem here. Let's take this doll over to the Peace Table, and you two can try to work out this problem.

Lydia: Rose, you weren't holding that doll or near that doll, so I thought you weren't using it.

Rose: Lydia, my baby was taking a nap, and I was doing some cooking while she slept. You can't take my baby.

Teacher: We have some new information. Rose was still using that doll, but Lydia thought she was done because Rose wasn't near the doll. What are we going to do about this problem?

Rose: I know. Lydia can have a turn when I'm done.

Teacher: What do you think about that, Lydia?

Lydia: No... I want a turn now. I know, Rose, you can be the mom and I can be the babysitter.

Rose: OK, and you can have a turn when I'm done.

Teacher: So Rose is going to be the mom and Lydia is going to be the babysitter, and Lydia will have the baby when Rose is done.

Lydia: We solved the problem!

Rose: Yeah.

Why did this episode end so peacefully? Does simply adding a Peace Table to a classroom insure there will be peaceful solutions to every problem? Actually, these two children have had two years of experience using the Peace Table at the University of Rhode Island Child Development Center as a safe and peaceful place to go to solve problems nonviolently with their peers. At first, children require a great deal of adult support and input in negotiating their problems, and often, it is the adult who guides the discussion. The steps which can be followed to guide these conflict resolution discussions are:

- *Initiate the mediation. It looks like there is a problem here.* Or, *what's happening here?*
- *Clarify each child's perspective.* In this step each child is given the opportunity to explain his/her perspective on the situation.
- *Summarize.* In this step, the teacher clearly articulates a summary of each child's perspective.
- *Generate alternative solutions. What can we do about this problem?* In this step, the teacher supports children's generation of alternative solutions.
- *Agree on a solution.* Here, both children agree on a solution to the problem. It is critical to allow sufficient time for children to arrive at a mutually satisfying solution.
- *Follow through.* The teacher checks with the children later to be sure that the solution actually satisfied everyone. *You had a problem with that doll before. You two solved that problem. Did your solution work?*

These discussions provide opportunities for everyone involved in a conflict to feel empowered and to participate in generating solutions to the problem. This process is effective with many types of problems and conflicts that arise daily in an early childhood classroom. Some of these conflicts involve possessions (two children want the same truck at the same time), position (two children want to sit on the teacher's left side at the same time), exclusion (*you can't play at the texture table with us*), and misunderstandings or accidents (*I didn't mean to hurt you when I stepped on your finger*). As time goes on and children gain more experiences with the problem-solving process, they are able to become more and more independent in clarifying misunderstandings and nonviolently solving their problems at the Peace Table.

The Peace Table is one tool used at the University of Rhode Island Child Development Center as part of the overarching approach to social interactions that encourages children to peacefully interact with each other. This method encourages children to accept diversity and to attempt to understand differing perspectives. This approach helps children to see all problems as solvable and scaffolds children in their attempts to "solve the problem." Within an environment where adults assist children to feel empowered to actively solve interpersonal problems, children like Lydia and Rose quickly become peacemakers.

Sue Warford is the coordinator of the University of Rhode Island's Child Development Center, a part of the Department of Human Development and Family Studies. She has worked at the CDC for 16 years, while also teaching courses in early childhood education. Sue has a Master's Degree in Education from the University of Massachusetts, Amherst.

SUMMARY

Psychosocial development is at the center of the early childhood curriculum. Planning for emotional, social, creative, and spiritual growth involves an understanding of how each develops in the young child and how they are interrelated. Children learn many skills in these areas as they interact with each other, with adults, and in the environment.

Planning curriculum for psychosocial growth calls upon teachers to play a supportive role, facilitating children's involvement with the materials and each other. Only then can children discover themselves, explore their relationships, develop the ability to use their imagination and resources, and explore deeper questions of self and spirit. Art is a special way to encourage psychosocial development in young children.

KEY TERMS

psychosocial domain	imaginary companions	social cognition
affective	social referencing	social action
emotional intelligence	socialization	coacting
basic emotions	sociocentric	convergent thinking
complex emotions	peer interactions	divergent thinking
social mores	undifferentiated	flexibility
positive stress	unilateral	fluency
self-regulation	reciprocal	aesthetics
superhero	social skills	

REVIEW QUESTIONS

1. Define the psychosocial domain and name the areas within it.

2. How can teachers help children articulate their feelings?

3. List some of the social skills that are learned in the major areas of the early childhood setting.

4. Write three examples of a child's divergent thinking and how teachers can encourage this type of creativity.

5. How can teachers nurture the spirit in nonsectarian environments?

LEARNING ACTIVITIES

1. How does your center promote positive self-concept? What else could be done?

2. Make behavioral definitions of emotions you think you will see in the children you teach. Observe the children; then check the accuracy of your definitions.

3. Observe a group of 4-year-olds at play. How do they decide what roles each one takes? Are they clear in their expectations of what sex roles are appropriate for boys and girls? Is there sex-role stereotyping?

4. Taking turns and sharing equipment and materials are difficult for young children. Cite three examples you have seen in which children used their social skills to negotiate a turn. Was teacher intervention necessary?

5. Name five people you consider creative. Match their skills with those we have identified in early childhood. How are they similar? Different?

6. Give three examples of children in your center trying to "break mental set." In what area of the classroom did it occur? What were the adults' responses?

7. How do teachers in your setting plan for creativity? What place does such expression take in the priority of the school philosophy?

8. If spirituality includes the embodiment of the highest human qualities, name three and offer an idea of how to put this into the curriculum.

HELPFUL WEBSITES

Collaborative to Advance Social and Emotional Learning   **http://www.casel.org**

Creative Curriculum   **http://www.teachingstrategies.com**

Cultural Survival   **http://www.cs.org**

Educators for Social Responsibility   **http://www.esrnational.org**

Institute of Noetic Sciences   **http://www.noetic.org**

M.U.S.I.C.   **http://learningfromlyrics.org**

Youth Peace Literacy/Atrium Society   **http://www.atriumsoc.org**

Society for Myth and Tradition   **http://www.parabola.org**

Southern Poverty Law Center   **http://www.teachingtolerance.org**

 Additional resources including the TeachSource Videos can be found on the premium website for this book. Go to **http://www.cengage.com/login** to register your access code.

REFERENCES

General

Berger, K. S. (2006). *The developing person through childhood and adolescence* (7th Ed). New York: Worth Publishers.

Berk, L. E. (2007). *Infants, children and adolescents* (7th Ed). Boston: Allyn & Bacon.

York, S. (2003). *Roots and wings: Affirming culture in early childhood programs* (2nd Ed). St. Paul, MN: Redleaf Press.

Emotional Growth

Bowling, J. H., & Rogers, S. (2001, March). The value of healing in education. *Young Children, 56*(2).

Bowman, B., & Moore, E. K. (Eds.). (2006). *School readiness and social-emotional development: Perspectives on cultural diversity.* Washington, DC: National Black Child Development Institute.

Breslin, D. (2005, January). Children's capacity to develop resiliency. *Young Children, 60*(1).

Bronson, M. R. (2000, March). Recognizing and supporting the development of self-regulation in young children. *Young Children, 55*(2).

Carlson, S. M., and Taylor, M. (2005). Imaginary companions and impersonated characters: Sex differences in children's fantasy play. *Merrill-Palmer Quarterly, 51,* 93-118.

Cook, J. W. (2001, January). Create and tell a story: Help young children who have psychological difficulties. *Young Children, 56*(1).

Cooper, R. M. (1992, November). The impact of child care on the socialization on African American children. Paper presented at the NAEYC Annual Conference, New Orleans, LA.

Curry, N. E., & Johnson, C. N. (1990). *Beyond self-esteem: Developing a genuine sense of human value.* Washington, DC: NAEYC.

Ginsburg, K. R. (2006). *Building resilience in children and teens: Giving your child roots and wings.* Elk Grove Village, IL: American Academy of Pediatrics.

Goleman, D. (1995). *Emotional intelligence.* New York: Bantam Books.

Hoffman, E. (2004). *Magic capes, amazing powers: Transforming superhero play in the classroom.* St. Paul, MN: Redleaf Press.

Kostelnik, M., Whiren, A. P., & Stein, L. G. (1986, May). Living with He-Man: Managing superhero fantasy play. *Young Children, 41*(4).

Marion, M. (2006). *Guidance of young children* (7th Ed). Columbus, OH: Merrill Publishers.

Marshall, H. H. (1989, July). Research in review: The development of self-concept. *Young Children, 44*(5).

Matsumoto, D. (2004). Reflections on culture and competence. In R. J. Sternberg & E. L. Grigorenko (Eds.), *Culture and competence: Contexts of life success.* Washington, DC: American Psychological Association.

McCormick, J. (1993). Family child care. In A. Gordon and K. W. Browne (Eds.), *Beginnings and beyond* (3rd Ed).Clifton Park, NY: Thomson Delmar Learning.

Nakahata, A. (2001, Fall). Identity is tied to culture. Interview by Marion Hironaka Cowee in *Connections: California AEYC Newsletter.*

Pool, C. R. (1997, May). Up with emotional health. *Educational Leadership, 54*(8).

Rofrano, F. (2002, January). "I care for you": A reflection on caring as infant curriculum. *Young Children, 57*(1).

Teaching Tolerance Project. (1997). *Starting small: Teaching tolerance in preschool and the early grades.* Montgomery, AL: Southern Poverty Law Center.

York, S. (1998). *Big as life: The everyday inclusive curriculum.* St. Paul, MN: Redleaf Press.

Social Growth

Blaska, J. K., & Lynch, E. C. (1998, March). Is everyone included? Using children's literature to facilitate the understanding of disabilities. *Young Children, 53*(2).

Bos, B. (1990). *Together we're better: Establishing a co-active learning environment.* Roseville, CA: Turn the Page Press.

Colker, L. (2007, November). News from the field: Preschoolers dance their way to social competence and success. *Teaching Young Children.* Washington, DC: NAEYC.

Coplan, R. J., & Armer, M. (2007 January). A "multitude" of solitude. *Child Development Perspectives,* 26-32.

Derman-Sparks, L., & Olsen Edwards, J. (2010). *Anti-bias education for young children and ourselves.* Washington, DC: NAEYC.

Gordon, A. M., & Browne, K. W. (1996). *Guiding young children in a diverse society.* Boston, MA: Allyn and Bacon.

Hawkins, J. D., Kosterman, R., Catalano, R. F., Hill, K.G., & Abbott, R.D. (2008). Effects of social development intervention in childhood 15 years later. *Archives of Pediatrics and Adolescent Medicine,* 162(12): 1133-1141.

Holland, H. (2000, Spring). These guys are fun! *Teaching Tolerance, 17.*

Katz, L. G., & McClennan, D. E. (1997). *Fostering children's social competence.* Washington, DC: NAEYC.

Kendall, F. E. (1996). *Diversity in the classroom: New approaches to the education of young children* (2nd Ed). New York: Teachers College Press.

Kostelnik, M. J., Whiren, A. P., Soderman, A. K., Stein, L. C., & Gregory, K. (2005). *Guiding children's social development: Theory to practice* (5th Ed).Clifton Park, NY: Delmar Cengage.

Lillard, A., & Curenton, S. (1999, September). Research in review: Do young children understand what others feel, want, and know? *Young Children* 54 (5).

Maniates, H., & Heath, M. (1998, Spring). Creating a climate for learning. *Early Childhood Resources.*

Paley, V. G. (1992). *You can't say you can't play.* Cambridge, MA: Harvard University Press.

Porro, B. (1996). *Talk it out: Conflict resolution in the elementary classroom.* Alexandria, VA: Association for Supervision and Curriculum Development.

Rubin, K. H., Bukowski, W., & Parker, J. G. (2006). Peer interactions, relationships and groups. In W. Damon and N. Eisenberg (Eds.), *Handbook of child psychology* (Vol. 3): *Social emotional and personality development,* (5th Ed). New York: Wiley.

Sawyer, W. E., and Comer, D. E. (1996). *Growing up with literature.* Clifton Park, NY: Thomson Delmar Learning.

Whitin, K. (2001, September). Kindness in a jar. *Young Children.* Washington, DC: NAEYC.

Creative Growth

Amabile, T. M. (1989). *Growing up creative.* New York: Crown.

Bos, B. (1978). *Don't move the muffin tins.* Roseville, CA: Turn the Page Press.

Bovard, K. (2000, Spring). The emotion map. *Teaching Tolerance, 17.*

Feinberg, S. G. (2003, May). All about art inside and out! *Scholastic: Early Childhood Today.*

Gillespie, C. W. (2000, January). Six Head Start classrooms begin to explore the Reggio Emilia approach. *Young Children, 55*(1).

Kellogg, R. (1969). *Analyzing children's art.* Palo Alto, CA: Mayfield Publishing.

Lopez-Morgan, C. (2002). *Creative arts for the young child.* Cupertino, CA: De Anza College.

Lowenfeld, V., & Brittain, W. L. (1975). *Creative and mental growth.* New York: Macmillan.

Schirrmacher, R., & Fox, J. (2009). *Art and creative development for young children* (6th Ed). Clifton Park, NY: Thomson Delmar Learning.

Taunton, M., & Colbert, C. (2000). Art in the early childhood classroom: Authentic experiences and extended dialogues. In N. Yelland (Ed.), *Promoting meaningful learning.* Washington, DC: NAEYC.

Spiritual Growth

Coles, R. (1990). *The spiritual life of children.* Boston, MA: Houghton-Mifflin.

Delattre, E. J. (1990, September 5). Teaching integrity: The boundaries of moral education. *Education Week.*

DeVries, R., & Zan, B. S. (1994). *Moral classrooms, moral children.* NY: Teachers College Press.

Dillon, J. J. (2000, Winter). The spiritual child: Appreciating children's transformative effects on adults. *Encounter: Education for Meaning and Social Justice, 13*(4).

Elkind, D. (1992, Spring). Spirituality in Education. *Holistic Education Review.*

Fitzpatrick, J. G. (1991). *Something more: Nurturing your child's spiritual growth.* New York: Viking Press.

Hart, T. (2000, Summer). Teaching for wisdom. *Encounter: Education for meaning and social justice, 14*(2).

Johnson, M. L. (1998). Trends in peace education. *ERIC Digest.* Bloomington, IN: ERIC Clearinghouse, ED417123.

Sandstrom, S. (1999, November). Dear Samba is dead forever. *Young Children, 54*(6), 14-16.

Saxton, R. R. (2004). A place for faith. In A. Gordon and K. W. Browne (Eds.), *Beginnings and beyond* (6th Ed). Clifton Park, NY: Thomson Delmar Learning.

Saxton, R. R., & McMurrain, M. K. (2002). *Spiritual diversity in the classroom.* Atlanta, GA: Georgia State University Research Project.

Wolf, A. D. (2000, January). How to nurture the spirit in nonsectarian environments. *Young Children, 55*(1).

How Do We Teach for Tomorrow?

© Cengage Learning

Issues and Trends in Early Childhood Education

PREVIEW QUESTIONS

- What are the most pressing issues facing early childhood educators today?

- How are the major themes of early childhood education reflected in the issues facing children, families, and teachers today?

- What are the major factors that diminish the importance of childhood in today's society?

- How do the values of family, culture, and school get transmitted in today's world?

- What standards and issues apply to professionalism of early childhood education?

NAEYC CODE OF ETHICAL CONDUCT

These Core Values and sections from the NAEYC Code of Ethical Conduct are addressed in this chapter. As you read, note how the Core Values, Ideals, or Principles listed here apply to the topics in this chapter. (Reprinted with permission from the National Association for the Education of Young Children.)

I-1.1   To be familiar with the knowledge base of early childhood care and education and to keep current through continuing education and in-service training.

P-1.5   We shall be familiar with the symptoms of child abuse, including sexual, physical, verbal and emotional abuse, and neglect. We shall know and follow state laws and community procedures that protect children against abuse and neglect.

P-1.6   When we have reasonable cause to suspect child abuse or neglect, we shall report it to the appropriate community agency and follow up to ensure that appropriate action has been taken.

I-2.2   To acknowledge and build upon strengths and competencies as we support families in their task of nurturing children.

I-2.3   To respect the dignity of each family and its culture, language, customs, and beliefs.

I-3C.2   To strive to secure equitable compensation (salary and benefits) for those who work with or on behalf of young children.

I-4.3   To work through education, research, and advocacy, toward an environmentally safe world in which all children receive adequate health care, food, and shelter, are nurtured, and live free from violence.

1-4.5   To work toward greater social acknowledgement of children's rights and greater social acceptance of responsibility for their well-being.

Changing Issues/ Changing Times

Early childhood education has undergone remarkable changes in the past 50 years, evolving from being an option for middle class preschool children to a necessity for millions of families with children from infancy through the primary years. Such a transformation is a reflection of the economic, social, and political climate of the times, as well as research in child development and early education. Changes in education historically have been linked to societal reform and upheaval. Issues of today and trends for tomorrow grow out of the problems and solutions of the past.

In the 1960s, social action and the War on Poverty captured the American interest and spirit. Head Start programs opened around the country and were the symbols of social action of that era. They also brought national attention to early childhood education. The 1970s brought changes related to economic crisis. The family unit was affected by the job market, the end of the Vietnam War, an energy crisis, inflation, rising divorce rates, and the feminist movement. All of these factors led more women into the workplace rather than remaining in the home. One of the expansions in public funding at this time was in the services to the handicapped and bilingual populations.

The 1980s meant further budget cuts and reduced services for children and families. Many children were now in group care for most of their waking hours. They grew up with change, rather than stability, as a constant in their lives. Child abuse became a national cause for alarm. The need for early child care and educational services was well established. The education reforms that

Courtesy of the author

Who are the children of tomorrow, and how do we meet their needs?

began in the early 1980s brought about some rethinking in early childhood education. Interest in young children flourished along with reforms at other grade levels. As the 1990s ended, there was an expanded acceptance of child care for children under age 5 and an increasing awareness of the needs of the whole child in the early primary years. The quality and cost of programs for young children became an issue.

To date, many of these issues are unresolved. Due to lack of funding, Head Start and Early Start can enroll only a small percentage of the children who need the programs. Government-mandated standards and testing are pressuring programs to put more emphasis on academics. Professionalism is making its way into early childhood certification. All these issues are making inroads into early childhood programs at every level.

It seems appropriate to discuss current issues in light of the history of the early childhood profession. Look back at Chapter 1. For all its diverse and varied past, early childhood education has had a consistent commitment to four major themes: the ethic of social reform, the importance of childhood, transmitting values, and

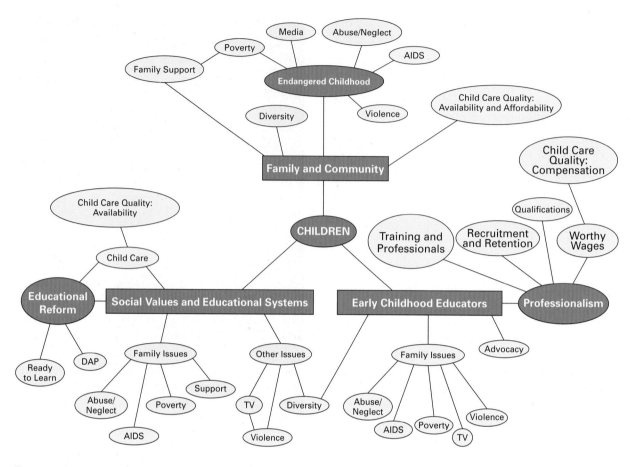

FIGURE 15-1 A web of influences and challenges for today's children and their families.

professionalism. These four themes are reflected in Figure 15-1 and are the same ones facing early childhood educators today:

- *Ethic of social reform:* the quality of programs and services needed for children under age 8 and the education reforms that provide it.
- *Importance of childhood:* children's health and welfare and the changes in family life.
- *Transmission of values:* challenges presented by the media culture, violence, disaster, and diversity.
- *Professionalism:* standards for children's programs and teacher preparation.

Ethic of Social Reform

The first theme suggests that schooling for young children will lead to social change and improvement. Maria Montessori, the McMillan sisters, Patty Smith Hill, and Abigail Eliot were pioneers in improving children's lives through a comprehensive approach to education. Today,

Marion Wright Edelman, by creating the Children's Defense Fund, is continuing the efforts started nearly 100 years ago. Louise Derman-Sparks and colleagues enlarged the issue when they published the *Anti-Bias Curriculum* in 1989 and challenged our thinking about bias as a social issue for young children.

Child Care

- Two out of three mothers with preschool and three out of four mothers with school-age children were in the labor force in 2007 (Children's Defense Fund, 2008).
- Between 1964 and 1999, enrollment rate in nursery schools rose from about 5 percent of the preschool population to about 50 percent, reflecting a significant societal shift (U.S. Census Bureau, 2008).
- Only 3 percent of the infants eligible are enrolled in Early Head Start, and 50 to 67 percent of those eligible for Head Start are enrolled (Children's Defense Fund, 2008).

■ In 1991, 52.8 percent of 3 to 5 year olds were enrolled in a center-based, out-of-home child care program. In 2005, the number rose to 57.2 percent (Children's Defense Fund, 2008).

Without question the need for child care has been firmly established. The significant increase in enrollment in child care centers over the last 40 years, underscored by the demographic facts, has had a profound impact on this country. In 1990, Congress passed the first comprehensive child care legislation in nearly 20 years; a year later Head Start funding was increased significantly (see Chapter 2 for more discussion on child care).

Quality and Cost

The key word is *quality*—the terms *good quality* and *high quality* identify specific features in early childhood programs as described in Chapter 2.

Two broad-based studies, one conducted in child care centers and the other in family day care settings, have examined the critical relationship between quality and cost and present a disturbing picture.

Inadequate child care was found to be rampant in the first study, which was conducted in hundreds of centers in California, Colorado, Connecticut, and North Carolina (Costs, Quality and Child Outcomes Study Team, 1995). In a dramatic conclusion, the study found that most child care centers provided mediocre services and that some were of such poor quality that they threatened children's emotional and intellectual development. Infants and toddlers were most likely to be at risk for poor care in these centers; nearly half of their settings failed to meet basic health and safety needs. Yet 90 percent of the parents rated the care as "good."

The report was the first of its kind to examine the relationship between the costs of child care and the nature of children's experiences in child care settings (quality). In centers in which researchers found high quality care, the center staffs were paid higher wages, there were more personnel, and more of them were trained in early childhood education. They were also programs that were subsidized in some way, by the government, a university, or employers of families using these services. The states that had more demanding licensing requirements had few poor quality programs. According to this report, these factors along with teachers' salaries and administrators' prior experience are strong determinants of quality.

A follow-up study, "The Children of the Cost, Quality, and Outcomes Study Go to School" (Peisner-Feinberg, et al., 1999), followed the children in the original study through second grade. The findings from this study reinforced the notion that high quality child care enhances cognitive and social skills that, in turn, help children be more prepared and successful in school.

The results of a major study of family day care are similarly distressing, highlighting uneven and poorly regulated conditions. Conducted by Galinsky and co-workers (1994), the study concluded that only 9 percent of the homes they observed were of good quality and that over one-third of the providers were indifferent to such an extent in their caregiving as to be harmful to children's development. More than 40 percent of the providers planned no activities for children in their care, and only half of the children showed signs of trust or attachment to the caregiver.

The more a provider was paid, the better the care; the licensed or regulated providers were more likely to be warm and attentive to children, communicate with parents, and provide a safe home. Look at NAEYC's criteria for high quality programs in Chapter 2 to see the relationship with the findings of these two studies. The good news is that between 1990 and 2002, licensing of family child care homes increased by 37 percent (The Children's Foundation, 2001).

© Cengage Learning

The quality of a child care program is directly related to the experience and training of the teachers.

These two forms of child care—child care centers and family day care—are equally popular; they are the programs of choice by America's working families, who, according to this research, either do not recognize what makes a quality program or who think they cannot demand it. The NACCRRA study of parental concerns cited in Chapter 2 further found that parents *assumed* caregivers were trained to work with young children and that most child care programs were regularly inspected (National Association of Child Care Resources and Referral Agencies, 2008). Quality is a function of group size, low teacher–child ratios, trained and experienced staff, adequate compensation, and safe and stimulating environments.

All of the studies share a common concern that parents must be able to distinguish good from poor quality centers and demand higher quality care before the centers will increase their fees to cover the costs of providing better care.

DAP

A National Crisis

Good, affordable, accessible child care that will meet the increasing needs of American families is one of today's most crucial issues. Quality care and education of young children has a cost that must be addressed. The cost of quality is directly related to the needs of the families served by the specific program, the added costs of helping families connect with the right resources and providing the necessary comprehensive services, and fee reductions and financial aid for low income families. The average cost of child care at a full time center for an infant is $4,542 to $14,591. The average cost for a 4-year-old in a family child care home is $3,380 to $9,164 and the average cost for a school-age child in a center is $2,500 to $8,600 (NACCRRA, 2008). Families who live at or near the poverty line and middle income families are hard-pressed to afford these fees.

Quality is significantly related to staff: how many adults there are compared with the number of children in a class; whether the salaries and benefits provide incentive for teachers to be retained for a number of years; and the level of staff education and training and their years of experience. These factors have created a staffing crisis of major proportion in the country today. Refer to the section "A Trilemma" in Chapter 2 for more discussion on the quality, cost, and compensation factors.

The difficulties of recruiting and retaining qualified staff for good early childhood programs profoundly affects program quality and is one of the most serious issues facing the early childhood field today. "Parents can't afford to pay; teachers can't afford to stay" succinctly sums up the situation according to Herzenberg and others (2005). Their study brings to light some of the reasons for this dilemma. In 1983, 43 percent of the teachers and administrators in early childhood programs had 4 or more years of colleges. In 2004, this number dropped to 30 percent, and the levels are lower for those who participate in home-based care. The aging of the most qualified teachers raises concerns about training and keeping the best qualified staff.

It is no wonder that the Center for the Child Care Workforce found that the national employee turnover rate stays at about 30 percent and that less than one-third of child care employees have health benefits. As noted above, the Center also reports that child care programs have difficulty recruiting and hiring qualified replacement staff for those who leave. This is understandable when the median wage for child care workers is between $13,970 and $21,000. Elementary school teachers, on the other hand, have starting salaries at $32,950 and can range up to over $66,000 (Children's Defense Fund, 2008). At the same time this is happening, there is an unprecedented demand for child care services. For further discussion, see Chapter 2 and the report *Then and Now: Changes in Child Care Staffing, 1994-2000* (Whitebook, Sakai, Gerber, & Howes, 2001).

Quality 2000: Advancing Early Child Care and Education is an initiative with the goal to provide high quality early care and education to all children from birth to age 5 by 2010 (Kagan & Neuman, 1997). Creating an early child care and education system requires a comprehensive vision that includes factors such as:

- Promoting cultural sensitivity and cultural pluralism
- Increasing the number of accredited programs
- Linking programs to support services and other community resources
- Creating three separate types of licenses for early childhood care and education workers and developing national licensing guidelines
- Focusing staff training and preparation on children and families, with respect to cultural and linguistic diversity

---

- Funding that is commensurate with per-child levels for elementary school children
- Establishing governance and accountability structures in every state and locality

These factors will help ensure that families have equal access to good programs in which consistent standards at a national and local level guarantee equality and excellence for all children. The most comprehensive description of quality implementation is that of developmentally appropriate practices (Bredekamp & Copple, 1997, Copple & Bredekamp, 2009).

Education Reform

One of the primary functions of the public school system in the United States is to prepare students for productive roles in society—to produce skilled workers who will enter the job market and contribute to a healthy, competitive economy worldwide.

The trend since the 1990s has been toward a national agenda. In 1989, a national summit on the future of American education resulted in the creation of eight national goals, the first of which was that by 2000, every child will start school *ready to learn*. It was the first time in history that we have had a national consensus on a vision of public education.

The first goal, *Ready to Learn*, included the provision that all children would have equal access to high quality and developmentally appropriate preschool programs that help prepare children for school. Strong parent involvement with training and support and comprehensive health care, primarily through enhanced prenatal health systems, were also a part of the agenda.

No Child Left Behind

As the new century began, a new administration passed the reauthorization of the Elementary and Secondary Education Act of 1965 to close the achievement gap between disadvantaged and minority students and their peers (U.S. Department of Education, 2001). Since then, a national education problem has been identified and a sense of urgency instilled in the public mind. By 2005, the Elementary and Secondary Education Act became known as the No Child Left Behind Act (NCLB).

The major provisions of the act pertaining to early childhood are:

- *Adequate annual progress:* Children will be assessed in reading and math (plus a third area by state choice) beginning in the third grade. As discussed in Chapters 6 and 10, the trickle down of inappropri-

ate testing or imbalanced curriculum for younger children is a valid concern of early educators.

- *Highly qualified teachers:* By the 2005-06 school year, all teachers in core academic subjects must have a B.A. degree and be fully certified (by state definition) in their areas of teaching assignment. The early learning field, plagued by high turnover and low pay, cannot meet these standards without significantly more funding.
- *Reading/literacy:* There are significantly increased funds aimed at having all children achieve reading proficiency by grade three. An early childhood concern is that other critical domains of child development will be undervalued or overlooked altogether.

Critics of NCLB cite many reasons to be concerned about this plan. They worry that the narrow focus on reading and literacy and math will create an imbalanced curriculum that loses focus on the whole child and that other critical domains of child development will be undervalued or overlooked altogether. Critics also question whether teachers will be forced to "teach to the test" in order for a school to avoid sanctions. The sanctions for not meeting the NCLB standards seem punitive to some and seem to impact the most seriously disadvantaged schools. Overall, there is the threat of facing sanctions without adequate resources or support to meet the requirements that are imposed by this plan.

Standards and high stakes testing are realities in the primary grades. Preschool educators are feeling these pressures as well. It remains to be seen how this complicated and ambitious plan will fare over the coming years and how it relates to early education from birth to age 5. The Obama administration seems sensitive to the issues facing the early childhood field, in particular the Secre-

---

TeachSource Video ▶⏸

Watch the TeachSource Video Case entitled, "Education Reform: Teachers Talk about No Child Left Behind." After you study the video clip and the artifacts and read the teacher interviews and text, reflect upon the following questions:

1. With which of the pros and cons of NCLB that are discussed in this case do you agree?

2. How are state standards used to individualize the program and the curriculum?

tary of the Department of Education, Arne Duncan. Early childhood professionals and school reform advocates are hopeful that Duncan's initial comments will be realized: "When you focus on basics like reading and math, when you embrace innovative new approaches to learning, and when you create a professional climate that attracts great teachers, you can make a difference for children" (Sorrentino, 2008).

Universal Preschool

Early learning opportunities are unavailable to many children who could benefit from a quality early childhood program. Families throughout the country put together a patchwork of child care situations. Programs are unequal in quality, and the low income working families who would benefit the most from quality child care are unable to afford it. There is a discrepancy between the need and demand for quality child care and the government's willingness to fund it.

Universal Preschool, called Preschool for All in some areas, is an effort in many states to address this inequality. If successful, it would mean that there would be universal access to publicly funded, high quality preschool education for one or two years prior to kindergarten. Three quarters of the states plus the District of Columbia currently have such initiatives; Georgia, Oklahoma, and Florida already provide voluntary preschool for all 4-year-olds. It would appear that this effort has every chance to succeed within the next few years as it is supported by the Secretary of Education, Duncan, who said:

> We believe that it is time for the United States to acknowledge society's stake in and responsibility for early education, as it long has for older children, by making publicly-funded prekindergarten, offered by a variety of providers, available to all children age 3 and over whose parents want them to participate. (Committee for Economic Development, 2005)

Universal preschool is also discussed in Chapter 2.

Reform Strategies

To meet the needs of working parents and ensure that children are ready to learn, reform strategies should be enlarged to include the following:

- *Link education and child care.* The dichotomy between care and education must be eliminated, as

learning in the early years includes both caregiving and educational aspects of teaching.

- *Establish continuity between early childhood programs and the early elementary years.* The perception that preschools are "only about play" and that primary schools are "all about academics" negates the whole child philosophy of the early childhood years.
- *Address children's nonacademic needs.* Unless more is done to meet the early health and social needs of children, school reform is likely to fail.
- *Promote developmental learning.* Get schools ready for young children as opposed to having children be pressured and pushed to get ready for school.
- *Initiate programs and policies that strengthen the family.* The family support for learning should be addressed by focusing on parental attitudes and involvement at home as well as at school and on the parents' responsibility for meeting the basic care and needs of their children.
- *Develop partnerships with the community and with business.* Coordinating with providers of child care services and collaborating with other community agencies that service young children and their families make better use of public funds and improve the quality of all programs (National Association of State Boards of Education, 1988).

DAP

The Importance of Childhood

The second theme of early childhood is the importance and uniqueness of childhood. In fact, the entire notion rests on the concept of the child as a special part of human existence and, therefore, a valuable part of the human life cycle. When a society values its children, it takes the responsibility for providing a quality of life for them.

The impact of social changes in the last 40 years has been hardest felt by the children. The increase in the divorce rate, poverty and homelessness, and the dangerous effects of the media culture, drugs, and worldwide violence have thrust children into adult situations with adult troubles. Dual-parent careers and single working parents, together with the lack of extended families, have meant that children's behavior is not as closely monitored as it once was.

DAP Closer relationships would support greater alignment so that curriculum, standards, and tests compliment and balance one another.

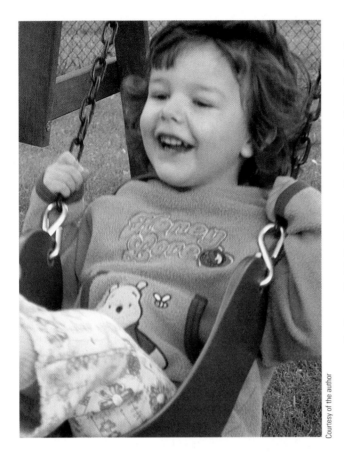

Every child has the right to a full and wondrous childhood.

Children and childhood have changed. Gone are the days when the majority of children arrived home from school to be greeted by Mom in the kitchen, serving milk and homemade cookies. Today's child spends the bulk of time in child care centers or elsewhere while the parent is at work. Too many children arrive at empty homes and spend the next few hours alone or caring for younger siblings. As often as not, the child of today lives with just one parent.

Childhood Stress

Common experiences that produce stress in young children are family related. Divorce, remarriage, a move to a new home, prolonged visits from a relative, and a new sibling are classic stress situations for children. Yet, there are less dramatic sources of stress—the simple everyday occurrences that children face: being told not to do something, not having a friend, being ignored by a parent, experiencing changes in the routine, not being able to read or zip a zipper or put a puzzle together.

Stress may also occur in families in which both parents pursue high-powered careers and children feel the need to live up to exceptional standards in academic achievement or sports proficiency. Apathetic parents, parents who ignore their children or have no time for them, and parents who push children into frantic schedules of activity also cause stress in their children. Stress can result from happy occasions as well—holidays, vacation, or a new puppy may be overanticipated, overstructured, and overstimulating to a child.

Children respond to stress in many ways. Signs of stress include sleeping problems (such as nightmares or sleepwalking), depression, regression to the behavior of an earlier stage, aches and pains, acting out, eating problems, and overreactions, as well as medical problems (such as headaches, upset stomach, and bleeding ulcers).

Brazelton and Greenspan (2000), in response to the overwhelmed, stressed-out life of children and parents today, defined seven irreducible needs of children:

1. The need for ongoing nurturing relationships
2. The need for physical protection, safety, and regulation
3. The need for experiences tailored to individual differences
4. The need for developmentally appropriate experiences
5. The need for limit setting, structure, and expectations

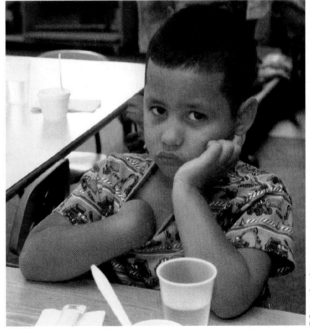

How do we help children cope with stress?

6. The need for stable, supportive communities and cultural continuity

7. Protecting the future (on behalf of the world's children)

Stress is a natural part of life and is a factor in every child's development. It needs to be identified and addressed by the families, teachers, and other adults who care for them. Chapter 14 discusses stress in detail.

Child Abuse and Neglect

More than 3 million children were reported as victims of **child abuse and neglect** in 2007, at the rate of one child every 35 seconds (Children's Defense Fund, 2008), and children ages birth to 3 are the most likely to experience abuse (Childhelp, 2009). Four children die every day as a result of child abuse and three out of four of those children are under the age of 4. One third of abused and neglected children will eventually victimize their own children, perpetuating the cycle (Childhelp, 2009). These horrendous statistics tell us that child abuse and neglect are significant problems in this country.

DAP

A neglected child may be one whose waking hours are mostly unsupervised by adults, in front of the television or simply unconnected with—and unnoticed by—parents or an important caregiver. **Child neglect** takes other, more hazardous, forms, however. When the basic needs of adequate food, clothing, shelter, and health are unmet, parents are being neglectful. Failure to exercise the care that children need shows an inattention to and lack of concern for children. Sixty-four percent of the reported child abuse in the United States is for neglect, 16 percent is physical abuse, and nearly 9 percent is sexual abuse (Children's Defense Fund, 2008).

Signs of various forms of child abuse often indicate one or more types of abuse. According to Childhelp (2009), the most obvious signs are:

- *Signs of neglect:* unsuitable clothing for weather, dirty or unbathed, extreme hunger, and an apparent lack of supervision
- *Signs of physical abuse:* unexplained burns, cuts, bruises, or welts in the shape of an object; bite marks, anti-social behavior, problems in school, fear of adults
- *Signs of emotional abuse:* apathy, depression, hostility or stress, lack of concentration, eating disorders

- *Signs of sexual abuse:* inappropriate interest or knowledge of sexual acts, nightmares and bed-wetting, drastic changes in appetite, overcompliance or excessive aggression, fear of a particular person or family member

The residual effects of child abuse, which occurs at every socioeconomic, ethnic, cultural, religious, and educational level, are equally dramatic. Children who have been sexually abused are two-and-one-half times more likely to abuse alcohol and nearly four times more likely to become addicted to drugs than nonvictims. Children who experience abuse and neglect have a 59 percent chance of being arrested as a juvenile and are 25 percent more likely to become pregnant as a teenager (Childhelp, 2009).

Potential Solutions

A national call to action to increase public awareness and understanding of child abuse is under way. Standardized licensing procedures, upgrading of the certification of child care workers, and national **accreditation** of all preschools are some of the most frequently mentioned solutions to the problem. Helping parents identify what qualities to look for when placing their children in someone else's care is another way to prevent child abuse in centers.

In 1996, NAEYC adopted a *Position Statement on the Prevention of Child Abuse in Early Childhood Programs and the Responsibilities of Early Childhood Professionals to Prevent Child Abuse.* The statement urges that early childhood programs in homes, centers, and schools adopt a set of policies based on guidelines such as:

- employing adequate staff and adequate supervision of staff
- environments that reduce the possibility of hidden places
- orientation and training on child abuse detection, prevention, and reporting
- defined and articulated policies for a safe environment
- avoidance of creating "no-touch" policies by the caregivers and staff

In regard to staff recruitment, NAEYC recommends that early childhood programs in the home, center, or school initiate policies that require personal interviews, verification of references and education background and

---

DAP Abuse and neglect must be viewed in the context of the culture, family life, and economic situation and needs.

qualifications, criminal record checks, and disclosure of previous convictions. New employees should serve a probationary period, and programs should have policies that provide for the removal of anyone whose performance is unacceptable. Procedures must also be in place for responding to an accusation of child abuse and provide due process for the accused (NAEYC, 1997).

All those involved in early childhood care and education would be well advised to secure a copy of the statement and use it to reflect on the effectiveness of their own program's policies and procedures.

Role of the Teacher

Reporting suspected child abuse is mandated by law in all states. Educators must assume the responsibility to inform the proper authorities if they suspect that a child in their care is being abused by anyone.

The mandate to report suspected child abuse applies to teachers, principals, counselors, school nurses, and staff members of child care centers and summer camps. Certain knowledge that abuse took place is not required; reports are legally required if there is reasonable cause to suspect a child has been mistreated. For the protection of anyone reporting abuse or neglect, the person filing the report is held immune from civil or criminal liability if the report was made in good faith. Figure 15-2 discusses the steps to take if child abuse is suspected.

Poverty

There is a group of Americans who are destined for limited participation in the social, political, and economic mainstream of national life. The children who are at risk for academic failure are likely to be: those who live in poverty, members of minority groups in racial isolation, children with various physical and mental disabilities, children with limited English proficiency, children from single-parent families, or children attending schools with a high concentration of students who live in poverty (Casey Foundation, 2006).

One out of five children is poor in the United States (see Figure 15-3).

- An American child is born into poverty every 43 seconds and one out of five children is poor during the first 3 years of life—the time of greatest brain development.

Reporting Child Abuse

What to Do If You Suspect Child Abuse

- Make notes of child's appearance—any bruises, marks, or behaviors that cause you concern.
- Inform the director of the program and/or your immediate supervisor; plan together who will inform the proper authorities and how to contact the parent(s).
- Discuss ways to support the staff members who make the report, the parent(s), and the child.
- Call the locally designated agency for child abuse. A written report may be required within 24 to 48 hours.
- Support the parent(s) throughout the investigation. Be available to the parent(s) and the child as they deal with the other agencies that are trained and equipped to handle this problem.
- Follow through with assistance or support if requested to do so by the child protective services agency. Help the family by working with others who are counseling them and performing parent support services.

What to Do If a Child Tells You He or She Has Been Abused

- Believe the child; children rarely lie about sexual abuse.
- Commend the child for telling you what happened.
- Convey your support for the child. Children's greatest fear is that they are at fault and responsible for the incident. It is important to help children avoid blaming themselves.
- Temper your own reactions, recognizing that your perspective and acceptance are critical signals to the child. Do not convey your own feelings about the abuse.
- Report the suspected abuse to the child's parent(s), the designated social service agency, and/or the police.
- Find specialized agencies that evaluate sexual abuse victims and a physician with the experience and training to detect and recognize sexual abuse.

FIGURE 15-2 Recommendations for teachers about child abuse. (Source: *Child Sexual Abuse Prevention*. Washington, DC: U.S. Department of Health and Human Services, 1998.)

Child Poverty in the United States

A child is born into poverty every 33 seconds.

A child is abused or neglected every 35 seconds.

A child is born uninsured every 39 seconds.

A child dies before his/her first birthday every 18 minutes.

A child or teen is killed by gunfire every 3 hours.

13,324,00 children are poor (18%).

5,768,000 children are living in extreme poverty (7.8%).

3,741,535 adults and children receive cash assistance from Temporary Assistance for Needy Families (TANF).

8,067,728 women and children receive Supplemental Nutrition Assistance (WIC).

30,129,883 children are in the School Lunch Program.

12,559,379 children receive food stamps.

65% percentage of eligible persons receive food stamps.

FIGURE 15-3 Poverty affects all children in America (Children's Defense Fund, "Children in the United States" Web version, www.cdf.org, November, 2008).

- Nearly 12 million children are poor and millions are hungry, at risk of hunger, living in worst case housing, or homeless.
- Almost 80 percent of poor children live in working households. (Children's Defense Fund, 2008)

There is a striking correlation between poverty and school failure. Children who start out at a disadvantage fall farther behind in academic achievement throughout their school years.

The changing school population suggests that these problems will only increase as the proportion of minority groups expands (because they are overrepresented among the poor), as a larger and larger percentage of children fall below the poverty line, and as traditional patterns of child rearing and marriage change so that fewer children will have the emotional and educational advantages of a two-parent family.

The National Institute of Child Health and Human Development Study of Early Child Care conducted a 3-year study of 1,000 children in 10 cities, examining maternal sensitivity, home environment, hours in child care and quality of child care. Children were then given a school readiness test, and the data were compared with children in similar settings. In a report entitled *Growing Up in Poverty* (Center for Children and Families, 2000), researchers from Berkeley, Columbia, Stanford, and Yale Universities found that early maternal employment had negative effects on children's intellectual development. Children whose mothers worked by the time the babies were 9 months old, had insensitive mothers, and had poor quality child care had scores significantly lower than those with sensitive mothers who were not employed by the ninth month and had good quality child care. While the study did not take into consideration such factors as father involvement or how much the mother wants to be employed, it certainly has serious implications for families at risk.

A dramatic and intensive reform effort is needed for these children, and a number of solutions are being considered. Too many of today's children will reach adulthood unhealthy, illiterate, and unemployable. This is a personal tragedy for everyone involved—the young people, their communities, and the nation.

Family Support

The family of today has many shapes, sizes, and styles. Chapter 8 elaborates on the many kinds of families in which children live and grow. In fact, the American family has evolved so extensively over the last few decades that the Children's Defense Fund (2008) reports:

- Two out of three preschoolers have a mother in the labor force.
- Three-quarters of mothers of school-age children are in the labor force; 6 out of 10 preschool-age children and 7 out of 10 school-age children have parents in the work force; 55 percent of working women provide half or more of the family's income.
- One out of two children will live in a single-parent family at some point in childhood.
- Families with children accounted for more than a third of the homeless Americans in urban areas who seek shelter.
- More than one out of six—13.3 million—children in the United States are poor. The federal poverty line for a family of four in 2008 is $21,200.
- The United States ranks first among industrialized countries in gross domestic product, but 18th in the income gap between rich and poor children.

The changing family structure and circumstances affect early childhood professionals in several ways. Chapter 8 discusses issues around the changing family and makes recommendations for the role of the teacher.

Divorce and Family Structures

Perhaps no one single change has affected children as much as the divorce rate. DelCampo and DelCampo (2006) note that, in some studies, "children rate divorce second only to the death of a parent as the most stressful event in their lives, and most of them end up not having a close relationship with one of their parents." The trend toward more divorce is significant. Nearly 50 percent of marriages end in divorce, and the American national average is at 31 percent overall, with the range within ethnic groups of 15 to 64 percent (Casey, 2006). One school child in three has parents who are divorced; 30 percent of these are children in stepfamilies and the other 70 percent live with their mothers or fathers alone. The effects of divorce are felt for years. Getting over divorce and on with a productive life is critical for both child and parent; teachers can help.

The effects of divorce are felt by children well before the event itself. Children exhibit "pre-divorce family stress" by increased impulsive or aggressive behavior, and parents show the stress with headaches, fatigue, mood swings, or depression. Children's initial reaction to their parents' separation is traumatic—shock and distress (the *Stage 1* responses to stress as described in Chapter 14). Even if parents are not in violent conflict with each other, no child is happy about divorce. After divorce, many parents become overworked and overwhelmed. Children are often neglected or left with less than what both parents could provide, including emotional and financial support.

> Among employed adults, unmarried women who support families have the greatest risk of living in poverty. ... Moreover, unmarried mothers often have time constraints that can affect their ability to supervise their children, offer emotional support, take an active part in their education, and arrange other activities for them. When children live with one parent, it is still most often the mother. (Casey Foundation, 2006)

Adjustment to divorce is difficult, and the psychological effects of divorce on children are often felt well into adulthood. "Divorce is a cumulative experience for the child. Its impact increases over time," writes Wallerstein (2002), reporting on a 25-year research project. For instance, of the people who were $2\frac{1}{2}$ to 6 years old when their parents divorced one-third did not pursue any education beyond high school, although 40 percent of those who attended college did graduate.

Growing up in a divorced home does not mean children cannot live happy lives. Fortunately, children are amazingly resilient. The age and gender of the children involved seem to have some bearing on their adjustment. Very young children recover more easily than older ones, and boys react more intensely than girls to the loss of their fathers from the home. The parents' ability to be caring and available makes a difference, as does the parents' relationship with each other and the quality of the children's relationship with both parents.

What can teachers do?

1. Read and understand the effects of divorce (DelCampo & DelCampo [2006] have an extensive suggested reading list).
2. Be informed about what to expect from children in a divorce cycle (see Chapter 14 about stress).
3. Help parents get access to outside help (parent support groups, community welfare services, or a parental stress hotline).
4. Plan strategies for family involvement that take into account the work demands, resources, and expertise of parents.
5. Provide a place and time to heal:

   - *Know your children.* Confer with families as often as possible and be aware of family stresses and crises.
   - *Talk about feelings.* Anger and sadness are predominant, along with guilt, loss, helplessness, and loneliness; an understanding teacher can go a long way to help a child feel less alone and can offer appropriate opportunities—through intimate moments, puppets and dolls, unstructured drawings, role playing, and creative drawing—for expression.
   - *Use bibliotherapy.* Books are powerful tools to connect with children with understanding and kindness. They are also wonderful resources for families.
   - *Keep aware of family diversity.* Be sure to include many family structures in the curriculum, during informal discussions, with any correspondence to home.
   - *Include open communication with parents and family members.* Divorce tends to complicate communication between teachers and parents. Make adjustments in conferences, newsletters, and notes about the child so both the primary and non-custodial parents are included as much as possible.

The Working Parent

More than two thirds of all preschool children under age 6 have mothers in the work force (Children's Defense Fund, 2008), and the percentage rises when considering school-aged children as well. Mothers at work affect the family and the teacher.

The implications for families are considerable. For women, the double roles of job or career and family nurturer can be overwhelming, creating great conflict and the stress of chronic fatigue. Men are looking at their role in a different light; many are learning about greater involvement in child rearing and how to adjust to a new financial provider role. For both parents, three issues loom large: the concern for good child care; the struggle to provide *quality time* with children and as a family unit; and the financial burden. Without parental leave, parents are forced to return to work during the critical early months of infancy or lose income and even their job. Further, while many mothers go to work from welfare, there are still few gains in the family's broader economic well-being. Women report still needing to use local food banks and taking second and third jobs. Self-sufficiency without income supports is rarely achieved.

For educators, working families have special new issues. As more parents are fully occupied with work during the school day, they are less available for direct participation in a classroom or on a constant basis. Teachers plan flexible opportunities for them to become involved in their children's education.

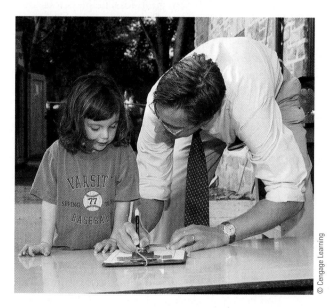

© Cengage Learning

When both parents work outside the home, new roles for fathers emerge.

In the public sector, several proposals gained momentum in the 1990s. The most successful so far, the ABC Bill of 1990, allotted federal dollars to the states to provide support for centers, improving the quality of children's services available. Child tax credits and pretax dependent care credits are government and employer supports. Leading pediatrician T. Berry Brazelton's Washington-based lobby group, Parent Action, is garnering support for family medical leave that would enable parents of newborns to take several months of unpaid leave from their jobs to be at home and establish an attachment bond and family setting so critical to infants' well-being and survival.

Public policy is a reflection of the attitude and values a nation holds toward children and families, and the inequities are glaring. Most European countries fund public programs for children and support services for parents at a much higher rate than that in the United States. We look toward a future trend of clearer and more supportive public policies.

Community and School Support

The relationship between schools and the community at large and the families they serve dictates the role schools play in the lives of families. The history of education in the United States is the story of the "progressive assumption" (Elkind, 1991). This means that the trend over time is for educational institutions to assume functions once performed by the family. There are difficulties in this progression, however, as schools are reluctant—perhaps unable—to assume some of these responsibilities, and parents are wary of giving them up. In addition, it is unclear if children gain from such a "handoff" of responsibility.

In colonial times, schools were primarily private, church-based programs for boys. After the American Revolution the government began forming a national public school system, based on the belief that a democracy demands literate participants. This trend continued as the "public" came to include women and people of color. The 21st century has seen governments provide subsidies to schools to provide free or low cost meals, medical and dental services, and physical education programs.

In the last 30 years, schools have continued to take on more child-rearing functions. Schools have a key role to play in nurturing parental involvement in education and family life, rebuilding the "**social capital**" (Coleman, 1991) both within the family and in the community. Drawing on an economic model, social capital refers to the richness and resources that social relationships provide for a child. The strength of these social relations helps shape a child's habits, establish norms of acceptable behavior, and encourage the development of children's character, long range goals, and even educational attainment.

One example of the school as a reflection of community life is the Reggio Emilia system (see Chapter 2). Founder Malaguzzi understood that the child cannot be thought of in the abstract, but as tightly connected to the world of relationships and experiences. Both Vygotsky (see Chapters 4 and 12) and Bronfenbrenner (see Chapter 2) emphasize these ties.

The issue today in the United States is to define a new role for schools. Some specific ways include taking a comprehensive approach to families, so that the early childhood program is fully integrated into the families it serves. School systems can help parents get needed medical, dental, mental, job-related, and social services by collaborating with other agencies and individuals. Head Start models this resource-rich type of program.

"It takes a village to raise a child." This old adage has new significance in today's society. The factors of positive experiences, relationships, opportunities, and personal qualities help children grow up to be healthy, caring, and responsible. These include both *external assets* (those positive experiences that young children receive from the people and institutions in their lives) of support, empowerment, boundaries and expectations, and constructive use of time and *internal assets* (the internal dispositions that guide children's choices and create a sense of centeredness and purpose) of commitment to learning, positive values, social competencies, and a positive identity.

Children who have positive family communication, have supervised time at home, and have stimulating activities outside of home in a community that is safe and that values children have experiences that enhance positive development. The roles that families, schools, congregations, neighborhoods, youth organizations, and others in communities play in shaping young people's lives contribute to both external and internal supports.

Early childhood programs can help articulate the shared values of the community and the support for diversity of the whole community. The trend is for the role of the teacher to become greater with families. Teaching is a two-client job: a teacher of the child and a resource for the family.

Transmitting Values

As with the other themes in early childhood education, the issue of transmitting values is not for the teacher or school alone. A deep and primary source of values is that of the family and culture. The school must work with the family to provide a sense of shared values; nonetheless, both parents and teachers must acknowledge other sources that shape children's values and behavior. Three other critical sources are the media culture, violence and disaster, and social diversity.

The Media Culture

In many homes, the television set has replaced adult supervision. Ninety-nine percent of American households contain at least one television, with more than two thirds containing two or more sets. Nielsen Media Research (2008) now reports that 111.4 million households in the United States have televisions. "Children and adolescents comprise between 10 percent and 20 percent of the prime time viewing audience, and they spend more time watching television (15,000 hours) than they do in school (11,000 hours). During this time they witness 180,000 murders, rapes, armed robberies, and assaults" (Johnson, 1996). The Nielsen Report on Television (1989) estimated that U.S. children age 2 to 5 viewed television approximately 27 hours per week, and children age 6 to 11 viewed more than 23 hours per week. Television and, for school-age children, the Internet and other media represent an influential force in the lives of children.

There are four basic concerns that parents and teachers express about children's viewing of media:

1. Media violence can lead to aggression and desensitization to violence.
2. Media viewing promotes passivity, slowing intellectual development and stifling imagination.
3. Media promote racist and sexist attitudes.
4. Television promotes materialistic consumerism.

Common Sense Media and the National Institutes of Health analyzed 173 studies about the effect of media consumption on children, finding a strong correlation between greater exposure and adverse health outcomes. "Couch potato does, unfortunately, sum it up pretty well," says Ezekiel J. Emanuel, chair of bioethics department at NIH. "The research is clear that exposure to media has a variety of negative health impacts on children and teens. ...We found very few studies that had any positive association for children's health" (Common Sense Media, 2008). This research highlights the powerful effects on children of the models they see, whether they be of children, adults, or fantasy characters (see Bandura, Chapter 4). The Center for Media Literacy

(1993) documented four effects of viewing media violence:

1. Increased aggressiveness and antisocial behavior. *"There is absolutely no doubt that higher levels of viewing violence on television are correlated with increased acceptance of aggressive attitudes and increased aggressive behavior."*
2. Increased fear of becoming a victim. *"Viewing violence increases the fear of becoming a victim of violence, with a resultant increase in self-protective behaviors and increased mistrust of others."*
3. Desensitization to violence and victims of violence. *"Viewing violence increases desensitization to violence, resulting in a calloused attitude toward violence directed at others and a decreased likelihood to take action on behalf of the victim when violence occurs."*
4. Interest in more violence in entertainment and real life. *"Viewing violence increases viewers' appetite for becoming involved with violence or exposing themselves to violence."*

In the area of bias and stereotyping, children's television is an arena "where boys are king" (Carter, 1991). Networks generally assert that boys will not watch female-lead shows, but girls will watch shows with a male lead. In children's television shows, the Euro-American and male attitudes and behaviors are reinforced.

Television and the lessons it teaches are and will be a part of children's lives. "Perhaps if parents [and teachers] could accept the inevitable, that television is not only here to stay but viewing choices are expanding almost daily, then society could move past this dichotomy of thinking of television as simply good or bad. Television viewing could be thought of as an active endeavor rather than a passive one" (DelCampo & DelCampo, 2006).

Families and teachers can use guidelines for television viewing and for dealing with the hazards of media culture (video games, computer games, assorted toys and games, etc.) (NAEYC, 1990).

1. *Set limits.* Know how many hours of television children watch and set limits. The American Academy of Pediatrics suggests a maximum of one to two hours daily. Keep the television turned off unless someone is actively viewing; television viewing can easily become more of a habit than a choice. Involve your children in discussions about video game systems or computer games; consider establishing rules (for instance, "Game-playing counts as 'screen time'" and "I can't play when a friend comes over").

Antidotes to television.

2. *Plan and participate.* Work together with children to decide what to watch. Help children choose shows with an age-appropriate viewing length, bias-free content, and peaceful action. Consider watching shows together, pointing out parts that are prosocial and asking about those parts you wonder about or disagree with. Use the "pause," "rewind," and "mute" buttons as part of the process. Watch carefully what children are doing with video and computer games.

3. *Resist commercials.* Children do not distinguish easily between the sales pitch commercial and the ordinary show. Help them become "critical consumers" by pointing out the exaggerated claims. Even 3-year-olds can answer the question "What are they trying to sell us?"

4. *Express your views.* Call a station that airs a show or commercial you find offensive or write a letter to the Children's Advertising Review unit of the Better Business Bureau. Action for Children's Television in Cambridge, Massachusetts, has been a leading public interest group for more than 20 years and has valuable suggestions for how adults can influence children's television programming.

Violence and Disaster

The trend of children's increasing exposure to violence is alarming. Families speak of what is shown in the media and the kinds and choices of toys that give them a sense of being out of control in limiting or influencing children's behavior. Teachers notice changes in children's play, commenting that the weapon and war play in classrooms is so single purpose and intense that it is difficult to redirect; rule setting and controlling overzealous play take an inordinate amount of teachers' energy.

When a catastrophe happens, whether personal or societal, children need help making sense of the calamity and then support in recovery. Shock, confusion, fear, anxiety, grief, anger, guilt, and helplessness are all common emotional responses to trauma. Such reactions will generate changes in behavior, both in adults and in the children we care for.

How much children are traumatized varies; research has shown that five factors seem to determine the amount of suffering children experience during war. The child's own biological and psychological makeup, the level of disruption of the family unit, the breakdown of the community, cultural influences (especially positive), and the intensity, suddenness, and duration of the war affect how deep the scars will be on one's childhood. How children see their parents and teachers react, a child's age, and how much destruction and/or death is seen will also make an impact (AACAP, 1993). Chapter 14 discusses children's reactions to stress and the role of the teacher in helping children process and cope with child trauma. Figure 15-4 gives suggestions for how to help children in case of a disaster.

The increasing violence of American society has so alarmed educators and parents alike that programs are being developed for children and for teachers (Levin, 1998). Organizations such as Adults and Children Together (ACT) Against Violence, the Educators for Social Responsibility, and the National Association for Mediation Educators serve as both clearinghouses for information and material and as training institutes for teachers.

Children act out what they see in their play. Should teachers allow aggressive pretend play unchecked or with limits and some kind of adult intervention? Or should this type of play be banned, contained, or otherwise redirected and altered? This dilemma illustrates children's play from two different viewpoints, a developmental one and a sociopolitical one.

The *developmental* viewpoint states that play, including war play, is the primary vehicle through which children work on developmental issues. Because children need to develop a sense of how the world works, of fantasy and reality, of good and bad, war play is an extension of superhero play (see Chapter 14), and is, therefore, a necessary part of children's play.

The *sociopolitical* view assumes that children learn basic social and political behavior at an early age and, therefore, will learn militaristic concepts and values through war play. This viewpoint contends that children learn about conflict and resolution, the use of fighting, and the meaning of friends and enemies in their play, and that allowing war play endorses the use of force (Carlsson-Paige & Levin, 2005).

These two ideas give teachers the basic building blocks for how to deal with the issue of developing shared values and for engaging in a dialogue with fellow teachers and parents. Whatever your viewpoint, remember that early learning is powerful. Exposure to violence is harmful, particularly when children are victims.

Moreover, when disaster strikes, what children need most is reassurance, to know they will be safe and that caring adults will still take care of them. Constancy and predictability, in the form of consistent routines and continued habits of behavior and tradition, will help children feel anchored in their lives. Listening carefully, answering children's questions in simple ways, and asking questions to elicit their thoughts all encourage communication and a dialogue about their feelings. Most educators and counselors also remind adults to monitor children's media exposure to war.

When a Child Experiences Disaster

Infants/Toddlers

*Resume normal routines & favorite rituals.

*Give limited exposure to media & adult conversations about crisis.

*Give special time at nap & bed time.

Preschoolers

*Reassure verbally that they will be OK.

*Make sure they know where you are at all times.

*Give opportunities to write/dictate stories and draw about their experiences.

With All Children

*Spend time with child, being observant of their behavior.

*Give reassurance and physical comfort.

*Provide consistent, predictable structure during the day.

*Adapt curriculum to include relaxing, therapeutic activities such as sand, water, clay, and play dough.

*Spend more time in physical activity for emotional release.

*Connect with families frequently; share observations and ideas.

School-Age Children

*Ask what is on their minds, and answer their questions honestly.

*Share emergency plans so children know safety measures for the future.

*Provide guided exposure to media; watch/listen with them.

*Offer ways to take action, such as helping them organize relief efforts.

FIGURE 15-4 A catastrophe such as an earthquake, hurricane, or fire or a disaster such as war or an act of terrorism is frightening to both adults and children.

Teachers help children find peaceful resolutions to their everyday conflicts, ensuring that, in their daily school life, war will not break out and take over (see Chapters 7 and 14 for suggestions):

- A family child care provider of infants and toddlers may spend extra time giving hugs and helping children share toys.
- A class of preschoolers may choose a cross-town child care center to exchange drawings and visits with, to increase their knowledge of their city neighbor.
- A first grade class might write letters to the President. ("I don't like it when you make war. My big sister says to use words when I have a problem and you should too.")

On an adult scale, teachers can:

- Talk about and decide on your viewpoint and values with parents and the school board.
- Develop guidelines that address your values and the needs of the children.
- Talk with parents about toys and the role of the media in the development of children's interests and the role of parents in helping children decide and choose what and how to play.
- Investigate peace education and building peaceable classrooms that have conflict resolution teaching as part of the curriculum (see Chapters 7 and 14).

Take care of yourselves as professionals; teachers need someone to talk to and may need to adjust the curriculum to give everyone more breathing room.

Social Diversity

Facing Reality

America as a "melting pot," into which all racial and cultural differences are smoothly mixed into one single blend, is a myth, both an unrealistic and unnecessary goal. Moreover, much of America's history can be characterized as **racist, classist, sexist,** and **ethnocentric** by one group or another. The discrepancy between our ideals of equal opportunity and freedom and the daily reality can be altered only if we recognize the problems and then set specific goals for change.

Today's **demographics** point to a trend of an increasingly diverse society (see Chapter 3). The issue is that attitudes do not yet parallel reality. Segregation of schools by color is still a reality by virtue of neighborhood configurations and of white families sending their children to private schools; indeed schools with high populations of African-American and/or Latino children almost without exception are also high poverty schools, which correlates with less qualified teachers, fewer classroom resources, and higher absenteeism among teachers and students (Frankenberg, Lee, & Orfield in Book, 2004).

Moreover, school reform efforts have done little to meet the educational needs of America's demographic profile.

Research shows a strong relationship between education attainment and economic well-being. Children who are provided a comprehensive, high quality education are less likely to be poor and more likely to find employment and receive higher wages than their less educated peers. In addition, we find that children from low income families are constantly outperformed by their wealthier peers across a broad range of academic measures. Poor children, therefore, often find themselves in a Catch-22 with their economic circumstances denying them access to the escape valve out of a life of poverty—a quality education. (Children's Defense Fund, 2008)

Figure 15-5 illustrates this point.

We know that children exhibit an awareness of racial and gender differences by age 3 (Derman-Sparks, et al., 1989) and are formulating rudimentary concepts about the meaning of those differences in the preschool years.

Reading and Math Achievement of Fourth graders

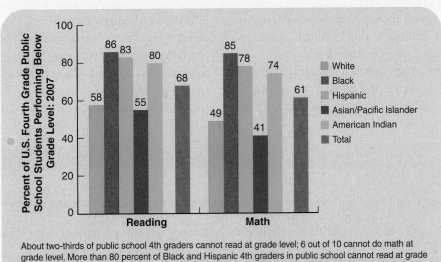

About two-thirds of public school 4th graders cannot read at grade level; 6 out of 10 cannot do math at grade level. More than 80 percent of Black and Hispanic 4th graders in public school cannot read at grade level, compared with 58 percent of their White peers. Eighty-five percent of Black 4th graders in public school cannot do math at grade level, compared with 78 percent of Hispanic and about half of White children.

FIGURE 15-5 The disparate levels of education in America's diverse cultures confirm that school reforms have not yet met the needs of all children. (Reprinted with permission from Children's Defense Fund, 2009. Sources: US Department of Education, National Assessment of Education Progress, The Nation's Report Card; calculations by Children's Defense Fund).

It is logical to conclude that, by the end of the early childhood years, children have consolidated their attitudes about race, ethnicity, gender, and (dis)ability, and are far along the path of **attitude crystallization.** Unless the social environment changes, children will re-create the prejudices of the current adult society. Teachers and families need to look with sensitivity to the meaning of diversity (see Figure 15-6).

Multicultural Education

Multicultural education is the system of teaching and learning that includes the contributions of all ethnic and racial groups. In other words, it is a comprehensive educational approach that reflects more than just the dominant culture's perspective, providing all children with a fuller, more balanced truth about themselves, their own history, and culture. This means responsiveness to the child's origins, habits at home, and ways of self-expression.

At high levels of education there are contrasting views about how to deal with diversity. One viewpoint is a separatist education in which education is taught from a particular viewpoint—European, Afro-centrist, or the like. Many assert that most public schooling is a European-dominant education. A second viewpoint is the more traditional pluralist approach in which education stresses the commonalities of varying peoples. Most early education programs follow the second approach.

Janice E. Hale (1993) offers another idea, that "a more culturally appropriate pedagogy would expose African American children to [both] Anglo-centric and Afro-centric literature at each grade level ... [T]o educate African American children in a culturally appropriate manner, there is a kind of dual educational process that is required." Hale sees the miseducation of black children as a form of "educational malpractice." In *Learning While Black* (2001), Hale notes that "academic failure, incarceration and unemployment are outcomes of the public schooling for African American boys." The hidden racism that permeates both private and public schools in the United States must be addressed.

What underlies these issues is how we see ourselves as a common culture. When we change the metaphor of "melting pot" to one of "mosaic" or "mixed salad," we encourage a way of thinking that might be termed **cultural pluralism**—the idea that we are all one people, but we do not necessarily divest ourselves of our ethnic origins. Based on DAP and DCAP (see Chapter 2), good early childhood programs can represent the best of multicultural education.

Bilingual Education

The goals and purposes of bilingual education remain controversial, for there are still disagreements over how to define bilingualism, how to determine who needs it, and who is to provide the services. Chapter 13 discusses bilingual education in light of language learning and curriculum development. This section highlights the broader issues and implications.

Bilingual education has been part of the American experience since before the Revolutionary War, when school was taught in any one of the more than 18 languages that were spoken by the colonists. Nonetheless, numerous cultures have been suppressed with regularity in the United States. Both Native American and immigrant groups have categorically faced discrimination. Speaking English is only part of bilingual education: At issue are the civil and educational rights of people who speak limited English, the respect or assimilation of their culture, and their participation and acceptance in society.

Social Diversity and Teacher Attitudes

1. Recognize developmentally equivalent patterns. Before judging a child as difficult, assume s/he is normal and look again.
2. Do not value some ways of achieving developmental milestones more highly than others. Remember different is not deficient.
3. Start teaching in ways that are familiar to children. You may not be fluent in a child's language, but you can learn key words and phrases.
4. School learning is most likely to occur when family values reinforce family expectations. Partner up with parents so that the child is the big winner.
5. Deal with discrepancies between home and school directly. Instead of ignoring the differences, ask about them.

FIGURE 15-6 There are several guidelines teachers can follow regarding diversity.

Changing populations and the influx of immigrants from Asia as well as from the Hispanic nations have brought with them new challenges to bilingual education. Bilingual programs serve primarily Spanish-speaking students. States that do not have bilingual programs still need to meet the needs of limited–English-proficient (LEP) students in schools through other means. The number of school-age Spanish-speaking children in the United States increased by 50 percent between 1980 and 2000, so all levels of education have been affected.

The School-Age Child. The questions about bilingualism for the school-age child are different from those for the young child. In elementary school, teachers and children are forced to deal with issues beyond those of receptive and expressive language. Learning graphic language (reading and writing), acquiring concepts in other subject areas through listening, and dealing with the more complex social patterns and interpersonal issues are just a few of these issues. Moreover, the age at which children should be taught a second language is highly controversial. Research shows that children can acquire native-like mastery of a second language if they learn to *speak* the language before age 5. At the same time, elementary school age appears to be an ideal time to be *taught* a second language.

Much research is centered on how children achieve second language competence and performance. We do know that, by age 5, children know most of the sounds and grammatical structure of their native tongue and appear to learn a second language in a similar way. With a bilingual child, the level of competence in both languages may be low while gaining mastery in the second language.

The two government actions that have most influenced the bilingual issue in our time are the passing of the 1968 Bilingual Education Act and the 1974 *Lau v. Nichols* Supreme Court decision. In that case, the Supreme Court determined that a lack of instruction in one's first language is a violation of children's civil rights.

Since 1968, Title VII programs (the Elementary and Secondary Education Act, also known as the Bilingual Education Act) addressed the needs of students with limited proficiency in English. State bilingual education laws followed, requiring special instruction for children who lack competence in English.

The result is that children are taught in public kindergarten and elementary schools by using both the primary language and English. For instance, children may be taught to read in their primary language first; once they have learned the reading process in their own language, they are then taught to decode in English. Yet, bilingual programs are so varied that it is difficult to assess them. Some work

to mainstream children into regular classrooms as quickly as possible; others try to maintain the child's native language. A more recent program, the *dual* or *bilingual immersion method*, attempts a blending of language instruction by putting both English speakers and those with limited English into class together and teaching *two-way* bilingual education. By bringing together both groups for language instruction, this method also indicates respect for both languages as assets. It shows promise as a truly multicultural tool for desegregation.

Still, the controversy continues. Another political backlash occurred in the late 1980s against non-English speakers. The U.S. Office of Education claimed that bilingual education programs have not helped children learn English. In 1998, a California initiative effectively ended publicly funded bilingual programs, to be replaced by shorter term, intensive English immersion programs at the elementary and secondary levels. Without consensus on the effectiveness and goals of bilingual education, educators must press for continuing research and clarity.

The Young Child. In preschools and child care centers, children are still taught in regular class settings, usually with little extra instruction. This type of instruction is known as an *immersion* system. The problem with this system lies in the risk that language-minority children in English-speaking schools will experience a substantial erosion of their native language ability and have difficulty communicating with their parents. Thus, parent–child relationships may be damaged and loss of culture may result.

The Plight of the Immigrant

Another serious challenge for schools is posed by the educational and socioeconomic needs of immigrant children. Attempting to immerse new children into a *national way* and to teach basic skills needed to succeed in the new country have been central functions of schools throughout history (see Chapter 1). In the United States, there are more than 2.5 million school-age immigrants and at least as many children under 5; one out of six children in the United States has a foreign-born mother (Children's Defense Fund, 2008). Immigrant enrollment in schools varies among the states and can reach as high as 95 percent in some schools.

Financial and social supports for legal immigrant children are a critical problem. Estimates are that 70 to 75 percent of the legal immigrants in this country are unaided by food stamps (Children's Defense Fund, 2008); the actual need is difficult to calculate.

The language barrier is the most immediate problem, followed by that of acceptance of the immigrants' native cultures. Further, many newcomers arrive from countries wracked with war, violence, and poverty. These children and families are under tremendous pressures and need help coping with the overwhelming stress and dislocation. Many young children in immigrant families do not have access to health and education services. Key issues are (Takanishi, 2006):

- Children's skills in kindergarten and their achievement at the end of third grade are important predictors of their future life prospects.
- Although well-designed early education and after-school programs hold promise to reduce ethnic group-related inequalities in children's cognitive skills and social competence, children in immigrant families are less likely to participate in these programs than are children in native-born families.
- Availability and access are important factors: When pre-kindergarten programs are offered in public schools, Hispanic and Asian-American children are more likely to participate.
- Family literacy programs are a promising strategy for improving language skills of children in immigrant families, as well as their parents. The way schools place and monitor immigrant children—both their educational progress and their general well-being—challenges educators and all American citizens to clarify the responsibilities our society has toward its newcomers. Chapter 8 describes the needs of immigrant families.

Inclusive Education

Since the 1970s, recognition of people with disabilities has been paired with public funding for education. The Americans with Disabilities Act (ADA) and its legislative authorization, the Individuals with Disabilities Education Act (IDEA), are designed "to reasonably accommodate individuals with disabilities in order to integrate them into the program to the extent feasible, given each individual's limitations" (Child Care Law Center, 1994). Key principles are:

- Individuality (understanding the limitations and needs of each individual).
- Reasonableness (of the accommodation to the program and the person).
- Integration (of the individual with others).

Accommodating a child with special needs is unreasonable only if it puts an undue burden on a program, would fundamentally alter the nature of the program, or poses a threat to the health or safety of the other children and staff. With these guidelines in mind, children with special needs will do best in the least restrictive environment, as fully included in a program as possible. Chapter 3 describes in detail the implications of ADA and IDEA for early childhood professionals.

Many programs, including all Head Start at the early childhood level, have welcomed children with special needs. All children, regardless of their abilities or disabilities, are more alike than different. Early intervention for children with special needs can minimize the effect of a condition or help such special needs from becoming more serious problems than need be.

Still, many children have special needs that remain undiagnosed. Many others have difficulty finding appropriate placement, particularly in programs for children under age 5. Early childhood special education is a relatively new area of our profession. Exemplary programs are those in which:

- Intervention is focused on specific and measurable child goals.
- Services are family-centered.
- Regular monitoring and adjustments of the intervention occur.
- Planning for transitions and changes occurs.
- Multidisciplinary services are provided.

Early childhood educators need support in learning about special needs and in understanding what it means to be inclusive of children with special needs without diminishing program quality for all children or overwhelming and exhausting staff. Programs that are engaged in developmentally appropriate practices already have activities and equipment that provide for a wide range of abilities, a schedule that emphasizes child-initiated play, and a curriculum that merges the children with the teachers' plans. Those teachers who are committed to an anti-bias approach will find that inclusion of children with special needs is another way to honor diversity.

Class Differences

In the 21st century, there are still great disparities in levels of poverty/affluence and schooling/achievement:

> In the United States, there are more poor White, non-Hispanic children than Black children. However, Hispanic and Black children are about three times as likely to live in poverty than White, non-Hispanic children. Children who live in inner cities, rural areas, in the South, or in female-headed families are more likely to be poor. (Children's Defense Fund, 2008)

Schools with the highest proportion of poor children have markedly fewer resources than schools serving affluent students, fewer books and supplies, and teachers with less training. Eighty-five percent of black fourth graders in public school cannot do math at grade level, compared to 78 percent of Hispanic children and about 50 percent of white children. Black and American-Indian children are more likely to be enrolled in classes for students with mental retardation, emotional disturbance, and learning disabilities.

Although no one likes to talk about it, the class differences cause many children, particularly children of poor and minority families, to get:

- Less in the way of experienced and well-trained teachers
- Less in the way of a rich and well-balanced curriculum
- Less actual instructional time
- Less in the way of well-equipped and well-stocked laboratories and libraries
- Less of what undoubtedly is most important of all—a belief that they can really learn (Haycock, 1991)

So what can teachers do? First, we will have to deal with the "lesses." All of us know what makes good schools work, and our work on developmentally appropriate practices, though still needing continual refinement, helps us articulate what makes good teaching and improved educational experiences for all children. Second, we must join with other community efforts in building support systems so families can thrive and help their children succeed. Third, we will need to engage in advocacy efforts (see "Professionalism") in speaking out about children's needs and pushing for adequate teaching conditions.

Equal Play and Gender Issues

There is ample research to confirm the widespread occurrence of gender segregation in childhood (American Association of University Women, 1992; Grossman & Grossman, 1994). Sex differences are less apparent in early childhood than is gender-based behavior (see Chapter 4). Although adults may not always directly contribute to biased development, teachers and parents are indirectly responsible for the inequity between the sexes in their children.

Look at unstructured play situations. Free play is the backbone of early education programs and most at-home play, in which children choose playmates and play situations that are comfortable to them. They will not, typically, choose those activities with which they have had little or no experience, nor will they ordinarily choose cross-sex playmates (particularly as peer pressure increases with age). Further, boys still get more attention than girls do at most grade levels and in most subject areas (Sadker & Sadker,

1994). This is not always an advantage to boys, as there is increasing concern that early education programs are becoming less compatible with active behavior or less developed fine motor skills. Sexist treatment in the classroom encourages the formation of patterns of power and dominance that occurs very early (Maccoby & Jacklin, 1985).

Adults must take an assertive role in recognizing this sexist bias and replacing it with more equitable experiences for all children. Summaries of wide-ranging research indicate that both our homes and schools are "gendered environments" that spell different expectations and conduct for children on the basis of their gender (Grossman & Grossman, 1994). If we are committed to an anti-bias education and environment (see Chapters 9 to 14), we must attempt to reduce gender-stereotypical behavior.

What are teachers to do? Educators Schlank and Metzger (1997) suggest that these guidelines be followed when trying to teach for change:

- *Begin with yourself.* Just as in other issues of diversity and anti-bias, it all begins with self-awareness and reflection on one's own behavior, responses, and attitudes.
- *What you say and do can make a difference.* Whenever possible, be gender inclusive or neutral, acknowledging positive behaviors and milestones by describing what you see and avoiding using gender designations (such as "all boys get your jackets" or "all girls go to the snack tables").
- *Watch your language.* Avoid descriptions of children such as "pretty/handsome" and treat the class as a group ("friends" rather than "boys and girls"); be careful of word choices that reflect gender bias (such as "He is confident/She is full of herself").
- *Establish rules and conduct for cooperation and gender equity.* Everybody may play everywhere with any toy; blocks are not just for boys and the house corner is not for girls only; no child may be kept from playing because of something she or he cannot change—skin color, disability, or gender.
- *Be ready to intervene and support.* If you hear a "No boys allowed" or "Girls can't do that," be ready to intervene in a supportive way, finding out why children think that, and what you think or what the class rule is.
- *Think about how to cope with superheroes and Barbie dolls.* Weapon and doll play can both be viewed in a "developmental versus sociocultural" way.

Expanding children's learning styles is helpful. Girls need more experiences with spatial exploration and gross motor coordination as well as quality attention from—without dependence on—adults. Boys in particular need experiences in flexibility, nurturance, and learning from modeling.

Eliminating stereotypical relationships is also important. Be sure that all members of a group have the opportunity to participate equally. For instance, try to reduce male dominance of females in mixed-gender situations. Keep a watchful eye in the environment to see that areas do not get labeled "off limits" by one gender, such as the blocks and tricycles that become "boy places" or the house corner and art "for girls only."

Encourage cross-gender interaction, and use cooperative learning activities. Whereas there is little research about the long term effects of these strategies, a combination of these techniques has been found effective to increase mixed-gender interactions, helping behavior and friendships. Help make and keep connections among children, so they do not get locked into narrow constraints.

Sexuality

One of the most complicated issues that touches the lives of early childhood educators is sexuality. Although human sexuality is not likely to be among typical early childhood curriculum topics, teachers are increasingly more likely to encounter issues of homosexuality in the following ways: working with gay or lesbian families or co-workers, dealing with aspects of femininity and masculinity in children's sex role identity, and having multicultural children's books about gay families.

Some experts estimate that approximately 10 percent of the children in our classes will grow up to be gay or lesbian adults (Corbett, 1993). Whether or not the estimates are accurate, gay issues are controversial and produce anxiety for many; it is difficult and risky and often seems easier to ignore the whole issue and conclude that it is an "adult problem." A number of studies suggest a possible genetic basis for homosexual behavior. "It is difficult, however, to conclusively establish genetic origins for any human behavior, and the study of homosexuality presents some unique problems" (Friemann, O'Hara, & Settel, 1996). Little direct research has been done with young children, and it is likely that, "while a handful may show early indications of seeming 'different' in some way, the vast majority will offer no clue to even the most observant eye" (Corbett, 1993).

If teachers are relinquishing stereotypes about ethnic, ability, and gender, they must also consider avoiding the rejection of a family for its choice of lifestyle or the criticism of a child on the basis of some notion of "femininity" or "masculinity." Researchers have failed to find evidence that parental characteristics determine sexual orientation (Berger, 2007). The homophobia at the root of such biased behavior, either subtle on the part of teachers or overt by other children, can be hurtful and harassing. Friemann and others (1996) offer steps for teachers to take that will sound familiar because they are similar to those dealing with other forms of bias:

> Teachers should examine their own feelings about homosexuality. ... [They] must honestly recognize any biases that they may have about children who are stigmatized as sissies [or tomboys], and keep those biases out of the classroom. ... Second, teachers should immediately handle any instances of students-to-student abuse and harassment, no matter how slight. ... [Third,] teachers should challenge negative remarks about gay people and other minority groups. ... Classroom meetings are a good tool to deal with harassment cases. Start with a "stem" phrase for the children to complete, such as "When I am teased it makes me feel ..." and help children focus on how people feel when they are harassed.

Our attitude ought to be one that children should never be made to feel ashamed about their family, their teachers, or themselves.

Professionalism

Every day, early childhood professionals open their doors to young children by the millions. As they do, they are influencing the course of our history in the 21st century. Consider this: A child born in 2010 will be a voting adult in 2028 and may live until the end of the century. We are teaching the children of the future!

If you are thinking about working with young children as a career, you may be wondering if early childhood education is a profession worthy of a lifetime commitment as a career. Can a person look forward to a challenging, intellectually stimulating, and rewarding future? To find those answers in today's world, we look at three issues: standards (for children's programs and teacher preparation), teaching for human values, and child advocacy.

Standards

Children's Programs

In Chapter 2, you read about the rich array of programs offered for children in group care from infancy through age 8. Because they are so diverse, it is often difficult to define and assess the standard of care and education with one set of guidelines. Consider these statistics:

■ Thirty-two states do not require prior training to teach in child care centers, and 39 and the District of Columbia do not require training of family child care providers (Children's Defense Fund, 2008).

■ A study of child–staff ratios found that fewer states met NAEYC recommended standards for 4-year-olds in 1995 than in 1981 (Snow, Teleki,& Reguero-de-Atiles, 1996).

■ Fifteen states allow child–caretaker ratios higher than the recommended maximum for infants; 31 states exceed the maximum for toddlers; and 35 states exceed the maximum for preschoolers. Seventeen states have no maximum requirements for group size for at least one of the age groups. (Children's Defense Fund, 2008)

The most comprehensive set of standards for quality education and care in early childhood is known as Developmentally Appropriate Practices (NAEYC, 2009). The National Academy of Early Childhood Programs (2009) reported that more than 10,000 programs are accredited, serving more than 1 million children.

We need a core set of standards and an assessment system to evaluate them. Early learning standards (Chapter 6) will connect teaching practice and curriculum to state and community guidelines. This will ensure that young children receive quality care and will help us to

achieve professional status. Chapter 2 also describes the criteria for evaluating programs on these standards.

Teacher Preparation

In Chapter 5, you read about the multiple roles of teachers and the "trilemma" regarding the connections between quality of program, availability for families, and compensation for professionals. The challenge is before all of us—the child care professionals, the parents, the leaders of business and industry, and the legislators on the local, state, and national scene. National efforts called "Worthy Wage Campaign" and "Full Cost of Quality in Early Childhood Education Programs Campaign" are leading the early childhood field in advocacy and in bringing the issues of the child care crisis to national attention (see "Education Reform" earlier in this chapter).

The quality of care in child development centers is linked to the training and education of the staff. Consequently, it is imperative that we attract and recruit to the field of early childhood education individuals who not only are dedicated to working with young children but also are skilled and competent. Many states are working on developing a career lattice and professional development plan for early childhood staff. Consideration must be given to developing a coordinated system that (1) welcomes people into the field from a variety of

A program that responds to diversity is one that invites acceptance and respect.

© Cengage Learning

points; (2) offers clear career pathways with articulated training and credentialing systems; and (3) provides a variety of incentives to stay in the field.

Further, teacher preparation institutions are embarking on a cycle of self-study and articulation of coursework and experience that is offered at both the community college and 4-year institutions in the United States. NAEYC's Standards for Programs (Hyson, 2003) is leading the charge, as are incentive programs such as California's Mentor Teacher Program. We look to continued efforts to articulate and upgrade the standards of care and education in early childhood programs. See Chapter 5 for a description of teacher preparation in the early childhood field.

A Reason to Teach

Teaching is a complex endeavor. Whenever something is taught, the choice of what and how to teach it implies the teacher's values. When a teacher prevents a child from hitting another, she shows a priority for peaceful conflict resolution. When a caregiver puts a crying child into his lap, he shows the value of responsive comforting.

When children are taught reading, given free play choices, or asked to sing, they are being given a sense of what is important.

Schools of the past could be concerned with simply academic and vocational learning, leaving the moral and personal responsibilities to the parents. The school of the present and future cannot afford that luxury. Look back at Chapter 4, and consider Brazelton and Greenspan's list of the irreducible needs of children in this chapter; this work helps educators identify key values. Professionals talk about what is important to teach. Ask yourself:

- Why am I teaching? Why young children? Why children at all?
- What made me choose early childhood education as my career?
- What do I stand for? Why?
- How did I come to have my beliefs?
- Do I allow others their beliefs?
- How do I state my values to children? To parents?
- How do I keep my values and integrity while allowing myself to grow and change?

THE MARINER'S STAR

Create caring communities of learners

Teach to enhance development and learning

Construct appropriate curriculum

Assess children's learning and development

Build reciprocal relationships with families

FIGURE 15-7 Five big ideas for effective practice; look up to the star and look within yourself (Hyson, 2000, and NAEYC, 1999).

Integrity, honesty, harmony, individuality, self-confidence, and responsibility can all be taught in authentic ways to young children. We prepare children to live successfully by embracing the willingness to change while at the same time holding to our beliefs of personal choice, equality, and opportunity.

Early childhood professionals need some guidelines as they decide, each moment, every day, through a year, how to teach. *The Code of Professional Ethics*, the principles and ideals of which open every chapter, is one guide. The second, built from in-depth study of Developmentally Appropriate Practices, is the *Mariner's Star* (see Figure 15-7).

Advocacy

Teachers are, by definition, advocates for children. They dedicate themselves to providing a better future for America's children. To be successful, early childhood teachers and caregivers need to learn how to advocate for families and schools and for themselves as a profession.

With the issues of diversity, distribution of resources, money, and educational reform of such immediate concern, teachers need to understand the forces that affect children. Teachers will have to educate themselves about the political process. They will need to know the rules and regulations regarding public funding sources. It is important to know how monies are allocated and with whom to work to affect the decisions regarding education. By becoming acquainted with legislation, teachers can rally support for bills that will help children, families, and schools.

Teachers have long kept out of the political process. But they have not been immune from its effects. As teachers, we must become informed to increase our power in the political and financial arenas of daily life. Just as we encourage children to help themselves, we must support each other in taking the initiative for our own profession's well-being. It was just such a coalition and coordinated effort among many people in child advocacy that secured the passage of the Child Care and Development Block Grants in 1990, the first such legislation to pass Congress in 20 years. Large-scale cooperation increased significantly the political success of that bill on behalf of all children.

Every teacher can become an advocate. By working for children and children's services, teachers advocate for themselves as well. By finding your voice and keeping focused, you express your commitment and make change for children more likely to be successful.

"You have chosen to enter the nation's most powerful profession. You will be the caretakers, educators, and teachers of your nation's future: our children" (Edelman, 2000). Jonah Edelman, executive director of Stand for Children, leads a grassroots membership that advocates for children to become a higher priority in our public agencies and our lives. Established in 1996 by the Children's Defense Fund, it challenges us to become effective advocates. How can you take these steps?

1. Make a personal commitment.
2. Keep informed.

Different Kinds of Child Advocacy

Personal advocacy: Sharing personal views and philosophies with others.
  Example: "Maria was concerned about the safety of the neighborhood playground. While pushing her toddler on the swing, she mentioned to the mother next to her that she was frustrated by the litter in the park including broken glass in the sandbox. The two women agreed to ask other parents and neighbors to come back the next day with trash bags and gloves to pick up litter while taking turns playing with the children" (Robinson & Stark, 2002).

Public policy advocacy: Influencing public policies and practices so that they are more responsive to children.
  Example: Frustrated with changes the state legislature was considering, the local child care planning council sent a letter to state legislators and the chair of the funding committee. They also attended a hearing to offer testimony about how the allocation of preschool funds would affect everyone.

Private-sector advocacy: Changing private policies to better support children, families, and teachers.
  Example: A group of teachers approached its local school board about the lack of technology in the schools. They talked to local businesses and the parents of the community, identified a collaborative committee of all three groups, and began volunteering their expertise about children and learning. Within 2 years, the school had a list of needs and priorities, has received donations of time and technical assistance from parents, and received a grant for computers in the classrooms.

▮ **FIGURE 15-8** Early childhood advocacy takes many forms.

How do adults become advocates to ensure a fulfilling life for children in the 21st century?

3. Know the process.
4. Express your views.
5. Let others know.
6. Be visible.
7. Show appreciation.
8. Watch the implementation.
9. Build rapport and trust.
10. Educate your legislators.

It seems sometimes as if our society has arranged its priorities to put making a living first, making more money second, and raising children a distant third place. By getting involved, early childhood educators could help our societies make child-friendly choices, which help today's children who will be tomorrow's parents. The teacher who works to ensure high quality programs and services for children and their families also increases the likelihood of achieving the improved working conditions, professional opportunities, and public recognition that the field of early childhood education so richly deserves. Every day, we open our doors to young children by the millions.

Is this profession a worthwhile one? The early years are a special time of life, and those who work with young children might reflect on the following aspects of professionalism:

- *Sense of identity.* Early childhood professionals see themselves as caregivers who strive to educate the whole child, taking into consideration the body, the mind, and the heart and soul (see Chapter 1).
- *Purpose to engage in developmentally appropriate practices (DAP).* Quality care and education calls for blending child development and learning the strengths, interests, and needs of each child, and the social and cultural contexts in which children live (see Chapter 2).
- *Commitment to ethical teaching and to child advocacy.* Being a professional means behaving with a child's best interests in mind, keeping confidentiality when discussing issues in the classroom and about families, upholding a code of ethics, and taking themselves and their work seriously (see Chapter 5 and Appendix A).
- *Participation in the work as a legitimate livelihood.* The people who provide care and education to young children deserve wages and working conditions that are worthy of their efforts (Chapters 5 and 15).

Ours is a profession that is constantly growing, branching out in many directions and ready to meet emerging challenges in flexible, innovative ways. We have professional organizations to guide us. The National Association for the Education of Young Children (NAEYC) is the largest professional organization. ACEI (Association for Childhood Education International) includes both preschool and elementary school. Children's Defense Fund (CDF) is a lobbying organization founded in 1973 by Marian Wright Edelman to advocate for children, particularly addressing the needs of poor and minority children and those with disabilities. All these efforts have resulted in important improvements in the status of children, and they have begun to outline standards and practices for the people who call themselves early childhood professionals.

What Do YOU Think? Which of the four themes of early childhood is most compelling to you? Which of the issues facing early childhood educators today are most applicable to you and the community in which you live? What steps are being taken to address these issues and how successful are they? How can *you* make a difference today?

Insights *from the field*

How Do We Teach for Tomorrow? *by Dr. Sharon L. Kagan*

Arguably, nothing—but nothing—in the field of early care and education deserves more attention than the way in which we teach young children. Not only are early childhood curriculum and early childhood pedagogy at the center of early childhood education, they are a key determinant of the enduring results young children will derive during and after their experiences in early care and education settings.

In speaking about how we teach for tomorrow, we must consider who the children of tomorrow will be. In a landmark volume, *Children of 2010*, Washington and Andrews (1998) clearly point out that tomorrow's children are not the children of today. Yes, of course at the core, children are children from one century to the next; their development proceeds in fairly predictable ways, they are more dependent than adults, and they always have and always will need love to thrive. Beyond these fundamentals, however, children of the future will be different in the aggregate and they will be different from children who grew up but a few short years ago.

In the aggregate, American children of the future will be more diverse, with many more being of color. They will come from families where, increasingly, the home language is not English. Many will come to early childhood programs having had no prior experience in the United States. Many will come from familial and community environments characterized by abuse, drugs, and violence.

Simultaneously, many young children will come from families where, for the first time in generations, mothers are working out of the home. Others will come from homes where technology is readily available, if not a pervasive element of the environment. Still others will come from families where substantial wealth has recently been amassed. All these children come to our doors, each with different, unique needs that require equally different and unique approaches in order to cohere their talents into a collective, well-functioning citizenry.

Given this diversity, what and how should early childhood teachers teach? Fortunately, we have some strong guidance on these matters. First, regarding *what* should be taught: The National Education Goals Panel has codified what children need to learn so that they will be ready to enter school. These necessary learnings are divided into five dimensions:

1. Physical and motor development.
2. Social and emotional development.
3. Approaches toward learning.
4. Language, literacy, and communication skills.
5. Cognition and general knowledge.

We know that learning in all five of these areas is equally important and that no one area should take precedence over the others, although at certain times in the developmental trajectory, it is important to focus a bit more on one domain than another. A rounded and high quality early childhood program must have exciting content that addresses each of these domains.

With regard to *how* young children should be taught, I suggest that if we simply understand how little children learn we will have the key to how they should be taught. For example, we know that little children cannot master abstract thinking until they have mastered concrete thinking. As a result, it is critical that all programs that serve young children (be they in museums, libraries, family child care homes, or early childhood centers) provide abundant opportunities for hands-on learning. It is true that little children learn by doing. It is also true that they are episodic learners; that is, they often learn something one day, only to "forget" it the next day. While they don't actually forget, little children do store knowledge, often retrieving it at odd time frames and in nonlinear ways. This is why it is inappropriate to rely on test results taken at a single point in time; children's learning is very variable. For the teachers, this means we must be keen and constant observers; we must be informants for parents who often worry unnecessarily about the natural fits and starts that characterize children's development.

We also know that young children learn according to their own timetables, with some learning some facts quickly and needing more time to master other facts. This means that as we teach, we must provide opportunities for different learning styles. We also know that children's learning is reinforced by repetition. This is why, innately, little children love to repeat stories, songs, and experiences; they derive pleasure (as do adults) from that which is familiar. Finally, we know that little children are constant learners; that is, they pick up ideas, facts, and gestures from all that is around them. This is why we must remember that as teachers, above all, we are role models. While it is axiomatic to early childhood educators that children learn by doing, it is also important to remember that children learn a great deal by watching.

All of this means that the early educators' task is enormous. Little children don't miss a trick; they want to learn, and they do learn. Our job as educators and caring adults is to be sure that *what* they are learning is important and that *how* they learn matches their developmental capacities and predilections to learning.

References

Washington, V., & Andrews, J. D. (Eds.). (1998). *Children of 2010*. Washington, DC: NAEYC.

Sharon Lynn Kagan is the Virginia and Leonard Marx Professor of Early Childhood and Family Policy at Teachers College, Columbia University, and a Professor Adjunct at Yale University's Child Study Center. Author of over 100 articles and 12 books, Kagan's research focuses on the institutions and policies that impact child and family life. Kagan consults with numerous federal and state agencies, Congress, governors, and legislators; is a member of 40 national boards; and is past president of the National Association for the Education of Young Children and Family Support America.

SUMMARY

How might we approach the future as we start this new century? By reflecting on our past and looking closely at the present, we are reminded of several important factors that illuminate today's issues:

1. Out of the past, we create a vision of the future. A backward glance along the timeline shows us that today we have a living, viable organism: a growing comprehensive vision of the field of early childhood; a growing definition of what early childhood means; a growing collaboration of early childhood professionals from all walks of life; a growing involvement in the education reform movement; a growing system of early childhood programs to serve the families of the 21st century; and a growing sense of our own effectiveness as advocates.

2. The ultimate goal seems timeless but bears frequent repetition. Our aim is to help all children learn so that they can live full and satisfying lives, to help them develop their talents and capabilities. What is our vision of the future for these children? Our vision is that they are prepared for the challenges and responsibilities of adult life.

3. Today's children are learning in a new century. The growing cultural diversity and global connectedness provides rich opportunities and new challenges from which to learn. Learning about the values and attributes of other cultures through meaningful and accurate experience becomes an imperative agenda for the children, families, and early childhood professionals of the 21st century.

KEY TERMS

ethic of social reform	child neglect	sexist
importance of childhood	accreditation	ethnocentric
transmission of values	social capital	demographics
professionalism	racist	attitude crystallization
child abuse	classist	cultural pluralism

REVIEW QUESTIONS

1. Using the four themes of early childhood education, list at least one of the pressing issues facing early childhood educators today.

2. What is the relationship between the quality of a child care program and the cost?

3. What are the signs that indicate child abuse?

4. What are the four major findings on research about viewing media violence and their implications for ECE teachers?

5. What standards apply to early childhood practice in regards to the "Mariner's Star"?

LEARNING ACTIVITIES

1. Interview teachers from a child care center, nursery school, and kindergarten about their salary scales and health benefits. How do they compare with one another? What conclusions can you draw from their information?

2. Interview teachers of a child care center, a nursery school, and a first grade about the policies for reporting suspected child abuse in their settings. Do they know what to do if they suspect child abuse? Are they aware of the signs that indicate abuse?

3. In addressing social diversity in ECE programs, interview at least two professionals and then describe how you would address the following issues:

   a. A group of children says "No boys (girls) allowed."

   b. Children in your center have several different home languages, and the class is typically taught by English-dominant staff.

   c. The board of your program has decided to fully include children with special needs this year.

4. How can you advocate for improving the working conditions for the early care and education workforce? Make a list of several concrete actions you can take in your community.

HELPFUL WEBSITES

Adults and Children Together Against Violence   http://www.ACTagainstviolence.org

American Academy of Pediatrics   http://www.aap.org

American Red Cross   http://www.redcross.org/disaster/masters/

Annie E. Casey Foundation/KidsCount   http://www.aecf.org

Center for the Child Care Workforce   http://www.ccw.org/

Centers for Disease Control and Prevention   http://www.cdc.gov

Child Maltreatment   http://www.acf.hhs.gov

Child Statistics   http://www.childtrends.org

Child Welfare League of America   http://www.cwla.org

Children's Defense Fund   http://www.childrensdefensefund.org

Common Sense Media   http://www.commonsensemedia.org

Coping with Disaster   http://www.counselingforloss.com

Developmental Assets   http://www.search-institute.org

Educators for Social Responsibility   http://www.esrnational.org

National Association for the Education of Young Children   http://www.naeyc.org

Child Welfare Information Gateway   http://www.childwelfare.gov

National Indian Child Welfare Association   http://www.nicwa.org

Prevent Child Abuse America   http://www.childabuse.org

Stand for Children   http://www.stand.org

U.S. Census Bureau   http://www.census.gov

U.S. Department of Education   http://www.ed.gov

U.S. Department of Health and Human Services   http://www.dhhs.gov

 Additional resources including the TeachSource Videos can be found on the premium website for this book. Go to http://www.cengage.com/login to register your access code.

REFERENCES

Ethic of Social Reform
Child Care

Bredekamp, S., & Copple, C. (Eds.). (1997). *Developmentally appropriate practice in early childhood programs serving children from birth through age 8*. Washington, DC: NAEYC.

Children's Defense Fund. (2008). *The state of America's Children*. Washington, DC: Children's Defense Fund.

Copple, C., & Bredekamp, S. (Eds.). (2009). *Developmentally appropriate practice in early childhood programs serving children from birth through age 8*. Washington, DC: NAEYC.

Costs, Quality and Child Outcomes Study Team. (1995). *Cost, quality and child outcomes in child care centers, executive summary*. Denver: Economics Department, University of Colorado at Denver.

Galinsky, E., Howe, C., Cantos, S., & Schinn, M. (1994). *The study of children in family child care and relative care: Highlight of findings*. New York: Families and Work Institute.

Herzenberg, S., Price, M., & Bradley, D. (2005). *Losing ground in early childhood education: Declining workforce qualifications in an expanding industry*. Washington, DC: Economic Policy Institute.

Kagan, S. L., & Neuman, M. J. (1997, September). Highlights of the Quality 2000 Initiative: Not by chance. *Young Children*: 54–62.

Peisner-Feinberg, E. S., Burchinal, M. R., Clifford, R. M., Culkin, M. L., Howes, C., Kagan, S. L., Yazejian, N., Byler, P., Rustici, J., & Zelazo, J. (1999). *The children of the cost, quality and outcomes study go to school: Technical report*. Chapel Hill, NC: University of North Carolina at Chapel Hill, Frank Porter Graham Child Development Center.

National Association of Child Care Resource and Referral Agencies (NACCRRA). (2009). *Child care in America: 2008 Fact Sheet*. Retrieved from website www.naccrra.org in March 2009.

The Children's Foundation. (2001). *Family child care licensing summary data*. Bloomington, IL.

U.S. Census Bureau. (2008). *School enrollment in the United States—Social and economic characteristics of students*. Washington, DC.

Whitebook, M., Sakai, L., Gerber, E., & Howes, C. (2001). *Then and now: Changes in child care staffing, 1994-2000*. Washington, DC: Center for the Child Care Workforce.

Education Reform

Committee for Economic Development. (2005). *Preschool for all*. Executive Summary. Pittsburgh.

National Association of State Boards of Education. (1988). *Right from the start*. Alexandria, VA: The report of the NABE Task Force on Early Childhood Education.

Sorrentino, J. (2008, December 17). *New secretary of education Arne Duncan: What it could mean for kids*. Retrieved from www.Education.com.

U.S. Department of Education. (2001). *The No Child Left Behind Act of 2001*. Executive Summary and Fact Sheet. Washington, DC: United States Department of Education.

The Importance of Childhood
Childhood Stress

Brazelton, T. B., & Greenspan, S. D. (2000, March). The irreducible needs of children. *Young Children*, 6–13.

Child Abuse and Neglect

Childhelp. (2009). *Signs of child abuse, 2006*. Retrieved from website www.childhelp.org/resources, March, 2009.

Childhelp. (2009). *Child abuse in America, 2006*. Retrieved from website www.childhelp.org/resources, March 2009.

Children's Defense Fund. (2008). *The state of America's children*. Washington, DC: Author.

National Association for the Education of Young Children. (1997, March). *Position statement on the prevention of child abuse in early childhood programs and the responsibilities of early childhood professionals to prevent child abuse* (42–46). Washington, DC: Author.

U.S. Department of Health and Human Services. (1998). *Child sexual abuse prevention—Tips to parents*. Washington, DC: Author.

Poverty

Casey Foundation. (2006). *Kids Count Data Book*. Baltimore: Annie E. Casey Foundation.

Center for Children and Families. (2000). *"Growing Up in Poverty" Project*. New York: Teachers College, Columbia University.

Children's Defense Fund. (2008). *The state of America's children*. Washington, DC: Author.

Family Support

Children's Defense Fund. (2002). *The state of children in America's union*. Washington, DC: Author.

DelCampo, D., & DelCampo, R. (2006). *Taking sides: Clashing views in childhood and society* (6th Ed). Dubuque, IA: McGraw-Hill. (See Issue 7: Does Divorce Create Long-Term Negative Effects for Children?)

Elkind, D. (1991, September). The family and education in the postmodern world. *Momentum.*

Wallerstein, J. (2002). *The unexpected legacy of divorce.* New York: Hyperion.

Transmitting Values
Media Culture
Carter, B. (1991, May 1). *Children's TV, where boys are king.* New York Times.

Center for Media Literacy. (1993, August). *Beyond blame: Challenging violence in the media:* Report from the American Psychological Association's Commission on Violence and Youth in America. Malibu, CA.

Common Sense Media and Department of Clinical Bioethics, National Institutes of Health. (2008, December). *Media + child and adolescent health: A systematic review.* www.commonsensemedia.org

DelCampo, D. S., & DelCampo, R. L. (2006). *Taking sides: Clashing views in childhood and society* (6th Ed). Dubuque, IA: McGraw-Hill. (See Issue 8: Is Television Violence Viewing Harmful for Children?)

Johnson, M. O. (1996, April). Television violence and its effect on children. *Journal of Pediatric Nursing,* 11(2).

Levin, D. (1998). *Remote control children?* Washington, DC: NAEYC.

Minow, N. (1991, June 19). Worth noting: Address to commemorate 30th anniversary of his "vast wasteland" speech. *Education Week.*

National Association for the Education of Young Children. (1990). *Media violence and children.* Washington, DC: Author.

Nielsen Media Research. (1989, 2008). *Nielsen Report on Television.* New York: Nielsen Media Research.

Violence and Disaster
Adults and Children Together Against Violence (ACT). (2002). *Violence prevention for families of young children.* Washington, DC: American Psychological Association.

Carlsson-Paige, N., & Levin, D. (2005). *The war play dilemma* (2nd Ed). New York: Teachers College.

Greenman, J. (2001). *What happened to the world? Helping children cope in turbulent times.* Portland, OR:

The Dougy Center, National Center for Grieving Children and Families.

Social Diversity
Bowman, B.T. (1991). Educating language-minority children. *ERIC Digest.* University of Illinois.

Child Care Law Center. (1994, November). *The ADA: A new way of thinking.* (Personal communication from M. Cruz, San Francisco, CA, 2001-02).

Children's Defense Fund. (2008). *The state of America's children.* Washington, DC: Author.

Derman-Sparks, L., & the ABC Task Force. (1989). *Anti-bias curriculum.* Washington, DC: NAEYC.

Frankenberg, E., Lee, C., & Orfield, G. (2004). A multiracial society with segregated schools; are we losing the dream? In S. Books, *Poverty & schooling in the U.S.* Cambridge, MA: Lawrence Erlbaum.

Hale, J. E. (1993). Culturally appropriate pedagogy and the African American child. In A. Gordon & K. W. Browne (Eds.), *Beginnings and beyond* (3rd Ed). Clifton Park, NY: Thomson Delmar Learning.

Hale, J. E. (2001). *Learning while black: Creating educational excellence for African American children.* Baltimore, MD: Johns Hopkins University Press.

Haycock, K. (1991, March). *Reaching for the year 2000.* Childhood Education.

Takanishi, R. (2006). *Leveling the playing field: Supporting immigrant children from birth to 8.* The future of children. Princeton, NJ: Brookings Institute.

Gender and Sexuality
American Association of University Women. (1992). *How schools short change girls.* Washington, DC: Author.

Corbett, S. (1993, March). A complicated bias. *Young Children.*

Friemann, B. B., O'Hara, H., & Settel, J. (1996, Fall). What heterosexual teachers need to know about homosexuality. *Childhood Education.*

Grossman, H., & Grossman, S. H. (1994). *Gender issues in education.* Boston: Allyn & Bacon.

Maccoby, E., & Jacklin, C. N. (1985, April). *Gender segregation in nursery school: Predictors and outcomes.* Paper presented to the National Society for Research in Child Development. Toronto, Ontario.

Sadker, M.,& Sadker, D. (1994). *Failing at fairness: How our schools cheat girls.* New York: Simon& Schuster.

Schlank, C. H., & Metzger, B. (1997). *Together and equal.* Boston, MA: Allyn & Bacon.

Professionalism

Children's Defense Fund. (2008). *The state of America's children.* Washington, DC: Author.

Edelman, J. (2000). Take a stand for children. In A. Gordon & K. W. Browne (Eds.), *Beginnings and beyond* (5th Ed). Albany, NY: Thomson Delmar Learning.

Hyson, M. (2000, November). Is it OK to have calendar time? Look up to the star … look within yourself. *Young Children,* 55(6).

National Association for the Education of Young Children. (1999). *Tools for teaching developmentally appropriate practice—the leading edge in early childhood education* [videos]. Washington, DC: Author.

National Association for the Education of Young Children. (2005). *Accreditation criteria and procedures of the National Academy of Early Childhood Programs.* Washington, DC: Author.

Robinson, A., & Stark, D. R. (2002). *Advocates in action: Making a difference for young children.* Washington, DC: NAEYC.

Snow, C. W., Teleki, J. K., & Reguero-de-Atiles, J. T. (1996, September). Child care center licensing standards in the United States: 1981 to 1995. *Young Children,* 36–41.

Code of Ethical Conduct and Statement of Commitment

A position statement of the *National Association for the Education of Young Children*

Revised April 2005

Preamble

NAEYC recognizes that those who work with young children face many daily decisions that have moral and ethical implications. The NAEYC Code of Ethical Conduct offers guidelines for responsible behavior and sets forth a common basis for resolving the principal ethical dilemmas encountered in early childhood care and education. The Statement of Commitment is not part of the Code but is a personal acknowledgement of an individual's willingness to embrace the distinctive values and moral obligations of the field of early childhood care and education. The primary focus of the Code is on daily practice with children and their families in programs for children from birth through 8 years of age, such as infant/toddler programs, preschool and prekindergarten programs, child care centers, hospital and child life settings, family child care homes, kindergartens, and primary classrooms. When the issues involve young children, then these provisions also apply to specialists who do not work directly with children, including program administrators, parent educators, early childhood adult educators, and officials with responsibility for program monitoring and licensing. (Note: See also the "Code of Ethical Conduct: Supplement for Early Childhood Adult Educators.")

Core Values

Standards of ethical behavior in early childhood care and education are based on commitment to the following core values that are deeply rooted in the history of the field of early childhood care and education. We have made a commitment to

- Appreciate childhood as a unique and valuable stage of the human life cycle.
- Base our work on knowledge of how children develop and learn.
- Appreciate and support the bond between the child and family.
- Recognize that children are best understood and supported in the context of family, culture,* community, and society.
- Respect the dignity, worth, and uniqueness of each individual (child, family member, and colleague).
- Respect diversity in children, families, and colleagues.
- Recognize that children and adults achieve their full potential in the context of relationships that are based on trust and respect.

Conceptual Framework

The Code sets forth a framework of professional responsibilities in four sections. Each section addresses an area of professional relationships: (1) with children, (2) with families, (3) among colleagues, and (4) with the community and society. Each section includes an introduction to the primary responsibilities of the early childhood practitioner in that context. The introduction is followed by (1) a set of ideals that reflect exemplary professional practice and (2) a set of principles describing practices that are required, prohibited, or permitted.

The **ideals** reflect the aspirations of practitioners. The **principles** guide conduct and assist practitioners in resolving ethical dilemmas.† Both ideals and principles are

---

* *Culture* includes ethnicity, racial identity, economic level, family structure, language, and religious and political beliefs, which profoundly influence each child's development and relationship to the world.

† There is not necessarily a corresponding principle for each ideal.

intended to direct practitioners to those questions which, when responsibly answered, can provide the basis for conscientious decision making. While the Code provides specific direction for addressing some ethical dilemmas, many others will require the practitioner to combine the guidance of the Code with professional judgment.

The ideals and principles in this Code present a shared framework of professional responsibility that affirms our commitment to the core values of our field. The Code publicly acknowledges the responsibilities that we in the field have assumed and in so doing supports ethical behavior in our work. Practitioners who face situations with ethical dimensions are urged to seek guidance in the applicable parts of this Code and in the spirit that informs the whole.

Often, "the right answer"—the best ethical course of action to take—is not obvious. There may be no readily apparent, positive way to handle a situation. When one important value contradicts another, we face an ethical dilemma. When we face a dilemma, it is our professional responsibility to consult the Code and all relevant parties to find the most ethical resolution.

Section I: Ethical Responsibilities to Children

Childhood is a unique and valuable stage in the human life cycle. Our paramount responsibility is to provide care and education in settings that are safe, healthy, nurturing, and responsive for each child. We are committed to supporting children's development and learning; respecting individual differences; and helping children learn to live, play, and work cooperatively. We are also committed to promoting children's self-awareness, competence, self-worth, resiliency, and physical well-being.

Ideals

I-1.1—To be familiar with the knowledge base of early childhood care and education and to stay informed through continuing education and training.

I-1.2—To base program practices upon current knowledge and research in the field of early childhood education, child development, and related disciplines, as well as on particular knowledge of each child.

I-1.3—To recognize and respect the unique qualities, abilities, and potential of each child.

I-1.4—To appreciate the vulnerability of children and their dependence on adults.

I-1.5—To create and maintain safe and healthy settings that foster children's social, emotional, cognitive, and physical development and that respect their dignity and their contributions.

I-1.6—To use assessment instruments and strategies that are appropriate for the children to be assessed, that are used only for the purposes for which they were designed, and that have the potential to benefit children.

I-1.7—To use assessment information to understand and support children's development and learning, to support instruction, and to identify children who may need additional services.

I-1.8—To support the right of each child to play and learn in an inclusive environment that meets the needs of children with and without disabilities.

I-1.9—To advocate for and ensure that all children, including those with special needs, have access to the support services needed to be successful.

I-1.10—To ensure that each child's culture, language, ethnicity, and family structure are recognized and valued in the program.

I-1.11—To provide all children with experiences in a language that they know, as well as support children in maintaining the use of their home language and in learning English.

I-1.12—To work with families to provide a safe and smooth transition as children and families move from one program to the next.

Principles

P-1.1—**Above all, we shall not harm children. We shall not participate in practices that are emotionally damaging, physically harmful, disrespectful, degrading, dangerous, exploitative, or intimidating to children.** *This principle has precedence over all others in this Code.*

P-1.2—We shall care for and educate children in positive emotional and social environments that are cognitively stimulating and that support each child's culture, language, ethnicity, and family structure.

P-1.3—We shall not participate in practices that discriminate against children by denying benefits, giving special advantages, or excluding them from programs or activities on the basis of their sex, race, national origin, religious beliefs, medical condition, disability, or the marital status/family structure, sexual orientation, or religious beliefs or other affiliations of their families. (Aspects of this principle do not apply in programs that have a lawful mandate to provide services to a particular population of children.)

P-1.4—We shall involve all those with relevant knowledge (including families and staff) in decisions concerning a child, as appropriate, ensuring confidentiality of sensitive information.

P-1.5—We shall use appropriate assessment systems, which include multiple sources of information, to provide information on children's learning and development.

P-1.6—We shall strive to ensure that decisions such as those related to enrollment, retention, or assignment to special education services, will be based on multiple sources of information and will never be based on a single assessment, such as a test score or a single observation.

P-1.7—We shall strive to build individual relationships with each child; make individualized adaptations in teaching strategies, learning environments, and curricula; and consult with the family so that each child benefits from the program. If after such efforts have been exhausted, the current placement does not meet a child's needs, or the child is seriously jeopardizing the ability of other children to benefit from the program, we shall collaborate with the child's family and appropriate specialists to determine the additional services needed and/or the placement option(s) most likely to ensure the child's success. (Aspects of this principle may not apply in programs that have a lawful mandate to provide services to a particular population of children.)

P-1.8—We shall be familiar with the risk factors for and symptoms of child abuse and neglect, including physical, sexual, verbal, and emotional abuse and physical, emotional, educational, and medical neglect. We shall know and follow state laws and community procedures that protect children against abuse and neglect.

P-1.9—When we have reasonable cause to suspect child abuse or neglect, we shall report it to the appropriate community agency and follow up to ensure that appropriate action has been taken. When appropriate, parents or guardians will be informed that the referral will be or has been made.

P-1.10—When another person tells us of his or her suspicion that a child is being abused or neglected, we shall assist that person in taking appropriate action in order to protect the child.

P-1.11—When we become aware of a practice or situation that endangers the health, safety, or well-being of children, we have an ethical responsibility to protect children or inform parents and/or others who can.

Section II: Ethical Responsibilities to Families

Families* are of primary importance in children's development. Because the family and the early childhood practitioner have a common interest in the child's well-being, we acknowledge a primary responsibility to bring about communication, cooperation, and collaboration between the home and early childhood program in ways that enhance the child's development.

Ideals

I-2.1—To be familiar with the knowledge base related to working effectively with families and to stay informed through continuing education and training.

I-2.2—To develop relationships of mutual trust and create partnerships with the families we serve.

I-2.3—To welcome all family members and encourage them to participate in the program.

I-2.4—To listen to families, acknowledge and build upon their strengths and competencies, and learn from families as we support them in their task of nurturing children.

I-2.5—To respect the dignity and preferences of each family and to make an effort to learn about its structure, culture, language, customs, and beliefs.

I-2.6—To acknowledge families' childrearing values and their right to make decisions for their children.

I-2.7—To share information about each child's education and development with families and to help them understand and appreciate the current knowledge base of the early childhood profession.

I-2.8—To help family members enhance their understanding of their children and support the continuing development of their skills as parents.

I-2.9—To participate in building support networks for families by providing them with opportunities to interact with program staff, other families, community resources, and professional services.

Principles

P-2.1—We shall not deny family members access to their child's classroom or program setting unless access is denied by court order or other legal restriction.

---

* The term *family* may include those adults, besides parents, with the responsibility of being involved in educating, nurturing, and advocating for the child.

P-2.2—We shall inform families of program philosophy, policies, curriculum, assessment system, and personnel qualifications, and explain why we teach as we do—which should be in accordance with our ethical responsibilities to children (see Section I).

P-2.3—We shall inform families of and, when appropriate, involve them in policy decisions.

P-2.4—We shall involve the family in significant decisions affecting their child.

P-2.5—We shall make every effort to communicate effectively with all families in a language that they understand. We shall use community resources for translation and interpretation when we do not have sufficient resources in our own programs.

P-2.6—As families share information with us about their children and families, we shall consider this information to plan and implement the program.

P-2.7—We shall inform families about the nature and purpose of the program's child assessments and how data about their child will be used.

P-2.8—We shall treat child assessment information confidentially and share this information only when there is a legitimate need for it.

P-2.9—We shall inform the family of injuries and incidents involving their child, of risks such as exposures to communicable diseases that might result in infection, and of occurrences that might result in emotional stress.

P-2.10—Families shall be fully informed of any proposed research projects involving their children and shall have the opportunity to give or withhold consent without penalty. We shall not permit or participate in research that could in any way hinder the education, development, or well-being of children.

P-2.11—We shall not engage in or support exploitation of families. We shall not use our relationship with a family for private advantage or personal gain, or enter into relationships with family members that might impair our effectiveness working with their children.

P-2.12—We shall develop written policies for the protection of confidentiality and the disclosure of children's records. These policy documents shall be made available to all program personnel and families. Disclosure of children's records beyond family members, program personnel, and consultants having an obligation of confidentiality shall require familial consent (except in cases of abuse or neglect).

P-2.13—We shall maintain confidentiality and shall respect the family's right to privacy, refraining from disclosure of confidential information and intrusion into family life. However, when we have reason to believe that a child's welfare is at risk, it is permissible to share confidential information with agencies, as well as with individuals who have legal responsibility for intervening in the child's interest.

P-2.14—In cases where family members are in conflict with one another, we shall work openly, sharing our observations of the child, to help all parties involved make informed decisions. We shall refrain from becoming an advocate for one party.

P-2.15—We shall be familiar with and appropriately refer families to community resources and professional support services. After a referral has been made, we shall follow up to ensure that services have been appropriately provided.

Section III: Ethical Responsibilities to Colleagues

In a caring, cooperative workplace, human dignity is respected, professional satisfaction is promoted, and positive relationships are developed and sustained. Based upon our core values, our primary responsibility to colleagues is to establish and maintain settings and relationships that support productive work and meet professional needs. The same ideals that apply to children also apply as we interact with adults in the workplace.

A. Responsibilities to Co-workers

Ideals

I-3A.1—To establish and maintain relationships of respect, trust, confidentiality, collaboration, and cooperation with co-workers.

I-3A.2—To share resources with co-workers, collaborating to ensure that the best possible early childhood care and education program is provided.

I-3A.3—To support co-workers in meeting their professional needs and in their professional development.

I-3A.4—To accord co-workers due recognition of professional achievement.

Principles

P-3A.1—We shall recognize the contributions of colleagues to our program and not participate in practices that diminish their reputations or impair their effectiveness in working with children and families.

P-3A.2—When we have concerns about the professional behavior of a co-worker, we shall first let that person know of our concern in a way that shows respect for personal dignity and for the diversity to be found among staff members, and then attempt to resolve the matter collegially and in a confidential manner.

P-3A.3—We shall exercise care in expressing views regarding the personal attributes or professional conduct of co-workers. Statements should be based on firsthand knowledge, not hearsay, and relevant to the interests of children and programs.

P-3A.4—We shall not participate in practices that discriminate against a co-worker because of sex, race, national origin, religious beliefs or other affiliations, age, marital status/family structure, disability, or sexual orientation.

B. Responsibilities to Employers

Ideals

I-3B.1—To assist the program in providing the highest quality of service.

I-3B.2—To do nothing that diminishes the reputation of the program in which we work unless it is violating laws and regulations designed to protect children or is violating the provisions of this Code.

Principles

P-3B.1 – We shall follow all program policies. When we do not agree with program policies, we shall attempt to effect change through constructive action within the organization.

P-3B.2—We shall speak or act on behalf of an organization only when authorized. We shall take care to acknowledge when we are speaking for the organization and when we are expressing a personal judgment.

P-3B.3—We shall not violate laws or regulations designed to protect children and shall take appropriate action consistent with this Code when aware of such violations.

P-3B.4—If we have concerns about a colleague's behavior, and children's well-being is not at risk, we may address the concern with that individual. If children are at risk or the situation does not improve after it has been brought to the colleague's attention, we shall report the colleague's unethical or incompetent behavior to an appropriate authority.

P-3B.5—When we have a concern about circumstances or conditions that impact the quality of care and education within the program, we shall inform the program's administration or, when necessary, other appropriate authorities.

C. Responsibilities to Employees

Ideals

I-3C.1—To promote safe and healthy working conditions and policies that foster mutual respect, cooperation, collaboration, competence, well-being, confidentiality, and self esteem in staff members.

I-3C.2—To create and maintain a climate of trust and candor that will enable staff to speak and act in the best interests of children, families, and the field of early childhood care and education.

I-3C.3—To strive to secure adequate and equitable compensation (salary and benefits) for those who work with or on behalf of young children.

I-3C.4—To encourage and support continual development of employees in becoming more skilled and knowledgeable practitioners.

Principles

P-3C.1—In decisions concerning children and programs, we shall draw upon the education, training, experience, and expertise of staff members.

P-3C.2—We shall provide staff members with safe and supportive working conditions that honor confidences and permit them to carry out their responsibilities through fair performance evaluation, written grievance procedures, constructive feedback, and opportunities for continuing professional development and advancement.

P-3C.3—We shall develop and maintain comprehensive written personnel policies that define program standards. These policies shall be given to new staff members and shall be available and easily accessible for review by all staff members.

P-3C.4—We shall inform employees whose performance does not meet program expectations of areas of concern and, when possible, assist in improving their performance.

P-3C.5—We shall conduct employee dismissals for just cause, in accordance with all applicable laws and regulations. We shall inform employees who are dismissed of the reasons for their termination. When a dismissal is for cause, justification must be based on evidence of inadequate or inappropriate behavior that is accurately documented, current, and available for the employee to review.

P-3C.6—In making evaluations and recommendations, we shall make judgments based on fact and relevant to the interests of children and programs.

P-3C.7—We shall make hiring, retention, termination, and promotion decisions based solely on a person's competence, record of accomplishment, ability to carry out the responsibilities of the position, and professional preparation specific to the developmental levels of children in his/her care.

P-3C.8—We shall not make hiring, retention, termination, and promotion decisions based on an individual's sex, race, national origin, religious beliefs or other affiliations, age, marital status/family structure, disability, or sexual orientation. We shall be familiar with and observe laws and regulations that pertain to employment discrimination. (Aspects of this principle do not apply to programs that have a lawful mandate to determine eligibility based on one or more of the criteria identified above.)

P-3C.9—We shall maintain confidentiality in dealing with issues related to an employee's job performance and shall respect an employee's right to privacy regarding personal issues.

Section IV: Ethical Responsibilities to Community and Society

Early childhood programs operate within the context of their immediate community made up of families and other institutions concerned with children's welfare. Our responsibilities to the community are to provide programs that meet the diverse needs of families, to cooperate with agencies and professions that share the responsibility for children, to assist families in gaining access to those agencies and allied professionals, and to assist in the development of community programs that are needed but not currently available.

As individuals, we acknowledge our responsibility to provide the best possible programs of care and education for children and to conduct ourselves with honesty and integrity. Because of our specialized expertise in early childhood development and education and because the larger society shares responsibility for the welfare and protection of young children, we acknowledge a collective obligation to advocate for the best interests of children within early childhood programs and in the larger community and to serve as a voice for young children everywhere.

The ideals and principles in this section are presented to distinguish between those that pertain to the work of the individual early childhood educator and those that more typically are collectively engaged on behalf of the best interests of children—with the understanding that individual early childhood educators have a shared responsibility for addressing the ideals and principles that are identified as "collective."

Ideal (Individual)

I-4.1—To provide the community with high-quality early childhood care and education programs and services.

Ideals (Collective)

I-4.2—To promote cooperation among professionals and agencies and interdisciplinary collaboration among professions concerned with addressing issues in the health, education, and well-being of young children, their families, and their early childhood educators.

I-4.3—To work through education, research, and advocacy toward an environmentally safe world in which all children receive health care, food, and shelter; are nurtured; and live free from violence in their home and their communities.

I-4.4—To work through education, research, and advocacy toward a society in which all young children have access to high-quality early care and education programs.

I-4.5—To work to ensure that appropriate assessment systems, which include multiple sources of information, are used for purposes that benefit children.

I-4.6—To promote knowledge and understanding of young children and their needs. To work toward greater societal acknowledgment of children's rights and greater social acceptance of responsibility for the well-being of all children.

I-4.7—To support policies and laws that promote the well-being of children and families, and to work to change those that impair their well-being. To participate in developing policies and laws that are needed, and to cooperate with other individuals and groups in these efforts.

I-4.8—To further the professional development of the field of early childhood care and education and to strengthen its commitment to realizing its core values as reflected in this Code.

Principles (Individual)

P-4.1—We shall communicate openly and truthfully about the nature and extent of services that we provide.

P-4.2—We shall apply for, accept, and work in positions for which we are personally well-suited and professionally qualified. We shall not offer services that we do not have the competence, qualifications, or resources to provide.

P-4.3—We shall carefully check references and shall not hire or recommend for employment any person whose competence, qualifications, or character makes him or her unsuited for the position.

P-4.4—We shall be objective and accurate in reporting the knowledge upon which we base our program practices.

P-4.5—We shall be knowledgeable about the appropriate use of assessment strategies and instruments and interpret results accurately to families.

P-4.6—We shall be familiar with laws and regulations that serve to protect the children in our programs and be vigilant in ensuring that these laws and regulations are followed.

P-4.7—When we become aware of a practice or situation that endangers the health, safety, or well-being of children, we have an ethical responsibility to protect children or inform parents and/or others who can.

P-4.8—We shall not participate in practices that are in violation of laws and regulations that protect the children in our programs.

P-4.9—When we have evidence that an early childhood program is violating laws or regulations protecting children, we shall report the violation to appropriate authorities who can be expected to remedy the situation.

P-4.10—When a program violates or requires its employees to violate this Code, it is permissible, after fair assessment of the evidence, to disclose the identity of that program.

Principles (Collective)

P-4.11—When policies are enacted for purposes that do not benefit children, we have a collective responsibility to work to change these practices.

P-4.12—When we have evidence that an agency that provides services intended to ensure children's well-being is failing to meet its obligations, we acknowledge a collective ethical responsibility to report the problem to appropriate authorities or to the public. We shall be vigilant in our follow-up until the situation is resolved.

P-4.13—When a child protection agency fails to provide adequate protection for abused or neglected children, we acknowledge a collective ethical responsibility to work toward the improvement of these services.

Statement of Commitment *

As an individual who works with young children, I commit myself to furthering the values of early childhood education as they are reflected in the ideals and principles of the NAEYC Code of Ethical Conduct. To the best of my ability I will

- Never harm children.
- Ensure that programs for young children are based on current knowledge and research of child development and early childhood education.
- Respect and support families in their task of nurturing children.
- Respect colleagues in early childhood care and education and support them in maintaining the NAEYC Code of Ethical Conduct.
- Serve as an advocate for children, their families, and their teachers in community and society.
- Stay informed of and maintain high standards of professional conduct.
- Engage in an ongoing process of self-reflection, realizing that personal characteristics, biases, and beliefs have an impact on children and families.
- Be open to new ideas and be willing to learn from the suggestions of others.
- Continue to learn, grow, and contribute as a professional.
- Honor the ideals and principles of the NAEYC Code of Ethical Conduct.

---

* This Statement of Commitment is not part of the Code but is a personal acknowledgement of the individual's willingness to embrace the distinctive values and moral obligations of the field of early childhood care and education. It is recognition of the moral obligations that lead to an individual becoming part of the profession.

Glossary

Accommodation. A concept in Piaget's cognitive theory as one of two processes people use to learn and incorporate new information; the person adjusts what is already known to "accommodate" new learning. Children usually will change their way of thinking into a "schema" once they see that their usual ways do not take new information into account; they then will add new thought patterns to handle the new knowledge.

Accountability. The quality or state of being answerable to someone or of being responsible for explaining exact conditions; schools often must give specific account of their actions to a funding agency to assure the group that the funds and operation of the school are being handled properly.

Accreditation. A system of voluntary evaluation for early childhood centers. The goal is to improve the quality of care and education provided for young children. Accreditation is administered by the National Academy, a branch of the National Association for the Education of Young Children.

Active Listening. A child guidance technique of reflecting back to the speaker what the listener thinks has been said.

Activity Centers. Similar to learning centers and interest areas; areas in a classroom or yard that are designed and arranged for various activities to take place. An early childhood setting will offer several centers, or stations, that are based on both children's interests and what the staff hopes for them to learn in class.

Advocate. One who maintains, defends, or pleads the cause of another; in early childhood terms, an advocate is someone who furthers the principles and issues of the field by speaking to others about such issues.

Aesthetics. Sensitivity to what is beautiful; the study of beauty.

Affective. Of, caused by, or expressing emotion or feeling; emotional.

After-School Care. Programs designed to care for children after the regular academic school day.

Age-Level Characteristics. Those features of children's development and behavior that are most common among a given age group.

Alignment. The act of matching the subject matter of the curriculum with the desired outcomes that the learning standards require.

Anti-bias. A phrase describing the development of curriculum that emphasizes an inclusive look at people and problems, extending the tenets of multicultural education and pluralism.

Articulation. The manner in which sounds and words are actually spoken.

Asperger's Syndrome. A developmental disorder linked to autism and characterized by a lack of social skills, poor concentration, self-absorption, and limited interests.

Assessment. An evaluation or determination of importance, disposition, or state of something or someone, such as in evaluating a child's skills, a teacher's effectiveness, or a classroom environment.

Assimilation. A concept in Piaget's cognitive theory as one of two processes people use to learn and incorporate new information; the person takes new information and puts it together with what is already known in order to "assimilate" the new information intellectually, such as when a toddler shakes a toy magnet first, as with all other toys, in order to get to know this new object. Children usually first try to put new experiences into the "schema," or categories, they already know and use.

Atelierista. A person trained in the arts who acts as a resource and teaches techniques and skills to children in the schools of Reggio Emilia, Italy.

Attachment/Attachment Behaviors. The relational bond that connects a child to another important person; feelings and behaviors of devotion or positive connection.

Attention-Deficit/Hyperactivity Disorder (ADHD). A condition affecting children and adults, making them prone to restlessness, anxiety, short attention spans, and impulsiveness.

Attitude Crystallization. To assume a definite, concrete form in one's attitudes; refers to the formation of a firm set of attitudes and behaviors about others' race, ethnicity, gender, and ability that may be prejudicial and difficult to change.

Auditory Learners. Those who prefer to listen to others and discuss what they learn.

Authentic Assessment. The quantitative and qualitative study of a child's work, activity, and interactions that focuses on the whole child within the context of family, school, and community. Such assessment occurs in a child's natural settings in which the child is performing real tasks. Viewed as a process rather than an end, authentic assessment includes collecting and organizing information over time, from multiple sources, and using a variety of methods.

Autonomy. The state of being able to exist and operate independently, of being self-sufficient rather than dependent on others.

Baseline. A picture of the status of a child, teacher, or environment that serves as the basis for evaluation and later comparison.

Basic Emotions. Those emotions that are present and observable in the newborn or within the first few months of life; they include happiness, interest, surprise, disgust, distress, fear, anger, and sadness.

Basic Needs. Conditions, described by Abraham Maslow and other humanists, that are necessary for growth; these needs, such as physiologic conditions and safety and security, are critical for a person's survival.

Behavior Model. A guidance and behavior technique based on the adult's actions and behavior as an example to follow.

Behaviorist Theory. A psychological theory developed in the United States in the 20th century, which states that all important aspects of behavior and people are learned and can be modified or changed by varying external conditions.

Bias. A tendency that prevents an unprejudiced consideration of a question, person, or action; a prejudice or favoritism that can affect one's thinking or behavior.

Bicognitive Development. A term coined by Ramirez and Casteneda (see Chapter 4) to describe a set of experiences and environments that promote children's ability to use more than one mode of thinking or linguistic system. Each of us grows up with a preferred cognitive style, such as global or analytic, field dependent or field independent, seeing the parts vs. seeing the whole, as well as a linguistic style. For true cultural democracy to take place, we need to develop a flexibility to switch learning styles or cognitive modes (i.e., develop bicognitive abilities) and have an awareness of and respect for differing cognitive styles.

Bilingualism. The acquisition of two languages during the first years of life; using or being able to use two languages.

Biracial. Having parents of two different races.

Brainstorming. The process of thinking that involves bringing up as many ideas as possible about a subject, person, event, etc.

Building Block Years. The phrase refers to the foundation years of early childhood; namely, the first eight years of life in which the basic skills of life and future learning is set, such as locomotor skills of walking and manipulating, cognitive skills of language/literacy and thinking, and affective skills of social interaction, personal identity, and self-expression.

Charter School. A public school operated independently of the local school board, often with a curriculum and educational philosophy different from the other schools in the system.

Checklist. A modified child study technique that uses a list of items for comparison, such as a "yes/no" checklist for the demonstration of a task.

Child Abuse. Violence in the form of physical maltreatment, abusive language, and sexual harassment or misuse of children.

Child Care Center. A place for care of children for a large portion of their waking day; includes basic caretaking activities of eating, dressing, resting, toileting, as well as playing and learning time.

Child-Centered Approach. The manner of establishing educational experiences that takes into consideration children's ways of perceiving and learning; manner of organizing a classroom, schedule, and teaching methods with an eye toward the child's viewpoint.

Child Neglect. The act or situation of parents' or other adults' inattention to a child's basic health needs of adequate food, clothing, shelter, and health care; child neglect may also include not noticing

a child or not paying enough attention in general.

Classical Conditioning. The most common and basic category of learning in behaviorist theory, involving an association between a stimulus and a response so that a reflex response (eye-blinking, salivating, etc.) occurs whenever a neutral and new stimulus is activated (a bell for a light, food, etc.); conditioned-response experiments conforming to the pattern of Pavlov's experiment, sometimes known as "stimulus substitution."

Classification. The ability to group like objects in sets by a specific characteristic.

Classist. A biased or discriminating attitude based on distinctions made between social or economic classes.

Clinical Method. An information-gathering technique, derived from therapy and counseling fields, in which the adult observes and then interacts with the client (in this case, children) by asking questions and posing ideas to the person or group being observed.

Coacting. A situation in which the participants simply act together in a spontaneous way; a goal is not required, as in cooperation, and may be one-on-one rather than in groups; a necessary prerequisite to cooperation is the ability to engage in coactivity.

Cognition. The act or process of knowing, thinking, and perceiving. Cognition involves perceptual, intellectual, and emotional skills that begin as a child makes connections among objects and people and later extends to formulating mental representations.

Cognitive Theory. The psychological theory developed by Jean Piaget and others; the theory focuses on thought processes and how they change with age and experience; this point of view contrasts with the stimulus-response aspects of behaviorist theory.

Competency-Based Assessment. Evaluation in which a teacher is judged or rated in comparison with a predetermined set of skills, or competencies, related to the job.

Complex Emotions. Those emotions that emerge in the child after infancy; these include shame, guilt, envy, and pride.

Comprehensive. Inclusive, covering completely, such as a program for children that concerns itself with the physical, intellectual, social, emotional, creative, and health needs of the children.

Concrete. Concerning the immediate experience of actual things or events; specific and particular rather than general or symbolic.

Connected Knowledge. That kind of knowledge and information that is connected to the child in ways that are real and relevant to that individual; also

known as meaningful knowledge in Piagetian terms, it is elaborated by Gilligan (see Chapter 4) and others.

Constructivism. A theory of learning, developed from the principles of children's thinking by Piaget and implemented in programs as those in Reggio Emilia, Italy, which states that individuals learn through adaptation. The "constructivist" model of learning posits that children are not passive receptacles into which knowledge is poured but rather are active at making meaning, testing out theories, and trying to make sense of the world and themselves. Knowledge is subjective as each person creates personal meaning out of experiences and integrates new ideas into existing knowledge structures.

Continuing Education. The commitment of teachers to learning new approaches and ideas and to continuing to challenge themselves to higher levels of learning and competence.

Continuum. Something that is continuous; an uninterrupted, ordered sequence.

Convergent Thinking. Thinking that brings together information focussed on solving a problem (especially solving problems that have a single correct solution).

Core Values. The basic purposes or issues a professional group acknowledges as common concerns to all its members.

Cortisol. Hormone released when the brain perceives a threat or stress.

Cultural Pluralism. A state or society in which members of diverse ethnic, racial, or cultural groups maintain participation in and development of their traditional culture within the common society.

Culturally Appropriate Curriculum. Curriculum that helps children understand the way individual histories, families of origins, and ethnic family cultures make us similar to and yet different from others.

Curriculum. A framework in which teachers define the content, the process, and the context for what is being taught and what children will learn.

Custodial. Those tasks relating to guardianship of a child's basic needs for food, clothing, and shelter; they include providing for eating, dressing, toileting, resting, and appropriate protection from physical hardships such as weather, danger, etc.

Daily Schedule. A plan or procedure that outlines the sequence and time periods for a children's day in a program.

Decoding. Converting from code into ordinary language; in terms of language development, decoding is the process of making sense out of printed letters or words.

Demographics. The statistical graphics of a population, especially showing average age, income, etc.

Dendrites. Branches of brain cells that reach out to make connections with other cells.

Developmentally Appropriate Practice (DAP). That which is suitable or fitting to the development of the child; refers to those teaching practices that are based on the observation and responsiveness to children as learners with developing abilities who differ from one another by rate of growth and individual differences, rather than of differing amounts of abilities. It also refers to learning experiences that are relevant to and respectful of the social and cultural aspects of the children and their families.

Dialect. A variation of a language, sufficiently different from the original to become a separate entity but not different enough to be considered as a separate language.

Diary Descriptions. A form of observation technique that involves making a comprehensive narrative record of behavior, in diary form.

Disability. A measurable impairment or incapacity that may be moderate to severe. The Individuals with Disabilities Act defines 13 categories that identify specific limitations or challenges, such as hearing, speech, visual, or orthopedic impairments. Individuals who are classified with one or more impairments may be eligible for early intervention and special education classes.

Discipline. Ability to follow an example or to follow rules; the development of self-control or control in general, such as by imposing order on a group. In early childhood terms, discipline means everything adults do and say to influence children's behavior.

Discrimination. To make a distinction in or between, such as being able to note or distinguish as different two or more objects, processes, persons, or actions.

Divergent Thinking. The processes of thought and perception that involve taking a line of thought or action different from what is the norm or common; finding ideas that branch out rather than converge and center on one answer.

Documentation. Keeping written records of events, progress, correspondence, etc.

Down Syndrome. A genetic abnormality that results in mongolism, one of the most common and easily identified forms of mental retardation.

Dramatic Play. Also known as imaginative play, this is a common form of spontaneous play in which children use their imagination and fantasy as part of the setting and activity.

Dual Language Learners. Young children who are learning a second language while still acquiring their first.

Dynamic. Having energy or effective action; a basic skill is one with consequences that will motivate the child, affecting development or stability.

Early Childhood Education. Education in the early years of life; the field of study that deals mainly with the learning and experiences of children from infancy through the primary years (up to approximately eight years of age).

Early Learning Standards. Statements that describe expectations for the learning and development of young children across the domains of: health and physical well-being; social and emotional well-being; approaches to learning; language development and symbol systems; and general knowledge about the world around them (CCSSO, 2005).

Ebonics. Term used to describe "black English" and the center of a controversy in the late 1990s over whether such language is a dialect of standard English or a separate language altogether.

Eclectic. Choosing what appears to be best in various doctrines, methods, styles; comprising elements drawn from various sources.

Educaring. A concept of teaching as both educating and care giving; coined by Magda Gerber in referring to people working with infants and toddlers.

Egocentric. Self-centered; regarding the self as the center of all things; in Piaget's theory, young children think using themselves as the center of the universe or as the entire universe.

Elaboration. The act of expanding language; developing language by building complex structures from simple ones and adding details.

Emergent Curriculum. A process for curriculum planning that draws on teachers' observations and children's interests. Plans emerge from daily life interests and issues. This approach takes advantage of children's spontaneity and teachers' planning.

Emergent/Early Literacy. The process of building upon prereading skills in a child-centered fashion, so that the ability to read evolves from children's direct experiences.

Emergent Writing. The early skills that help children learn to write, such as scribbling and invented spelling.

Emotional Framework. The basic "feeling" structure of a classroom that determines the tone and underlying sensibilities that affect how people feel and behave while in class.

Emotional Intelligence. An understanding of how to feel, interpret, and express emotions.

Employer-Sponsored Child Care. Child care supported in some way by the parents' employers. Support may be financial (as an employee benefit or subsidy) or physical (offering on-site care).

Entry Level. The level of development or behavior that a child shows on beginning a program or group experience; usually an observation-based informal assessment after the first few weeks of school.

Environment. All those conditions that affect children's surroundings and the people in them; the physical, interpersonal, and temporal aspects of an early childhood setting.

Environmental Adaptation. Forces that are not innate or hereditary aspects of development; in early childhood terms, environmental aspects of growth are all those influences of physical conditions, interpersonal relationships, and world experiences that interact with a person to change the way he or she behaves, feels, and lives.

Equilibration. To balance equally; in Piaget's theory, the thinking process by which a person "makes sense" and puts into balance new information with what is already known.

Ethic of Social Reform. The quality of programs and services needed for children under eight and the education reforms that provide it.

Ethics. A theory or system of oral principles and standards; what is "right and wrong"; one's values; the principles of conduct governing both an individual teacher and the teaching profession.

Ethnocentric. Having one's race as a central interest, or regarding one's race or cultural group as superior to others.

Evaluation. A study to determine or set significance or quality.

Event Sampling. An observation technique that involves defining the event to be observed and coding the event to record what is important to remember about it.

Exceptionalities. The preferred expression for the term *disabilities*, which are measurable impairments or incapacities that may be moderate to severe.

Experimental Procedure. An observation technique that gathers information by establishing a hypothesis, controlling the variables that might influence behavior, and testing the hypothesis.

Expressive Language. Those aspects of language development and skill that deal with expression: pronunciation, vocabulary, and grammar, as well as speaking and articulation.

Extended Discourse. Denoting written or spoken communication that goes on for longer than most; in the case of language development, this is meant to be a conversation between child and adult that serves to extend the child's expressive language skills.

Extrinsic. Originating from or on the outside; external, not derived from one's essential nature.

Faith-Based Programs. Those programs that teach the religious dogma of the sponsoring organization.

Family Child Care. Care for children in a small, homelike setting; usually six or fewer children in a family residence.

Feedback Loop. In terms of evaluation, feedback loop is used to describe the process whereby an evaluator gives information to a teacher, who in turn uses this information to improve teaching skills.

Fine Motor. Having to do with the smaller muscles of the body and the extremities, such as those in the fingers, toes, and face.

Flexibility. Capable of modification or change; willing or easily moved from one idea to another.

Fluency. The ability to produce many ideas; an easy and ready flow of ideas.

Formal Assesments. Evaluation instruments that are administered in a conventional, "test-like" atmosphere that have standardized measures and have statistics that are compared to data on other children and are usually described as standards or percentiles. They may or may not be developed commercially.

Four "I"s. The four components (I, Initiative, Independence, and Interaction) of early childhood curriculum for building self-esteem.

Frames of Mind. A theory of intelligence developed by Gardner that refers to intelligence as a host of different skills and abilities.

Full Inclusion. Providing the "least restrictive environment" for children with physical limitations.

Gender Differences. A distinction of characteristics, behaviors, or attitudes typically associated as being either male or female such that the differences are attributed with the sex that a person identifies with.

Gender Identity. The characteristics determining who or what a person is; in this case, those social and cultural differences around being male and female.

Gender Role. The function or part played by a person according to the social and cultural expectations of being male and female.

Genes. The biological elements that transmit hereditary characteristics.

Gifted and Talented Children. Children who have unusually high intelligence, as characterized by: learning to read spontaneously; being able to solve problems and communicate at a level far advanced from their chronological age; excellent memory; extensive vocabulary; and unusual approaches to ideas, tasks, people.

Gross Motor. Having to do with the entire body or the large muscles of the body, such as the legs, arms, and trunk.

Group Times. Those parts of the program in which the whole class or group is together during one activity, such as music, movement, fingerplays, or stories.

Growth Needs. Conditions, as described by Abraham Maslow and other humanists, that are important to a person's well-being; these needs, such as love and belonging, self-esteem and respect for others, playfulness, truth, beauty, etc., while not critical to a person's survival, are necessary for growth.

Guidance. The ongoing system by which adults help children learn to express and manage their feelings, solve their problems, and learn the difference between acceptable and unacceptable behavior.

Holistic. A viewpoint that takes into account several conceptions of a child or situation to form a wider, more rounded description; in early childhood terms, this view includes a child's history, present status, relationships with others, and the interrelationships of development to arrive at a picture of the child; in medicine, this view includes dealing with a person's mental and emotional state, relationships, etc., as well as body signs.

Humanist Theory. The psychological theory of Abraham Maslow and others; it involves principles of motivation and wellness, centering on people's needs, goals, and successes.

Hypothesis. A tentative theory or assumption made to draw inferences or test conclusions; an interpretation of a practical situation that is then taken as the ground for action.

Identity Crisis. A period of uncertainty or confusion in which a person's sense of self becomes insecure.

IEP. An individualized education plan is a process of planning for the education of children with special needs that involves joint efforts of specialists, teachers, and parents.

Imaginary Companions. Also known as imaginary friends, these are pretend characters often created by children.

Importance of Childhood. Children's health and welfare and the changes in family life.

Inclusion. When a child with a disability is a full-time member of a regular classroom with children who are developing normally as well as with children with special needs.

Inclusive Curriculum. Those aspects of a program that reflect awareness of and sensitivity to a person's culture, home language, religion, gender, and abilities.

Independent. Not controlled or influenced by others; thinking for oneself and autonomous.

Individualized Curriculum. A course of study developed and tailored to meet the needs and interests of an individual, rather than those of a group without regard for the individual child.

Inductive Guidance. A guidance process in which children are held accountable for their actions and are called on to think about the impact of their behavior on others. Reasoning and problem-solving skills are stressed.

Inference. A conclusion reached by reasoning from evidence or after gathering information, whether direct or indirect.

Initiative. An introductory step; in early childhood terms, the energy, capacity, and will to begin taking action.

Inquiry. A questioning process that is a seeking or request for information, knowledge, or truth.

Integrated Curriculum. A set of courses designed to form a whole; coordination of the various areas of study, making for continuous and harmonious learning.

Integrated Day. A school schedule with no prescribed time periods for subject matter, but rather an environment organized around various interest centers among which children choose in organizing their own learning experiences.

Intelligence. The cluster of capabilities that involves thinking (see Chapter 13 for details.)

Interaction. Acting on one another, as in the interplay or reciprocal effect of one child upon another.

Interdependence. Dependence on one another, as in the relationship between teachers' experience in the areas of discipline and their competence at knowing and using appropriate language for discipline.

Interest Areas. Similar to learning centers and activity areas; one way to design physical space in a classroom or yard, dividing the space into separate centers among which children move about, rather than assigning them desks.

Interpersonal. Relating to, or involving relationships with, other people; those parts of the environment that have to do with the people in a school setting.

Interracial. Relating to, involving, or representing different races.

Intervention. Entering into a situation between two or more persons or between a person and an object; to interpose oneself into another's affairs, such as when teachers enter into children's interactions when their behavior calls for some action on the part of an adult.

Intrinsic. Belonging to the essential nature of or originating from within a person or body, such as intrinsic motivation, whereby one needs no external reward in order to do something.

Intuition. The direct perception of a fact or truth without any reasoning process; immediate insight.

Invented Spelling. Children's first attempts at spelling words the way they sound to them, based on their current knowledge of letters and sounds. Far from "correct" ("scnd" for second, "grrn" for green, or "relly" for really), invented spelling becomes more conventional over time.

Job Burnout. Exhaustion and stress from one's job, characterized by a wearing down of body and attitude.

Kindergarten (Children's Garden). A school or class for children four to six years old; in the United States, kindergarten is either the first year of formal, public school or the year of schooling before first grade.

Kindergartners. (1) A modern term to describe the children who are attending kindergarten programs; (2) a term used in 19th-century America to describe early childhood practitioners who worked in kindergartens patterned after Froebelian models.

Laboratory Schools. Educational settings whose purposes include experimental study; schools for testing and analysis of educational and/or psychological theory and practice, with an opportunity for experimentation, observation, and practice.

Learning Centers. Similar to interest areas and activity areas; hubs or areas in a classroom designed to promote learning; the classroom is arranged in discrete areas for activity, and children move from one area to another rather than stay at an assigned desk or seat.

Learning Styles. A child's preferred method of integrating knowledge and experiences.

Least Restrictive Environment (LRE). Under the Individuals with Disabilities Education Act (IDEA), a child with identified special needs is entitled to a placement into an environment that is most like that of other children in which the child can succeed; this refers to the physical location of the child's learning and how the child will be taught, so the preference is that the child be included in regular education activities as much as possible.

Licensing. The process of fulfilling legal requirements, standards and regulations for operating child care facilities.

Limits. The boundaries of acceptable behavior beyond which actions are considered misbehavior and unacceptable conduct; the absolute controls an adult puts on children's behavior.

Linchpin. Something that serves to hold together the elements of a situation.

Log/Journal. A form of observation technique that involves making a page of notes about children's behavior in a cumulative journal.

Logical Mathematical Knowledge. One of three types of knowledge in Piagetian theory; the component of intelligence that uses thinking derived from logic.

Looping. The practice of keeping a teacher and a group of children in a class together for two or more years.

Magnet Schools. A public school offering a specialized curriculum, often with high academic standards, to a student body representing a cross-section of the community.

Mainstreaming. The process of integrating handicapped children into classrooms with the nonhandicapped.

Maturation. The process of growth whereby a body matures regardless of, and relatively independent of, intervention such as exercise, experience, or environment.

Maturation Theory. A set of ideas based on the notion that the sequence of behavior and the emergence of personal characteristics develop more through predetermined growth processes than through learning and interaction with the environment; the theory of growth and development proposed and supported by Dr. Arnold Gesell and associates.

Meaningful Knowledge. The form of knowing that is learned within the context of what is already known; that knowledge that has meaning because it has particular significance of value to an individual.

Methode Clinique. A kind of information-gathering technique, first used extensively by Jean Piaget, that involves observing children and asking questions as the situation unfolds. The purpose of this technique is to elicit information about how children are thinking as they behave naturally.

Misbehavior. Improper behavior or conduct.

Mixed-Age Groups. The practice of placing children of several levels, generally one year apart, into the same classroom. Also referred to as family grouping, heterogeneous grouping, multiage grouping, vertical grouping, and ungraded classes.

Modeling. A part of behavior theory, modeling is a way of learning social behavior that involves observing a model (either real, filmed, or animated) and mimicking its behavior, thus acquiring new behavior.

Multiple Intelligences. A theory of intelligence, proposed by Howard Gardner, that outlines several different kinds of intelligence, rather than the notion of intelligence as measured by standardized testing, such as the IQ (see Frames of Mind).

Multiracial. Having ancestors of several or various races.

Myelination. The forming of the myelin sheath, the material in the membrane of certain cells in the brain; the development of the myelination of the brain seems to parallel Piagetian stages of cognitive development.

Narratives. A major observation technique that involves attempting to record nearly everything that happens, in as much detail as possible, as it happens. Narratives include several subtypes such as baby biographies, specimen descriptions, diary descriptions, and logs or journals.

Naturalistic Assessments. Methods of appraisal or child evaluations done in the usual natural surroundings.

Nature/Nurture Controversy. The argument regarding human development that centers around two opposing viewpoints; nature refers to the belief that it is a person's genetic, inherent character that determines development; nurture applies to the notion that it is the sum total of experiences and the environment that determine development.

Negative Reinforcement. Response to a behavior that decreases the likelihood that the behavior will recur; for instance, a teacher's glare might stop a child from whispering at group time, and from then on, the anticipation of such an angry look could reinforce not whispering in the future.

Norm. An average or general standard of development or achievement, usually derived from the average or median of a large group; a pattern or trait taken to be typical of the behavior, skills, or interests of a group.

Norm-Referenced Tests. Standardized tests that compare the child's performance to a large sample of similar children (the norm sample) that represents the general population. There are strict procedures to be followed when administering the test.

Objectivity. The quality or state of being able to see what is real and realistic, as distinguished from subjective and personal opinion or bias.

Observational Learning. Any acquired skills or knowledge having to do with interacting with others; in Bandura's Social Learning theory, observational learning occurs when children watch other people directly or in film, etc., and imitate what they have seen in the model.

Open-ended. Activities or statements that allow a variety of responses, as opposed to those that allow only one response; anything organized to allow for variation.

Open School. A style of education, developed in progressive American schools and in the British infant schools, that is organized to encourage freedom of choice and that does not use predetermined roles and structure as the basis of education; an educational setting whose ultimate goal and base for curriculum is the development of the individual child, rather than of programmed academic experiences.

Operant Conditioning. A category of learning in behavior theory that involves a relation between a stimulus and a response. The response is learned, rather than reflexive, and is gradually and carefully developed through reinforcement of the desired behavior as it occurs in response to the stimulus; behavior leading to a reward.

Organic Reading. A system of learning to read, popularized by Sylvia Ashton-Warner, that lets children build their own vocabulary with the words they choose.

Parent Cooperative Schools. An educational setting organized by parents for their young children, often with parental control and/or support in the operation of the program itself.

Pedagogista. A person trained in early childhood education who meets weekly with the teachers in the schools of Reggio Emilia, Italy.

Pediatrician. A medical specialist in pediatrics, the branch of medicine dealing with children, their development, care, and diseases.

Peer Interactions. Associations with people of the same age group or with those one considers equals.

Perceptual-Motor Development. The growth of a person's ability to move (motor) and perceive (perceptual) together; perceptual-motor activity involves the body and the mind together, to co-ordinate movement.

Performance-Based Assessment. Evaluation based on observable, specific information on what a teacher actually does (performance while on the job).

Philosophy. Concepts expressing one's fundamental beliefs; in early childhood educational terms, the beliefs, ideas, and attitudes of our profession.

Phobia. A strong, exaggerated, and illogical fear of an object or class of things, people, etc.; one of several reactions children often have to divorce.

Phonemes. Language sounds; the smallest units of meaningful speech; two examples of phonemes are /a/ (as in hat) and /p/ (as in sip).

Phonemic Awareness. Having knowledge or perception of the distinct units of sounds that distinguish one word from another; in English this would include buh [b], puh [p], and sss [s], among others.

Physical Environment. Having to do with equipment and material, room arrangement, the outdoor space, and facilities available.

Physical Knowledge. One of three types of knowledge in Piagetian theory; that knowledge that is learned through external, sensory experiences.

Portfolio. An intentional compilation of materials and resources, collected over a period of time that provides evidence for others to review.

Portfolio-based Assessment. An evaluation of a teacher's work using materials, journals, and other resources compiled over a period of time.

Positive Reinforcement. A response to a behavior that increases the likelihood that the behavior will be repeated or increased; for instance, if a child gets attention and praise for crawling, it is likely that the crawling will increase—thus, the attention and praise were positive reinforcers for crawling.

Positive Stress. Refers to an amount of strain or tension that encourages a person to be active and challenged rather than overwhelmed or discouraged.

Precedent. Something done or said that serves as an example or rule to authorize or justify other acts of the same or similar kind; an earlier occurrence of something similar.

Precursor. What precedes and indicates the approach of another; predecessor or forerunner.

Prejudices. Ideas and attitudes that are already formed about other people, situations, ideas, etc., before hearing or experiencing full or sufficient information; in teaching terms, those attitudes or biases that may be based less on mature thought and reasoning than on incomplete or nonexistent personal experiences.

Prepared Environment. The physical and interpersonal surroundings of an educational setting that are planned and arranged in advance with the group of children in mind.

Prerequisite. Something necessary or essential to carrying out an objective or performing an activity; when early childhood teachers determine what skills children will need in order to successfully engage in an activity, they are clarifying the prerequisites for that activity.

Private (Inner) Speech. The language children use for self-guidance and self-direction, as well as for helping them think about their behavior and plan for action; once known as "egocentric speech," it is used for self-regulation.

Professional. One engaged and participating in a profession and accepting the technical and ethical standards of that profession; in early childhood terms, one who has accumulated methods, course work, and teaching experience with young children along with attitudes of competency, flexibility, and continual learning.

Professional Confidentiality. Spoken, written, or acted on in strict privacy, such as keeping the names of children or schools in confidence when discussing observations.

Professional Organizations. Those associations developed for the purpose of extending knowledge and teaching/learning opportunities in the field of education.

Professional Standards. The level of requirement, excellence, or attainment mandated by a professional group, organization, or association for its membership.

Professionalism. The competence or skill expected of a professional; in early childhood education, this includes a sense of identity, purpose to engage in developmentally appropriate practices, a commitment to ethical teaching and to child advocacy, and participation in the work as a legitimate livelihood.

Project Approach. An in-depth study of a particular subject or theme by one or more children. Exploration of themes and topics over a period of days or weeks. Working in small groups, children are able to accommodate various levels of complexity and understanding to meet the needs of all the children working on the project.

Prosocial. Behaviors that are considered positive and social in nature, such as sharing, inviting, including, and offering help or friendship.

Psychodynamic Theory. The psychological theory of Dr. Sigmund Freud and others; it asserts that the individual develops a basic personality core in childhood and that responses stem from personality organization and emotional problems as a result of environmental experiences.

Psychosocial. Those psychological issues that deal with how people relate to others and the problems that arise on a social level; a modification by Erikson of the psychodynamic theories of Freud with attention to social and environmental problems of life.

Psychosocial Domain: The area of development that includes the development of emotions, temperament, social skills, creativity, and spiritual development.

Punishment. The act of inflicting a penalty for an offense or behavior.

Racist. Attitudes, behavior, or policies that imply either a hatred or intolerance of other race(s) or involving the idea that one's own race is superior and has the right to rule or dominate others.

Rating Scale. A modified child study technique similar to a checklist that classifies behavior according to grade or rank, such as using the descriptors "always, sometimes, never" to describe the frequency of a certain behavior.

Readiness. The condition of being ready, such as being in the state or stage of development so that the child has the capacity to understand, be taught, or engage in a particular activity.

Receptive Language. Those aspects of language development and skill that deal with the ability to receive messages: listening, understanding, and responding.

Reciprocal. The stage of children's friendship in which friendship is given or felt by each toward the other; a kind of give-and-take or two-way relationship, this is the stage most often seen in the latter part of the early childhood years.

Reinforcement. A procedure, such as reward or punishment, that changes a response to a stimulus; the act of encouraging a behavior to increase in frequency.

Reinforcers. Rewards in response to a specific behavior, thus increasing the likelihood that behavior will recur; reinforcers may be either social (praise) or nonsocial (food) in nature and may or may not be deliberately controlled.

Rote Knowledge. A form of knowing that is learned by routine or habit and without thought of the meaning.

Roughhousing. Rough and disorderly, but playful, behavior.

Routines. Regular procedures; habitual, repeated or regular parts of the school day; in early childhood programs, routines are those parts of the program schedule that remain constant, such as indoor time followed by cleanup and snack, regardless of what activities are being offered within those time slots.

Running Record. The narrative form of recording behavior; this kind of descriptive record of one's observations involves writing down all behavior as it occurs.

Scaffolding. A useful structure to support a child in learning. A child who gets advice or hints to help master an activity is said to have scaffolding learning, a term Vygotsky used.

Schema. A plan, scheme, or framework that helps make an organizational pattern from which to operate; in Piaget's theory, cognitive schemas are used for thinking.

Screening. Evaluations to determine a child's readiness for a particular class, grade, or experience.

Self-Actualization. The set of principles set forth by Abraham Maslow for a person's wellness or ability to be the most that a person can be; the state of being that results from having met all the basic and growth needs.

Self-Awareness. An awareness of one's own personality or individuality; in teaching terms, an ability to understand one's self and assess personal strengths and weaknesses.

Self-Care. A current description for latchkey children (see Latchkey Children).

Self-Concept. A person's view and opinion of self; in young children, the concept of self develops as they interact with the environment (objects, people, etc.); self-concept can be inferred in how children carry themselves, approach situations, use expressive materials such as art, etc.

Self-Correcting. Materials or experiences that are built or arranged so that the person using them can act automatically to correct errors, without needing another person to check or point out mistakes.

Self-Efficacy. The feelings or thoughts about how competent a person perceives him/herself to be.

Self-Esteem. The value we place on ourselves; how much we like or dislike who we are; self-respect.

Self-Help. The act of helping or providing for oneself without dependence on others; in early childhood terms, activities that a child can do alone, without adult assistance.

Self-Regulation. The term used to describe a child's capacity to plan and guide the self. A disposition or part of the personality (rather than a skill or behavior such as self-control), self-regulation is a way of monitoring one's own activity flexibly over changing circumstances.

Sensorimotor. Relating to or functioning in both sensory and motor aspects of body activity.

Sensory. Having to do with the senses or sensation, as in an awareness of the world as it looks, sounds, feels, smells, tastes.

Separation Process. The act and procedure that occur when parents leave a child at school.

Seriation. The process of sequencing from beginning to end or in a particular series or succession.

Sex Differences. The biological differences between males and females.

Sex-Role Stereotyping. A standardized mental picture or set of attitudes that represents an oversimplified opinion of people's abilities or behavior according to their sex; overgeneralizing a person's skills or behavior on the basis of an inequitable standard of sex differences.

Sexist. Attitudes or behavior based on the traditional stereotype of sexual roles that includes a devaluation or discrimination based on a person's sex.

Shadow Study. A modified child study technique that profiles an individual at a given moment in time; similar to diary description, the shadow study is a narrative recorded as the behavior happens.

Simultaneous/Successive Acquisition. The two major ways second-language learning occurs. Simultaneous acquisition happens if a child is exposed to two languages from birth. Successive acquisition occurs as a child with one language begins to learn another language.

Social Action. Individual or group behavior that involves interaction with other individuals or groups, especially organized action toward social reform.

Social Capital. The richness and resources that social relationships provide for a child.

Social Cognition. The application of thinking to personal and social behavior; giving meaning to social experience.

Social Competence. The ability to successfully deal with social interactions and problems; the skills and personal knowledge to deal with others.

Social Knowledge. One of three types of knowledge in Piagetian theory; that knowledge that is learned about and from people, such as family and ethnic culture, group behavior, social mores, etc.

Social Learning Theory. A psychological theory developed in the 20th century by Albert Bandura of Stanford University, which states that learning often takes place by observing and modeling others.

Social Mores. Standards of conduct and behavior that are determined by society, as opposed to those established by family or personal preference.

Social Referencing. The process used to gauge one's own response to a situation by relying on another person's emotional reaction, such as a child who looks to a teacher after falling down before crying or getting up.

Social Reform. The ethic of social reform is a major theme in early childhood education and history, and refers to the idea that schooling for young children will lead to social change and improvement.

Social Skills. Strategies children learn to enable them to respond appropriately in many environments.

Socialization. The process of learning the skills, appropriate behaviors, and expectations of being part of a group, particularly society at large.

Sociocentric. Oriented toward or focused on one's social group rather than on oneself.

Sociocultural. Aspects of theory or development that refer to the social and cultural issues; key descriptor of Vygotsky's theory of development.

Sociodramatic Play. At least two children participating in dramatic play or play that involves two basic elements; imitation and make-believe.

Software. The programs used to direct the operation of a computer, as opposed to the physical device on which they are run (known as "hardware").

Spatial. Having to do with the nature of space, as in the awareness of the space around a person's body.

Special-Needs Children. Children whose development and/or behavior require help or intervention beyond the scope of the ordinary classroom or adult interactions.

Specimen Description. A form of narrative observations technique that involves taking on-the-spot notes about a child (the "specimen") to describe behavior.

Spontaneous Play. The unplanned, self-selected activity in which a child freely participates.

Standardized Testing. Formal assessment techniques whose results have been tabulated for many children and thus have predetermined standards, or norms, for evaluating the child being tested.

Standards. The degree or level of requirement, excellence, or attainment, mandated by local or national government agencies that describe the learning outcomes for various age groups.

Stimulus–Response. The kind of psychological learning, first characterized in behavior theory, that makes a connection between a response and a stimulus; that is, the kind of learning that takes place when pairing something that rouses or incites an activity with the activity itself in such a way that the stimulus (such as a bell) will trigger a response (such as salivating).

Stress. The physical and emotional reactions and behaviors that come from having to cope with difficult situations beyond one's capabilities.

Superhero. Those characters who embody a higher nature and powers beyond ordinary human abilities, such as Superman, Wonder Woman, etc.

Support System A network of people who support each other in their work and advancement.

Tabula Rasa. A mind not affected yet by experiences, sensations, and the like. In John Locke's theory, a child was born with this "clean slate" upon which all experiences were written.

Tactile. Perceptible or able to be learned through the sense of touch.

Tactile Learners. Those who are full, active-body learners and learn by hands-on activities.

Teaching Objectives. A set of goals teachers set for themselves as they plan activities for children; these goals remind teachers what they will do to help children learn.

Team Teaching. Group-based manner of teaching, where a group composed of people with varying skills, experience, and training teach jointly.

Temporal. Having to do with time and time sequence; in the early childhood setting, refers to scheduling and how time is sequenced and spent, both at home and in school.

Theory. A group of general principles, ideas, or proposed explanations for explaining some kind of phenomenon; in this case, child development.

Time Sampling. A form of observational technique that involves observing certain behavior and settings within a prescribed time frame.

Traditional Nursery School. The core of early childhood educational theory and practice; program designed for children aged two-and-a-half to five years of age, which may be a part- or an all-day program.

Transactional Model. A model of education that describes the interaction of an individual with one or more persons, especially as influenced by their assumed roles. This model implies that the role of parent, child, or teacher has an effect on what and how information is taught and learned.

Transcurricular. Able to be used or applied in a variety of situations or activities.

Transformative Curriculum. The process of viewing events and situations from diverse perspective to gain new insights and ways of thinking in order to create more culturally appropriate curriculum.

Transitions. Changes from one state or activity to another; in early childhood terms, transitions are those times of change in the daily schedule (whether planned or not), such as from being with a parent to being alone in school, from playing with one toy to choosing another, from being outside to being inside, etc.

Transmission Model. A model of education describing the transference of information directly from one person to another, such as in the sense of passing on knowledge directly from teacher to child.

Transmitting Values. A major theme in early childhood education and history, helping children learn and accept basic values of the family and community has been one of the reasons for education for centuries.

Trauma. A deeply distressing or disturbing experience.

Unconscious. Not conscious, without awareness, occurring below the level of conscious thought.

Undifferentiate The stage of children's friendships in which children do not distinguish between "friend" and "person I'm playing with," considered the first stage, usually from infancy into the preschool years.

Unilateral. The stage of children's friendships in which children think of friendship as involving one side only; that is, a one-way situation in that a "friend" is "someone who does what I want him to do," usually spanning the preschool years and into early primary.

Universal Infection Control Precautions. These are procedures to be followed by all teaching staff who are caring for an injured or ill child who might be harboring a highly contagious, dangerous pathogen that is transmitted in blood, blood products, and other body fluids. Universal precautions were described in directives and guidelines issued by the CDC in the late 1980s.

Vertical Groupings. See Mixed-Age Groups.

Visual Learners. Those who prefer to lean through pictures, photos, charts, and graphs and represent their learning through reading, writing, and drawing.

Webbing. A process through which teachers create a diagram based on a topic or theme. It is a planning tool for curriculum and includes as many resources as teachers can name.

Whole Language. The area of graphic language development that refers to a particular way in which language, particularly reading and writing, is learned; whole language refers to that movement within primary education that emphasizes an integrated and literary-based approach rather than a phonics, decoding-skills approach.

Word Pictures. Descriptions of children that depict, in words, norms of development; in this text, these are age-level charts that describe common behaviors and characteristics, particularly those that have implications for teaching children (in groups, for curriculum planning, with discipline and guidance).

Working Portfolio. A type of child portfolio that is used and added onto regularly, documenting a child's skills and behavior over time. Rather than one that collects only a child's exemplary work or everything a child has done, this type of portfolio attempts to capture key documentation to demonstrate a child's growth.

Zone of Proximal Development. The term in Vygotskys sociocultural theory that defines which children can learn. Interpersonal and dynamic, the zone refers to the area a child can master (skill, information, etc.) with the assistance of another skilled person; below that, children can learn on their own; above the limit are areas beyond the child's capacity to learn, even with help.

Subject Index

Psychosocial domain, 459–460, 476
Psychosocial theories of child development, 109–112, 145
Punishment, 115, 244–245
Puppet shows, 451

Q

Quality 2000: Advancing Early Child Care and Education, 518–519

R

RAND Corporation study, 63
Rating methods, 205–207, 210
Ratios
  in child care, 537
  in family child care, 49
Readiness, 10
Reading, social diversity and, 531
Reauthorization Act, 51
Receptive language, 421, 429, 433, 436
Record keeping, 169–170
Recording observations, 200–212
Redirecting activity, 251, 256
Reggio Emilia, 29, 196–197, 268, 322–323, 364–366, 497, 498
  as community life, 527
Reinforcement, positive and negative, 113–115, 251, 256
Reinforcer, 114
Rest areas, 304
Rote knowledge, 396–397
Roughhousing, 292
Rousseau, Jean Jacques, 3, 7, 11–12
Routines, 315–317, 474, 487–489, 499
Ruggles Street Nursery School, 8
Running record, 201–202, 210

S

Safety, 296–300
  automobile safety, 301
Sanitation, 296–297
Schemas, 117
School-age children
  bilingualism and, 533
  child care, 60
  disasters and, 530
Schools
  charter schools, 262
  family support by, 524–527
  family-friendly, 266
  "Free School," 24
  German system of, 10
  homeschooling, 61
  Infant Schools, 29
  laboratory, 17, 28
  laboratory schools, 17, 28, 52–53
  magnet schools, 262
  Montessori Schools, 3, 7, 13–14, 25, 366–367
  nursery schools, 20–22, 46–47
  open school, 29
  parent cooperative schools, 53
  social capital and, 526–527
  traditional nursery school (preschool), 20–22, 46–47
  universal preschools, 52
  values transmission in, 527–536
Schurtz, Margaretha, 19
Screening, 225–227
Self care, 60
Self-actualization, 129–130
Self-awareness, 172
Self-concept, 385–386
Self-discipline, 244, 246
Self-efficacy, 113
Self-esteem, 130, 292, 461–462
Self-evaluation, 179–180, 182
Self-help environments, 286, 291–292

Self-regulation, 468
Sensitivity, 495
  cultural awareness and, 183
  cultural sensitivity, 98–99, 183, 431
  desensitization, to violence, 527–528
Sensory awareness, 379
Sensory styles, 342
Separation process, 273–274
Seriation, 402, 404
Sesame Street, 9, 128
Setting limits, 252–253
Sex differences, 138–139
Sex role stereotyping, 382–383, 535–536
Sexist attitudes, 531–532, 535–536
Sexual abuse, 522–523
Shadow study, 207–208, 210
Sharing, 358, 488, 490
Simultaneous acquisition, 425
Six- and seven-year-olds
  cognitive development, 86
  creative development, 86
  cultural identity development, 86
  developmental milestones, 86
  language development, 86
  physical-motor development, 86
  social-emotional development, 86
  word pictures, 86
Skills acquisition, planning for, 347
Skinner, B. F., 113, 144
Slavery, children and, 16–17
Social action, 484
  conflict resolution, 480–482, 485, 488, 490–492, 508
Social capital, 526–527
Social cognition, 482
Social competence, 475, 477–478, 486
Social diversity
  attitude crystallization, 531–532
  bilingual education, 532–533
  class differences, 534–535
  cultural pluralism, 532
  equal play and gender issues, 535–536
  facing reality, 531–532
  immigrants and, 271–272, 533–534
  inclusive education, 534
  math and, 531, 534–535
  multicultural education, 532
  racist attitudes, 531–532
  reading and, 531
  sexist attitudes, 531–532, 535–536
  sexuality, 536
  teacher attitudes and, 532
Social growth, 345
  adults, skills learned with, 483
  common social challenges, 479–482
  curriculum planning, 486–493
  early childhood, social skills in, 490
  group, skills learned in a, 483
  individual, skills learned as an, 483–484
  peer relationships, 480–482
  peers, skills learned with, 483
  skills, 482–484
  social action, 484
  social cognition, 482
  social competence, 475, 477–478, 486
  social development, 478–479
  social intelligence, 482
  social knowledge and understanding, 486–488
  socialization, 477
  sociocentric viewpoint, 480
  undifferentiated level, 481
  unilateral level, 481
Social knowledge, 396
Social mores, 463
Social referencing, 470
Social reform, 10, 516–520
  child care, 516–519

ethic of, 30–31
Social skills, 482
Social world, knowledge of, 401, 404
Social-emotional development, 79, 80–87
  eight-year-olds, 87
  five-year-olds, 85
  four-year-old, 84
  infant, 80
  six- and seven-year-olds, 86
  three-year-olds, 83
  toddler, 81
  two-year-olds, 82
Socialization, 113, 477
Sociocultural, 44, 123
Sociocultural theory
  application, 124–125, 145
  bicognitive development, 124
  private (inner) speech, 124
  scaffolding, 123
  Vygotsky, Lev, 122–125
  Vygotsky's sociocultural theory, 123–125
  zone of proximal development (ZPD), 123–125
Sociodramatic play, 136
Sociopolitical view, of violence, 529
Solitary play, 134–135, 202
Spanking, 240
Spatial awareness, 378
Spatial intelligence, 127, 339, 342
Spatial relationships, 403, 404
Special needs children
  art adaptations for, 507
  Asperger syndrome (AS), 93
  Attention-Deficit/Hyperactivity Disorder (ADHD), 92–93
  bias and stereotypes, 97
  bipolar disorder, 92
  children with exceptionalities/multiple exceptionalities, 90–91
  cultural, racial, and ethnic considerations, 96–99
  definition of, 90
  Down syndrome, 91
  dyslexia, 91
  family support for, 93
  Gardner's MI, 97
  gifted and talented children, 96–97
  Head Start, 50, 93
  inclusive classroom for, 94–96, 534
  individualized program (IEP), 93–94
  learning disabilities, 91–92
  mainstreaming, 94–96
  oppositional defiant disorder (ODD), 92
  physical growth/motor development and, 375–377
  P.L. 94-42, 376
  P.L. 94-142 (Education for All Handicapped Children Act), 93–94, 225
  P.L. 99-457 (Education of the Handicapped Amendments Act), 94, 225, 268
  P.L. 101-336 (Americans with Disabilities Act) (ADA), 9, 94, 534
  P.L. 101-576 (Individuals with Disabilities Education Act) (IDEA), 94
  public recognition, 93–94
  race and, 535
  teacher and parental role, 93–98
Specimen descriptions, 202, 210
Spiritual development
  children as a spiritual resource, 503–504
  issues, 502–503
  teacher's role, 503
Spock, Benjamin, 8, 26
Staff, 66
Standards
  in curriculum, 350–352

Name Index

Where to Find the *NAEYC Standards for Early Childhood Professional Preparation* in This Text

Note: The Code of Ethical Conduct, Developmentally Appropriate Practices, and Issues of Cultural Diversity are integrated into *every* chapter in the text.